PROGRAMMING
ASSEMBLER LANGUAGE

PROGRAMMING ASSEMBLER LANGUAGE

IBM® 370 Series Architecture and Assembly Language

Third Edition

PETER ABEL
British Columbia Institute of Technology

PRENTICE HALL, Englewood Cliffs, New Jersey 07632

Library of Congress Cataloging-in-Publication Data

ABEL, PETER
    Programming assembler language : IBM 370 series architecture and
assembly language / Peter Abel. — 3rd ed.

    p.   cm.
    Includes index.
    ISBN 0-13-728924-3
    1. Assembler language (Computer program language)   2. IBM 370
(Computer)—Programming.   I. Title.
    QA76.73.A8A23 1989
    005.2′25—dc 19   88-28144
                                                                        CIP

Editorial/production supervision and
  interior design: Kathleen Schiaparelli
Cover design: Ben Santora
Manufacturing buyer: Mary Noonan

 © 1989, 1984, and 1979 by Prentice-Hall, Inc.
A Division of Simon & Schuster
Englewood Cliffs, New Jersey 07632

The author and publisher of this book have used their best efforts in preparing this
book. These efforts include the development, research, and testing of the theories
and programs to determine their effectiveness. The author and publisher make no
warranty of any kind, expressed or implied, with regard to these programs or the
documentation contained in this book. The author and publisher shall not be liable
in any event for incidental or consequential damages in connection with, or arising
out of, the furnishing, performance, or use of these programs.

IBM is a registered trademark of International Business Machines Corporation.

Printed in the United States of America

10 9 8 7 6 5 4 3 2

ISBN 0-13-728924-3

PRENTICE-HALL INTERNATIONAL (UK) LIMITED, *London*
PRENTICE-HALL OF AUSTRALIA PTY. LIMITED, *Sydney*
PRENTICE-HALL CANADA INC., *Toronto*
PRENTICE-HALL HISPANOAMERICANA, S.A., *Mexico*
PRENTICE-HALL OF INDIA PRIVATE LIMITED, *New Delhi*
PRENTICE-HALL OF JAPAN, INC., *Tokyo*
SIMON & SCHUSTER ASIA PTE. LTD., *Singapore*
EDITORA PRENTICE-HALL DO BRASIL, LTDA., *Rio de Janeiro*

CONTENTS

5 DATA DEFINITION   79

Part IV   Special Applications   247

10   INPUT/OUTPUT MACROS   247

11   EXPLICIT USE OF BASE REGISTERS   269

12 LOGICAL OPERATIONS AND BIT MANIPULATION   311

13 SUBPROGRAM LINKAGE   340

PREFACE

Assembler language is the fundamental "low-level" language of the IBM 370 series of computers, which includes such recent models as the 434x, 438x, 308x, and 309x. As such, assembler language is directly translatable into machine language, such that one assembler instruction typically generates one machine code instruction. High-level languages like COBOL and PL/I, by contrast, are easier to learn and to use. Why, then, learn assembler language? An understanding of assembler language can help a programmer in a number of ways:

- Programs (or even parts of programs) written in assembler may be considerably more efficient in storage space and execute time, a useful consideration if such programs are run frequently.
- A knowledge of assembler can facilitate learning of any other language, including high-level languages and other assembly languages. And with a background in assembler, the user can more clearly understand what the computer is doing.
- A knowledge of assembler can help a programmer become more efficient. High-level languages like COBOL and PL/I can be deceptive and appear to execute in some mysterious fashion. A programmer familiar with assembler can code high-level languages with an understanding of what machine code they generate and which is the more efficient technique. For example, why

in COBOL does the use of COMPUTATIONAL (BINARY), COMPU-
TATIONAL-3 (PACKED DECIMAL), and SYNC have considerable effect
on a program's efficiency? What is the significance in PL/I of the DECIMAL
FIXED, ALIGNED, and DEFINED attributes? With knowledge of assembler, a programmer can examine the generated code to determine more efficient ways to write certain routines.

- Although most high-level languages provide extensive debugging aids, there
  are times when a programmer needs assembler knowledge to delve into generated machine code or to examine storage dumps.

- Some specialized areas, such as technical support and data communications,
  require an extensive knowledge of assembler.

Although the material in this text has been used successfully as an introduction
to programming, more educational institutes do not teach assembler as an introductory language. Generally, the concepts of logic and programming style are
easier to learn when there is less need for concern with rigorous rules and field
sizes. The text does not, however, assume that the reader has had much, if any,
programming experience. The approach of the text is to introduce simple input
and output processing, beginning with character data. Chapter 5 covers the character, packed, and binary formats and their general programming requirements so
that users of the text may concentrate on the formats that best suit them. In this
way, programming concepts are introduced early, and users are soon writing re-
alistic programs.

The book should serve as both a practical guide for the assembler student
and a useful later reference. These objectives are accomplished in two ways:

- The step-by-step presentation begins with simple material and progresses to
  more complex material. Many practical examples of complete and partial
  programs illustrate concepts as they are introduced.

- Chapters are organized by logical topics, such as character, packed, and binary
  data and input/output. The user can concentrate on mastering one programming area at a time, and most related material is contained in its own chapter.

The complexities of base/displacement addressing and file definition are delayed through use of several simple macros, similar to those used in many educational institutions. Appendix E provides a listing of the macros for readers who
want to catalog them on their own system. The text discontinues these macros
by Chapter 6, where the technical material is covered in detail.

The two major IBM operating systems are DOS and OS. The text covers
the differences between them, giving examples for both.

Part I. Chapters 1 and 2 cover computers and programming in general.
This material could act as a review for readers who are already familiar with it.

Part II. Chapters 3, 4, 5, and 6 cover material on control sections, directives, data declaratives, program assembly, and base registers that is basic to most assembler programs.

Part III.   Chapters 7, 8, and 9 provide for the processing of character, packed decimal, and binary fixed-point data, respectively.

Part IV.   Chapters 10 through 16 cover a variety of special topics: input/output, explicit use of base registers, logical operations, subprograms, macro writing, debugging strategy, and floating-point operations.   Chapters 10 (input/output) and 11 (explicit use of base registers) could be taken first; the other chapters may be taken in any sequence or omitted.   Chapter 15 on debugging may be referenced at any time.

Part V.   This part is concerned with external storage and file processing. It is not expected that readers will write large assembler programs that process disk and tape files, but an understanding of the material in these chapters gives considerable insight into the design and use of files.   Chapter 17, which covers the details of disk and tape hardware, should be covered first.   The usual procedure would be to cover sequential processing in Chapter 18 next and then to read in any sequence (or omit) Chapters 19 (VSAM) and 20 (ISAM).   ISAM is treated lightly because VSAM has largely replaced it in IBM installations.

Chapter 21 provides additional material on operating systems, the supervisor, and input/output for advanced programmers and systems programmers.

The following diagram indicates the oganization of chapters.   Thus Chapters 1 and 2 on computers and programming in general (if not already familiar) would be covered first, in that sequence.   Chapters 3, 4, 5, and 6 on basic assembler features are to be covered next, also in that sequence.   At that point, readers have mastered the basics of the language and may proceed to any of Chapters 7 (character data), 8 (packed decimal data), 9 (binary fixed-point data), 10 (input/output), or 15 (debugging strategy).

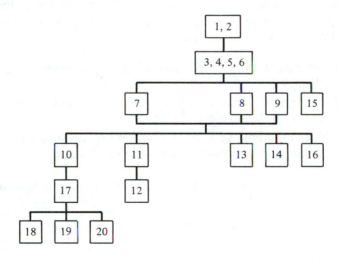

Many users of earlier versions of this text worked ahead of the course, experimenting with binary operations, macro writing, and subprogram linkage. Such motivation is commendable and should be encouraged.

The IBM manuals concerned with the material in this text require a bookshelf about 5 feet long. Readers should not expect, therefore, that this or any other single book will provide all there is to know about the assembler language and related topics. Eventually the IBM manuals have to be referenced for current detailed information. The following IBM manuals or their equivalent are especially recommended:

IBM FORM NUMBER	TITLE
GA22-7000	IBM System/370 Principles of Operation (system organization, machine instructions, input/output)
GC33-4010	OS/VS-DOS/VS-VM/370 Assembler Language (assembler statements and macros)
GC28-6646	OS Supervisor Services and Macro Instructions
GC26-3746	OS Data Management Services Guide
GC26-3794	OS Data Management Macro Instructions
GC24-5138	DOS/VSE Data Management Concepts
GC24-5139	DOS/VSE Macro User's Guide
GC24-5140	DOS/VSE Macro Reference

Other useful manuals include those on job control, disk file organization, tape labels, disk labels, the operating system, and virtual storage.

Note on the Third Edition

Since the first edition of *Programming Assembler Language,* the computer world has changed dramatically. The most notable change has been the increase in microcomputer technology and a renewed interest in assembler language. As well, authors evolve their thinking and approaches to programming. This third edition reflects these changes:

- Programming style and structured programming are introduced earlier, in Chapter 2.
- Parts and chapters have been reorganized, and stronger emphasis has been placed on data types.
- More program examples and further explanations are given, especially at the beginning, when students have the most trouble.

I hope that this revision satisfies your needs, at least until new technology replaces the IBM 370-based assembler.

The author is grateful for the assistance from all who contributed typing, reviews, and suggestions and to IBM for permission to reproduce some of their copyrighted materials. The following materials are reprinted with permission and with modifications from publications copyrighted in 1973 and 1981 by International Business Machines Corporation as IBM form numbers GA22-7000, GX20-1850, and GC29-1649: Figure 17-5, Appendix C. and Appendix F.

Special thanks for the thoughtful review of the manuscript by Arline Sachs, Northern Virginia Community College.

Peter Abel

PROGRAMMING
ASSEMBLER LANGUAGE

1

THE COMPUTER

OBJECTIVE

To review the internal characteristics of the digital computer, its basic operations, and the function of the stored program.

This chapter discusses computer concepts and systems in general terms and then introduces basic technical material concerned specifically with the IBM 370-series computers.

The purpose of computers, like other automated devices, is to replace repetitive human labor. The two main classes of computers are analog and digital. An analog computer, which measures physical variables such as rotation speed, water pressure, and electric current, usually indicates the result by an approximation. Examples of analog computers are traditional speedometers, pressure gauges, barometers, and slide rules. A digital computer works with digits to perform calculations. A useful comparison of analog and digital is the watch: An analog watch has a sweep hand that indicates the time, whereas a digital watch uses digits to display the time.

A unique characteristic of a digital computer is that it is usually capable of performing more than one function. The feature that provides this multifunction ability is the *stored program*, which is a set of instructions that is temporarily stored in the computer's memory and that the computer executes. To perform a different function, you can replace the program with another one. In this text, the term *computer* means the common digital computer, and the term *program* means the stored program.

A computer has the ability to deal with data in the form of numeric values and alphabetic characters. The computer can perform arithmetic on numeric values and can make comparisons on numeric values and on alphabetic characters. Consider, for example, a computer installation that maintains data about customers on disk storage in the form of a record for each customer. Each record contains customer number, customer name and address, balance owed, and credit limit. If programmed accordingly, a stored program in the computer can successively read each customer record from disk into its memory. It can compare the balance owed against the credit limit and display all records where the balance is greater. It can also add all customer balances and display a final total.

But a computer has limitations. It can process data only that it has received externally, and then it can process the data only according to the instruction steps that a programmer provides in the stored program.

COMPUTER GENERATIONS

The first generation of digital computers was introduced in the early 1950s. These computers were characterized by many vacuum tubes and relatively slow processing speeds.

The second generation of computers, introduced in 1958, used transistorized circuitry that permitted smaller size, higher-speed storage, and lower cost.

The third generation of computers, introduced in 1964, replaced transistors with integrated circuits and featured higher speed, greater storage capacity, more facilities, and greater reliability. IBM introduced System/360 to replace and improve upon a variety of then existing IBM computers. The 360 provided a single computer designed to serve effectively for both business and scientific applications. The 360's greater speed and capacity enabled it to perform larger and more complex applications.

An important feature of the 360 (and of many other computers) was its use of an *operating system*, which facilitates the use of libraries for storing program and data files, continuous processing of programs with limited operator intervention, and automatic error handling and recovery.

In 1970 IBM introduced System 370, with significant improvements in computing performance over the 360 but with full compatibility. In 1977 the 370 was further extended into more advanced computer systems, the 303x series. Other advances have been the 4300 series in 1979, the 308x series in the early 1980s, and the 309x series in the mid-1980s.

The distinction between generations is no longer clear-cut. Because of ongoing technological improvements in large-scale integration, it is generally conceded that the early 1970s ushered in the fourth generation of computers. This text follows the convention of referring to this generation of IBM computers as the 370 series. Throughout the various enhancements to the original computer line, the basic assembler language has remained much the same.

Let's now examine the components of the computer, beginning with the smallest unit, binary numbers.

THE BINARY NUMBER SYSTEM

Binary numbers constitute the basic numbering system of computers. It may be worthwhile to compare binary numbers with our common decimal number system. A decimal (base 10) number has ten digits, 0 through 9, whereas a binary (base 2) number has only two digits, 0 and 1. For example, the decimal number 10 does not equal the binary number 10 ("one-zero").

For any number system, the position of a digit determines its value. Consider the decimal number 1111 (which has a base of 10), with the value of each digit determined by its position and the power of 10:

$$\text{decimal } 1111 = (1 \times 10^3) + (1 \times 10^2) + (1 \times 10^1) + (1 \times 10^0)$$

$$= 1000 \quad\quad + 100 \quad\quad + 10 \quad\quad + 1$$

Now consider the binary number 1111, which uses the power of 2. You can convert it to its decimal equivalent as follows:

$$\text{binary } 1111 = \text{decimal } (1 \times 2^3) + (1 \times 2^2) + (1 \times 2^1) + (1 \times 2^0)$$

$$= 8 \quad\quad\quad + 4 \quad\quad + 2 \quad\quad + 1 = 15$$

Let's examine a binary number that contains some zeros. Because a zero digit in any base evaluates to zero, you simply add the values for the nonzero digits. For example, the binary number 1100 converts to its decimal equivalent as follows:

$$\text{binary } 1100 = \text{decimal } (1 \times 2^3) + (1 \times 2^2) + (0 \times 2^1) + (0 \times 2^0)$$

$$= 8 \quad\quad\quad + 4 \quad\quad + 0 \quad\quad + 0 = 12$$

In this way, a binary number, using only the digits 0 and 1, can represent any decimal value. For example, the binary number 101101 equals

$$2^5 + 0^4 + 2^3 + 2^2 + 0^1 + 2^0$$

$$= \text{decimal } 32 + 0 + 8 + 4 + 0 + 1 = 45$$

You can also represent binary (binal) points and negative numbers, but we'll leave that discussion until Chapter 9.

The K and M Measures

The well-known measurement K, as in 256K, has the value 2^{10}, or 1,024 (a close approximation to 1,000). Thus

$$256K = 256 \times 1,024 = 262,144$$

The measurement M (also known as *meg*) has the value 2^{20}, or 1,048,576, and is commonly used to describe disk capacities, such as 100M.

A computer internally represents the digits 0 and 1 as "off" and "on" conditions. It is this simplicity that makes binary the important numbering system of computers, as the next section explains.

BITS AND BYTES

A single storage location in a computer is known as a *byte*, which consists of a specified number of *bits*. A bit, which is an abbreviation for *binary digit*, can be either "off" (the value 0) or "on" (the value 1). On most computers, including the 370 series, each storage location (byte) consists of 8 bits to represent data. Each of the 8 bits has a value of 0 or 1 and a number to represent its position. In the following representation of a byte, each bit is set to zero:

Bit value:	128	64	32	16	8	4	2	1	
On/off setting:	0	0	0	0	0	0	0	0	(storage location, byte)

In a byte, all bits off (00000000) means a zero value. If only the bit numbered 1 (the rightmost bit) is on, the byte appears as 00000001, and the value of its contents is 1. If only the bit numbered 2 is on, the byte appears as 00000010, and the value is 2. If both bits numbered 1 and 2 are on, the byte contains 00000011, and its value is 3. In this way, combinations of zero bits and one bits provide values 0 through 255 in an 8-bit byte.

On most computers, each byte has one extra bit, called the parity bit, that is used to ensure the integrity of the data bits. On IBM 370-series computers, which require odd parity, the parity bit ensures that each byte always contains an odd number of bits that are on. For example, a byte contains the value 7: Bits numbered 4, 2, and 1 are on. Because this is an odd number of on bits (3), the computer sets the parity bit to off:

Bit value:	P	128	64	32	16	8	4	2	1	
On/off setting:	0	0	0	0	0	0	1	1	1	(parity bit off)

Now assume that the value in a byte is 9: Bits numbered 8 and 1 are on, an even number of on bits. To force odd parity, the computer sets the parity bit to on:

Bit value:	P	128	64	32	16	8	4	2	1	
On/off setting:	1	0	0	0	0	1	0	0	1	(parity bit on)

Setting bits on and off is an entirely automatic process over which programmers have no control. Occasionally, although rarely, a bit is somehow "lost" and the parity in a byte becomes even. When processing the contents of a byte, the computer automatically checks its parity. If the parity is even, the computer signals a warning to the operator that the computer may require servicing.

A reference to byte capacity does not include the parity bit. Thus the previous example would be an 8-bit code, which can represent 2^8, or 256, characters.

A byte contains a specified number of bits that represent numbers and characters in storage. One or more adjacent bytes may represent a *data item*, or *field*. For example, a program could treat two adjacent bytes as a binary field. If the contents are binary 00001010 00101000, the value as a decimal number would be 2,600—try it. One or more adjacent related fields may constitute a *record*.

The contents of a byte have no intrinsic meaning to a computer. Your program defines data as a specific format and has to handle it accordingly. Thus some instructions process character data, others process binary data, others process packed data, and still others process floating-point data.

HEXADECIMAL REPRESENTATION

The purpose of the hexadecimal numbering system is to represent the contents of main storage. The hexadecimal base is 16, and the numbers used are 0 through 9 and A through F to represent the decimal values 0–15. Hexadecimal (or hex) is only a representation, and at no time does the computer actually work in base 16. One hex digit represents 4 bits in a byte, and two hex digits represent all 8 bits in a byte. Figure 1-1 shows the related decimal and binary values for the hexadecimal digits 0 through 15.

Decimal	Binary	Hexadecimal	Decimal	Binary	Hexadecimal
0	0000	0	8	1000	8
1	0001	1	9	1001	9
2	0010	2	10	1010	A
3	0011	3	11	1011	B
4	0100	4	12	1100	C
5	0101	5	13	1101	D
6	0110	6	14	1110	E
7	0111	7	15	1111	F

Figure 1-1   Decimal, binary, and hexadecimal representation.

The 370-series computers use an 8-bit code to represent data in one storage location (byte) that allows up to 256 different characters. As can be seen from Fig. 1-1, one hex digit represents 4 bits; as a result, two hex digits can represent the contents of any byte.

You can use the hexadecimal format to display the contents of any type of data on the system. For example, the hexadecimal representation of the binary number 00001010 00101000 is 0A 28. To express a hex value, this text uses the common notation X'0A28'.

Among the uses for hexadecimal format are the following:

- The assembler converts your symbolic source program to machine code. It prints the locations of instructions and their object code entirely in hex format.
- To facilitate tracing program bugs, you can instruct the supervisor to print a storage dump, which shows the contents of each storage location as two hex digits per byte.
- Special-purpose characters perform various functions; for example, some control the printer for line feeds and form feeds, and others edit numeric data fields for comma, decimal point, and sign. You use hex values to represent these special characters in your program.

Each position of a hex number determines its value, based on the powers of 16. Here is how you would convert X'15E' to its decimal equivalent:

$$15E = (1 \times 16^2) + (5 \times 16^1) + (14 \times 16^0)$$
$$= 256 + 80 + 14 = 350$$

Our discussion of data formats later in this chapter will provide more details on the hexadecimal representation of various data types.

Hexadecimal Arithmetic

You can perform arithmetic on hex numbers, and in assembler you may have occasions to do so. Note how X'F' overflows when you add 1 to it:

DECIMAL VALUE	HEX VALUE
15	F
+ 1	+ 1
16	10

Thus X'10' equals the decimal value 16. Also note that X'5' + X'5' = X'A' and X'8' + X'8' = X'10'. The following examples illustrate more hex addition:

21	385	412A	53A6
+15	+385	+ 94	+ 92A
36	70A	41BE	5CD0

Appendix A provides a useful reference for converting hexadecimal numbers to decimal and vice versa. Understanding hex notation is especially important in assembler programming, and you are urged to grasp it fully.

Let's now examine the components of a computer system.

THE COMPUTER SYSTEM

Since the first primitive models, computers have evolved radically but although there are many makes and models, their basic structure has remained much the same. Figure 1-2 illustrates the main components of a computer: input/output, main storage (memory), and the central processing unit (CPU).

Input/Output

To access new data, a computer "reads" data into its main storage from input devices such as terminal keyboards and disk storage. Also, to communicate its results to users, the computer "writes" data from main storage onto devices such as video display screens, printers, and disk storage.

I/O devices are controlled by special control units. A disk controller may control a number of disk drives, and a tape controller may control a number of tape drives. The CPU directs data from main storage via an I/O channel to a controller, which in turn directs it to an external device. Conversely, the CPU directs a controller to read data from an external device, which is then routed via a channel to main storage.

Main Storage

Main storage is the work area of a computer system. Think of it this way: If the books on the shelves in a library are like a computer's external disk storage, your notebooks and scratchpads are like a computer's main (or internal) storage. Main storage is also known as memory, primary storage, and internal storage. Micro-computer aficionados may recognize this component as RAM.

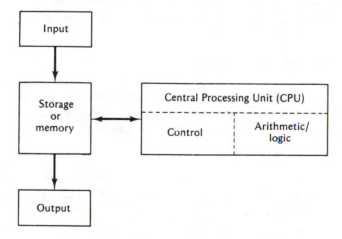

Figure 1-2   Basic computer components.

A computer program consists of instructions (such as read, add, and compare) and data (numbers used in calculations and areas used to develop answers and to accept input data). The program is usually stored on a disk device; whenever it is needed, a user enters a command to the computer system to read the program from disk into the computer's main storage, a process known as *loading a program*. The stored program now directs the computer to read input data, make calculations, and write output data.

A stored program is only temporarily in main storage; the current program erased the one that previously executed and will in turn be erased by the next program that is to execute.

The amount of available main storage is expressed in sizes such as 256K and 512K, where K = 1,024 bytes. Depending on the computer model, the storage varies considerably, up to sizes as large as 16,000K.

In a program, an instruction may require only a few bytes, whereas an area for data may require hundreds of bytes. Each byte has a specific address, numbered consecutively from location 0, the first one. Through this address the computer's central processing unit can locate stored instructions and data areas as required. Instructions in a stored program that are suitable for execution are called *machine language*.

Figure 1-3 illustrates a possible organization of a stored program in main storage. Assume that you have already written the program and have stored it on disk. You then enter special job control entries to request the computer's operating system to load that program from the disk into main storage. Let's say that the program calculates employees' wages. You then request your program to execute. The program—if written correctly—requests that you enter hours worked and rate of pay into a terminal keyboard. You reply by keying in the two values. The system directs the values to an input area, where the program calculates wage by multiplying hours times rate. The program then displays the calculated wage on the terminal video screen. You can even write the program to "loop back" to repeat its instructions requesting input so that you can process any number of employee wages.

The Central Processing Unit

The central processing unit (CPU) consists of an arithmetic/logic unit, a control unit, and a number of special-purpose and general-purpose registers. The arithmetic/logic unit performs addition, subtraction, multiplication, division, shifting,

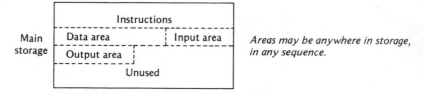

Figure 1-3 Map of program in main storage.

and moving data within main storage. Its logic capability enables you to code instructions that can compare one value in storage to another and permits the program to change the sequence of instruction execution; for example, a program can "loop back" to reexecute instructions.

The control unit directs and coordinates the system. It controls the arithmetic/logic unit, input/output units, the transfer of data into and out of main storage, and the location of instructions and data to be executed. Access time, which is the time required to transfer data, is measured in millionths of a second (microseconds) and even in billionths of a second (nanoseconds). The type and number of input/output devices, the type and complexity of arithmetic/logic circuitry, the size of storage, and the access time vary considerably by computer model.

The Registers

The 370-series computers support three sets of registers, all of which are contained in special circuitry.

1. The 16 general-purpose registers are numbered 0 through 15 and have two main purposes: performing binary arithmetic and addressing storage locations. Every reference that an instruction makes to main storage is by means of a base address in one of the registers and a displacement from that address. With some minor exceptions, you may use any of the 16 registers for either binary arithmetic or addressing. A reference in this text to the term *register* is always to a general-purpose register, except in Chapter 16 on floating-point operations.

2. The four floating-point registers are numbered 0, 2, 4, and 6 and provide for floating-point data and operations.

3. The 16 control registers are used by the operating system to control the operation of the computer and are not generally available to the programmer.

The Program Status Word

The program status word (PSW) is a 64-bit hardware feature in the control section of the CPU. The PSW contains the current status of the computer and controls the sequence of instructions being executed. One field, the 24-bit instruction address, contains the address of the next instruction to be executed.

One feature of the PSW that is important to a programmer is the 2-bit condition code that indicates the result of an arithmetic test (minus, zero, or plus) or a logical comparison (low, equal, or high). A program can test the result of arithmetic or a comparison in order to perform special action.

The condition code and the instruction address are in these bit positions of the PSW:

	condition code		instruction address
0———17	18–19	20———39	40———63

EXECUTION OF INSTRUCTIONS

The following illustrates an instruction, AR, that adds the contents of two registers. Let's say that AR is to add the contents of register 7 to that of register 9. The instruction in source language (what you code) would be AR 9,7. The machine code instruction (as translated by the assembler program) that the computer executes would be two bytes, or four hex digits: 1A 97.

On execution, the machine code is in main storage. The computer reads the instruction from storage and decodes it. The first byte is the operation (add registers) and the second byte for AR contains the two operands: the 9 is operand 1 and the 7 is operand 2. Suppose that registers 7 and 9 contain hex 0005 and hex 0013, respectively:

        register 7:   0005   register 9:   0013

The operation adds the contents of register 7 to register 9 and leaves the contents of register 7 unchanged:

        register 7:   0005   register 9:   0018

The operation tells the computer what function to perform. The operands specify which registers or storage locations the operation is to process. You need not concern yourself for now why the machine code for AR is hex 1A or how the machine code got into main storage.

A computer program consists of instructions and data areas, all kept temporarily in main storage during execution. As discussed earlier, a machine instruction consists of at least two parts: (1) the operation—the function that the computer is to perform, such as read, add, or move—and (2) one or more operands—the addresses of data areas, input/output units, or even other instructions.

The computer extracts an instruction from main storage and delivers it to the CPU for execution. For example, the instruction could be the add in the previous example: 1A 97. The CPU executes this instruction, and the computer then delivers to the CPU the instruction immediately following it in storage. Depending on the type of instruction, a machine instruction is always 2, 4, or 6 bytes, and includes such operations as read, move, add, compare, and write.

The computer sequentially extracts instructions until it encounters an instruction that specifies a *branch* operation. This operation directs execution to another instruction in the program that is not in the normal sequence, such as an instruction that branches back to the beginning of the program to reexecute a series of instructions. Another example of branching is execution of a compare instruction that uses the logic unit to check the sign of an arithmetic field. If the sign is plus, control is to continue with the next sequential instruction following the compare, and if it is minus, control is to branch to an instruction elsewhere in the program.

INPUT/OUTPUT DEVICES

This section briefly examines a number of the more important input/output devices.

Video Display Terminals

The common video display terminal shown in Fig. 1-4 typically contains a type-writerlike keyboard and an 80-column screen. Most installations provide terminals so that the programmers can enter their programs through the keyboard. Most installations also require that users "log on" to the terminal using a special password and "log off" when they have finished a session.

If your installation operates under a system such as IBM's Conversational Monitor System (CMS), you should be able to key in your assembler programs, test them, store them in a disk library, and recover them for further changes and tests. The system has an associated screen editor, XEDIT, that facilitates full-screen editing. You can develop a program on the terminal by entering each assembler statement one after another and can move the cursor freely about to change any statement on a line.

When you fill the screen (about 25 lines), some systems require that you enter a special command to continue on a fresh screen, whereas other systems automatically scroll up the lines so that the top lines appear to disappear off the top of the screen.

Presumably, your system provides for tab stops that you can set at convenient columns on the screen. Typical tab stops for an assembler program are:

10   16   41   72

You can also set tab stops to any other desirable locations.

Disk Storage Devices

The circular tracks of these flat, rotating disks can contain millions of bytes of data and are used for storing programs and storing data files, such as customer records.

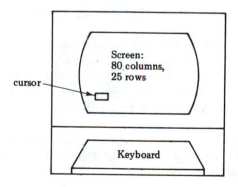

Figure 1-4 Video display terminal.

Computer installations store (or catalog) their assembler translator, operating system, and programs on disk for ready execution.

Magnetic Tape Drives

Magnetic tape, which is similar to that used in a home music system, can store millions of bytes of data on one reel. Tape is used for recording data files and storing backup files, kept for historical and security purposes.

Printers

Printers include those that use inked ribbons and those that use a laser. Printing speeds range from a few hundred to several thousand lines per minute. Typical printing capacity is 10 or more characters per inch and 80 to 160 characters per line.

The paper used for printing is called continuous forms. These forms often contain horizontal perforations every 11 inches to facilitate separating the sheets after printing. Manufacturers supply these forms in various sizes, usually 11 or 15 inches wide and 11 inches long. At 6 lines per inch, this length permits up to 60 lines of print per page.

DATA FORMATS

Although some instructions can access bits or half-bytes, a byte is considered the smallest data length. In an assembler program, you may represent data in bytes in character or arithmetic format.

Character Data

Character format is for descriptive information such as titles and names and is not intended for arithmetic processing. A character field requires one byte for each character. The 8 bits in a byte can represent 256 (2^8) possible characters, including the letters A through Z, the numbers 0 through 9, and special characters such as $, %, and #. For example, the on bits 1100 0001 represent the letter A, and 1111 0001 represents the number 1.

The character code on the 370 series is called the Extended Binary-Coded Decimal Interchange Code (EBCDIC) and is shown in detail in Appendix E. Another common character code on minicomputers and microcomputers is the American Standard Code for Information Interchange (ASCII). Although the two formats differ, programs can perform translation when passing data between different systems.

For example, a typical computer system represents character data as one character per byte. The following is the EBCDIC code for the characters A through Z and 0 through 9:

CHARACTER	BINARY	HEXADECIMAL
A–I	11000001–11001001	C1–C9
J–R	11010001–11011001	D1–D9
S–Z	11100001–11101001	E2–E9
0–9	11110001–11111001	F0–F9

A blank character appears in storage as hex 40. Thus an alphanumeric item defined in a program as JUNE 17 would appear in main storage as the following 7 bytes:

Character:	J	U	N	E	b	1	7
Hexadecimal:	D1	E4	D5	C5	40	F1	F7

Arithmetic Data

The assembler supports three types of arithmetic data: binary, decimal (packed), and floating-point.

1. *Binary Format.* For binary arithmetic, addressing, and special features, each bit represents a binary 0 or 1. For example, the binary value 0100 0111 (or X'47') equals the decimal value 71—check it.

2. *Decimal or Packed Format.* For ordinary decimal arithmetic, the digits 0 through 9 are "packed" two digits per byte. The sign (+ or −) requires a half-byte on the right. The common plus sign is binary 1100, or X'C'. For example, the packed value 125 would require 2 bytes as 12 5C.

   Note that to represent the value 1, character format requires a full byte (1111 0001), packed format requires a byte for the digit and sign (0001 1100), and binary format requires one bit (1).

3. *Floating-Point Format.* Floating point is used for representation and processing of extremely small or large values or values of which the magnitude is uncertain. The computer performs all floating-point operations in the four floating-point registers. Unlike binary or packed formats, the computer keeps track of the decimal point.

THE OPERATING SYSTEM

The 370-series computers come equipped with an operating system, which is a set of programs that the manufacturer supplies. The operating system is stored on disk and controls the various jobs that need to be run, such as execution of programs and handling communications with remote users. The two main IBM operating systems are DOS (Disk Operating System) for medium-sized installations and OS (Operating System) for large installations.

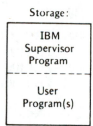

Figure 1-5   Supervisor program in main storage.

The heart of the operating system, the *supervisor*, is always loaded and resident in main storage whenever the system is up and running, as Fig. 1-5 illustrates. For example, if a program that is executing has trouble and "crashes," the supervisor takes control of the computer and terminates the program. The supervisor then arranges for the processing of next program.

Here are some of the functions of a typical supervisor:

- Determining priority for the programs waiting to be executed
- Handling the steps between jobs that are to be run
- Loading programs into main storage for execution
- Performing job accounting for the time taken by each program that executes
- Checking for requests from users at terminals

Programmers and operators notify the supervisor as to what job to perform by means of job control, which consists of commands to the operating system on disk or as entries keyed into a terminal. Typical job control commands request translating an assembler program, executing a program, and sorting records on disk. Appendix D describes job control commands in detail.

Program Interruption

The program status word contains bits that record the status of the currently running program. Among these conditions are bits to record program interrupts. An interrupt occurs when your program requests the operating system to perform a special task, such as input or output. Your program is interrupted, and control passes to the supervisor program. An interrupt also occurs when the computer encounters a serious error, such as an attempt to perform arithmetic on invalid data. The supervisor may have to flush the interrupted program and resume with the next job that is waiting to be run.

KEY POINTS

- The stored program is a set of instructions, temporarily stored in the computer's memory, that the computer executes. To perform a different function, you can replace the program with another one.

- Because of ongoing technological improvements in large-scale integration, it is generally conceded that the early 1970s ushered in the fourth generation of computers.

- Binary numbers constitute the basic numbering system of computers. A decimal (base 10) number has ten digits, 0 through 9, whereas a binary (base 2) number has only two digits, 0 and 1.

- A single storage location in the 370 series is known as a byte, which consists of 8 bits used to represent data. A bit (short for *binary digit*) can be either off (the value 0) or on (the value 1). Each of the 8 bits has a value of 0 or 1 and a number to represent its position.

- One or more adjacent bytes may represent a data item or field, and one or more adjacent related fields may constitute a record.

- The contents of a byte have no intrinsic meaning to a computer. Your program defines data as character, binary, packed, or floating-point and has to handle it accordingly.

- A hexadecimal numbering system uses base 16 for its representation. Hex numbers use 0 through 9 and A through F to represent the decimal values 0–15. One hex digit represents 4 bits in a byte, and two hex digits represent all 8 bits in a byte. Hexadecimal is only a representation of main storage, and at no time does the computer actually work in base 16.

- The main components of a computer are main storage (memory), the central processing unit (CPU), and input/output.

- Instructions in a stored program that are suitable for execution are called machine language.

- The central processing unit (CPU) consists of an arithmetic/logic unit, a control unit, and a number of special-purpose and general-purpose registers.

- The two main purposes of the 16 general-purpose registers (GPRs) are performing binary arithmetic and addressing storage locations.

- Every reference that an instruction makes to main storage is by means of a base address in one of the registers and a displacement from that address.

- The program status word (PSW) contains the current status of the computer and controls the sequence of instructions being executed.

- A machine instruction consists of the operation (the function that the computer is to perform, such as read, add, or move) and the operands (addresses of data areas, input/output units, or other instructions).

- You may represent data in bytes in character or arithmetic format. Character format is for descriptive information such as titles and names and is not intended for arithmetic processing. The three types of arithmetic data are binary, decimal or packed, and floating-point.

- The 370-series computers come equipped with an operating system, which controls the various jobs to be run. The two main IBM operating systems are DOS for medium-sized installations and OS for large installations. The heart of the operating system, the supervisor, is always loaded and resident in main storage.

PROBLEMS

1-1. What is the difference between a digital computer and an analog computer?

1-2. What is a stored program?

1-3. What are the advantages of computers (if any)?

1-4. Express the following binary numbers as decimal numbers: (a) 0111; (b) 1101; (c) 11001; (d) 101110.

1-5. Express the following decimal numbers as binary numbers: (a) 6; (b) 8; (c) 18; (d) 26.

1-6. Give the hexadecimal representation for the following decimal values: (a) 10; (b) 15; (c) 18; (d) 21; (e) 32; (f) 255; (g) 256.

1-7. Add the following hex numbers: (a) 9 + 2; (b) 8 + 7; (c) 9 +9; (d) 12 + 6; (e) 12 + 8; (f) 1B + 3; (g) 1C + 26.

1-8. Distinguish between a bit and a byte.

1-9. What is the purpose of the parity bit?

1-10. What are the three main components of a computer system?

1-11. How many bytes is (a) 64K; (b) 512K?

1-12. What are the main units of the CPU and their purpose?

1-13. What is machine language?

1-14. What is a branch instruction?

1-15. What are the two parts of a machine instruction?

1-16. Name five input devices and five output devices.

1-17. What are the three types of arithmetic data that the assembler supports?

1-18. Show the contents of a byte in both binary and hexadecimal formats for the value 5 as (a) character; (b) binary; (c) packed.

1-19. (a) Given the character format, provide the representation for hexadecimal and binary (for example, for ABC the hex is C1C2C3 and the binary is 1100 0001 1100 0010 1100 0011): (a) 370; (b) IBM; (c) Sam (note lowercase); (d) @#*.

1-20. Given the hexadecimal format, provide the representation for character and binary of (a) C2E4C7; (b) E2C1D4; (c) 5B406B; (d) 4E5060.

1-21. Given the binary format, provide the representation for character and hexadecimal of (a) 1101 0111 1100 0001 1110 0011; (b) 0100 0000 1111 1001 1111 0000; (c) 0100 1101 0100 0000 0101 1101.

1-22. What is an operating system? Describe the role of the supervisor.

2

PROGRAMMING REQUIREMENTS

OBJECTIVE

To present the basic requirements for designing, coding, and testing programs.

This chapter describes the use of records and files, the various levels of programming languages, and the basic steps involved in designing, coding, and testing programs.

As a professional computer programmer, you'll require knowledge and skills beyond just a program language, much of which is outside the scope of this book. Areas of knowledge and skills include:

- Familiarity with your company's business so that you can understand and even initiate program assignments
- Ability to apply the features of a programming language to an assignment so that it is likely to work correctly and be easily maintained
- Willingness to follow the standards and practices of your installation
- Familiarity with the hardware of the computer system, the operating system, and file organization methods

- Willingness to suspect flaws in the program's logic and to perform rigorous tests to identify them
- Awareness of new developments in your company's business and in computer technology

FIELDS, RECORDS, AND FILES

A *field* consists of one or more related bytes. Some fields, such as customer name, contain alphabetic (or character) data. Other fields, such as customer number or billing amount, contain numeric data. Fields may also contain *subfields:* A date field, for example, could contain subfields for month, day, and year.

A *record* consists of one or more related fields. A record may also contain unused positions, available for future expansion.

A *file* consists of a number of related records. A typical program defines the files to be accessed and the records and fields to be processed and uses instructions to read a record from external storage, to process the contents of its fields, and to write the revised record onto external storage.

Figure 2-1 shows an 80-byte record containing fields for a customer. There would be one record for each customer and any number of records in the file. This file could be kept on a disk or tape device and may be viewable on a terminal.

customer number	customer name	address-1	address-2	balance due	unused
1 − 5	6 − − − − − 27	28 − − − − − 49	50 − − − − − 71	72 − − 78	79 − − 80

Figure 2-1   Sample record.

LANGUAGES

The 370-series computers come equipped with a set of executable machine instructions similar in all models. Instructions include the ability to read input data, to move data in storage, to add and subtract the contents of storage locations, to compare, and to print or display output data.

Machine Language

The computer executes only instructions that are in main storage and are in *machine language*. You provide a special job control command to instruct the supervisor to enter or "load" the machine instructions from disk into main storage, where they become the stored program. Each storage location (byte) has a unique numeric address; the operands of the instructions reference the addresses of storage locations by their number. For example, Chapter 1 illustrated a machine instruction 1A 97 that adds the contents of register 7 to the contents of register 9.

Symbolic Language

Because of the complexity of machine language, programmers code in *symbolic languages*, which are special languages that the manufacturers design to facilitate program coding. Instead of coding machine instructions and actual storage locations, you use symbolic names. For example, you would code the machine language instruction 1A 97 in symbolic assembler language as AR 9,7. You then use the assembler translator program to translate the AR operation and the operands into a machine code instruction.

Assembler Language

Assembler is a low-level language in which each symbolic instruction translates directly into one machine instruction, on a one-for-one basis. (A compiler such as COBOL or PL/I may generate dozens of machine instructions for one symbolic statement.)

Assembler is directly related to a particular computer and its architecture. Consequently, a program written in IBM assembler language will not run on most other computers. But since there are many similarities among computer designs, there are many similarities among assembler versions.

Note that when you write a program in assembler language, you use the IBM assembler translator program to convert it to machine-executable code. The translators for high-level languages are known as compilers.

Macro Instructions

In assembler language, each symbolic instruction translates into a machine language instruction. But the assembler also has provision for *macro instructions*, which are specially written instructions that the assembler recognizes. Depending on its requirements, a macro instruction causes the assembler to generate one or more machine language instructions. IBM supplies special macros such as CALL, GET, and RETURN to facilitate supervisor and input/output operations.

In contrast to the low-level assembler language are high-level languages such as COBOL and PL/I, which you code entirely with macro instructions. Chapter 14 describes how you can write and execute your own macro instructions.

PROGRAMMING STEPS

Programming consists of much more than merely coding instructions for a computer to execute. There are usually five distinct phases: specification, design, coding, testing, and implementation.

In a small installation, the same person may handle a project through all of the phases, whereas in a large installation, an analyst may handle the specification and design phases and then pass the project on to the programmers for coding and testing.

The following explains the steps in programming, from coding through assembling and execution.

The Specification Phase

The first phase, specification, often requires that you interview people concerned with a programmable problem, determine their objectives, assess its economic feasibility, and determine how it may integrate with the present system. You then study the input data that the program is to process, identify the major processing and logic requirements, and determine the required output. When management approval is received, you may proceed to the design phase.

The Design Phase

The design phase may involve designing input and output record formats and display screens. If input data is on source documents, you may have to design an input record to contain the data. If other existing programs use the same input data or can make use of the output, the new program must be integrated with the present system. Also, you have to design output formats for printed reports or screen layouts, depicting each position that the program is to print or display.

A common format for showing the contents of records is the *data element list*. Figure 2-2 provides a typical data element list for customer records, divided into fields for customer number, name, address, and balance owing. The figure shows the position of each field in the employee record, the item name, the format (A for alphanumeric and N for numeric), and, for numeric format, the number of decimal places. (Alphanumeric format allows a mixture of alphabetic and numeric data.) Some data element lists show a COBOL-like picture in place of the format shown, such as X(5) to indicate five alphanumeric characters.

Data Element List Customer Record			
Positions	Item Name	Format	Decimals
01-05	Customer number	A	
06-27	Customer name	A	
28-49	Customer address-1	A	
50-71	Customer address-2	A	
72-78	Balance due	N	2

Figure 2-2   Data element list.

A print layout form typically consists of a grid of 80 to 132 columns and 65 lines on which you enter all the headings, detail lines, total lines, and other information that the program is to produce. Specify every item in the exact position

customer number	customer name	address-1	address-2	balance due
xxxx	x − − − − x	x − − − − − − x	x − − − − − − x	xx,xxx.xx
7 − 11	15 − − 36	41 − − − − 62	67 − − − − 88	93 − − 101

Figure 2-3 Sample output layout.

that the program is to reference, and, for readability, arrange the information properly centered and spaced.

To print or display the contents of this customer record, you normally design a print layout. Figure 2-3 provides a typical print layout form showing an arrangement for printing information based on the data element list in Fig. 2-2. As Fig. 2-3 shows, the output fields are spaced apart for readability. Note that the balance due field in the print layout is two characters longer to allow for a comma and decimal point.

The next step in the design phase involves determining the detailed logic required by the program and all of its processing steps. Various support tools such as pseudocode and hierarchy charts are available for this purpose and are described in detail later in this chapter.

The Coding Phase

Based on your definition of the problem and the required output, code your source program in symbolic language. The *source program* consists of assembler instructions and data areas.

Watch carefully for coding characters that are similar. Although there is no universal standard, you could use the following to distinguish among certain easily confused characters:

- Code the digit zero as 0, and the letter O with a slash (some use the opposite convention).
- Code the digit 1 and letter I clearly.
- Code the letter Z with a bar to distinguish it from the digit 2.
- Code carefully to avoid confusion between the digit 5 and letter S, between the left parenthesis and the letter C, and between the letters U and V.

Having coded and checked the source program, you next key in the statements for storage on disk. Modern computer systems provide visual display terminals and text editing programs to facilitate keying in source programs and data.

You also have to provide special job commands that instruct the system to assemble and link the assembly source program and to execute any test data. The job commands are inserted before and after the source program and before and after the test data. Appendix D covers job control language in some detail, although you should note that it varies considerably from one system to another.

The Testing Phase

To test a source program, you first have to request, through job control commands, that the system assemble it into an *object program* and link-edit it into an *executable module*:

$$\text{Source program} \longrightarrow \text{object program} \longrightarrow \text{executable module}$$

The supervisor loads the assembler translator program from disk into storage. The assembler reads your source program and checks for spelling mistakes and violation of the language rules. You have to correct any assembly errors and reassemble the source program. The assembler creates an object program on disk.

The next step is to request, through job control commands, that the supervisor link-edit the object program. For this purpose, the supervisor loads the *linkage editor* program from disk into main storage. The linker reads the object program and, among other tasks, includes any required input/output modules that are already cataloged on disk. The linker creates an executable module, which may be executed any number of times.

For testing the program, arrange suitable input data that tests the program logic thoroughly. The test data may be in the form of records, in the exact format that the program expects. Note that the assembler cannot recognize errors in your program logic—these errors you must locate through testing and debugging.

Early attempts to test a program are almost certain to have bugs in job control, in the source program statements, or in the data. This text provides considerable aid in debugging, especially in Chapter 15.

A common practice for a large program is to test it as the coding is developed. That is, you write the main logic first, test and debug it, and then add to it various routines that you test in turn.

The Implementation Phase

Implementation occurs when the programs have been fully tested, if such a state is possible. The system developers (one programmer or a team of analysts and programmers) at this point provide the users with any necessary procedures. The developers then install the completed programs along with required job control and follow their progress through the first live production.

Documentation

Documentation is an activity that occurs throughout all phases and involves establishing a permanent record of relevant information, all properly dated. The documentation enables you or other programmers subsequently to make changes to the program. The documentation file contains the following items:

- The initial request for the program
- All requests for subsequent modifications
- Any pseudocode or other logic chart used for its development, along with any descriptions of complex computations and logic
- Any layouts for records, printer, and screen
- A current listing of the assembled program

STRUCTURED PROGRAMMING

Structured programming originated as a response to the need for more readable programs. In established computer installations, 60 to 80 percent of programming effort has been devoted to correcting and revising existing programs. In many cases, programs are found to be virtually incomprehensible, with peculiar names and little apparent organization. To remedy this situation, a systematic approach to programming was required, and what developed was structured programming.

Structured programming is a style that clarifies a program's form (the relationship of its parts) as much as possible by limiting control logic to just three basic control structures—sequence, selection, and repetition—that can perform any function. According to the structure theorem, you can write any *proper program* using only these three control structures. A proper program conforms to the following two requirements:

1. It has only one entry point and one exit point.
2. Execution leads from the entry point through every part of the program to the exit. Thus there are no endless loops or sections that the program can never execute.

"Program" in this context means a complete program or any portion of a program that can be viewed as a complete routine that the program calls. An example is a payroll program that consists of routines for pension, income tax, and so forth, each of which may be viewed as a proper program.

Assembler language lends itself well to only some of the structured programming requirements, which are better facilitated by high-level languages.

The three basic control structures are described next.

1. *Simple Sequence of Functions.* One operation directly follows another, with no tests to change the sequence. Unless coded otherwise, a computer executes statements in the order in which they appear.

A simple example is "move data to the print area" and "display the contents of a line." In the following diagram, process A and process B may be single executable statements or complete routines, and both processes must be proper programs as described earlier.

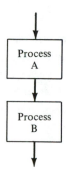

Because process **A** and process B have only one entry and exit point, their combination could also be viewed as a proper program, as the following diagram shows:

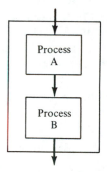

2. *Selection.*   Based on a condition, the program executes one of two actions and returns.   This is known as a IF-THEN-ELSE structure.   Assembler expresses this logic by means of compare and branch.

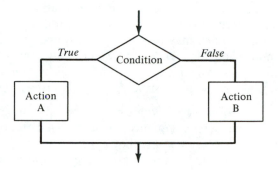

Note that actions A and B in the diagram have one entry and one exit.   Either action could be "null"—that is, if the condition is true, do action A; otherwise, do nothing.   For example, if a customer's balance due is greater than the credit limit (true), display a warning message. The false condition, where the balance is not greater than the credit limit, is not important to this test.

3. *Repetition.* The program executes an operation or a series of operations a number of times. The diagram on the left is a known as a DOWHILE: Continue processing and looping while a certain condition is true. DOWHILE tests at its start, and if the condition is already false, the controlled code (process A) does not execute at all.

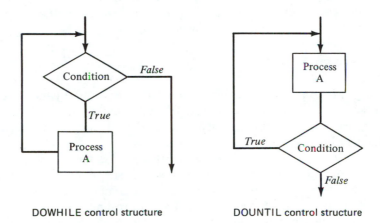

DOWHILE control structure   DOUNTIL control structure

The variation on the right is known as DOUNTIL, which continues processing and looping until a certain condition is true. Since DOUNTIL first executes the controlled code (process A) before testing, it will always execute at least once, whether the condition is true or false.

A proper program, then, always consists of a simple sequence and may contain selection and repetition according to the requirements for solving a problem.

Elimination of GO TO Statements

The GO TO statement in high-level languages is said to be the greatest cause of program complexity because it encourages forward and backward jumps between routines. Structured programming has been called "GO TO–less" programming, although the elimination of GO TOs is more a result of proper programming than a goal. Basically, the flow of execution should be forward, step by step, in such a way that the mind can grasp and follow what the program is supposed to accomplish.

The assembler's unconditional branch (B) instruction is equivalent to the GO TO statement of high-level languages. Although there are some artificial ways to avoid the use of the branch statement, in general, it is an integral part of assembler coding, and the examples in this text do not attempt to eliminate it. However, assembler programming can readily adapt itself to the other features of structured programming.

Organization into Logical Routines

Larger programs should consist of a section of main logic and various subsidiary routines of related logic. The routines, such as to calculate income tax or net pay, are localized so that each one performs only operations that are relevant to that routine. The main logic calls the subsidiary routines as required, and the subsidiary routines can call other routines at a lower level.

Each routine has one entry point (at the top) and one exit (at the end), as described earlier. Each routine is restricted to about 60 lines that may appear on a printed page, or fewer on a display terminal.

Top-Down Approach

Large programs are generally complex and are often organized, coded, and tested as separate routines. The program is designed around a main logic routine with various subsidiary routines at lower levels. A typical organization is illustrated later in Fig. 2-5.

The main logic, the highest level, provides the skeleton (or scaffold) of the program and should be coded and tested first. Even if there is little output, the test helps to validate the overall logic. As you develop routines of the next lower levels, you attach them to the main logic for testing. Since the main logic is known to work, you can readily locate any error in a subsidiary routine. Routines of lower levels are added and tested until a working program is complete.

A common practice is to code lower-level routines as program stubs that consist of only a few statements. For example, an income tax routine for a payroll project has not yet been developed, so the routine arbitrarily calculates 10 percent of income. There are two advantages to this approach. First, the analysts and system users can verify earlier that the output is what is required and appears to be correct to that point. Second, the approach facilitates locating and correcting bugs as the project is developed, whereas the alternative is to debug the entire project at the end, in a state of panic.

Coupling and Cohesion

A structured program is divided into logical modules (or routines), and you may measure the success of this division by the terms *coupling* and *cohesion*.

Coupling refers to the relationship between modules. The objective is to achieve low coupling, in which modules are (relatively) unrelated and independent. Thus a change to one module has little or no effect on other modules. Also, low coupling means that you can more likely read and understand any given module without having to examine other modules. For example, a highly coupled program could have several modules involved with handling customer discounts.

Cohesion refers to the consistency within a module. The objective is to achieve high cohesion, in which all statements in a module are dedicated to only one purpose. For example, all the statements within a particular module are concerned only with handling customer discounts. All the programs in this text (other than a few trivial examples that have no subroutines) apply the concept of cohesion.

A program in which modules consist of low coupling and high cohesion is easier to understand, debug, and maintain.

Self-documenting Code

You can improve the readability of a program by the use of descriptive names. As names of data items, A, B, X, AMTA, and SWITCH1 are legal in an assembler program but would be meaningless to a programmer trying to revise the program. A program is more self-documenting if the names of data items, such as NETPAY, DISCOUNT, and TOTSALES, describe their purpose.

Structured Walkthroughs

A structured walkthrough involves an evaluation of a project or program or even a program module. The walkthrough may occur at any stage in a program's development and is attended by all those involved. Its purpose is to locate errors in interpretation of the problem or implementation of the solution.

The emphasis of a walkthrough should be on evaluating the program (not the programmer) and on detecting errors (and not on criticizing or providing corrections).

PROGRAMMING OBJECTIVES

The objectives of a computer program are accuracy, relevance, efficiency, robustness, and maintainability. Accuracy and efficiency result from a thorough working knowledge of the computer and its language and from painstaking care in coding and testing. Maintainability results from a programming attitude involving clarity, organization, coding techniques, and flexibility.

Accuracy

First, a program should produce correct results, because an inaccurate program is useless.

Relevance

A program should produce the information that is required and in the manner that the recipient wants. Thus a program not only should be accurate but also should produce the desired results.

Efficiency

Subject to the time allowed to get it working accurately, a program should be reasonably efficient. A skillful programmer can code a problem that uses less storage and execution time while spending little (if any) additional coding time.

Robustness

A robust program can recover from unexpected and incorrect input. In effect, a user at a keyboard can accidentally (or otherwise) press any sequence of keys. If the input is improper, the program either ignores it or displays a message. A weak program is likely to collapse when a user enters unexpected input.

Maintainability

Programs are revised continually to meet new conditions and reflect new technology. As a result, write a program with the awareness that it will eventually have to be rewritten.

Clarity. To improve a program's clarity, use comments wherever necessary to explain what a routine is supposed to accomplish, especially calculations and logic. Use meaningful descriptive names for data items, and adopt standards regarding the names of data items, documentation, and programming style. Keep in mind that a simple solution is usually the best one.

Later chapters introduce other features that enhance program clarity, including labeling conventions (the names of routines) and the assignment of registers for specific purposes.

Organization. As discussed earlier, organize a program into logical routines with related operations together. Limit routines to about one page (60 lines or so), and arrange them in a logical sequence with the more commonly performed routines first and less commonly performed routines last.

Coding techniques. Whereas organization is concerned with an approach to programming, coding techniques involve the use of instructions. The more elegant programs are simple and clear and avoid the use of complicated, tricky routines to solve relatively simple problems.

Flexibility and expandability. Write a program knowing that requirements change over time. For example, field sizes may have to be enlarged because of increases in the volume of business and price levels. Define the length of data items to provide for larger values in the future. In general, main storage is cheaper than programmer time, and defining a few extra positions for larger field lengths is low-cost insurance against program revisions.

PROGRAM DEVELOPMENT

The following questions often occur at the outset of a new program:

1. **What is the required output?** Since you must know what output is required, designing report formats and screen displays is one of the first steps in programming.
2. **What is the required input?** The input data may already be available as a file in the system, or it may require that an operator enter the data from a new source.
3. Given the required input, what processing must the program perform to achieve the required output? This step involves solving how to translate the available input data into output information:

The input, processing, and output stages are the essence of a computer program. Among the various techniques for tracing the logic of a program are pseudocode, flowcharts, IPO charts, and hierarchy charts, all of which have their function and their adherents. These development tools have numerous advantages:

- You need only knowledge of basic computer operations rather than a knowledge of a programming language.
- A noncomputer person such as the user of the application can examine the design to ensure that it will do the job it is supposed to do.
- The tools help define and clarify the problem being programmed. Being more general and less technical than the coding, they facilitate defining and simplifying the logic of the problem.
- They act as useful documentation when a program has to be reviewed or modified.

All narrative within the development tools should be simple, clear, and free of technical terminology—in effect, suitable to any programming language and readable by anyone. Commonly accepted notations include these:

+	Add	=	Equal
−	Subtract	≠	Not equal
× *or* *	Multiply	<	Less than
/	Divide	>	Greater than
**	Exponentiation	:	Compare
EOF	End of file	EOJ	End of job

The next sections explain logic by means of the traditional flowchart, the structured flowchart, and pseudocode.

Flowcharts

A flowchart consists of standard symbols that trace the logic of a solution to a programming problem. These symbols provide for all possible computer operations: read input, make logical decisions, perform arithmetic, move data, and write results.

As a rule, the flow of logic through the symbols is vertically downward or horizontally to the right. Other than the terminal symbol that denotes the start and end of processing, every symbol has a line that provides an entry into the symbol and a line that provides an exit out of the symbol. Neither a flowchart nor a program may have dead ends.

Structured Flowcharts

Structured flowcharts were designed to represent structured programming style. They consist of three symbols that relate directly to the three control structures of structured programming discussed earlier in this chapter, sequence, selection, and repetition, respectively:

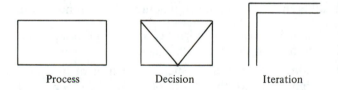

Process   Decision   Iteration

The process symbol represents the regular inline execution steps, such as input/ output, transfer of data, and arithmetic. The decision symbol provides for alternative action that results from tests and is equivalent to the IF-ELSE selection structure. The iteration symbol provides for looping and repetitive operations and is equivalent to the DOWHILE repetition structure. The left portion of the symbol provides for the path that the repetition is to follow until the tested condition is satisfied.

When combined, these symbols represent all the operations of a program in both high-level and low-level diagrams. You design (and read) structured flowcharts from top to bottom and from left to right.

Pseudocode

Pseudocode is a shortcut for sketching an initial program or part of a program. Although there are few conventional rules, a common practice is to indent all code that is subject to a condition, such as the result of a decision or instructions that are executed repetitively.

Sample Flowcharts

As a simple example, consider a program that has to read a file of inventory records and produce a report of stock value (quantity times unit cost). The program reads a record (from any type of input device), calculates the value, moves the data to an output area and displays the output information. The program repeats the routine to process the new input record and continues in this manner until it has exhausted all the input data. The pseudocode for this example follows:

```
Begin program:
    Read first stock record.
    Do repetitively while there is still input data:
        Calculate stock value = quantity x unit cost.
        Display results.
        Read next stock record.
    End Do.
End program.
```

The traditional flowchart in Fig. 2-4 for the same program shows a beginning point, BEGIN, to indicate the start of execution, and a termination point, EOJ, to indicate "end of job" or end of execution. The structured flowchart also in Fig. 2-4 requires only process and iteration symbols.

The program logic shows two read operations: An initial read is executed only once at the start, whereas the second read is executed repetitively until all input data has been read. A special end-of-file test actually follows each read operation in a program. The methods of signaling the end of input data vary according to the type of input device.

Except for terminal input, an operating system automatically tests for the end-of-file record and directly links to a designated end-of-file address in your program.

As the flowchart shows, the end-of-file test occurs immediately after a read operation. Consequently, the read operation has two symbols: The first symbol represents the transfer of data (if any) from the input device into main storage, and the second symbol represents the automatic logic test for end-of-file. An EOF test immediately follows the initial read operation in case there is no input data. Following is a loop that calculates, prints, and reads. After the second read is another EOF decision symbol: If not end-of-file, loop back to process the new input record; if end-of-file, terminate execution.

Hierarchy Charts

When a program consists of a variety of subroutines, it is often useful to design a hierarchy chart (or structure chart) to indicate the dependency of subroutines. Figure 2-5 shows a hierarchy chart for a payroll program that is organized into independent subroutines, following the rules of coupling and cohesion. Note its

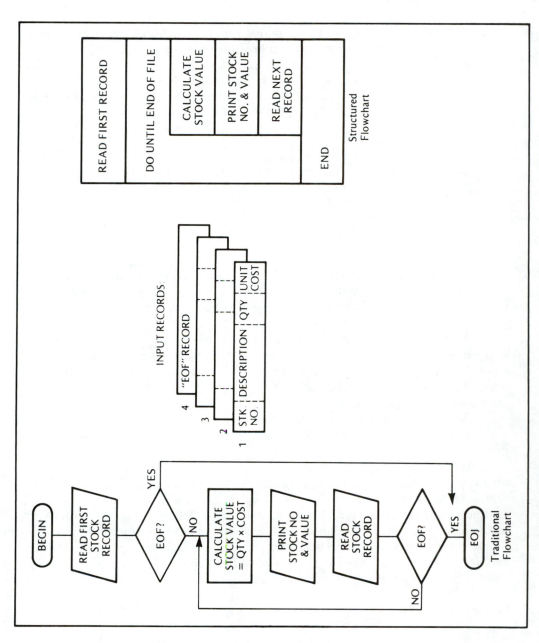

Figure 2-4 Flowcharts to read, process, and write. (Peter Abel, COBOL PRO-GRAMMING: A Structured Approach, 3/E, ©1989, p. 23. Reprinted by permission of Prentice-Hall, Inc., Englewood Cliffs, NJ.)

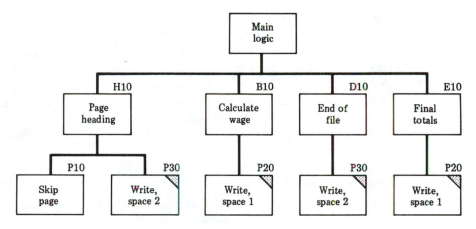

Figure 2-5 Hierarchy chart.

similarity to an organization chart.   Each box represents a logical unit of related code and contains a description of its purpose.

The top box indicates the program's main logic, which directly calls the subroutines in the line below: page heading, wage calculation, end-of-file, and final totals.   Each of these subroutines also calls one or more subroutines indicated in boxes in the line below.   According to the chart, the main logic does not link directly to the bottom level.

Hierarchy charts vary by personal preference but are a useful planning tool in program design.

KEY POINTS

- A field consists of one or more related bytes, a record consists of one or more related fields, and a file consists of a number of related records.   Fields may also contain subfields: A date field, for example, could contain subfields for month, day, and year.   Some fields contain alphabetic (or character) data, whereas other fields contain numeric data.

- A typical program defines the files to be accessed and the records and fields to be processed and uses instructions to read a record from external storage, to process the contents of its fields, and to write the revised record onto external storage.

- The five distinct phases involved in designing, coding, and testing programs are specification, design, coding the instructions, testing, and implementation.

- When a program consists of a variety of routines, it is often useful to design a hierarchy chart (or structure chart) to indicate the dependency of routines.

- Structured programming is a style that clarifies a program's form (the relationship of its parts) by limiting control logic to just three basic control structures—sequence, selection, and repetition—that can perform any function.

- A structured walkthrough, which involves an evaluation of a project or program, may occur at any stage in a program's development.
- Coupling refers to the relationship between modules. The objective is low coupling, in which modules are unrelated and independent. A change to one module has little or no effect on other modules, and you can more likely read and understand any given module without having to examine other modules. Cohesion refers to consistency within a module. The objective is high cohesion, in which all statements in a module are dedicated to only one purpose.
- The objectives of a computer program are accuracy, relevance, efficiency, robustness, and maintainability.
- Input, processing, and output are the essence of a computer program and are often solved in general terms before coding by such development tools as flowcharts, hierarchy charts, and pseudocode.
- The levels of program languages include low-level machine language that a computer executes and high-level symbolic languages that a programmer codes that must be translated into machine language for execution.
- Every computer comes equipped with a set of executable machine instructions that vary by manufacturer and model.
- The assembler treats your source program like input data and translates it into object code. The linkage editor translates an object program into an executable module, which may be executed any number of times.

PROBLEMS

2-1. Define the following: (a) field; (b) record; (c) file.

2-2. Explain (a) machine language instruction; (b) symbolic instruction; (c) macro instruction.

2-3. Identify three activities in the specification phase when developing a program.

2-4. What is a data element list?

2-5. Explain each term: (a) source program; (b) object program; (c) executable module.

2-6. What is the role of the linkage editor?

2-7. Identify and describe the three basic control structures involved in structured programming.

2-8. Distinguish between coupling and cohesion.

2-9. Explain the purpose and advantages of a structured walkthrough.

2-10. What are the primary objectives of a computer program?

PART II

Basic Assembler Features

3

ASSEMBLER GROUND RULES

OBJECTIVE

To cover the basic statements necessary for assembler programs, requirements of the coding form, and the assembly process.

This chapter covers the assembler translator program and the requirements for coding and assembling a source program in assembler language.

Assembler language, with which this text deals, is the fundamental language for the 370 series and is reasonably standardized for all models. There are several assembler versions at the time of this writing:

DOS/360 D	Standard DOS version
OS/360 F	Standard OS version
DOS/VSE	DOS version for VS users
OS/VS-VM/370	OS version for VS/VM users

Although you code programs in symbolic assembler language, the computer cannot execute such instructions. You require the assembler translator program to assemble, or translate, the symbolic language of the source program into the machine language of the object program.

To make computer programs more comprehensible and more easily maintained, this text advocates standard coding practices, such as naming conventions for fields and for files.

TYPES OF ASSEMBLER STATEMENTS

An assembler source program consists of four types of statements: comments, directives, declaratives, and instructions.

1. A *comment* is any descriptive information that you code as documentation to make your program clearer. The assembler includes comments on the assembled listing but deletes them from the object program.
2. A *directive* is a special command such as TITLE, START, or END that notifies the assembler to take special action during the assembly process. Directives generate no object code.
3. A *declarative* is a command identified by DS and DC that defines data items in the program. Technically, a declarative is a special type of directive that reserves an area of storage or defines an initial constant value for a data item.
4. An *instruction* is a statement such as MVC (move), AP (add), and CP (compare) that the assembler converts into object code.

The assembler ignores comments, acts on directives, and converts declaratives and instructions into object code. An assembler program typically consists of executable instructions and declaratives coded in separate sections. The declaratives contain the various constants, workareas, and input/output areas that the instructions process.

PREDEFINED CODING FORMAT

Figure 3-1 depicts a format for coding assembler source programs. The convention, as shown, is to begin names in position 1, instructions and directives in position 10, and operands in position 16.

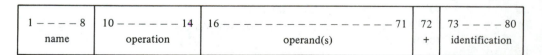

1 – – – 8	10 – – – – – 14	16 – – – – – – – – – – – – – – 71	72	73 – – – 80
name	operation	operand(s)	+	identification

Figure 3-1 Coding format.

Positions 1-8: Name. You assign a name to each declarative and a label to each instruction that you intend to reference in your program. The rules governing names and labels are as follows:

- The name must be unique in the program, defined only once.
- The name may be 1 to 8 characters long. The first character must be a letter A through Z (and $, #, or @, although these special characters are not recommended). Remaining characters in the name may be letters or digits, such as PROG25. A name may not contain blank characters.

Following is a declarative named FIELD that reserves 5 bytes of storage:

name	operation	operand
FIELD	DS	CL5

If column 1 is blank, the assembler assumes that the instruction or declarative has no name, and if column 1 contains an asterisk (*), the assembler assumes that the entire line is a comment.

Positions 10-14: Operation. The operation is the only required entry and provides the symbolic operation code for an instruction, declarative, directive, or macro, which the assembler must be able to recognize. Examples include MVC, DC, and EJECT. There must be at least one blank position between Operation and the next field, Operand.

The following sample statement tells the assembler to space three lines on the listing of the assembled program.

name	operation	operand
	SPACE	3

Positions 16-71: Operand. The operand identifies data on which the operation is to act. Depending on the operation, there may be none, one, or more operands. A comma separates each operand, with no blank spaces (except within quotes) either within operands or between them; the assembler assumes that a blank ends the operands. In the following instruction, the name is A20ADD, the

operation is AP (add), and the operand is ACCUM,FIVE. The instruction means add FIVE to ACCUM, and both ACCUM and FIVE would be defined as declaratives:

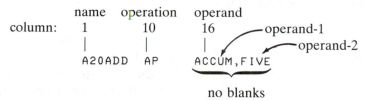

```
          name   operation   operand
column:    1        10         16        ┌─operand-1
           |         |          |      ╱ ┌─operand-2
         A20ADD     AP        ACCUM,FIVE
```

no blanks

Any characters following the operands are treated as a comment.

Position 72: Continuation. Operands and comments may not continue past column 71. If an operand requires more positions, code any nonblank character in column 72. This text uses a plus (+) sign; others may use X or C. Continue coding the statement on the next line beginning in column 16. Depending on the version, the assembler permits one or more continuations. When you do use a continuation character, be especially careful on a terminal system to code it in column 72.

Positions 73–80: Identification Sequence. You can use this optional field to identify your program with a name and a sequence number in ascending sequence. On terminal systems such as IBM's CMS, the editor can automatically assign and reassign sequence numbers, thus making the sequence field somewhat redundant.

The assembler accepts coding that is "free-form"—that is, you do not have to begin operation and operand in the defined positions. However, there is usually little need to vary from the defined positions, and there is a need for standardized, legible programs.

COMMENTS

The use of comments in a program can often help clarify the purpose of the instructions and is especially useful in assembler programs, which are not by nature self-documenting.

An asterisk in column 1 means that the entire line is a comment, as in the following example:

```
column 1:
   |
   *    This routine validates input data
```

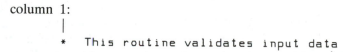

You may also code a comment on a line following an instruction, with at least one blank between the operand and the comment. For readability and to facilitate data entry, the programs in this text align comments beginning in column 41. The next example illustrates a comment following a multiply instruction:

```
column:  10      16              41   comments
          |       |               |
         MP      VALUE,RATE      Calculate bond interest
```

When translating symbolic instructions to machine code, the assembler ignores your comments. As a result, you may include as many comments as you want, with no effect on the size of the assembled object program.

CONTROL SECTIONS

Every assembler program consists of one or more control sections, or CSECTs. Small programs, like those in this text, almost always consist of one control section. The first (or only) control section begins with the directive START or CSECT and terminates with the directive END, as follows:

```
column: 1        10              16
        name     operation       operand
         |        |               |
        progname START           [location counter value]
                  . . .
        [instructions -- executable code]
                  . . .
        [declaratives -- defined constants and workareas]
                  . . .
                 END             progname
```

In this case, both START and END are directives that begin in column 10. Column 1 of START also includes the name of the program, which may be any unique name up to 8 characters long beginning with a letter A through Z. A later section provides more details of name conventions.

START tells the assembler that this point is the beginning of a control section, and END tells the assembler that this point is the end of the control section. For a program with one control section, START and END also indicate the beginning and end of the assembly. The convention is to code the program name in the END operand to inform the system where the program is to begin execution.

The operand may contain an optional starting value (decimal or hex). The usual practice is to code 0 or omit it.

An assembler source program consists of executable instructions and declaratives for the defined input/output devices and constants. Carefully separate the declaratives from the executable instructions so that there is no chance of program execution running inadvertently into the declaratives.

In the formats for statements throughout this text, a name or operand between brackets is optional and may be either coded or omitted.

DIRECTIVES

The assembler translates instructions such as AP (Add) or MVC (Move) into machine language executable code.   But the assembler recognizes directives such as START, TITLE, and END as requests to perform certain operations only during the assembly and generates no machine code.   Included next are some of the more common directives.

The TITLE Directive

The purpose of the TITLE directive is to identify an assembly listing.   This is its general format:

Name [name]	Operation TITLE	Operand 1-100 characters, between apostrophes

The name field is optional.   The operand field contains any descriptive title that you want printed at the top of each page of the assembled listing, such as the following:

```
column:10        16
        |         |
               TITLE   'VALIDATION PROGRAM'
```

You enclose the title in apostrophes to denote its start and end.   The maximum length is 100 characters.   If the title exceeds 56 characters, you have to continue it on the next line: Code a continuation character (any nonblank character) in column 72 and continue the title on the next line in column 16.

When used in a directive, the apostrophe (') and the ampersand (&) have special meaning to the assembler.   If you need to use them in your title, code them as two adjacent apostrophes (' ') or ampersands (&&).   The assembler stores and prints only one.   The following example contains both apostrophes and ampersands:

```
TITLE   'JEAN && SAM''S PROGRAM'
```

The START Directive

The START directive designates the beginning of a control section, although technically you may code TITLE, EJECT, and SPACE directives before START.

Here is its general format:

Name	Operation	Operand
progname	START	blank or numeric value

The name field contains the name of the program and must match the entry in the operand of the END directive. Some systems load programs from disk into storage for execution beginning at fixed, predictable locations; however, most systems load programs into one of a number of locations, depending on where there is sufficient space; check the requirements for your own system.

	NAME	OPERATION	OPERAND
Fixed starting address:	progname	START	numeric value
Unknown starting address:	progname	START	0 or blank

The EJECT Directive

After printing a full page of a program listing, the assembler automatically ejects to the top of the next page. However, you may want to eject a page before it is full, for example, to start printing a new major routine or a section of declaratives. To cause the assembler to eject the forms to a new page of the program listing, code EJECT in the Operation column:

Name	Operation	Operand
[blank]	EJECT	[blank]

The SPACE Directive

The SPACE directive tells the assembler to space one or more blank lines on the program listing. Code the number of lines to be spaced (up to three) in the operand field. If you leave the operand blank, the assembler assumes a space of one line.

Name	Operation	Operand	Comment
[blank]	SPACE		Space 1 line
[blank]	SPACE	1	Space 1 line
[blank]	SPACE	2	Space 2 lines
[blank]	SPACE	3	Space 3 lines

The assembler acts on EJECT and SPACE but does not print them. It does, however, increment the statement (STMT) number on the listing.

The PRINT Directive

The PRINT directive controls the general format of a program listing, and contains any or all of the following three operands, in any sequence. Here is the general format:

```
NAME     OPERATION   OPERAND
                     ( ON,  )  ( GEN,   )( DATA   )
          PRINT      {      }  {        }{        }
                     ( OFF, )  ( NOGEN, )( NODATA )
```

ON	Print the program listing from this point on.
OFF	Do not print the listing.
GEN	Print all statements that macros generate.
NOGEN	Suppress statements that macros generate. For example, OPEN is a macro; since its generated code is seldom of interest, you normally suppress its listing.
DATA	Print the full hexadecimal contents of constants (on the left side of the assembly listing, under OBJECT CODE).
NODATA	Print only the leftmost 8 bytes (or 16 hex digits) of constants. Since the full printed hex contents of constants are of little interest, a common practice is to code NODATA.

A common requirement is

```
PRINT ON,NOGEN,NODATA
```

The END Directive

The END directive must be the last statement of an assembler control section.

Name	Operation	Operand
[blank]	END	[progname]

You normally code the operand with a symbolic address, such as END PROG25. The operand PROG25 in this case designates an address in the program where execution is to begin and is therefore normally the program's first executable instruction.

Remember that these directives simply tell the assembler how to handle your source program and generate no machine code. This section provides the most commonly required information. Later chapters cover other directives such as EQU, LTORG, and USING. All the assembler directives are summarized in Appendix H.

DECLARATIVES

A declarative is a nonexecutable statement that defines constants, accumulators, and input/output areas. The two types of declaratives are DS and DC:

Name	Operation	Operand
[name]	DS	operand denoting type and length
[name]	DC	operand denoting type, length, and constant

For both DS and DC, the name entry is optional but must contain a name if your program references the field. An operand such as CL5 means a character (C) field 5 bytes long (L5).

DS: Define Storage

A DS declarative defines an area of storage within a program, such as an input/output area. The following declarative defines a field named RECDIN, character (C) format, and a length (L) of 80 bytes:

```
RECDIN   DS   CL80
```

When a program first executes, the contents of a DS are unpredictable and could contain "garbage." (Actually, a DS contains the contents of the last program that happened to occupy the same storage locations.) It is up to you to move data into the area as required in the program. For example, your program could read data into this area using the macro instruction

```
GET   FILEIN,RECDIN
```

The GET macro reads a record from a file named FILEIN into the input area RECDIN in main storage and erases any previous contents.

DC: Define Constant

A DC declarative defines an area containing an initial constant. For example, the declarative

```
HEADING   DC   C'PHASAR ELECTRONICS'
```

defines a field named HEADING containing a character constant used for a report heading. In this example, a program would not normally change the contents of HEADING during its execution. But a program would change other constants, such as an accumulator initialized to zero and used to count the number of lines displayed on a screen.

For any declarative, the name (if any) references the leftmost byte of the field that it defines, and all names in a program must be unique. However, a name is optional, and in situations where a program never references a field, you may omit the name.

All the assembler declaratives are summarized in Appendix G.

SAMPLE PROGRAM

The simple program in Fig. 3-2 skips to the top of a new page and prints two headings—that's all! The following explains the program statements:

- Statements beginning with an asterisk in column 1 are all comments and have no effect on the final executable program.
- Beginning in column 41 are various comments that explain the action of the executable instructions.
- The TITLE directive provides a description for the program.
- The PRINT directive specifies a printed listing (ON), only the leftmost 16 hex digits of object code (NODATA), and no generated macro statements (NOGEN).
- The SPACE directive causes the assembler to space one line when listing the source program.
- The START directive provides the starting point for program execution.
- The INIT macro in this example generates some initializing instructions required at the start of every assembler program.
- The OPEN macro makes the printer available to the program during execution.
- The first PUTPR macro skips to the top of a new page.
- The second PUTPR macro prints the first heading line.
- The third PUTPR macro prints the second heading line.

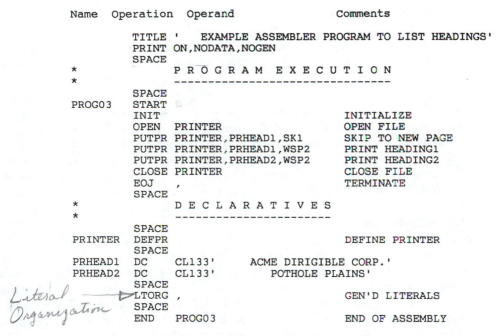

```
Name   Operation  Operand                    Comments
              TITLE  '   EXAMPLE ASSEMBLER PROGRAM TO LIST HEADINGS'
              PRINT  ON,NODATA,NOGEN
              SPACE
*                    P R O G R A M   E X E C U T I O N
*                    --------------------------------
              SPACE
PROG03        START
              INIT                            INITIALIZE
              OPEN   PRINTER                  OPEN FILE
              PUTPR  PRINTER,PRHEAD1,SK1      SKIP TO NEW PAGE
              PUTPR  PRINTER,PRHEAD1,WSP2     PRINT HEADING1
              PUTPR  PRINTER,PRHEAD2,WSP2     PRINT HEADING2
              CLOSE  PRINTER                  CLOSE FILE
              EOJ    ,                        TERMINATE
              SPACE
*                    D E C L A R A T I V E S
*                    -----------------------
              SPACE
PRINTER       DEFPR                           DEFINE PRINTER
              SPACE
PRHEAD1       DC     CL133'    ACME DIRIGIBLE CORP.'
PRHEAD2       DC     CL133'       POTHOLE PLAINS'
              SPACE
              LTORG  ,                        GEN'D LITERALS
              SPACE
              END    PROG03                   END OF ASSEMBLY
```

Literal Organization

Figure 3-2   Program: printing headings.

- The CLOSE macro releases the printer to the system.
- The EOJ macro terminates program execution and returns control to the supervisor.
- Under DECLARATIVES are the name of the printer device, PRINTER, and two heading lines named PRHEAD1 and PRHEAD2 that the executable instructions print.
- LTORG defines the start of a literal pool for unnamed data generated within the program.
- The END directive ends the assembly, and PROG03 in the operand indicates the starting point for execution (see START).

The rest of this chapter and the next chapter should clarify the details.

CODING CONVENTIONS

This text uses clear and meaningful conventions to define the names of declaratives and the labels of instructions.

Declarative Names

Always assign unique, descriptive names to declaratives. Since a name may be up to 8 characters long, it is clearer, for example, to define a name such as EX-PENSE rather than EXP. Also, it is often helpful to identify a packed field with a suffix PK, such as RATEPK, and a binary field with a suffix BIN, such as RATEBIN. You may assign an input area with a descriptive name such as REC-DIN and an output area with a name such as PRINT or DISPLINE (display line).

In the case of the declarative PRINT, do not confuse it with the directive PRINT that controls the assembled listing. This example illustrates how you can legally use the name of a directive for the name of a declarative; the assembler can tell from its context whether the symbol references a declarative or a directive.

Instruction Labels

Give an instruction a name (or rather, a *label*) if you reference it elsewhere in your program. This text uses a convention in which the first character of an instruction label is an alphabetic letter, A through Z. The next two or three characters are digits, for example, A20, D35, and P200. In the first main logical section of the program, labels begin with A. Instruction labels, where required, are numbered within this section starting with A10, then increasing by intervals of 10: A20, A30, and so forth.

The next logical section of the program and all others begin with a letter higher than the previous, such as B10, E10, and R10. Each section uses digits starting with 10 and increasing by intervals of 10. The first label of a section has a descriptive name, such as C10TAX or E10PENSN. This practice facilitates the following:

- Since all labels are sequential, they are easy to locate.
- There is less chance of using duplicate labels in a program.
- You can easily insert additional labels where required, such as B12 and B16.

An examination of the programs throughout this text should make clear the advantages of such coding conventions. Note, however, that there are other methods, and you should adopt the convention of your own installation.

THE ASSEMBLY PROCESS

Through job control commands, you request that the supervisor assemble your source program. For this purpose, the supervisor loads the assembler translator program from disk into main storage. The assembler translator then reads your source program as data into main storage and performs the following:

- Accounts for the amount of storage that each instruction and data area requires and assigns storage locations to them in the sequence in which you have coded them.
- Supplies messages for programming errors, such as the invalid use of an instruction and spelling errors.
- Includes any required routines that are already cataloged on disk.
- Prints the original symbolic coding and the translated machine language on a printer form. This printout is useful for debugging a program and for making subsequent changes.
- Writes the assembled object program onto disk.

Correct any errors that the assembler signals, and reassemble your program. The next step prior to execution is to request, through job control commands, that the supervisor link-edit the assembled object program and produce an executable load module, which you use for executing your test data.

Chapter 4 covers assembly and link-editing in detail, along with job control requirements.

Location Counter

The assembler uses a *location counter* to account for the length of each data field and instruction. If the assembler has just assigned a 4-byte instruction starting at location 10024, the location counter now contains 10028, the starting address of the next instruction. The assembler always assigns an address to the leftmost byte of a data field or an instruction.

ASSEMBLED PROGRAM LISTING

Figure 3-2 illustrated a small program that simply prints two heading lines. The instructions were keyed as a source program via a terminal onto disk, and special job control commands requested its assembly. The assembler translator program translated the source program into object code and printed a listing of the assembled program, as shown in Fig. 3-3.

The first page of the listing provides an external symbol dictionary (ESD) containing information about "external symbols" that the program has used. These are the names of items that the system must recognize outside of the assembled program. The first entry, PROG03, is the actual name of the program; the supervisor requires this name in order to transfer to its address in main storage to begin execution of the program.

The second strange-looking entry, IJDFYZIW, is the name of a printer module contained in the system disk library. The system automatically includes a special module for each input/output device that the program references. To

```
          EXTERNAL SYMBOL DICTIONARY

SYMBOL     TYPE          ID   ADDR    LENGTH LD-ID
PROG03     SD (CSECT)    001  000000  0002DC
IJDFYZIW   ER (EXTRN)    002

                 EXAMPLE ASSEMBLER PROGRAM TO LIST HEADINGS

LOC    OBJECT CODE      ADDR1 ADDR2   STMT  SOURCE STATEMENT
                                        2         PRINT ON,NODATA,NOGEN
                                        4 *     P R O G R A M   E X E C U T I O N
                                        5 *     -------------------------------
000000                                  7 PROG03  START
                                        8         INIT                   INITIALIZE
                                       14         OPEN  PRINTER          OPEN FILE
                                       23         PUTPR PRINTER,PRHEAD1,SK1    SKIP TO NEW PAGE
                                       30         PUTPR PRINTER,PRHEAD1,WSP2   PRINT HEADING1
                                       37         PUTPR PRINTER,PRHEAD2,WSP2   PRINT HEADING2
                                       45         CLOSE PRINTER          CLOSE FILE
                                       53         EOJ   ,                TERMINATE
                                       57 *     D E C L A R A T I V E S
                                       58 *     -----------------------
                                       60 PRINTER DEFPR                  DEFINE PRINTER
0001B3 404040404C1C3D4                 90 PRHEAD1  DC   CL133'  ACME DIRIGIBLE CORP.'
000238 40404040404040                  91 PRHEAD2  DC   CL133'  POTHOLE PLAINS'
                                       93         LTORG ,                GEN'D LITERALS
0002C0 5B5BC2D6D7C5D540                94         =C'$$BOPEN '
0002C8 5B5BC2C3D3D6E2C5                95         =C'$$BCLOSE'
0002D0 00000078                        96         =A(PRINTER)
0002D4 000001B3                        97         =A(PRHEAD1)
0002D8 00000238                        98         =A(PRHEAD2)
00000                                 100         END  PROG03            END OF ASSEMBLY

          DIAGNOSTICS AND STATISTICS

NO ERRORS FOUND

END OF ASSEMBLY

Output:-

          ACME DIRIGIBLE CORP.
          POTHOLE PLAINS
```

Figure 3-3 Assembler program listing.

perform an input/output operation, the program temporarily exits to the supervisor, which performs all I/O including printing. You don't have to know the names of these I/O modules.

You will seldom, if ever, have to refer to the ESD. If you are processing under full OS, you will get a lot of additional diagnostics that you can safely ignore for now.

The next page of the assembler listing is shown here overlapped with page 1 to save space. It contains the listing of the assembled program. The first line lists the contents of the TITLE statement (if any) at the top of each page (there could be more than one page) and the page number to the right.

The second line contains the following information:

- Under LOC (for location or, technically, assembler location counter) is the location or address of the leftmost byte of each declarative. The notation is in hexadecimal format. Note, for example, that the address of PRHEAD1 begins at X'0001B3', where X implies a hex number. The program actually "begins" at location X'000000', and the macros INIT, OPEN, PUTPR, CLOSE, and EOJ occupy the locations up to X'1B3'. Since PRHEAD1 is defined as 133 bytes (CL133), then PRHEAD2 should begin 133 (X'85') bytes following PRHEAD1:

Location of PRHEAD1:	X'0001B3'
Add 133:	+ X'000085'
Location of PRHEAD2:	X'000238'

  If you check the listing in Fig. 3-3, you will see that the location of PRHEAD2 is indeed at X'000238'.

  The reason that no entries appear under LOC before PRHEAD1 is that every preceding statement is a macro instruction. For macros, the instruction PRINT NOGEN causes the assembler to omit listing their generated object code. PRINT GEN causes the generated object code to print, and you may want to experiment with this feature, although at this point you won't find the generated code very useful.

- OBJECT CODE shows the contents of instructions (but not macros in this case) and defined constants. In the case of constants, the directive PRINT NODATA causes only the first 8 bytes (16 hex digits) to print. PRHEAD1, for example, begins with five blanks (X'40') and the three letters ACM:

  40 40 40 40 40 C1 C3 D4
   b   b   b   b   b   A   C   M

  To print the entire contents of constants (not recommended because of the added space required to list the program), code PRINT DATA.

- ADDR1 and ADDR2 refer to the addresses that instructions reference. No addresses appear here because PRINT NOGEN has suppressed the generated code for all the macro instructions. Subsequent programs, however, all contain conventional instructions and show addresses under LOC, OBJECT CODE, ADDR1, and ADDR2.
- STMT provides the number that the assembler has assigned to each statement and accounts for all entries, including code that macros generate. TITLE is actually the first statement. Statement 3 does not show because it contains the directive SPACE, which tells the assembler to space one line.
- SOURCE STATEMENT shows the original instructions in the source program, exactly as keyed in. But there is one exception: Immediately following the directive LTORG are some addresses such as =C'$$BOPEN' that the assembler has generated to facilitate input/output. Technically, these addresses are *literals*, which you may ignore for now. Note, however, that the assembler automatically generates these literals—do not code them yourself!

Execution

You provide a special job control command to instruct the supervisor to execute this program as a job. The system loader program brings the load module (not the object program) into main storage, and execution begins at the address of PROG01, wherever it happens to be located in storage. The computer executes the instructions generated by the macros INIT, OPEN, PUTPR, CLOSE, and EOJ. EOJ causes termination of the program's execution and return to the supervisor, which then checks for the next job to process.

Admittedly, to examine even a simple program, a lot of miscellaneous detail must be covered. However, the next sections and Chapter 4 explain this material, and further, most of it is common to all the programs in this text.

ASSEMBLER DIAGNOSTIC MESSAGES

Unless your program is especially small or you are especially clever, chances are that your first assembly will result in a number of coding errors. To help you get started making errors, Fig. 3-4 provides the assembled program listing, similar to the previous example, with a random assortment of coding errors. Immediately following the program is a list of errors that the assembler has identified, along with a statement number and an explanation. Check this section immediately on receiving a listing of your assembled program. (The code numbers under ERROR can also help you locate further explanations in the IBM assembler manual, although you may rarely need to reference it.)

The assembler denotes some (but not all) errors to the left of an invalid

```
LOC OBJECT CODE    ADDR1 ADDR2    STMT    SOURCE STATEMENT
                                   2            PRINT ON,NODATA,NOGEN
                                   4    *               P R O G R A M   E X E C U T I O N
                                   5    *        --------------------------------------
                                   7      PROG3A
                                   8            INIT                              INITIALIZE
                                  14            OPEN    PRTR                      OPEN FILE
                                  23            PUTPR   PRINTER,PRHEAD1,SK1       SKIP TO NEW PAGE
                                  30            PUTPR   PRINTER,PRHEAD1,WSP2      PRINT HEADING1
                                  37            PUTPR   PRINTER,PRHEAD2,WSP2      PRINT HEADING2
                                  45            CLOSE   PRINTER                   CLOSE FILE
                                  53            EOJ                               TERMINATE
                                  56            SAPCE
*** ERROR ***
                                  57    *               D E C L A R A T I V E S
                                  58    *
0001B3 404040404040C1C3D4         60  PRINTER   DEFPR                             DEFINE PRINTER
*** ERROR ***
                                  90  PRHEAD1   DC      CL133'        ACME DIRIGIBLE CORP.'
                                  91  PRHEAD2   DC      CL133
*** ERROR ***
000238                            93            LTORG                            GEN'D LITERALS
000238 5B5BC2D6D7C5D540           94                    =C'$$BOPEN '
000240 5B5BC2C3D3D6E2C5           95                    =C'$$BCLOSE'
000248 00000078                   96                    =A(PRINTER)
00024C 000001B3                   97                    =A(PRHEAD1)
000250 00000000                   98                    =A(PRHEAD2)
*** ERROR ***
                                 100            END     PROG03                   END OF ASSEMBLY
*** ERROR ***

         DIAGNOSTICS AND STATISTICS

STMNT  ERROR   SEV  MESSAGE
    7  IPK097    8  UNDEFINED OP CODE 'STRAT', OR MACRO NOT FOUND
   20  IPK156    8  SYMBOL 'PRTR' UNDEFINED
   38  IPK156    8  SYMBOL 'PRHEAD2' UNDEFINED
   56  IPK097    8  UNDEFINED OP CODE 'SAPCE', OR MACRO NOT FOUND
   91  IPK128    8  CONSTANT FIELD MISSING OR PRECEDED BY INVALID FIELD, ''
   98  IPK156    8  SYMBOL 'PRHEAD2' UNDEFINED
  100  IPK144   12  INVALID END OPERAND
  100  IPK149    8  SYMBOL 'PROG03' NOT PREVIOUSLY DEFINED
```

Figure 3-4 Assembler diagnostic messages.

statement with ✳✳✳ ERROR ✳✳✳. Before reading the following explanation, try
to identify the cause of each error message in the figure.

STATEMENT	CAUSE
7	The directive should be coded START.
20	The message refers to the OPEN macro in which the un-defined name PRTR appears. (Statement 60 defines the printer device as PRINTER.) The use of PRINT NOGEN has caused the assembler to suppress printing statements generated by macros.
38	Since PRHEAD2 is invalidly defined in statement 91, the assembler generates an error message for any reference to it.
56	The directive should be coded as SPACE.
91	A DC instruction must contain a defined constant between apostrophes.
98	The PUTPR macro at statement 37 has generated the address of PRHEAD2, but the instruction that defines PRHEAD2 is invalid. Such instances of one error causing another error are common.
100	The operand should be PROG3A to match the program name in the START directive. In this case, the one error has generated two diagnostic messages.

If the computer attempts to execute this program, it will crash on an unpredictable error. Before executing a program, be sure to correct all error diagnostics
and reassemble it.

ADDRESSING

The first location in main storage is numbered zero, with subsequent bytes numbered consecutively from that address. Therefore, a storage size of 65,536 bytes
has addresses numbered zero through 65,535. The amount of storage in this case
would be 64K, where 1K equals 1,024 bytes.

The computer performs its addressing by means of the rightmost 24 bits of a
register, which provide a capacity of 2^{24}, or 16,777,216 addressable bytes of storage.
Machine code uses a two-part system for addressing main storage, consisting of

1. A *base register* (an available general-purpose register). The base register
contains the beginning address of an area in storage where the program resides
and provides a reference point for 4,096 bytes of storage. Programs larger
than 4,096 bytes (4K) may require more than one base register.

2. A *displacement*, or the number of bytes from zero to 4095, from the first byte of the storage area. Thus the first byte of a program (or rather, control section) has a displacement of 0, the second byte has a displacement of 1, and so forth.

When you code an assembler program, you do not know, or need to know, where in storage your instructions and declaratives will reside. You code in symbolic language, assigning names to the various instructions and data fields. For example, an instruction may have the label B20CALC, and an accumulator that counts the number of pages printed may have the name PAGECTR. The name you give refers only to a single storage location, the leftmost byte of the field.

For example, the contents of PAGECTR may be 3 bytes long, and the assembler assigns it to locations 10516, 10517, and 10518. A reference to PAGECTR is to a 3-byte field beginning in location 10516. In the following illustration, PAGECTR contains the packed decimal value 00015C, where C is a plus sign:

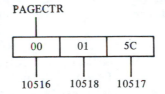

At this point you do not have to understand base/displacement addressing; a full discussion is provided in Chapter 6.

Relative Addressing

You may reference a storage position relative to a symbolic address. For example, you could define an area of 80 bytes named RECDIN for reading and storing 80-byte records. The following definition uses the declarative DS (Define Storage) to define this 80-byte area:

```
RECDIN   DS   CL80
```

The name RECDIN refers to the first (leftmost) byte of the area. You could reference it as RECDIN + 0. Accordingly, you may reference the second byte as RECDIN + 1, the third byte as RECDIN + 2, through to the 80th byte as RECDIN + 79:

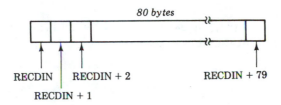

You can reference any location in a program by similar relative addressing, although its use tends to make a program difficult to maintain.

INSTRUCTION FORMAT

The assembler translates your symbolic instructions into machine code object instructions, with correct format and length. The assembler aligns the first byte of every instruction on an even-numbered storage location. The first byte is the operation code, such as add, move, or compare, and provides for 256 possible operations. When the computer executes a machine instruction, it accesses the operation code (the first byte) from main storage and analyzes it for the instruction's format and length.

An instruction usually contains one or more operands that involve a reference to a storage location or a register. There are five basic instruction formats, with lengths of 2, 4, and 6 bytes. Depending on its format, an instruction may transfer data between registers, between a register and storage, or between storage locations.

The five main instruction formats are RR (register-to-register), RX (register-to-indexed-storage), RS (register-to-storage), SI (storage immediate), and SS (storage-to-storage), as Fig. 3-5 shows. A special sixth type, S-format, which uses 2 bytes for the operation code, is used mainly by the operating system.

Format	Length (Bytes)	Typical Use
RR (register-to-register)	2	Data movement between registers
RX (register-to-indexed storage)	4	Data movement between a register and storage
RS (register-to-storage)	4	Data movement between a register and storage
SI (storage immediate)	4	Data movement from a one-byte constant in the instruction to storage
SS (storage-to-storage)	6	Data movement between two storage locations

Figure 3-5 Assembler instruction formats.

For example, you can use an RR format instruction, AR, to add the contents of register 8 to register 6, coded as

```
              AR              6,8  ← operand-2
               |               ↑
           operation       operand-1
```

The machine code for AR is X'1A'. The assembler translates the symbolic instruction AR to two bytes of object code, in hexadecimal as 1A 68. This instruction is relatively simple because it addresses only registers. The object code for instructions that reference storage is more complex because the assembler has to convert their addresses to base/displacement format.

Let's examine the format for the MVC (move characters) instruction, which uses SS format. Both operands reference a location in main storage, and the length of operand 1 governs the number of bytes moved. Here's the machine language format for MVC:

$$
\text{bit:}\ \left|\ \begin{array}{c} 0\text{--}7 \\ \text{op} \end{array}\ \right|\ \begin{array}{c} 8 \text{------} 15 \\ \text{length} \end{array}\ \left|\ \begin{array}{cc} 16 \text{------} 31 \\ \text{B1} \quad | \quad \text{D1} \end{array}\ \right|\ \begin{array}{cc} 32 \text{------} 47 \\ \text{B2} \quad | \quad \text{D2} \end{array}\ \right|
$$

- Byte 1 (bits 0–7) contains the operation code, X'D2' for MVC.
- Byte 2 (bits 8–15) contains a length code, the number of bytes to be moved.
- Bytes 3 and 4 (bits 16–31) contain the base/displacement reference for operand 1
- Bytes 5 and 6 (bits 32–47) contain the base/displacement reference for operand 2.

When you code a symbolic instruction such as

```
MVC    PRINTAREA,HEADING      (Move heading to print area)
```

the assembler converts it into its object code format. Chapter 6 covers instruction formats in detail.

KEY POINTS

- An assembler source program consists of four types of statements: comments, directives, declaratives, and instructions.
- A comment is any descriptive information that you code as documentation to make your program clearer.
- A directive is a special command such as TITLE, START, or END that notifies the assembler to take special action during the assembly process. Directives generate no object code.
- A declarative is a command defined by DS and DC that provides for data items in the program. A DS simply reserves an area of storage, whereas a DC defines an area with a constant value.
- An instruction is a statement such as MVC (move), AP (add), and CP (compare) that the assembler converts into machine language.

- You assign a name to each instruction and declarative that you intend to reference in your program. The name must be unique and may be 1 to 8 characters long. The first character must be a letter A through Z (or $, #, or @); the remaining characters may be letters or digits, as in PROG25.

- The operation provides the symbolic operation code for an instruction, declarative, directive, or macro, which the assembler must be able to recognize.

- The operand identifies data on which the operation is to act.

- The END directive is the last statement of an assembler program and causes termination of the assembly. You may code the operand with a symbolic address, such as END PROG25, where PROG25 designates an address where execution is to begin.

- A label is a name that you give to an instruction if you reference it elsewhere in your program.

- The computer performs its addressing by means of the rightmost 24 bits of a register, which provide a capacity of 2^{24}, or 16,777,216 addressable bytes of storage.

- Machine code uses a two-part system for addressing, consisting of a base register (an available general-purpose register) and a displacement, the number of bytes from 0 to 4095, from the first byte of the storage area.

- The five main instruction formats are RR (register-to-register), RX (register-to-indexed-storage), RS (register-to-storage), SI (storage immediate), and SS (storage-to-storage).

PROBLEMS

3-1. One type of assembler statement is a comment. What are the other three types?

3-2. In the assembler coding format, what does an asterisk in column 1 indicate? What would it indicate in column 72?

3-3. In the coding format, what fields begin in columns 1, 10, 16, 72, and 73?

3-4. What is the first statement required in an assembler control section?

3-5. What statement terminates a control section?

3-6. Does the EJECT directive cause the printer to skip to the top of a page during an assembly, during program execution, or both?

3-7. What statement causes an assembled program listing to space three lines?

3-8. Indicate for the following whether they are acted on during assembly, link edit, or execution: (a) directives, (b) declaratives, (c) machine instructions.

3-9. How can you cause the generated code for a macro to appear on an assembled listing?

3-10. What is a declarative? How do DS and DC differ?

3-11. Distinguish between a name and a label.

3-12. Comment on the validity of the following assembler names: (a) W25; (b) START-UP; (c) READDEVICE; (d) $AMT; (e) TOT AMT; (f) *TOTAL; (G) 25CENTS.

3-13. How does the assembler account for the address of each instruction and declarative?

3-14. Distinguish between a source program and an object program.

3-15. What do the following mean on an assembled program listing: (a) LOC; (b) OBJECT CODE; (c) ADDR1 and ADDR2; (d) STMT?

3-16. What are the two parts of the addressing scheme that the system uses for referencing main storage locations?

3-17. Indicate which instruction formats you use to move data (a) between registers; (b) between storage locations; (c) between registers and storage.

4

ASSEMBLY
AND EXECUTION
OF A PROGRAM

OBJECTIVE

To cover the requirements for assembling and executing a program.

Chapter 3 covered the requirements for coding an assembler program. This chapter covers the basic instructions for executing an assembler language program: initialization, the defining of files, and the input/output macros. Also covered are introductory job control requirements and details of the two-pass assembler.

PROGRAM INITIALIZATION

The first statements in an assembler program may vary depending on the version of the assembler being used and the requirements of the operating system. Under DOS, you would normally code at least the following instructions to initialize addressing for a program:

Name	Operation	Operand
[label]	BALR	3,0
[label]	USING	*,3

The BALR instruction physically loads a base address in register 3 (which could be any other available register). The address that BALR loads is that of the instruction that immediately follows. (Not USING, however, which is a directive and not part of the assembled object program.) USING tells the assembler to begin displacements for addressing from this point—the address of the instruction that follows.

Under OS, you would have to code not only these instructions but also a number of others concerned with returning to the supervisor program at the end of execution.

To facilitate getting started, the early programs in this text use a special macro instruction, INIT, which replaces the BALR/USING pair and which you code as the first executable instruction:

Name	Operation	Operand
[label]	INIT	[blank]

You may supply a name for the operation or leave it blank. Chapter 6 covers the precise methods of initializing an assembler program and explains the requirements for both DOS and OS.

DEFINING INPUT AND PRINTER FILES

Let's begin with the simplest processing of input/output files: input from a terminal or system reader and output on a terminal or printer. A program must define the names of these input and output files. In the early chapters, two special macros handle this definition: DEFIN (Define Input) and DEFPR (Define Printer). These macros generate some complex assembler code. (Chapter 10 covers the standard IBM file definition macros DTFCD, DTFPR, and DCB.) The input/output macros such as OPEN and GET reference these files by their defined names.

Name	Operation	Operand
inputfile	DEFIN	end-of-file-address
printfile	DEFPR	[blank]

DEFIN defines an input file with any valid unique name, preferably descriptive. The operand specifies an address in your program where the system is to link on encountering the end of input data. Under DOS, the last record of input data for the system reader or CMS terminals is a job control entry containing /* in columns 1–2. As it reads each data record, the system checks the first two positions. If they contain /*, the system directs the program to your end-of-file address, typically the name of a routine that may print final totals and terminate program execution.

The logic looks like this:

```
Read a record
End-of-file?
       If yes, branch to EOF address
       If no, continue....
```

DEFPR defines any unique name for the printer file. Because the printer is an output file, it has no associated end-of-file.

OPENING AND CLOSING FILES

Most computer systems require a program at its start to activate (open) the files that are to be accessed and at its end to deactivate (close) them. The normal function of OPEN is to make a file available to the program, since it may be out of service or in use by another program. At the end of program execution, CLOSE releases the file for use by other programs.

The formats differ for DOS and for OS:

DOS Version:

Name	Operation	Operand
[label]	OPEN	inputfile,printfile
[label]	CLOSE	inputfile,printfile

OS Version:

Name	Operation	Operand
[label]	OPEN	(inputfile,(INPUT),printfile,(OUTPUT))
[label]	CLOSE	(inputfile,,printfile)

For both OPEN and CLOSE, the operands are the input and printer file names defined by DEFIN and DEFPR. Under larger systems, a program may omit the OPEN and CLOSE of system reader and printer files.

Under OS, you code OPEN and CLOSE with the operands in brackets. Also, OPEN must indicate whether the file is INPUT or OUTPUT, although CLOSE may omit this reference.

For either DOS or OS, you may use one statement to OPEN or to CLOSE one or more files. The advantage of a separate OPEN statement for each file is that you may more easily identify which file is invalid if the OPEN fails.

READING INPUT RECORDS

The GET macro causes an input record to be read into main storage. There are two operands: operand 1 designates the file name defined by DEFIN (or by the IBM macro DCB or DTFCD); operand 2 is the name of an input area in main storage. For the system reader, the record and the input area typically are 80 bytes.

Name	Operation	Operand
[label]	GET	filename,inputarea

GET causes the named device to read (or attempt to read) a record. The input area may have any unique name. If a record is available, the operation transfers its contents to the input area, erasing the previous contents. If the record indicates end-of-file, the operation transfers control to the end-of-file address defined in the DEFIN macro.

Figure 4-1 illustrates the use of the macros introduced so far for DOS and for OS.

```
DOS Version:

                    OPEN    READER             Open input file
                    GET     READER,INAREA      Read a record
                    ...
        D10EOF      CLOSE   READER             Close input file
                    ...
        READER      DEFIN   D10EOF             Define input file
        INAREA      DS      CL80               Define input area
                    ...

OS Version:

                    OPEN    (READER,(INPUT))   Open input file
                    GET     READER,INAREA      Read a record
                    ...
        D10EOF      CLOSE   (READER)           Close input file
                    ...
        READER      DEFIN   D10EOF             Define input file
        INAREA      DS      CL80               Define input area
                    ...
```

Figure 4-1   Use of the input macros.

PRINTING LINES

Commands to a printer during program execution may involve printing with spacing one or more lines or spacing lines without printing. Keep the difference clear between printing during execution time and the use of the SPACE and PRINT directives that control the listing of an assembled program. To simplify the requirements involved in handling the printer, the early chapters in this text use a special macro, PUTPR.

Name	Operation	Operand
[label]	PUTPR	printfile,printarea,command

Operand 1 is the name of the printer file defined by DEFPR (or by the IBM macros DCB or DTFPR). Operand 2 is the name of your print area that contains data to be printed. Your program may have any number of uniquely named print areas. Operand 3 specifies printer forms control, as follows:

COMMAND	OPERATION
WSP0	Write, no space
WSP1	Write, space 1 line
WSP2	Write, space 2 lines
WSP3	Write, space 3 lines
SK1	Skip (eject) to top of a new page
SP1	Space 1 line without printing
SP2	Space 2 line without printing
SP3	Space 3 line without printing

The following macro instruction causes a program to print the contents of PRLINE and to space to the next line on the printer form:

```
PUTPR PRINTER,PRLINE,WSP1
```

You may use WSP0 occasionally for underlining or double-printing important information. SK1, SP1, SP2, and SP3 simply move the printer form with no printing on the page, regardless of the contents of the print area.

PUTPR uses the first byte of the print area to insert a special forms control character, which replaces any character that you may have already stored there:

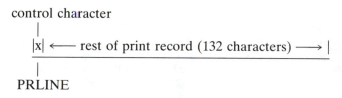

If you have defined the print area as

```
PRLINE  DC      CL133' '
```

then PRLINE+0 is the position that the control character uses. The remaining positions, PRLINE+1 through PRLINE+132, are available for storing your output data. As discussed in Chapter 10, the standard IBM macro, PUT, requires that you define and insert the proper control character.

The DOS example in Fig. 4-2 prints and spaces one line. OS requires slightly modified OPEN and CLOSE statements, as discussed earlier.

```
        OPEN    PRINTER                     Open file
        ...
        PUTPR   PRINTER,PRLINE,WSP1         Print a line
        ...
        CLOSE   PRINTER                     Close file
        ...
PRINTER DEFPR                               Define printer device
PRLINE  DC      CL133' '                    Define print area
```

Figure 4-2   Use of the output macros.

TERMINATING EXECUTION

After closing the files, you terminate program execution under DOS with the EOJ macro, which causes a return to the supervisor program.

Name	Operation	Operand
[label]	EOJ	[blank]

Under OS, termination involves the RETURN macro. Appendix E provides an EOJ macro for OS users.

Advanced programs are written to check for invalid data in input records and to cancel processing if any is found. The CANCEL macro not only terminates processing but also flushes any remaining input records. Under OS, the macro equivalent of CANCEL is ABEND (abnormal end).

Name	Operation	Operand	
[label]	CANCEL	, or ALL	(DOS abnormal termination)
[label]	ABEND	code	(OS abnormal termination)

The comma in the operand of CANCEL is used if you want to omit an operand but include a comment to the right.

END OF ASSEMBLY

EOJ and CANCEL are concerned with terminating a program's execution, and may appear at any logical place in a program. To terminate a program assembly, the last statement in a program must be the END directive, which tells the assembler that there are no more statements.

The operand of END indicates the address of the first executable statement in the program, usually the program name, as here:

Name	Operation	Operand	Comment
PROG48	START		Start of execution
	...		
	END	PROG48	End of program

SAMPLE PROGRAM: READING AND PRINTING ONE RECORD

Figure 4-3 combines the preceding assembler macros into a program that prints a heading, reads one record, prints its contents, and terminates execution. The GET macro reads a record from the file named FILEIN and transfers the record into an 80-byte field defined as RECORDIN. In this program, the label for the end-of-file address is A90END. The instruction following GET is MVC (Move Characters) that moves (actually copies) the contents of RECORDIN to the print area:

```
MVC DATAPR,RECORDIN
```

DATAPR is defined within PRINT. Note that PRINT is defined as 0CL133, the zero indicating that the assembler is not to increment its location counter. Consequently, the following 10-byte field (unnamed) is aligned at the same location as PRINT, and all the fields are defined within PRINT:

```
| — 10 — | ——— 80 ——— | —— 43 —— |
|          |
PRINT     DATAPR
```

In effect, PRINT is a record consisting of three fields that total 133 bytes. A reference to PRINT is to the entire 133-byte record, and a reference to DATAPR is to an 80-byte field within PRINT.

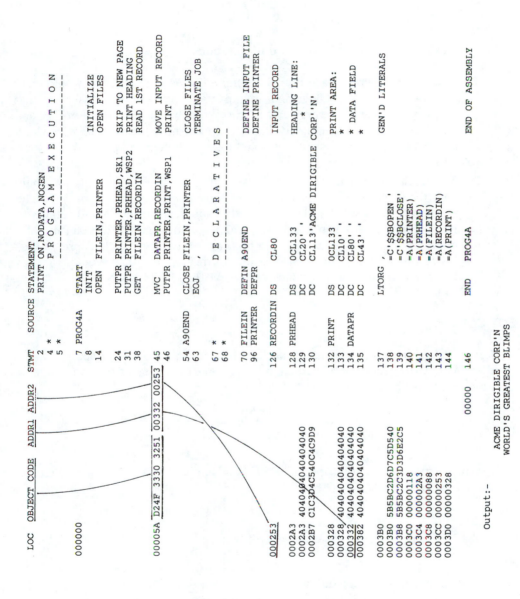

Output:-

ACME DIRIGIBLE CORP'N
WORLD'S GREATEST BLIMPS

Figure 4-3 Program: reading and printing one record.

The program was coded to run under DOS. An OS program would code the OPEN and CLOSE macros as follows:

```
OPEN  (FILEIN,(INPUT),PRINTER,(OUTPUT))
CLOSE (FILEIN,,PRINTER)
```

Now, consider the following two propositions:

1. What if the program was run with no input data? The program would open the files, print the heading, and attempt to read a record. Assuming that the job control entries were correct, the system would signal end-of-file, and the program would immediately link to its end-of-file address A90END, where it closes the files and terminates. In effect, although the program does not read or print a record, there is no error.

2. What if the program was run with two input records? The program would open the files, print the heading, read the first record, and print it. The program then closes the files, and EOJ terminates execution and returns to the supervisor. The supervisor would expect a job control entry at this point in the job stream but instead would encounter the second data record. Since this record would be incomprehensible to the supervisor, it would print (or display) a warning message such as INVALID STATEMENT.

OBJECT CODE

Let's now examine the generated machine object code for this program. Since the MVC (Move Character) instruction is not a macro, the assembler has listed its object code to the left, as follows:

```
    LOC       OBJECT CODE    ADDR1 ADDR2
  00005A   D24F 3330 3251   00332 00253
```

The instruction begins at location X'00005A'—that is, the first byte of object code containing X'D2':

```
         D2  4F  3330  3251
         |   |   | |   | |
        5A   | 5C|   5E |
            5B   5D    5F
```

The actual machine code is 6 bytes and consists of operation, length code, and two operands. Note that this explanation applies to an MVC instruction and not necessarily to other assembler instructions.

     D2   The machine code for MVC. MVC always generates this code for its first byte.

4F   The length in hex of this move operation. Actually, X'4F' is decimal value 79, not 80 (look it up!), but the assembler always deducts 1 from the length, and the computer when executing always adds 1.

3330   The address of operand 1 (DATAPR) in terms of the computer's addressing scheme, where register 3 is a base register and 330 is a displacement.

3251   The address of operand 2 (RECORDIN) in terms of the computer's addressing scheme, where register 3 is a base register and 251 is a displacement.

These two operand addresses consist of a reference to a base register and a displacement. A full discussion of this topic is delayed until Chapter 6, since there's enough to wrestle with learning symbolic code first.

Under ADDR1 and ADDR2 are two values that the assembler lists for informative purposes and are not part of the actual machine code. The value 00332 indicates the location (LOC) of operand 1, DATAPR, and the value 00253 indicates the location of operand 2, RECORDIN. If you trace down the column under LOC, you will find these two values, and sure enough, they are the lines that define DATAPR and RECORDIN, respectively.

You may want to examine a few other op codes, lengths, and addresses in your own programs, but expect to understand this material fully only after you've written a few programs.

JOB CONTROL

To assemble and execute a program, you submit job control commands that tell the operating system what action to perform. A job may consist of one or more programs (roughly, job steps) that are to execute along with any required data. The system recognizes the start of a job by means of the first job control command, which contains an entry such as // JOB jobname. The entries that specify the job and the action to perform comprise the job control language (JCL).

Basically, job control for assembling and executing a program consists of three major steps: assembly, link edit, and execution. Here is a simplified example:

1.	`// JOB jobname`	Specify job name
2.	`// EXEC ASSEMBLY`	Request assembly
3.	`[source program]`	Your assembly source program
4.	`/*`	End of source program
5.	`// EXEC LNKEDT`	Request link edit
6.	`// EXEC [program-name]`	Execute your linked program
7.	`[data]`	Your input data
8.	`/*`	End of input data
9.	`/&`	End of your job

The following explains each of these job steps:

1. You supply to the system a name for this job.
2. The system loads the assembler program from disk into storage.
3. The assembler reads your source program as input data and converts its symbolic code into machine object code.
4. On encountering the end of the source program, the assembler completes conversion to object code and writes it as a disk file.
5. The system loads the linkage editor program from disk into storage. The linkage editor reads the assembled object program and includes any required cataloged input/output modules (and if necessary combines any separately assembled programs). The linker writes the executable load module onto disk.
6. The loader brings the load module from disk into storage and begins execution.
7. The executable module reads and processes your input data.
8. When your program reads the end-of-file indication, it prepares to terminate execution and returns control to the system.
9. The system terminates your job and returns control to the supervisor.

Job control language varies considerably for the two main IBM systems, DOS and OS. Appendix D gives sample job control for typical situations, but check the particular requirements for your own installation.

Let's now find out how to process any number of input records.

LOOPING

Most programs involve reading and processing a number of input records. The program has to perform looping, or repetitive processing, until reaching end-of-file, as shown in Fig. 4-4.

```
          . . .                        Initialization
          GET    first-record          If EOF, exit to A90EOF;
                                          else drop through to next
- - - - - - - - - - - - - - - - - - - - - - - - - - - - - - - - - - - -
A10LOOP   . . .   (process record)      Processing
          GET    next-record           If EOF, exit to A90EOF;
          B      A10LOOP                  else transfer to A10LOOP
- - - - - - - - - - - - - - - - - - - - - - - - - - - - - - - - - - - -
          . . .
A90EOF    . . .                         End-of-file processing
```

Figure 4-4 Program looping.

This text has adopted a structured programming technique in which an initial GET instruction reads only the first record. The program processes the record (including perhaps performing an output operation), then executes another GET. This GET is followed by a branch (B) instruction that says, in effect, to branch to the address A10LOOP, which is coded after the initial GET. The loop processes and reads continuously until GET senses the end-of-file condition. At this point, the program automatically links to the end-of-file address, in this case assumed to be A90EOF.

SAMPLE PROGRAM: READING AND PRINTING MULTIPLE RECORDS

Figure 4-5 provides an example that combines the program in Figure 4-3 that reads one record with the preceding material on looping. This program reads and processes any number of records.

Input. The three input records contain a company's name and address.

Processing. The program performs initialization, opens the reader and printer files, skips to a new page, and prints a heading line. It next reads the first record of the file. The processing loop begins at the MVC instruction labeled A10LOOP, where the program moves data from the input record to the print line, prints the line, reads the next input record, and branches to the MVC instruction at A10LOOP.

On reaching end-of-file, the program automatically branches to A90END, where it skips to a new page, closes the files, and terminates processing.

Output. Printed output consists of a heading line and the data from the three input records.

CROSS-REFERENCE LISTING

The program in Fig. 4-5 supplied one additional feature: a cross-reference listing of the defined symbols in alphabetic sequence, shown separately in Fig. 4-6. In this case, "symbol" means any declarative and name in the program. The listing is useful for complex programs where you want to locate quickly all the instructions that reference a particular declarative.

Some of the symbols are not immediately recognizable. For example, symbols beginning with IJC and IJJ are special entries that the assembler has included to handle reading and printing. Immediately following are three entries for buffer areas that the system generates to facilitate input/output. Also, the assembler has generated literals for addresses concerned with I/O. These begin with equal signs,

```
LOC     OBJECT CODE  ADDR1 ADDR2  STMT  SOURCE STATEMENT

                                   3          PRINT  ON,NODATA,NOGEN
                                   5    *          I N I T I A L I Z A T I O N
                                   6    *          ---------------------------
000000                             8  PROG4B  START
                                   9          INIT                              INITIALIZE
                                  15          OPEN   FILEIN,PRINTER             OPEN FILES

                                  25          PUTPR  PRINTER,PRHEAD,SK1         SKIP TO NEW PAGE
                                  32          PUTPR  PRINTER,PRHEAD,WSP2        PRINT HEADING
                                  39          GET    FILEIN,RECORDIN            READ 1ST RECORD

                                  46    *          R E A D   &   P R I N T   R O U T I N E
                                  47    *          -----------------------------------------
00005A D24F 3358 3279 0035A 0027B 49  A10LOOP MVC    DATAPR,RECORDIN            MOVE INPUT RECORD
                                  50          PUTPR  PRINTER,PRINT,WSP1         PRINT
                                  57          GET    FILEIN,RECORDIN            READ NEXT RECORD
000084 47F0 3058      0005A       63          B      A10LOOP                    LOOP

                                  65    *          E N D - O F - F I L E   R O U T I N E
                                  66    *          -----------------------------------------
                                  68  A90END  PUTPR  PRINTER,PRINT,SK1          SKIP PAGE
                                  75          CLOSE  FILEIN,PRINTER             CLOSE FILES
                                  84          EOJ                               TERMINATE JOB
```

Figure 4-5 Program: processing multiple records.

```
                      D E C L A R A T I V E S
                      -----------------------

         88  *
         89  *

00027B   91  FILEIN    DEFIN  A90END              DEFINE INPUT FILE
        117  PRINTER   DEFPR                      DEFINE PRINTER

0002CB  147  RECORDIN  DS     CL80                INPUT RECORD

0002CB  149  PRHEAD    DS     0CL133              HEADING LINE:
0002CB 4040404040404040      150            DC     CL10' '              *
0002D5 C3D6D4D7C1D5E840      151            DC     CL123'COMPANY NAME AND ADDRESS'

000350  153  PRINT     DS     0CL133              PRINT AREA:
000350 4040404040404040      154            DC     CL10' '              *
00035A 4040404040404040      155  DATAPR    DC     CL80' '              * DATA FIELD
0003AA 4040404040404040      156            DC     CL43' '              *

0003D8  158            LTORG  ,                    GEN'D LITERALS
0003D8 5B5BC2D6D7C5D540      159            =C'$$BOPEN '
0003E0 5B5BC2C3D3D6E2C5      160            =C'$$BCLOSE'
0003E8 00000140      161            =A(PRINTER)
0003EC 000002CB      162            =A(PRHEAD)
0003F0 000000B0      163            =A(FILEIN)
0003F4 0000027B      164            =A(RECORDIN)
0003F8 00000350      165            =A(PRINT)

00000   167            END    PROG4B              END OF ASSEMBLY
```

Output:-

```
COMPANY NAME AND ADDRESS
ACE ELECTRONICS CORPORATION
4325 SUNNYHILL ROAD
FONZDALE, CALIFORNIA
```

Figure 4-5 (continued)

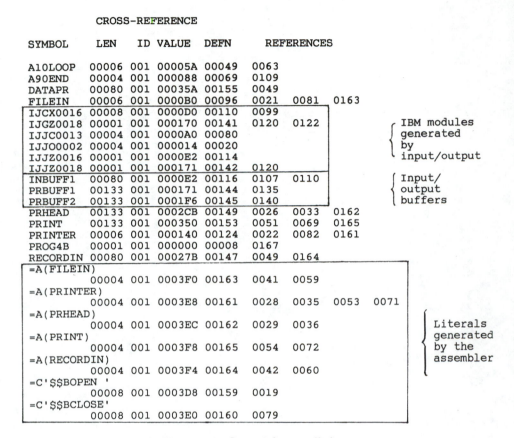

CROSS-REFERENCE

SYMBOL	LEN	ID	VALUE	DEFN	REFERENCES			
A10LOOP	00006	001	00005A	00049	0063			
A90END	00004	001	000088	00069	0109			
DATAPR	00080	001	00035A	00155	0049			
FILEIN	00006	001	0000B0	00096	0021	0081	0163	
IJCX0016	00008	001	0000D0	00110	0099			
IJGZ0018	00001	001	000170	00141	0120	0122		
IJJC0013	00004	001	0000A0	00080				
IJJO0002	00004	001	000014	00020				
IJJZ0016	00001	001	0000E2	00114				
IJJZ0018	00001	001	000171	00142	0120			
INBUFF1	00080	001	0000E2	00116	0107	0110		
PRBUFF1	00133	001	000171	00144	0135			
PRBUFF2	00133	001	0001F6	00145	0140			
PRHEAD	00133	001	0002CB	00149	0026	0033	0162	
PRINT	00133	001	000350	00153	0051	0069	0165	
PRINTER	00006	001	000140	00124	0022	0082	0161	
PROG4B	00001	001	000000	00008	0167			
RECORDIN	00080	001	00027B	00147	0049	0164		
=A(FILEIN)	00004	001	0003F0	00163	0041	0059		
=A(PRINTER)	00004	001	0003E8	00161	0028	0035	0053	0071
=A(PRHEAD)	00004	001	0003EC	00162	0029	0036		
=A(PRINT)	00004	001	0003F8	00165	0054	0072		
=A(RECORDIN)	00004	001	0003F4	00164	0042	0060		
=C'$$BOPEN '	00008	001	0003D8	00159	0019			
=C'$$BCLOSE'	00008	001	0003E0	00160	0079			

IBM modules generated by input/output

Input/output buffers

Literals generated by the assembler

Figure 4-6 Cross-reference listing.

such as =A(FILEIN), meaning the address of the input file. You may cheerfully ignore these entries.

- The column headed LEN provides the length in decimal notation of instructions and declaratives. For example, the instruction at A10LOOP, the MVC, is 6 bytes long. Of more relevance is the length of declaratives; for example, the length of PRHEAD is 133.
- The column headed VALUE contains the location of the symbol. For example, the "value" of A10LOOP is X'00005A', which relates directly to the LOC column in the assembler listing.
- The column headed DEFN indicates the statement number of the symbol. For example, the DEFN of A10LOOP is 00049, which agrees with its number under STMT in the assembled listing.
- REFERENCES identifies all the other statements in the program that refer to the symbol. For example, A10LOOP is defined in 49 and referenced in

63. PRHEAD is defined in 149 and is referenced by macros in 26 and 33 and by a literal in 162.

TWO-PASS ASSEMBLER

Most assemblers adopt a similar approach to assembling a program. Typically, an assembler requires two passes through a source program, although the second pass involves a modified version of the program.

An assembler has to handle and integrate such diverse features as location counter, base registers, symbolic instructions, literals, explicit base/displacement addressing, declaratives, directives, macro instructions, input/output files, and linkage to other programs.

To deal with these features, the assembler has two basic types of tables. The first type provides for words that are already known to the assembler. One assembler table includes entries for symbolic instructions, such as MVC and ZAP. Associated with each table entry is its machine code and general format. Another assembler table of this type provides for declaratives and directives, such as DC, EQU, START, and USING. Associated with each table entry is an address of a routine that processes the statement. The assembler compares each operation code of your program against these two tables; if the word is not in the table and is not a macro, the assembler tags the operation as an error.

The second type of table is constructed by the assembler for your own data names, literals, and instruction labels and is known as a symbol table.

Because the assembler cannot readily handle all the many forward and backward references in a source program, it requires a second pass. For example, consider the following instruction:

```
MVC CODE,FIVE
```

The reference to the operands CODE and FIVE appears before their definition at the end of the program. As a consequence, the assembler cannot complete the object code for the MVC instruction until it knows the length and relative location of the operands. As pass 1 progresses through the source program, the assembler determines the length and relative location of each statement that generates machine code and constructs the symbol table in a format such as this:

NAME	LOCATION	LENGTH
...	...	...
CODE	0126	02
...	...	...
FIVE	0315	02
...	...	...

Pass 1 generates a modified source program that now includes the location counter setting and statement number. This phase terminates on encountering the END directive. Pass 2 then reads through the modified file and completes the object code. It converts symbolic operation codes to machine code, operands to base register and displacement, and DC constants to hexadecimal. Since a DS is not converted, its contents at the time of execution will be whatever data happens to be in storage.

Pass 2 generates an optional source listing file and object file. The source listing file, as you have seen, contains your original source statements plus a statement number and a representation of the generated object code. The object file consists of four sections:

1. *External Symbol Dictionary (ESD).* An external symbol is any name that the system must recognize outside the program. One symbol that always appears in an ESD is the name of the program itself. Other names include input/output modules cataloged on disk and the names of separately assembled modules that this program calls for execution.
2. *Text (TXT) Entries.* Text entries provide the object code instructions and constants. All the information in the program listing under the heading OBJECT CODE appears in this section.
3. *Relocation Dictionary (RLD) Entries.* The RLD concerns address-dependent code that is affected when the system relocates the program for execution. The entries include all address (A-type) and external address (V-type) constants. The RLD also provides references for each external symbol in the ESD.
4. *END Entry.* END supplies the address of the first instruction that is to execute when the program is run.

You may catalog object modules on disk so that they are available for linkage with other object modules.

Linkage Editor

The next step, if requested, is link editing, in which the linkage editor program processes the object program. It examines the ESD entries to determine what I/O modules to include and, if there is more than one object program to link together, to complete any linkage addresses between them. The linker then writes an executable load module onto disk under its assigned name, where it is available for execution any number of times.

You may catalog load modules permanently on disk so that they are available for execution at any time.

Loader

When requested, the system loader program reads the load module from disk (where the linker stored it) into an available area in main storage.

The loader is also concerned with address constants in the relocation dictionary. Since the assembler deals with relative locations only from a starting point, when it defines an address constant, the address is only a displacement, such as X'35A'. But since the program loads for execution at a specific location in storage, such as X'20440', a reference to the constant during execution would be X'20440' + X'35A', or X'2079A'.

The loader secures a *load point address* (also known as *entry point address* and *relocation factor*) from the operating system, loads the program into storage beginning at the load point, and adds this relocation factor to each address constant in the relocation dictionary. It then transfers control to the entry in the END section, and at last your program begins execution.

You may execute a load module any number of times in a job, because it resides on disk during the session. Each execution of the load module causes it to read into storage, erasing the previous version.

Figure 4-7 provides the flow of assembly, linkage, and execution of a program.

DEBUGGING TIPS

- A disastrous error is caused by incorrectly coding GET or PUT, as, for example, GET RECDIN,FILEIN. The computer may end up executing outside of the program area, perhaps even executing garbage in the supervisor.

- Even a simple program stands a good chance of containing errors. Check first the diagnostics immediately following the assembled program for any errors that the assembler has located. The most common error that the assembler identifies is spelling mistakes: An operation is misspelled, such as MCV for MVC, or an operand is not spelled the way it is defined. Such errors may cause the assembler to generate a dummy instruction of hex zeros that cause an operation exception if executed. Failure to initialize with INIT (or the USING directive) causes a large number of addressability errors.

KEY POINTS

- Early programs in this text use a special macro instruction, INIT, which replaces the BALR/USING pair and which you code as the first executable instruction.

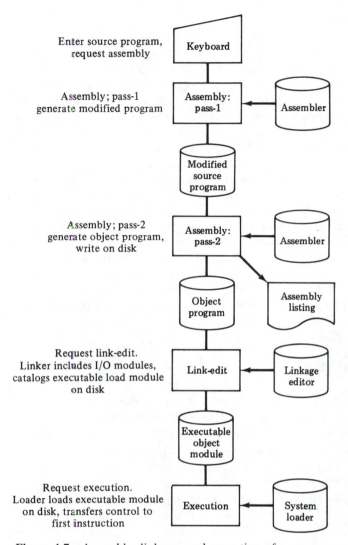

Figure 4-7   Assembly, linkage, and execution of a program.

- This text begins with simple processing of input from a terminal or system reader and output on a terminal or printer and uses two special macros to handle their definition: DEFIN (Define Input) and DEFPR (Define Printer).
- The OPEN macro makes a file available to the program, since it may be out of service or in use by another program.   At the end of program execution, the CLOSE macro releases the file for use by other programs.
- The GET macro causes the system to read an input record into main storage.

- To simplify the requirements involved in handling the printer, in the early chapters this text uses a special macro, PUTPR.

- After closing the files, you terminate program execution under DOS with the EOJ macro, which causes a return to the supervisor program.

- To assemble and execute a program, you submit job control commands that tell the operating system what action to perform. A job may consist of one or more programs (roughly, job steps) that are to execute along with any required data.

- Most programs involve reading and processing a number of input records. The program has to perform looping, or repetitive processing, until reaching end-of-file.

- The assembler supplies a cross-reference listing of the defined symbols in alphabetic sequence.

- The assembler requires two passes through a source program, although the second pass involves a modified version of the program and generates an object program.

- The linkage editor processes the object program. It includes I/O modules and, if there is more than one object program to link together, it completes any linkage addresses between them. The linker then writes an executable load module onto disk, where it is available for execution.

- The system loader program reads the load module from disk (where the linker stored it) into main storage for execution.

PROBLEMS

4-1. This text uses an INIT macro for initializing addressing for a program. What two statements does it replace?

4-2. An input file is named FILEIN and an output file is named FILEPR. The end-of-file address is E90EOF. Provide the DEFIN and DEFPR macros for these files.

4-3. For the files defined in Problem 4-2, provide (a) the OPEN statement for both DOS and OS; (b) a properly defined area for input records; (c) the GET statement; (d) a properly defined area for print records; (e) the write statement necessary to write and space two lines; (f) the CLOSE statement for both DOS and OS.

4-4. Provide the print macros for FILEPR defined earlier for (a) print and space one line; (b) print and space no line; (c) space two lines with no print; (d) skip to a new page.

4-5. The first character of a print line is reserved for what special purpose?

4-6. What macro provides normal termination of a program? What happens as a result of its execution?

4-7. For an MVC instruction, the length of operand 1 is 8 bytes, both operand 1 and operand 2 are subject to base register 3, and the displacements for the data items defined by the operands are X'163' and X'18A', respectively. Provide the 6-byte machine code for this MVC.

4-8. Identify and explain (a) source program; (b) object program; (c) load module.

4-9. Explain and distinguish the job control commands for (a) EXEC ASSEMBLY; (b) EXEC LNKEDT; (c) EXEC (with an optional program name).

4-10. An instruction is labeled C20STEP, as

```
C20STEP   MVC     RECDOUT,RECDIN
```

Your program has to get to this instruction in a way other than normally dropping into it. What would be the required instruction for this purpose?

4-11. What does the cross-reference listing contain, and what is its purpose?

4-12. What do pass 1 and pass 2 of the assembly accomplish?

4-13. What are the four sections of the assembled object file? What are their contents?

4-14. What are the two main functions of the linkage editor?

4-15. What is the function of the system loader?

4-16. What is the load point address? What is another name for it?

4-17. Code, assemble, link, and test a program that reads any number of records and prints their contents. You can define the print area as follows:

```
PRINT     DS      0CL133
          DC      CL20' '
RECOUT    DS      CL80
          DC      CL33' '
```

5

DATA DEFINITION

OBJECTIVE

To provide the definition of the basic data formats and
an overview of the ways of handling such data.

This chapter covers the basic rules for defining data items by means of the DS and
DC directives. It also introduces each of the assembler data types (other than
floating point) along with its related instruction set. In this way, you get an
overview of where and in what way you would use each data type. You also get
to examine the contents of data in main storage for both defined data and input/
output areas.

After mastering the material in this chapter, you may proceed with Chapter
6 for base register addressing and the instruction format, and then with any of
Chapters 7 (character data), 8 (packed data), or 9 (binary data) as required.

Declaratives are statements that the assembler recognizes and assigns storage
locations. They do not generate an executable instruction. Declaratives provide
for the entry of data to a program in two ways:

1. The declarative DS (Define Storage) defines areas for a program to receive
   data that varies in content, such as an input area.

2. The declarative DC (Define Constant) defines constants, such as a title for a report heading, the numeric value 1 to add to a count of pages being printed, or an accumulator initially set to zero.

You may define any data type as DS or DC. The types of declaratives are as follows:

A	address
B	binary digits
C	character
D	double-precision floating-point
E	single-precision floating-point
F	fullword fixed-point binary
H	halfword fixed-point binary
L	extended-precision floating-point
P	packed decimal
Q	symbol naming a DXD or DSECT
S	address in base/displacement format
V	external defined address
X	hexadecimal digits
Y	address
Z	zoned decimal

INPUT DATA

An input record is normally divided into fields of data, such as identification number, name, and balance due for a customer. A collection of all related records, such as for all customers, comprises a file, or, in OS terminology, a data set. Records are usually recognized by a control field, or key—in this case, customer number.

Character data is a common format for fields on records to represent the numbers 0 through 9, the letters A through Z, and special characters such as $, %, #, and @. The combination of 8 bits in a byte provides 2^8, or 256, possible characters, although many printers can print only about 60 different characters.

Figure 5-1 provides some of the common printable characters. As can be seen in the figure, the representation of a blank character is binary 0100 0000, or hex 40. The letter A would appear in storage as 1100 0001, or X'C1', and the numbers 0 through 9 are 1111 0000 through 1111 1001, or X'F0' through X'F9'.

You need not memorize these representations. When necessary, refer to this figure or to Appendix F, which provides the representation of all 256 codes from X'00' through X'FF'.

A keyboard and the system reader deliver input data into main storage normally only in character format, and a terminal screen and a printer also display

Dec	Hex	Binary	Symbol
64	40	0100 0000	blank
75	4B	0100 1011	. (decimal point
91	5B	0101 1011	$ (dollar sign)
92	5C	0101 1100	* (asterisk
107	6B	0110 1011	, (comma)
193	C1	1100 0001	A
.	.		.
.	.		.
201	C9	1100 1001	I
209	D1	1101 0001	J
.	.		.
.	.		.
217	D9	1101 1001	R
226	E2	1110 0010	S
.	.		.
.	.		.
232	E9	1110 1001	Z
240	F0	1111 0000	0 (zero)
.	.		.
.	.		.
249	F9	1111 1001	9 (nine)

Figure 5-1   Representation of selected EBCDIC characters.

output in this format.   An input record containing alphabetic and numeric data read from a terminal or the system reader is read into an input area defined in a program, entirely in character format.   To perform arithmetic on a numeric field, however, you must convert it into packed or binary format.

Here are the contents of an imaginary input record:

COLUMN	FIELD	CONTENTS
01–02	Record code	01
03–05	Customer number	427
06–18	Customer name	JP MCKINNON (left-adjusted, followed by blanks)
19–25	Balance due	0127450 (represents $1,274.50, but the dollar sign, comma, and decimal point are not stored)
26–80	Unused	Blank

Assume that the name of the input file is FILEIN and the name of the 80-byte input area is RECDIN.   The relevant instructions to read a customer record are as follows:

```
                        GETCARD
              GET       FILEIN,RECDIN
              ...
FILEIN        DEFIN     A90EOF
RECDIN        DS        CL80
```

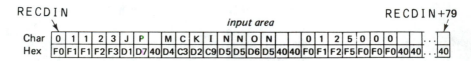

Figure 5-2   Representation of an input record in storage.

The GET macro reads the 80-character input record into the 80-byte area in the program, byte for byte, as shown in Fig. 5-2.

Compare the hexadecimal and character representations, two hex digits for each character in storage.   The numbers 0 through 9 appear as X'F0' through X'F9'.   Also, each blank position appears in storage as X'40' (binary 0100 0000).

You may assign a symbolic name to each field in an input area.   To process the data, you refer to the symbolic names of the fields.   You may move the customer number, name, and balance due to an output area for printing.   And you could convert the balance due into packed (decimal) format in order to accumulate the total balance for all customers.

Internal Representation

Let's examine the contents of data in storage.   Consider the following hex contents of three fields:

$$F0F1F2F3E9D6D6C3D3C3$$

Before looking ahead for the solution, try to answer the following two questions. (1) The length of each field is respectively 4, 3, and 3 bytes.   What are the character contents of each field?   (2) The address of the leftmost byte is X'80046'.   What are the hex addresses of each of the three fields?   The solutions: (1) The character representation is 0123 ZOO CLC.   (2) The addresses are X'80046', X'8004A', and X'8004D', respectively.

DS (DEFINE STORAGE)

The DS statement reserves an area of storage, for example, to define areas for reading records and for printing.   DS does not define a constant value, and at execution time its contents are whatever happens to be in main storage.   Consequently, DS is typically used for defining an area or field that the program is sure to initialize.

The general format of the DS statement is

Name	Operation	Operand
[name]	DS	dTLn 'comments'

- name is an optional entry. If the program needs to refer to a field by name, assign a name in columns 1–8. The name refers to the first (leftmost) byte of the field. Chapter 3 gives the requirements for symbolic names.

- d is an optional duplication factor that tells the assembler how many repetitions of the same area are required. If you omit the factor, the assembler assumes 1. If you specify 2, the assembler creates two adjacent areas; the name (if any) refers to the first area.

- T is a required type of format, such as C for character, P for packed, or F for fullword. You code the type that you expect the field to contain, but note that the assembler is not concerned with its actual contents, and technically the field may contain any type of data.

- Ln is an optional length of the field in bytes (n), positive values only. For example, L3 designates a 3-byte field. If length and comments are omitted (as in DS C), the assembler assumes a length of one byte. The maximum length of a DS field varies by the type (T) of format.

- 'comments' is an optional description between apostrophes of the purpose of the field. If you omit the length (Ln), the assembler assumes that the length is the number of bytes between the apostrophes. For example, the statement DS C'LIZ' defines a 3-byte area but generates no constant value; the contents are uninitialized.

Figure 5-3 provides various DS statements defined as character, packed, and binary. Note the headings on the assembler listing.

- SOURCE STATEMENT in the center lists the original source symbolic language code.

```
  LOC        STMT     SOURCE STATEMENT
Hex address of leftmost
 byte of defined field
  |
003600         5 CHARFLD1 DS     1CL5              5 BYTES NAMED CHARFLD1

003605         7 CHARFLD2 DS     CL5               5 BYTES NAMED CHARFLD2

00360A         9          DS     C  \ Byte         1 BYTE

00360B        11 INAREA   DS     CL80              80 BYTES FOR INPUT

00365B        13 PACKFLD  DS     3PL4  12 Byte     3 4-BYTE FIELDS

003667        15 DATE     DS     CL8'DD/MM/YY'     8 BYTES.   CONTENTS
              16 *                                 DOCUMENTATION ONLY
003670        17 FULLFLD  DS     F Full word Type  A FULLWORD

003674        19 HALFFLD  DS     H Half word Type  RESERVE A HALFWORD
```

Figure 5-3 DS statements in various formats.

- STMT, immediately to the left, gives the statement number of each source statement, as generated by the assembler. CHARFLD1, for example, is statement 5. (Statement 6 is suppressed; it contains the directive SPACE, which causes the assembler to space one line.)
- LOC at the far left is the contents of the location counter that lists the hexadecimal address location of each statement. CHARFLD1 is a 5-byte field beginning in location X'003600'. CHARFLD2 begins immediately following in X'003605'. The assembler defines statements in the same sequence that they are coded, in locations directly one after the other.
- OBJECT CODE lists the assembled machine code: object code instructions and the contents of DCs. DS lists no object code because it merely reserves space, and at assembly time the contents are unknown.
- ADDR1 and ADDR2 refer to instructions, not declaratives.

Each declarative is explained next. Comments to the right of each statement describe the defined area.

Statement 5: CHARFLD1 is a 5-byte DS beginning in location X'003600'. The duplication factor 1 may be omitted, as shown in CHARFLD2 next.

Statement 7: CHARFLD2 at X'003605' immediately follows CHARFLD1.

Statement 9: The address of this unnamed DS is X'360A' because CHARFLD2 at X'3605' is 5 bytes: X'3605' + 5 = X'360A' (5 + 5 = 10, or A in hex).

Statement 11: INAREA defines an 80-byte area to be used for input.

Statement 13: PACKFLD defines three 4-byte fields for packed data. A reference to the name PACKFLD is to the leftmost byte of the first 4-byte field.

Statement 15: DATE illustrates the use of comments. The programmer expects to store the date in the field in the specified format.

Statement 17: FULLFLD defines a 4-byte (fullword) field for binary data.

Statement 19: HALFFLD defines a 2-byte (halfword) field for binary data.

Let's now resolve three questions:

1. Where in storage will a field reside? The assembler assigns a field's location and accounts for the length of every instruction, storage area, and constant. For this task it uses a location counter (see Chapter 3).
2. How does the computer know the location of the field and its length? The assembler translates the symbolic addresses into machine object addresses. If it has assigned, say, CHARFLD1 with the address X'3600', any instruction's

reference to CHARFLD1 is to address X'3600'. For certain instructions, the assembler stores the length of the field as part of the instruction.

3. What are the contents of the field? The contents of a DS field are unknown because the assembler merely reserves the defined area. At the start of program execution, a DS area may contain data from a previous program. Therefore, you may have to initialize DS fields with valid data. The only purpose of DS is to define an area of storage with a specified length. The fact that the field's format is defined as a character, packed, and so on is irrelevant, because at execution time a DS may contain data in any format. The defined format is merely a convenient reminder of the format you expect the field to contain. A major use of DS is to define input and output areas, covered next.

Input Areas

To define fields within a record, code the DS for the record with a zero duplication factor, as DS 0CL80, and define the fields immediately following.

The set of DSs in Fig. 5-4 fully defines the input fields for a customer record. The first DS defines RECDIN as an 80-byte record. However, because of the zero duplication factor in 0CL80, the assembler does not increment its location counter. Consequently, the assembler assigns the next field, CODEIN, with the same location as RECDIN, X'4101'. CODEIN, however, is a 2-byte field that increments the location counter. Although both RECDIN and CODEIN begin at X'4101', a reference to RECDIN is to an 80-byte field, whereas a reference to CODEIN is to the first 2 bytes of RECDIN.

Each DS following RECDIN defines a field within the RECDIN area. To account for the full record length that reads into the program's storage area, the sum of their lengths should equal 80, the length of RECDIN. You may now refer by name to the entire 80-byte record or to any field defined within the record.

In the statement GET FILEIN,RECDIN, the GET macro reads an 80-byte record into an 80-byte area that the program defines as RECDIN. On input, position 1 of the record reads into the leftmost byte of RECDIN (location X'4101' on the assembled DS statement), position 2 reads into the next byte (X'4102'), and position 80 reads into the 80th byte (X'4150').

```
     LOC        STMT    SOURCE STATEMENT

   004101       25 RECDIN   DS    0CL80      80-BYTE INPUT AREA:
   004101       26 CODEIN   DS    CL2        *    RECORD CODE
   004103       27 ACCTIN   DS    CL3        *    ACCOUNT NUMBER
   004106       28 NAMEIN   DS    CL13       *    NAME
   004113       29 BALANIN  DS    CL7        *    BALANCE OWING
   00411A       30         DS    CL55       *    REST OF RECORD
```

Figure 5-4   Area defined for an input record.

A read operation enters all bytes from an input record, even if some positions contain blanks, which enter storage as X'40' in the input area. Also, a read operation erases the previous contents of the input area.

Output Areas

Whereas a read operation erases the previous contents of the input area, a write operation leaves the contents of the output area unchanged. Therefore, if you use DS to define the output area, ensure that the storage positions do not contain garbage from a previous program. At the beginning of program execution, clear the output area to blanks (X'40'), or use DC to define the output area with an initial constant containing blanks. You may also have to clear the print area after writing a line so that it is blank for the next line to be printed.

Although the number of print positions varies with the printer used, a common requirement is to define a 133-byte print area as follows:

```
           PRINT DS CL133      (uninitialized)
or         PRINT DC CL133' '   (initialized)
```

The leftmost byte of the print area acts as a printer forms control character, which controls forms movements such as print and space one line or skip to a new page. You may use the other 132 positions to store data to be printed.

You may also define the print area with a zero duplication factor, as PRINT DS 0CL133, with a declarative to define each field within the output record. Alternatively, you may reference PRINT by relative addressing. (You may use relative addressing to reference any field in main storage.) Since the leftmost byte (the position labeled PRINT) is reserved for the control character, you may refer to the first printable position as PRINT + 1, to the second as PRINT + 2, and so forth:

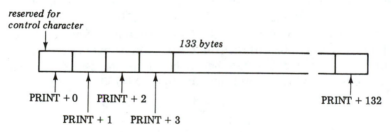

DC (DEFINE CONSTANT)

The DC statement, like DS, reserves storage of a defined length. In addition, DC defines a constant (or value) such as a heading to be printed on a report. DC may define a constant in any format—character, binary, or packed—and in various lengths. The general format for a DC statement is as follows:

Name	Operation	Operand
[name]	DC	dTLn 'constant'

- name is an optional entry. If the program needs to refer to a field by name, assign a name in columns 1–8. The name refers to the first (leftmost) byte of the field.

- d is an optional duplication factor that tells the assembler how many repetitions of the same area are required. If you omit the factor, the assembler assumes 1. If you specify 2, the assembler creates two adjacent areas; the name (if any) refers to the first area.

- T is a required type of format, such as C for character, P for packed, or F for fullword.

- Ln is an optional length of the field in bytes (n), positive values only. If Ln is omitted, the assembler assumes the field length to be the number of bytes defined by the constant. The maximum length of a DC field varies by the type (T) of format.

- 'constant' is the required constant that is to be defined, written between apostrophes. If you omit the length (Ln), the assembler assumes that the length is the number of bytes between the apostrophes. For a constant that continues past column 71, enter any nonblank character in column 72 and resume the constant in column 16 of the next line.

A declarative may define any number of fields, such as

```
DC        C'SAM',P'125', ...
```

Figure 5-5 provides DCs defined as character, packed, and binary with explanations. Note the object code generated by each statement on the assembler listing. LOC gives the hex address of the first byte of each constant. Under OBJECT CODE are the hex contents up to the first 8 bytes (16 hex digits) of the constant. (You can use the directive PRINT DATA to cause the assembler to print the entire hex contents for constants exceeding 8 bytes.)

```
LOC    OBJECT CODE        STMT    SOURCE STATEMENT

004201 C1E2E2C5D4C2D3C5    35 CHARCON1 DC      C'ASSEMBLER'    CHARACTER
00420A F2F5                36 CHARCON2 DC      CL2'25'         CHARACTER
00420C 00025C              37 PACKCON  DC      PL3'25'         PACKED
00420F 00            ——— Setting Up For A Fullword ———
004210 00000019            38 FULLCON  DC      F'25'           FULLWORD
004214 0019                39 HALFCON  DC      H'25'           HALFWORD
```

Figure 5-5 DC statements in various formats.

- CHARCON1 defines a character constant containing 'ASSEMBLER'.
- CHARCON2 defines a character constant containing the number 25.
- PACKCON defines a packed constant containing the number 25.
- FULLCON defines a binary fullword constant containing the number 25. The assembler converts your decimal number into binary format.
- HALFCON defines a binary halfword constant containing the number 25.

Note the difference in the generated constant for each of the data types for the number 25. Character 25 is X'F2F5', packed 25 is X'025C' (where C is a plus sign), and binary 25 is X'0019'.

HEXADECIMAL CONSTANTS

Two hexadecimal digits can represent any of the 256 different characters. You can use hexadecimal (X) format to define values that cannot easily be defined in formats such as character, packed, zoned, or binary. A major use is in defining edit word constants, covered in Chapter 8. The following rules apply to hexadecimal constants:

- They may be defined in length from 1 byte (two hex digits) to 256 bytes (512 hex digits).
- They may contain only the hex digits 0 through 9 and A through F.
- A length (Ln), if defined, specifies the number of bytes, one byte for each pair of hex digits. The assembler right-adjusts hex constants. Therefore, if the defined length is less than the constant, the assembler truncates the constant on the left. If the defined length is longer, the assembler pads hex zeros to the left.

See Fig. 5-6 for examples of hex DCs. Compare the defined constant to the object code:

HEX1 defines a DC that requires 2 bytes of storage.

HEX2 defines a length of 1 byte but the constant is 2 bytes. This is a possible coding error, because the assembler has truncated the constant on the left.

HEX3 specifies a length as 3 but the constant is 2 bytes. The assembler pads zeros on the left.

HEX4 defines a constant with three hex digits: 1½ bytes. The assembler pads a hex zero to the left, resulting in a 2-byte constant.

HEX5 illustrates the duplication factor and defines three constants each containing X'FF'. The name HEX5 refers to the first constant with a length of 1 byte.

```
LOC    OBJECT CODE      STMT     SOURCE STATEMENT

004216 1A76             46 HEX1     DC    X'1A76'
004218 76               47 HEX2     DC    XL1'1A76'       TRUNCATE
004219 001A76           48 HEX3     DC    XL3'1A76'       PAD ZEROS
00421C 012C             49 HEX4     DC    X'12C'          PAD ZERO
00421E FFFFFF           50 HEX5     DC    3X'FF'          3 CONSTANTS
```

Figure 5-6 Declaratives in hexadecimal format.

Do not confuse hex constants with constants of other formats. Note the difference between the following character and hexadecimal definitions:

FORMAT	CONSTANT	BYTES	HEX REPRESENTATION
Character	DC C'ABCD'	4	|C1|C2|C3|C4|
Hexadecimal	DC X'ABCD'	2	|AB|CD|

LITERALS

The use of literals is a shortcut way of writing a DC. A literal begins with an equal (=) sign followed by a character for the type of constant and then the constant between apostrophes ('). The basic rules that apply to DCs apply to literals as well.

The following example compares using a DC and using a literal:

```
Use of a DC:       HEADING   DC    C'INVENTORY'
                             MVC   PRINT+20(9),HEADING
Use of a literal:            MVC   PRINT+20(9),=C'INVENTORY'
```

Both operations accomplish the same results. However, the use of the literal ='INVENTORY' saves you writing the line of coding for the DC.

The assembler recognizes that an operand beginning with an equal sign is a literal. The assembler creates an object code constant, assigns an address, and stores the constant as part of the program in an unnamed *literal pool*. Two or more literals defined identically within a program are usually set up as only one constant in the literal pool. Literals generated by input/output macros, such as OPEN and GET, are also included in the pool.

The Literal Pool

The assembler organizes the literal pool into four sections and within these sections stores the literals in order of their appearance in the program:

SECTION	CONTENTS
1	All literals whose length is a multiple of 8
2	All remaining literals whose length is a multiple of 4
3	All remaining literals whose length is a multiple of 2
4	All odd-length literals

Unless directed otherwise, the assembler stores the literal pool at the end of the control section and prints it immediately following the END statement. However, the LTORG directive can cause the assembler to store literals anywhere in a program. Whenever you use LTORG, the assembler stores and prints the literals up to that point, from either the start of the program or from the previous LTORG.

Name	Operation	Operand
[name]	LTORG	[not used, omit]

Figure 5-7 depicts various uses of literals. Note that the sequence of the literals in the literal pool after LTORG is different from the sequence in which they were originally coded. (Chapter 8 covers the ZAP and AP instructions.)

```
LOC     OBJECT CODE       STMT     SOURCE STATEMENT
004222  D207 3C40 3C58    57              MVC    SAVLIT,=C'COMPUTER'          MOVE CONSTANT
004228  F820 3C48 3C68    58              ZAP    PAGECT,=P'0'                 ZERO PAGECT
00422E  FA10 3C4B 3C69    59              AP     LINECT,=P'1'                 ADD TO LINECT
004234  D205 3C4D 3C60    60              MVC    VALUEPR,=X'40204B202060'     MOVE CONSTANT
00423A  D201 3C53 3C66    61              MVC    ASTERPR,=C'**'               MOVE CONSTANT
                          62      *               . . .

004240  4040404040404040  63      SAVLIT  DC     CL8' '
004248  00000C            64      PAGECT  DC     PL3'0'
00424B  000C              65      LINECT  DC     PL2'0'
00424D                    66      VALUEPR DS     CL6
004253                    67      ASTERPR DS     CL2
004258                    68              LTORG
004258  C3D6D4D7E4E3C5D9  69                     =C'COMPUTER'          ⎧ Literal
004260  40204B202060      70                     =X'40204B202060'      ⎪ pool
004266  5C5C              71                     =C'**'                ⎨ generated
004268  0C                72                     =P'0'                 ⎪ by the
004269  1C                73                     =P'1'                 ⎩ assembler
```

Figure 5-7 Use of literals.

DATA TYPES

This section describes the major data types used in assembler programming.

Character Format

Character format may contain any of the characters in the instruction set, including the blank, but is usually restricted to those that can be keyed in or displayed. Typical uses are for descriptive information, for input from external devices, and for output on the printer or display screen. The maximum length of a character constant is 256 bytes. A sample 35-character declarative for a heading is

```
HEADING  DC  C'International Balloon Manufacturers'
```

Zoned Format

Zoned decimal data is similar to character data but is of limited use. You could use a zoned format to define a field containing data that will later be packed, such as a numeric field read from an input record. The length may be defined from 1 to 16 bytes. The constant may contain only the digits 0 through 9, a sign (+ or −), and a decimal point. A sample zoned declarative for a 5-byte input field is

```
RATEIN  DS  ZL5
```

Packed Format

Packed format is used for ordinary decimal arithmetic. The plus or minus sign is the rightmost half-byte of the field. Each other packed byte contains two digits, one in each half-byte. For example, the packed value +250 requires 2 bytes, as |25|0C|, where C is a plus sign. The length may be defined from 1 to 16 bytes. The following packed declarative initializes an accumulator to zero:

```
TOTAL  DC  PL4'0'
```

Binary Data Types

You may define binary data in one of three ways, depending on your requirements. Fullword (F) and halfword (H) fixed-point formats define binary data for arithmetic purposes, always performed in the general registers. Binary (B) format defines actual bits in main storage, which you could use, for example, to store on/off conditions or for Boolean operations.

Fullword format defines a 4-byte binary data item aligned on a fullword boundary (evenly divisible by 4). An example is

```
FULLCON  DC  F'15'
```

Halfword format defines a 2-byte binary data item aligned on a halfword boundary (evenly divisible by 2).   An example is

```
HALFCON   DC   H'15'
```

The less used binary (B) format defines each bit in a string.   The following example defines a byte's worth of bits:

```
BITCON    DC   B'01011001'
```

Address Constants

An address constant may occasionally be used to define an address in a program. One example is to modify an address to step through a table, although you can handle this situation by other means.   Another situation involves transferring an address from a program to a subprogram to make data recognized in both programs. An address constant is a fullword and is coded within parentheses:

```
ADDRCON   DC   A(TABLE)
```

DATA MOVEMENT

The major data formats have an associated instruction set for data movement, comparison, conversion, and, where applicable, arithmetic.

Character Data

The MVC instruction is designed to move character and zoned data in main storage, although technically it can move any type of data.   The following MVC copies the contents of CHRFLD1 to CHRFLD2:

```
           MVC   CHRFLD2,CHRFLD1
           ...
CHRFLD1 DC   C'TOTAL'
CHRFLD2 DS   CL5
```

Packed Data

The ZAP (Zero Add Packed) instruction is designed to transfer packed data.   The following ZAP instruction replaces the contents of TOTAL with packed zeros:

```
           ZAP   TOTAL,=P'0'
```

Operand 2 must contain packed data, but operand 1 may contain anything.

Fullword and Halfword Data

Since binary arithmetic is performed in registers, your concern is transferring the data between main storage and registers and between two registers. The following examples refer to these declaratives:

```
FULLWD   DS      F
HALFWD   DS      H
```

Storage to register:

```
L        6,FULLWD        Load fullword in register
L        7,=A(TABLE)     Load fullword in register
LH       8,HALFWD        Load halfword in register
```

Register to register:

```
LR       5,9     Load register 9 into 5
```

Register to storage:

```
ST       6,FULLWD        Store fullword in storage
STH      8,HALFWD        Store halfword in storage
```

Use the MVC instruction to move these declaratives from one storage location to another.

Symbol Length Attribute

The assembler permits explicit lengths coded absolutely, as already described, and symbolically. The symbol length attribute uses L' followed by a symbolic name. The following uses the definitions of FIELD1 and FIELD2 and compares the two methods:

```
FIELD1   DS      CL5
FIELD2   DS      CL5
```

Absolute explicit length: MVC FIELD1(5),FIELD2
Symbolic explicit length: MVC FIELD1(L'FIELD2),FIELD2

The intention in this example is to move 5 bytes. Since the length of FIELD2 is 5, the assembler understands the explicit length to be 5.

DATA COMPARISON AND BRANCHING

The logical ability of a computer enables a program to compare the contents of one field to another, to check if a numeric value is positive, negative, or zero, and to check for an arithmetic overflow in which a numeric field is too small for a calculated result.   On the 370 series, comparing fields and performing arithmetic sets the condition code, which consists of 2 bits in the program status word (PSW). The following shows the results of these operations on the condition code:

RESULT	CONDITION CODE	
Equal or zero	00	(0)
Low or minus	01	(1)
High or plus	10	(2)
Arithmetic overflow	11	(3)

Branching

With normal processing, the computer executes instructions in storage, one after another.   *Conditional branch* instructions permit a program to test what condition was set and to branch to different addresses in the program.   You may therefore code your program to test, for example, for valid record codes.   If a record does not contain the correct code in a specified column, you may branch to an error routine that prints a warning message.

The condition code remains set until another comparison or arithmetic operation changes it.   Thus using a branch instruction to test the condition code does not change it.

To test the condition code to determine what action to take (for example, was the result of a comparison high, low, or equal?), use the following conditional branch instructions:

CONDITION CODE	CONDITIONAL BRANCHES	
0 = Equal/zero	BE (branch equal)	BNE (branch not equal)
1 = Low/minus	BL (branch low)	BNL (branch not low)
2 = High/plus	BH (branch high)	BNH (branch not high)

Similarly, a program may test the condition code after an arithmetic operation to determine whether the result is zero (0), negative (1), positive (2), or an overflow:

CONDITION CODE	CONDITIONAL BRANCHES	
0 = Equal/zero	BZ (branch zero)	BNZ (branch not zero)
1 = Low/minus	BM (branch minus)	BNM (branch not minus)
2 = High/plus	BP (branch plus)	BNP (branch not plus)
3 = Overflow	BO (branch overflow)	BNO (branch not overflow)

BE and BZ are the same, BL and BM are the same, and so forth. Each of the preceding conditional branch instructions is called an extended mnemonic and is a unique use of the Branch on Condition (BC) instruction, explained in detail in Chapter 6.

Two other branch instructions are *unconditional branch* (B), and *no operation* (NOP). The unconditional branch tests if any condition (high, low, equal) exists. Since there is always at least one condition, use B if a branch is always required. For example, after processing an input record, you may return to process the next record by means of an unconditional branch:

```
A10LOOP
        ...                     Process the record
        GET    RECDIN           Read the next record
        B      A10LOOP          Loop back
```

NOP, which tests no condition, has specialized uses. You could use one or more NOP instructions where you later expect to insert different machine code.

Character Data

The CLC instruction, used for comparing character and zoned data, makes a *logical* comparison—that is, it compares, bit for bit, from left to right and does not consider an arithmetic sign.

For example, a program expects a file of customer records to be in sequence by customer number. It sequence-checks each record by comparing the customer number on the input record just read against the customer number on the record that was previously read and processed. The possibilities are as follows:

NEW CUSTOMER NUMBER READ	CONDITION CODE SETTING	DECISION
Equal	0	Same customer as previous
Low	1	Out of sequence
High	2	Next customer

The following example compares two fields and, if the result is high, branches to another address:

```
     CLC   NEW,PREV   Compare the contents of NEW to PREV.
     BH    R20HIGH    If NEW is higher, branch to R20HIGH (an address
                      of a routine in the program).
     ...
NEW  DS    CL4        Contains the account number just read.
PREV DS    CL4        Contains the previous account number read.
```

Interpret the preceding instructions as follows: Compare the new account (assume 1347) to the previously read account (assume 1208). Since NEW's contents are higher than PREV's, the condition code is set to high (2).   Next, BH tests if the high condition code is set.   Because the code is high, the program branches to R20HIGH.   If the code was not high, the computer would execute the next sequential instruction (NSI) following the BH.

Packed Data

The CP instruction, used for comparing packed data, makes an *algebraic* comparison—that is, its comparisons consider the arithmetic sign.   Thus any positive nonzero value is greater than zero, and zero is greater than any negative value. The following CP instruction compares a packed amount; if equal to zero, the program branches to the instruction labeled X10ZERO:

```
          CP        TOTALPK,=P'0'
          BE        X10ZERO
```

The following ZAP instruction also sets the condition code, and BM tests for a negative value in AMNT1:

```
          ZAP       AMNT1,AMNT1
          BM        X10MINUS
```

Binary Data

The fixed-point binary instructions C, CH, and CR also make algebraic comparisons—that is, the comparisons consider the arithmetic sign.   The following instructions compare binary data, and each could be followed by a conditional branch, such as BH or BE:

```
    C         7,FULLWD1  Compare register to fullword
    CH        8,HALFWD1  Compare register to halfword
    CR        7,8        Compare registers
```

Programming Style

Unnecessary branching may cause a program to be less readable.   For example, a program has to print a warning if customers' balances exceed their credit limit. The following example contains unnecessary branch operations that work but are poor programming practice:

```
              CP        CUSTBAL,CREDLIM
              BH        D30
    D20       B         D40
    D30       MVC       MSGOUT,=C'OVER LIMIT'
              B         D20
    D40       ...
```

The next example remedies the unnecessary branches:

```
                   CP        CUSTBAL,CREDLIM
                   BNH       D20
                   MVC       MSGOUT,=C'OVER LIMIT'
        D20        ...
```

DATA CONVERSION

A program often has to convert data from one format to another. For example, numeric data entered from a keyboard would be in character or zoned format and would have to be converted to packed for arithmetic purposes.

Character or Zoned to Packed Format

The PACK instruction converts character and zoned data from operand 2 into packed format in operand 1, as the following example shows:

```
              PACK    .PACKFLD,ZONEFLD    (operand 1←operand 2)
              ...
   ZONEFLD    DC      ZL5'12345'          |F1|F2|F3|F4|F5|
   PACKFLD    DS      PL3                 |12|34|5F|
```

The operation reduces the zoned value X'F1F2F3F4F5' to packed X'12345F'.

Packed to Binary Format

The CVB instruction converts packed data into binary format. The packed field must be in an 8-byte field, usually defined as a doubleword (D format). The following example zaps a packed field into DBLWORD, and CVB converts it into binary format in register 6:

```
              ZAP     DBLWORD,PACKFLD
              CVB     6,DBLWORD           (operand 1←operand 2)
              ...
   PACKFLD DS PL3
   DBLWORD DS D
```

Binary to Packed Format

The CVD instruction converts binary data into packed (decimal) format. The packed field must be in an 8-byte field, usually defined as a doubleword (D format). The following example converts the binary contents in register 7 (operand 1) into packed format in DBLWORD (operand 2):

```
        CVD     7,DBLWORD           (operand 1→operand 2)
```

Packed to Character or Zoned Format

The UNPK instruction converts packed data from operand 2 into character or
zoned format in operand 1, as the following example shows:

```
              UNPK     ZONEFLD,PACKFLD  (operand 1←operand 2)
              ...
PACKFLD       DC       P'12345'         |12|34|5C|
ZONEFLD       DS       ZL5              |F1|F2|F3|F4|F5|
```

The operation expands the packed value X'12345F' to zoned X'F1F2F3F4F5'. The
ED (edit) instruction provides a more powerful way to unpack packed data.

THE EQUATE DIRECTIVE: EQU

The EQU directive is used to equate one symbolic address to another.   The
assembler only acts on EQU and does not generate executable code.

Name	Operation	Operand
[name]	EQU	an expression

You may assign more than one symbolic name to a field, just as a person
may have a full name and a nickname.   In the following example, the assembler
assigns the identical attributes to P as it has to PRINT:

```
PRINT    DC      CL133' '   Define PRINT
P        EQU     PRINT      Equate P to PRINT
```

You may now use either symbol to reference the same location, with a length of
133 bytes.   However, the assembler requires that you define the symbol in the
EQU operand field, PRINT, before the EQU statement.   DOS assembler allows
only one operand, whereas OS allows three, separated by commas.
        You can use the assembler's location counter reference to equate an address.
An asterisk as an operand is a reference to the current value in the location counter:

```
LOC:   X'3012'    SAVE   DS    CL3
       X'301A'    KEEP   EQU   *5
```

After the assembler processes SAVE, its location counter contains X'3012' + 3,
or X'3015'.   The address of KEEP is equated to the "address" in the operand,

*+5, meaning the contents of the location counter plus 5. KEEP is therefore assigned the address X'3015' plus 5, or X'301A' and has a length attribute of 1.

SET LOCATION COUNTER: ORG

The ORG directive tells the assembler to alter or reoriginate the value of the location counter during assembly. You can use ORG to redefine data areas in the program, that is, one on top of the other.

Name	Operation	Operand
[name]	ORG	[not used, omit]

The name is normally used only in macro writing and is otherwise omitted. The operand, if any, is a symbolic address with or without relative addressing (for example, A30 or A30 + 1000) or a reference to the location counter itself (such as *+20). The assembler sets the location counter to the value of the expression. The operand may not be an absolute address, such as 8192 or X'2000'.

If you omit the operand, the assembler sets the location counter to the maximum value that it has been set up to this point. Beware of ORG with no operand, because the assembler may mistakenly use a comment for its operand. In the following example, the assembler uses the asterisk in column 41 as the ORG operand. Instead of setting the location counter to the previous high setting, it is set incorrectly to the current setting of the location counter:

```
column: 10      16                          41
                                            |
         ORG                                * Reset location counter
```

The solution is either to omit the asterisk or to insert a comma in column 16, which tells the assembler explicitly that there is no operand:

```
         ORG       ,                        * Reset location counter
```

The following defines an input record and uses ORG to redefine the input area for definition of a second record format:

```
         RECDIN    DS      0CL80
         NAMEIN    DS      CL20
         ADDR1IN   DS      CL30
         ADDR2IN   DS      CL30
                   ORG     RECDIN
         NUMBIN    DS      CL10
```

The last declarative defines only the first 10 bytes of RECDIN. Advance the assembler location counter to the end of the 80-byte input area by means of another DS or an ORG:

```
        DS     CL70       (Define 70 more bytes)
  or    ORG    ,          (Set to previous high setting)
  or    ORG    *+70       (Set to present location + 70)
  or    ORG    RECDIN+80  (Set to RECDIN + 80)
```

SAMPLE PROGRAM: DEFINED INPUT FIELDS

The program in Fig. 5-8 reads and prints any number of records. The program is similar to the one in Fig. 4-5 except that this program defines fields within the input and output records.

Input.   Any number of records in the following format:

01–05	Part number
06–20	Part description
21–24	Quantity on hand

Processing.   The program reads records and moves part number, description, and quantity to the output area for printing.

Output.   The program prints a heading at the start and prints each record in this format:

11–15	Part number
21–35	Part description
41–44	Quantity on hand

A STORAGE DUMP OF DATA AREAS

Figure 5-9 shows the hexadecimal contents of the declaratives defined in the preceding program from the first byte of RECORDIN through QTYPR, as at the end of processing. The program listing shows RECORDIN beginning at location (LOC) X'293'. In this particular execution, the program happened to load in storage

```
LOC     OBJECT CODE       STMT   SOURCE STATEMENT
                             3       PRINT ON,NODATA,NOGEN
                             5  *    ----- I N I T I A L I Z A T I O N -----
                             6  *
000000                       8  PROG05   START                            INITIALIZE
                             9           INIT                             OPEN FILES
                            15           OPEN   FILEIN,PRINTER            SKIP TO NEW PAGE
                            25           PUTPR  PRINTER,PRHEAD,SK1        PRINT HEADING
                            32           PUTPR  PRINTER,PRHEAD,WSP2       READ 1ST RECORD
                            39           GET    FILEIN,RECORDIN

                            46  *    R E A D   &   P R I N T   R O U T I N E
                            47  *
00005A  D204 3370 3291      48  A10LOOP  MVC    PARTPR,PARTIN             MOVE PART NO.,
000060  D20E 337A 3296      49           MVC    DESCPR,DESCIN            * DESCRIPTION
000066  D203 338E 32A5      50           MVC    QTYPR,QTYIN             * QUANTITY
                            51           PUTPR  PRINTER,PRLINE,WSP1       PRINT
                            58           GET    FILEIN,RECORDIN           READ NEXT RECORD
000090  47F0 3058           64           B      A10LOOP                   LOOP

                            66  *    E N D - O F - F I L E   R O U T I N E
                            67  *
                            68  A90EOF   PUTPR  PRINTER,PRHEAD,SK1        SKIP PAGE
                            75           CLOSE  FILEIN,PRINTER            CLOSE FILES
                            84           PDUMP  RECORDIN,QTYPR+4
                            90           EOJ    ,                         TERMINATE JOB

                            94  *    D E C L A R A T I V E S
                            95  *
                            96  FILEIN   DEFIN  A90EOF                    DEFINE INPUT
                           122  PRINTER  DEFPR                            DEFINE PRINTER

                                                                          INPUT RECORD:
000293                     152  RECORDIN DS     OCL80
000293                     153  PARTIN   DS     CL05                    * PART #
000298                     154  DESCIN   DS     CL15                    * DESCRIPTION
0002A7                     155  QTYIN    DS     ZL04                    * QUANTITY
0002AB                     156           DS     CL56                    * UNUSED
```

Figure 5-8 Program: defined input and output fields.

Figure 5-8 *continued on next page.*

```
0002E3                          158  PRHEAD  DS   0CL133            HEADING LINE:
0002E3  4040404040404040        159          DC   CL10' '          *
0002ED  D3C9E2E340D6C640        160          DC   CL123'LIST OF PARTS FOR ACE ELECTRONICS'

000368                          162  PRLINE  DS   0CL133            PRINT AREA:
000368  4040404040404040        163          DC   CL10' '          *
000372                          164  PARTPR  DS   CL05             *  PART #
000377  4040404040            165          DC   CL05' '          *
00037C                          166  DESCPR  DS   CL15             *  DESCRIPTION
00038B  404040404040            167          DC   CL05' '          *
000390                          168  QTYPR   DS   ZL04             *  QUANTITY
000394  4040404040404040        169          DC   CL89' '

0003F0                          171          LTORG ,
0003F0  5B5BC2D6D7C5D540        172                =C'$$BOPEN '     GEN'D LITERALS
0003F8  5B5BC2C3D3D6E2C5        173                =C'$$BCLOSE'
000400  5B5BC2D7C4E4D4D7        174                =CL8'$$BPDUMP'
000408  0000029300000394        175                =A(RECORDIN,QTYPR+4)
000410  00000158                176                =A(PRINTER)
000414  000002E3                177                =A(PRHEAD)
000418  000000C8                178                =A(FILEIN)
00041C  00000293                179                =A(RECORDIN)
000420  00000368                180                =A(PRLINE)

000482                          182          END  PROG05            END OF ASSEMBLY
```

Output:-   LIST OF PARTS FOR ACE ELECTRONICS

```
10436    TERMINALS        0023
10927    MODEMS           0120
24322    REGULATORS       0152
33569    MICROPROCESSORS  0022
```

Figure 5-8 (*continued*)

```
84F300                              404040F3  F3F5F6F9    D4C9C3D9  D6D7D9D6  C3C5E2E2  D6D9E2F0
84F320    F0F2F240  40404040  40404040  40404040    40404040  40404040  40404040  40404040
84F340    40404040  40404040  40404040  40404040    40404040  40404040  4040408B  40404040
84F360    40404040  40D3C9E2  E340D6C6  40D7C1D9    E3E240C6  D6D940C1  C3C540C5  D3C5C3E3
84F380    D9D6D5C9  C3E24040  40404040  40404040    40404040  40404040  40404040  40404040
84F3A0    40404040  --SAME--
84F3E0    09404040  40404040  4040F3F3  F5F6F940    40404040  D4C9C3D9  D6D7D9D6  C3C5E2E2
84F400    D6D9E240  40404040  F0F0F2F2  40404040
```

Figure 5-9　Hexadecimal dump of storage.

beginning at X'84F078'.　Consequently, the actual location of RECORDIN during execution would be

Starting point of program	X'84F078'
Location (LOC) of RECORDIN	X'000293'
Actual storage location	X'84F30B'

You can locate the contents of RECORDIN in the storage dump beginning with the first hex characters on the top line.　At the extreme left is the address of the leftmost byte of each line.　The first line starts at X'84F300':

If you count across each pair of hex digits (or where digits would appear) as one byte, you'll find that X'84F30B' is the actual storage location of RECORDIN, just as was calculated.　The blank columns are only for readability.

RECORDIN contains the last input record.　PARTIN occupies the first 5 bytes containing X'F3F3F5F6F9' or 33569, and DESCIN occupies the next 15 bytes containing MICROPROCESSORS, continuing on the second line.　The dump also shows the contents of PRHEAD.

Note that if X'84F300' is the leftmost byte, the address of the byte beginning the right half of the dump is X'84F310'.

Lines such as the one at X'84F3A0' that show

```
40404040  --SAME--
```

contain the same value in every byte, in this case X'40'.

Chapter 15 further develops storage dumps and explains how to generate your own.

DEBUGGING TIPS

- Violating the rules of declaratives is common, such as defining a DS with a constant, which is treated as a comment, and defining a DC without a constant. Watch for defining a constant length (Ln) that does not agree with the defined constant, as CL3'DATE'.
- A program, when corrected and reassembled, may cause errors during execution. Be sure that the input definition agrees exactly with the actual input record format—any difference causes incorrect results.
- A difficult error to detect is caused by incorrect branching—reversing operands 1 and 2 or using, say, BNH instead of BNL.

KEY POINTS

- The DS statement reserves an area of storage, for example, to define areas for reading records and for printing. A DS does not define a constant value, and at execution time its contents are whatever happens to be in main storage.
- The DC statement defines a constant in any format, such as character, binary, and packed, and in various lengths.
- Hexadecimal (X) format can define values that cannot easily be defined in formats such as character, packed, zoned, or binary.
- A literal is a shortcut way of writing a DC. A literal begins with an equal (=) sign followed by a character for the type of constant and a constant between apostrophes. The assembler assigns an address and stores the constant in a literal pool.
- Character format may contain any of the characters in the instruction set, including the blank. Typical uses are for descriptive information, for input from external devices, and for output on the printer or display screen.
- Zoned format can be used to define a field containing data that will be later packed, such as a numeric field read from an input record.
- Packed format is used for ordinary decimal arithmetic.
- You may define binary data as fullword (F) and halfword (H) fixed-point formats for arithmetic performed in the general registers or binary (B) format as actual bits.
- An address constant may be used to define an address in a program.
- The MVC instruction moves character and zoned data in main storage, although technically it can move any type of data. The ZAP (Zero Add Packed) instruction is designed to transfer packed data. The load and store instructions transfer binary data between main storage and registers and between two registers.

- Comparing fields and performing arithmetic set the condition code, which consists of 2 bits in the program status word (PSW). Conditional branch instructions permit a program to test what condition was set and to branch to different addresses in a program.
- The PACK instruction converts character and zoned data into packed format. The CVB instruction converts packed data into binary format. The CVD instruction converts binary data into packed format. The UNPK instruction converts packed data into character or zoned format.

PROBLEMS

5-1. Define the following declaratives:
   (a) A declarative named SAM1 that reserves 12 bytes of storage for character data
   (b) A declarative named SAM2 that reserves 4 bytes of storage for packed data
   (c) A declarative named SAM3 that reserves a halfword of storage for binary data
   (d) A 2-byte packed constant named DAN1 containing 150
   (e) A character constant named DAN2 containing SPACE AGE CORP
   (f) A fullword constant named DAN3 containing 35
   (g) A hexadecimal constant named DAN4 containing X'53C7'

5-2. Determine which instruction you would use to perform each of these functions:
   (a) Transfer character data between two storage locations
   (b) Transfer packed data between two storage locations
   (c) Transfer binary data from a fullword to a register
   (d) Transfer binary data from a halfword to a register
   (e) Transfer binary data from one register to another
   (f) Compare the contents of two registers
   (g) Compare the contents of two packed fields
   (h) Compare the contents of two character fields
   (i) Compare the contents of a register to a fullword
   (j) Convert zoned to packed format
   (k) Convert packed to binary in a register

5-3. A field is tested and found to be negative. What is the condition code setting?

5-4. Refer to the defined data and explain the coding error in each of the instructions:

```
            CHARA   DC      CL4'ADAM'
            PACKB   DC      PL3'12345'
            FULLC   DS      F
    (a)             MVC     CHARA,PACKB
    (b)             ZAP     PACKB,CHARA
    (c)             MVC     7,FULLC
    (d)             ZAP     PACKB,=C'25'
    (e)             LH      5,FULLC
    (f)             PACK    PACKB,PACKB
    (g)             CLC     CHARA,=P'1250'
    (h)             CVB     7,CHARA
```

5-5. This is a partial hex dump of storage:

| 03251C | C1C4C1D4 | 000200 |

(a) The first field begins at X'352C5' in storage and is 3 bytes long. The second field is 4 bytes, and the third field is 3 bytes. What are their addresses?

(b) The first field is packed, the second is character, and the third is in binary format. Give the character contents or decimal value of each field.

5-6. Code and test a program that reads and prints any number of customer records. The record format is as follows:

01–05	Customer number
06–25	Customer name
26–45	Street address
46–65	City/state
66–71	Balance due (two decimal places)

Print a suitable heading, and arrange the output data evenly in the print area.

6

BASE REGISTERS
AND
SUBROUTINES

OBJECTIVE

To explain the assigning and loading of base registers,
the instruction format, and the use of subroutines.

The 16 general-purpose registers are numbered from 0 through 15 and are referenced by number. Each register contains 32 data bits, numbered from left to right as 0 through 31. They provide two main functions:

1. *Binary Arithmetic*. The general registers perform all binary arithmetic. For binary values, bit 0 (to the left) is the sign bit and bits 1–31 are data. Chapter 9 covers the details of binary arithmetic.

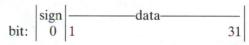

2. *Addressing*. The general registers perform all the addressing involved in referencing main storage. A register when used for addressing purposes is known as a base register. Although extended architecture on the largest models provides 31 bits for addressing, on most models addressing uses only

the rightmost 24 bits (bits 8–31), giving a maximum address of $2^{24} - 1$, or 16,777,215:

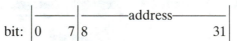

$$\text{bit: } \begin{array}{|c|c|}\hline 0 \quad\quad 7 & 8 \quad\quad\quad\quad\text{address}\quad\quad\quad\quad 31 \\\hline\end{array}$$

Certain instructions of RX format have the facility to modify or index an address, and a register when used for this purpose is known as an index register.

Some of the registers have special functions, and the following restrictions apply:

REGISTER	RESTRICTION
0–1	You may use register 0 and 1 freely for temporary calculations, but supervisor operations such as CALL and GET destroy their contents. Also, because the supervisor uses register 0 as its own base register, the system does not permit you to assign it as a base register for your programs.
2	Register 2 is available as a base register or for binary arithmetic, with one exception: The TRT instruction uses it to store a generated value, thus limiting its use as a base register.
3–12	Registers 3–12 are always available as base registers or for binary arithmetic.
13	Control program routines including the input/output system use register 13. Use it only when performing linkage to a subprogram.
14–15	Control program and subprogram routines also use these registers. Their use is restricted, as for 0 and 1, for temporary calculations.

You may use the EQU directive to assign a name to a register. For example, the statement LINKREG EQU 7 tells the assembler to substitute the value 7 for each reference to the name LINKREG in the program. Thus the instruction

```
BAL LINKREG,H10PAGE
```

becomes

```
BAL 7,H10PAGE
```

CONTROL SECTIONS

For practical purposes, only ten registers, 3 through 12, are available for use as base registers. It would appear, then, that because a displacement is limited to 4K of storage, the largest program you can assemble and execute is 10 × 4K, or

40K, although up to 16 million bytes may be available. However, the common practice is to write large programs in separate control sections (CSECTs). You assemble the control sections with their own sets of base registers and link-edit them into one executable load module.

By definition, a control section is "a block of coding that can be relocated (independent of other coding) without altering the operating logic of the program." Neither the assembler nor the linkage editor recognizes a program as such—each processes one or more control sections.

Either the START or CSECT directive identifies the first or only control section of a program, and CSECT identifies subsequent control sections. An END directive or another CSECT terminates a CSECT, and END terminates an entire program. Chapter 13 covers features of program sectioning and CSECT.

If you know where the program will be loaded for execution, you may code START with an initial value (evenly divisible by 8) for the assembler location counter. However, under most systems, you do not know where programs will reside. You omit the initial value from the START, and the assembler sets its location counter at 0.

The following examples illustrate various uses of START and CSECT:

1. The control section is named PROGA and the location counter is set to 0. This coding practice is common when it is not known in advance where programs will reside during execution.

```
PROGA    START
```

2. The name of the control section is PROGB. The assembler sets the location counter to X'4800' or 18432, where, presumably, the program will be loaded:

```
PROGB    START   X'4800'
```

3. The control section is unnamed and the location counter is set to 18432:

```
START   18432
```

4. The name of the control section is PROGC and the location counter is set to 0:

```
PROGC    CSECT
```

OS, but not DOS, permits a value in the CSECT operand for the location counter.

The system loader program on execution relocates each control section in main storage.

Consider a system in which the load address is not known. You would code START with a blank or 0 operand, and the assembler would begin its location counter at 0. Thus the first statement on the assembler listing would begin at location 0. Let's say that the program actually loads into storage for execution at X'14200', where the first instruction would begin. When using a storage dump to debug the program, you have to reconcile the listing with the dump. For example, an instruction listed under LOC at X'0048' is in storage at X'14200' + X'0048', or X'14248'.

BASE REGISTER ADDRESSING

For addressing locations in main storage, the 370-series computers use a common design feature that splits addresses into two parts: a base address and a displacement from that address.

1. *Base Address*. The base address references the beginning of a storage area. You code a BALR instruction to load the address into a register and a USING directive to tell the assembler that this register is to be the base register containing the address of the start of the control section. (The INIT macro has performed these functions up to now.) You can allocate any register, preferably 3 through 12, for the base address and subsequently may not use it for any other purpose.

2. *Displacement*. For each instruction and declarative in the program, the assembler calculates its displacement, the number of bytes from the base address.

The effective address of a main storage location is determined by two parts: the contents of a base register combined with a displacement.

There are two major advantages to base/displacement addressing:

1. The instruction length is reduced because each address requires only 2 bytes rather than 3.

2. The system facilitates program relocatability. Instead of assigning specific storage addresses, the assembler determines each address relative to a base address. At execute time, the base address, which may be almost anywhere in storage, is loaded into a base register. For example, the program may execute today beginning at location X'64200' and tomorrow at location X'A3500'.

The purpose of program relocatability is to facilitate multiprogramming, which involves the concurrent execution of two or more programs in storage. Note, however, that the computer can execute only one instruction at a time, and it flip-flops between programs as available time permits.

Addressing with One Base Register

Refer now to Fig. 6-1(a), which shows a small program in main storage. Assume that register 3 is the base register and now contains the value X'4200', which is the location of the first byte of the program in main storage. A BALR instruction would have loaded this value into the register.

Within the program, every location is relative to the first byte, X'4200'. For example, since location X'4502' is X'302' bytes from the start, its displacement is X'302'. The computer references location X'4502' by means of the base address plus the displacement:

Base address:	X'4200'
Displacement:	+ X'0302'
Effective address:	X'4502'

Any instruction that references location X'4502' does so by combining the contents of base register 3 plus the displacement.

The assembler uses its location counter to calculate the displacement for every instruction and directive in the program. For every instruction that references a storage location, the assembler forms an operand in object code comprised of the base register number and the displacement and stores them as 2 bytes within the instruction:

$$| \quad B \quad | D \ D \ D \ |$$
$$\text{bits:} \quad 0\text{—}3 \quad 4\text{———}15$$

Bits 0–3 provide 4 bits to reference a base register, as X'0' through X'F'. Bits 4–15 provide for a displacement from X'000' through X'FFF', in effect up to 4095. In Fig. 6-1(a), an instruction referencing X'4502' would contain as its operand the hex value

$$| \ 3 \ | \ 302 \ |$$

An MVC instruction containing this object code for operand 1 would move data to the address of base register 3, X'4200', plus the displacement, X'302', or X'4502'.

Addressing with More than One Base Register

Since the maximum displacement is X'FFF' or 4,095, the area covered by a base register and its displacement is X'000' through X'FFF', giving X'1000' or 4,096 bytes. Each 4,096 (4K) bytes of program being executed requires a base register. A program up to 12K bytes in size requires three base registers, as shown in Fig. 6-1(b).

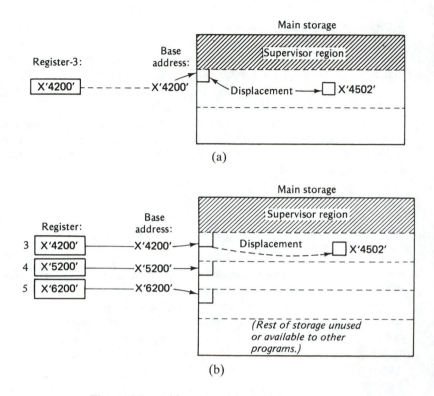

Figure 6-1   Addressing with one base register.

In the example, the three base registers assigned for addressing are 3, 4, and 5. These registers are arbitrarily chosen, and any other legal registers in any sequence could have been chosen.

The first 4K area begins at base address X'4200', and any location referenced within this area is subject to base register 3 and a displacement relative to the base address.

The second 4K area begins at a location X'1000' higher, at X'5200'. Any location referenced within this area is subject to base register 4 and a displacement relative to this base address.

The third 4K area begins at a location X'1000' higher, at X'6200'. Any location referenced within this area is subject to base register 5 and a displacement relative to this base address.

ASSIGNING BASE REGISTERS

You have to notify the assembler which registers are available for addressing. Subject to the restrictions discussed earlier, you may assign any general register, usually 3 through 12, and your program should not subsequently use them for any other purpose.   When coding a program, you can only guess how much storage is required; assume about 25 coding sheets for each 4K of storage, excluding any large declaratives.   You'll need one base register for each 4K, and if your program is especially large, you may consider organizing it into a number of control sections. In any event, even if you are unsure of its size, the assembler informs you with "addressability errors" when your program does not provide enough registers.

You code the USING directive to tell the assembler which registers to use for base addressing.   Note that USING, like other directives, generates no machine code.   Its general format is

Name	Operation	Operand
[blank]	USING	s1,r1,...,rn

s1 in the operand designates the address from which the assembler calculates displacements.   r1, . . . , rn specifies the base registers and their sequence.   Consider the following three examples:

1. This typical USING format tells the assembler from this point on (for the next 4,096 bytes) to assign register 3 as the base register:

```
USING *,3
```

The asterisk in the operand refers to the current value in the assembler's location counter.   In effect, the assembler inserts a 3 as the base register into any object code address that references this region.   The assembler also calculates displacements from this beginning address and inserts the displacement into the object code instruction.

2. For this example, register 5 becomes the assigned base register, and the assembler calculates displacements from the address of A10, which immediately follows it:

```
          USING A10,5
A10       MVC   NAMEPR,NAMEIN
```

It happens that the current value of the location counter is also the address of A10, and you could get the same effect coding USING *,5.

3. This example assigns three base registers, which the assembler applies in the exact sequence as coded:

```
USING *,3,9,4
```

Since each 4,096 bytes of storage referenced by a program requires a base register, this USING provides for a size up to 12K. The assembler applies register 3 to the first 4K of storage, register 9 to the second 4K, and register 4 to the third 4K. The effect would look like this:

register 3:	4K
register 9:	4K
register 4:	4K

Note that assigning base registers is only half the story; you still have to load addresses in them at execute time.

LOADING BASE REGISTERS

USING merely notifies the assembler which base registers to apply during the assembly process. It is your responsibility to code the program to load base registers with the proper addresses at execute time. This section covers the way in which a DOS program typically handles base register addressing; the OS method differs somewhat and is covered in the next section.

The instruction for loading the first or only base register is BALR. BALR is an RR (register-to-register) instruction with this format:

Name	Operation	Operand
[label]	BALR	r1,r2

- Both operands specify any general register.
- BALR loads bits 32–63 of the program status word into the operand 1 register. The leftmost 8 bits contain the instruction length code, condition code, and program mask, which are ignored for addressing purposes. The rightmost 24 bits contain the address of the next instruction, which is the portion used for addressing:

<pre>
base register: |ilc.cc.pm.|────────address────────|
position: |0   7| 8   31|
</pre>

BALR generates two bytes of object code, the first of which is machine code 06. Thus the symbolic instruction BALR 3,0 becomes hex 0630. If BALR is the first executable instruction in a program, it loads the address of the next instruction in base register 3. For example, if the program loads at X'253A0', the address stored in base register 3 is X'253A2':

```
|06|30|xx|xx|xx|...
|            |
X'253A0'     |
         X'253A2'
```

- If operand 2 specifies register 0 (a common practice), the computer assumes no register reference; that is, the operand is ignored. The following example loads the address of the next sequential instruction in register 3 and continues processing with the next instruction, MVC:

```
BALR   3,0
USING  *,3
MVC    NAMEPR,NAMEIN
```

This is the most common use of BALR, in which operand 2 means no register. Note that the USING is a message to the assembler and is long gone at execute time.

- If operand 2 specifies registers 1 through 15, the instruction branches to the address in the register. There has to be an address already in the register. The following example loads the address of the next instruction in register 6 and branches to the address presumably in register 9:

```
BALR   6,9
```

You'll seldom need this use of BALR, and it isn't particularly relevant to loading base registers. However, it is covered here to complete the discussion of BALR.

Another instruction, BASR (branch and save register), is available only on advanced models. BASR works just like BALR and may be used in its place. The difference is that BALR inserts data from the PSW in bits $0-7$ of the operand 1 register, whereas BASR inserts X'00'.

Not yet covered is how to load more than one base register. At this stage, your programs won't exceed 4K in size, and we can delay the method until the LM instruction in Chapter 9 and the LA instruction in Chapter 11.

COMBINING ASSIGNING AND LOADING BASE REGISTERS

Figure 6-2 shows how to combine BALR and USING at the beginning of a program to initialize and assign a base register. This is a skeleton program for illustrative

```
 LOC   OBJECT CODE   ADDR1 ADDR2   STMT     SOURCE STATEMENT
                                    2              PRINT ON,NODATA,NOGEN
000000                              3 PROG06  START
000000 0530                         4          BALR   3,0      LOAD BASE REG
                      00002         5          USING  *,3      ASSIGN BASE REG

000002 D20E 302B 3008 0002D 0000A   7          MVC    HDGPR,HEADING
                                    8 *        .
                                    9 *        .
                                   10 *        .
                                   11          EOJ

                                   15 *        DECLARATIVES
00000A C9D5E5D6C9C3C540            16 HEADING  DC     CL15'INVOICE LISTING'
000019                             17 PRINT    DS     0CL133
000019 4040404040404040            18          DC     CL20' '
00002D                             19 HDGPR    DS     CL15
00003C 4040404040404040            20          DC     CL98' '

                      00000        22          END    PROG06
```

Figure 6-2   Base register initialization.

purposes, and normally other instructions would follow the MVC.   Be careful to distinguish between operations that occur at assembly time and at execute time.

At Assembly Time

In Fig. 6-2, the START directive initializes the location counter to 0 since the starting address of the program will be unknown at execute time.   Other than telling the assembler that this is the beginning of a control section and providing a starting value for the location counter, START has nothing to do with initializing base registers or loading a program.

Under LOC, the listing shows the initial value of the location counter as 000000, and it is incremented for the length of each instruction and declarative. The first executable instruction, BALR, is RR format.   The assembler generates 2 bytes of object code, 0530, in which 05 is the operation code and 30 represents registers 3 and 0, respectively.

Because BALR is 2 bytes long, the assembler increments the location counter to 000002.   The USING directive tells the assembler from this point (000002) to apply register 3 as the base register.   Note that 000002 is a relative location within the program, not the location where the program loads for execution.   USING generates no machine code.

The next instruction, MVC HDGPR,HEADING, begins at 000002 and has the following object code:

$$|D2| \; 0E| \; 302B \; | \; 3008|$$
$$(a) \; (b) \quad (c) \qquad (d)$$

(a) D2 is the machine operation code for MVC.

(b) The implicit length of operand 1, HDGPR, is 15.   The assembler deducts 1 from this length and stores 14 (X'0E') in the second byte of the object code. For any instruction that references main storage, the length in object code is always 1 less than the actual length.   On execution, the computer automatically increments the length by 1.

(c) Operand 1, X'302B', references HDGPR.   The assembler inserts 3 for base register 3 in the next half-byte of object code.   It now has to calculate a displacement for this operand.   The location counter shows HDGPR at X'00002D', and USING is at X'000002', from which point displacements are calculated:

HDGPR:	X'00002D'
USING:	− X'000002'
Difference:	X'00002B'

The displacement of HDGPR from the USING directive at X'000002' is therefore X'02B', which the assembler inserts in the object code for operand 1.

(d) Operand 2, X'3008', references HEADING.   The assembler inserts 3 for base register 3 in the next half-byte of object code.   It now calculates a displacement for this operand.   The location counter shows HEADING at X'00000A':

HEADING:	X'00000A'
USING:	− X'000002'
Difference:	X'000008'

The displacement of HEADING from the USING directive is therefore X'008', which the assembler inserts in the object code for operand 1.

At Execution Time

After assembly and link edit, the program is ready to execute.   Assume that this program actually loads in storage beginning at location X'9800'.   The contents of storage would appear in hexadecimal as follows:

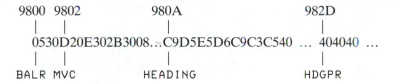

The first instruction, BALR, loads into register 3 the instruction address in the PSW containing the address of the next instruction, X'9802'.   When executing the

MVC, the computer calculates the effective addresses for its two operands as follows:

	OPERAND 1 (HDGPR)	OPERAND 2 (HEADING)
Contents of base register 3:	X'9802'	X'9802'
Displacement:	+X'002B'	+X'0008'
Effective address:	X'982D'	X'980A'

These are the effective addresses for the locations of PRHDG and HEADING, respectively. On execution, the computer also adds 1 to the length (14 + 1 = 15) and moves 15 bytes beginning at X'980A' to the location beginning at X'982D'.

You must reserve base registers and ensure that they are loaded with proper addresses. The assembler cannot check that base registers are correctly initialized. It is possible to get an error-free assembly that still references the wrong locations at execute time. One way to cause such an error is to code USING before BALR. In this case, the assembler sets the location counter after the USING to 000000 instead of 000002 and calculates displacements from 000000. But at execute time, BALR loads the base register with an address such as X'9802', making all displacements in object code incorrect by 2.

OS INITIALIZATION

Both DOS and OS require the usual BALR and USING pair for initializing base registers. However, OS is a more complex system, and it treats all users' programs like subprograms. You have to provide additional code for the linkage between the supervisor and your program. Figure 6-3 illustrates initializing an OS program.

```
1    PROGNAME    START                    Begin control section
2                SAVE    (14,12)          Store supervisor's registers
3                BALR    3,0              Base register initialization
4                USING   *,3
5                ST      13,SAVEAREA+4    Store register 13
6                LA      13,SAVEAREA      Load address of SAVEAREA
7                OPEN    ...
             ...
8                CLOSE   ...
9                L       13,SAVEAREA+4    Reload register 13
10               RETURN  (14,12)          Reload registers, return to supervisor
             ...
11   SAVEAREA    DS      18F              Save area, 18 fullwords
12               END     PROGNAME
```

Figure 6-3 OS base register initialization.

- Statement 1 is the usual START directive, omitting the operand under OS. At execute time, the system prints a location factor that tells you where the program has loaded.

- Statement 2 is a special SAVE macro that immediately saves the contents of the registers for the supervisor. The program changes the register contents for its own purposes but restores the original values before returning to the supervisor.

- Statements 3 and 4 are conventional BALR and USING instructions, coded after SAVE.

- Statements 5 and 6 are concerned with a special save area named SAVE-AREA (defined in statement 11) and the contents of register 13. Register 13 is important for linkage between programs and should not be used for any other purpose. There is continual traffic between a user program and the supervisor for I/O operations and program checks. Statement 5 stores the contents of register 13, and statement 6 loads into register 13 the address of SAVEAREA.

- Statements 9 and 10 are coded following the CLOSE at the end of all processing and are equivalent to the DOS EOJ macro. The L (Load) instruction reloads the registers that were saved at the start, and the RETURN macro returns control to the supervisor.

- Statement 11 defines SAVEAREA as 18 fullwords (each 4 bytes long) for storing the contents of the 16 general registers and two other values.

    Another version of OS initialization, which has the same effect, looks like this:

Program entry:

```
PROGNAME START                      Begin control section
         STM    14,12,12(13)        Store supervisor's registers
         LR     3,15                Load base register 3
         USING  PROGNAME,3
         LA     14,SAVEAREA         Load address of SAVEAREA
         ST     13,4(14)            Store register 13
         ST     14,8(13)
         LR     13,14
         OPEN   ...
```

Program termination:

```
         CLOSE  ...
         L      13,4(13)            Reload register 13
         LM     14,12,12(13)        Reload other registers
         BR     14                  Return to supervisor
```

When using OS linkage, be sure to code it as illustrated, in the same sequence. The assembler does not check your logic, and an improper variation could be disastrous at execute time.

Later chapters cover these register operations in detail, and Chapter 13 explains subprogram linkage.

PROBLEMS WITH INITIALIZING BASE REGISTERS

These are some common errors involving the use of base register assignment and initialization:

- Omission of either BALR or USING. Omitting BALR causes an unpredictable error at execution time, and omitting USING causes the assembler to generate addressability errors for instructions that require a base register reference.
- Failure to assign and load enough base registers for a large program. The assembler generates addressability errors for the unassigned 4K areas.
- Loading the second and third base registers with incorrect values.
- Using a base register for some other purpose in a program, thereby destroying the base address reference.
- Reversing BALR and USING. BALR will load the base register with a value of 2 greater than the assembler expects when calculating displacements. If you code USING/BALR, you could use the following instructions to adjust the base register to the correct value:

```
USING    *,3
BALR     3,0
BCTR     3,0        Decrement register 3 by 1
BCTR     3,0        Decrement register 3 by 1
```

INSTRUCTION FORMATS

This section examines the instruction formats in detail to clarify how the assembler converts symbolic instructions to object code and how it stores base registers and displacements. Each format has a specific function, as shown in Fig. 6-4. RR format processes data between registers; RS and RX process data between registers and storage; and SS and SI process data between storage locations. A sixth type, S format, is available only to the supervisor.

The object code for the instruction formats also varies, as shown in Fig. 6-5. The first column, headed Format, contains the general instruction format.

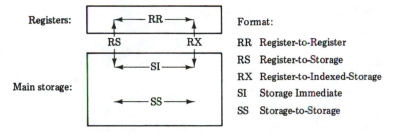

Figure 6-4　Relationship of instruction formats.

The second column gives the length of the object code in bytes.　The symbols in the other columns mean the following:

> B = base register
>
> D = displacement
>
> I = immediate operand
>
> L = length (number of bytes processed)
>
> R = register
>
> X = index register

　　The hex representation of machine language is in the column headed Object Code Format—the format in which the assembler converts from symbolic code. The first byte, bits 0–7, contains the operation code.　For example, the code for CLC is X'D5'.　One other instruction type, S format, uses the first 2 bytes for the operation code and is not covered here.　The convenient IBM reference card, Form GX20-1850, contains all instruction codes and formats.

　　The next sections explain the remaining bytes in the instruction format.

Format	Length in bytes	Explicit symbolic operands	Object code format					
RR	2	R1, R2	OP	R1R2				
RS	4	R1, R3, D2(B2)	OP	R1R3	B2D2	D2D2		
RX	4	R1, D2(X2, B2)	OP	R1X2	B2D2	D2D2		
SI	4	D1(B1), I2	OP	I I	B1D1	D1D1		
SS(1)	6	D1(L,B1), D2(B2)	OP	L L	B1D1	D1D1	B2D2	D2D2
SS(2)	6	D1(L1, B1), D2(L2, B2)	OP	L1L2	B1D1	D1D1	B2D2	D2D2
		Bits	0–7	8–15	16–23	24–31	32–39	40–47
		Byte	1	2	3	4	5	6

Figure 6-5　Details of instruction formats.

RR (Register-to-Register) Format

RR format is used to process data between registers, so that both operands reference registers, as LR 7,9. The object code for RR format is 2 bytes. The operation code occupies the first byte and the operands, a half-byte each, occupy the second byte. The half-byte capacity is therefore X'0' through X'F', or 0 through 15. Because of the fixed length of registers, the assembler implicitly knows the length, and thus no length indication is required or permitted.

The instruction AR 6,8 adds the contents of register 8 to register 6. The operation code, 1A, occupies the first byte, and the operands occupy the second byte. The result is

$$| 1A | 68 |$$

As another example, the instruction AR 10,11 converts to

$$| 1A | AB |$$

An exception to the regular RR format is BCR (Branch on Condition), which is specified as M1,R2. Operand 1 is a mask or a reference to the condition code in the PSW rather than a register.

RS (Register-to-Storage) Format

RS format provides the facility to process data between registers and storage. RS also permits three operands and requires 4 bytes of object code.

For example, you may code the Load Multiple instruction as LM 5,7,FIELDS, which means load registers 5, 6, and 7 with the three fullword fields beginning at the address of FIELDS. The operation code, 98, occupies the first byte, the two registers occupy the second byte, and the reference to storage occupies the third and fourth bytes. The result is

$$| 98 | 57 | BD | DD |$$

The assembler fills the last 2 bytes, BDDD, with a base register (B) and a displacement (DDD) for the operand FIELDS.

Some RS instructions, such as shift, use only two operands. For these, you omit R3, as shown in Fig. 6-5, and the assembler inserts a 0 in the object code position. The computer recognizes 0 as no register rather than register 0.

RX (Register-to-Indexed Storage) Format

RX format also processes data between registers and storage and is similar to RS format. RX also requires 4 bytes of object code. Two RX instructions that add binary data in storage to a register are A (Add Fullword) and AH (Add Halfword). The general object code format is

$$op\ R1X2\ B2D2\ D2D2$$

where R1 is a register, X2 is an index register, and B2D2D2D2 is a base/displacement reference. (An index register is just a special use of a general register.)

Consider an A instruction that adds the contents of FULLWD to register 7:

```
                         A      7,FULLWD
                         ...
            FULLWD       DC     F'5'
```

The length of FULLWD is understood to be 4 bytes and the register length is also 4 bytes. The operation code for A is 5A. Let's say that FULLWD is subject to base register 3 and has a displacement of X'2B2'. The object code looks like this:

| 5A | 70 | 32 | B2 |

In this case, no index register is involved, so the assembler plugs a 0 in its position. As before, a reference to register 0 means no register.

Considering that the entire RX format provides for indexing, you would expect it to have many uses, but such is not the case. One instruction that you may occasionally use with an index register is LA, but we'll delay its discussion until Chapter 12.

An exception to the regular RX format is BC (Branch on Condition), which is specified as M1,D2(X2,B2). Operand 1 is a mask or a reference to the condition code in the PSW rather than a register.

SI (Storage Immediate) Format

For SI format, operand 1 references a storage location and operand 2 represents a one-byte immediate constant. Two examples of SI format are MVI (Move Immediate) and CLI (Compare Immediate). In object code, the first byte contains the operation code, the second byte contains the immediate value, and the third and fourth bytes contain a base/displacement reference, as

op II B1D1 D1D1

Since immediate operations are defined as one byte, no length indication is required. For example, the following MVI instruction moves an asterisk to ASTERPR:

```
            MVI ASTERPR,C'*'
```

Let's say that ASTERPR is subject to base register 3 and has a displacement of X'6C4'. The object code, with the asterisk as X'5C', looks like this:

| 92 | 5C | 36 | C4 |

SS (Storage-to-Storage) Format

For SS format, both operands reference storage locations. The two types of SS instructions are character instructions of the form D1(L,B1),D2(B2), which provide a length only for operand 1, and packed operations of the form D1(L1,B1),D2(L2,B2), which provide a length for both operands.

    1. *Character Instructions.* Two examples of this format are MVC (Move Character) and CLC (Compare Character). In object code, the first byte contains the operation code, and the second byte contains the length of operand 1. The third and fourth bytes contain a base/displacement reference for operand 1, and the fifth and sixth bytes contain a base/displacement reference for operand 2, as

$$| \text{ op } | \text{ L } | \text{ B1D1 } | \text{ D1D1 } | \text{ B2D2 } | \text{ D2D2 } |$$

For example, the following MVC instruction moves the contents of CONAME to TITLEPR:

```
MVC TITLEPR,CONAME
```

Let's say that TITLEPR is subject to base register 3 and has a displacement of X'40A' and that CONAME is subject to base register 3 and has a displacement of X'42C'. The length of TITLEPR is 14 bytes. The object code looks like this:

$$| \text{ D2 } | \text{ 0D } | \text{ 34 } | \text{ 0A } | \text{ 34 } | \text{ 2C} |$$

- D2 is the operation code for MVC.
- 0D (13) is the implicit length of TITLEPR after the assembler has deducted 1. At execute time, the computer increments this length by 1.
- The third and fourth bytes contain a base/displacement reference for operand 1: base register 3 and displacement 40A.
- The fifth and sixth bytes contain a base/displacement reference for operand 2: base register 3 and displacement 42C.

    At execute time, the computer automatically increments the length by 1, to 14. Also, it combines the contents of base register 3 with the displacements. For example, if register 3 contains X'28400', the effective addresses of the two operands are:

	OPERAND 1	OPERAND 2
Contents of base register 3:	X'28400'	X'28400'
Displacement:	+ X'0040A'	+ X'0042C'
Effective address:	X'2880A'	X'2882C'

    2. *Packed Instructions.* Two examples of this format are AP (Add Packed) and CP (Compare Packed). In object code, the first byte contains the operation code, and the second byte contains the length of operand 1 and the length of operand 2. The third and fourth bytes contain a base/displacement reference for operand 1, and the fifth and sixth bytes contain a base/displacement reference for operand 2, as

| op | L1L2 | B1D1 | D1D1 | B2D2 | D2D2 |

For example, the following AP instruction adds the contents of AMOUNT to TOTAL:

                              AP TOTAL,AMOUNT

Let's say that TOTAL is 4 bytes long, is subject to base register 3, and has a displacement of X'50A'. Also, AMOUNT is 3 bytes long, is subject to base register 3, and has a displacement of X'52C'. The object code looks like this:

                         | FA | 32 | 35 | 0A | 35 | 2C|

- FA is the operation code for AP.
- 32 is the implicit lengths of TOTAL and AMOUNT after the assembler has deducted 1 from each. At execute time, the computer increments these lengths by 1.
- The third and fourth bytes contain a base/displacement reference for operand 1: base register 3 and displacement 50A.
- The fifth and sixth bytes contain a base/displacement reference for operand 2: base register 3 and displacement 52C.

At execute time, the computer automatically increments the lengths by 1, to 3 and 4, respectively. Also, it combines the contents of base register 3 with the displacements. For example, if register 3 contains X'28400', the effective addresses of the two operands are as follows:

	OPERAND 1	OPERAND 2
Contents of base register 3:	X'28400'	X'28400'
Displacement:	+X'0050A'	+X'0052C'
Effective address:	X'2890A'	X'2892C'

Length Code

Let's now see why only SS format instructions require length codes.

RR format. This format references registers, whose lengths are always understood to be 4 bytes; for example:

            LR   9,12   Load register 9 with contents of 12

RS and RX formats. These formats reference registers (always 4 bytes) and also storage locations, which are either 4 bytes (a fullword) or 2 bytes (a halfword). The system can tell from context which length applies; for example:

```
AH   5,HALFWORD      Add a halfword to register 5
A    5,FULLWORD      Add a fullword to register 5
```

SI format. This format always processes one byte, such as

```
CLI CODE,C'*'      Does CODE contain an asterisk?
```

In this case, CODE would be defined as one byte.

SS format. This format references storage locations that may involve various lengths. The format differs for character and for packed operations.

- Character instructions like CLC and MVC are governed by the length of operand 1. The following example compares the contents of AREA1 to AREA2:

```
               CLC     AREA1,AREA2
               . . .
        AREA1  DS      CL30
        AREA2  DS      CL30
```

Since operand 1, AREA1, is defined as CL30, the comparison is 30 bytes, regardless of the length of AREA2. The assembler stores the length as 29, and at execution time the computer increments the length by 1. The object code for the instruction provides one byte for the length, making the maximum X'FF', or 255. Since the computer increments the length at execution time, the effective maximum is 256.

- Packed instructions, such as CP and AP, are governed by the lengths of both operands. The following example compares the contents of CUSTLIM, OVERLIM:

```
        CP       CUSTLIM,OVERLIM       Compare CUSTLIM to OVERLIM
        . . .
CUSTLIM DC       PL3'123.45'           3-byte packed field
OVERLIM DC       PL2'215.00'           2-byte packed field
```

The CP instruction makes an algebraic comparison of the 3-byte field to the 2-byte field. The object code contains one byte for the two lengths, a half-byte for operand 1 and a half-byte for operand 2, each decremented and then stored as 21. The maximum length in object code is X'F', or 15. Since the computer increments the lengths at execution time, the effective maximum is 16.

S Format Instructions

A sixth instruction type, S format, is involved with more advanced operations, largely to do with privileged supervisor functions. Unlike other instruction types, the operation code is 2 bytes long:

$$\text{bits:} \quad \left| \begin{array}{c|c|c} \text{operation} & \text{B2} & \text{D2} \\ 0\text{------}15 & 16\text{--}19 & 20\text{------}31 \end{array} \right|$$

EXTENDED MNEMONICS

The instructions for comparisons such as B, BE, BH, and BL are known as *extended mnemonics*. Technically, these are special variations on the BC (Branch on Condition) instruction, which has the general format

```
BC M1,D2(X2,B2)
```

M1 is a mask, a reference to the condition code in the program status word (PSW). You could, for example, code the unconditional branch (B) instruction or a conditional branch (BH) instruction either of two ways:

	EXTENDED MNEMONIC	BRANCH ON CONDITION (BC)
Unconditional branch:	B addr	BC 15,addr
Conditional branch:	BH addr	BC 2,addr

The BCR (Branch on Condition Register) instruction has the general format

```
BCR    M1,R2
```

A common extended mnemonic for BCR is the BR instruction, which causes an unconditional branch to an address in a register. You could code the instruction using either BR or BCR as follows:

	EXTENDED MNEMONIC	BRANCH ON CONDITION REGISTER (BCR)
Unconditional branch:	BR reg	BCR 15,reg

The two bits in the condition code represent the following:

CONDITION CODE	VALUE	INDICATION
00	0	Equal/zero
01	1	Low/minus
10	2	High/plus
11	3	Overflow

Figure 6-6 provides the 4-bit mask for the nine common branch conditions. You can use, for example, either BE addr or BC 8,addr to test for equal/zero. The assembler translates the 8 to binary 1000 in the object code mask position. Note that bits are numbered from left to right, beginning with 0 for the leftmost bit, as 0, 1, 2, 3. On execution, the computer checks the mask—binary 1000 asks if bit 0 is on, meaning, does the condition code value equal zero?

For not equal, you could code either BNE addr or BC 7,addr. The assembler translates the 7 to binary 0111 in the mask. On execution, the computer checks the mask:

If bit number 1 is on, does the condition code value equal 1?
If bit number 2 is on, does the condition code value equal 2?
If bit number 3 is on, does the condition code value equal 3?

If any one of these conditions is true, the condition is not equal. The assembler provides the extended mnemonics to save you memorizing trivial information and to make programs more readable. Either way, however, the assembler generates the same object code.

In the interests of clarity and minimizing program bugs, this text recommends

The 4-bit Mask

Condition	Eq/zero 0	Low/min 1	High/plus 2	Over-flow 3	Branch on condition	Extended mnemonic
0 = Equal/zero	1	0	0	0	BC 8,addr	BE addr BZ addr
1 = Low/minus	0	1	0	0	BC 4,addr	BL addr BM addr
2 = High/plus	0	0	1	0	BC 2,addr	BH addr BP addr
3 = Overflow	0	0	0	1	BC 1,addr	BO addr
No branch	0	0	0	0	BC 0,addr	NOP addr
1,2,3 = Not equal	0	1	1	1	BC 7,addr	BNE addr BNZ addr
0,2,3 = Not low	1	0	1	1	BC 11,addr	BNL addr BNM addr
0,1,3 = Not high	1	1	0	1	BC 13,addr	BNH addr BNP addr
0,1,2,3 = Any	1	1	1	1	BC 15,addr	B addr

Figure 6-6   Branch on condition mask.

use of the extended mnemonics. An understanding of the mask and the condition is useful, however, as an aid in deciphering object code.

SUBROUTINE LINKAGE

A subroutine is a section of program coding that acts almost as an independent part of a program. Sometimes more than one part of the main program uses the subroutine. For example, you can treat the section of coding for page overflow as a separate part of the main program. Each time a line is printed, the program can check whether the maximum number of lines per page has been reached. If so, the program branches, or links, to the subroutine. The subroutine executes the following:

- Skips to a next page
- Prints the heading
- Initializes the line counter
- Adds 1 to the page count
- Returns, or links, to the point of invocation in the main program

Subroutines adhere to the principles of coupling and cohesion discussed in Chapter 2. Coupling refers to the relationship between modules, in which modules are (relatively) unrelated and independent. Thus a change to one module has little or no effect on other modules. Cohesion refers to the consistency within a module, in which all statements in a module are dedicated to only one purpose. Thus all the statements within the page overflow module are concerned only with handling page overflow.

The use of subroutines has several advantages: (1) It simplifies program writing. Commonly used routines, or complex routines, may be separated from the main program. The main program logic then is simplified. (2) A subroutine may be written once, then cataloged as a permanent part of the system, available for use by other programs. (3) It helps teams of programmers working on one program.

Subroutine Linkage: BAL and BR

The two instructions used to perform subroutine linkage, BAL and BR, reference a register and have this format:

Name	Operation	Operand
[label]	BAL	R1,X2 *or* R1,D2(X2,B2)
[label]	BR	R1

Branch and link: BAL.   BAL is similar to the BALR instruction covered earlier. The rules for BAL are as follows:

- Operand 1 specifies a register to be used for subroutine linkage.
- Operand 2 references an address, generally that of a subroutine.
- On execution, BAL loads bits 32–63 of the program status word into the operand 1 register. The leftmost 8 bits contain the instruction length code, condition code, and program mask, which are ignored for addressing purposes. The rightmost 24 bits contain the address of the next instruction, which is the portion used for addressing. Then BAL branches unconditionally to the operand 2 storage address.

For example, the instruction BAL 8,P10PAGE means: Load the address of the next instruction in register 8, and branch to the address of P10PAGE.

Another instruction, BAS (Branch and Save), is available only on advanced models. BAS works just like BAL except that BAL inserts data from the PSW in bits 0–7 of the operand 1 register, whereas BAS inserts X'00'.

Branch on condition register: BR.   BR is an unconditional branch to an address in a register and is commonly used to return from a subroutine. For example, the instruction BR 8 branches unconditionally to an address stored in register 8. BR is an extended mnemonic and is actually a BCR (Branch Condition Register) operation.

Use of Linkage

You may allocate any available register for subroutine linkage, for now let's say registers 6-12 only. But be careful not to change the contents of the register between the time BAL loads the address and the time BR returns from the subroutine. In Fig. 6-7, the main program has two linkages, at statements 1 and 5, to the subroutine, P10PAGE.

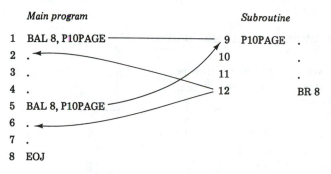

Figure 6-7   Subroutine linkage.

The program executes as follows:

STATEMENT	DESCRIPTION
1	BAL loads the address of the next instruction, statement 2, into register 8 and branches to P10PAGE, statement 9.
9–12	The subroutine, P10PAGE, is executed. At statement 12, the program branches to the address stored in register 8, statement 2.
2–4	Statements 2, 3, and 4 are executed.
5	BAL loads the address of the next instruction, statement 6, into register 8 and branches to P10PAGE, statement 9.
9–12	The subroutine, P10PAGE, is executed. At statement 12, the program branches to the address stored in register 8, statement 6.
6–8	Statements 6 and 7 are executed, and statement 8 terminates program execution.

Ensure that the subroutine is a separate part of the program. The only way this subroutine should be normally entered is with BAL 8,P10PAGE. The program should enter a subroutine only by means of BAL, with no inadvertent drop-through into it. The normal exit in this example is back through register 8.

In this way, a subroutine can return to any number of addresses. The standard practice is to enter a subroutine at its top and to exit from its bottom. In the case of a serious error in the data, however, the program may have to exit from a subroutine earlier.

Some programmers prefer to use EQU to name registers, as in the following manner:

```
LINKREG1    EQU    6
LINKREG2    EQU    7
```

LINKREG1 would be the register designated for the first level of subroutines, and LINKREG2 would be for the second (deeper) level of subroutines. For example, if P10PAGE is at the first level, the instructions to link and to return would be

```
        BAL    LINKREG1,P10PAGE       Link to subroutine
          .
          .
          .
P10PAGE   .
          .
        BR     LINKREG1               Return from subroutine
```

A convention would be to assign a specific register for each level, for example, register 6 for level 1 and register 7 for level 2. If the program contains a subroutine that is referenced from both levels, you could set it at the third level and link to it by, say, register 8.

SAMPLE PROGRAM: PROCESSING INVENTORY RECORDS

The program in Fig. 6-8 illustrates the use of base register addressing and a subroutine.

Input. Input records for inventory parts consist of the following fields:

COLUMN	CONTENTS
01–05	Part number
06–20	Part description
21–24	Quantity on hand

Input data is the following:

```
Part No.   .Description........   Qty.
10436      TERMINALS...........   0023
10927      MODEMS..............   0120
24322      REGULATORS..........   0152
33569      MICROPROCESSORS.....   0022
```

Processing. At the start, the program prints a heading to identify each printed field for the input records and reads the first record. At this point is a looping routine:

```
A10LOOP       BAL       7,B10PROC
              GET       FILEIN,RECORDIN
              B         A10LOOP
```

The BAL instruction links to B10PROC, where the program moves the input fields to the output area and prints the record. BR then returns control to the main routine. The program repeats looping at A10LOOP until end-of-file. At that point, control passes to A90EOF, where the program ejects the printer form to the next page and terminates execution.

Output. In the print line, the fields are spaced apart for better readability, as follows:

```
          Part No.    Description         Qty.
          XXXXX       X———————X           XXXX
          |           |                   |
column 10             20                  40
```

```
  LOC    OBJECT CODE        STMT     SOURCE STATEMENT
                             3                  PRINT ON,NODATA,NOGEN
000000                       4  PROG06   START
000000 0530                  5           BALR  3,0                  INITIALIZE
                             6           USING *,3                     ADDRESSABILITY
                             7           OPEN  FILEIN,PRINTER        OPEN FILES
                            17           PUTPR PRINTER,PRHEAD,SK1    SKIP TO NEW PAGE
                            24           PUTPR PRINTER,PRHEAD,WSP2   PRINT HEADING
                            32           GET   FILEIN,RECORDIN       READ 1ST RECORD
00004E 4570 308E            38  A10LOOP  BAL   7,B10PROC            MAIN PROCESSING
                            39           GET   FILEIN,RECORDIN       READ NEXT RECORD
000062 47F0 304C            45           B     A10LOOP

                            47  A90EOF   PUTPR PRINTER,PRHEAD,SK1    SKIP PAGE
                            54           CLOSE FILEIN,PRINTER        CLOSE FILES
                            63           EOJ   ,                     TERMINATE JOB

                            67  *                   M A I N   P R O C E S S I N G
                            68  *                   -----------------------------

000090 D204 3360 3281       70  B10PROC  MVC   PARTPR,PARTIN        MOVE PART NO.,
000096 D20E 336A 3286       71           MVC   DESCPR,DESCIN          *  DESCRIPTION
00009C D203 337E 3295       72           MVC   QTYPR,QTYIN            *  QUANTITY
                            73           PUTPR PRINTER,PRLINE,WSP1   PRINT
0000B6 07F7                 80           BR    7                     RETURN

                            82  *                   D E C L A R A T I V E S
                            83  *                   -----------------------

                            85  FILEIN   DEFIN A90EOF               DEFINE INPUT
                           111  PRINTER  DEFPR                      DEFINE PRINTER

000283                     141  RECORDIN DS    0CL80                INPUT RECORD:
000283                     142  PARTIN   DS    CL05                  *  PART #
000288                     143  DESCIN   DS    CL15                  *  DESCRIPTION
000297                     144  QTYIN    DS    ZL04                  *  QUANTITY
00029B                     145           DS    CL56                  *  UNUSED

0002D3                     147  PRHEAD   DS    0CL133               HEADING LINE:
0002D3 4040404040404040    148           DC    CL10' '                   *
0002DD D3C9E2E340D6C640    149           DC    CL123'LIST OF PARTS FOR ACE ELECTRONICS'

000358                     151  PRLINE   DS    0CL133               PRINT AREA:
000358 4040404040404040    152           DC    CL10' '                   *
000362                     153  PARTPR   DS    CL05                  *  PART #
000367 4040404040          154           DC    CL05' '                   *
00036C                     155  DESCPR   DS    CL15                  *  DESCRIPTION
00037B 4040404040          156           DC    CL05' '
000380                     157  QTYPR    DS    ZL04                  *  QUANTITY
000384 4040404040404040    158           DC    CL89' '

0003E0                     160           LTORG ,                    GEN'D LITERALS
0003E0 5B5BC2D6D7C5D540    161                 =C'$$BOPEN '
0003E8 5B5BC2C3D3D6E2C5    162                 =C'$$BCLOSE'
0003F0 00000148            163                 =A(PRINTER)
0003F4 000002D3            164                 =A(PRHEAD)
0003F8 000000B8            165                 =A(FILEIN)
0003FC 00000283            166                 =A(RECORDIN)
000400 00000358            167                 =A(PRLINE)

                           169           END   PROG06              END OF ASSEMBLY
```

Figure 6-8 Program: processing inventory records.

Output:-
```
LIST OF PARTS FOR ACE ELECTRONICS

10436      TERMINALS            0023
10927      MODEMS               0120
24322      REGULATORS           0152
33569      MICROPROCESSORS      0022
```

Figure 6-8   (*continued*)

Note instruction alignment: All the instructions begin on an even storage location, as shown under LOC (location).

KEY POINTS

- The general registers perform all binary arithmetic. For binary values, bit 0 (to the left) is the sign bit, and bits 1–31 are data.

- The general registers perform all the addressing involved in referencing main storage. A register when used for addressing purposes is known as a base register. On most models, addressing uses only the rightmost 24 bits (bits 8–31).

- For practical purposes, only registers 3 through 12 are available for use as base registers. A common practice is to write large programs in separate control sections (CSECTs). You assemble the control sections with their own sets of base registers and link-edit them into one executable load module.

- For addressing locations in main storage, the base address references the beginning of a storage area. A BALR instruction loads the address into a register, and a USING directive tells the assembler that this register is to be the base register containing the address of the start of the control section.

- For each instruction and declarative in the program, the assembler calculates its displacement, the number of bytes from the base address.

- Each instruction format has a specific function. RR format processes data between registers, RS and RX process data between registers and storage, and SS and SI process data between storage locations.

- Character instructions, such as CLC and MVI, are governed by the length of operand 1. The object code for the instruction provides one byte for the length, making the maximum X'FF', or 255. Since the computer increments the length at execution time, the effective maximum is 256.

- Packed instructions, such as CP and AP, are governed by the lengths of both operands, making the maximum X'F', or 15. Since the computer increments the length at execution time, the effective maximum is 16.

- You use BAL to link to a subroutine and BR to return from it. Subroutines adhere to the principles of coupling and cohesion. Coupling refers to the relationship between modules, in which modules are (relatively) unrelated and independent. Cohesion refers to the consistency within a module, in which all statements in a module are dedicated to only one purpose.

PROBLEMS

6-1. Explain the uses and restrictions for the following registers: (a) 0; (b) 1; (c) 2; (d) 3 through 12; (e) 13; (f) 14; (g) 15.

6-2. If only registers 3 through 12 are available as base registers, what would be the maximum size of a control section? If the program exceeds this size, what is a possible solution?

6-3. When would a program include a value in the operand of START, and when would it omit the value?

6-4. What are the two major advantages to base/displacement addressing?

6-5. Code the base register initialization for a program that assigns base register 10.

6-6. Explain which instructions take effect at assembly time and at execute time: (a) START; (b) BALR; (c) USING.

6-7. A program is 18K in size. Explain how many base registers it requires.

6-8. Provide the object code for the following instructions, and assume that the assigned base register in all cases is 4:

(a) RR:
```
               AR   12,5
```
(b) RS:
```
               LM   8,11,FULLWDS
```
(FULLWDS has a displacement of X'2CD'.)

(c) RX:
```
               A    12,FULLWORD
```
(FULLWORD has a displacement of X'2E3'.)

(d) SI:
```
               MVI  SAVEIT,C'#'
```
(SAVEIT has a displacement of X'82F'.)

(e) SS character:
```
               MVC  NAMEPR,NAMEIN
                 . . .
       NAMEPR  DS   CL20     (displacement is X'2F8')
       NAMEIN  DS   CL20     (immediately follows NAMEPR)
```
(f) SS packed:
```
               AP   ACCUM,NUMBER
                 . . .
       ACCUM   DC   PL5'0'   (displacement is X'5FD)
       NUMBER  DC   PL3'8'   (immediately follows ACCUM)
```

6-9. Consider the following code. Is there a bug? If so, explain it.
```
               BALR  3,0
               USING *,3
               BAL   3,P10PAGE
                 . . .
       P10PAGE ...
               BR    3
```

6-10. Consider the following code. Is there a bug? If so, explain it.

```
          BALR     3,0
          USING    *,3
          BAL      5,P10PAGE
          ...
P10PAGE   ...
          BR       3
```

6-11. Give the extended mnemonics for the following: (a) BC 8,C50; (b) BC 2,D50; (c) BC 11,E50; (d) BC 15,F50.

6-12. Code the following in machine language, assuming that the base register is 3 and B30 is at displacement X'A38': (a) B B30; (b) BNL B30; (c) BAL 5,B30; (d) BR 7.

6-13. Explain how the instruction format limits (a) the number of registers to 16; (b) character lengths to 256; (c) packed lengths to 16; (d) displacements to 4,096 bytes.

6-14. Consider the following pair of related instructions. Explain the effect of their execution.

```
          BALR     8,0
          BR       8
```

7

PROCESSING CHARACTER DATA

OBJECTIVE

To cover the definition and uses of character data.

This chapter covers in detail the defining and processing of character data. The first part describes the assembler declaratives that define the character fields for areas in storage to handle input and output records and constants such as report headings. Character data consists of a 4-bit zone portion and a 4-bit numeric portion:

	←——zone——→				←——numeric——→			
bits	0	0	0	0	0	0	0	0
position	0	1	2	3	4	5	6	7

Because programs must manipulate data that is read or defined, the next sections cover the basic instructions to move and compare data. A sample program illustrates the use of these instructions and how you may organize them into a working program.

CHARACTER DECLARATIVES

Chapter 5 covered the use of DS to assign an area of storage and DC to define a constant. The following rules govern character constants:

1. Their length may be defined from 1 to 256 characters.
2. They may contain any character that may be keyed or printed, including blanks.
3. If the length (Ln) is not coded, the assembler assumes that the field length is that of the defined constant. Thus DC C'SAM' defines a 3-character constant.
4. If the length (Ln) is specified, the following may occur:
   (a) The defined length equals the length of the constant:

```
FIELDA DC CL5 'APRIL'
```

   The length of FIELDA is 5 bytes. The assembler generates APRIL.
   (b) The defined length is less than the length of the constant:

```
FIELDB DC CL4 'APRIL'
```

   The defined length, 4, overrides the length of the constant. The length of FIELDB will be 4 bytes. The assembler left-adjusts the constant and truncates rightmost characters that exceed the defined length. APRI is generated.
   (c) The defined length is greater than the length of the constant:

```
FIELDC DC CL6 'APRIL'
```

   The length of FIELDC will be 6 bytes. The assembler left-adjusts the constant and pads rightmost bytes with blanks. In this case, APRIL followed by one blank is generated.
5. The apostrophe (') and the ampersand (&) have special meaning to the assembler. If you define them within a constant, code them as two adjacent characters, although the assembler counts and prints only one.

Figure 7-1 provides various character declaratives with explanations.

BLANK1 generates a 5-byte field containing five blanks. Under OBJECT CODE are the 5 bytes of blanks (X'40's).
BLANK2 defines 5 one-byte blank fields; the implicit length is that of the first field, one byte.

```
 LOC     OBJECT CODE        STMT   SOURCE STATEMENT                              Constant Generated:
                              7   *        DEFINE BLANKS:                        --------------------
                              8   *
004301  4040404040            9   BLANK1   DC   CL5' '                           '     ' ( 5 BLANKS )
004306  4040404040           10   BLANK2   DC   5CL1' '                          5 1-BYTE BLANKS

                             12   *        DEFINE NUMBERS:
00430B  F0F0F0F0F0           13   ZERO1    DC   C'00000'                         '00000'
004310  F04040404040         14   ZERO2    DC   CL5'0'                           '0'
004315  F0F0F0F0F0           15   ZERO3    DC   5C'0'                            '0','0','0','0','0'
00431A  F5                   17   FIVEA    DC   CL1'5'                           '5'
00431B  F5                   18   FIVEB    DC   C'5'                             '5'
00431C  F0F5                 19   FIVEC    DC   C'05'                            '05'

                             21   *        DEFINE ALPHABETIC:
00431E  5BF16BF0F0F04BF0     22   AMT      DC   C'$1,000.00'                     '$1,000.00'
004327  C1C2C3C44040         23   PADBLANK DC   CL6'ABCD'                        'ABCD'
00432D  40D1D6C5405040C6     24   AMPERSND DC   C' JOE && FLO''S '               ' JOE & FLO'S '
00433A  C1C2C1C2             25   TRUNCATE DC   2CL2'ABCD'                       2 CONSTANTS = 'AB','AB'
00433E  F0F7D1E4D3E8         26   JULY     DC   C'07',C'JULY'                    2 CONSTANTS = '07','JULY'
004344  404040C940D540E3     27   TITLE    DC   C' INTERNATIONAL BUSINESS MAC+
                                            HINES'                                            continuation

                             29   *        DEFINED ERRORS:
               *** ERROR *** 30   ERRORA   DC   CL3                              MISSING 'CONSTANT'
               *** ERROR *** 31   ERRORB   DC   ' '                              MISSING FORMAT
               *** ERROR *** 32   ERRORC   DC   CL'123'                          MISSING LENGTH N
               *** ERROR *** 33   ERRORD   DC   CL300' '                         LENGTH EXCEEDS 256 BYTES
```

DIAGNOSTICS AND STATISTICS

```
STMNT ERROR  SEV  MESSAGE
  30  IPK128  8   CONSTANT FIELD MISSING OR PRECEDED BY INVALID FIELD, ' '
  31  IPK123  4   INVALID TYPE SPECIFICATION, ' '
  32  IPK129 12   INVALID DUPLICATION FACTOR OR MODIFIER, ''123''
  33  IPK140  8   INVALID LENGTH MODIFIER
```

Figure 7-1 Declaratives in character format.

The second group defines numeric values, although note that you cannot perform arithmetic on character data:

ZERO1 generates a 5-byte field containing five zeros.   Note that a character zero is X'F0'.

ZERO2 is also a 5-byte field.   But because only one zero is specified, the assembler left-adjusts the zero and fills the remaining bytes with blanks.   This is a common coding error, where a field of all zeros was intended.

ZERO3 generates 5 one-byte fields, each containing a zero.

FIVEA and **FIVEB** show two ways to define a one-byte field containing the value 5 (X'F5').

FIVEC generates 05, or X'F0F5'.

The third group defines alphabetic fields:

AMT generates a field with a dollar sign (X'5B'), a comma (X'6B'), and a decimal point (X'4B').

PADBLANK left-adjusts the constant and pads two blanks to the right.

AMPERSND illustrates the use of the ampersand (&) and apostrophe ('), both of which must be defined twice.   The generated constant in this case is 13 bytes long, although the assembler prints only the first 8 bytes under OBJECT CODE.

TRUNCATE defines two constants, each 2 bytes long.   The assembler truncates the constant ABCD on the right to 2 bytes (because of the length L2) and generates AB twice (see the hex object code).

JULY shows one statement that defines two character constants, separated by a comma.   A reference to the name JULY is to the first 2-byte field.

TITLE illustrates the continuation character, in this case a plus sign (+) in column 72.   The constant continues on the next line in column 16.   (Even though there is an assembler directive TITLE, you can use TITLE for the name of a field.)'

The last group defines some common coding errors.   (The comments on the right explain the cause of the error.)   The assembler prints ERROR instead of the object code and gives the cause at the end of the program listing.   Any instruction in the program that references one of these invalid constants also causes an error message for that instruction.

CHARACTER INSTRUCTIONS

The next sections cover the movement and comparison of fields in character format. The contents of these fields are made available to the program from an input record or declared as a constant value. A program must often move the contents of one field to another. Fields in the input area must be moved to other areas in order to save them from erasure by the next record that the program reads. Also, constants, headings, and calculated values must be moved to the print area for printing.

The two instruction formats that process data in main storage are storage-to-storage (SS) and storage immediate (SI). SS format processes data between two fields in main storage, whereas SI format processes between a one-byte constant built into the instruction and a location in main storage.

The following instructions move fields, bytes, and half-bytes from one storage location to another: Move Character (MVC), Move Numerics (MVN), Move Zones (MVZ), Move Immediate (MVI), and Move with Offset (MVO). This chapter describes MVC and MVI. Since MVN, MVZ, and MVO have uses connected with packed data, they are covered in Chapter 8.

Some instructions reference data in main storage only, others process data between main storage and the registers, and others process in registers only. Storage-to-storage (SS) format references only storage locations. In an instruction like MVC (Move Character), the operands are represented as S1,S2, meaning that both operand 1 (S1) and operand 2 (S2) reference main storage. Another representation in symbolic form is

```
MVC  D1(L,B1),D2(B2)
```

- D1(L,B1) means that the operand 1 address consists of a base register (B1) and a displacement (D1).
- L means that the length of operand 1 controls the number of bytes processed.
- D2(B2) means that the operand 2 address consists of a base register (B2) and a displacement (D2).

MOVE CHARACTERS: MVC

MVC is a storage-to-storage (SS) instruction that may move data in any format, although its use is normally confined to character fields.

Name	Operation	Operand
[label]	MVC	S1,S2 *or* D1(L,B1),D2(B2)

Its rules are as follows:

1. MVC may move from 1 to 256 bytes, usually character data but technically in any format.

2. Data beginning in the byte specified by operand 2 is moved one byte at a time to the field beginning with the byte specified by operand 1. The move does not affect the contents of the operand 2 field; the bytes are copied into the operand 1 field. Thus the instruction MVC FLDA,FLDB copies the contents of FLDB into FLDA.

3. The length of the operand 1 field determines the number of bytes moved. Since the MVC instruction format contains a length code (L) for operand 1 only, the length of operand 2 is irrelevant to the operation. If the operand 1 field is 5 bytes long and operand 2 is 6 bytes, MVC moves only the first 5 bytes of operand 2 (from left to right one byte at a time) to the operand 1 field. If the operand 1 field is 6 bytes and operand 2 is 5, MVC moves all 5 bytes of operand 2, plus 1 byte immediately to its right.

Field Length

You may specify the number of bytes to be moved by either implicit or explicit length. Assume these DCs for the examples that follow:

Name	Operation	Operand
FIELD1	DC	C'JUNE'
FIELD2	DC	C'APRIL'

Implicit length. The following MVC instruction uses implicit length:

```
MVC FIELD1,FIELD2
```

Operand 1, FIELD1, is implicitly defined as a 4-byte constant. Since the assembler recognizes that a reference to FIELD1 is to a 4-byte field, the MVC moves only the first 4 bytes of FIELD2, APRI. The contents of FIELD2 are unaffected. The following shows the contents of FIELD1 and FIELD2 before and after the move operation:

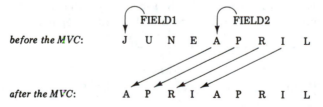

Explicit length. The following MVC instruction uses explicit length to move 3 bytes:

```
MVC FIELD1(3),FIELD2
```

Operand 1 has an explicit length (3) that overrides the defined length of FIELD1. Therefore, MVC moves only the first three bytes of FIELD2 (APR) into the first three bytes of FIELD1.   The fourth byte of FIELD1 is unaltered, as shown.

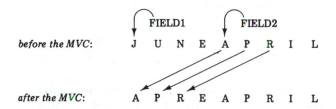

Because of the MVC instruction format, only operand 1 may contain an explicit length.

Explicit length.   The following MVC instruction also uses explicit length to move 5 bytes:

```
MVC FIELD1(5),FIELD2
```

The operation moves APRI into FIELD1.   The L is moved into the next byte to the right, the first byte of FIELD2, which in this example immediately follows FIELD1:

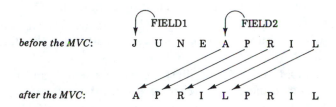

Relative Addressing

Any operand that references main storage may use relative addressing.   If you have to refer to a byte that has no name, you may refer to its position relative to a byte that has a name.   For example, suppose you want to use the following MVC instruction to move the third and fourth bytes of FIELD2 to the second and third bytes of FIELD1:

```
MVC FIELD1+1(2),FIELD2+2
```

The operation moves as follows:

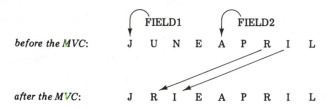

FIELD1   FIELD2

before the MVC: J U N E A P R I L

after the MVC: J R I E A P R I L

To move 2 bytes, the instruction uses an explicit length (2) in operand 1. A relative address of +1 refers to the second byte, and +2 refers to the third byte.

Figure 7-2 depicts unrelated MVC operations. Note the object code generated for each statement. The assembler lists under ADDR1 and ADDR2 the addresses of operand 1 and operand 2, respectively. For example, statement 12 is MVC X,Y. The address of X, a 3-byte field, is 03002, and the address of Y, a 5-byte field, is 03005. You could interpret this instruction as: Move the first 3 bytes of Y, starting in location 03005, to the field named X, starting in location 03002. The object code instruction is 6 bytes long, beginning in location 003012.

Chapter 6 gives the interpretation of this machine language. These examples illustrate some extreme cases, and although important to understand, most data movement is directly from one field to another field defined with the same length.*

MOVE1: Operand 1, X, is shorter than operand 2, Y. The implicit length (3) of X governs the number of bytes moved.

MOVE2: Operand 1, Z, is longer than operand 2, X. The implicit length (8) of Z governs the number of bytes moved.

MOVE3: The explicit length (3) overrides Z's implicit length of 8; only 3 bytes are moved. With symbol length attribute, the statement could be MVC Z(L'X),X.

MOVE4 and MOVE5 illustrate explicit length and relative addressing. In each case the explicit length overrides the defined implicit length.

MOVE6 shows how to copy a character a specified number of positions to the right. The leftmost byte of X contains 'A', which MVC copies 4 bytes to the right. It is possible to propagate any character in this fashion because MVC moves one character at a time, from left to right. This technique is useful, for example, to clear areas to blanks.

MOVE7 shifts data one byte to the left. You may find it helpful to check the operation by following the data movement one byte at a time.

MOVE8 intends to move 3 bytes, but it is erroneously coded with an explicit length of 3 in operand 2 instead of operand 1. The assembler generates 6 bytes of hex zeros as the object code "instruction." These bytes will cause

---

*For illustrative purposes, some examples use declarative names such as X,Y,and Z, although this text does not advocate such cryptic names in programs.

```
LOC    OBJECT CODE      STMT    SOURCE STATEMENT       ACTION OF MOVE:          RESULT:
                                                       ---------------          -------
                          9  *
                         10  *

003000 D202 4030 4033    12  MOVE1   MVC  X,Y           1ST 3 BYTES OF Y INTO   X:  'DEF'
                                                          1ST 3 BYTES OF X
003006 D207 4038 4030    13  MOVE2   MVC  Z,X           ALL BYTES OF X &        Z:  'ABCDEFGH'
                                                          Y INTO Z
00300C D202 4038 4030    14  MOVE3   MVC  Z(3),X        1ST 3 BYTES OF X INTO   Z:  'ABCLMNOP'
                                                          1ST 3 BYTES OF Z
003012 D202 403A 4030    15  MOVE4   MVC  Z+2(L'X),X    3 BYTES OF X INTO       Z:  'IJABCNOP'
                                                          BYTES 3-5 OF Z
003018 D201 403B 4032    16  MOVE5   MVC  Z+3(2),X+2    3RD BYTE OF X & 1ST     Z:  'IJKCDNOP'
                                                          BYTE OF Y INTO Z
00301E D203 4031 4030    17  MOVE6   MVC  X+1(4),X      X TO X+1, X+1 TO X+2,   X:  'AAA'
                                                          X+2 TO Y, & Y TO Y+1  Y:  'AAFGH'
003024 D202 4030 4031    18  MOVE7   MVC  X,X+1         LEFT SHIFT. MOVES X+1 TO X,
                                                          X+2 TO X+1, Y TO X+2  X:  'BCD'
00302A 0000 0000 0000    19  MOVE8   MVC  Z,X(3)        MVC DOES NOT PERMIT EXPLICIT LENGTH IN
                                                          OPERAND-2

             *** ERROR ***

003030 C1C2C3            20  *                 ..:                THESE FIELDS
003033 C4C5C6C7C8        21  X    DC  C'ABC'                      ARE ADJACENT
003038 C9D1D2D3D4D5D6D7  22  Y    DC  C'DEFGH'                    IN STORAGE
                         23  Z    DC  C'IJKLMNOP'


                           DIAGNOSTICS AND STATISTICS

STMNT  ERROR    SEV  MESSAGE
  19   IPK173    8   DISPLACEMENT VALUE IN OPERAND 2 NOT ABSOLUTE
```

Figure 7-2 Unrelated MVC operations.

a program interrupt if the program is executed.   MOVE3 shows the instruction correctly written.

DUPLICATING CHARACTERS

This section describes how you can duplicate any character or group of characters through storage.   Consider the following two declaratives defined at locations 5800 and 5801, respectively:

```
5800   ASTER   DC   C'*'
5801   FIELD   DC   CL3' '
```

To duplicate the contents of ASTER through the next 3 bytes of FIELD, code the following instruction:

```
MVC FIELD,ASTER
```

The MVC moves one byte at a time from left to right.   Initially, operand 1 references 5801 and operand 2 references 5800.   The length of the move is 3 bytes, which is stored in machine code as 1 less, that is, 2.   The MVC works as follows:

1. Copies the contents of ASTER at 5800 into the first byte of FIELD at 5801:

```
        *   *   b   b
        |   |
      5800  5801
```

Since the length is not equal to zero, the operation deducts 1 from the length (it is now 1) and increments the operand 1 address to 5802 and the operand 2 address to 5801.

2. Copies the contents of 5801 into 5802:

```
      *   *   *   b
          |   |
        5801  5802
```

Since the length is still not equal to zero, the operation deducts 1 from the length (now 0) and increments the operand 1 address to 5803 and the operand 2 address to 5802.

3. Copies the contents of 5802 into 5803:

```
      *   *   *   *
              |   |
            5802  5803
```

Since the length is now zero, the operation terminates.

The MVC has now propagated the 1-byte ASTER through the 3-byte contents of FIELD. Now suppose that you want to repeat two characters (/ and -) across a line that is to display on a video screen. The following provides the code:

```
            MVC    DISPLAY,STRING
            ...
STRING      DC     C'/-'
DISPLAY     DS     CL80
```

The MVC initially moves the first / character to DISPLAY and the first - to DISPLAY + 1. The operation continues copying these characters across the entire 80 bytes from DISPLAY to DISPLAY + 2, DISPLAY + 1 to DISPLAY + 3, up to DISPLAY + 77 to DISPLAY + 79.

In this fashion, you can copy any character or string of characters through any number of bytes. One common application is the clearing of an output area to blank. The only requirement is that the characters to be copied must immediately precede the receiving field.

COMPARE LOGICAL CHARACTER: CLC

It is often necessary to determine whether the contents of one field are equal to, greater than, or less than the contents of another field. Here are situations in which the need to compare character fields arises:

- Testing for valid codes
- Checking for valid dates on records
- Testing for ascending sequence of account numbers in an input file (In this test, sequence-checking, the new account number just read is compared to the previously processed account number.)

The instructions to compare character fields are CLC (Compare Logical Characters) and CLI (Compare Logical Immediate). Another logical compare operation, CLCL (Compare Logical Long), has rather limited use. All comparison instructions and certain others set the condition code described in Chapter 5. As a result of the operation, the condition code is set as high, low, or equal and may be tested with a conditional branch instruction. CLC may compare data in any format, but you normally confine its use to comparing character fields.

Name	Operation	Operand
[label]	CLC	S1,S2 *or* D1(L,B1),D2(B2)

The following example compares the contents of NAMEIN (unknown) to that of NAMETST (initialized as JONES):

```
          CLC   NAMEIN,NAMETST
          . . .
NAMEIN    DS    CL5
NAMETST   DC    C'JONES'
```

The rules for CLC are as follows:

1. CLC may compare fields from 1 to 256 bytes long.
2. CLC compares data beginning in the byte specified by operand 1 to the data beginning with the byte specified by operand 2.   Comparison is left to right, one byte at a time.   The condition code is set as follows:

COMPARISON	CONDITION CODE SETTING
Operand 1 equals operand 2.	0 (equal)
Operand 1 is lower.	1 (low)
Operand 1 is higher.	2 (high)

3. The operation terminates comparison as soon as an unequal condition is encountered or, if none, by the explicit or implicit length of operand 1.

Comparison is based on the binary contents of the bytes, and all possible bytes are valid.   The lowest value is binary zeros (X'00'), and the highest is binary ones (X'FF').   A character field contains what is called *logical* (unsigned, non-arithmetic) data.

Carefully examine the examples of CLC instructions in Fig. 7-3.

COMP1: Both compared fields, FIELD1 and FIELD2, have the same length and contents.   The CLC operation sets the condition code to equal.

COMP2: The operand 1 field, FIELD3, is shorter.   CLC compares the 3 bytes of FIELD3 against the first 3 bytes only of FIELD2.   Because the data in FIELD3 is logically greater than that of FIELD2 the condition code is set to high.

COMP3: The operand 1 field is longer.   CLC compares the 5 bytes of FIELD2 against the 3 bytes of FIELD3 plus the next rightmost 2 bytes of FIELD4 (two asterisks).   Operand 1 is lower.

COMP4: Operand 1 uses relative addressing and explicit length.   CLC compares bytes 3, 4, and 5 of FIELD2 against FIELD3.

COMP5: The instruction is similar to COMP4, with the explicit length omitted.   The implicit length of operand 1 is therefore 5.

```
LOC     OBJECT CODE          STMT    SOURCE STATEMENT                          DATA COMPARED:        RESULT:
                                                                               --------------        ------
                             30  *                                             'ABCDE' = 'ABCDE'     EQ
                             31  *                                             'FGH'   > 'ABC'       HI
003040 D504 406A 406F        32  COMP1     CLC   FIELD1,FIELD2                  'ABCDE' < 'FGH**'     LO
003046 D502 4074 406F        33  COMP2     CLC   FIELD3,FIELD2                  'CDE'   < 'FGH'       LO
00304C D504 406F 4074        34  COMP3     CLC   FIELD2,FIELD3                  'CDEFG' < 'FGH**'     LO
003052 D502 4071 4074        35  COMP4     CLC   FIELD2+2(3),FIELD3            '**'    < 'AB'        LO
003058 D504 4071 4074        36  COMP5     CLC   FIELD2+2,FIELD3
00305E D501 4077 406F        37  COMP6     CLC   FIELD4,FIELD2                  NO EXPLICIT LENGTH
003064 0000 0000 0000        38  COMP7     CLC   FIELD3,FIELD2+2(3)            IN OPERAND-2
                             39  *
         *** ERROR ***                                                         THESE
                             40  *                                             FIELDS
00306A C1C2C3C4C5            41  FIELD1    DC    C'ABCDE'                       ARE ADJACENT
00306F C1C2C3C4C5            42  FIELD2    DC    C'ABCDE'                       IN STORAGE
003074 C6C7C8               43  FIELD3    DC    C'FGH'
003077 5C5C                 44  FIELD4    DC    C'**'


                             DIAGNOSTICS AND STATISTICS


STMNT ERROR    SEV MESSAGE
   38  IPK173    8 DISPLACEMENT VALUE IN OPERAND 2 NOT ABSOLUTE
```

Figure 7-3 Unrelated CLC operations.

COMP6: An asterisk (X'5C') is lower than character A (X'C1'), so the operation terminates as "low" after comparing only the first byte.

COMP7: The example illustrates erroneous use of explicit length in operand 2; omitting the length corrects the error.

To minimize program bugs, be sure that you compare fields that are defined with the same length and format, and avoid the use of relative addressing wherever possible.

Branching

CLC makes a comparison and sets the condition code, as described in Chapter 5. The following conditional branch instructions test the condition code to determine what action to take:

BE (Branch Equal)   BNE (Branch Not Equal)
BL (Branch Low)   BNL (Branch Not Low)
BH (Branch High)   BNH (Branch Not High)

The following examples assume that declaratives X, Y, and Z contain data and are each defined as DS CL4.

Example 1.   If X is greater than or equal to Y, branch to J10HIEQ (an address elsewhere in the program):

```
CLC    X,Y         Compare contents of X to Y
BH     J10HIEQ     Branch if high
BE     J10HIEQ     Branch if equal
```

You could code this example more efficiently as follows:

```
CLC    X,Y         Compare contents of X to Y
BNL    J10HIEQ     Branch if X is not lower (high or equal)
```

Example 2.   If X is greater than Z, branch to J20HI.   If Z does not equal Y, branch to J30NEQ.

```
CLC    X,Z         Compare X to Z
BH     J20HI       Branch if high
CLC    Z,Y         Compare Z to Y
BNE    J30NEQ      Branch if unequal
```

LOGIC EXAMPLE

Records for a file of employees contain (among other fields) the following data: employee number, employee name, monthly salary, male/female code, and de-

partment code.   A program is to read each record and display these fields if the
following conditions are all true: (1) monthly salary is greater than \$2,000.00, (2)
the employee is female (F), and (3) she is employed in department 27.
The skeleton code in Fig. 7-4 shows the logic.

```
EMPREC   DS      0CL100             Employee record:
EMPNO    DS      CL05                  Number
EMPNAME  DS      CL25                  Name
MFCODE   DS      CL01                  M/F code
EMPDPT   DS      CL02                  Department
MTHSAL   DS      CL07                  Monthly salary
         DS      CL60                  Rest of record
         ...
         GET     FILEIN,EMPREC      Read first record
C20      CLC     MTHSAL,=C'0200000'  Salary > 2,000.00?
         BNH     C30                   No - exit
         CLC     MFCODE,=C'F'            Female?
         BNE     C30                   No - exit
         CLC     EMPDPT,=C'27'       Department 27?
         BNE     C30                   No - exit
         [display employee record]  Display
C30      GET     FILEIN,EMPREC      Read next record
         B       C20                Loop
```

Figure 7-4   Program logic.

STORAGE IMMEDIATE (SI) FORMAT

Unlike storage-to-storage (SS) format, storage-immediate (SI) format references
only one field.   The immediate instructions MVI (Move Immediate) and CLI
(Compare Logical Immediate) are useful where you want to move or compare a
one-byte character.   The assembler stores the immediate constant in the second
byte of the object code instruction.

Name	Operation	Operand
[label]	MVI	S1,I2 *or* D1(B1),I2
[label]	CLI	S1,I2 *or* D1(B1),I2

The rules for MVI and CLI are similar to those for MVC and CLC, with the
following exceptions:

- Operand 1 references a single main storage location.   The operand does not
  permit an explicit length code because the number of bytes is always 1.

- Operand 2 contains a one-byte immediate constant. The immediate constant value may be character (C), hexadecimal (X), binary (B), or a decimal digit, but not zoned (Z) or packed (P).

Figure 7-5 provides some typical uses of immediate operations:

- MOVIMM1 moves a one-byte dollar sign defined in character format. Note that the object code for MOVIMM1 is 925B4089: The machine code for MVI is hex 92, and the dollar sign, X'5B', is in the next (second) byte.
- MOVIMM2 shows a definition of a hexadecimal dollar. Both this and the preceding statement generate identical object code, although C'$' provides better clarity.
- COMIMM1 compares the contents of a one-byte field, CODEIN, to an immediate operand. Because both contain the character value 5, the condition code is set to equal.
- MOVIMM3, MOVIMM4, COMIMM2, and COMMI3 illustrate common coding errors that the assembler recognizes. MOVIMM4 incorrectly attempts to use a literal.

```
LOC   OBJECT CODE    STMT    SOURCE STATEMENT
                     48 *       ----------------------
    MVI $            49 ***       MVI    MOVE IMMEDIATE
     | |             50 *       ----------------------
00307A 925B 408A     51 MOVIMM1   MVI    SAVE,C'$'      SAVE= |5B|F0|F0|
00307E 925B 408A     52 MOVIMM2   MVI    SAVE,X'5B'     X'5B'IS SAME AS C'$'
003082 0000 0000     53 MOVIMM3   MVI    SAVE(1),C'?'   LENGTH IN OPERAND-1
    *** ERROR ***
003086 0000 0000     54 MOVIMM4   MVI    SAVE+1,=C'$'   CANNOT USE LITERALS
    *** ERROR ***
                     55 *          ...
00308A F0F0F0        56 SAVE      DC     C'000'         SAVE= |F0|F0|F0|

                     57 *       ---------------------------------
    CLI 5            58 ***       CLI    COMPARE LOGICAL IMMEDIATE
     | |             59 *       ---------------------------------
00308E 95F5 409A     60 COMIMM1   CLI    CODEIN,C'5'    SETS COND'N CODE EQ
003092 0000 0000     61 COMIMM2   CLI    CODEIN(1),C'5' LENGTH IN OPERAND-1
    *** ERROR ***
003096 0000 0000     62 COMIMM3   CLI    CODEIN,P'5'    ERROR: PACKED IMMEDIATE
    *** ERROR ***
                     63 *          ...
00309A F5            64 CODEIN    DC     C'5'
```

```
                    DIAGNOSTICS AND STATISTICS
    STMNT ERROR  SEV
       53 IPK173    8 DISPLACEMENT VALUE IN OPERAND 1 NOT ABSOLUTE
       54 IPK131   12 ILLEGAL USE OF LITERAL
       61 IPK173    8 DISPLACEMENT VALUE IN OPERAND 1 NOT ABSOLUTE
       62 IPK116    8 INVALID SELF-DEFINING TERM, 'P'5''
```

Figure 7-5 Unrelated MVI and CLI operations.

You may use EQU to give a symbolic name to an immediate operand:

```
CODE   EQU   C'5'          Assign '5' to the name CODE.
CLI    RECDNO,CODE          Compare RECDNO to C'5'.
```

You may now use CODE in place of C'5' in an immediate operand. The assembler recognizes that CODE is a reference to a value C'5' and substitutes C'5' wherever it encounters the operand CODE.

This technique facilitates program modifications. You may have to change the value of the immediate operand, but rather than change many instructions in the program, merely change the operand in the EQU statement and reassemble the program.

CHARACTER LITERALS

Immediate instructions, such as MVI and CLI, have a one-byte constant in operand 2. A literal, however, is preceded by an equal sign and generates a constant elsewhere in storage. For one-byte nonarithmetic constants, immediate instructions are more efficient.

The following example compares the use of a literal and an immediate operand:

```
Use of a literal:        MVC    DOLLARPR,=C'$'
Use of immediate:        MVI    DOLLARPR,C'$'
```

Although both operands accomplish identical results, note that (1) MVC requires a length (1) in operand 1 if DOLLARPR is not defined with a length of 1; (2) MVC uses a literal—the assembled address of operand 2 will contain the location of the constant ($); (3) MVI contains the $ as part of the assembled instruction; (4) MVI is more efficient coding here because it is only 4 bytes long, whereas MVC requires 6 bytes for the instruction plus 1 byte for the constant defined by the literal = C'$'.

SAMPLE PROGRAM: READING AND PRINTING CUSTOMER RECORDS

The program in Fig. 7-6 reads customer records and prints selected fields. Although relatively simple, the program is still organized into logical routines for initialization, main processing, end-of-file, and errors. Also, the program has been made more readable by the use of comments and clear, meaningful instruction labels and data names.

```
                   READ AND PRINT CUSTOMER RECORDS
    LOC    OBJECT CODE       STMT     SOURCE STATEMENT
                              2               PRINT ON,NOGEN,NODATA

000000                        4 PROG07   START
000000 0530                   5          BALR  3,0                INITIALIZE
                              6          USING *,3                  ADDRESSING
000002 4570 3092              7          BAL   7,C10INIT          INITIALIZATION
000006 4570 3032              8 A10LOOP  BAL   7,B10PROC          PERFORM MAIN PROCESS
                              9          GET   FILEIN,CRECDIN     READ NEXT
00001A 47F0 3004             15          B     A10LOOP            LOOP

                             17 A90EOF   CLOSE FILEIN,PRINTER     END-OF-FILE
                             26          EOJ

                             30 ***            M A I N   P R O C E S S I N G
                             31 *              ----------------------------
000034 95F3 3319             32 B10PROC  CLI   CCODEIN,CCODE      VALID RECORD CODE?
000038 4780 3042             33          BE    B20               *  YES - BYPASS
00003C 4580 3110             34          BAL   8,R20INVRC        *  NO  - ERROR
000040 47F0 3090             35          B     B90
000044 D504 331E 34B2        36 B20      CLC   CUSTIN,PREVCUST    CUST NO. IN SEQ?
00004A 4720 3054             37          BH    B30               *  YES - BYPASS
00004E 4580 311A             38          BAL   8,R30SEQER        *  NO  - ERROR
000052 47F0 3090             39          B     B90
000056 D204 34B2 331E        40 B30      MVC   PREVCUST,CUSTIN    SAVE NEW CUST#
                             41 *                                 MOVE TO PRINT:
00005C D201 341C 3345        42          MVC   CENTSPR,BALIN+4    *  CENTS POSITIONS
000062 924B 341B             43          MVI   DECPR,C'.'         *  DECIMAL POINT
000066 D203 3417 3341        44          MVC   DOLLPR,BALIN       *  DOLLAR POSITIONS
00006C D213 3401 3323        45          MVC   NAMEPR,NAMEIN      *  NAME
000072 D204 33FA 331E        46          MVC   CUSTPR,CUSTIN      *  CUSTOMER NO.

                             48          PUTPR PRINTER,CUSLINE,WSP1 PRINT CUST RECORD
00008C D284 33EF 33EE        55          MVC   CUSLINE,BLANK      CLEAR PRINT LINE
000092 07F7                  56 B90      BR    7                  RETURN

                             58 *              I N I T I A L I Z A T I O N
                             59 *              ----------------------------
                             60 C10INIT  OPEN  FILEIN,PRINTER
0000A6 D284 33EF 33EE        69          MVC   CUSLINE,BLANK      CLEAR PRINT AREA
                             71          PUTPR PRINTER,HDGLINE,SK1 SKIP TO NEW PAGE
                             78          GET   FILEIN,DRECDIN     READ DATE RECORD
0000D0 95C4 3319             84          CLI   DCODEIN,DCODE      VALID DATE CODE?
0000D4 4780 30DA             85          BE    C20               * YES - BYPASS
0000D8 4580 3106             86          BAL   8,R10NODAT        * NO -- ERROR
0000DC D211 33A2 3320        87 C20      MVC   DATEPR,ALFDTIN     STORE DATE
                             88          PUTPR PRINTER,HDGLINE,WSP2 PRINT HEADING
                             95          GET   FILEIN,CRECDIN     READ 1ST CUST
000106 07F7                 101          BR    7                  RETURN

                            103 ***            E R R O R   R O U T I N E S
                            104 *              ----------------------------
000108 D211 33A2 3474       105 R10NODAT MVC   DATEPR,DATEMSG     MISSING DATE
00010E 47F0 312C            106          B     R90

000112 D215 3421 3486       108 R20INVRC MVC   MESSAGPR,RECDMSG   INVALID RECORD
000118 47F0 3120            109          B     R80

00011C D215 3421 349C       111 R30SEQER MVC   MESSAGPR,SEQMSG    OUT-OF-SEQUENCE
```

Figure 7-6 Program: reading and printing customer records.

```
000122 D213 3401 3323   113 R80      MVC    NAMEPR,NAMEIN         MOVE NAME &
000128 D204 33FA 331E    114          MVC    CUSTPR,CUSTIN          CUST NO. TO PRINT
                         115 R90      PUTPR  PRINTER,CUSLINE,WSP1  PRINT ERROR MESSAGE
000142 D284 33EF 33EE    122          MVC    CUSLINE,BLANK         CLEAR PRINT LINE
000148 07F8              123          BR     8                     RETURN

                         125 ***               D E C L A R A T I V E S
                         126 *                  -----------------------

                         128 FILEIN   DEFIN  A90EOF               DEFINE INPUT FILE
                         154 PRINTER  DEFPR                       DEFINE PRINT FILE

00031B                   184 DRECDIN  DS     0CL80                DATE RECORD:
00031B                   185 DCODEIN  DS     CL01                 * CODE (D)
00031C                   186 NUMDTIN  DS     CL06                 * NUMERIC DATE
000322                   187 ALFDTIN  DS     CL18                 * ALPHA DATE
000334                   188          DS     CL55

00036B                   190          ORG    DRECDIN              RESET LOC'N CTR
00031B                   191 CRECDIN  DS     0CL80                CUSTOMER RECORD:
00031B                   192 CCODEIN  DS     CL01                 01-01 CODE(3)
00031C                   193          DS     CL04                 02-05
000320                   194 CUSTIN   DS     CL05                 06-10 CUST. NO.
000325                   195 NAMEIN   DS     CL20                 11-30 CUST NAME
000339                   196          DS     CL10                 31-40
000343                   197 BALIN    DS     ZL06                 41-46 BALANCE
000349                   198          DS     CL34                 47-80

00036B                   200 HDGLINE  DS     0CL133               HEADING LINE:
00036B 4040404040404040  201          DC     CL11' '              * ----------
000376 C3E4E2E37B4040D5  202          DC     CL29'CUST#   NAME'    *
000393 C2C1D3C1D5C3C540  203          DC     CL17'BALANCE'        *
0003A4                   204 DATEPR   DS     CL18                 *
0003B6 4040404040404040  205          DC     CL58' '              *

0003F0 40                207 BLANK    DC     C' '                 BLANK TO CLEAR PRINT
0003F1                   208 CUSLINE  DS     0CL133               CUST PRINT LINE:
0003F1 4040404040404040  209          DC     CL11' '              * -------------
0003FC                   210 CUSTPR   DS     CL05                 *   CUST. NO.
000401 4040              211          DC     CL02' '              *
000403                   212 NAMEPR   DS     CL20                 *   NAME
000417 4040              213          DC     CL02' '              *
000419                   214 DOLLPR   DS     ZL04                 *   $ POSITIONS
00041D                   215 DECPR    DS     CL01                 *   DECIMAL POINT
00041E                   216 CENTSPR  DS     ZL02                 *   CENTS POS'NS
000420 404040            217          DC     CL03' '              *
000423 4040404040404040  218 MESSAGPR DC     CL22' '              *   ERROR MESSAGE
000439 4040404040404040  219          DC     CL61' '              *

000476 D5D640C4C1E3C540  221 DATEMSG  DC     CL18'NO DATE RECORD'
000488 C9D5E5C1D3C9C440  222 RECDMSG  DC     CL22'INVALID RECORD CODE'
00049E D9C5C3D6D9C440D6  223 SEQMSG   DC     CL22'RECORD OUT OF SEQUENCE'

0004B4 0000000000        225 PREVCUST DC     XL5'00'              PREV. CUST. NO.

                         227 DCODE    EQU    C'D'                 DATE REC CODE
                         228 CCODE    EQU    C'3'                 CUST REC CODE
```

Figure 7-6 *(continued)*

```
0004C0                  230        LTORG
0004C0 5B5BC2C3D3D6E2C5 231                   =C'$$BCLOSE'
0004C8 5B5BC2D6D7C5D540 232                   =C'$$BOPEN '
0004D0 00000150         233                   =A(FILEIN)
0004D4 0000031B         234                   =A(CRECDIN)
0004D8 000001E0         235                   =A(PRINTER)
0004DC 000003F1         236                   =A(CUSLINE)
0004E0 0000036B         237                   =A(HDGLINE)
0004E4 0000031B         238                   =A(DRECDIN)
                        239        END        PROG07
```

Output:-

```
      CUST#   NAME                      BALANCE          JANUARY 28, 1995

      12345   KE ANDERSON               1234.56
      24680   D  BAKER                  5432.10
      33333   JW COUSTON                3333.33
      34567   AB DONOVAN                0025.00
      42312   KM EDWARDS                0001.25
      99999   WM FISHER                 3456.32
```

Figure 7-6   (*continued*)

Input.   Two record formats for a date record and a file of customer records in sequence by customer number.   The customer record format is

COLUMN	DESCRIPTION
01	Record Code
06–10	Customer number
11–30	Customer name
41–46	Balance due

Processing.   The program consists of a main procedure and three subroutines.

Main procedure.   The routine initializes the base registers and links to C10INIT for opening files and reading the date record and the first customer record. At A10LOOP is a looping routine: BAL to B10PROC, read the next record, and loop back to A10LOOP.   The program repeats looping until end-of-file. At that point, control passes to A90EOF, where the program terminates execution.

B10PROC.   After the date record, the rest of the file must be customer records (record code '3').   If the code is invalid, a routine prints an error message.   To ensure that each record is in ascending sequence (one record per customer), the program compares the current customer (CUSTIN) to the previously processed customer number (PREVCUST).   If the new customer number is higher, the program stores CUSTIN in PREVCUST for the next input test.   An equal or low customer number causes an error message.   For valid customer records, the program moves customer name, number, and balance due to the print area and inserts a decimal point in the balance field. BR then returns control to the main routine.

C10INIT.   After opening the files, the initialization routine reads the first record.   If the record is the date (record code 'D'), the program moves the date from the record to the heading and prints it.   If not a date record, the program prints an error message and cancels processing.

Error routines.   The labels R10NODAT, R20INVRC, and R30SEQER begin routines that issue error messages.

Output.   The program prints a heading and the contents of each record:

11———15	16—17	18————37	38—39	40———46
Cust. No.		Customer Name		Balance Due

Immediately before PRINT is a one-byte constant named BLANK.   After printing, the program propagates the contents of BLANK through the 133 bytes of PRINT, clearing the entire field.   (See the section "Duplicating Characters" for an explanation.)

Redefining the Input Area

The program uses the ORG directive to redefine the input area for the two types of input records, as follows:

```
00031B    DRECDIN    DS     0CL80     Define date record
00031B    DCODEIN    DS     CL01      *
00031C    NUMDTIN    DS     CL06      *
000322    ALFDTIN    DS     CL18      *
000334               DS     CL55      *

          ORG        DRECDIN    Redefine
00031B    CRECDIN    DS     0CL80     Define customer record
00031B    CCODEIN    DS     CL01      *
00031C               DS     CL04      *
000320    CUSTIN     DS     CL05      *
                     . . .
```

Sequence Checking

The program initializes PREVCUST, the previously stored customer number, with hexadecimal zeros (XL5'00').   This value represents 5 bytes of binary zeros, the lowest possible value on a computer.   The blank character, X'40', for example is higher than X'00', and there is no single key on a keyboard that can enter X'00'. Under normal conditions, it would be virtually impossible for a data record to contain hex zeros in its customer number field.   As a consequence, the customer number in the first input record is always higher than the contents of PREVCUST. If you define PREVCUST as CL5" or C'00000', the first customer number could conceivably contain blanks or zeros.   The program would then treat the customer number as equal to PREVCUST, resulting in an invalid error message.

MOVE INVERSE: MVCIN

The MVCIN instruction, available on more advanced models, has specialized uses. Like MVC, it can copy up to 256 characters from one location to another, but it moves them in reverse sequence.   Thus operand 1 references the rightmost byte of the receiving field, and characters are moved from right to left.

Name	Operation	Operand
[label]	MVCIN	S1,S2 *or* D1(L,B1),D2(B2)

In the following example, MVCIN stores the character string in NEWSEQ in reverse sequence, as ATAD TUPNI:

```
                MVCIN     NEWSEQ,OLDSEQ
                 . . .
        OLDSEQ  DC        CL10'INPUT DATA'
        NEWSEQ  DS        CL10
```

Uses for MVCIN could include reversing the data sequence for I/O devices that require it and encrypting data.

DEBUGGING TIPS FOR CHARACTER DATA

• A common programming error is caused by omitting the explicit length from an MVC or CLC used with relative addressing, as here:

```
                MVC     PRINT+95,=C'DATE'
                 . . .
        PRINT   DC      CL133
```

The instruction moves 133 bytes, starting from the first byte of the literal 'DATE'—perhaps a good reason to minimize (or avoid) use of relative addressing.   The areas following PRINT will be clobbered, with often spectacular results that may not appear until later in the execution.

- Be careful with the use of literals that are associated with character data. Consider the following definition:

```
AMOUNTIN     DS     CL7
```

Suppose you want to check whether AMOUNTIN contains all blanks. The instruction CLC AMOUNTIN,=C' ' assumes the length of operand 1, 7 bytes. The comparison is all 7 bytes of AMOUNTIN to the 1-byte literal plus the 6 bytes immediately following in the literal pool, whatever they may contain. To correct the error, change the literal to =7C' ' or =CL7' '.

- Suppose you also want to check whether AMOUNTIN contains all zeros. The instruction CLC AMOUNTIN,=C'0' causes the same error as the 1-byte blank. Let's try a 7-byte literal, =CL7'0'. Watch out for this one! The assembler generates a 7-byte literal with the 0 left-adjusted and six blanks filled to the right, as '0bbbbbb'. The correct literal is =7C'0' or =C'0000000'.

Appendix B contains a list of program-check interrupts that can occur during program execution, along with possible causes of the errors.

KEY POINTS

- Character constants may be from 1 to 256 characters long, and they may contain any character, including blanks. If the length (Ln) is not coded, the assembler assumes that the field length is that of the defined constant. It is easy to code a constant incorrectly; for example, the constant DC CL5'0' generates '0bbbb' rather than '00000'.
- MVC is a storage-to storage (SS) instruction that may move up to 256 bytes in any format, although its use is normally confined to character fields.
- CLC is a storage-to storage instruction that compares up to 256 bytes in any format, although its use is normally confined to character fields. As a result of the operation, the condition code is set as high, low, or equal and may be tested with a conditional branch instruction.
- The immediate instructions MVI and CLI are useful where you want to move or compare a one-byte character. The assembler stores the immediate constant in the second byte of the object code instruction.
- Operand 1 of an MVI or CLI or operand 2 of an MVC or CLC may not have an explicit length.

PROBLEMS

7-1. *Define Storage.* Define each of the following as a DS:
  (a) An 80-byte area named OUT to be used for output
  (b) A 100-byte area that does not increment the location counter
  (c) Five 10-byte areas defined with one statement
  (d) An area named DATE, subdivided with three 2-byte fields called MONTH, DAY, and YEAR, respectively

7-2. *Define Constant.* Define each of the following as a DC:
  (a) A field named ASTER, one byte long, containing an asterisk
  (b) A field of ten blanks, named BLANKS
  (c) A constant containing SAM'S
  (d) A constant of ten character zeros
  (e) Three 5-byte constants all containing blanks, defined with one statement

7-3. *Move Character.* Given the declaratives shown, code the following unrelated questions. Show the contents of both fields after completion of the operation.

```
A    DC    C'123'    These fields are defined
B    DC    C'4567'   adjacent in storage
C    DC    C'XY'
```

Example: Move the contents of C to the leftmost 2 bytes of A: MVC A(2),C.
  (a) Move the contents of C to the second and third bytes of B.
  (b) Move the rightmost byte of A to the third byte of B.
  (c) Move A to the bytes starting at the third byte of B.
  (d) Use one MVC to change all the contents of A, B, and C to character 1s.
  (e) Use one MVC to shift both A and B one byte to the left, as follows:

```
before:   1 2 3 4 5 6 7
          ✓ ✓ ✓ ✓ ✓ ✓
after:    2 3 4 5 6 7 7
          |         |
          A         B
```

7-4. *Compare and Branch.* Given the declaratives, code the following:

```
D    DC    C'ANN'
E    DC    C'MAC'
F    DC    C'SAL'
```

  (a) If E is less than or equal to F, branch to X40.
  (b) If D is greater than E but not less than F, branch to X50.

7-5. *Condition Code.* Indicate the condition code (high, low, or equal) set by the following. Declaratives D, E, and F refer to the DCs in Problem 7-4. Explain if an invalid assembly or execute operation arises.

(a) CLC	D,F	
(b) CLC	F,E	
(c) CLC	D,=C'DAN'	
(d) CLI	E,C'P'	
(e) CLI	F,C'F'	
(f) CLI	D(1),=C'A'	

7-6. *Program Assignment.*   A program that reads inventory records and prints selected data is required.

   Input:

COLUMN	CONTENTS
01	Record code ('4')
04–08	Stock number
09–28	Description
29–30	Month
31–35	Quantity on hand
36–42	Value (xxxxx.xx)

Output (including heading):

```
STOCK NO   DESCRIPTION MONTH   QUANTITY    VALUE
XXXXX      X————————X  XX      XXXXXX     XXXXX.XX
```

Procedure.

(a) Check the record code (4) to ensure that the program processes only valid records. Bypass invalid records and print a message 'INVALID RECORD'.

(b) To ensure that the records are in proper order, sequence-check them on stock number.   If out of sequence, print an error message 'OUT OF SEQUENCE'.

(c) Provide input data that tests for invalid record code and out-of-sequence condition.

(d) Print the fields as shown, in any suitable print positions.   As an optional extra, code the program to convert the numeric input month into alphabetic for printing (i.e., convert '01' to 'JANUARY').

(e) Analyze, code, and test the program.   Be sure to use the programming standards for your installation.

8

PROCESSING PACKED DECIMAL DATA

OBJECTIVE

To cover the requirements for processing data in
packed format.

The programs to this point covered the use of data in character format. Few
programs are written using just this format, because generally they need to perform
arithmetic. A common format for arithmetic is packed decimal. The instructions
MVN and MVZ, although technically character operations, are covered here because they are used mostly with packed data. This chapter, then, covers the basic
operations for packing, unpacking, comparing, and decimal arithmetic.

ZONED DECIMAL DATA

Zoned decimal format is similar to character and may be used as a DS to define
a field containing data that will later be packed, such as a numeric field read from

an input record.   Zoned data, like character, consists of a 4-bit zone portion and a 4-bit numeric portion:

```
                ←——zone——→ │ ←—numeric—→
   bits:       │ 0 │ 0 │ 0 │ 0 │ 0 │ 0 │ 0 │ 0 │
   position:     0   1   2   3   4   5   6   7
```

The following rules govern zoned declaratives:

1. The length may be defined from 1 to 16 bytes.
2. The constant may contain only the digits 0 through 9, a sign (+ or −), and a decimal point.   The assembler does not translate or store the decimal point—you code it only for documentation, where you intend the decimal to be.
3. You may define more than one zoned constant with one DC, separated by commas.
4. Except for the rightmost digit of the constant, the assembler converts each zoned digit 0 through 9 to X'FO' through X'F9'.   If the constant is positive, the assembler generates a plus sign, X'C', and if negative, a minus sign, X'D'. In the following example, the rightmost byte X'C5' contains the plus sign in the zone portion:

```
        DC  Z'123.45'     | F1 | F2 | F3 | F4 | C5 |
```

5. Code the sign (+ or −) to the left of the constant, such as DC Z' − 1.25'. To represent a positive value, code a + sign or omit the sign altogether.
6. You may specify a length (Ln) as for other formats.   If the constant is shorter than the specified length, the assembler right-adjusts the constant and pads leftmost zeros:

```
        DC  ZL3'25'       | F0 | F2 | C5 |
```

If the constant is longer than the specified length, the assembler truncates the constant on the left:

```
        DC  ZL2'1234'     | F3 | C4 |
```

Figure 8-1 illustrates zoned declaratives explained as follows:

ZONE0 defines a DS as 5 bytes long, to be used for zoned data.
ZONE1 is a DC with a decimal point in the constant.   Note the generated object code on the left.

```
LOC      OBJECT CODE      STMT    SOURCE STATEMENT
003000                     7 ZONE0    DS    ZL5                5-BYTE AREA
003005  F1F2F3C5            8 ZONE1    DC    Z'123.5'           IGNORES DECIMAL
003009  F5F0F0F0D0          9 ZONE2    DC    Z'-500.00'         MINUS SIGN
00300E  F0F1F2C3           10 ZONE3    DC    ZL4'123'           PADS ZEROS LEFT

003012  F2C3               12 ZONE4    DC    ZL2'123'           TRUNCATES LEFT
003014  F0C0F0C0F0C0       13 ZONE5    DC    3ZL2'0'            3 CONSTANTS
00301A  F1F2C3C4F6C7       14 ZONE6    DC    Z'123,4,67'        3 CONSTANTS
```

Figure 8-1 Declaratives in zoned format.

ZONE2 shows a DC with a minus sign coded to the left. The assembler stores the sign in object code on the right as X'D'.

ZONE3 and **ZONE4** use the length indication (Ln). In ZONE3, X'F0' is padded on the left, and in ZONE4 the constant is truncated.

ZONE5 defines three identical constants. A reference to ZONE5 is to the first 2-byte constant.

ZONE6 defines three constants, each separated by a comma. The comma is not stored. A reference to ZONE6 is to the first 3-byte constant.

Note the difference between the generated constants for the following character and zoned DCs. The comma in the zoned example generates two constants:

```
Character:    DC  C'1,234.56'    | F1 | 6B | F2 | F3 | F4 | 4B | F5 | F6 |
Zoned:        DC  Z'1,234.56'    | C1 | F2 | F3 | F4 | F5 | C6 |
```

PACKED DECIMAL DATA

Ordinary decimal arithmetic is performed on fields in packed format. You may either define these fields initially as packed or use the PACK instruction to translate character or zoned data into packed. The plus or minus sign is the rightmost half-byte of the field. Each other packed byte contains two digits, one in each half-byte. For example, the packed value +125 requires 2 bytes, as in

| 12 | 5C |

The binary representation of this field is

| 0001 | 0010 | 0101 | 1100 |

Packed fields must conform to the following rules:

- All digit positions (all half-bytes other than the rightmost sign) contain only digits 0 through 9 (binary 0000 through 1001).

- The rightmost half-byte contains a sign. There are four valid plus signs and two valid minus signs:

BINARY	HEX	SIGN
1010	A	+
1011	B	−
1100	C	+ (standard plus sign)
1101	D	− (standard minus sign)
1110	E	+
1111	F	+ (a common plus sign)

The standard plus sign is X'C' or binary 1100, and the standard minus sign is X'D' or binary 1101. The X'F' plus sign is common in input fields.

- Packed fields may be a minimum of 1 byte long (one digit plus a sign) and a maximum of 16 bytes (31 digits plus a sign).

Packed Decimal Constants

Constants are defined as packed for use in decimal arithmetic. The rules for packed, which are similar to zoned, are as follows:

- The length may be defined from 1 to 16 bytes.
- A packed constant may contain only the digits 0 through 9 and, optionally, a decimal point (.) and a sign (+ or −). The assembler does not store the decimal point, which serves only as documentation.
- One DC may define more than one packed constant, each separated by a comma.
- You may also use length indication (Ln). The assembler right-adjusts the constant to permit padding leftmost zeros or truncation on the left.
- The rightmost half-byte (numeric portion) of the assembled constant contains the sign, X'C' for plus and X'D' for minus. For example, DC PL3'1234' is converted to packed as | 01 | 23 | 4C | .
- All other half-bytes contain a digit. Other than the rightmost byte, which has a digit and a sign, all bytes contain two digits. A packed constant, therefore, always has an odd number of digits, 1 to 31.

Figure 8-2 depicts packed DCs, explained as follows:

PACK1 packs three digits into 2 bytes. The plus (+) sign is optional.
PACK2 defines a negative constant.
PACK3 packs four digits into 3 bytes. The assembler inserts a zero digit in

```
LOC    OBJECT CODE      STMT    SOURCE STATEMENT
003020 370C             21 PACK1   DC    P'+370'          PLUS SIGN
003022 500D             22 PACK2   DC    P'-500'          MINUS SIGN
003024 01234C           23 PACK3   DC    P'12.34'         IGNORES DEC
003027 0012345C         24 PACK4   DC    PL4'12345'       PADS ZERO

00302B 345C             26 PACK5   DC    PL2'12345'       TRUNCATES
00302D 000C000C000C     27 PACK6   DC    3PL2'0'          3 CONSTANTS
003033 125C215C387C     28 PACK7   DC    PL2'125,215,387' 3 CONSTANTS
003039 007CD1E4D3E8     29 PACK8   DC    P'07',C'JULY'    2 CONSTANTS
```

Figure 8-2 Declaratives in packed format.

USED FOR TABLE PROCESSING

the leftmost half-byte. Note that a packed constant defined as an even number of digits results in an odd number of packed digits. Also, the decimal point acts as a comment and is not stored.

PACK4 defines the length longer than the constant. The assembler pads zeros on the left.

PACK5 defines the length shorter than the constant. The assembler truncates the leftmost digit.

PACK6 defines three identical constants containing zeros.

PACK7 defines three constants, each separated by a comma, which is not stored. A reference to PACK7 is to the first 2-byte field.

PACK8 defines two constants, the first packed and the second character. A reference to PACK8 is to the first field, the 2-byte packed constant.

MOVE NUMERIC (MVN) AND MOVE ZONES (MVZ)

The main use of the MVN and MVZ instructions is to manipulate half-bytes for decimal arithmetic. The rules for both instructions are similar to those for MVC, with the following exceptions:

- MVN and MVZ may move from 1 to 256 half-bytes in any format.
- MVN moves only the numeric portion of the half-byte, the rightmost 4 bits, numbered 4 to 7. From 1 to 256 numeric portions may be moved. The zone portion is undisturbed.
- MVZ moves only the zone portion of the half-byte, the leftmost 4 bits, numbered 0 to 3. From 1 to 256 zones may be moved. The numeric portion is undisturbed.
- Data beginning in the byte specified by operand 2 is copied one half-byte at a time to the field beginning with the byte specified by operand 1. The move does not affect the contents of the operand 2 field.
- The length of the operand 1 field determines the number of half-bytes moved.

Since the instruction formats contain a length code (L) for operand 1 only, the length of operand 2 is irrelevant to the operation.

Name	Operation	Operand
[label]	MVN	S1,S2 *or* D1(L,B1),D2(B2)
[label]	MVZ	S1,S2 *or* D1(L,B1),D2(B2)

The following four unrelated MVN and MVZ examples use this defined data:

```
FLDA      DC      C'123'        | F1 | F2 | F3 |
FLDB      DC      X'45678C      | 45 | 67 | 8C |
```

1. Move the numeric portion of each byte of FLDA to the numeric portion of each byte of FLDB:

```
                                    | F1 | F2 | F3 |
                                    |    |    |    |
          MVN      FLDB,FLDA        | 41 | 62 | 83 |
```

2. The next MVN illustrates relative addressing and explicit length, and moves two numerics, starting from FLDA to FLDB + 1:

```
                                       | F1 | F2 | F3 |
                                       |    |    |
          MVN      FLDB+1(2),FLDA    | 45 | 61 | 82 |
```

3. Move the zone portion of each byte of FLDA to the zone portion of each byte of FLDB:

```
                                    | F1 | F2 | F3 |
                                    |    |    |    |
          MVZ      FLDB,FLDA        | F5 | F7 | FC |
```

4. Move one zone from FLDB + 1 to FLDB + 2:

```
                                       | 45 | 67 | 8C |
                                       |
          MVZ      FLDB+2(1),FLDB+1  | 45 | 67 | 6C |
```

PACKED OPERATIONS: PACK AND UNPK

The computer can perform arithmetic only on valid numeric fields (packed decimal and binary).   Since input data from a terminal or the system reader is in character format, it is necessary to convert into packed, using the PACK operation.   In packed format, operations such as AP, SP, and ZAP can perform arithmetic, and CP can perform comparisons.   The UNPK operation and ED (discussed later in this chapter) convert the packed data into printable characters.

Packing Fields: PACK

Data normally appears in packed format by (1) a constant defined as packed or (2) an instruction, PACK, that converts character or zoned fields into packed. The standard steps to process decimal arithmetic are as follows:

1. Read input data.   Regardless of your definition, numeric fields from a terminal or system reader are read in character format.

2. Convert (PACK) character amount fields into packed.

3. Perform decimal arithmetic on packed fields.

4. Prepare the output area.   Output on tape and disk may be in any format. Output on a printer or video screen is usually in character format; the packed fields must be either unpacked or edited into the print area.

5. Write or display the output data.

Name	Operation	Operand
[label]	PACK	S1,S2 or D1(L1,B1),D2(L2,B2)

Although PACK is normally used to convert character and zoned to packed, PACK executes regardless of the format.   There is no checking for valid data, and PACK can easily generate garbage if applied to the wrong data field.   The rules for PACK are as follows:

- The maximum length of each operand is 16 bytes.   Both operands may specify an explicit length (L1 and L2).

- Bytes referenced by operand 2 are packed one byte at a time from right to left into the operand 1 field.   In the rightmost byte, the half-bytes are reversed.   The zone portion of the rightmost byte of operand 2 (X'F') is placed in the numeric portion of the rightmost byte of operand 1.   The numeric portion of operand 2 (X'5') is placed in the zone portion of operand 1.   It becomes the rightmost, or units, digit.

operand-2: | F | 5 |

operand-1: | 5 | F |

```
LOC     OBJECT CODE      STMT     SOURCE STATEMENT
003000  F224 401E 4021     8 PACKA    PACK   G,H              G= |12|34|5C|
003006  F222 401E 4026     9 PACKB    PACK   G,J              G= |00|12|3F|
00300C  F225 401E 4029    10 PACKC    PACK   G,K              G= |23|45|6C|

003012  F244 4021 4021    12 PACKD    PACK   H,H              H= |00|00|12|34|5C|
003018  F212 402C 4022    13 PACKE    PACK   K+3(2),H+1(3)    K= |F1|F2|F3|23|4F|C6|
                          14 *               ...
00301E                    15 G         DS     PL3
003021  F1F2F3F4C5        16 H         DC     Z'12345'         H= |F1|F2|F3|F4|C5|
003026  F1F2F3            17 J         DC     C'123'           J= |F1|F2|F3|
003029  F1F2F3F4F5C6      18 K         DC     Z'123456'        K= |F1|F2|F3|F4|F5|C6|
```

Figure 8-3   Unrelated PACK operations.

- Other than the rightmost byte, all other zones of operand 2 are ignored. PACK extracts numeric portions from operand 2 one at a time from right to left and places them adjacent to one another in the operand 1 field. The following instruction packs the contents of ZONED into PACKED:

```
           PACK       PACKED,ZONED
             . . .
ZONED   DC       Z'12345'        |F1|F2|F3|F4|C5|

PACKED  DS       PL3             |12|34|5C|
```

Note that the zoned sign F becomes the packed sign. The zoned 5 becomes the rightmost digit, and each other numeric ZONED digit is extracted and placed in PACKED. PACKED now contains data on which you may perform decimal arithmetic.

- PACK terminates when all digits are transmitted. If operand 1 is too short to receive all the digits, the operation ignores the remaining leftmost digits of operand 2. If operand 1 is longer than necessary to receive all the digits, the operation fills its leftmost bytes with zeros (X'0'). In any event, PACK fully erases the previous contents of the receiving field.

Figure 8-3 gives various unrelated PACK examples, explained as follows:

PACKA illustrates a conventional PACK operation. H, a 5-byte zoned field, requires 3 bytes when converted to packed format.

PACKB's operand 1, G, is one byte longer than necessary for the PACK operation. PACK pads zeros in the leftmost byte.

PACKC depicts a common programming error. A 6-byte field, K, is packed into a 3-byte field, G. PACK proceeds from right to left, terminating before packing all the digits in G.

PACKD shows the effect of packing a field into itself. Although the operation works correctly, this practice is not always desirable. First, the field is defined as zoned but now contains packed data. Second, the defined length is 5 bytes, but the field now contains only 3 bytes of significant data. For consistency and maintainability, it is preferable to pack into a field defined with the correct format and length.

PACKE illustrates valid use of relative addressing and explicit lengths. The second, third, and fourth bytes of H are packed into the fourth and fifth bytes of K; the other bytes are not affected by the operation. The example is illustrative, because there are few practical reasons to code in this way.

Blank Input Fields

What if a numeric input field is blank? PACK actually packs any kind of data, even blanks. Consider the following definitions and PACK operation:

```
            PACK   RATEPK,RATEIN      Pack rate
            ...
RATEIN  DS     ZL5                Input field
RATEPK  DS     PL3                Packed field
```

If RATEIN is blank (X'4040404040'), the result of packing RATEPK is X'000004'. Since the rightmost digit is supposed to be a valid sign, an attempt to perform arithmetic on RATEPK causes a data exception.

One way to avert such an error is to assign zeros to a blank input field, as follows:

```
        CLC    RATEIN,=CL5' '       Blank field?
        BNE    D50                  No - bypass
        MVC    RATEIN,=CL5'00000'   Yes - insert zeros
D50     PACK   RATEPK,RATEIN        Pack rate
```

Packing a blank input field now results in RATEPK containing X'00000F', a valid signed field of packed zeros.

Unpacking Fields: UNPK

UNPK performs the reverse of PACK. Its main purpose is to convert data into zoned in order, for example, to print the zoned field. Since there is no checking for validity of data, UNPK may be used to manipulate data in any format. However, unpacking data that is not packed may result in garbage.

Name	Operation	Operand
[label]	UNPK	S1,S2 or D1(L1,B1),D2(L2,B2)

The rules for UNPK are as follows:

- The maximum length for each field is 16 bytes. Both operands may specify an explicit length (L1 and L2).
- Bytes referenced by operand 2 are unpacked one byte at a time from right to left into the operand 1 field.
- As done also by PACK, the half-bytes of the rightmost byte of the operand 2 field are reversed in the operand 1 field.
- UNPK successively places all other digits in operand 2 from right to left in the numeric portion of each byte in operand 1. The zone portions are filled with hex 'F'. The following unpacks PACKED into ZONED:

```
              UNPK      ZONED,PACKED
              ...
      PACKED  DC        PL3'12345'          | 12 | 34 | 5C |

      ZONED   DS        ZL5                 | F1 | F2 | F3 | F4 | C5 |
```

Note that UNPK reverses the PACKED sign C and the digit 5 in the receiving field, ZONED. All other digits are placed in ZONED with a zone 'F'. The data in ZONED is now in a format that you can print, whereas PACKED contains bytes that are unsuitable for printing. Rather than use UNPK to translate packed data for printing, the normal practice is to use the ED operation (to be explained shortly).

- UNPK normally terminates when all digits are transmitted. If the operand 1 field is too short to receive all the digits, the remaining leftmost bytes of operand 2 are ignored. If the operand 1 field is longer than necessary to receive all the digits, its leftmost bytes are filled with character zeros (X'F0').

Consider the UNPK examples in Fig. 8-4.

```
LOC      OBJECT CODE        STMT      SOURCE STATEMENT

003030  F342 4057 4054       25 UNPACK1    UNPK   M,L          M=  | F1 | F2 | F3 | F4 | C5 |
003036  F352 405C 4054       26 UNPACK2    UNPK   N,L          N=  | F0 | F1 | F2 | F3 | F4 | C5 |
00303C  F322 4062 4054       27 UNPACK3    UNPK   P,L          P=  | F3 | F4 | C5 |

003042  F342 405D 4054       29 UNPACK4    UNPK   N+1(5),L     N=  | F9 | F1 | F2 | F3 | F4 | C5 |
003048  F322 4054 4054       30 UNPACK5    UNPK   L,L          L=  | F3 | F4 | C5 |
00304E  F344 4065 4065       31 UNPACK6    UNPK   Q,Q          Q=  | FF | F7 | F7 | F8 | C9 |
                             32 *          ...
003054  12345C               33 L          DC     P'12345'     L=  | 12 | 34 | 5C |
003057                       34 M          DS     ZL5
00305C  F9F9F9F9F9C9         35 N          DC     Z'999999'    N=  | F9 | F9 | F9 | F9 | F9 | C9 |
003062                       36 P          DS     CL3
003065  123456789C           37 Q          DC     P'123456789' Q=  | 12 | 34 | 56 | 78 | 9C |
```

Figure 8-4 Unrelated UNPK operations.

UNPACK1 unpacks a 3-byte field into a 5-byte field, the correct size.

UNPACK2's operand 1 is one byte longer than necessary. The unpack fills a character zero (X'F0') to the left.

UNPACK3's operand 1 is 2 bytes too short to receive all the unpacked data. Therefore, the two leftmost digits of the operand 2 field are not unpacked.

UNPACK4 depicts the use of relative addressing and explicit length, fancy but risky coding.

UNPACK5 attempts to unpack a 3-byte field called L into itself. Because L contains five digits, which cannot fully unpack into a 3-byte field, the two leftmost digits (1 and 2) are erased. This works correctly only if the field is 1 or 2 bytes long. However, UNPACK5 and UNPACK6 process fields that exceed this limit.

UNPACK6 unpacks a 5-byte field called Q also into itself, propagating an error. The error can be best understood if you consider the rule of UNPK: One byte at a time is extracted and unpacked from right to left:

- The zone and numeric portions of Q+4, C9 are reversed.
- Q+3 containing 78 is extracted. F8 is stored in Q+3, and F7 is stored in Q+2. Q now contains | 12 | 34 | F7 | F8 | 9C | .
- Q+2 now contains F7 and is extracted. F7 is stored in Q+1, and FF is stored in Q, as follows: | FF | F7 | F7 | F8 | C9 | . The operation, having filled all 5 bytes, is now complete but incorrect.
- The computer continues processing with no indication that an error has occurred.

PACKED DECIMAL ARITHMETIC: ZAP, AP, AND SP

The computer performs decimal arithmetic in main storage using valid packed data and the appropriate packed decimal instructions. The ZAP (Zero and Add Packed) instruction transfers packed data, just as you use MVC to transfer character data. However, if the receiving field is longer than the sending field, ZAP fills the leftmost bytes with zeros. You use AP (Add Packed) and SP (Subtract Packed) for addition and subtraction of packed fields.

Name	Operation	Operand
[label]	ZAP	S1,S2 *or* D1(L1,B1),D2(L2,B2)
[label]	AP	S1,S2 *or* D1(L1,B1),D2(L2,B2)
[label]	SP	S1,S2 *or* D1(L1,B1),D2(L2,B2)

The rules for ZAP, AP, and SP are as follows:

- The maximum length of each field is 16 bytes. Both operands may contain an explicit length (L1 and L2), up to 16.

- The operand 2 sending field must be a packed field with a valid sign (hex 'A' to hex 'F'). If the field is not valid, a program interrupt "data exception" occurs.

- For AP and SP, the operand 1 receiving field must be a packed field with a valid sign. In the case of ZAP, the operand 1 (receiving) field may be in any format.

- If the operand 1 field is shorter than the operand 2 field, a program interrupt overflow may occur. Normally, an arithmetic field should be defined so that it can contain the largest answer that could ever occur, plus a byte for insurance.

- The rules of algebra determine the resulting sign. Positive and zero sums yield a plus (hex 'C') sign, and negative sums yield a minus (hex 'D') sign. An arithmetic operation changes an X'F' sign to X'C'. If an input field contains the value '12345', its hex representation in main storage is X'F1F2F3F4F5'. If you pack the field, it becomes X'12345F', still with the F sign. If you perform any arithmetic on this packed field, its sign changes to X'C' if positive, X'D' if negative. This feature is algebraically correct but confusing to a learner.

- ZAP, AP, and SP set the condition code so that you may test the results if necessary. The following conditional branches may then test for these conditions:

CONDITION CODE		CONDITIONAL BRANCHES	
0 = Equal/zero	BZ (branch zero)		BNZ (branch not zero)
1 = Low/minus	BM (branch minus)		BNM (branch not minus)
2 = High/plus	BP (branch plus)		BNP (branch not plus)
3 = Overflow	BO (branch overflow)		BNO (branch not overflow)

The following example performs an addition and tests the condition code. Assume that the contents of ACCUM and TOTAL are unknown. If the result of adding the contents of ACCUM to TOTAL is negative, the program branches to P10NEG. If the result is positive or zero, the program continues with the next instruction.

```
              AP      TOTAL,ACCUM      Add and set condition code
              BM      P10NEG           Branch if negative
              . . .
ACCUM   DC    PL2'0'
TOTAL   DC    PL3'0'
```

```
 LOC   OBJECT CODE      STMT    SOURCE STATEMENT
                          4  *           ------------------------
                          5  ***         ZAP    ZERO ADD PACKED
                          6  *           ------------------------
003000 F821 404A 4048     7  ZAP1        ZAP    P2,P1           P2= |00|12|3C|
003006 F823 404A 404D     8  ZAP2        ZAP    P2,P3           ERROR - OVERFLOW IN P2
00300C F822 404A 404D     9  ZAP3        ZAP    P2,P3(3)        ERROR - NO SIGN IN OP-2
003012 F822 404A 404E    10  ZAP4        ZAP    P2,P3+1(3)      P2= |90|12|3C|
003018 F811 4048 4048    11  ZAP5        ZAP    P1,P1           COND'N CODE HIGH/PLUS
00301E F810 4048 40C6    12  ZAP6        ZAP    P1,=P'0'        P1= |00|0C|

                         14  *           --------------------
                         15  ***         AP     ADD PACKED
                         16  *           --------------------
003024 FA21 404A 4048    17  ADD1        AP     P2,P1           P2= |04|69|0C|
00302A FA12 4048 404A    18  ADD2        AP     P1,P2           ERROR - OVERFLOW IN P1
003030 FA21 404D 4048    19  ADD3        AP     P3(3),P1        ERROR - NO SIGN IN OP-1
003036 FA11 4048 40C0    20  ADD4        AP     P1,=P'999'      P1= |12|2C| OVERFLOW

                         22  *           --------------------------
                         23  ***         SP     SUBTRACT PACKED
                         24  *           --------------------------
00303C FB21 404A 4048    25  SUBTR1      SP     P2,P1           P2= |04|44|4C|
003042 FB11 4048 4048    26  SUBTR2      SP     P1,P1           P1= |00|0C|
                         27  *           ...
003048 123C              28  P1          DC     P'123'          P1= |12|3C|
00304A 04567C            29  P2          DC     P'4567'         P2= |04|56|7C|
00304D 0890123C          30  P3          DC     P'890123'       P3= |08|90|12|3C|
```

Figure 8-5   Unrelated ZAP, AP, and SP operations.

Figure 8-5 provides various unrelated ZAP, AP, and SP examples:

ZAP1, ADD1, and **SUBTR1** illustrate conventional ZAP, AP, and SP operations.

ZAP2 and **ADD2** depict a coding error in which operand 1 is shorter than operand 2.   The result at execute time is an overflow condition.

ZAP3 and **ADD3** are also coding errors not recognized by the assembler.   The explicit length P3(3) causes processing of only the first 3 bytes.   Since there is no sign in the explicitly defined field, the instruction will "bomb" with a data exception.

ZAP4 shows how you may correctly use explicit length and relative addressing.

ZAP5 tests the contents of a packed field.   If you ZAP a field into itself, the value is unchanged, but the condition code is set.   Since P1 contains a positive value, the operation sets the condition code to high/plus.

ZAP6 and **SUBTR2** both clear a field to packed zeros.   Subtracting a field from itself, as in SUBTR2, is more efficient but requires valid packed data in operand 1.   ZAP requires a constant defined for operand 2, in this case a literal =P'0'.

ADD4 depicts a common coding error caused by an operand 1 field that is too short:

Contents of P1:		12	3C	
Add 999:	+	99	9C	
Total (overflow):		12	2C	

Because P1 is only 2 bytes and the total requires 3, an overflow interrupt occurs, and the answer is 122 instead of 1,122.

FORMATTING THE PRINT AREA

No problem was encountered in earlier chapters printing character data. Packed fields, however, contain nonprintable characters and must be unpacked for printing. However, a small problem arises when printing unpacked data. Consider reading an input field QTYIN containing the value 12345 (F1F2F3F4F5). Pack QTYIN into QTYPK, add '50', and unpack QTYPK into QTYOUT for printing:

```
        PACK    QTYPK,QTYIN      QTYPK:  | 12 | 34 | 5F |
        AP      QTYPK,=P'50'     QTYPK:  | 12 | 39 | 5C |
        UNPK    QTYOUT,QTYPK     QTYOUT: | F1 | F2 | F3 | F9 | C5 |
        ...
QTYIN   DS      ZL5
QTYPK   DS      PL3
QTYOUT  DS      ZL5
```

The AP operation has changed the plus sign in QTYPK from X'F' to X'C'. Now, because the printer graphic for X'C5' is the letter E, QTYOUT displays or prints as 1239E. In order to print the correct value 12395, you have to convert X'C5' to X'F5'. To accomplish this, move an F zone into the units zone position of QTYOUT, which now prints correctly as 12345:

```
  MVZ   QTYOUT+4(1),=X'F0'     | F1 | F2 | F3 | F9 | C5 |     X'F0'
```

Another problem arises if a field is negative. Assume that QTYOUT contains | F1 | F2 | F3 | F9 | D5 | . Inserting an F zone to replace the D zone changes the field's value from negative to positive. If you want the field to print, if positive as 12395, and if negative as 12395−, you may use the routine shown in Fig. 8-6.

Alas, this is a cumbersome procedure. To the rescue comes an instruction that facilitates printing the unit position digit and the minus sign. ED, described later in this chapter, does just that, and much more.

```
34                   PACK  QTYPK,QTYIN            PACK QTYIN
35                   AP    QTYPK,=P'50'           ADD 50 TO QTYPK
36                   BNM   D10                    NOT MINUS?  BYPASS
37 *                                              MINUS:
38                   MVI   QTYOUT+5,C'-'          * SET MINUS SIGN
39 D10               UNPK  QTYOUT,QTYPK           UNPACK QTYPK
40                   MVZ   QTYOUT+4(1),=X'F0'     CORRECT SIGN POS'N
41 *                    .
42 *                    .
43 *                    .
44 QTYIN             DS    ZL5                    ZONED INPUT FIELD
45 QTYPK             DS    PL3                    PACKED FIELD
46 QTYOUT            DS    ZL5                    ZONED OUTPUT FIELD
```

Figure 8-6   Formatting signs in unpacked amounts.

COMPARISON OF PACKED DECIMAL FIELDS: CP

A program often has to test whether a packed field is plus, minus, or zero and to compare the result of one calculation to another.   You use CP (Compare Packed) to compare packed decimal fields.

Name	Operation	Operand
[label]	CP	S1,S2 *or* D1(L1,B1),D2(L2,B2)

The rules for CP are as follows:

- Maximum field lengths are 16 bytes.   Either operand may contain an explicit length (L1 and L2).
- Both operands must contain valid packed data.   Invalid data results in a program interrupt (data exception).
- If the fields are not the same length, CP extends the shorter field (in the CPU, not in storage) with leftmost zeros The value is not changed algebraically, and the test is still valid.   There can be no overflow.
- CP compares the contents of operand 1 algebraically to that of operand 2. That is, the positive value P'+001' is algebraically greater than P'−001'. (However, +0 is equal to −0.)   CP sets the condition code, which you may then test with conditional branches.

COMPARISON	CONDITION CODE	BRANCH
Operand 1 = operand 2	0 (equal/zero)	BE, BZ
Operand 1 < operand 2	1 (low/minus)	BL, BM
Operand 1 > operand 2	2 (high/plus)	BH, BP

Example: Contrast CP and CLC. The following illustrates why you should use the correct operation for the data format, CLC for character data and CP for packed:

```
          PACK    AMTPACK,AMTCHAR
          CP      AMTPACK,=P'123'       Compare packed
          CLC     AMTPACK,=P'123'       Compare character
          . . .
AMTCHAR   DC      C'123'              | F1 | F2 | F3 |
AMTPACK   DS      PL2                 | 12 | 3F |
```

AMTCHAR packed into AMTPACK gives the hex value | 12 | 3F | . Both CP and CLC compare AMTPACK to a literal, =P'123', which generates a constant | 12 | 3C | . For CP, | 12 | 3F | and | 12 | 3C | are algebraically equal (+123), and the condition code is set to equal. For CLC, the two fields do not contain identical bits, and because F is greater than C, the condition code is set to high.

Figure 8-7 illustrates various CP operations:

COMP1 compares A to B. Because A's algebraic value is less, the condition code is set to low/minus.

COMP2 shows that CP correctly compares packed fields of unequal length.

COMP3 compares a positive amount in A against a negative value in D. A's value is algebraically higher.

COMP4 uses relative addressing and explicit length to compare the 2 bytes of B against the second and third bytes of C.

COMP5 compares A to a literal containing packed zero.

```
LOC     OBJECT CODE    STMT    SOURCE STATEMENT
                        53  *                          DATA COMPARED:      RESULT:
                        54  *                          --------------      ------
003080  F911 40B0 40B2  55  COMP1   CP   A,B           '012+'  <  '345+'    LOW
003086  F921 40B4 40B0  56  COMP2   CP   C,A           '05000+'>  '012+'    HIGH
00308C  F911 40B0 40B7  57  COMP3   CP   A,D           '012+'  >  '025-'    HIGH
003092  F911 40B2 40B5  58  COMP4   CP   B,C+1(2)      '345+'  >  '000+'    HIGH

003098  F910 40B0 40C6  60  COMP5   CP   A,=P'0'       '012+'  >  '0+'      HIGH
00309E  F911 40B0 40B9  61  COMP6   CP   A,E           '012+'  =  '012+'    EQUAL
0030A4  F911 40B4 40B2  62  COMP7   CP   C(2),B        ERROR - NO SIGN IN OP-1
0030AA  F911 40B0 40C4  63  COMP8   CP   A,=C'12'      ERROR - NO SIGN IN OP-2
                        64  *            . . .
0030B0  012C            65  A       DC   P'12'         | 01 | 2C |
0030B2  345C            66  B       DC   P'345'        | 34 | 5C |
0030B4  05000C          67  C       DC   P'5000'       | 05 | 00 | 0C |
0030B7  025D            68  D       DC   P'-25'        | 02 | 5D |
0030B9  012A            69  E       DC   X'012A'       | 01 | 2A |
```

Figure 8-7 Sample CP operations.

COMP6 compares A against a hex constant, E, containing valid packed data. The sign in E is X'A', which, though a valid plus sign, is rarely used.

COMP7 depicts a programming error made with packed data: Operand 1 as used does not contain valid packed data. The operand should be coded with no explicit length, because C(2) means the first 2 bytes of C, containing no sign.

COMP8's character literal does not define valid packed data. The literal should be defined as packed, =P'12'. Although these last two instructions assemble with no error message, at execute time they would cause a program interrupt.

SUM OF DIGITS CALCULATION

The routine in Fig. 8-8 adds the sum of the digits from 1 to 10: $1 + 2 + 3 + \cdots + 10$. The example defines two fields: CTRPK is an accumulator that the routine increments by 1 for each iteration $(1, 2, 3, \ldots, 10)$, and SUMPK is the accumulator for the sum of the digits and increments by the value in CTRPK for each iteration: $1, 3, 6, 10, \ldots, 55$. You may find it worthwhile tracing the arithmetic and logic.

```
LOOP      AP      CTRPK,=P'1'        1, 2, 3, 4, . . . , 10
          AP      SUMPK,CTRPK        1, 3, 6, 10, . . . , 55
          CP      CTRPK,=P'10'       Looped 10 times?
          BNE     LOOP                  No - continue
          . . .                         Yes - done
CTRPK     DC      PL2'0'             Counter
SUMPK     DC      PL2'0'             Sum digits
```

Figure 8-8 Sum of the digits.

EDITING: ED

The purpose of the ED instruction is to make packed data suitable for printing and displaying. ED converts packed data into character format and provides for punctuation, sign, and zero suppression.

Name	Operation	Operand
[label]	ED	S1,S2 or D1(L,B1),D2(B2)

Editing consists of two operations:

1. Define an edit word, or pattern, that indicates where you want commas,

decimal point, and sign to print or display.   Use MVC to move the edit word
to the required output positions.

2. Then use ED to modify the packed field according to the edit word definition.
   ED unpacks the amount field and inserts the commas, decimal point, and
   sign and suppresses leftmost zeros if required.

The following simple example edits a 2-byte (three-digit) packed field named
COUNT into an output field named COUNPR.   There is no provision for commas
or decimal point.

```
           MVC    COUNPR,=X'40202020'      Move edit word to output
           ED     COUNPR,COUNT             Edit packed field
           . . .
COUNT      DC     PL2'001'                 3-digit packed field
COUNPR     DS     CL4                      Output field
```

The MVC moves the edit word into COUNPR.   The ED operation uses the
leftmost hex '40' as a fill character and processes through the two operands from
left to right.   The operation replaces the two leading zeros from COUNT with
X'40' in COUNPR and converts the packed 1 to character 1.   The result, X'404040F1',
prints as bbb1.

Significant Digits and Zero Suppression

A significant digit is a nonzero digit.   In the value 00025, the 2 is the first significant
digit.   The fill character X'40' suppresses the leftmost zeros by replacing them with
blanks.   For example, zero-suppressing 00025 converts it to bbb25.   Editing may
also suppress commas, so that 0012345 edits as bbb123.45 instead of bb,123.45.
You may also force significance so that a leftmost zero prints as bb0.25 instead of
bbb.25.

Edit Word

An edit word consists of pairs of hex digits that represent one output position.
The commonly used edit characters are as follows:

HEX	NAME	PURPOSE
40	Fill character	X'40' is is the normal fill character used for zero suppression, to replace leftmost unwanted zeros with blanks. You may use any other character, such as asterisk (X'5C').

HEX	NAME	PURPOSE
20	Digit selector	Each X'20' in an edit word represents a packed digit to be printed. Since a packed field always contains an odd number of digits, the edit word contains an odd number of X'20's (including X'21's, if any). ED unpacks one packed digit in each X'20' position. However, if the digit is a leading (leftmost) zero, ED replaces the X'20' with the X'40' fill character.
21	Significance starter	X'21' acts like a digit selector, but in addition, it forces significance, so that all characters to the right, including leading zeros, are forced to print. An edit word requires only one X'21'.
6B	Comma (,)	Code X'6B' in an edit word wherever a comma is to appear.
4B	Decimal point (.)	Code X'4B' in an edit word wherever a decimal point is to appear.
60	Minus sign (−)	For possible negative values, code X'60' to print a minus sign to the right of an edited amount.
C3D9	Credit (CR)	Code X'C3D9' to print CR instead of minus.
22	Field separator	You can use X'22' to edit more than one field in one operation. It is seldom used because it tends to make a program unreadable.

Basic Rules of Editing

Following are the basic steps for editing:

- You move the required edit word into the output area.   The maximum length is 256 bytes.
- Operand 1 of the ED instruction references the leftmost byte of the edit word in the output area.   Operand 2 references the packed field to be edited. Only operand 1 may have an explicit length.   Editing proceeds from left to right through both fields.
- The operation assumes that the leftmost hex byte is the fill character, normally but not necessarily X'40'.

- For each X'20' (or X'21'), ED selects a packed digit. A nonzero digit is unpacked and replaces the X'20'. If significance has not been encountered, a zero digit is replaced by the fill character. Either a significant digit or the significance starter forces significance.
- If the hex byte is X'6B' (comma) or X'4B' (decimal) and significance has been encountered, the operation preserves them. If significance has not been encountered, ED replaces them with the fill character.
- If the packed field is negative, the operation preserves any CR or minus (X'60'). If positive, ED replaces them with the fill character. The condition code is set for minus, zero, or plus.
- The length of operand 1 terminates the operation.

Sample Edit Operation

An edit word for a 3-byte (five-digit) packed field is to provide for decimal point, minus sign, and suppression of the leftmost three digits:

```
PACKAMT  DC      PL3'7'                  | 00 | 00 | 7C |
EDWORD   DC      X'402020214B202060'
   P     DC      CL133' '                  ' '
```

EDWORD provides the necessary sign and punctuation control, with a X'20' or X'21' for each packed digit. The instructions to edit are as follows:

```
MVC     P+90(8),EDWORD         | 40 | 20 | 20 | 21 | 4B | 20 | 20 | 60 |
ED      P+90(8),PACKAMT        | 40 | 40 | 40 | 40 | 4B | F0 | F9 | 40 |
                                 |    |    |    |    |    |    |    |
                            P+90  |+92    |+94    |+96    |
                                P+91   +93     +95     +97
```

ED replaces the edit word with the edited value. The explicit length (8) in the ED operand refers to the length of the edit word, not to the length of PACKAMT. Editing starts at P+90 and proceeds from left to right:

P+90   X'40', assumed to be the fill character, is not changed.

P+91   Because the position contains X'20', ED examines the first digit of PACKAMT. Since it is zero, ED replaces the X'20' with X'40':

| 40 | 40 | 20 | 21 | 4B | 20 | 20 | 60 |

P+92   Because the position contains X'20', ED examines the second digit of PACKAMT. Since it is zero, ED replaces the X'20' with X'40':

| 40 | 40 | 40 | 21 | 4B | 20 | 20 | 60 |

P + 93   Since X'21' is the significance starter, all characters to the right are to be forced.   ED also examines the third digit of PACKAMT, a zero, and replaces the X'21' with X'40':

| 40 | 40 | 40 | 40 | 4B | 20 | 20 | 60 |

P + 94   Since X'21' has signaled to force printing, ED does not replace the X'4B' (decimal point) (without the X'21', the fill character would have replaced the X'4B'):

| 40 | 40 | 40 | 40 | 4B | 20 | 20 | 60 |

P + 95   The X'20' causes ED to examine the fourth digit of PACKAMT, a zero.   Since significance has been forced, ED unpacks the zero and replaces X'20' with X'F0':

| 40 | 40 | 40 | 40 | 4B | F0 | 20 | 60 |

P + 96   The X'20' causes ED to unpack the fifth digit of PACKAMT, 7, and to replace X'20' with X'F7':

| 40 | 40 | 40 | 40 | 4B | F0 | F7 | 60 |

P + 97   The X'60' in the edit word tells ED to check the next digit of PACKAMT for a minus (X'D').   Because PACKAMT is positive (X'C'), ED replaces the X'60' with the fill character:

| 40 | 40 | 40 | 40 | 4B | F0 | F7 | 40 |

At this point, the length of operand 1 is exhausted, and the operation terminates.   The edited amount prints as bbbb.70.   If EDWORD had contained X'402021204B202060', the result would be bbb0.70.

Figure 8-9 illustrates three edit operations:

- EDWD1 edits a 4-byte (seven-digit) packed field with zero suppression, comma, decimal point, and minus sign.   X'20' or X'21' in the edit word matches each digit in the packed field.
- EDWD2 illustrates use of the CR symbol, commonly used in financial statements.
- EDWD3 is explained in the next section.

Dollar Sign and Asterisk

The dollar sign (X'5B') and the asterisk (X'5C') can cause a few problems when used in edit words.   The normal purpose of the dollar sign ($) is printing checks

```
 8  *                    COMMA, DECIMAL, MINUS SIGN:
 9  *                    ---------------------------
11             MVC       P+30(11),EDWD1          |40|20|20|6B|20|20|21|4B|20|20|60|
12             ED        P+30(11),AMOUNT         |40|40|F2|6B|F3|F4|F5|4B|F0|F0|60|
13  *                    ...
14  P          DC        CL133' '
15  AMOUNT     DC        P'-2345.00'             |02|34|50|0D|
16  EDWD1      DC        X'4020206B2020214B202060'

18  *                    CREDIT (CR) SIGN:
19  *                    -----------------
20             MVC       P+50(12),EDWD2          |40|20|20|6B|20|21|20|4B|20|20|C3|D9|
21             ED        P+50(12),TOTAL          |40|40|40|40|40|40|F0|4B|F0|F5|C3|D9|
22  *                    ...
23  TOTAL      DC        P'-0000.05'             |00|00|00|5D|
24  EDWD2      DC        X'4020206B2021204B2020C3D9'

26  *                    ASTERISK AND DOLLAR SIGN:
27  *                    -------------------------
28             MVC       P+70(10),EDWD3          |5B|40|20|20|21|4B|20|20|60|5C|
29             ED        P+71(08),ACCUM          |5B|40|40|F1|F2|4B|F3|F4|40|5C|
30  *                    ...
31  ACCUM      DC        P'12.34'                |01|23|4C|
32  EDWD3      DC        X'5B402020214B2020605C'
```

Figure 8-9 Sample ED operations.

for employees and suppliers and bills for customers, with the $ to the left of the amount. If you code X'5B' on the left of an edit word, ED improperly uses it as the fill character. Also, a standard in many installations is to print asterisks (*) to the right of an amount field to indicate the total level:

*	Minor total
**	Intermediate total
***	Major total

If you code one or more X'5C's to the right of an edit word, ED leaves the asterisks intact only if the amount is negative. If positive, ED replaces the asterisks with the fill character, thus erasing them.

One solution is to omit X'5B' and X'5C' from the edit word and use separate operations to move them to the output area. Another solution is the technique that EDWD3 uses in Fig. 8-9, in which the $ and * are defined as part of the edit word but do not participate in the ED operation. MVC moves the full edit word, starting at P+70, but the ED operation begins at P+71, leaving the $ intact. Further, although the MVC moved 10 bytes, ED specifies editing only 8. The operation terminates just prior to the asterisk at P+79, leaving it also intact.

Another instruction, EDMK, which provides for floating dollar sign and asterisk, is covered in Chapter 11.

MULTIPLY PACKED: MP

The purpose of MP is to multiply one packed field (the multiplicand) by another (the multiplier). Common examples include multiplying hours by rate of pay for payroll and multiplying quantity by unit cost for inventory.

Name [label]	Operation MP	Operand S1,S2 *or* D1(L1,B1)D2(L2,B2)

The rules for MP are as follows:

- The operand 1 field is the *multiplicand*, containing valid packed data. The operation develops the *product* in this field and replaces the multiplicand:

$$
\begin{array}{ll}
\text{before:} & |\,0000000\text{multiplicand}\,| \\
\text{after:} & |\,\text{———product———}\,|
\end{array}
$$

- The maximum length of operand 1 is 16 bytes, or 31 digits. A standard practice is to define the field large enough to accommodate the largest possible product that the operation can develop, generally the length in bytes of the multiplicand plus the multiplier.
- Operand 2 references the *multiplier*, containing valid packed data. The maximum length is 8 bytes, or 15 digits.
- Either operand may contain an explicit length (L1 and L2).
- MP is governed by the normal rules of algebra: Like signs yield a positive product and unlike signs yield a negative product. MP does not set the condition code.

Product Length

A standard practice is to define the product length equal at least to the length in bytes of the multiplicand plus the multiplier. From another point of view, prior to execution of the MP, for each byte in the multiplier, the product field must contain one byte of zeros to the left of the significant digits in the multiplicand.
Consider the following MP example:

```
            ZAP     PRODUCT,MULTPLD        | 00 | 00 | 12 | 34 | 56 | 0C |
            MP      PRODUCT,MULTPLR        | 01 | 17 | 28 | 32 | 00 | 0C |
                    . . .
MULTPLD     DC      PL4'1234560'
MULTPLR     DC      PL2'950'
PRODUCT     DS      PL6
```

Since MULTPLD is 4 bytes and MULTPLR is 2, PRODUCT is defined as 6 bytes, although it could be longer. A ZAP instruction initializes the multiplicand in the product area. After the MP, PRODUCT contains a 6-byte product. If PRODUCT were shorter than 6 bytes, the MP operation would cause a program interrupt.

Decimal Precision

Neither the assembler nor the computer handles decimal positions. With decimal arithmetic, you must provide for the implied decimal point. The following is a useful rule: The number of decimal positions in the product equals the number of decimals in the multiplicand plus multiplier. For example, if the multiplicand has three decimals and the multiplier has two, the product would have five decimal positions:

Multiplicand: XXX.XXX

Multiplier: XX.XX

Product: XXXXX.XXXXX

Multiplication Examples

The first example in Fig. 8-10 multiplies a 2-byte field, QTY, by a 2-byte field, PRICE. The product, AMT, is therefore defined as 4 bytes in length. Since PRICE has two decimals and QTY none, the generated product has two implied decimal positions. No rounding is required for the two-decimal answer.

    The second example in Fig. 8-10 multiplies a 3-byte field, HRS, by a 2-byte field, RATE. The product, WAGE, is therefore defined as 5 bytes in length. Since HRS has one decimal and RATE has two, the generated product has three implied decimal positions. Because only two decimal places are required, the

```
40  *                MULTIPLY, GENERATE 2 DECIMALS, NO ROUND:
41  *                ---------------------------------------------
43         ZAP       AMT,QTY      |00|00|47|5C|
44         MP        AMT,PRICE    |01|66|25|0C|  = 1662.50
45  *                ...
46  QTY    DC        P'475'       |47|5C|
47  PRICE  DC        P'3.50'      |35|0C|
48  AMT    DS        PL4

50  *                MULTIPLY, GENERATE 3 DECIMALS, ROUND:
51  *                -----------------------------------------
52         ZAP       WAGE,HRS     |00|00|01|20|5C|
53         MP        WAGE,RATE    |00|10|30|27|5C|  MULTIPLY
54         SRP       WAGE,63,5    |00|01|03|02|8C|  SHIFT/ROUND
55  *                ...
56  HRS    DC        P'120.5'     |01|20|5C|
57  RATE   DC        P'8.55'      |85|5C|
58  WAGE   DS        PL5
```

Figure 8-10   Sample MP operations.

example rounds the unwanted rightmost decimal digit.   An SRP (Shift and Round Packed) operation shifts the product one digit to the right, leaving two decimal places, as explained in the next section.

SHIFTING AND ROUNDING

Basically, rounding consists of adding 5 to the first unwanted decimal position and dropping all the unwanted positions to the right.   For a negative product, subtract 5.   The following two examples round a three-decimal value and a five-decimal value:

1. Round a three-decimal value:

Value:	123.456
Add 5:	+ .005
Result:	123.461

   For a two-decimal result, shift off the rightmost digit 1: 123.46.

2. Round a five-decimal value:

Value:	123.45678
Add 500:	+ .00500
Result:	123.46178

   For a two-decimal result, shift off the rightmost three digits: 123.46.

Assembler provides two ways to perform rounding and shifting.   The first way involves the SRP (Shift and Round Packed) instruction, and the second way involves the AP and MVO (Move with Offset) instructions.   The next two sections examine these methods.

SHIFT AND ROUND PACKED: SRP

The purpose of the SRP instruction is to shift packed data to the left or right.   For right shifts, SRP can also provide rounding.

Name	Operation	Operand
[label]	SRP	S1,S2 *or* D1(L,B1),D2(B2),I3

Although an SS format instruction, SRP has three operands, coded, for example, as

       SRP   AMTPK,2,0   Shift left 2 digits

- Operand 1 denotes a packed field, AMTPK, to be shifted and optionally rounded.
- Operand 2 is a displacement that indicates the number of digits that are to shift. The maximum size of a packed field, 31 digits, sets the limit to the shift.
- Operand 3 contains a value 0–9 to be used for rounding. You normally code 0 for left shifts to indicate no rounding and 5 for right shifts with conventional rounding.

The operation sets the condition code to indicate zero, minus, and plus.

Left Shift

A *positive* value as a shift factor implies a left shift. Consider the following SRP instruction:

```
              SRP    AMTPK,3,0      12 34 00 0C
              ...
      AMTPK   DC     P'0001234'     00 01 23 4C
```

Operand 2 of the SRP means shift left 3 digits (not bytes). The operation fills zeros in the rightmost vacated positions.

Right Shift

A *negative* value as a shift factor implies a right shift. However, because the shift factor is technically a displacement, you cannot code SRP, for example, as

       SRP   AMTPK,-2,5   (invalid shift factor)

You have to represent the negative number in a form that the assembler will accept and that the computer will interpret as a negative shift—as a negative 6-bit binary number. For example, the representation for +2 in binary is 000010. To express this value in binary as −2, you have to convert it to its *two's complement form* by reversing the bit values and adding 1:

	BINARY	HEX	DECIMAL
Initial value:	000010	02	2
Reverse bits:	111101	3D	61
Add 1:	111110	3E	62

You can use either of the following SRP examples to shift right and round two digits:

```
                   SRP     AMTPK,X'3E',5      | 00 | 12 | 34 | 6C |
or

                   SRP     AMTPK,62,5         | 00 | 12 | 34 | 6C |
                   ...
        AMTPK      DC      P'1234589'         | 12 | 34 | 58 | 9C |
```

The SRP operation adds the rounding factor 5 to the last digit that it shifts off, as follows:

Original value:	| 12 | 34 | 58 | 9C |
Shift first digit:	| 01 | 23 | 45 | 8C |
Add 5:	| 01 | 23 | 46 | 3C |
Shift second digit:	| 00 | 12 | 34 | 6C |

A shift and round is correct regardless of the sign of the packed field. For example, if the original value of AMTPK was negative, the result would be 00 12 34 6D.

Here are some examples of factors for right shifts:

SHIFT FACTOR	BINARY	TWO'S COMPLEMENT	HEX	DECIMAL
1	000001	111111	3F	63
2	000010	111110	3E	62
3	000011	111101	3D	61
...				
31	011111	100001	21	33

You don't have to understand how a right shift works! Simply insert the correct decimal or hex value into operand 2. For example, a right shift of four digits would be

```
                   SRP     AMTPK,60,5
```

Chapter 9 explains two's complement representation of binary numbers, and Chapter 11 covers other technicalities of the SRP instruction.

SAMPLE PROGRAM: LOAN REPAYMENT SCHEDULE

The program in Fig. 8-11 illustrates most of the instructions covered to this point: PACK, ZAP, AP, SP, CP, ED, MP, and SRP. The program contains definitions

```
 3                 PRINT ON,NODATA,NOGEN
 5  *                       M A I N   P R O C E S S I N G
 6  *                       ---------------------------
 7  PROG8A    START
 8            BALR  3,0                      INITIALIZE
 9            USING *,3                      ADDRESSABILITY
10            OPEN  PRINTER                  OPEN FILE
18            PUTPR PRINTER,PRHEAD,SK1       SKIP TO NEW PAGE
25            PUTPR PRINTER,PRHEAD,WSP2      PRINT HEADING
32            BAL   6,B10CALC               CALC SCHEDULE
33            CLOSE PRINTER
41            EOJ   ,                        TERMINATE

45  *                       L O A N   S C H E D U L E
46  *                       -------------------------
47  B10CALC   PACK  PAYPK,PAYMENT
48            PACK  BALPK,BALANCE
49            PACK  RATEPK,RATE
50  B20       ZAP   CALCPK,BALPK
51            MP    CALCPK,RATEPK            BAL X RATE
52            SRP   CALCPK,60,5              SHIFT & ROUND
53            ZAP   INTPK,CALCPK+4(4)

55            MVC   MONPR,EDMON              EDIT:
56            ED    MONPR,MONPK                 MONTH
57            MVC   OLDBPR,EDAMT
58            ED    OLDBPR,BALPK                OLD BALANCE

60            SP    BALPK,PAYPK              CALCULATE
61            AP    BALPK,INTPK              *   NEW BALANCE
62            BNM   B30                      NEG BALANCE?
63            AP    PAYPK,BALPK              YES - ADD TO PAY'T
64            SP    BALPK,BALPK                 CLEAR BALANCE

66  B30       MVC   PAYPR,EDAMT              EDIT:
67            ED    PAYPR,PAYPK                 PAYMENT
68            MVC   INTPR,EDAMT
69            ED    INTPR,INTPK                 INTEREST
70            MVC   NEWBPR,EDAMT
71            ED    NEWBPR,BALPK                NEW BALANCE
73            PUTPR PRINTER,PRLINE,WSP1      PRINT

80            AP    MONPK,=P'1'              ADD TO MONTH
81            CP    BALPK,=P'0'              SCHEDULE ENDED?
82            BE    B90                      YES - EXIT
83            CP    INTPK,PAYPK              INTEREST : PAY'T
84            BL    B20                      *  LOWER - CONTINUE
85  B90       BR    6                        RETURN

87  *                       D E C L A R A T I V E S
88  *                       -----------------------

 90  PRINTER  DEFPR                          DEFINE PRINTER FILE
120  PRHEAD   DS    0CL133                   HEADING LINE:
121           DC    CL25' '                  *
122           DC    CL42'MONTH     OLD BAL.       INTEREST'
123           DC    CL66'PAYMENT        NEW BAL.'
```

Figure 8-11 Program: loan repayment schedule.

```
125 PRLINE    DS    0CL133                PRINT AREA:
126           DC    CL26' '               *
127 MONPR     DS    ZL04                  *    MONTH
128           DC    CL04' '               *
129 OLDBPR    DS    ZL11                  *    OLD BALANCE
130           DC    CL04' '               *
131 INTPR     DS    ZL11                  *    PAYMENT
132           DC    CL04' '               *
133 PAYPR     DS    ZL11                  *    INTEREST
134           DC    CL04' '               *
135 NEWBPR    DS    ZL11                  *    NEW BALANCE
136           DC    CL43' '               *

138 BALANCE   DC    Z'5000.00'            ORIGINAL BAL.
139 PAYMENT   DC    Z'500.00'             REGULAR PAY'T
140 RATE      DC    Z'.0125'              INTEREST RATE

142 MONPK     DC    PL2'1'                PACKED FIELDS:
143 BALPK     DS    PL4                   *
144 PAYPK     DS    PL4                   *
145 RATEPK    DS    PL4                   *
146 INTPK     DS    PL4                   *
147 CALCPK    DS    PL8                   *

149 EDMON     DC    X'40202020'           EDIT WORDS:
150 EDAMT     DC    X'4020206B2020214B202060'
151           LTORG ,
152                 =C'$$BOPEN '
153                 =C'$$BCLOSE'
154                 =A(PRINTER)
155                 =A(PRHEAD)
156                 =A(PRLINE)
157                 =P'1'
158                 =P'0'
159           END   PROG8A
```

Output:-

MONTH	OLD BAL.	INTEREST	PAYMENT	NEW BAL.
1	5,000.00	62.50	500.00	4,562.50
2	4,562.50	57.03	500.00	4,119.53
3	4,119.53	51.49	500.00	3,671.02
4	3,671.02	45.89	500.00	3,216.91
5	3,216.91	40.21	500.00	2,757.12
6	2,757.12	34.46	500.00	2,291.58
7	2,291.58	28.64	500.00	1,820.22
8	1,820.22	22.75	500.00	1,342.97
9	1,342.97	16.79	500.00	859.76
10	859.76	10.75	500.00	370.51
11	370.51	4.63	375.14	.00

Figure 8-11   (*continued*)

of loan balance outstanding, monthly payment, and monthly rate of interest and generates a loan repayment schedule.   For brevity, the program uses defined data instead of reading input data.   A more complete program would accept these values from a terminal and would produce any number of loan schedules.

The calculation for each month's interest is the following:

$$\text{Interest} = \text{old balance} \times \text{rate of interest}$$

The calculation for each month's new balance is

New balance = old balance + month's interest − monthly payment

The schedule continues for each month until the balance of the loan is fully paid. Calculations and logic are straightforward, with two exceptions:

1. The interest rate may be so high or the monthly payment so low that the first calculation of interest exceeds the monthly payment. In such a case, the loan schedule would never end. On recognizing this situation, the program terminates the schedule after one month.

2. It is unlikely that the scheduled payment for the last month will be exact. For each calculation of a new balance, the program checks if it is overpaid. For example, the last payment in the output contains the following results:

Old balance:	370.51
Plus interest:	+ 4.63
	375.14
Less payment:	− 500.00
New balance:	− 124.86

The last payment should be smaller by the amount that the new balance would be overpaid. The solution is to add the new balance to the scheduled payment and clear the new balance to zero—see the last line of the program's output.

MOVE WITH OFFSET: MVO

For completeness, this section covers the MVO (Move With Offset) instruction, which was used for shifting and rounding packed digits prior to the introduction of SRP on the 370. The rounding technique involves adding rightmost unwanted decimal digits to themselves, so that any value less than 5 does not overflow and any value greater than 5 does overflow, as the following two examples show.

1. The product has three decimal places and two are required:

Product:	123.456	
Add 6:	+ .006	
Rounded result:	123.462	(shift to 123.46)

2. The product has five decimal places and two are required:

Product:	123.45678−	
Add 678−:	+ .00678−	
Rounded result:	123.46356−	(shift to 123.46−)

Because of the presence of the sign in a packed field, you may adjust only an odd number of unwanted decimal positions. For example, the value 123.4567 (12 | 34 | 56 | 7C) is to be rounded and shifted to two decimal places. You cannot add the 67C—only 7C or 567C. You can use MVO to shift an odd number of digits to the right. In this case, MVO can shift the preceding value one digit to the right—01 | 23 | 45 | 6C—and you may now add the 6C.

Name	Operation	Operand
[label]	MVO	S1,S2 *or* D1(L1B1),D2(L2,B2)

The rules for MVO are as follows:

- The maximum length of each operand is 16 bytes. Either operand may specify an explicit length (L1 and L2).
- MVO moves the operand 2 data to the operand 1 field and shifts to the right an odd number of half-bytes. (Two MVOs are required to shift an even number of bytes.) MVO may be used to shift half-bytes in any format.
- The operation fills leftmost shifted half-bytes with X'0'.
- The length of operand 2 determines how many bytes MVO moves into the operand 1 field.

Figure 8-12 provides examples of the MVO instruction:

- MVO1 moves the first 4 bytes of X into Y. The packed digits from X are right-shifted, one half-byte, to the rightmost half-byte of Y.

```
 3 ***              MOVE WITH OFFSET:
 4 *                ----------------
 5 MVO1    MVO      Y,X(4)          |01|23|45|67|8C| SHIFT 1 DIGIT
 6 MVO2    MVO      Y,X(3)          |00|01|23|45|6C| SHIFT 3 DIGITS
 7 MVO3    MVO      Y,X(2)          |00|00|01|23|4C| SHIFT 5 DIGITS
 8 *       ...
 9 X       DC       P'123456789'    |12|34|56|78|9C|
10 Y       DC       PL5'0'          |00|00|00|00|0C|

12 *                MULTIPLY, GENERATE 4 DECIMALS, ROUND TO 2:
13 *                -------------------------------------------
14         ZAP      PAY,HOUR        |00|00|00|20|5C|
15         MP       PAY,RATEPY      |00|16|91|25|0C| MULT    169.1250
16         MVO      PAY,PAY(4)      |00|01|69|12|5C| SHIFT   169.125
17         AP       PAY,PAY+4(1)    |00|01|69|13|0C| ROUND   169.130
18         MVO      PAY,PAY(4)      |00|00|16|91|3C| SHIFT   169.13
19 *       ...
20 HOUR    DC       P'20.5'         |20|5C|
21 RATEPY  DC       P'08.250'       |08|25|0C|
22 PAY     DS       PL5
```

Figure 8-12 Sample MVO operations.

- MVO2 moves the first 3 bytes of X into Y and right-shifts 3 half-bytes, to the rightmost half-byte of Y.
- MVO3 moves the first 2 bytes of X into Y and right-shifts 5 half-bytes, to the rightmost half-byte of Y.

Figure 8-12 also illustrates a multiply operation that generates four decimal positions. Because only two positions are required, two MVOs are used to shift the unwanted two decimal places. The rounding operation, AP, immediately follows the first MVO because rounding must begin with the first unwanted decimal position, in this case, 5.

DIVIDE PACKED: DP

The DP (Divide Packed) instruction divides one packed field (the dividend) by another (the divisor). Common examples include dividing inventory value by quantity to determine the unit cost and computing ratios and percentages.

Name	Operation	Operand
[label]	DP	S1,S2 *or* D1(L1B1),D2(L2,B2)

The rules for DP are as follows:

- The maximum length of operand 1 is 16 bytes and of operand 2, 8 bytes. Either operand may specify an explicit length (L1 and L2).
- Operand 1 is the *dividend*, which must contain valid packed data. The operation generates the *quotient* and *remainder* in this field and erases the dividend. Both quotient and remainder contain a sign. Operand 1 should be defined large enough to accommodate the largest possible quotient plus remainder:

  Before division: [——dividend——]
  After division: [quotient | remainder]

- Operand 2 is the *divisor*, which must contain valid packed data.
- The length of the generated remainder is the length of the divisor.
- DP is governed by the normal rules of algebra: Like signs yield a positive product and unlike signs yield a negative product. DP does not set the condition code.
- A zero divisor causes a program interrupt.

Here is a typical DP example:

```
              ZAP        RESULT,DIVDND
              DP         RESULT,DIVSOR
              ...
DIVDND        DS         PL4                    Dividend
DIVSOR        DS         PL1                    Divisor
RESULT        DS         PL5                    Quotient/remainder
```

Quotient Length

Since you do not normally know the contents of numeric fields, provide for the worst possible case, in which the divisor contains the value 1. (Zero divisors are not permitted.) A divisor of 1 means that the quotient will equal (and cannot exceed) the value of the dividend. The following illustrates this:

$$\frac{\text{Dividend}}{\text{Divisor}} \quad \frac{1234567}{1} = 1234567 \text{ (quotient = dividend)}$$

A convention is to provide the length of the quotient equal at least to that of the dividend. Also, the length of the remainder always equals that of the divisor. The following rule always provides for adequate field lengths: Define the length of the operand 1 field at least equal to that of the dividend plus divisor. If the quotient is longer than necessary, DP inserts leftmost zeros. If the quotient field is too short to contain all the generated digits, an overflow interrupt occurs.

Let's examine the preceding DP example in more detail.

```
              ZAP        RESULT,DIVDND          | 00 | 12 | 34 | 56 | 7C |
              DP         RESULT,DIVSOR          | 04 | 11 | 52 | 2C | 1C |
              ...
DIVDND        DC         PL4'1234567'           Dividend
DIVSOR        DC         PL1'3'                 Divisor
RESULT        DS         PL5                    Quotient/remainder
```

Since DIVDND contains 4 bytes and DIVSOR 1, RESULT (to be used for the quotient and remainder) should contain at least 5 bytes, although it may be longer. The ZAP instruction initializes the dividend in RESULT. After the DP, the first 4 bytes of RESULT contain the quotient, with a sign, and the fifth byte contains the remainder, also with a sign. The remainder is 1 byte, the same length as the divisor.

Decimal Precision

You have to provide for an implied decimal point and can use the following rule: The number of decimal places in a quotient equals the number in the dividend minus the number in the divisor.

For example, if the dividend contains four decimal places and the divisor contains one, then the quotient has three, as shown next:

$$\text{dividend} \longrightarrow \frac{\text{xx.xxxx}}{\text{x.x}} = \text{xx.xxx} \leftarrow \text{quotient}$$
$$\text{divisor} \longrightarrow$$

If a dividend does not already contain sufficient decimal places for a planned division, you may use SRP to generate additional positions by shifting the dividend to the left. Thus 12.34 is the same algebraic value as 12.3400, provided that your program accounts for the new implied decimal point.

You can mentally clear the divisor of decimal positions first. For example, you can clear the following divisor of its decimal places with no programming steps, by definition:

$$\frac{12.3400}{1.23} = \frac{1234.00}{123}$$

Rounding, or Half-adjusting

In the earlier example that divided DIVSOR into DIVDND, the remainder was 1/3, not 0.1. You usually do not round or even need the remainder. You often have to round the quotient, just as you round a product. To get additional precision for rounding, you simply shift the dividend to the left. Note that after a left shift, the dividend is longer, so the quotient has to be correspondingly longer.

Consider a 3-byte dividend and a 2-byte divisor. Shifting the dividend two digits (1 byte) makes the dividend effectively 4 bytes, so the quotient/remainder should be 6 bytes. You may generate one more decimal position than you need and round it off. The following three examples each divide 246.79 by 31:

1. A one-decimal quotient is required (with no left shift):

$$\frac{246.79}{31} = 7.96 \text{ (may be rounded to 8.0)}$$

2. A two-decimal quotient is required—shift left one digit:

$$\frac{246.79}{31} = \frac{246.790}{31} = 7.960 \text{ (may be rounded to 7.96)}$$

3. A three-decimal quotient is required—shift left two digits:

$$\frac{246.79}{31} = \frac{246.7900}{31} = 7.9609 \text{ (may be rounded to 7.961)}$$

Our next example calculates speed by dividing distance by time. Distance contains one decimal place and time contains none, and the result is to have one decimal place after rounding.   If you were to divide directly with no left shift of distance, the speed would be in terms of one decimal place, with no provision for rounding.   Consequently, the example shifts distance one digit to the left prior to dividing.   This step converts the dividend from 1128.9 to 1128.90, and the division generates a quotient of 53.75.   The result after the round and shift is 53.8.

```
            ZAP      SPEED,DIST         00 00 00 11  28 9C
            SRP      SPEED,1,0          00 00 01 12  89 0C
                                        —quotient:— |rmdr:
            DP       SPEED,TIME         00 05 37 5C |01 5C
            SRP      SPEED(4),63,5      00 00 53 8C |01 5C
            ...
DIST        DC       P'1128.9'          11 28 9C
TIME        DC       P'021'             02 1C
SPEED       DS       PL6
```

Note that after the left shift, the size of the dividend is 4 bytes.   Since the remainder is 2 bytes, the defined length of the quotient/remainder field is (at least) 6 bytes.

Each increase in precision provides a more accurate result, although required precision varies by application.

The examples in Fig. 8-13 divide distance (DIST) by gallons (GALS) to calculate miles per gallon.   Both DIST and GALS contain one decimal position.

ANS1 illustrates a direct divide of DIST by GALS.   Since both fields contain one decimal place, the quotient, 15, has no decimal places.

ANS2 requires a result that has no decimal places after rounding.   The example shifts the dividend to the left one digit so that 2356.5 becomes 2356.50. This is now the dividend that you consider when defining the quotient/remainder area.   Since the divisor (GALS) is 3 bytes and the dividend is now 4 bytes, the answer area (ANS2) is defined as 7 bytes.

ANS3 requires a result that has one decimal place after rounding.   The dividend is shifted to the left two digits to become 2356.500.   Since the divisor is 3 bytes and the dividend is now 4 bytes, ANS3 is defined as 7 bytes.

ANS4 requires a result that has two decimal places after rounding.   The dividend is shifted to the left three digits to become 2356.5000.   Since the divisor is 3 bytes and the dividend is now 5, ANS4 is defined as 8 bytes.

This example also illustrates redefining the answer area.   ANS4 is defined with a zero duplication factor, 0PL8, and contains two subfields: QUOT defines the 5-byte quotient area, and RMDR defines the 3-byte remainder.   You may reference by name the entire area, ANS4, or the subfield QUOT.

```
 9 DIST      DC     P'2356.5'              |23|56|5C|
10 GALS      DC     P'150.0'               |01|50|0C|

12 *                DIVIDE, NO DECIMAL, NO ROUNDING:
13 *                --------------------------------
14           ZAP    ANS1,DIST              |00|00|00|23|56|5C|
15 *                                        --QUOT-- |--RMDR--
16           DP     ANS1,GALS              |00|01|5C|01|06|5C|
17 *                ...
18 ANS1      DS     PL6

20 *                DIVIDE, ROUND TO NO DECIMALS:
21 *                -----------------------------
22           ZAP    ANS2,DIST              |00|00|00|00|23|56|5C|
23           SRP    ANS2,1,0               |00|00|00|02|35|65|0C|
24 *                                        ---QUOT----|--RMDR--
25           DP     ANS2,GALS              |00|00|15|7C|00|15|0C| DIVIDE 15.7
26           SRP    ANS2(4),63,5           |00|00|01|6C|00|15|0C| SHIFT  16
27 *                ...
28 ANS2      DS     PL7

29 *                DIVIDE, ROUND TO ONE DECIMAL:
30 *                -----------------------------
31           ZAP    ANS3,DIST              |00|00|00|00|23|56|5C|
32           SRP    ANS3,2,0               |00|00|00|23|56|50|0C|
33 *                                        ---QUOT----|--RMDR--
34           DP     ANS3,GALS              |00|01|57|1C|00|00|0C| DIVIDE 15.71
35           SRP    ANS3(4),63,5           |00|00|15|7C|00|00|0C| SHIFT  15.7
36 *                ...
37 ANS3      DS     PL7
38 *                DIVIDE, ROUND TO TWO DECIMALS:
39 *                -----------------------------
40           ZAP    ANS4,DIST              |00|00|00|00|00|23|56|5C|
41           SRP    ANS4,3,0               |00|00|00|02|35|65|00|0C|
42 *                                        -----QUOT-----|--RMDR--
43           DP     ANS4,GALS              |00|00|15|71|0C|00|00|0C|  15.710
44           SRP    QUOT,63,5              |00|00|01|57|1C|00|00|0C|  15.71
45 *                ...

46 ANS4      DS     0PL8      ZERO DUPLICATION FACTOR
47 QUOT      DS     PL5       QUOTIENT AREA
48 RMDR      DS     PL3       REMAINDER AREA
```

Figure 8-13   Sample DP operations.

PAGE OVERFLOW

The standard 11-inch printer form provides for up to 60 lines of printing. Up to now we have not considered the possibility that the printer would reach the bottom of the form. Unless action is taken, the program will continue printing lines to the bottom of the page, over the horizontal perforation, and onto the top of the next page. Desirably, the program should know when printing has reached the bottom of the page, and the forms should eject to the top of the next page. Then the routine that printed the heading at the beginning of the program should be repeated, and normal printing of detail lines should be resumed.

The procedure to accommodate page overflow is for the program to count the lines that have been printed or spaced. The count is compared to some number, such as 40 or 50, that has been deemed the maximum number of print lines on a page. If the count exceeds this maximum, the program is directed to repeat the heading routine. The program in the next section provides for page overflow.

SAMPLE PROGRAM: INVENTORY CALCULATION

The program in Fig. 8-14 calculates unit costs for inventory records.

```
 5 PROG8B   START
 6          BALR   3,0                    INITIALIZE
 7          USING  *,3                      ADDRESSING
 8          OPEN   FILEIN,PRTR
17          BAL    7,P10PAGE              PERFORM HEADING
19          GET    FILEIN,RECDIN          1ST RECORD

26 A10LOOP  CLC    STOCKIN,PREVSTK        STOCK NO. SEQUENCE?
27          BH     A30                    *    HIGH -- BYPASS
28          MVC    MSGPR,SEQERR           OUT-OF-SEQUENCE STOCK
30 A30      BAL    6,B10PROC              PROCESS RECORD
31          MVC    PREVSTK,STOCKIN        STORE STOCK IN PREV
32          GET    FILEIN,RECDIN          READ NEXT
38          B      A10LOOP                LOOP

40 A90EOF   BAL    6,F10FINAL             FINAL TOTALS
41          CLOSE  FILEIN,PRTR
50          EOJ

54 *               C A L C U L A T E   N E W   U N I T   C O S T
55 *        -------------------------------------
56 B10PROC  CP     LINEPK,=P'10'          END OF PAGE?
57          BL     B20                    NO  - BYPASS
58          BAL    7,P10PAGE              YES - HEADING
59 B20      PACK   COSTPK,COSTIN          *
60          PACK   QTYPK,QTYIN            *
61          ZAP    UNCOSTPK,=P'0'         CLEAR UNIT-COST FIELD
62          ZAP    QTYPK,QTYPK            STOCK QUANTITY = 0?
63          BZ     B30                    *    YES - BYPASS DIVIDE
64          ZAP    UNCOSTPK,COSTPK        |00|00|00|00|XX|XX|X.X|XC|
65          SRP    UNCOSTPK,1,0           |00|00|00|0X|XX|XX|.XX|0C|
66          DP     UNCOSTPK,QTYPK         |00|00|XX|.XX|XC|XX|XX|XC|
67          SRP    UNCOSTPK(5),63,5       |00|00|0X|X.X|XC|XX|XX|XC|

69 B30      MVC    COSTPR,EDCOST          EDIT STOCK FIELDS
70          ED     COSTPR,COSTPK          *    COST

72          MVC    UNCOSPR,EDUNIT         *
73          ED     UNCOSPR,UNCOSTPK+2     *    UNIT COST

75          MVC    QTYPR,EDQTY            *
76          ED     QTYPR,QTYPK            *    QUANTITY

78          MVC    DESCRPR,DESCRIN        *
79          MVC    STOCKPR,STOCKIN        *
```

Figure 8-14 Program: inventory calculation.

```
 81              PUTPR  PRTR,STKLINE,WSP1          PRINT STOCK RECORD
 88              AP     LINEPK,=P'1'
 89              MVC    STKLINE,BLANK
 90              AP     FINCOSPK,COSTPK            ADD COST TO TOTAL
 91              BR     6                          RETURN

 93 *                  P R O C E S S   F I N A L   T O T A L
 94 *                  ------------------------------------
 95 F10FINAL MVC    FINTOTPR,EDCOST
 96              ED     FINTOTPR,FINCOSPK          EDIT FINAL TOTAL COST
 97              MVI    ASTERPR+1,C'*'
 98              PUTPR  PRTR,TOTLINE,WSP1          PRINT FINAL TOTAL
112              BR     6                          RETURN

114 *                  P A G E   H E A D I N G
115 *                  ----------------------
116 P10PAGE  PUTPR  PRTR,HDG1LINE,SK1          SKIP NEXT PAGE
123              MVC    PAGEPR,EDPAGE             EDIT
124              ED     PAGEPR,PAGEPK               PAGE NO.
125              PUTPR  PRTR,HDG1LINE,WSP2        PRINT HEADING-1
132              PUTPR  PRTR,HDG2LINE,WSP2        *   HEADING-2
139              AP     PAGEPK,=P'1'              ADD TO PAGE NUMBER
140              ZAP    LINEPK,=P'0'              CLEAR LINE COUNTER
141              BR     7                          RETURN

143 *                  D E C L A R A T I V E S
144 *                  -----------------------
146 FILEIN   DEFIN  A90EOF                    DEFINE INPUT FILE
172 PRTR     DEFPR                            DEFINE PRINTER FILE

202 RECDIN   DS     0CL80                     INPUT RECORD COLUMNS:
203 CODEIN   DS     CL02                      01-02   RECORD CODE
204 STOCKIN  DS     CL04                      03-06   STOCK NO.
205 DESCRIN  DS     CL16                      07-22   DESCRIPTION
206 QTYIN    DS     ZL04                      23-26   QUANTITY
207 COSTIN   DS     ZL07'00000.00'            27-33   COST
208          DS     CL47                      34-80   *
210 *                                         HEADING-1:
211 HDG1LINE DC     CL24' '                   ---------
212          DC     CL53'I N V E N T O R Y   U N I T   C O S T   R E P O R T'
213          DC     CL05'PAGE'
214 PAGEPR   DS     ZL04
215          DC     CL47' '

217 HDG2LINE DC     CL22' '                   HEADING-2:
218          DC     CL23'STOCK  DESCRIPTION'  *--------
219          DC     CL88'QUANTITY    UNITCOST        COST'

221 BLANK    DC     C' '                      BLANK TO CLEAR PRINT AREA
222 STKLINE  DS     0CL133                    STOCK PRINT LINE:
223          DC     CL23' '                   *--------------
224 STOCKPR  DS     CL04                      *   STOCK NO.
225          DC     CL02' '                   *
226 DESCRPR  DS     CL16                      *   DESCRIPTION
227 QTYPR    DS     ZL08                      *   QUANTITY
228          DC     CL04' '                   *
229 UNCOSPR  DS     ZL07                      *   UNIT COST
230          DC     CL01' '                   *
231 COSTPR   DS     ZL12                      *   COST
232 MSGPR    DC     CL31' '                   *
233          DC     CL25' '                   *
```

Figure 8-14   (*continued*)

```
235 TOTLINE   DS    0CL133              FINAL TOTAL LINE:
236           DC    CL31' '             *---------------
237           DC    CL34'FINAL TOTAL'   *
238 FINTOTPR  DS    ZL12                *
239 ASTERPR   DC    CL01'*'             *
240           DC    CL55' '             *

242 COSTPK    DC    PL4'0'              *
243 FINCOSPK  DC    PL4'0'              *
244 QTYPK     DC    PL3'0'              *
245 UNCOSTPK  DC    PL8'0'              *
246 LINEPK    DC    PL2'0'              *
247 PAGEPK    DC    PL2'1'              *

249 SEQERR    DC    CL38'EQ/LO SEQUENCE'
250 PREVSTK   DC    XL4'00'             PREVIOUS STOCK NO.
251 *                                   EDIT WORDS :
252 EDCOST    DC    X'4020206B2020214B2020C3D9',C'**'
253 EDUNIT    DC    X'402020214B2020'
254 EDQTY     DC    X'402020202020C3D9'
255 EDPAGE    DC    X'40202020'

257           LTORG
258                 =C'$$BOPEN '
259                 =C'$$BCLOSE'
260                 =CL8'$$BPDUMP'
261                 =A(RECDIN,PREVSTK+4)
262                 =A(FILEIN)
263                 =A(RECDIN)
264                 =A(PRTR)
265                 =A(STKLINE)
266                 =A(TOTLINE)
267                 =A(HDG1LINE)
268                 =A(HDG2LINE)
269                 =P'10'
270                 =P'0'
271                 =P'1'
272           END   PROG8B
```

Output:-

```
   I N V E N T O R Y   U N I T   C O S T   R E P O R T     PAGE     1

STOCK   DESCRIPTION      QUANTITY      UNITCOST       .COST

 1214   PLYWOOD 1/4         50           3.05         152.50
 1218   PLYWOOD 3/8        150           5.50         825.00
 1222   PLYWOOD 1/2         5CR          3.05          15.25CR
 1234   PLYWOOD 3/4        155           5.48         850.00
 1470   SHIPLAP           155           5.48         850.00
 2476   HAMMERS            10           3.05          30.50
 1222   PLYWOOD 1/2         5CR          3.05          15.25CR EQ/LO SEQUENCE
 2560   WRENCHES                         .00           .00
 2633   PLIERS              1           6.50          6.50

        FINAL TOTAL                                 2,684.00   **
```

Figure 8-14 (*continued*)

Input.   Input data consists of inventory records in sequence by stock item number. There may be only one record for each stock item. Equal or out-of-sequence conditions cause an error.

COLUMN	DESCRIPTION
01–02	Record code
03–06	Stock item number
07–22	Stock description
23–26	Quantity on hand
27–33	Cost of item (two decimal places)

Processing.   The program consists of the following routines:

Main logic.   The program opens the files and links to P10PAGE to print the first headings. It reads the first record and then performs a loop: Link to B10PROC and read a record. At end-of-file, the program links to F10FINAL to print final totals.

B10PROC.   For each stock item, the program calculates unit cost (cost ÷ quantity), prints the result, and adds cost for a final total.

F10FINAL.   The routine prints final total cost.

P10PAGE.   The routine skips to a new page, prints the headings, adds to the page number, and resets the line count.

Output.   The program prints two heading lines, the details for each inventory record, and a final total cost at end-of-file.

REPRESENTATION IN STORAGE

Figure 8-15 shows the hexadecimal contents at the end of processing of the declaratives defined in the preceding program from the first byte of RECDIN through PREVSTK. The program listing shows RECDIN beginning at location (LOC) X'35B'. In this execution, since the program happened to load in storage beginning at X'02C078', the actual location of RECDIN during execution is determined as follows:

Starting point of program:	X'02C078'
Location (LOC) of RECDIN:	+ X'00035B'
Actual storage location:	X'02C3D3'

You can locate the contents of RECDIN in the storage dump beginning with the first hex characters on the top line. At the extreme left is the address of the

```
02C3C0                                                        404040F1  F1F2F6F3  F3D7D3C9  C5D9E240
02C3E0    40404040  40404040  40FCF0F0  F1F0F0F0    F0F6F5F0  40404040  40404040  40404040
02C400    40404040  --SAME--
02C420    40404011  40404040  40404040  40404040    40404040  40404040  404040C9  40D540E5
02C440    40C540D5  40E340D6  40D940E8  4040E440    D540C940  E3406040  C340D640  E240E340
02C460    40D940C5  40D740D6  40D940E3  40404040    D7C1C7C5  40404040  F1404040  40404040
02C480    40404040  --SAME--
02C4A0    40404040  40404040  11404040  40404040    40404040  40404040  40404040  4040E2E3
02C4C0    D6C3D240  40C4C5E2  C3D9C9D7  E3C9D6D5    40404040  40D8E4C1  D5E3C9E3  E8404040
02C4E0    40E4D5C9  E3C3D6E2  E3404040  404040C3    D6E2E340  40404040  40404040  40404040
02C500    40404040  --SAME--
02C5A0    40404040  40404040  40404040  40404040    40404009  40404040  40404040  40404040
02C5C0    40404040  40404040  40404040  40404040    4040C6C9  D5C1D340  E3D6E3C1  D3404040
02C5E0    40404040  40404040  40404040  40404040    40404040  4040F26B  F6F8F44B  F0F04040
02C600    5C5C4040  40404040  40404040  40404040    40404040  40404040  40404040  40404040
02C620    40404040  40404040  40404040  40404040    40404040  40404040  0000650F  0268400C
02C640    00001C00  0000650C  00000C00  9C002CC5    D8E4C1D3  61D3D6E6  40E2C5D8  E4C5D5C3
02C660    C540D6D5  40E2E3D6  C3D24040  40404040    40404040  40F2F6F3  F3402020
```

Figure 8-15   Hexadecimal representation of storage.

leftmost byte of each line.   The first line starts at X'02C3C0' with a half-row of blanks:

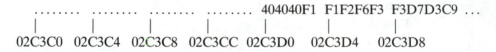

If you count across each pair of hex digits as one byte, you will find that X'02C3D3' is the actual storage location of RECDIN, just as was calculated.   RECDIN contains the last input record.   CODEIN, the first byte, contains X'F1F1', or 11, and STOCKIN occupies the next 4 bytes, X'F2F6F3F3', or 2633.   DESCRIN is the next 15 bytes, containing PLIERS, and continues on the second line.

Note that if X'02C3C0' is the leftmost byte, the address of the byte beginning the right half of the dump is X'02C3D0'.

The dump also shows the contents of the defined declaratives COSTPK through to PREVSTK.   As at the end of processing, COSTPK should contain 00650.   Let's check whether this is true:

Starting point of program:	X'02C078'
Location (LOC) of COSTPK:	+ X'0005C0'
Actual storage location:	X'02C638'

To find this value in the dump, trace down the leftmost column until you reach X'02C620'.   Starting at this location, count across until you reach the center at X'02C630', then count eight more pairs.   You should be at the value X'0000650F', the correct contents of COSTPK.

DEBUGGING TIPS FOR PACKED DATA

- Expect considerably more bugs in both the assembly and execution phases as your programs become larger and involve arithmetic data. Finding a bug for the first time is often time-consuming, but in time you can become proficient at tracing errors, especially if you have enough of them.

- New assembly errors can involve coding packed DCs with characters other than 0–9, decimal point, and sign. Watch for coding hex constants: For example, DC XL3'FF' generates '0000FF', not 'FFFFFF'.

- More likely are errors during program execution. Packing a field that contains a blank (X'40') in its rightmost position generates a packed field with an invalid sign (X'04'); an attempt to perform arithmetic using this field will cause a data exception. A likely cause is a blank input field or an improperly defined input record. Another popular cause of data exceptions is adding to a field that has not been initialized as a DC or is defined as character, so that it contains invalid packed data.

- Watch out also for using MVC and CLC on packed data (incorrect execution) or ZAP and CP on character data (data exceptions). Improper relative addressing and missing explicit lengths are common causes of bugs.

- The system is designed to terminate processing on a program check interrupt, such as a data exception or an operation exception. (Appendix B contains a complete list.) The supervisor's error diagnostics vary considerably by operating system. See Chapter 15 for details.

- The ED operation provides many opportunities for bugs. Allow in the edit word X'20's and an X'21' for each packed digit to be edited. There should be an odd number.

- For MP, the product field must be at least the length of the multiplicand plus multiplier. If the field is too short, a data exception occurs.

- For DP, the quotient/remainder area must be at least as long as the dividend (after scaling) plus divisor. Another pitfall is trying to divide by a zero value. Both errors cause a decimal divide exception.

- If you cannot locate a bug, rerun the program with a request for a storage dump. The error may be in logic or in the data. Sometimes there is no error and you think there is—this is the most difficult of all to trace.

KEY POINTS

- Ordinary decimal arithmetic is performed on fields in packed format. The plus or minus sign is the rightmost half-byte of the field. Each other packed byte contains two digits, one in each half-byte.

- The main use of the MVN and MVZ instructions is to manipulate half-bytes for decimal arithmetic.
- The PACK operation converts character data into packed. In the rightmost byte, the half-bytes are reversed. Other than the rightmost byte, PACK extracts numeric portions from all other bytes one at a time from right to left and places them adjacent to one another in the operand 1 field.
- UNPK converts packed data into zoned. The half-bytes of the rightmost byte of the operand 2 field are reversed in the operand 1 field. UNPK places all other digits in operand 2 from right to left in the numeric portion of each byte in operand 1 and fills the zone portions with hex 'F'.
- The ZAP instruction transfers packed data; AP and SP add and subtract packed fields.
- The CP instruction compares packed decimal fields algebraically.
- ED converts packed data into character format and provides for punctuation, sign, and zero suppression. The fill character X'40' zero suppresses the leftmost zeros by replacing them with blanks. X'20's in an edit word represent each packed digit to be printed. X'21' acts like a digit selector, but in addition, it forces printing of all characters to the right.
- MP multiplies packed fields. Define the product length equal at least to the length in bytes of the multiplicand plus the multiplier.
- The SRP instruction shifts packed data to the left or right. For right shifts, SRP can also provide rounding.
- The DP instruction divides packed fields. Operand 1 is the dividend, and the operation generates the quotient and remainder in this field. Define the length of the operand 1 field at least equal to that of the dividend plus divisor.

PROBLEMS

8-1. *MVN and MVZ.*   Given the following declaratives, code the unrelated questions below them.   Give results in hex and character.

```
HAM      DC       C'HAL'
EGGS     DC       C'2472'
TOAST    DC       X'C9E2C4E0'
```

(a) Move the first 3 numeric half-bytes of TOAST to the numerics of HAM.
(b) Move the zone half-bytes of TOAST to those of EGGS.

8-2. Complete the hex representation for the following.   Except for (a) and (b), questions are unrelated.

```
                         CH1       DC        C'345678'
                         CH2       DC        C'1234'
                         ZN1       DC        Z'123'
                         PK1       DC        P'-123'
                         PK2       DC        P'12.34'
```

(a) { PACK   PK1,ZN1
         { UNPK   CH1,PK1

(b) { PACK   PK2,CH1
         { UNPK   ZN1,PK2

(c)   PACK   PK2+1(2),ZN1+1(2)
(d)   PACK   PK1,=CL2' '
(e)   PACK   CH2,CH2
(f)   UNPK   PK1,PK1
(g)   ZAP   PK2,PK1
(h)   ZAP   PK1,PK2
(i)   AP   PK2,=P'5'
(j)   AP   PK2,=X'5F'

8-3. Determine the condition code set by the following. Symbolic names refer to Problem 8-2. Explain if invalid.

(a) CP   PK1,PK2
(b) CP   PK2,PK1
(c) CP   CH2,PK2
(d) CLC   CH2,ZN1

8-4. *Editing.* (a) What characters other than X'40' may be used as a fill character? (b) The field defined as ACCUM DC PL3'0' currently contains a zero value. Define an edit word that causes ACCUM to print as all blanks. (c) Why does an edit word contain an odd number of X'20's and X'21's?

8-5. Complete the following edit words and edit operations as indicated.

(a) Use comma, decimal point, and minus sign. If zero, the edited field should print as .00.

```
                         MVC       PRINT+25...
                         ED        ...
                         ...
              VALUE1     DS        PL4
              EDWD1      DC        X'....
```

(b) Use commas, decimal point, and minus sign. If zero, the edited field should print as 0.00.

```
                         MVC       PRINT+45...
                         ED        ...
                         ...
              VALUE2     DS        PL5
              EDWD2      DC        X'....
```

(c) Use $, commas, decimal point, CR, and two asterisks. If zero, the edited field should print as .00.

```
                        MVC       PRINT+65...
                        ED        ...
                        ...
        VALUE3   DS     PL4
        EDWD3    DC     X'....
```

8-6. *Multiply Packed.* Code the instructions as indicated and show the results in hex representation. Define a product field named PRODUCT for each example.

```
        AMT1     DC     P'73.5'
        AMT2     DC     P'837.5'
        AMT3     DC     P'69.75'
        AMT4     DC     P'93.345'
```

(a) Multiply AMT1 by AMT2; round and shift to one decimal place.
(b) Multiply AMT2 by AMT3; round and shift to two decimal places.
(c) Multiply AMT2 by AMT4; round and shift to two decimal places.
(d) Multiply AMT3 by AMT4; round and shift to two decimal places.
(e) Explain the error, if any: MP AMT3,=P'2'

8-7. *Divide Packed.* Code the instructions as indicated and show the results in hex representation. Define a quotient/remainder field named RESULT for each example.

```
        AMTA     DC     P'018'
        AMTB     DC     P'131.5'
        AMTC     DC     P'612.54'
        AMTD     DC     P'931.277'
```

(a) Divide AMTB by AMTA and round to one decimal place.
(b) Divide AMTC by AMTB and round to two decimal places.
(c) Divide AMTD by AMTA and round to one decimal place.
(d) Divide AMTD by AMTB and round to zero decimal places.
(e) Explain the error, if any: DP AMTD,=P'3'

8-8. *Program Assignment.* A program is required to read sales records, print the detail, and accumulate totals.

 Input. Data records in the following format:

COLUMN	DESCRIPTION
01	Record code (3)
02–6	Sales agent number
07–26	Sales agent name
27–29	Category (type of sale: TV, VCR, appliance. etc.)
31–33	Commission rate (e.g., .175 = 17.5%)
34–47	Category description
48–53	Selling price (2 decimals)
54–59	Cost price (2 decimals)

Processing.   (a) Check for valid record code (3).   (b) Sequence-check the file according to sales agent number.   (c) For each record, calculate

$$\text{Gross profit} = \text{selling price} - \text{cost (may be negative)}$$

$$\text{Percent gross profit} = \frac{\text{gross profit}}{\text{cost}}$$

$$\text{Commission} = \text{gross profit} \times \text{commission rate}$$

(d) Test input data should test all possible conditions in the program.

Output.   Print suitable page headings and provide for page overflow.   Print the details from each record and final totals of sales, cost, gross profit, and commission.

9

PROCESSING BINARY DATA

OBJECTIVE

To cover the uses of binary data and the programming requirements.

Chapter 6 introduced the use of registers for base addressing. You may also use the registers for performing binary arithmetic and for manipulating data in binary format. Indeed, binary arithmetic is done only in the registers, and, conversely, the registers perform arithmetic only in binary format. This chapter covers basic binary and register operations: first the representation of binary data and then the instructions that perform binary arithmetic.

Binary data may enter a program in several ways:

- Defined in storage as a constant, as binary (B type), fullword (F type), and halfword (H type)
- Generated in a register by such instructions as CVB, LA, BAL, and EDMK
- Received from an external source such as disk or tape, where the data was recorded in binary format

Although processing binary data in registers is fast, additional steps may be required in converting character input to packed and to binary and then into printable format: binary to packed to edited character. Binary format does have many useful applications, however, especially in manipulating addresses for table searching, covered in Chapter 11.

BINARY DATA REPRESENTATION

Binary numbers are defined in storage by types B, F, and H constants or used in the general registers. For reference, bits are numbered from left to right, with the leftmost bit numbered zero:

Binary value: 000000000
Position: 012345678 etc.

The sign is the leftmost bit, position 0, where a zero bit indicates a positive value and a one bit indicates negative. A zero value is always positive.

Binary Addition

The following examples illustrate the rules of binary addition:

```
                            1
    0        0       1      1
  +0       +1      +1     +1
 ─────    ─────   ─────  ─────
    0        1      10     11
```

In the following three examples of decimal and binary addition, the leftmost bit is the sign:

DECIMAL	BINARY	DECIMAL	BINARY	DECIMAL	BINARY
4	00000100	7	00000111	7	00000111
+2	00000010	+2	00000010	+7	00000111
6	00000110	9	00001001	14	00001110

Negative Binary Numbers

Negative numbers are expressed in what is known as two's complement form. To express a negative binary number, reverse all the bits of its positive value (a zero bit becomes 1, and a one bit becomes 0), and add 1. The same procedure converts negative values to positive values.

Consider the binary representation of −7:

Decimal value +7:   00000111
Reverse bits: 11111000
Add 1:   11111001 (two's complement of −7)

For subtraction, convert the field being subtracted to its two's complement and then add the fields. The following subtracts 7 from 9:

Decimal value: +9   00001001
Add −7:   −7   11111001 (two's complement of −7)

Result: 2   00000010

Since there is a carry into and out of the sign position, the result is correct, not an overflow.

Invalid Overflow Conditions

Invalid overflows occur on the following two conditions, based on 8-bit examples.

  1. Overflow caused by a carry into the sign position:

Decimal value: 89   01011001
Add 49:   +49   00110001

Result: 138   10001010 (negative value, −118)

There is a carry into the sign position but none out. The sum is an incorrect negative value. To determine the value of 10001010, reverse the bits and add 1. Since the value is +118, the result is −118 but should have been +138.

  2. Overflow caused by a carry out of the sign position:

Decimal value: −89   10100111
Add: +(−49)   11001111

Result: −138   01110110 (positive value, +118)

There is no carry into the sign position but one out. The sum is an incorrect positive value, 118, but should have been −138.

BINARY DECLARATIVES

The three types of binary declaratives are B (ordinary binary), F (fullword fixed-point), and H (halfword fixed-point). The following sections describe DCs for these formats; DS statements are written similarly except that the constant is optional and acts as a comment.

Binary Constants

Type B constants define binary ones and zeros as a string of bits. A common use is as operands for the immediate instructions NI, OI, XI, and TM, covered in Chapter 12. Although the format has some specialized uses, the binary arithmetic instructions are designed to work with the F and H formats.

Name	Operation	Operand
[name]	DC	dBLn'constant'

- d (duplication factor) is optional and defaults to 1 if omitted.
- B specifies a binary constant.
- Ln provides for an optional length in bytes, with a maximum of 256.
- The constant consists of zero and one bits. If the length of the defined constant differs from the specified length (Ln), the assembler pads with zeros or truncates the constant on the left.

Here are three examples of B-type declaratives:

			LENGTH	ASSEMBLED AS	VALUE
BIN1	DC	B'00010011'	1	00010011	19
BIN2	DC	B'110'	1	00000110	6
BIN3	DC	BL2'100010011'	2	00000001 00010011	275

You may also code B format in an immediate operand, as in

           CLI   CODE,B'10110010'

Binary Fixed-Point Constants: F and H

Fixed-point constants (F and H formats) are commonly used for register arithmetic.

Name	Operation	Operand
[name]	DC	dFLn'constant'
[name]	DC	dHLn'constant'

- d (duplication factor) is optional and defaults to 1 if omitted.
- Type F defines a fullword and H defines a halfword. A fullword is a 4-byte field aligned on a fullword boundary (evenly divisible by 4). A halfword is a 2-byte field aligned on a halfword boundary (evenly divisible by 2). These are the standard formats for binary arithmetic.
- Ln provides for an optional length in bytes, which is used only in specialized situations. If you code a length, the assembler does not attempt to align the constant on a fullword or halfword boundary, as you will see later in this section.
- You code a decimal number as the defined constant, which the assembler converts to binary. If the length of the constant is greater than its implicit or explicit length, the assembler truncates it on the left.

With bit 0 (the leftmost) as the sign, the maximum and minimum binary values are as follows:

FORMAT	BITS	MAXIMUM	MINIMUM
Halfword	16	$2^{15} - 1 = 32,767$	$-2^{15} - 1 = -32,768$
Fullword	32	$2^{31} - 1 = 2,147,483,647$	$-2^{31} - 1 = -2,147,483,648$

Figure 9-1 provides a number of declaratives in fullword and halfword formats.

BINVAL1 is a DS that simply causes the location counter to align on a fullword boundary. (Check the hex address for this statement.)

BINVAL2 defines a 2-byte field aligned on a halfword boundary.

BINVAL3 defines two adjacent fullwords; a reference to the name BINVAL3 is to the first fullword.

BINVAL4 is a halfword that defines the decimal value 25. The assembler converts 25 to binary 00011001, shown in object code on the left as X'19'.

BINVAL5 defines a fullword containing -5. Note the generated hex con-

```
LOC    OBJECT CODE     STMT    SOURCE STATEMENT
003800                    7 BINVAL1   DS     0F        ALIGNS ON FULLWORD ADDR.
003800                    8 BINVAL2   DS     H         HALFWORD AREA
003804                    9 BINVAL3   DS     2F        2 FULLWORD AREAS
00380C 0019              10 BINVAL4   DC     H'25'     HALFWORD WITH POS. VALUE
00380E 0000
003810 FFFFFFFB          11 BINVAL5   DC     F'-5'     FULLWORD WITH NEG. VALUE
003814 8001              12 BINVAL6   DC     H'32769'  EXCEEDS MAXIMUM OF 32767
         *** ERROR ***

STMNT  ERROR  SEV
  12   IPK189   8 DATA ITEM TOO LARGE IN CONSTANT 1
```

Figure 9-1 Fullword and halfword declaratives.

stant.   Try converting 5 to its two's complement and see if you get the same answer.

BINVAL6 illustrates a coding error: The constant exceeds the halfword maximum of 32,767.   This maximum is a trivial amount for many computer problems and is easily exceeded.

In storage, these declaratives would appear as follows:

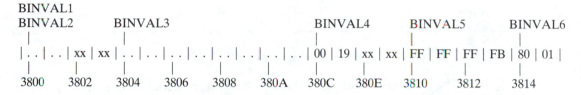

Both BINVAL1 and BINVAL2 align on the same halfword address, x'3800'. Since BINVAL3 is a fullword, the assembler aligns it on a fullword boundary, X'3804'; consequently, bytes X'3802' and X'3803' are unused ("slack" bytes).   Similarly, BINVAL5 begins at X'3810' and leaves slack bytes at X'380E' and X'380F'.

Overriding the alignment.   You may have occasions to define a binary H or F field without the assembler's automatic alignment.   One case occurs when an input or output record for disk or tape contains a binary field.   Consider the following disk input record:

```
Loc      Name        Operation   Operand
8420    RECORDIN        DS        0CL29
8420    ACCTIN          DS        CL05
8428    AMTIN           DS        F          (fullword alignment here)
842C    NAMEIN          DS        CL20
```

The assembler's location counter for ACCTIN is at X'8420'.   Since ACCTIN is a 5-byte field, the next field, AMTIN, would normally begin at X'8425'.   But AMTIN is defined as DS F, so the assembler aligns its address on the next fullword boundary, X'8428'.   There are now 3 slack bytes between the two fields, and the record is now defined as 32 bytes instead of the expected 29.   An input operation would read a 29-byte record byte for byte beginning at RECORDIN.   The first 3 bytes of the binary amount in the input area will now be the slack bytes, and the program will reference incorrect data in AMTIN and NAMEIN.

A simple remedy is to override the assembler's alignment by coding the fullword with an explicit length, as follows:

```
8425    AMTIN           DS        FL4        (no fullword alignment)
```

Address Constants

A declarative may also define an address constant. For example, you code BALR to initialize the first base register and may code address constants to initialize additional registers. Of the four types of address constants, this chapter discusses only the common A type.

Name	Operation	Operand
[name]	DC	A(address-1,address-2,...,address-n)

The rules for address constants are as follows:

- The address constant is enclosed within parentheses. You may define more than one address, each separated by a comma. The constant may be either an absolute value (rarely used) or a symbolic name.
- The assembler generates a fullword constant, aligned on a fullword boundary, provided you do not code a length indication. The constant is right-adjusted in the field, and the maximum is $2^{31} - 1$, the highest fullword value.

Figure 9-2 gives a number of examples:

ADDRESS1 defines an address constant with an absolute value, a rare procedure, since you do not normally know where a program resides for execution.

ADDRESS2 defines the address of DECLAR. The object code address generated by the statement (X'3806') is the same as the address of DECLAR.

ADDRESS3 defines the address of A10. Compare the object code address constant with that of the actual address of A10.

ADDRESS4 illustrates a relative address, A10+4096. The assembler con-

```
   LOC    OBJECT CODE          STMT     SOURCE STATEMENT
003800 0530                      20 BEGIN     BALR  3,0                INIT'IZE BASE REG 3
                                 21           USING *,3,4,5,6          ASSIGN BASE REGS
003802 9846 3026                 22 A10       LM    4,6,ADDRESS5       LOAD REGS 4, 5, 6
                                 23 *         .
                                 24 *         .
003806 C1C4C4D9C5E2E240          25 DECLAR    DC    C'ADDRESS CONSTANTS'
00380E C3D6D5E2E3C1D5E3
003816 E2
003817 00
003818 00004E20                  26 ADDRESS1 DC    A(20000)            ADDR OF 20000
00381C 00003806                  27 ADDRESS2 DC    A(DECLAR)           ADDR OF DECLAR
003820 00003802                  28 ADDRESS3 DC    A(A10)              ADDR OF A10
003824 00004802                  29 ADDRESS4 DC    A(A10+4096)         ADDR OF A10+X'1000'
003828 0000480200005802          30 ADDRESS5 DC    A(A10+4096,A10+2*4096,A10+3*4096)
003830 00006802
                                 31 ***                                A10+X'1000', A10+X'2000', A10+X'3000'
```

Figure 9-2 Address constants.

verts 4096 to X'1000', and the object code address becomes X'3802' + X'1000' = X'4802'.

ADDRESS5 illustrates three address constants separated by commas. Note the use of assembler arithmetic: 2*4096 = 8192.

Figure 9-2 also shows how to assign and load more than one base register. BALR loads the first base register, register 3, and USING tells the assembler to allocate registers 3, 4, 5, and 6 as base registers, in that order. The LM (load multiple register) instruction

                    LM   4,6,ADDRESS5

loads registers 4, 5, and 6 with the three fullword addresses beginning at ADDRESS5— A10 + X'1000', A10 + X'2000', and A10 + X'3000', respectively. For this operation to work correctly, however, ADDRESS5 must be defined within the first 4K of the program so that LM can actually access it.

BINARY FIXED-POINT INSTRUCTIONS

Instructions whose operands are aligned require fewer machine cycles and execute faster. For example, operand 2 for CVB and CVD is normally aligned on a doubleword; operand 2 for L, A, C, and D is normally aligned on a fullword, and operand 2 for LH, AH, and CH is normally aligned on a halfword. However, only channel command words and operands of certain privileged instructions must align on integral boundaries.

The following sections contain binary instructions for such operations as conversion between binary and packed formats and arithmetic operations. Figure 9-3 provides a summary of these instructions by their formats.

Operation	RR	RX (fullword)	RX (halfword)	RS
Convert			CVB, CVD	
Load	LR	L	LH	LM
Load complement	LCR			
Load negative	LNR			
Load positive	LPR			
Load and test	LTR			
Store		ST	STH	STM
Add	AR	A	AH	
Subtract	SR	S	SH	
Compare	CR	C	CH	
Multiply	MR	M	MH	
Divide	DR	D		
Shift left				SLA, SLDA
Shift right				SRA, SRDA

Figure 9-3 Table of binary instructions.

CONVERSION OF DECIMAL AND BINARY DATA: CVB AND CVD

The CVB and CVD instructions are involved with converting data between packed decimal and binary formats. CVB (convert to binary) converts packed decimal data from storage into binary format in a register. The packed data is contained in an 8-byte field, preferably defined as a doubleword, aligned on a doubleword boundary. For this purpose, you would normally use the DS D definition. (Note that a D-type DC is used for defining floating-point values, but a DS may store data in any format.) Similarly, CVD (convert to decimal) converts binary data from a register into packed decimal format in storage.

You would typically use CVB to convert packed data to binary in a register, perform binary arithmetic, use CVD to convert the binary data to packed, and then edit the packed value for output. The formats for CVB and CVD are

Name	Operation	Operand
[label]	CVB	R1,X2 *or* R1,D2(X2,B2)
[label]	CVD	R1,X2 *or* R1,D2(X2,B2)

For CVB, operand 1 specifies a general register, and operand 2 references a storage location defined as a doubleword containing packed data. For CVD, operand 1 specifies a general register, and operand 2 references a storage location defined as a doubleword. Note a significant difference between these two instructions: CVB converts data from operand 2 (storage) to operand 1 (a register), whereas CVD converts data from operand 1 (a register) to operand 2 (storage).

In the following example, the packed field, AMTPK, is zapped into a doubleword field, DBLWD1, and CVB converts the packed contents of DBLWD1 to binary format in register 6. Subsequently, CVD converts the binary contents of register 6 to packed format in DBLWD2:

```
           ZAP     DBLWD1,AMTPK       Packed to doubleword
           CVB     6,DBLWD1           Convert to binary
           ...
           CVD     6,DBLWD2           Convert to packed
           ...
AMTPK      DC      P'125'             Packed field
DBLWD1     DS      D                  Doubleword
DBLWD2     DS      D                  Doubleword
```

LOADING REGISTERS: L, LH, LR, LM, LA

The computer provides a number of instructions for loading binary fullwords and halfwords in registers. The most common load instructions are L (Load Fullword), LH (Load Halfword), LR (Load Register), LM (Load Multiple), and LA (Load

Address).   These instructions do not set the condition code.   The next section gives a number of less used load instructions: LCR, LNR, LPR, and LTR.

Name	Operation	Operand
[label]	L	R1,X2 *or* R1,D2(X2,B2)
[label]	LH	R1,X2 *or* R1,D2(X2,B2)
[label]	LR	R1,R2
[label]	LM	R1,S2 *or* R1,R3,D2(B2)
[label]	LA	R1,X2 *or* R1,D2(X2,B2)

Load Fullword (L)

The L instruction loads a binary fullword value from main storage into a register. The rules are as follows:

- Operand 1 specifies any general register.
- Operand 2 references a fullword in storage, typically aligned on a fullword boundary.
- The operation loads the contents of the fullword into the specified register, replacing the previous contents.

Let's now examine four L operations:

1. Load a fullword literal into register 2.   The literal is aligned on a fullword boundary and, although defined with a decimal value, contains a binary value:

```
        L         2,=F'123456'
```

2. Load a fullword constant into register 8:

```
                    L         8,FULLWORD
                    . . .
        FULLWORD    DC        F'6936'
```

3. Load an address constant (a literal) into register 5:

```
        L         5,=A(TABLE)
```

4. Load a halfword constant—an error, since the operand should reference a fullword.   The assembler does not generate an error message, and at execute time, the operation loads the halfword plus the 2 bytes immediately following:

```
        L         1,=H'287'      (coding error)
```

Load Halfword (LH)

The LH instruction loads a binary halfword value from main storage into a register. The rules are as follows:

- Operand 1 specifies any general register.
- Operand 2 references a halfword in storage, typically aligned on a halfword boundary.
- The operation loads the contents of the halfword into the rightmost 16 bits of the specified register and then propagates the sign bit (the leftmost bit of the halfword) through the 16 leftmost bits of the register. A positive value, with a zero bit, remains positive, and a negative value, with a one bit, remains negative, maintaining the proper two's complement format.

Let's examine three LH operations:

1. Load a halfword literal into register 9:

```
        LH        9,=H'500'
```

2. Load a halfword constant into register 0:

```
            LH        0,HALFWORD
            . . .
HALFWORD    DC        H'595'
```

3. Load a fullword constant—an error, since the operand should reference a halfword. The assembler does not generate an error message, and at execute time, the operation loads only the first 2 bytes of FULLWORD, causing an error that may be difficult to locate:

```
    LH        1,FULLWORD      (coding error)
```

Load Register (LR)

Both operands of the LR instruction reference a register. LR loads the contents of the register referenced by operand 2 into the register referenced by operand 1.

The following LR example loads (L) the contents of FULLWORD into register 8 and then uses LR to copy the contents of register 8 into register 7:

```
    L       8,FULLWORD      Load fullword
    LR      7,8             Load register 8 into 7
```

Load Multiple (LM)

The LM instruction can load data from main storage into more than one register in one operation. LM has two common uses. One use is to restore registers that were saved when the program linked to a subprogram (covered in Chapter 13). The second use is for base register initialization, covered later in this chapter.

LM is an RS-format instruction with three operands. The rules are as follows:

- Operands 1 and 2 specify registers that represent a span of registers; for example, 7,10 means registers 7, 8, 9, and 10.
- Operand 3 references a fullword address in storage, the first of a number of adjacent fullword values, one for each register that LM is to load successively into the registers. Technically, the data need not be fullwords at all; the operation begins at the designated storage location and stores groups of 4 bytes into the registers.

Let's examine two LM examples:

1. Load registers 6, 7, and 8 with the contents of FULLWD1, FULLWD2, and FULLWD3, respectively:

```
          LM        6,8,FULLWD1      Load 3 fullwords
          ...
FULLWD1   DC        F'7342'          3 fullwords
FULLWD2   DC        F'4855'          *
FULLWD3   DC        F'5126'          *
```

2. Load registers 15, 0, and 1 with the contents of FULLWD1, FULLWD2, and FULLWD3, respectively. The example shows how the operation may "wrap around" registers:

```
          LM        15,1,FULWD1
```

Use of LM to Load Additional Base Registers

You used BALR earlier to initialize the first base register, and you may use LM to initialize subsequent registers with base addresses, although LM is restricted to loading consecutive registers. Here is an example that uses BALR to load register 3 and LM to load registers 4, 5, and 6 with addresses that are successively 4,096 higher:

```
          BALR      3,0              Initialize register 3
          USING     *,3,4,5,6        Allocate registers 3-6
A10       LM        4,6,BASEADDS     Load registers 4, 5, 6
          ...
BASEADDS  DC        A(A10+4096)      Address constant
          DC        A(A10+2*4096)    *
          DC        A(A10+3*4096)    *
```

After the BALR executes, only base register 3 is initialized, and consequently LM executes correctly only if the constant BASEADDS is defined within the first 4K of the program.

Load Address (LA)

LA is a convenient RX instruction for loading base registers and for initializing an address in a register for table searching.   The rules are as follows:

- Operand 1 specifies any general register.
- Operand 2 references a storage address in the form D2(X2,B2).
- LA loads the operand 2 address into bits 8–31 of the operand 1 register and clears bits 0–7 to zero.
- LA is a logical instruction like MVC that treats data as unsigned.

Here are four examples of the LA instruction:

1. Load the address of A10ADDR in register 9:

                    LA   9,A10ADDR

Assume that A10ADDR is subject to base register 3 containing X'9800' with a displacement of X'260'.   The object code instruction is

                    | 41 | 90 | 32 | 60 |
                     (a) (b)(c)   (d)

(a) The machine code for LA is X'41'.
(b) The operand 1 register is 9.
(c) The index register is 0, since none was coded.
(d) The base register is 3 and the displacement is X'260'.
    The operation adds the contents of the base register (X'9800') plus the displacement (X'260').   The sum of X'9A60' (supposedly the address of A10ADDR) is loaded into register 9.
2. Load an explicit value into register 5.   This example illustrates explicit use of base and displacement values (covered fully in Chapter 11):

                    LA   9,5(0,0)

The object code for this instruction is

                    | 41 | 90 | 00 | 05 |

For execution, assume no base register, no index register, but load the displacement X'005' into register 9.   In effect, the operation loads the value 5 into the register.   But note that because the 5 is a displacement, it must be a positive number less than 4,096.

3. Load an explicit value into register 5:

```
LA        9,5
```

The assembler treats operand 2 as if it were coded like the previous example, that is, 5(0,0).   This is a convenient way to load a positive value into a register, up to 4,095.

4. Load a base value and a displacement:

```
LA        9,1(0,9)
```

The generated object code for the instruction is

| 41 | 90 | 90 | 01 |

For execution, operand 2 references base register 9, no index register, and displacement X'001'.   In effect, the operation increments the contents of register 9 by 1.   This method of adding to a register, though efficient, works correctly only for increments up to 4,095 and only if the value in the register is positive and does not exceed 24 bits.

Use of LA to Load Additional Base Registers

Our next example illustrates an efficient way to load additional base registers by means of LA's index register feature.   BALR loads the first base register with, say, X'5802', and LA instructions load registers 4, 5, and 6:

```
                          Reg-3  Reg-4  Reg-5  Reg-6
BALR    3,0               5802   ----   ----   ----
USING   *,3,4,5,6
LA      6,2048            5802   ----   ----   0800
LA      4,2048(6,3)       5802   6802   ----   0800
LA      5,2048(6,4)       5802   6802   7802   0800
LA      6,2048(6,5)       5802   6802   7802   8802
```

The first LA loads register 6 with 2048, or X'800'.   The second LA loads register 4 with X'6802' based on

Contents of base register 3:	X'5802'
Contents of index register 6:	+ X'0800'
Displacement:	+ X'0800'
Total generated address:	X'6802'

Note that X'800' plus X'800' equals X'1000'. The example loads registers 5 and 6 in a similar manner.

Other Load instructions: LCR, LNR, LPR, and LTR

You may find occasional uses for these load register (RR-format) instructions. Each sets the condition code.

Load complement register (LCR). LCR loads the contents of the operand 2 register into the operand 1 register and reverses the sign. The following example loads the contents of register 8 into register 5, reverses the sign, and sets the condition code:

```
           LCR       5,8
```

Load negative register (LNR). LNR loads the contents of the operand 2 register into the operand 1 register and sets its value to negative. The condition code is set to 0 for a zero value or 1 for a nonzero negative value.

The following example loads the contents of register 5 into register 5, forces a negative sign, and sets the condition code:

```
           LNR       5,5
```

Load positive register (LPR). LPR loads the contents of the operand 2 register into the operand 1 register and sets its value to positive. The condition code is set to 0 for a zero value or 2 for a nonzero positive value.

The following example loads the contents of register 7 into register 9, forces a positive sign, and sets the condition code:

```
           LNR       9,7
```

Load and test register (LTR). LTR loads the contents of the operand 2 register into the operand 1 register, just like LR, but in addition it sets the condition code for zero, minus, or plus.

The following example loads the contents of register 4 into register 4 and sets the condition code, a useful technique for testing the sign in a register:

```
           LTR       4,4
```

STORING REGISTERS: ST, STH, STM

A large program may require the use of many registers for base addressing, binary calculations, subroutine linkage, and input/output operations. You can use the binary store instructions, ST, STH, and STM, to store or save the contents of registers, use them for other purposes, and then use L or LM to reload them.

Name	Operation	Operand
[label]	ST	R1,X2 *or* R1,D2(X2,B2)
[label]	STH	R1,X2 *or* R1,D2(X2,B2)
[label]	STM	R1,S2 *or* R1,R3,D2(B2)

The store instructions act like a mirror image of L, LH, and LM, respectively. They store the contents of registers in fullword or halfword fields in storage. Like CVD, these instructions move the contents of operand 1 (a register) to operand 2 (storage).

Store Fullword (ST)

ST stores the contents of the operand 1 register into the fullword in storage referenced by operand 2. The following example stores the contents of register 5 in a fullword:

```
              ST        5,SAVEFULL       Store fullword
              . . .
SAVEFULL      DS        F                Fullword
```

Store Halfword (STH)

STH stores the rightmost 16 bits of the operand 1 register into the halfword in storage referenced by operand 2. The following example stores the rightmost 16 bits of register 6 in a halfword:

```
              STH       6,SAVEHALF       Store halfword
              . . .
SAVEHALF      DS        H                Halfword
```

Store Multiple (STM)

For STM, R1 and R3 specify a span of registers to be stored. STM stores the fullword contents of R1 and the fullword contents of each register up to and including R3 consecutively, starting at the operand 2 address. If R1 references a higher register than R3 (such as 14,3), the registers stored are 14, 15, 0, 1, 2, and 3.

In the following example, an LM instruction first initializes registers 4, 5, and 6 with fullword values. The first STM stores the contents of registers 4, 5, and 6

in three fullwords labeled THREEFW. The second STM stores the contents of
registers 15, 0, 1, 2, and 3 in five fullwords labeled FIVEFW:

```
            LM       4,6,FULLA        Load registers 4, 5, 6
            STM      4,6,THREEFW      Store registers 4, 5, 6
            STM      15,3,FIVEFW      Store registers 15-3
            ...
FULLA       DC       F'3157'          Fullword
            DC       F'4521'          *
            DC       F'1548'          *
THREEFW     DS       3F               3 fullwords
FIVEFW      DS       5F               5 fullwords
```

Use of STM and LM for Saving Registers

STM is useful for saving the contents of a number of registers, and LM is useful
for reloading them. The following example links to a subroutine named R10SUB
and uses STM to save registers 6 through 12 in SAVEADD. Assume that the
subroutine then uses registers 6 through 12 for its own purposes. On exit, the
subroutine uses LM to reload the saved registers.

```
            BAL      9,R10SUB         Link to subroutine
            ...
R10SUB      STM      6,12,SAVEADD     Save registers 6-12
            ...
            LM       6,12,SAVEADD     Reload registers 6-12
            BR       9                Return to caller
            ...
SAVEADD     DC       7A(0)            Area for saving registers
```

BINARY ARITHMETIC: A, S, AH, SH, AR, SR

The following instructions perform binary addition and subtraction in registers.
These operations treat the leftmost sign bit as a plus (zero bit) or minus (one bit)
sign, not data. For valid results, the data must be in binary format and should be
defined in normal fullword and halfword format. These instructions set the condition code (to zero, minus, and plus), which the usual conditional branch operations may test.

Name	Operation	Operand
[label]	A	R1,X2 *or* R1,D2(X2,B2)
[label]	S	R1,X2 *or* R1,D2(X2,B2)
[label]	AH	R1,X2 *or* R1,D2(X2,B2)
[label]	SH	R1,X2 *or* R1,D2(X2,B2)
[label]	AR	R1,R2
[label]	SR	R1,R2

Add and Subtract Fullword (A and S)

The A instruction adds a fullword in storage to a register, and the S instruction subtracts a fullword in storage from a register. Operand 1 references a register, and operand 2 references a fullword storage location, containing data in binary format. All 31 data bits of the fullword are algebraically added to or subtracted from the contents of the register.

In the following example, an L instruction loads the fullword value 125 in register 5, A adds the fullword value 70, and S subtracts a fullword literal containing 50. Although notation is in decimal format, the fields and registers actually contain binary values.

```
         L       5,FWD1        Load fullword
         A       5,FWD2        Add fullword
         S       5,=F'50'      Subtract fullword
         ...
FWD1     DC      F'125'
FWD2     DC      F'70'
```

Add and Subtract Halfword (AH and SH)

The AH instruction adds a halfword in storage to a register, and the SH instruction subtracts a halfword in storage from a register. Operand 1 references a register, and operand 2 references a halfword storage location, containing data in binary format. Before the add or subtract, the operation expands the halfword to a fullword by filling the sign bit through the 16 leftmost bit positions. All 31 data bits are then algebraically added to or subtracted from the contents of the register.

In the following example, an L instruction loads the halfword value 125 in register 8, AH adds a halfword literal containing 50, and SH subtracts a halfword literal containing 25.

```
         L       8,FWD1        Load fullword
         AH      8,=H'50'      Add halfword
         SH      8,=H'25'      Subtract halfword
         ...
FWD1     DC      F'125'
```

Add and Subtract Register (AR and SR)

The AR instruction adds the contents of a register to a register, and the SR instruction subtracts the contents of a register from a register. All 31 data bits of the operand 2 register are algebraically added to or subtracted from the contents of the operand 1 register.

In the next example, the statement DS 0D forces doubleword alignment so that the following two packed fields (both 8 bytes) are effectively doublewords. The two CVB instructions convert the packed values into binary format in registers

1 and 0. (These registers are available for temporary calculations.) AR adds the contents of register 1 to 0, and SR clears register 1 to zero. CVD then converts the binary contents of register 0 to packed format.

```
          CVB      1,DBPK1          Convert to binary
          CVB      0,DBPK2          Convert to binary
          AR       0,1              Add register
          SR       1,1              Subtract register
          CVD      0,DBPK1          Convert to packed
          ...
          DS       0D               Align doubleword
DBPK1     DC       PL8'250'         Packed
DBPK2     DC       PL8'075'         Packed
```

BINARY COMPARISON: C, CH, CR

The C, CH, and CR instructions are used to compare binary data. The operations algebraically compare the contents of operand 1 to operand 2 and set the condition code to equal, low, or high.

Name	Operation	Operand
[label]	C	R1,X2 *or* R1,D2(X2,B2)
[label]	CH	R1,X2 *or* R1,D2(X2,B2)
[label]	CR	R1,R2

You may test the condition code with conditional branches:

COMPARISON	CONDITION CODE	BRANCH
Operand 1 = operand 2	0 (equal/zero)	BE, BZ
Operand 1 < operand 2	1 (low/minus)	BL, BM
Operand 1 > operand 2	2 (high/plus)	BH, BP

Compare Fullword (C)

The C instruction compares the contents of operand 1 (a register) to operand 2 (a fullword in storage). The following example loads a fullword into register 6 and compares it to another fullword. The condition code is set to low.

```
          L        6,FWD1           Load fullword
          C        6,FWD2           Compare fullwords
          BL       ...              Branch if low
          ...
FWD1      DC       F'1250'
FWD2      DC       F'2575'
```

Compare Halfword (CH)

The CH instruction compares the contents of operand 1 (a register) to operand 2 (a halfword in storage). Before the compare, CH expands the halfword to a fullword by filling the sign bit through the 16 leftmost bit positions.

The following example loads a halfword into register 7 and compares it to another halfword. The condition code is set to high.

```
        LH      7,HWD1      Load halfword
        CH      7,HWD2      Compare halfwords
        BH      . . .       Branch if high
        . . .
HWD1    DC      F'365'
HWD2    DC      F'215'
```

Compare Register (CR)

The CR instruction compares the contents of operand 1 (a register) to operand 2 (a register). Both operands reference a register. In the following example, L instructions load fullwords into registers 8 and 9. CR compares registers 8 and 9 and sets the condition code to high.

```
        L       8,FWD3      Load fullword
        L       9,=F'975'   Load fullword
        CR      8,9         Compare registers
        BH      . . .       Branch if high
        . . .
FWD3    DC      F'1250'
```

EXAMPLE OF USE OF BINARY ARITHMETIC

The example in this section uses binary data to add the sum of digits from 1 to 10: $1 + 2 + 3 + \cdots + 10$. The routine uses three registers:

5:   The value 1 to act as an increment

6:   A counter that increments by 1 for each loop

7:   An accumulator for the sum of digits (The routine adds register 6, the counter, to this register.)

```
        LH      5,=H'1'     Set increment
        SR      6,6         Clear counter
        SR      7,7         Clear sum
LOOP    AR      6,5         Count: 1, 2, 3, 4, . . .
        AR      7,6         Sum: 1, 3, 6, 10, . . .
        CH      6,=H'10'    Looped 10 times?
        BNE     LOOP          No - continue
        . . .                 Yes - end
```

At the end, the sum in register 7 should be 55. If only two registers are available, the routine could add the literal =H'1' to register 6, as

```
        LOOP    AH      6,=H'1'
```

A more efficient technique uses LA with a displacement of 1:

```
        LOOP    LA      6,1(0,6)
```

Note that RR-format instructions such as AR execute faster than RX-format instructions such as AH that have to reference storage.

BINARY MULTIPLICATION: M, MH, MR

The binary instructions M, MH, and MR multiply fields in binary format. They do not set the condition code.

Name	Operation	Operand
[label]	M	R1,X2 *or* R1,D2(X2,B2)
[label]	MH	R1,X2 *or* R1,D2(X2,B2)
[label]	MR	R1,R2

The maximum value in a single register is $2^{31} - 1$, or 2,147,483,647. Certain binary operations require a pair of registers to express values that exceed this maximum. The registers are an even-odd numbered pair, such as 4 and 5 or 8 and 9, with the sign bit in the leftmost bit of the even register and the 63 data bits allowing values up to $2^{63} - 1$.

Both M and MR require an even-odd pair of registers. You load the multiplicand in the odd-numbered register. The multiply operation develops the product in the pair of registers, with one sign bit and 63 data bits.

	EVEN REGISTER	ODD REGISTER
Before execution:	(garbage)	multiplicand
After execution:	(product)	product

In many cases, only one register (the odd one) is sufficient to contain the product. In this case, the leftmost bit of the odd register contains the correct sign, that of the even register.

Multiply Fullword (M)

The M instruction multiplies the contents of a register by a fullword in storage. Operand 1 specifies the even register of an even-odd pair. The even register need not be initialized to zero because the operation ignores its contents. The odd register contains the multiplicand. Operand 2 references a fullword in storage containing the multiplier. The product is developed in the even-odd pair and erases the multiplicand.

In the following example, the even-odd pair is registers 4 and 5. An L instruction loads a fullword in register 5 (the multiplicand). M references register 4 (the even register) and multiplies the multiplicand in 5 by a fullword in storage. The product is generated in registers 4 and 5. In this case, register 4 will contain zeros and register 5 will contain X'00066660'.

```
             L      5,MULTCAND     Load multiplicand
             M      4,MULTPLER     Multiply by fullword
             . . .
MULTCAND     DC     F'3333'        Multiplicand
MULTPLER     DC     F'20'          Multiplier
```

Multiply Halfword (MH)

The MH instruction requires only one register. Operand 1 specifies any register, not necessarily an even one, and contains the multiplicand. Operand 2 references a halfword in storage containing the multiplier. The 32-bit product is developed in the operand 1 register and erases the multiplicand.

In the following example, an L instruction loads a fullword in register 7 (the multiplicand). MH multiplies the multiplicand in 7 by a halfword in storage. The product, generated in register 7, is X'00009999'.

```
             L      7,MULTCAND     Load multiplicand
             MH     7,MULTHALF     Multiply by halfword
             . . .
MULTCAND     DC     F'3333'        Multiplicand
MULTHALF     DC     H'3'           Multiplier
```

Multiply Register (MR)

The MR instruction multiplies the contents of one register by another register. Operand 1 specifies the even register of an even-odd pair. The even register need not be initialized to zero because the operation ignores its contents. The odd register contains the multiplicand. Operand 2 references a register containing the multiplier, which may be the even register. The product is developed in the even-odd pair and erases the multiplicand.

In the following example, the even-odd pair is registers 8 and 9. Two L instructions load fullwords in register 5 (the multiplier) and register 9 (the multiplicand). MR references register 8 (the even register) and multiplies the multiplicand in 9 by register 5. The product is generated in registers 8 and 9. In this case, register 8 will contain zeros and register 9 will contain X'00066660'.

```
                L         5,MULTPLER       Load multiplier
                L         9,MULTCAND       Load multiplicand
                MR        8,5              Multiply registers
                ...
MULTCAND        DC        F'3333'          Multiplicand
MULTPLER        DC        F'20'            Multiplier
```

You can also store the multiplier in the even register. In the next example, the multiplier is loaded in register 8 and the multiplicand in register 9. MR 8,8 here means multiply the contents of the multiplicand in odd register 9 by the multiplier in register 8. The product erases both multiplier and multiplicand.

```
        L         8,MULTPLER       Multiplier in even
        L         9,MULTCAND       Multiplicand in odd
        MR        8,8              Multiply registers
```

How about squaring a number that is in only one register? Both multiplicand and multiplier reference the same register. If both are in register 9, this MR should do the trick:

```
        MR        8,9       Square a number
```

Some additional programming may be involved when a product is so large that it requires both registers. This will be covered later in this chapter.

REGISTER SHIFT INSTRUCTIONS: SRA, SLA, SRDA, SLDA

You can shift binary data in a register left or right a specified number of bit positions. This feature is useful for clearing unwanted bit positions from a field and for multiplying or dividing a field by a power of 2, regardless of the sign.

The following operations shift the bit contents of registers other than the leftmost sign bit, which is unaffected. Bits shifted out of registers are lost, and the condition code is set.

Name	Operation	Operand
[label]	SRA	R1,S2 *or* R1,D2(B2)
[label]	SLA	R1,S2 *or* R1,D2(B2)
[label]	SRDA	R1,S2 *or* R1,D2(B2)
[label]	SLDA	R1,S2 *or* R1,D2(B2)

For each shift operation, if operand 2 contains 0, the instruction executes without shifting but does set the condition code. An example is SRA 5,0.

Shift Right Algebraic (SRA)

SRA performs a right algebraic shift. Operand 1 specifies a register whose 31-bit data contents are to shift to the right. Operand 2 indicates the number of bits to shift, usually a decimal number less than 32. Bits shifted off to the right are lost, and the sign bit replaces leftmost shifted bits. No overflow or program interrupt can occur.

SRA is useful for dividing the contents of a register by a power of 2. For example, shifting right one bit is equivalent to dividing by 2, shifting right two bits is equivalent to dividing by 4, and so forth. Consider the following 8-bit-register examples initially containing (a) 00001000 and (b) 11111111, and three unrelated shifts:

	(A) CONTENTS	(B) CONTENTS
Initial value	00001000 (8)	11111000 (-8)
Shift right 1	00000100 (4)	11111100 (-4)
Shift right 2	00000010 (2)	11111110 (-2)
Shift right 3	00000001 (1)	11111111 (-1)

The following example shifts the contents of register 9 two bits to the right. The operation is equivalent to dividing by 4.

```
         L      9,FULLWD1      Load fullword
         SRA    9,2            Shift 2 bits right
         ...
FULLWD1  DC     F'17191'
```

Shift Left Algebraic (SLA)

SLA performs a left algebraic shift. Operand 1 specifies a register whose 31-bit data contents are to shift to the left. The sign bit is unaffected. Operand 2 indicates the number of bits to shift, usually a decimal number less than 32. Bits shifted off to the left are lost, and zero bits replace rightmost shifted bits. A leftmost bit shifted out that is different from the sign bit may cause an overflow and interrupt.

SLA is useful for multiplying the contents of a register by a power of 2. Shifting left one bit is equivalent to multiplying by 2, shifting left two bits is equivalent to multiplying by 4, and so forth.

The following example shifts left the value 5 two bits; the result is 20.

```
         L      7,=F'5'        Load fullword: 00000101 (5)
         SLA    7,2            Shift left 2:   00010100 (20)
```

Shift Right Double Algebraic (SRDA)

SRDA performs a right algebraic shift of two registers as a single unit and is
commonly used with binary divide operations. Operand 1 specifies the even-
numbered register of an even-odd pair, and the sign bit in the even register is
treated as the sign for the pair. Operand 2 indicates the number of bits to shift,
usually a decimal number less than 64. Bits shifted off to the right are lost, and
the sign bit replaces leftmost shifted bits in both registers. No overflow or program
interrupt can occur.

In the following example, LM loads registers 6 and 7 with fullwords. SRDA
shifts the pair of registers 4 bits to the right.

```
                  LM        6,7,FULLWD1       Load 2 fullwords
                  SRDA      6,4               Shift 4 bits right
                  . . .
    FULLWD1       DC        F'319'            Fullwords
                  DC        F'17191'          *
```

Shift Left Double Algebraic (SLDA)

SLDA performs a left algebraic shift of two registers as a single unit. Operand 1
specifies the even-numbered register of an even-odd pair, and the sign bit in the
even register is treated as the sign for the pair. The sign bit is unaffected. Operand
2 indicates the number of bits to shift, usually a decimal number less than 64. Bits
shifted off to the left are lost, and zero bits replace rightmost shifted bits. A
leftmost bit shifted out that is different from the sign bit may cause an overflow
and interrupt.

In the following example, LM loads register 8 and 9 with fullwords. SLDA
shifts the pair of registers 18 bits to the left.

```
                  LM        8,9,FULLWD1       Load 2 fullwords
                  SLDA      8,18              Shift 18 bits left
                  . . .
    FULLWD1       DC        F'319'            Fullwords
                  DC        F'17191'          *
```

Varying the Shift Factor

If you want to vary the number of bits shifted throughout a program's execution,
you may use the base/displacement facility of operand 2: D(B). For example,
register 5 contains the value 12. The following instruction shifts right the contents
of register 9 according to the contents of register 5, that is, 12:

```
                  SRA       9,0(5)            Shift n bits right
```

Sum of the Digits by Formula

An earlier example added the sum of digits from 1 to 10. You can also calculate the sum using the formula

$$\text{Sum of digits} = \frac{n^2 + n}{2}$$

where n is any whole number. For example, if $n = 10$, the sum of the digits from 1 to 10 is

$$\frac{10^2 + 10}{2} = \frac{110}{2} = 55$$

Let's use binary multiplication and shift instructions to perform the calculation. The first instruction loads the value n, 10, in register 12:

```
                                                      reg-9
         LH     12,=H'10'      Load limit
         LR     9,12           Initialize n        10
         MR     8,12           Square n           100
         AR     9,12           Add n              110
         SRA    9,1            Divide by 2         55
         ST     9,SUMDIGIT     Store sum
         ...
SUMDIGIT DS     F
```

BINARY DIVISION: D AND DR

The binary instructions D and DR divide fields in binary format. Both operations require the use of a doubleword of 63 bits plus a sign in an even-odd pair of registers. They do not set the condition code. Unexpectedly, there is no DH instruction.

Name	Operation	Operand
[label]	D	R1,X2 *or* R1,D2(X2,B2)
[label]	DR	R1,R2

Operand 1 specifies the dividend in an even-odd pair of registers. Operand 2 references a fullword—in storage for D and in a register for DR. After execution, the remainder is in the even register and the quotient is in the odd register. Both contain 31 data bits and a leftmost sign bit. A quotient that exceeds 31 bits plus the sign causes an overflow and program interrupt.   Dividing by 0 is one way to cause this condition.

	EVEN REGISTER	ODD REGISTER
Before execution	dividend	dividend
After execution	remainder	quotient

The dividend in the even-odd pair of registers may have been loaded in by a program or generated by an M or MR operation.   If your program loads a fullword dividend into the odd register, be sure to initialize its sign into the even register.   You may use the following technique to force similar signs:

1. Load the dividend into the *even* register.
2. Use SRDA to shift the dividend 32 bits out of the even register into the odd register.   The even register is now cleared of garbage from any previous operation and is initialized with the correct sign.   If the sign is positive, the even register now contains zero bits; if the sign is negative, the even register now contains one bits.

Divide Fullword (D)

In the following D example, the even-odd pair of registers is 0 and 1.   L loads a fullword dividend into register 0, and SRDA shifts it into register 1, leaving register 0 correctly initialized.   D divides the doubleword pair by a fullword in storage.

```
              L       0,DIVD      Load dividend in register 0
              SRDA    0,32        Shift into register 1
              D       0,DIVSR     Divide
              . . .
      DIVD    DC      F'4569'     Dividend
      DIVSR   DC      F'14'       Divisor
```

Register 0 now contains the remainder, 5, and register 1 contains the quotient, 326.   This is a true remainder, not a decimal fraction.

Divide Register (DR)

In the following DR example, the even-odd pair of registers is 10 and 11.   The first L loads a fullword divisor into register 12.   The second L loads a fullword dividend into register 10, and SRDA shifts it into register 11, leaving register 10 correctly initialized.   DR divides the doubleword pair by register 12.

```
            L          12,DIVSR       Load divisor in register 12
            L          10,DIVD        Load dividend in register 10
            SRDA       10,32          Shift into register 11
            DR         10,12          Divide
            . . .
    DIVD    DC         F'4569'        Dividend
    DIVSR   DC         F'14'          Divisor
```

Register 10 now contains the remainder, 5, and register 11 contains the quotient, 326.

Scaling and Rounding

The computer performs arithmetic only on integers and in effect does not consider decimal-place precision.   To handle scaling, that is, to provide for the decimal point, you have to account mentally for the implied decimal point.   It simplifies programming to think of binary values as decimal values.

Figure 9-4 gives two examples that divide distance by gallons to calculate miles per gallon, with different precision.   Initially, both dividend and divisor are in packed format and are zapped into doublewords to facilitate conversion to binary format.

The first example, DIVID10, is a direct divide operation with no scaling for decimal point.   A CVB instruction converts gallons into binary in register 9, and a second CVB converts distance into binary in register 6.   Registers 6 and 7 are to contain the dividend, distance.   To initialize register 6 with the correct zero or one bit sign, an SRDA instruction shifts all 32 bits of distance from register 6 into register 7.   Since distance in this example is positive, register 6 now contains all zero bits.   A DR instruction next performs the division, and CVD converts the quotient to packed in main storage.

The second example, DIVID20, requires generating a two-decimal quotient after rounding.   Since both distance and gallons contain one decimal position (which cancel each other), the example has to generate three additional decimal positions.

To generate three decimal places, multiply by 1,000.   (Note that shift operations, such as SLA, multiply by powers of 2, not 10.)   LTR performs two functions.   First, it loads the quotient from register 7 into register 6; this action erases the unwanted remainder and sets up a second divide operation.   Second, LTR sets the condition code to be tested for rounding: if positive, add 5; if negative, subtract 5.   An SRDA instruction shifts the quotient from register 6 back into

```
36 DIVIDE     ZAP    DISTDW,DISTPK      REG CONTENTS AS DEC FORMAT:
37                   ZAP    GALSDW,GALSPK

39 *          DIVIDE, NO ROUNDING:
40 *          --------------------
41 DIVID10    CVB    9,GALSDW           9: 0000001500
42                   CVB    6,DISTDW    6: 0000023565
43                   SRDA   6,32        6: 0000000000   7: 0000023565
44                   DR     6,9         6: 0000001065   7: 0000000015
45                   CVD    7,ANSWPK    ANSWER = PACKED 15

47 *          DIVIDE & ROUND TO TWO DECIMALS :
48 *          --------------------------------
49 DIVID20    CVB    9,GALSDW           9: 0000001500
50                   CVB    6,DISTDW    6: 0000023565
51                   SRDA   6,32        6: 0000000000   7: 0000023565
52                   MH     7,=H'1000'  6: 0000000000   7: 0023565000
53                   DR     6,9         6: 0000000000   7: 0000015710
54                   LTR    6,7         LOAD QUOTIENT INTO REG-6,
55                   BM     DIVID22     *     TEST CONDITION CODE
56                   AH     6,=H'5'     6: 0000015715   7: 0000015710
57                   B      DIVID24
59 DIVID22    SH     6,=H'5'
60 DIVID24    SRDA   6,32               6: 0000000000   7: 0000015715
61                   D      6,=F'10'    6: 0000000005   7: 0000001571
62                   CVD    7,ANSWPK    ANSWER = PACKED 15.71
63 *          ...
64 DISTPK     DC     P'2356.5'
65 GALSPK     DC     P'150.0'
66 DISTDW     DS     D
67 GALSDW     DS     D
68 ANSWPK     DS     D
```

Figure 9-4   Binary division with decimal point scaling.

register 7, thereby initializing register 6 with the correct sign.   Finally, the division by 10 adjusts the quotient for the required number of decimal places.

LTR cleared the remainder from register 6 because of the subsequent division by 10.   If the remainder were left in the register, the second division would treat the contents of registers 6 and 7 as one large 63-bit value.

The contents of the registers and fullwords are in binary format.   However, coding in decimal format is a convenient way to express binary values.

PARTIAL SAMPLE PROGRAM: FINANCE CHARGE REBATES

For some types of loans, finance charges are precomputed; that is, the amount of interest for the term of the loan is predetermined and added to the amount of the loan.   For example, $500.00 is borrowed for a term of 6 months, with a precomputed finance charge of $30.00.   The sum of $530.00 is repayable in six equal installments of $88.33.   A borrower who repays the full amount of the balance remaining before the end of the term is entitled to a partial rebate on the precomputed finance charge. You can use the "sum of digits" formula to calculate the rebate:

$$R = \frac{(r^2 + r)/2}{(t^2 + t)/2} \times F = \frac{r^2 + r}{t^2 + t} \times F$$

where R = rebate, r = remaining term in months, t = original term in months, and F = precomputed finance charge.

Here's a sample calculation of a rebate, where $t = 6$, $r = 5$, and $F = \$30.00$:

$$\text{Rebate} = \frac{5^2 + 5}{6^2 + 6} \times 30.00 = \frac{30}{42} \times 30.00 = \$21.42$$

Figure 9-5 gives the program routine that calculates the rebate. The routine initially saves registers 5 through 9, uses them for temporary calculations, and restores them on exiting. The program also checks for a minimum finance charge of \$10.00, so that finance charge less rebate equals at least \$10.00. For example, \$30.00 − \$21.42 = \$8.58. Since \$8.58 is less than \$10.00, the rebate is \$30.00 − \$10.00 = \$20.00.

CONVERSION OF DOUBLE-PRECISION BINARY TO DECIMAL FORMAT

Binary multiplication may develop a product that exceeds the capacity of one register. The result is a double-precision, or two-register, product. Conversion of the product to decimal format involves some additional programming.

Consider a situation in which registers 4 and 5 contain only 4 bits and the following values. The sign is in the leftmost bit of register 4:

REGISTER 4   **REGISTER 5**

0011   0111

Individually, the registers contain the values 3 and 7, respectively. However, the decimal value in the pair of registers would be 32 + 16 + 0 + 4 + 2 + 1 = 55. A technique is required that converts the contents of the pair or registers to decimal format. The value 7 in register 5 is correct, but you have to adjust the value 3 in register 4:

Contents of register 4:	3
Multiply register 4 by 16:	× 16
Product:	48
Add contents of register 5:	+ 7
Correct decimal value:	55

```
 2 *                                      REG: DEC FORMAT:
 3 *          CALCULATE R SQUARED + R:
 4 CALCREB   STM    5,9,SAVEREGS
 5           L      9,REMGTERM          9: 05
 6           LR     7,9
 7           MR     6,9                 7: 25
 8           AR     7,9                 7: 30

10 *          MULTIPLY BY FINANCE CHARGE:
11           L      8,FINCHGE           8: 030.00
12           MR     6,8                 7: 900.00
13           M      6,=F'100'           7: 900.0000   SHIFT LEFT

15 *          CALCULATE T SQUARED + T:
16           L      9,ORIGTERM          9: 06
17           LR     5,9                 5: 06
18           MR     4,9                 5: 36
19           AR     5,9                 5: 42

21 *          DIVIDE TO CALCULATE REBATE:
22           DR     6,5                 7: 21.4285
23           AH     7,=H'50'            7: 21.4335   ROUND
24           SR     6,6                              CLEAR REMDR
25           D      6,=F'100'           7: 21.43     SHIFT RIGHT

27 *          CHECK FOR $10.00 MINIMUM CHARGE:
28           LR     9,8                 9: 30.00
29           SR     8,7                 8: 08.57
30           C      8,=F'1000'
31           BNL    B10NOTLO
32           S      9,=F'1000'          9: 20.00
33           LR     7,  9               7: 20.00

35 B10NOTLO  ST     7,  REBATE          7: 20.00
36           LM     5,9,SAVEREGS
37 *          ...

38 SAVEREGS  DS     5F                  REGISTER SAVEAREA
39 ORIGTERM  DC     F'06'
40 REMGTERM  DC     F'05'
41 FINCHGE   DC     F'03000'            030.00
42 REBATE    DS     F                   XXX.XX
```

Figure 9-5   Calculation of finance charge rebate.

You multiply register 4 by 16 because it is only 4 bits in size and its maximum value is 2^4, or 16.   You would multiply an 8-bit register by 2^8, or 128, and so forth.

Consider an example of a negative value, -59.   Its binary representation is 1100 0101.

	REGISTER 4	REGISTER 5
Binary value:	1100	0101

The leftmost bit of register 4 is the minus sign, a one bit.   Individually, the registers contain the values −4 and 7, respectively. The value 5 in register 5 is correct, but you have to adjust the value in register 4:

Contents of register 4:	− 4
Multiply register 4 by 16:	× 16
Product:	− 64
Add contents of register 5:	+ 5
Correct decimal value:	− 59

Once again, multiplying register 4 by 16 and adding register 5 gives the correct decimal value. However, a problem arises when the odd register contains a 1 in its leftmost bit, because CVD treats it as negative. Consider an example of a positive value, +40. Its binary representation is 0010 1000.

	REGISTER 4	REGISTER 5
Binary value:	0010	1000

Individually, the registers contain the values 2 and −8, respectively. Let's try the correction technique:

Contents of register 4:	2
Multiply register 4 by 16:	× 16
Product:	32
Add contents of register 5:	− 8
Incorrect decimal value:	24

This time the result, 24, is incorrect. You can use LTR to test the sign of the odd register. For a zero bit, the nonminus condition code is set, and you can convert the data as already described. For a one bit, the minus condition code is set, and you can perform the following procedure:

Contents of register 4:	2
Add 1:	+ 1
New contents of register 4:	3
Multiply register 4 by 16:	× 16
Product:	48
Add contents of register 5:	− 8
Correct decimal value:	40

```
16 *                                          REG-6 HEX  REG-7 HEX        DECIMAL
17 *                                          ---------  ---------        -------
18 E10DOUBL CVB      6,DATA1                   0001E240
19          CVB      7,DATA2                   0001E240  FF8907AB
20          MR       6,6                       FFFFFFF2  DEB1E0C0
21          LTR      7,7
22          BNM      E20
23          AH       6,=H'1'                   FFFFFFF3  DEB1E0C0

25 E20      CVD      6,PRODPK+8                PRODPK:                        013-
26          MP       PRODPK,CONSTANT           PRODPK:           55,834,574,848-
27          CVD      7,DBLWD                   DBLWD :              558,767,936-
28          AP       PRODPK,DBLWD              PRODPK:           56,393,342,784-
29 *        ...
30 DBLWD    DS       D
31 DATA1    DC       PL8'0123456'
32 DATA2    DC       PL8'-456789'
33 PRODPK   DC       PL16'0'
34 CONSTANT DC       P'4294967296'
```

Figure 9-6 Conversion of double-precision binary to packed.

The incorrect answer was 24 instead of 40, a difference of 16. But the addition of 1 to the even register was equivalent to incrementing the double-precision value by 2^4, or 16. The additional step of testing the even register for minus and adding 1 provides the correct answer in all cases.

Figure 9-6 gives the programming for this technique, in which a multiplication of binary values produces a double-precision product. CVB operations convert the packed fields DATA1 and DATA2 into binary format in registers 6 and 7. The MR operation generates a product that exceeds the capacity of register 7. Since register 7 appears to contain a negative value, an AH instruction adds 1 to register 6. A CVD instruction converts the contents of register 6 to decimal format into PRODPK. The constant used to multiply is no longer 24, but 2^{32}, or 4,294,967,296. A second CVD operation converts the contents of register 7 to decimal format in DBLWD, which is then added to PRODPK. The final result, $-56,393,342,784$, is correct.

MOVE LONG AND COMPARE LONG: MVCL AND CLCL

MVCL (Move Long) moves data areas that exceed 256 bytes; a major use is to clear large areas of storage. CLCL (Compare Long) compares data areas that exceed 256 bytes; a major use is to determine whether the contents of a record have been changed.

Name	Operation	Operand
[label]	MVCL	R1,R2
[label]	CLCL	R1,R2

Both MVCL and CLCL require the use of four registers. Operand 1 and operand 2 both reference the even-numbered register of an even-odd pair, for example 6 and 7 or 10 and 11:

```
         operand 1                      operand 2
   |address-1|  |length-1|        |address-2|  |pad length-2|
      even         odd               even           odd
```

Operand 1. The even register (bits 8–31) references the address of the receiving field for MVCL or the comparing field for CLCL. The odd register (bits 8–31) provides the length of this field.

Operand 2. The even register (bits 8–31) references the address of the sending field for MVCL or the compared field for CLCL. The odd register (bits 8–31) provides the length of this field, as well as an optional "padding" character (bits 0–7).

Since 24 bits are available for the operations, you may move or compare fields of virtually any length.

Move Long (MVCL)

Consider an MVCL instruction that is to move a 512-byte record using the register pairs 6 and 7 and 10 and 11:

```
          LA      6,RCVADR        Load address of receiving field
          L       7,=F'512'       Load length of receiving field
          LA      10,SNDADR       Load address of sending field
          L       11,=F'512'      Length of sending field (or LR 11,7)
          MVCL    6,10            Move sending to receiving
          ...
RCVADR    DS      CL512           Receiving field
SNDADR    DS      CL512           Sending field
```

MVCL moves from the address specified by register 10 to the address specified by register 6, from left to right. For each byte moved, the instruction deducts 1 from the length in registers 7 and 11 and adds 1 to the addresses in registers 6 and 10. For example, assume that the actual location of RCVADR is X'10000' and that the location of SNDADR is X'20000'. On completion of the move of 512 bytes (X'200'), the four registers contain

REGISTER	CONTENTS
6	10200
7	0
10	20200
11	0 (bits 8–31)

An additional feature is the use of the padding character if the receiving length is greater than that of the sending field. You may insert any character in bits 0–7 of the register with the length of the sending field. Typical padding characters are X'40' and X'00'. For example, if the receiving field is 512 bytes and the sending field is 500 bytes, MVCL fills the padding character in the rightmost 12 bytes of the receiving field.

MVCL does not permit overlapping of the receiving and sending fields; the two designated fields should be distinctly separate. If the fields do overlap, the operation sets condition code 3 (overflow), which you may test using BO.

You could use MVCL where field lengths are unknown at the time of assembly, one example being variable-length records.

Compare Long (CLCL)

Consider a CLCL instruction that is to compare two 512-byte records using the register pairs 4 and 5 and 8 and 9:

```
        LA      4,COMP1         Load address of comparing field
        L       5,=F'512'       Load length of comparing field
        LA      8,COMP2         Load address of compared field
        LR      9,5             Load length of compared field
        CLCL    4,8             Compare
        BNE     address         Branch if not equal
        ...
COMP1   DS      CL512           Comparing field
COMP2   DS      CL512           Compared field
```

CLCL compares logically from left to right beginning with the address in the two even registers. As long as the compared bytes are equal, the operation deducts 1 from the lengths in the two odd registers and adds 1 to the addresses in the two even registers. Unequal compared bytes cause the operation to terminate with the addresses of the unequal bytes in the even registers and the condition code appropriately set for high or low.

If the lengths of the compared fields are unequal, you may insert any padding character in bits 0–7 of the register with the length of operand 2 (in the example, register 9). Typical padding characters are X'40' and X'00'. The operation uses the padding character for the remaining rightmost bytes of the shorter field.

KEY POINTS

- Negative binary numbers are expressed in two's complement form: Reverse the bits of the positive value (a zero-bit becomes 1, and a one-bit becomes 0), and add 1. The same procedure converts negative values to positive values.

- An invalid overflow occurs when there is a carry into the sign position but none out or a carry out of the sign position but none in.
- The maximum and minimum binary values are 32,767 and −32,768 for half-word and 2,147,483,647 and −2,147,483,648 for fullword.
- CVB (Convert to Binary) converts packed decimal data from storage into binary format in a register. The packed data is contained in an 8-byte doubleword field. CVD (Convert to Decimal) converts binary data from a register into packed decimal format in a doubleword in storage.
- The L instruction loads a binary fullword value from main storage into a register. LH loads a binary halfword value from main storage into a register. LR loads the contents of the register referenced by operand 2 into the register referenced by operand 1. LM loads fullwords from main storage into a span of registers in one operation. LA is useful for loading base registers and for initializing an address in a register for table searching.

    For many operations, the selection of the correct instruction is vital. Consider the following load instructions that assemble with no error but on execution may produce unexpected results:

```
LR  7,4      Load into register 7 contents of register 4.
L   7,4      Load into register 7 contents of storage locations 4–7.
LH  7,4      Load into register 7 contents of storage locations 4 and 5.
LA  7,4      Load into register 7 the displacement value 4.
```

- The ST instruction stores the contents of a register into a fullword in storage. STH stores the rightmost 16 bits of a register into a halfword in storage. STM stores the contents of a span of registers into fullwords in storage.
- The A instruction adds a fullword in storage to a register, and S subtracts a fullword in storage from a register. AH adds a halfword in storage to a register, and SH subtracts a halfword in storage from a register. AR adds the contents of a register to a register, and SR subtracts the contents of a register from a register.
- C, CH, and CR algebraically compare the binary contents of operand 1 to operand 2 and set the condition code to equal, low, or high.
- For binary multiplication (M and MR), operand 1 designates an even register of an even-odd pair. The multiplicand is in the odd register, and the operation develops the product in the even-odd pair.
- SRA, SLA, SRDA, and SLDA shift the bit contents of registers other than the leftmost sign bit, which is unaffected. Bits shifted out of registers are lost, and the condition code is set.
- For binary division (D and DR), operand 1 designates an even register of an even-odd pair containing the dividend. The operation develops the remainder in the even register and the quotient in the odd register. Initialize the even register with the same sign as the odd register.

PROBLEMS

9-1. Express the following as 8-bit binary numbers:

(a)	7	(b)	8	(c)	9	(d)	8	(e)	−9
	+4		+5		−6		+(−5)		−8
	11		13		3		3		−17

9-2. Explain halfword, fullword, and doubleword alignment.

9-3. Given the following declaratives, explain concisely what each of the unrelated operations does.   Check also for coding errors.

```
FULLWD1  DC        F'285'
FULLWD2  DC        F'394
DOUBWD1  DS        D
```

(a) L 7,FULLWD1	(b) LR 6,4	(c) CVB 7,=P'370'
(d) LA 7,FULLWD1	(e) LA 11,5000	(f) LM 7,8,FULLWD1
(g) ZAP 7,=P'25'	(h) LH 9,=H'35'	(i) MVC FULLWD1,FULLWD2
(j) CVD 7,DOUBWD1	(k) ST 10,FULLWD2	(l) LH 9,FULLWD1

9-4. Use the same declaratives as in Problem 9-3 to explain the following unrelated instructions.   Check also for coding errors.

(a) SH 9,=H'7'	(b) S 9,FULLWD1	(c) SR 7,8
(d) CR 7,8	(e) C 8,FULLWD2	(f) S 9,=F'12'
(g) SH 9,FULLWD2	(h) M 9,FULLWD1	(i) MH 9,=H'21'
(j) MR 6,7	(k) SRA 7,8	(l) SLDA 6,7

9-5. Code the multiply instructions as indicated and show the results in hex representation.

```
FULL1    DC        F'73.5'
FULL2    DC        F'837.5'
FULL3    DC        F'69.75'
FULL4    DC        F'93.345'
```

(a) Multiply FULL1 by FULL2; round and shift to one decimal place.
(b) Multiply FULL2 by FULL3; round and shift to two decimal places.
(c) Multiply FULL2 by FULL4; round and shift to two decimal places.
(d) Multiply FULL3 by FULL4; round and shift to two decimal places.
(e) Code all additional instructions to convert the product in (d) to packed format.

9-6. Explain the effect of the following operations.   Parts (a), (b), and (c) are unrelated. FULLA is defined as DC F'285'.

(a) SR 6,6	(b) L 7,FULLA	(c) L 7,FULLA
L 7,=F'25'	SRA 7,2	SLA 7,3
MR 6,7	ST 7,FULLA	ST 7,FULLA

9-7. Given the following declaratives, explain what each of the unrelated operations does. Check also for coding errors. FULLWD1 is defined as DC F'285'.
(a) D   6,FULLWD1; (b) DR   6,7; (c) DR   6,6.

9-8. Code the divide instructions as indicated and show the results in hex.

```
FULLA      DC        F'018'
FULLB      DC        F'131.5'
FULLC      DC        F'612.54'
FULLD      DC        F'931.277'
```

(a) Divide FULLB by FULLA and round to one decimal place.
(b) Divide FULLC by FULLB and round to two decimal places.
(c) Divide FULLD by FULLA and round to one decimal place.
(d) Divide FULLD by FULLB and round to zero decimal places.
(e) Code all additional instructions to convert the quotient in (d) to packed format.

9-9. Two fields, BINAM and EXPON, are defined as DC H. BINAM contains a value to be raised to a power n, stored in EXPON. Compute $BINAM^n$ by performing repetitious multiplication of BINAM n times. Provide for a double-precision product and print the final result.

9-10. A program receives as input item number, quantity sold, and unit cost in the following record format:

COLUMN	DESCRIPTION
01–05	Item number
06–10	Quantity (xxxx.x)
11–16	Unit cost (xxxx.xx)

Read each record and convert item number, quantity, and unit cost to binary format. Check that each item number is successively higher than the previously processed item number. (But watch out for the first record.) Calculate value = quantity × unit cost, rounded. Accumulate total value and print it as a final total.

Organize the program into a main logic routine and subroutines containing related processing.

9-11. A program reads input records containing data for sales representatives:

COLUMN	DESCRIPTION
01–03	Sales rep number
04–23	Sales rep name
24–26	Commission rate (.xxx)
27–30	Quantity sold
31–36	Selling price (xxxx.xx)
37–42	Unit cost (xxxx.xx)

For each input record, calculate and print

Amount of sale $=$ quantity $\times$ selling price

Cost of sale $=$ quantity $\times$ unit cost

Gross profit $=$ amount of sale $-$ cost of sale (may be negative)

$$\% \text{ gross profit} = \frac{\text{gross profit}}{\text{cost of sale}} \text{ (rounded)}$$

Commission $=$ gross profit $\times$ commission rate (rounded)

Accumulate and print final totals for amount of sale, cost of sale, gross profit, and commission. Do all calculations in binary format.

PART IV

Special Applications

10

INPUT/OUTPUT MACROS

OBJECTIVE

To cover the requirements for using the file definition and imperative macros for sequential input and output.

Input/output on the 370-series computers is significantly complex, and for this reason its discussion has been delayed until now. This chapter covers the more important technical material for the simpler I/O devices, and Chapters 18, 19, and 20 cover I/O for disk and tape devices.

Early computers transmitted data directly between storage and external devices and accordingly read data directly into a storage area and wrote directly out of storage. Systems like those considerably delayed processing, especially when many devices were attached. I/O processing has been improved in three significant ways:

- The use of buffers at the software level
- Faster I/O devices

• Overlapping of CPU processing with data transmission (For example, while a print operation transmits data to the printer, the CPU continues executing instructions. This advantage is covered by the use of a hardware feature, channels.)

INPUT/OUTPUT CONTROL SYSTEM

A 370-series computer always executes in one of two states: The *supervisor state* executes the supervisor program, and the *problem state* executes a user's program. The supervisor handles the transition between jobs and all interrupts, which include program checks and machine checks and all input/output operations. A problem program cannot actually issue an I/O operation—these are privileged instructions that only the supervisor can execute. The PSW indication is in bit 15, in which 0 means the supervisor and 1 means the problem program is executing. A privileged instruction executes only when the system is in the supervisor state. For its input/ output requirements, a problem program has to perform an interrupt and transfer control to the supervisor.

For I/O operations, the supervisor uses the privileged instructions Start I/O, Test I/O, Halt I/O, and Test Channel. You can, though rarely, code I/O operations for the channel program by linking to the supervisor with SVC (supervisor call) and CCW (channel command word). This detailed level requires that you synchronize I/O operations with the program and provide for channel scheduling and interrupts. Rather than code at this level, you normally use a generalized input/ output control system, known as IOCS under DOS and data management services under OS. The two main forms of IOCS are physical IOCS (PIOCS) and logical IOCS (LIOCS).

Physical IOCS

The PIOCS level is still close to the actual machine operation, and coding is similar to that already discussed. You code the channel program using the macros EXCP (execute channel program), WAIT, and CCB (command control block). This level initiates execution of channel commands and handles I/O interrupts and channel scheduling, but you still have to synchronize I/O operations with your program. Chapter 21 provides more information on physical IOCS.

Logical IOCS

The LIOCS level uses the capabilities of physical IOCS but provides many more features. On input, LIOCS locates the required record and delivers it to the program as a logical record. On output, LIOCS delivers the logical record to the channel program. LIOCS handles end-of-file conditions and other functions not yet discussed, including:

- Switching (flip-flopping) between I/O areas (buffers) if more than one buffer is specified
- Blocking and deblocking disk and tape records
- Writing and checking disk and tape labels

To get a record using logical IOCS, simply define a file definition macro and code the usual GET and PUT macros (or READ and WRITE in special cases). IOCS saves you from coding the complex but repetitious input/output routines.

The rest of this chapter covers programming using logical IOCS. You have already used logical IOCS for OPEN, CLOSE, and GET operations. This chapter explains these and other macros in detail.

REGISTER USAGE

The operating system makes full use of the linkage registers 0, 1, 13, 14, and 15 for the following purposes:

0 and 1: Logical IOCS macros, supervisor macros, and other IBM macros use these registers to pass addresses.

13: Logical IOCS and other supervisor routines use register 13 to address an area used to save the contents of your registers and to restore them on return to your program.

14 and 15: Logical IOCS uses these registers for linkage. A GET or PUT automatically loads the address of the following instruction into register 14 to facilitate return from the I/O operation and automatically loads register 15 with the address of the actual I/O routine (and uses it when executing that routine as a base register). For debugging from a storage dump, you can check the contents of register 14 to see what was the last I/O operation that executed.

BUFFERS

Under an unbuffered input/output system, you would read a record, process it, then read another record:

Read-1	Process-1	Read-2	Process-2	Read-3	· · ·

time $\longrightarrow$

A system can achieve better efficiency by overlapping reading and writing with processing.   For example, the system can read a record, then while processing this record, read the next record into a buffer:

Read-1	Process-1	Process-2	Process-3	· · ·
	Read-2	Read-3	Read-4	· · ·

time $\longrightarrow$

As can be seen, reading and processing are overlapped.   The system reads input records into areas in your program called buffers or I/O areas.   You can extend this facility by increasing the number of buffers, up to 2 for DOS and 256 for OS. Similarly, writing can be overlapped with processing.   Under DOS, the programmer designates the buffer areas, but OS supplies them automatically.

The two types of input/output macros are *file definition macros* and *imperative macros*.

FILE DEFINITION MACROS

Up to now, program examples have used two special shortcut macros, DEFIN and DEFPR, to define files.   However, the proper input/output macros, DTF for DOS and DCB for OS, require more elaborate definitions.   A file definition macro may define, for example, the symbolic name of the file, the length of records, the buffers, and the actual device to be used.   Based on this definition, the assembler is able to construct a table of applicable channel commands.

The DOS DTF and OS DCB macros are keyword macros.   That is, you code entries with specific names, and you may code them in any sequence.   The keyword is followed by an equal sign (=) and a parameter, such as EOFADDR = A90END. The conventional coding is one entry per line, immediately followed by a comma to separate entries and a continuation character in column 72 to indicate that the macro continues on the next line, beginning in column 16.   The following partial DTF defines entries for a printer file:

Name	Operation	Operand	Continuation
filename	DTFPR	DEVADDR = SYSLST, DEVICE = 3203, . . .	+ +

You may also code several entries on a line, although this practice makes the listing more difficult to read and to change.   The entries may be in any sequence, and the last entry has no comma or continuation.

You may omit some entries; in these cases, the assembler assumes a default value. Since precise entries and defaults vary by version of the operating system, you may have to refer to your own installation's requirements.

File Definition for DOS

Under DOS, you use the DTFnn (define the file) macro to define a file. For example, DTFSD defines a sequential disk file, and DTFPR defines a printer file. Here is an outline of common entries for a DTF:

Name	Operation	Operand	Continuation
filename	DTFnn	BLKSIZE=size,	+
		DEVADDR=SYSnnn,	+
		DEVICE=device,	+
		EOFADDR=eofaddress,	+
		IOAREA1=buffer1,	+
		IOAREA2=buffer2,	+
		RECFORM=format,	+
		TYPEFLE=INPUT or OUTPUT,	+
		WORKA=YES or IOREG=(r)	

BLKSIZE gives the length of a block of data.

DEVADDR identifies the file's symbolic name. The primary system input device is SYSIPT or SYSRDR, depending on the system. The primary listing device is SYSLST. You may also designate a programmer logical unit, SYSnnn, for disk and tape devices.

DEVICE defines a particular I/O unit, such as a 3380 disk device.

EOFADDR provides the end-of-file address for input files that are to be read sequentially.

IOAREA1 is a required entry that specifies a unique name for the first or only buffer for the file. A directive defines this buffer elsewhere.

IOAREA2 is an optional entry that specifies a unique name for a second buffer for the file. A directive defines this buffer elsewhere.

RECFORM defines the format of the records, such as FIXUNB for fixed-length unblocked or FIXBLK for fixed-length blocked. Records on the system reader and printer are normally in this format, but disk and tape records may be variable in length and blocked with several records to a block. Omission of this entry causes the assembler to assume FIXUNB.

TYPEFLE (watch the spelling) indicates whether processing is INPUT or OUTPUT.

WORKA tells IOCS to process records in a workarea rather than directly in a buffer. IOCS is to transfer records from the buffers to the workarea, as specified by the GET macro, such as GET FILEIN,RECDIN. In this case, RECDIN is the workarea, defined elsewhere. You may omit the workarea entirely, but if so, you specify an alternate entry as IOREG = (r) and process the input records directly in the buffers.

Other entries are available, many of which are covered in Chapters 18, 19, and 20. The supervisor manual for each system gives more specific details.

File Definition for OS

Under OS, you use the DCB (data control block) macro to define a file. Because OS has considerable device independence capability, a common and recommended approach is to define all data sets as disk in order to facilitate this feature. Many entries required for a DOS DTF are omitted for DCBs. Under OS, you may specify additional I/O attributes at execute time by means of the DD (data definition) job control commands. This feature permits some programming changes related to I/O without a need for reassembling the program.

The assembler completes as much of the data control block as possible from the DCB entries. Prior to execution, the system checks for missing entries and accesses them, if possible, from the DD command. If some information is not provided, the system may make a default assumption, or if not possible, the program could crash when attempting an I/O operation.

Here is an outline of common entries for a DCB:

Name	Operation	Operand	Continuation
filename	DCB	BLKSIZE=size,	+
		DDNAME=symbolic-name	+
		DEVD=device,	+
		DSORG=organization,	+
		EODAD=eofaddress,	+
		MACRF=(nn)	

BLKSIZE gives the length of a block of data.

DDNAME identifies the file's symbolic name, such as SYSIN for the primary system input device and SYSPRINT for the primary listing device.

DEVD defines a particular I/O unit, such as DA for a data set that is "direct access," or disk.

DSORG identifies the data set organization; for example, PS means physical sequential, in which the data set is organized as sequential, rather than as, say, indexed sequential. This entry may appear only in a DCB macro and not in a DD job command.

EODAD provides the end-of-file address for input files that are to be read sequentially.

MACRF defines the type of input operation; for example, MACRF = (GM) means get and move to a workarea. (The coding is to be GET FILEIN,workarea.)

You may use DD job commands to provide other definitions at execute time, such as assigning the actual device to be used (disk, tape, printer, etc.). Also, you use DD commands to define the buffers rather than use entries in the DCB. Omission of a request causes OS to assume a default of two buffers.

IMPERATIVE MACROS: OPEN, CLOSE, GET, PUT

You have already been using the imperative macros OPEN, GET, and CLOSE for input/output. These macros, as well as PUT, relate to the generalized DTF or DCB channel commands and link to the supervisor to issue data transmission. Under OS, these macros are part of QSAM (queued sequential access method).

The OPEN Macro

OPEN makes a file available to a program. Control is passed to the supervisor, which checks that the file exists and that it is available. Note that the system does considerably more when opening disk and tape files. One OPEN statement may open up to 16 files.

Consider the following OPEN statements for DOS and for OS:

DOS coding for OPEN:

```
          OPEN FILEIN,PRINTER
          ...
FILEIN    DTFCD...    Define input file
PRINTER   DTFPR...    Define output file
```

OS coding for OPEN:

```
          OPEN (FILEIN,(INPUT),PRINTER,(OUTPUT))
          ...
FILEIN    DCB  ...    Define input file
PRINTER   DCB  ...    Define output file
```

The CLOSE Macro

CLOSE deactivates all previously opened files that you no longer require. (IOCS performs many additional features when closing a tape or disk file.) You may close a file at any time, and you should close all files before terminating program execution. Also, once you close a file, you may process it further only by reopening it. The coding for DOS and for OS differs:

> DOS: CLOSE FILEIN,PRINTER
> OS: CLOSE (FILEIN,,PRINTER)

In a multiprogramming system, be sure to close a file promptly once it is fully processed. The device and file are then available to other programs in the system.

The GET Macro

GET makes available the next record from a sequential input file. The input record erases the previous contents of the input area. Here are the general formats for GET:

Name	Operation	Operand
[label]	GET	filename,workarea
[label]	GET	filename
[label]	GET	(1),(0)

The filename is that of the DTF or DCB for the file. The system delivers the record to the workarea specified in operand 2. In the following example, the filename is FILEIN and the workarea is RECDIN:

```
          GET    FILEIN,RECDIN       Read a record into RECDIN
          ...
FILEIN    DTFCD or DCB ...           Define the input file
RECDIN    DS     CL80                Define the input area
```

Subject to your DTF or DCB definition, you may also code GET without specifying a workarea, as GET FILEIN. This practice is known as locate mode and is covered in a later section.

You may also load the DTF or DCB address and the workarea address into registers 1 and 0, as follows:

```
          LA     1,FILEIN            Load address of FILEIN
          LA     0,RECDIN            Load address of RECDIN
          GET    (1),(0)             Read a record into RECDIN
```

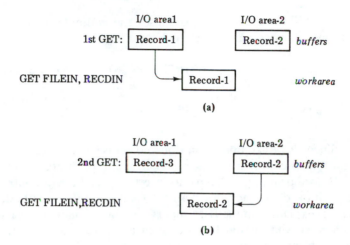

Figure 10-1   (a) Reading the first two records. (b) Reading the third record.

Figure 10-1(a) illustrates the relationship of the GET statement to two buffers. The first GET issued by the program reads record 1 into the first buffer, I/O area 1.   The system transfers record 1 from buffer 1 to RECDIN, where it is available for processing.   Then, while the program processes the record in RECDIN, the system reads record 2 into the second buffer, I/O area 2.

In Figure 10-1(b), the second GET issued by the program transfers record 2 from the buffer to RECDIN, and while the program processes the record in REC-DIN, the system reads record 3 into the first buffer.

Your DTF or DCB has to inform the system where to branch when it encounters the end-of-file.   If the file is from the system reader, the system reads the /* job command directly into a buffer.   When a GET attempts to transfer the /* to your workarea, the system instead automatically directs the program to the end-of-file address.

The PUT Macro

PUT writes a record from your output workarea.   The rules for coding PUT are similar to those for GET.   The general format for PUT is as follows:

Name	Operation	Operand
[label]	PUT	filename,workarea
[label]	PUT	filename
[label]	PUT	(1),(0)

The following PUT macro causes the contents of the workarea PRINT to write onto a device named PRINTER:

```
        PUT       PRINTER,PRINT        Write a record
        ...
PRINTER DTFPR or DCB ...               Define the print file
PRINT   DC        CL133' '             Define print workarea
```

Since the PUT operation does not erase the contents of the workarea and the buffers, a common practice is to clear the print area after writing.

Before printing, you have to insert a special forms control character into the first position of the print workarea. (An alternative method, using the CNTRL macro, is explained in the IBM supervisor macro manuals.) The character informs the channel what action to take, such as print, space, or eject. These are the common forms control characters:

X'0B'	Space 1 line, no write
X'13'	Space 2 lines, no write
X'1B'	Space 3 lines, no write
X'8B'	Skip to new page, no write
X'09'	Write, space 1 line
X'11'	Write, space 2 lines
X'19'	Write, space 3 lines
X'89'	Write, skip to new page

The first four control characters in the list space or eject without printing, regardless of the contents of the print area.

The following example writes and spaces two lines:

```
        MVI       CTLPR,X'11'          Insert control character
        PUT       PRINTER,PRINT        Print & space 2 lines
        ...
PRINT   DS        0CL133               Print area:
CTLPR   DS        XL1                  * control character
        DC        CL132' '             * rest of print area
```

The ASA Control Character

An alternative forms control character set that is more universal for different computers is the American Standards Association (ASA) set, which is less efficient on the 370 series. To request this format, code CTLCHR = ASA in the DTFPR. These are common characters:

blank	Space 1 line, then print
0	Space 2 lines, then print
–	Space 3 lines, then print
+	Print without spacing
1	Skip to the next page, then print

Note that execution involves spacing before printing, whereas the IBM code spaces after printing. As an example, the following instructions initialize an ASA control character for spacing two lines before printing:

```
MVI    CTLPR,C'0'      Insert control character
PUT    PRTR,PRINT      Space 2 and print
```

In order to space without printing, clear the print area to blanks; the PUT operation then "prints" a blank line.

SAMPLE PROGRAMS

Figures 10-2 and 10-3 illustrate the same program, using DOS and OS file definition and imperative macros, respectively. The programs simply read and print input records. For initialization, they load register 3 as the base register and open the files.

At P10PAGE the program skips to a new page to print a heading. Note that CTLCHAR is defined as the first position of the print line. In the loop routine B10LOOP, a record is read into RECDIN, which is then moved to the print area and printed. The line counter is incremented and checked for page overflow, as was done in previous programs.

When all the input records have been read and processed, IOCS recognizes the end-of-file (a /* trailer record under DOS) and directs the program to the end-of-file address, A90END, where the files are closed and execution terminates.

The DOS Program

The program in Fig. 10-2 provides the requirements for IOCS under DOS. The file definition macros are DTFCD for the system reader and DTFPR for the printer.

DTFCD: Define the card file. DTFCD is suitable for defining an input file on the system reader, which may be a terminal under CMS. The name of the file

```
  2                PRINT ON,NOGEN,NODATA
  3  ***              I N I T I A L I Z A T I O N
  4  PROG10  START
  5          BALR  3,0                    INITIALIZE BASE REGISTER
  6          USING *,3
  7          OPEN  FILEIN,PRINTER         ACTIVATE FILES
 16          GET   FILEIN,RECDIN          READ 1ST RECORD
 22          BAL   8,P10PAGE             HEADING ROUTINE
 23  A10LOOP BAL   7,B10PROC             MAIN PROCESSING
 24          GET   FILEIN,RECDIN          READ NEXT
 30          B     A10LOOP               LOOP

 32  A90EOF  CLOSE FILEIN,PRINTER        DE-ACTIVATE FILES
 41          EOJ

 45  ***            M A I N   P R O C E S S I N G
 46  B10PROC CP    LINECT,=P'50'         END OF PAGE?
 47          BNH   A20
 48          BAL   8,P10PAGE             PAGE HEADING
 49  A20     MVC   RECDPR,RECDIN         MOVE RECORD TO PRINT AREA
 50          MVI   CTLCHAR,X'09'
 51          PUT   PRINTER,PRINT         PRINT, SPACE 1 LINE
 57          AP    LINECT,=P'1'          ADD TO LINE COUNT
 58          BR    7                     RETURN

 60  ***            P A G E   O V E R F L O W
 61  P10PAGE MVI   CTLCHAR,X'8B'
 62          PUT   PRINTER,PRINT         SKIP TO NEW PAGE
 68          ZAP   LINECT,=P'0'          CLEAR LINE COUNT
 69          BR    8                     RETURN

 71  ***            D E C L A R A T I V E S
```

```
 73 FILEIN    DTFCD BLKSIZE=80,           DEFINE INPUT FILE        +
                    DEVADDR=SYSIPT,                                +
                    DEVICE=2540,                                   +
                    EOFADDR=A90EOF,       EOF ADDRESS              +
                    IOAREA1=IOARIN1,                               +
                    IOAREA2=IOARIN2,                               +
                    RECFORM=FIXUNB,                                +
                    TYPEFLE=INPUT,                                 +
                    WORKA=YES
 98 IOARIN1   DC    CL80' '              INPUT BUFFER 1
 99 IOARIN2   DC    CL80' '              INPUT BUFFER 2
```

```
101 RECDIN    DS    CL80                INPUT WORKAREA
```

```
103 PRINTER   DTFPR BLKSIZE=133,          DEFINE PRINTER FILE      +
                    CTLCHR=YES,                                    +
                    DEVADDR=SYSLST,                                +
                    DEVICE=3203,                                   +
                    IOAREA1=IOARPR1,                               +
                    IOAREA2=IOARPR2,                               +
                    RECFORM=FIXUNB,                                +
                    WORKA=YES
130 IOARPR1   DC    CL133' '            PRINT BUFFER 1
131 IOARPR2   DC    CL133' '            PRINT BUFFER 2
```

Figure 10-2   Program: full input/output under DOS.

```
133 PRINT     DS      0CL133              PRINT AREA :
134 CTLCHAR   DS      XL01                *    CONTROL CHAR POSITION
135           DC      CL19' '             *
136 RECDPR    DS      CL80                *      RECORD PRINT AREA
137           DC      CL33' '             *

139 LINECT    DC      PL2'0'              LINE COUNTER

141           LTORG
142                   =C'$$BOPEN '
143                   =C'$$BCLOSE'
144                   =A(FILEIN)
145                   =A(RECDIN)
146                   =A(PRINTER)
147                   =A(PRINT)
148                   =P'50'
149                   =P'1'
150                   =P'0'
151           END     PROG10
```

Figure 10-2   (*continued*)

in Fig. 10-2 is FILEIN, although any other unique name may be given. An explanation of the entries follows:

> **BLKSIZE = 80** tells IOCS that the size of each input data block is 80 characters.
>
> **DEVADDR = SYSIPT** identifies the primary system input device.
>
> **DEVICE = 2540** provides the model number of the reader device.
>
> **EOFADDR = A90END** provides the end-of-file address for IOCS.
>
> **IOAREA1 = IOARIN1** specifies the unique name of the first input buffer. A directive defines the buffer as IOARIN1 DC CL80.
>
> **IOAREA2 = IOARIN2** specifies the name of the optional second input buffer. A directive defines the buffer as IOARIN2 DC CL80.
>
> **RECFORM = FIXUNB** means that the record format is fixed-length and unblocked.
>
> **TYPEFLE = INPUT** identifies the file as input.
>
> **WORKA = YES** tells IOCS to deliver records to a workarea; that is, the GET macro is to be of the form GET file,workarea.

> **DTFPR: Define the printer file.**   DTFPR defines a file for the printer. The name of the file in Fig. 10-2 is PRINTER, although any other unique name may be given. Here is an explanation of the entries:

> **BLKSIZE = 133** tells IOCS that the size of each output data block is 133 characters, of which the first is reserved for the forms control character. The maximum block length depends on the particular printer device.
>
> **CTLCHR = YES** means that the program uses the standard 370-series forms

control character set.   Alternatively, coding CTLCHAR = ASA stipulates the ASA character set, but watch out—ASA codes differ from IBM codes.

DEVADDR = SYSLST identifies the primary system printing device.

DEVICE = 3203 provides the model number of the printer device.

IOAREA1 = IOARPR1 specifies the unique name of the first print buffer.   A directive defines the buffer as IOARPR1 DC CL80.

IOAREA2 = IOARPR2 specifies the name of the optional second print buffer. A directive defines the buffer as IOARPR2 DC CL80.

RECFORM = FIXUNB means that the record format is fixed-length and unblocked.

TYPEFLE = INPUT identifies the file as input.

WORKA = YES tells IOCS to accept records from a workarea; that is, the PUT macro is to be of the form PUT file,workarea.

The OS Program

The program in Fig. 10-3 provides the requirements for input/output under OS. The file definition macro is DCB for any type of device.   Some of the DCB entries may appear in DD job control commands.

DCB for the input file.   The name of the input file in Fig. 10-3 is FILEIN, although any other unique name may be given.   Here is an explanation of the entries:

BLKSIZE = 80 gives the length of a block of data.

DDNAME = SYSIN identifies the file's symbolic name for the primary system input device.

DEVD = DA means that the records may be spooled onto a direct access device for input.

DSORG = PS identifies the data set organization as physical sequential.

EODAD = A90EOF provides the end-of-file address for the input file.   Data management directs the program to this address on encountering the end-of-file.

MACRF = (GM) defines the type of input operation as get and move to a workarea.   (The coding is to be GET FILEIN,INAREA.)

DCB for the printer file.   The name of the printer file in Fig. 10-3 is FILEOT, although any other unique name may be given.   Here is an explanation of the entries:

BLKSIZE, DEVD, and **DSORG** are similar to the definitions for the input data set.

```
PROG10B  START  0
         SAVE   (14,12)                     Save regs for supervisor

         BALR   3,0                         Initialize base register
         USING  *,3

         ST     13,SAVEAREA+4               Save addresses for return
         LA     13,SAVEAREA                 *    to supervisor

         OPEN   (FILEIN,(INPUT),FILEOT,(OUTPUT))
         BAL    6,P10PAGE                   Page heading
         GET    FILEIN,INAREA               Read 1st record

***            M A I N   P R O C E S S I N G

A10LOOP  CP     LINECT,=P'50'               End of page?
         BNH    A20                         No - bypass
         BAL    6,P10PAGE
A20      MVC    RECPR,INAREA                Move record to print area
         MVI    CTLCHPR,X'09'               Move control character
         PUT    FILEOT,PRINT                Print, space 1 line
         AP     LINECT,=P'1'                Add to line count
         GET    FILEIN,INAREA               Read next
         B      A10LOOP                     Loop

***            E N D - O F - F I L E

A90EOF   CLOSE  (FILEIN,,FILEOT)
         L      13,SAVEAREA+4               End-of-job, return
         RETURN (14,12)                     *    to supervisor

***            P A G E   O V E R F L O W

P10PAGE  MVI    CTLCHPR,X'8B'               Forms control character
         PUT    FILEOT,PRINT                Skip to new page
         ZAP    LINECT,=P'0'                Clear line count
         BR     6

***            D E C L A R A T I V E S
```

```
FILEIN   DCB    BLKSIZE=80,                 Define input file          +
                DDNAME=SYSIN,                                          +
                DEVD=DA,                                               +
                DSORG=PS,                                              +
                EODAD=A90EOF,                                          +
                MACRF=(GM)
INAREA   DS     CL80                        Input workarea
```

```
FILEOT   DCB    BLKSIZE=133,                Define output file         +
                DDNAME=SYSPRINT,                                       +
                DEVD=DA,                                               +
                DSORG=PS,                                              +
                MACRF=(PM),                                            +
                RECFM=FM
```

```
PRINT    DS     0CL133                      Print area:
CTLCHPR  DS     XL01                        *    control character
         DC     CL19' '                     *
RECPR    DS     CL80                        *    record print area
         DC     CL33' '                     *

SAVEAREA DS     18F                         Register save area
LINECT   DC     PL2'0'                      Line counter
         LTORG
         END    PROG10B
```

Figure 10-3   Program: full input/output under OS.

DDNAME = SYSPRINT identifies the file's symbolic name for the primary system printing device.

MACRF = (PM) defines the type of output operation as put and move from a workarea. (The coding is to be PUT FILEOT,PRINT.)

RECFM = FM tells the system that the file is fixed (F) unblocked and machine (M) code, the format for the normal print control characters. The requirements for other installations may differ from this example. Some systems block print records onto disk prior to printing, and the entry may be FBM or FBSM.

INPUT/OUTPUT MODULES

For each file, the linkage editor includes an input/output logic module immediately following the program. A macro such as PUT PRINTER,PRINT links to the file definition macro, which in turn links to the printer logic module. In the following illustration, the two modules are DTFCD and DTFPR.

Program
DTFCD module
DTFPR module

The input/output modules are preassembled and cataloged in disk libraries, and the linkage editor includes the appropriate modules with all programs that require input/output.

You can determine the size and location of these modules from the linkage editor map. Chapter 21 provides an example map and the names of the input/output logic modules.

LOCATE MODE

You may process records in workareas or directly in the buffers. This latter method is known as *locate mode*. The (rather minor) advantage of processing in buffers is that you need not define a workarea. You code GET and PUT without specifying a workarea, as

```
GET   FILEIN
PUT   FILEOT
```

The DTF and DCB requirements differ. For the DTF, the entry IOREG = (reg) replaces WORKA and indicates an available register. IOCS is to load the register with the address of the buffer that contains the current record to be processed,

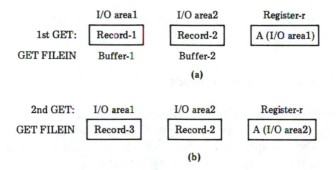

Figure 10-4 (a) First GET for locate mode. (b) Second GET for locate mode.

and you use that register to address the buffer. The DCB entry to denote locate mode is MACRF = (GL) for input and MACRF = (PL) for output. The system uses register 1 for the address of the buffer that contains the current record to be processed.

The example in Figure 10-4(a) shows the first GET executed. The system reads record 1 into buffer 1 and loads the address of buffer 1 into register r (register r here means the specified register for the DTF or register 1 for the DCB). Then, while the program processes the record in buffer 1, the system reads record 2 into buffer 2.

Figure 10-4(b) shows the second GET executed. The system loads the address of buffer 2 (which contains record 2) into register r. Then, while the program processes record 2, the system reads record 3 into buffer 1.

Processing continues flip-flopping between the two buffers (or more under OS). After execution of a GET, the register contains the address of the first byte of the current input record. For your purposes, the simplest action is to move the contents of the buffer to a workarea for processing. You can use the address in the register explicitly in an MVC operation immediately following the GET. The symbolic form of MVC is

```
MVC D1(L,B1),D2(B2)
```

You can use explicit addressing of the base/displacement in either operand. Since register r contains the address of the buffer, you can code the following:

```
GET    FILEIN          Read record, load register with buffer address
MVC    INAREA,0(r)     Move buffer to workarea
```

The MVC instruction works in this manner: Using the address in register r (base register r, no displacement), move from the referenced buffer to INAREA. Given that INAREA is an ordinary defined area of 80 bytes, this would be an 80-byte move.

The GET operation is similar for DOS and for OS, although OS requires the use of register 1 only. The PUT macros and file definitions for the two systems differ, however.

DOS Coding for Locate Mode

The following examples for DOS compare the conventional use of a workarea with the requirements to process in a buffer (locate mode). For input using locate mode, the example arbitrarily selects register 4 for the input register, and IOREG replaces the WORKA entry. Any available register will work, but be sure not to assign the program's base register.

```
USING A WORKAREA              USING LOCATE MODE
GET    FILEIN,RECDIN          GET    FILEIN
...                           MVC    RECDIN,0(4)
DTFCD                         ...
       WORKA=YES              DTFCD
                                     IOREG=(4)
```

For printing, the OPEN macro establishes in register 5 (in this case) the address of the first available print buffer. Before the PUT, move the contents of the print area to the buffer. Operand 1 of the MVC, coded as 0(133,5) uses a displacement of 0, a length of 133, and register 5 explicitly to move the contents of PRINT to the designated buffer. The PUT statement then initializes register 5 with the address of the next available buffer.

```
USING A WORKAREA              USING LOCATE MODE
PUT    PRTR,PRINT             MVC    0(133,5),PRINT
...                           PUT    PRTR
DTFPR                         ...
       WORKA=YES              DTFPR
                                     IOREG=(5)
```

OS Coding for Locate Mode

The following examples for OS compare the conventional use of a workarea with the requirements to process in a buffer (locate mode). The DCB entry for locate mode for an input data set is MACRF=(GL) (Get Locate).

```
USING A WORKAREA              USING LOCATE MODE
GET    FILEIN,RECDIN          GET    FILEIN
...                           MVC    RECDIN,0(1)
DCB                           ...
       MACRF=(GM)             DCB
                                     MACRF=(GL)
```

The DCB entry for locate mode for an output data set is MACRF = (PL) (Put Locate). PUT inserts into register 1 the address of the first byte of the buffer that is to receive the next output record. You code PUT to locate the output buffer, and then you can use register 1 explicitly to move data into the buffer. But note that under OS, unlike DOS, you code the PUT macro before the MVC.

```
USING A WORKAREA            USING LOCATE MODE
PUT     PRTR,PRINT          PUT     PRTR
...                         MVC     0(133,1),PRINT
DCB                         ...
    MACRF = (PM)            DCB
                                MACRF = (PL)
```

If you use standard workareas, the system performs these functions automatically. Locate mode involves extensive use of explicit base and displacements, a topic covered in detail in Chapter 11. The discussion of DSECT in Chapter 13 provides a sophisticated method of processing within a buffer and giving names to the various fields in that area. Meanwhile, feel free to continue using workareas, which is the common approach for handling input/output.

ABNORMAL TERMINATION

Both DOS and OS provide macros that you may use for abnormal termination when a program encounters a serious error condition. Both produce a hexadecimal dump of the registers and program storage area.

The DOS DUMP Macro

Under DOS, DUMP terminates program execution and produces a storage dump.

Name	Operation	Operand
[label]	DUMP	[ignored, use for comments]

As a rule, PDUMP is more convenient when testing a program because it continues processing. The CANCEL macro also terminates processing and flushes all remaining input records through to the /& job end command. If you precede program execution with a // OPTION DUMP (or PARTDUMP) job command, the supervisor automatically produces a storage dump after the CANCEL.

The OS ABEND Macro

To provide for a serious error condition under OS where you want an abnormal end for execution, code the ABEND macro.

Name	Operation	Operand
[label]	ABEND	completion code,DUMP

The operand includes a *completion code,* which is any decimal value up to 4,095, as ABEND 25,DUMP.   If the program contains a number of ABENDs, the completion code identifies which one caused the termination.   The DUMP operand invokes the ABDUMP (abnormal dump) macro, which prints a hexadecimal dump of the registers and relevant parts of main storage.

TERMINAL I/O

Under DOS, DTFCN (define console) provides the file definition for a terminal with keyboard input and either screen or printer output.   For input/output, you can define the usual GET and PUT macros.   Another macro, PUTR (PUT with Reply) allows a program to display a message that stays on the screen until the operator replies.   PUTR is useful for prompting a user to enter data and requires DTFCN entries DEVADDR = SYSLOG, INPSIZE = len, and TYPE-FLE = CMBND.

The following provide parameters for DTFCN:

DEVADDR	Code SYSLOG (normally) or SYSnnn.
BLKSIZE	The length of the I/O area.
INPSIZE	The length of the input part of the I/O area for the PUTR macro.
IOAREA1	The name of the buffer. For PUTR, the first part is reserved for the output message and the second part for the input reply.
RECFORM	The entry is FIXUNB or UNDEF (undefined).
RECSIZE	Use this parameter if RECFORM = UNDEF. For output, set the length in any register 2-12, and code this entry as (reg). For input, IOCS loads the actual length into the specified register.
TYPEFLE	INPUT allows both input and output; OUTPUT allows output only; use CMBND for the PUTR macro.
WORKA	Code WORKA = YES if GET or PUT designates a work-area.

Other DOS file definition macros include these:

DTFDR	3886 optical character reader
DTFDU	Diskette
DTFMR	Magnetic ink character reader
DTFOR	Optical scan reader

KEY POINTS

- For its input/output requirements, a problem program has to perform an interrupt and transfer control to the supervisor.
- The two main forms of IOCS are physical IOCS (PIOCS) and logical IOCS (LIOCS).
- The PIOCS level initiates execution of channel commands and handles I/O interrupts and channel scheduling, but you still have to synchronize I/O operations with your program.
- The LIOCS level uses the capabilities of physical IOCS but provides many more features. On input, LIOCS locates the required record and delivers it to the program as a logical record. On output, LIOCS delivers the logical record to the channel program. LIOCS handles end-of-file conditions and other functions not yet discussed, including flip-flopping between buffers, blocking and deblocking disk and tape records, and writing and checking disk and tape labels.
- Logical IOCS macros, supervisor macros, and other IBM macros use registers 0 and 1 to pass addresses. Logical IOCS and other supervisor routines use register 13 to address an area used to save the contents of your registers and to restore them on return to your program. Logical IOCS uses registers 14 and 15 for linkage.
- The use of buffers can help a system achieve better efficiency by overlapping reading and writing with processing.
- The two types of input/output macros are file definition macros and imperative macros.
- The file definition macros, DTF for DOS and DCB for OS, may define, for example, the symbolic name of the file, the length of records, the buffers, and the actual device to be used.
- The imperative macros OPEN, GET, PUT, and CLOSE relate to the generalized DTF or DCB channel commands and link to the supervisor to issue data transmission.
- OPEN makes a file available to a program. Control is passed to the supervisor, which checks that the file exists and that it is available.

- CLOSE deactivates all previously opened files that you no longer require.
- Since the PUT operation does not erase the contents of the workarea and the buffers, a common practice is to clear the print area after writing.
- Before printing, you insert a special forms control character into the first position of the print workarea. The character informs the channel what action to take, such as print, space, or eject.
- For each file, the linkage editor includes an input/output logic module immediately following the program.
- You may process records in workareas or directly in the buffers. This latter method is known as locate mode. You code GET and PUT without specifying a workarea, as GET FILEIN and PUT FILEOT.

PROBLEMS

10-1. Distinguish between supervisor and problem state.

10-2. What is a privileged instruction?

10-3. What advantage do buffers provide?

10-4. What is a file definition macro and an imperative macro for input/output?

10-5. Provide the file definition macro for an input device named READER, an end-of-file address X90END, a 2540 device, and a workarea. If you use DOS, define also two buffers.

10-6. What is the purpose of (a) OPEN; (b) CLOSE?

10-7. Provide the file definition macro for a printer named PRTR, a 3203 device, and a workarea of 133 bytes. If you use DOS, define also two buffers.

10-8. Code the MVI and the PUT statements to print and space three lines, using a file named PRTR and a workarea named PRINT.

10-9. Redefine the file in Problem 10-5 for locate mode and also provide the GET macro.

10-10. Redefine the file in Problem 10-7 for locate mode and provide also the PUT and MVI for print and space two lines.

10-11. Recode any previous program using full IOCS, and replace any special macros such as PUTPR, DEFCD, and DEFPR.

11

EXPLICIT USE
OF BASE REGISTERS

OBJECTIVE

To cover applications such as table handling that involve the explicit use of base registers in instructions.

A number of instructions to this point contain an explicit length reference that overrides an implicit length. In the following example, the explicit length of 2 overrides the defined implicit length of PRINT, which is 133:

```
              MVC     PRINT+30(2),=C'**'
              . . .
    PRINT     DC      CL133' '
```

In a similar manner, you may explicitly use a base register to override an implicit (assigned) base register. You may use a base register explicitly in any operand that references storage, with a reference to a base register, as B1 or B2. The instruction formats for explicit base addressing are shown in Fig. 11-1.

Format	Explicit operands	Object code format					
		1	2	3	4	5	6
RR	R1,R2	op	R1R2				
RX	R1,R3,D2(B2)	op	R1R3	B2D2	D2D2		
RS	R1,D2(X2,B2)	op	R1X2	B2D2	D2D2		
SI	D1(B1),I2	op	I	B1D1	D1D1		
SS(1)	D1(L,B1),D2(B2)	op	L1L1	B1D1	D1D1	B2D2	D2D2
SS(2)	D1(L1,B1),D2(L2,B2)	op	L1L2	B1D1	D1D1	B2D2	D2D2
	Byte						

B = base register   R = register
D = displacement   S = storage
I = immediate   X = index register
L = length

Figure 11-1 Instruction Formats.

Since a base register contains the address of an area of storage, you may override the program's normal base register with another register that contains the address of another area in storage. This chapter uses base registers explicitly to facilitate such operations as EDMK and COMRG and to modify addresses for searching through tables.

EXPLICIT BASE ADDRESSING FOR CHARACTER INSTRUCTIONS

Figure 11-2 shows three different ways to move a field named ASTERS to the print area. The figure depicts the explicit use of register 8 to override the implicit base register 4. Assume that the BALR instruction has initialized register 4 with X'8002'. Although this example uses MVC to illustrate explicit base addressing, you may use this feature with any instruction that references main storage. ASSGN1 in Fig. 11-2 illustrates a conventional move operation, with both operands implicitly subject to base register 4:

```
        MVC     PRINT+60(2),ASTERS
```

The assembled object code for operand 1 (PRINT + 60) is 4056, or base register 4, displacement X'056'. The effective address of operand 1 is therefore X'8058':

Contents of base register 4:	X'8002'
Displacement:	+ X'0056'
Effective address:	X'8058'

```
LOC   OBJECT CODE      ADDR1 ADDR2   STMT    SOURCE STATEMENT
008000                                  3 PROG11     START X'8000'
008000 0540                             4            BALR  4,0
                              08002     5            USING *,4

                                        7 *          IMPLICIT BASE REGISTER:
                                        8 *          ----------------------
008002 D201 4056 409F 08058 080A1       9 ASSGN1     MVC   PRINT+60(2),ASTERS

                                       11 *          EXPLICIT BASE REGISTER:
                                       12 *          ----------------------
008008 4180 4056            08058      13 ASSGN2     LA    8,PRINT+60
00800C D201 8000 409F 00000 080A1      14            MVC   0(2,8),ASTERS

                                       16 *          EXPLICIT BASE/DISPL'T:
                                       17 *          ----------------------
008012 4180 401A            0801C      18 ASSGN3     LA    8,PRINT
008016 D201 803C 409F 0003C 080A1      19            MVC   60(2,8),ASTERS
                                       20 *          .
                                       21 *          .
                                       22 *          .
00801C 4040404040404040               23 PRINT      DC    CL133' '
0080A1 5C5C                           24 ASTERS     DC    C'**'
                              08000    26            END   PROG11
```

Figure 11-2 Explicit use of base registers.

ASSGN2 in Fig. 11-2 illustrates explicit use of a base register:

```
LA      8,PRINT+60
MVC     0(2,8),ASTERS
```

An LA operation loads the address of PRINT + 60 (X'3058') into register 8. The MVC then explicitly uses the address in register 8 to override the implied register 4. Since the symbolic format for an MVC is D1(L,B1),D2(B2), you can code the operand 1 explicitly with a zero displacement, a length of 2, and base register 8:

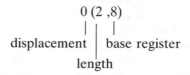

The assembled object code for operand 1 is 8000, or base register 8 and displacement zero. The effective address of operand 1 is also X'8058':

Contents of base register 8:	X'8058'
Displacement:	+ X'0000'
Effective address:	X'8058'

ASSGN3 in Fig. 11-2 illustrates the use of both explicit base addressing and displacement. LA loads the address of PRINT into register 8. Since the MVC is to reference PRINT + 60, you need a displacement of 60, coded in operand 1 as 60(2,8):

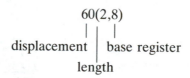

The assembled object code for operand 1 is 803C, or base register 8 and displacement 03C. The effective address is again X'8058':

Contents of base register 8:	X'801C'
Displacement:	+ X'003C'
Effective address:	X'8058'

As another example, consider a program that has stored a last name and one or two initials in the following fields:

```
SURNAMPR   DS   CL20      Surname such as BROWN
INITPR     DS   CL02      Initials such as JL
```

The program is to move the initials with a comma and periods immediately to the right of the surname, as BROWN, J.L.

The routine in Fig. 11-3 provides the logic. The first step is to scan the surname from left to right for a blank, which denotes the end of the name. At this point, the routine inserts a comma, and moves the first initial two positions to the right followed by a period, as BROWN, J. If the second initial is nonblank, the routine moves the initial and another period immediately to the right, as BROWN, J.L.

```
 6              LA      6,SURNAMPR          ADDRESS OF NAME
 7 M10          CLI     0(6),C' '           SCAN NAME
 8              BE      M20                     FOR BLANK
 9              AH      6,=H'1'
10              B       M10

11 M20          EQU     *
12              MVI     0(6),C','           INSERT COMMA
13              MVC     2(1,6),INITPR       INSERT 1ST INITIAL
14              MVI     3(6),C'.'           INSERT 1ST PERIOD
15              CLI     INITPR+1,C' '       2ND INITIAL BLANK?
16              BE      M30                 YES - EXIT
17              MVC     4(1,6),INITPR+1     NO  - INSERT 2ND
18              MVI     5(6),C'.'           INITIAL & PERIOD
19 M30          EQU     *
20 *            ...
21 *            ...
22 SURNAMPR     DS      CL30                SURNAME
23              DC      CL01' '             BLANK
24 INITPR       DS      CL02                INITIALS
```

Figure 11-3 Adjusting name and initials.

The TRT instruction (discussed in Chapter 12) could replace the instructions that scan the surname for a blank.

EXPLICIT BASE ADDRESSING FOR PACKED INSTRUCTIONS

Instructions such as MVC and CLC provide an explicit length only for operand 1. The packed instructions, however, permit lengths for both operands, as

$$D1(L1,B1),D2(L2,B2)$$

Consider a program that is to convert kilograms into pounds. The conversion is roughly 1 kg = 2.2 lb. These are the required declaratives and instructions:

```
        ZAP     POUNDS,KGS          Move KGS to POUNDS
        MP      POUNDS,CONVRN       Multiply by CONVRN:   27.566
        SRP     POUNDS,63,5         Shift and round:      27.57
        ...
KGS     DC      PL3'12.53'
CONVRN  DC      PL2'2.2'
POUNDS  DS      PL5
```

As a first example of explicit registers, let's initialize three registers with the address of each declarative and use explicit base addressing to perform the conversion:

```
LA      6,KGS               Address of KGS
LA      7,CONVRN            Address of conversion
LA      8,POUNDS            Address of pounds
ZAP     0(5,8),0(3,6)       Move KGS to POUNDS
MP      0(5,8),0(2,7)       Multiply by CONVRN:   27.566
SRP     0(5,8),63,5         Shift and round:      27.57
```

Since the three declaratives are defined consecutively beginning with KGS, you could also use one base register and an explicit displacement to reference each declarative, as follows:

```
LA      6,KGS               Address of KGS
ZAP     5(5,6),0(3,6)       Move KGS to POUNDS
MP      5(5,6),3(2,6)       Multiply by CONVRN:   27.566
SRP     5(5,6),63,5         Shift and round:      27.57
```

EXPLICIT BASE ADDRESSING FOR EDMK, COMRG, TIME, AND SRP

Some instructions require explicit use of base registers. These include the assembler instructions EDMK and the IBM macros COMRG and TIME. The following sections examine these operations in detail.

Edit and Mark (EDMK)

Without any special action, a seven-digit field containing only five significant digits, such as 123.45, would print as $bbb123.45. It is usually desirable on printed checks and on customer bills to provide check protection to prevent anyone from forging a leading digit. You may use the EDMK instruction to print a dollar sign immediately to the left of the first significant digit, as $123.45.

The general format of EDMK is

Name	Operation	Operand
[label]	EDMK	S1,S2 or D1(L1,B1),D2(B2)

EDMK is identical to the ED instruction except that it inserts into register 1 the address of the first significant digit of the edited field. After EDMK, you may decrement register 1 by 1, since the dollar sign is to appear one position to the left

```
31              LA     R1,AMTPR+4        Field in       LOAD ADDRESS OF SIGNIFICANT
32  *                                    Print         *    START CHARACTER +1
                                          Buffer
33              MVC    AMTPR,EDWORD                |40|20|20|21|4B|20|20|
34              EDMK   AMTPR,AMOUNT               |40|40|40|F3|4B|F5|F2|
35              SH     R1,=H'1'                    DECREMENT REG1 (OR BCTR 1,0)
36              MVI    0(R1),C'$'                  |40|40|5B|F3|4B|F5|F2|
37  *                  .                             $  3  .  5  2
38  *                  .
39  *                  .
40  EDWORD      DC     X'402020214B2020'
41  AMOUNT      DC     P'003.52'            WILL EDIT AS $3.52
42  AMTPR       DS     CL7
```

Figure 11-4 Sample EDMK operation.

of the first significant digit. You then use register 1 explicitly to move a dollar sign into the required print position.

In the following example, the edited field contains bb12345:

    Address in register 1 after EDMK: bb123.45
                                                   |

    Decrement register 1 by 1:   bb123.45|
    Move $ sign: b$123.45

If the significance start character (X'21') forces a zero digit to be printed, EDMK does not store the address in register 1. As a result, you should ensure against this possibility by initially loading into register 1 the address of the significance starter plus 1. After the EDMK operation, you still deduct 1 from register 1; if the significance starter forced the first printed digit, register 1 is known to contain the address of the significance starter, where the dollar sign should appear.

The example in Fig. 11-4 first loads the address of AMTPR+4 into register 1. The MVC instruction moves the editword into AMTPR. The address of the X'21' is therefore at AMTPR+3. After execution of the EDMK instruction, register 1 contains the address of the first significant digit at AMTPR+3. Decrementing register 1 results in the address of AMTPR+2, where an MVI instruction inserts a dollar sign. The final edited value is $3.52.

The COMRG and TIME Macros

The communication region is a storage area in the supervisor. The first 8 bytes contain the date as initialized each day by the computer operator. The format of the date, including the slashes, is mm/dd/yy or dd/mm/yy, depending on the installation. The address of the communication region varies by operating system and computer model, but both DOS and OS macros may access it.

DOS version. The DOS COMRG macro asks the supervisor for the address. The supervisor places the address of the communication region in register 1, which you can then explicitly use to reference it.

The following example extracts the date and stores it in an item named DATE:

```
        COMRG                    Locate address of communication region
        MVC     DATE,0(1)        Move date from communication region
        . . .
DATE    DS      CL8'MM/DD/YY'    Area to store date
```

(handwritten annotations: "user reg 1" pointing to COMRG, "column 10" above)

OS version. The OS TIME macro returns the date in packed format in register 1, as /00/YY/DD/DC/. The day (D) is in Julian format (that is, the day of the year), and C is a sign digit. As well, TIME stores the time of day in register 0.

The following example extracts the date from register 1 and stores it in an item named DATE:

```
        TIME    DEC              TIME packs date in register 1
        ST      1,FULLWORD       Store packed date in FULLWD
        UNPK    DATE,FULLWD      Unpack into DATE
        . . .
FULLWD  DS      F                Fullword area
DATE    DS      CL7              Field for unpacked date 00YYDDD
```

The ST instruction used for this purpose requires that operand 2 be a fullword (even though the contents of the register is technically in packed format). The UNPK instruction then unpacks the packed value in FULLWD into character format in DATE.

Shift and Round Packed (SRP)

The SRP instruction facilitates the rounding of values and the shifting of digits either to the left or right. Its general format is as follows:

Name	Operation	Operand
[label]	SRP	S1,S2 *or* D1(L,B1),D2(B2)I3

Although in SS format, SRP has three operands:

Operand 1   The field containing packed data to be shifted and optionally rounded.

Operand 2   A base/displacement reference that indicates the number of digits to be shifted. The maximum shift is 31 digits.

Operand 3   The value 0 through 9 to be used for rounding; a left shift usually has 0 to indicate no rounding, and a right shift usually has a 5 to indicate rounding. SRP sets the condition code for zero, minus, and plus.

```
                              46 *                          HEX REPRESENTATION
                              47 *      SHIFT LEFT 2 DIGITS:  RESULT IN AMOUNT:
                              48 *      --------------------  -----------------
003082 48E0 30C0              49 SHIFL2A  LH    14,=H'2'
003086 F040 3096 E000         50         SRP    AMOUNT1,0(14),0    12 34 56 70 0C
00308C F040 3096 0002         52 SHIFL2B  SRP    AMOUNT1,2(0),0    12 34 56 70 0C
003092 F040 3096 0002         54 SHIFL2C  SRP    AMOUNT1,2,0       12 34 56 70 0C
                                          ...
003098 001234567C             59 AMOUNT1  DC    PL5'1234567'       00 12 34 56 7C
```

Figure 11-5 Use of SRP for left shifts.

Left shift.   A positive value as a shift factor indicates a left shift.   For example, +2 means shift left two digits (digits, not bytes).   You may load the shift factor in a register and then code SRP to reference the register explicitly, as shown in Fig. 11-5.   More conveniently, code the shift factor as an explicit displacement using base register 0 (that is, no base register), as shown by SHIFL2B and SHIFL2C.

You may use any one of these three examples to shift two digits left.   Because shifting off a significant digit (1–9) left sets the decimal overflow condition but does not cause termination, you can use the BO (Branch Overflow) instruction to test if a significant digit was lost.

Right shift.   A negative shift factor indicates a right shift.   As shown by the first example in Fig. 11-6, you may load the negative factor into a register and code SRP to reference the register explicitly.

Although it is more convenient to code a shift factor as a displacement rather than load a base register, you cannot code such a right shift as SRP AMOUNT,−2,5. The reason is that the assembler does not accept negative "displacements"—that is, −2(0) for D2(B2).   You can solve the problem by representing −2 as a hexadecimal value.   SRP can shift up to a maximum of 31 decimal digits, which 6 bits can represent (5 data bits plus a sign bit: 011111 = 31).   The value 2 as six binary digits is 00 0010, and −2 in two's complement notation is 11 1110.   The hex representation of this binary number is X'3E', which, as SHIFR2B in Fig. 11-6 shows, you can use directly as a shift factor.

```
                              10 *      SHIFT RIGHT 2 ROUND:  RESULT:
                              11 *      --------------------  ------
00309D 00
00309E 48E0 30C2              12 SHIFR2A  LH    14,=H'-2'
0030A2 F045 30B2 E000         13         SRP    AMOUNT2,0(14),5    00 00 12 34 6C

0030A8 F045 30B2 003E         15 SHIFR2B  SRP    AMOUNT2,X'3E',5   00 00 12 34 6C

0030AE F045 30B2 003E         17 SHIFR2C  SRP    AMOUNT2,62,5      00 00 12 34 6C
                              18 *        ...
0030B4 001234567C             19 AMOUNT2  DC    PL5'1234567'       00 12 34 56 7C
```

Figure 11-6 Use of SRP for right shifts.

You can use any one of these three examples to shift two digits right and round. Note that right shifts include

1 = X'3F' or 63
2 = X'3E' or 62
3 = X'3D' or 61
4 = X'3C' or 60, up to a shift of 31 decimal digits

COMMON ERRORS

A common error that programmers make when using explicit base/ displacement addressing is in confusing the formats for character and packed decimal instructions. The following illustrates the two formats:

FORMAT	EXAMPLES	EXPLICIT NOTATION
Character	MVC, CLC, ED	D1(L,B1),D2(B2)
Packed decimal	ZAP, AP, PACK	D1(L1,B1),D2(L2,B2)

If you mistakenly code a length in operand 2 of an MVC as in

```
MVC     RATE,0(3,5)      (error)
```

the assembler signals an error message. However, if you omit the length in operand 2 for a ZAP as in

```
ZAP     RATEPK,0(5)      (another error)
```

the assembler assumes that you intended the operand to be 0(5,0). That is, a length of 5 bytes and base register 0. Actually, the zero means no base register, and the instruction will fail on a data exception or possibly protection exception.

TABLE DEFINITION

Many programs involve the use of tables, which contain a set of related data arranged so that each item can be referenced according to its location in the table. There are basically two types of tables. A *static table* contains defined data, such as income tax steps, inventory stock prices, and supplier names and addresses. A *dynamic table* consists of a series of adjacent blank or zero fields defined to store or accumulate related data.

The contents of a table may be descriptive (as the names of departments in a company), numeric (as in an income tax table), or a combination of descriptive and numeric. A table in which all the entries have the same length and format is also known as an array.

A simple example of a table is one that stores the numeric and the alphabetic month. A program could use the numeric month from an input record to locate the alphabetic month in the table and use it for printing in a heading. The table could appear in this format, the letter *b* here indicating a blank position:

```
MONTHTAB  DC   C'01','JANUARYbb'
          DC   C'02','FEBRUARYb'
          DC   C'03','MARCHbbbb'
          ...
          DC   C'12','DECEMBERb'
```

Note that each entry in the table is in its correct sequence and is the same length, that of the longest name, September.

Terminology

In the sample table, the numeric month is called the *table argument* and the alphabetic month is called the *function*. The numeric month from the input record used to compare against the table is known as the *search argument*. A function may contain more than one field. Each table argument in a table normally has the same format and length, as does each function. Table arguments are usually, but not necessarily, arranged in ascending sequence.

Within a table, the arguments are arranged in one of two ways, as unique entries or as steps.

Tables with Unique Entries

The following partial table contains unique entries in which one function (price) relates directly to one argument (stock number):

```
STOCKTAB  DC    C'203',P'3.10'
          DC    C'206',P'4.15'
          DC    C'240'.P'0.67'
          DC    C'265',P'3.56'
          ...
```

Table arguments need not be consecutive (one argument immediately following another, as 7, 8, 9) or sequential (each argument higher than the preceding one, as 2, 5, 8), although a sequential arrangement is more common. Each argument value, however, should occur only once in the table. A table with duplicate arguments, such as a stock item with two different prices, would be ambiguous.

To search through the table, compare the search argument successively against each table argument. The result of each comparison is as follows:

SEARCH ARGUMENT	RESULT OF COMPARISON
Equal	Argument is found; extract the function.
High	Argument may be higher in the table; continue searching.
Low	Argument is not in the table (determined because arguments are in ascending sequence).

The last result, low, merits further examination. Consider table argument entries 203, 206, 240, and 265. If the search argument is 187, the result of the first comparison is low, and you can tell by definition that the argument is not in the table because all arguments are higher. If the search argument is 204, the first comparison is high but the second is low, and once again all remaining arguments are higher.

A search argument may be higher than any table argument. With no special arrangement for terminating, the search could continue comparing past the end of the table. A common way to force termination of a table search is to store the highest possible value as the last table argument. The value depends on the data format:

Format	Highest Value
Character	Hex Fs
Packed	Packed 9s
Binary	Binary 1s if unsigned

For many applications, 20 percent of the table items involve 80 percent of the activity. Consequently, it may be more efficient to insert the most commonly referenced items at the start of the table. Since the table is no longer arranged in ascending sequence, the compare should test only for an equal or unequal condition. Determining whether an item is not in the table involves a search against all arguments through to the end. Alternatively, you could define two tables, the first containing active items and the second containing inactive items.

Tables with Steps

In a table with arguments arranged in steps, the arguments represent a range of values. Consider the following income tax table:

ANNUAL TAXABLE INCOME	TAX FORMULA
Up to $5,000	10% of taxable income
$5,001 to $10,000	12% of taxable income less $100
$10,001 to $16,000	15% of taxable income less $400
$16,001 to $24,000	19% of taxable income less $1,040
$24,001 to $40,000	24% of taxable income less $2,240
$40,001 and over	30% of taxable income less $4,640

The income tax table involves steps, such as all values up to $5,000, all values from $5,001 to $10,000, from $10,001 to $16,000, and so forth. The argument is the taxable income, and the function is the tax formula, consisting of tax rate and adjustment. To find the tax on a taxable income of, say, $12,000, multiply this amount by 15% ($12,000 × 0.15 = $1,800) and subtract the $400 adjustment factor ($1,800 − $400 = $1,400).

The adjustment occurs because the rates are "progressive." Consider the income of $12,000, broken down into its three steps:

STEP		TAXED AT	AMOUNT OF TAX
First	$ 5,000	10%	$ 500
Second	5,000	12%	600
Balance of	2,000	15%	300
	$12,000		$1,400

The calculated tax, $1,400, agrees with our previous calculation by table argument and function.

For a program, arrange the arguments in a table with the high number from each step, for example:

```
TAXTAB  DC   P'05000.00',P'.10','P'0000.00'
        DC   P'10000.00',P'.12','P'0100.00'
        DC   P'16000.00',P'.15','P'0400.00'
        DC   P'24000.00',P'.19','P'1040.00'
        DC   P'40000.00',P'.24','P'2240.00'
        DC   P'99999.99',P'.30','P'4640.00'
```

To search through the table, compare the taxable income successively against each table argument. The result of each comparison is as follows:

TAXABLE INCOME	RESULT OF COMPARISON
Equal	Argument found, extract function.
High	Argument may be higher in table; continue search.
Low	Argument found, extract function.

In this case, both equal and low comparisons locate the function, and because the highest possible defined value, $99,999.99, ends the table, every search argument can be located.

TABLE SEARCHING

A table search involves repetitive processing. You may initialize the search by loading the address of the table in an available register, which you then use explicitly as a base register. You then compare the search argument against the first table argument. To compare against successive table arguments, you have to increment the address in the register by the length of the table arguments and functions. When you compare a search argument to a table argument, there are three possibilities:

1. The search argument is equal. The required function has been located, and you may terminate the search.
2. The search argument is high. Continue the search by examining the next table entry.
3. The search argument is low. The action depends on the type of table. If the table contains steps, such as a tax table, the required function has been found in this step. If the table contains unique entries such as inventory stock numbers, the required table argument does not exist. You will have to check for this condition in your programs.

Termination of the Loop

If you make no provision to end a search, your program may compare a very high search argument against all the entries in the table and against any data following the table. You may use several ways to force termination of a search:

- Assign the last table argument with the highest possible value, such as hex Fs for character and binary fields and nines for packed fields. Because the search argument cannot exceed this value, an equal (found) or low (found or nonexistent argument) will always occur. An example appears in Fig. 11-7.
- If you know the number of entries in the table, you may code the program to count each time it makes a comparison. Terminate the search when the count exceeds the number of entries. An example appears in Fig. 11-9.
- If you know the address of the last table argument, compare the address being modified against this address. If the modified address exceeds the address of the last argument, you know that the table argument does not exist. An example appears in Fig. 11-10.
- If you know the value in the last table argument, compare the value of the

search argument to this value. If the value of the search argument exceeds the known value, you know that the table argument does not exist, and you need not perform the search.

Table Search with High Argument

The example in Fig. 11-7 performs a table search on the numeric month discussed earlier. These are some features:

- The table consists of a 2-character numeric month and a 9-character alphabetic month. The last table argument contains hex Fs.
- For initialization, an LA instruction loads the address of the table, MONTAB (at location X'3020'), into register 8, to be used explicitly as a base register. Note that LA loads the address of the table, not its contents.
- At C10LOOP, the CLC instruction compares the 2-character search argument, MONIN, against the first 2 bytes of the table:

```
C10LOOP    CLC    MONIN,0(8)
```

Operand 2 of CLC has the form D2(B2), and the coding references base register 8 and zero displacement, giving X'3020'.

- If the comparison is equal, the month is found, and the program branches to C20EQUAL.

```
LOC      OBJECT CODE        STMT    SOURCE STATEMENT
                            4               USING  *,4,5
003000 4180 4020            5               LA     8,MONTAB           INIT ADDR OF TABLE
003004 D501 40A6 8000       7  C10LOOP CLC    MONIN,0(8)         INPUT MONTH: TABLE?
00300A 4780 401A            8               BE     C20EQUAL           *   EQ - FOUND
00300E 4740 50BA            9               BL     R10INV             *   LO - NOT IN TAB
003012 4A80 4290           10               AH     8,=H'11'           INCR FOR NEXT ENTRY
003016 47F0 4004           11               B      C10LOOP            *   IN THE TABLE
00301A D208 40A8 8002       13  C20EQUAL MVC    MONOUT,2(8)        MOVE MONTH TO PRINT
                           14  *               ...
003020 F0F1D1C1D5E4C1D9     15  MONTAB  DC     C'01JANUARY  '     TABLE OF NUMERIC &
00302B F0F2C6C5C2D9E4C1     16          DC     C'02FEBRUARY '     *    ALPHA MONTHS
003036 F0F3D4C1D9C3C840     17          DC     C'03MARCH    '     *
003041 F0F4C1D7D9C9D340     18          DC     C'04APRIL    '     *
00304C F0F5D4C1E8404040     19          DC     C'05MAY      '     *
003057 F0F6D1E4D5C54040     20          DC     C'06JUNE     '     *
003062 F0F7D1E4D3E84040     21          DC     C'07JULY     '     *
00306D F0F8C1E4C7E4E2E3     22          DC     C'08AUGUST   '     *
003078 F0F9E2C5D7E3C5D4     23          DC     C'09SEPTEMBER'     *
003083 F1F0D6C3E3D6C2C5     24          DC     C'10OCTOBER  '     *
00308E F1F1D5D6E5C5D4C2     25          DC     C'11NOVEMBER '     *
003099 F1F2C4C5C3C5D4C2     26          DC     C'12DECEMBER '     *
0030A4 FFFF                27          DC     X'FFFF'            *    END OF TABLE
0030A6                     29  MONIN   DS     CL2               SEARCH ARGUMENT
0030A8 404040404040404040  30  MONOUT  DC     CL9' '            PRINT AREA
```

Figure 11-7 Table search on character data.

- If the comparison is low, the month is not in the table, and the program branches to an error routine. This error could occur if the search argument contained a value less than 01 or higher than 12. Since all search arguments will be lower than hex Fs at the end of the table, a low condition is always an error.

- If the comparison is high, the routine examines the next table argument. It increments register 8 by 11, the length of each entry. Register 8 now contains X'302B', where table argument 02 resides. The program then branches back to C10LOOP, where CLC compares the search argument against table argument 02.

- At C20EQUAL, an MVC instruction moves the found function, the alphabetic month, to the print area:

```
C20EQUAL    MVC   MONOUT,2(8)
```

Operand 1 indicates an implicit move of 9 bytes, and operand 2 references register 8, which contains the address of the found table argument. The displacement is 2 because the function is 2 bytes from the first position of the table argument (the address in register 8).

Table Search on Packed Data

A table may also contain arguments defined in packed format. Figure 11-8 provides the assembler instructions for calculating customers' discounts based on quantity sold. For example, there is no discount on quantity ordered up to 20 units, a 5% discount for orders between 21 and 50 units, a 10% discount for orders between 51 and 100 units, and so on. The maximum discount is 15% for quantities over 250, as indicated by nines in the last table argument.

In the comparison of quantity ordered to table quantity, an equal/low con-

```
LOC     OBJECT CODE      STMT     SOURCE STATEMENT
0030B2  4180 40CE         34              LA      8,DSCTAB          ADDR OF TABLE
0030B6  F922 40E7 8000    35 D10          CP      QTYIN,0(3,8)      QTY SOLD : TABLE
0030BC  47D0 40C8         36              BNH     D20               * LO/EQ - EXIT
0030C0  4A80 4292         37              AH      8,=H'5'           * HIGH CONTINUE
0030C4  47F0 40B6         38              B       D10

0030C8  F811 40EA 8003    40 D20          ZAP     DSCRATE,3(2,8)    EXTRACT RATE
                          41 *            ...
0030CE  00020C000C        42 DSCTAB       DC      P'00020',P'.000'  TABLE OF
0030D3  00050C050C        43              DC      P'00050',P'.050'    PACKED
0030D8  00100C100C        44              DC      P'00100',P'.100'    DATA
0030DD  00250C125C        45              DC      P'00250',P'.125'
0030E2  99999C150C        46              DC      P'99999',P'.150'

0030E7                    48 QTYIN        DS      PL3               QTY SOLD
0030EA                    49 DSCRATE      DS      PL2               DISCOUNT RATE
```

Figure 11-8 Table search on packed data.

dition in this example means that the discount rate has been found, and the routine extracts the rate from the table. Further instructions would involve calculating discount amount by multiplying sales amount by discount rate.

Table Search Using a Count: BCT, BCTR, BXLE, and BXH

This section examines two ways of performing a table search using the techniques for termination described earlier. You may use the following instructions to decrement a count and test termination of a search. None of these instructions changes the condition code.

Name	Operation	Operand
[label]	BCT	R1,X2 or R1,D2(X2,B2)
[label]	BCTR	R1,R2
[label]	BXLE	R1,S2 or R1,R3,D2(B2)
[label]	BXH	R1,S2 or R1,R3,D2(B2)

Branch on Count (BCT and BCTR)

Before using BCT or BCTR, you normally load a count in a register, such as the number of entries in the table. The routine may then use branch on count in the loop to decrement the count by 1 and to check if the count has been reduced to zero. The rules are as follows:

- Operand 1 specifies any available register containing a count.
- Operand 2 references an address in storage if BCT or a register containing an address if BCTR. On execution, the computer decrements the contents of the operand 1 register by 1. If the result is nonzero, the program branches to the operand 2 address. If the result is zero, the operation continues with the next instruction. Since the operation performs no other checking, you must ensure that the initial count is a positive nonzero value.
- For BCTR, if operand 2 specifies register 0, the operation decrements 1 from the operand 1 register but makes no test and takes no branch. This use of BCTR is a convenient way of decrementing the value in any register.

In the following three examples, assume that register 7 contains a positive value:

Example 1. Decrement register 7 by 1 and if nonzero branch to address K50:

```
BCT    7,K50
```

Example 2.   Decrement register 7 by 1 and if nonzero branch to the address in register 9, K50:

```
              LA      9,K50
              BCTR    7,9
```

Example 3.   Decrement register 11 by 1 and continue with the next instruction:

```
              BCTR    11,0
```

Figure 11-9 provides a table search using two registers and BCT.   The search argument is a 3-character field named JOBNO.   The table, named JOBTABLE, contains 60 five-byte entries consisting of a 3-character job number as the table argument and a 2-byte packed rate as the function.   The function, when found, is to be stored in a field named RATE.

The example loads the number of entries in the table, 60, into a register, subsequently to be decremented by BCT.   If the loop is performed 60 times, the count is reduced to zero, and the required argument is known not to be in the table.   An advantage of this method is that table arguments need not be in ascending sequence, so the most commonly referenced arguments could be first.

If another register is available, you could make the loop more efficient by replacing the BCT instruction with BCTR, since RR-type instructions such as BCTR execute faster than other types.   Add one instruction at the start to initialize the address of K10LOOP:

```
              LA    10,K10LOOP
```

```
LOC     OBJECT CODE        STMT     SOURCE STATEMENT
0030EC  4160 4115           53              LA      6,JOBTABLE     ADDR OF JOB TABLE
0030F0  4190 003C           54              LA      9,60           LOAD NO. OF ENTRIES
0030F4  D502 4110 6000      56  K10LOOP     CLC     JOBNO,0(6)     INPUT JOB# : TABLE JOB#?
0030FA  4780 410A           57              BE      K20EQUAL       *   EQUAL - FOUND
0030FE  4160 6005           58              LA      6,5(0,6)       INCREMENT FOR NEXT ENTRY
003102  4690 40F4           59              BCT     9,K10LOOP      DECR REG 9. NOT ZERO, LOOP
003106  47F0 50BA           60              B       R10INV         *   ZERO, NOT IN TABLE

00310A  F811 4113 6003      62  K20EQUAL    ZAP     RATE,3(2,6)    GET RATE FROM TABLE
                            63  *                   .
                            64  *                   .
                            65  *                   .
003110                      66  JOBNO       DS      CL3            JOB NO. (SEARCH ARG'T)
003113                      67  RATE        DS      PL2            RATE FOR FOUND FUNCTION
003115  F0F0F6585C          69  JOBTABLE    DC      C'006',P'5.85' *   JOB# 3 BYTES,
00311A  F0F1F2715C          70              DC      C'012',P'7.15' *   RATE 2 BYTES
00311F  F0F1F5830C          71              DC      C'015',P'8.30' *
003124                      72              DS      57CL5          *   REST OF TABLE
```

Figure 11-9   Table search using a count and BCT.

and replace the BCT with BCTR as follows:

```
BCTR    9,10
```

In fact, if the LA immediately precedes K10LOOP, you could replace it with a BALR instruction

```
BALR 10,0
```

that loads the address of the next instruction (K10LOOP) into register 10 and continues with the next instruction. Figure 11-10 shows the revised version, more efficient but less clear than the previous example.

Branch on Index Low or Equal (BXLE)

The BXLE instruction requires the use of three registers, two of which are an even-odd pair, such as 10 and 11. Before executing BXLE, be sure to initialize all three registers. BXLE is an RS-format instruction with three operands. The instruction is used like this:

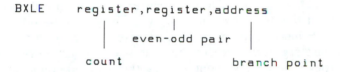

- Operand 1 specifies a register containing, generally, a count or an address.
- Operand 2 normally denotes the even-numbered register of an even-odd pair. The even-numbered register contains a value used to increment or decrement the operand 1 register. The operation adds all 31 bits as in normal binary addition. The odd-numbered register, which you do not code in the operands, contains the limit or address against which operand 1 is compared.
- Operand 3 references a storage address, which is the branch point for low/equal conditions.

On execution, BXLE adds the contents of the operand 2 even register to the

```
75              LA      6,JOBTABLE      LOAD ADDR OF JOB TABLE
76              LA      9,60            LOAD NO. OF ENTRIES
77              BALR    10,0            INIT'ZE ADDR OF LOOP
78 K10LOOP2 CLC         JOBNO,0(6)      INPUT JOB# : TABLE JOB# ?
79              BE      K20EQU2         *   EQUAL - FOUND
80              LA      6,5(0,6)        INCREMENT FOR NEXT ENTRY
81              BCTR    9,10            DECR REG 9. NOT ZERO, LOOP
82              B       R10INV          *   ZERO, NOT IN TABLE.
83 K20EQU2  ZAP         RATE,3(2,6)     GET RATE FROM TABLE
```

Figure 11-10   Table search using a count and BCTR.

```
 92              LA      6,JOBTABLE          LOAD ADDR OF JOB TABLE
 93              LA      8,5                 LOAD LENGTH OF ENTRY
 94              LA      9,JOBTABLE+59*5     LOAD ADDR OF LAST ENTRY

 96  L10LOOP     CLC     JOBNO,0(6)          INPUT JOB# : TABLE JOB# ?
 97              BE      L20EQUAL            *     EQUAL - FOUND
 98              BXLE    6,8,L10LOOP         INCR REG 6, REG 6 : 9?
 99  *                                      *   LO/EQ - BRANCH
100              B       R10INV              *   HIGH  - NOT IN TABLE

102  L20EQUAL    ZAP     RATE,3(2,6)         GET RATE FROM TABLE
```

Figure 11-11   Table search using BXLE.

operand 1 register.   The operation then compares operand 1 to the unreferenced odd register.   If the operand 1 contents are low or equal, the program branches to the address in operand 3.   If the contents are high, the program continues with the next instruction.

If the register in operand 2 is odd rather than even, the operation compares directly to this register.   In this case, the operand 2 register would be both the increment or decrement and the limit.

Figure 11-11 uses the BXLE instruction for a table search.   The table, JOB-TABLE, is the same one defined in Fig. 11-9.   The three LA instructions load the address of the table into register 6, the length of each entry (5) into register 8, and the address of the last table entry into the odd register, 9, respectively. BXLE increments the address of base register 6 by the constant 5 in register 8. If base register 6 exceeds the address of the last entry, the program has stepped through the table without locating the required argument.

Branch on Index High (BXH)

BXH is similar to BXLE except that whereas BXLE branches if not high (low or equal), BXH branches if high.   You could use BXH to search through a table from the last argument through to the first argument, that is, to perform a reverse scan.

The preceding examples give some of the common methods of terminating a table search.   The commonest and simplest method is to define the last table argument with a high value.   The methods using BCT and BXLE are efficient if enough registers are available.

OTHER TABLE-HANDLING ROUTINES

You may want to process a table for reasons other than a search for a function. For example, you may need to accumulate the contents of a table to determine the total and its mean average.   Following are two other techniques used in table processing. Consider the definitions of two tables both containing valid packed data:

```
TABLE1    DC    50PL5'0'
TABLE2    DC    50PL6'0'
```

The following routine adds the contents of TABLE1 to TABLE2 entry for entry:

```
        LA    10,TABLE1            Initialize address
        LA    11,TABLE2               of tables
        LA    12,50               Initialize for 50 entries
LOOP1   AP    0(6,11),0(5,10)     Add entries
        AH    10,=H'5'            Increment for
        AH    11,=H'6'               next entries
        BCT   12,LOOP1            Loop 50 times
```

Now let's code a loop to clear the contents of TABLE1 to zeros:

```
        LA    10,TABLE1            Initialize address
        LA    12,50               Initialize for 50 entries
LOOP2   SP    0(5,10),0(5,10)     Clear an entry
        AH    10,=H'5'            Set for next entry
        BCT   12,LOOP2            Loop 50 times
```

Another common practice is to print the entire contents of a table by initializing its address and extracting each entry one at a time.

ERRORS IN TABLE HANDLING

Among the many errors that programmers tend to make when using tables are these:

- Arguments are missing from the table, or the functions are incorrect.
- Arguments and functions are not consistently the same length.
- The increment value for stepping through the table is incorrect.
- The program has no way to terminate the search.
- The branch instruction that returns to perform the next compare goes instead to the instruction that initializes the search, so the program loops endlessly, like this one:

```
W30SRCH   LA    9,TABLE       Endless loop
          CLC   ...
          ...
          B     W30SRCH
```

DIRECT TABLE ADDRESSING

Table arguments arranged, for example, as 03, 07, 12, 15, 18, . . . are sequential but are not consecutive. If table arguments are both sequential and consecutive, such as 03, 04, 05, 06, . . . , you could omit defining the arguments in the table and can use direct table addressing instead of table searching. With just a table of functions, the function for argument 05, for example, would be the fifth entry in the table. To locate a required function, you calculate its relative location. Since no repetitive looping and comparing is required, direct table addressing is a particularly efficient way of locating functions.

Figure 11-7 illustrated a table of months in which the numeric month was the argument and the alphabetic month was the function. Since the arguments are both sequential and consecutive, for direct addressing, you can omit the argument, so the table appears like this:

```
MONTHTAB    DC    C'JANUARYbb'
            DC    C'FEBRUARYb'
            DC    C'MARCHbbbb'
            . . .
            DC    C'DECEMBERb'
```

The revised table contains only the functions for the 12 months. Figure 11-12 provides both a full definition of the table and the program logic for direct table addressing. For example, consider that the search argument, MONTHIN, contains 04 for April. The routine first checks that the month is valid (between 01 and 12, inclusive).

Here are the program steps:

Numeric value for April:	04
Deduct 1:	− 1
Decremented value:	03
Multiply by length of entries:	× 9
Relative location of April:	27, *or* X'001B'
Add address of table:	+ X'4030'
Actual location of April in storage:	X'404B'

The program has to deduct 1 from the search argument because the first entry is at table location 0, the second entry is at table location 1, and so forth.

For this technique, make sure that the search argument is valid. For example, if a search argument is incorrectly entered as 14, the program will calculate an address that is outside the table limits.

```
LOC    OBJECT CODE        STMT  SOURCE STATEMENT
004000 F271 50A8 509C     110          PACK  DBLEWORD,MONTHIN  MONTH IN DBLEWORD
004006 F970 50A8 50C4     111          CP    DBLEWORD,=P'1'    IS MONTH < 1 ?
00400C 4740 50BA          112          BL    R50LOW               YES - ERROR

004010 F971 50A8 50C0     114          CP    DBLEWORD,=P'12'   IS MONTH > 12 ?
004016 4720 50BA          115          BH    R60HIGH              YES - ERROR

00401A 4F70 50A8          117          CVB   7,DBLEWORD        CONVERT TO BINARY
00401E 0670               118          BCTR  7,0               DECREMENT MONTH BY 1
004020 4C70 50C2          119          MH    7,=H'9'           MULTIPLY BY LENGTH
004024 5A70 50A0          120          A     7,ADDRTAB         ADD TABLE ADDRESS
004028 D208 50B0 7000     121          MVC   MNTHPR,0(7)       GET ALPHA MONTH
                          122 *        ...
004030                    123          DS    0D                FORCE ALIGNMENT
004030 D1C1D5E4C1D9E840   124 MONTABLE DC    C'JANUARY  '      TABLE OF 12
004039 C6C5C2D9E4C1D9E8   125          DC    C'FEBRUARY '      * 9-CHARACTER
004042 D4C1D9C3C8404040   126          DC    C'MARCH    '      * ALPHABETIC
00404B C1D7D9C9D3404040   127          DC    C'APRIL    '      * MONTHS
004054 D4C1E84040404040   128          DC    C'MAY      '      *
00405D D1E4D5C540404040   129          DC    C'JUNE     '      *
004066 D1E4D3E840404040   130          DC    C'JULY     '      *
00406F C1E4C7E4E2E34040   131          DC    C'AUGUST   '      *
004078 E2C5D7E3C5D4C2C5   132          DC    C'SEPTEMBER'      *
004081 D6C3E3D6C2C5D940   133          DC    C'OCTOBER  '      *
00408A D5D6E5C5D4C2C5D9   134          DC    C'NOVEMBER '      *
004093 C4C5C3C5D4C2C5D9   135          DC    C'DECEMBER '      *

00409C                    137 MONTHIN  DS    CL2               INPUT MONTH
00409E 0000
0040A0 00004030           138 ADDRTAB  DC    A(MONTABLE)       ADDRESS OF TABLE
0040A8                    139 DBLEWORD DS    D                 SEARCH ARG
0040B0                    140 MNTHPR   DS    CL9               SAVE MONTH
```

Figure 11-12 Direct table addressing.

Calculation of the Direct Address

Consider the following values that you may use to calculate a direct address:

$$A(F) = \text{address of the required function}$$
$$A(T) = \text{address of the table}$$
$$SA = \text{value of the search argument}$$
$$L = \text{length of each function}$$
$$N = \text{value of the table argument representing the first,}$$
$$\text{or lowest, function in the table } (SA \geq N)$$

The following formula locates the table function:

$$A(F) = A(T) + [(SA - N) \times L]$$

In the routine in Fig. 11-12 that locates an alphabetic month, $A(T) = X'4030'$,

L = 9, and N = the input month. Given search arguments of 01, 02, and 12, respectively, the calculations for A(F) are as follows:

SA	CALCULATION OF A(F)		
01	X'4030' + [(01 - 1) × 9]	X'4030'	(January)
02	X'4030' + [(02 - 1) × 9]	X'4039'	(February)
12	X'4030' + [(12 - 1) × 9]	X'4093'	(December)

Check the logic of the formula and the calculations of A(F) against the table in Fig. 11-12.

LINKED LISTS

Although a table may contain any type of data, we'll examine the use of binary data in a linked list. A linked list contains data in what are called cells, like entries in a table but in no specified sequence. Each cell contains a pointer to the next cell in the list. (A cell may also contain a pointer to the preceding cell so that searching may proceed in either direction.) The method facilitates additions and deletions to a list without the need for expanding and contracting it.

For our purposes, the linked list contains cells with three words: part number, part price, and a pointer to the next cell in the list. The pointer is a displacement from the start of the list. The following linked list begins at displacement 0000, the second item is at 0036, the third item is at 0048, and so forth:

Displacement	Part no.	Price	Next address
0000	0103	12.50	0036
0012	1720	08.95	0024
0024	1827	03.75	0000
0036	0120	13.80	0048
0048	0205	25.00	0012

The item at displacement 0024 contains zero as the next address, either to indicate the end of the list or to make it circular.

The program in Fig. 11-13 uses the contents of the defined linked list, LINKLST, to create a sequential table of part numbers and prices, SEQTAB. Register usage is as follows:

5	Address of LINKLST
6	Address of SEQTAB
7	Used to load part number from LINKLST
8	Used to load price from LINKLST
9	Used to load next address from LINKLST

The first instructions initialize registers 5 and 6 with addresses and register 9 with

```
              LA    5,LINKLST
              LA    6,SEQTAB
              SR    9,9
LOOP          L     7,0(9,5)              Load part #
              L     8,4(9,5)              Load price
              L     9,8(9,5)              Load next address
              STM   7,8,0(6)              Store part & price
              AH    6,=H'8'
              C     9,=F'0'
              BNE   LOOP
              MVC   0(4,6),=4X'FF'
              ...


*             DECLARATIVES
LINKLST       DC    F'0103',F'12.50',F'0036'
              DC    F'1720',F'08.95',F'0024'
              DC    F'1827',F'03.75',F'0000'
              DC    F'0120',F'13.80',F'0048'
              DC    F'0205',F'25.00',F'0012'
SEQTAB        DC    24F'0'
```

Figure 11-13 Use of a linked list.

zeros.   Register 9 is initialized because it is also used as an index register.   In the loop, an L instruction loads from LINKLST the part number, price, and next address into registers 7, 8, and 9, respectively.   Note the use of explicit notation for L, an RX-type instruction:

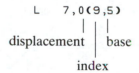

On the first execution, the operation combines the contents of index register 9, zero, with that of register 5, the address of LINKLST, and loads the first part number.   The second L uses a displacement of 4 to load the price, and the third L uses a displacement of 8 to load the next address.

Since register 9 now contains the next address, it becomes the index value for subsequent load operations.   (LM was not used because it does not have indexing capability.)   STM stores the part number and price in SEQTAB, and AH sets up the address of SEQTAB for the next STM.   The C instruction checks the next address in register 9; if it contains the ending indicator, zeros, MVC stores hex Fs in SEQTAB as a table stopper.

SORTING TABLE ENTRIES

Computer manufacturers supply a sort utility program, which is used to sort disk and tape records into a predefined sequence.   The sort program reads a number of the records into storage, sorts them into a new sequence, and writes them onto another device.   It reads and sorts more records and merges them with the previously sorted records until eventually the entire file is sorted.

You may have occasion to sort table entries for which you can write your own routine.   The table may be arranged in a random sequence and you have to sort it into argument sequence.   You may sort entries into either ascending (1, 2, 3, . . .) or descending (10, 9, 8, . . .) order.

The two sample programs in this section both sort the same table of five 5-character descriptions and on completion produce a hex dump of the table.   The programs use the DOS PDUMP macro for the dump; an OS user would use the SNAP macro, described in Chapter 15.

You could improve these sorts by generalizing them for any number of entries and any length.   One way is to use the EX instruction to permit modifying the lengths for MVC and CLC.

A Simple Sort

The program in Fig. 11-14 sorts a table of character data into ascending sequence.   To this end, it compares successively entry 1 to entry 2, entry 2 to entry 3, entry

```
 5 SORT1      START
 6            BALR   10,0                  INITIALIZE
 7            USING  *,10
 8            BAL    4,S10SORT
 9            PDUMP  TABLE,SAVENT+5
15            EOJ                          TERMINATE

19 S10SORT    MVI    XCHANGED,C'0'         CLEAR INDICATOR
20            LA     6,TABLE               INIT ADDRESS OF TABLE
21 S20        EQU    *
22            C      6,=A(TABLE+4*LEN)     END OF TABLE?
23            BE     S40                     YES - CHECK IF DONE
24            CLC    0(LEN,6),LEN(6)       COMPARE ADJACENT ENTRIES
25            BNH    S30                     EQUAL/LOW- BYPASS
26            MVC    SAVENT,0(6)            HIGH - EXCHANGE
27            MVC    0(LEN,6),LEN(6)                 ENTRIES
28            MVC    LEN(LEN,6),SAVENT
29            MVI    XCHANGED,C'1'           SET INDICATOR
30 S30        EQU    *
31            LA     6,LEN(0,6)            INCREMENT ADDRESS
32            B      S20                   REPEAT
33 S40        EQU    *
34            CLI    XCHANGED,C'1'         ANY EXCHANGED?
35            BE     S10SORT                 YES - REPEAT
36            BR     4                       NO -- RETURN

38 *                 ------------------------
39 *                 D E C L A R A T I V E S
40 *                 ------------------------
41 LEN        EQU    5                     ENTRY LENGTH
42 TABLE      DC     C'SORT '
43            DC     C'TABLE'
44            DC     C'STACK'
```

Figure 11-14 Simple sort program.

```
45              DC      C'LIST '
46              DC      C'DUMP '
47 SAVENT       DS      CL5                     TEMP'Y SAVE
48 XCHANGED     DC      C'0'                    EXCHANGE INDICATOR
50              LTORG
51                      =CL8'$$BPDUMP'
52                      =A(TABLE,SAVENT+5)
53                      =A(TABLE+4*LEN)
54              END     SORT1
```

Dump of sorted table:-

```
02C0C0                                    C4E4D4D7    40D3C9E2 E340E2D6 D9E340E2 E3C1C3D2
02C0E0   E3C1C2D3 C5D3C9E2 E340F000
              |                              |
           SAVENT                     Start of table
```

Figure 11-14 (*continued*)

3 to entry 4, and entry 4 to entry 5, exchanging entries where the first is higher than the second:

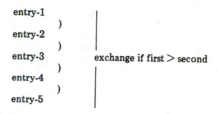

The routine uses an indicator named XCHANGED to determine when entries are fully in sequence. Each initialization of the program loop sets XCHANGED to 0, and whenever the routine exchanges entries, it sets XCHANGED to 1. On completion of a pass through the table, the routine tests if any entries were exchanged: Does XCHANGED contain 1? If any entries were swapped, the routine reinitializes the table address, sets XCHANGED to 0, and performs another pass through the table. If no entries were swapped, the routine recognizes that the table is now in sequence and dumps its contents.

The advantage of this sort, other than its simplicity, is that it exits quickly if entries are already in or near sequence.

Some tables may have arguments with equal values. If so, be sure that your routine exchanges only if the first entry is higher than the second. If you exchange on not low (high/equal), you'll exchange equal entries. Since the routine sets XCHANGED to 1, the sort will run endlessly.

Straight Insertion

Let's now examine a more sophisticated and efficient sort technique known as straight insertion. In effect, the technique steps through the table only once but

```
    5 SORT2       START
    6             BALR   10,0                         INITIALIZE
    7             USING  *,10
    8             BAL    4,S10SORT
    9             PDUMP  TABLE,SAVENT+5
   15             EOJ                                 TERMINATE

   19 S10SORT     STM    5,8,SAVEREGS                 SAVE REGISTERS
   20             LA     L,LEN(0)                     SET LENGTH OF ENTRY
   21             LA     J,TABLE                      INIT ADDRESS OF TABLE
   22 S20         EQU    *
   23             LR     I,J                          MOVE J TO I
   24             AR     J,L                          INCR J TO NEXT
   25             MVC    SAVENT,0(J)                  SAVE ENTRY(J)
   26 S30         EQU    *
   27             CLC    SAVENT,0(I)                  SAVE : ENTRY(I)?
   28             BNL    S40                            NOT LO -- BYPASS
   29             MVC    LEN(LEN,I),0(I)                LO -- MOVE ENTRY(I) TO NEXT
   30             SR     I,L                          DECREMENT I
   31             C      I,=A(TABLE-LEN)              BEFORE START TABLE?
   32             BNE    S30                            NO -- REPEAT
   33 S40         EQU    *
   34             MVC    LEN(LEN,I),SAVENT              YES - STORE SAVE IN ENTRY
   35             C      J,=A(TABLE+LEN*4)            AT END OF TABLE?
   36             BNE    S20                            NO -- REPEAT
   37             LM     5,8,SAVEREGS                 RESTORE REGISTERS
   38             BR     4                            RETURN

   40 *                  ----------------------
   41 *                  D E C L A R A T I V E S
   42 *                  ----------------------
   43 J           EQU    6                            ADDR OF FORWARD REG
   44 I           EQU    7                            ADRR OF BACKWARD REG
   45 L           EQU    8                            REG WITH LENGTH
   46 LEN         EQU    5                            ENTRY LENGTH
   47 TABLE       DC     C'SORT TABLESTACKLIST DUMP '
   48 SAVENT      DS     CL5                          TEMP'Y SAVE
   49 SAVEREGS    DS     4F

   51             LTORG
   52                    =CL8'$$BPDUMP'
   53                    =A(TABLE,SAVENT+5)
   54                    =A(TABLE-LEN)
   55                    =A(TABLE+LEN*4)
   56             END    SORT2
```

```
Dump of sorted table:-
                                        Start of table
                                               |
02C0C0                                   07F4C4E4    D4D740D3 C9E2E340 E2D6D9E3 40E2E3C1
02C0E0   C3D2E3C1 C2D3C5C4 E4D4D740 00000000
                 |
              SAVENT
```

Figure 11-15 Sort with straight insertion.

always backfills earlier entries. As a result, the search automatically terminates on reaching the end of the table.

In simple terms, here's how it operates. Consider an array containing the values D, C, B, and A, in that sequence. Select and save entry 2, C. Compare it to entry 1, D. Since C is lower, move D to entry 2 and move the saved C to entry 1:

entry 1	D	C	(first two entries
entry 2	C	D	now in sequence)
entry 3	B		
entry 4	A		

Now select and save entry 3, B. Compare it to entry 2, D. Since B is lower, move D to entry 3. Next compare the saved B to entry 1, C; since B is lower, move C to entry 2 and move the saved B to entry 1:

entry 1	C	B	(first three
entry 2	D	C	entries now
entry 3	B	D	in sequence)
entry 4	A		

Now select and save entry 4, A. Compare it to entry 3, D. Since A is lower, move D to entry 4. Next compare the saved A to entry 2, C; since A is lower, move B to entry 2 and move the saved A to entry 1:

entry 1	B	A	(all four
entry 2	C	B	entries
entry 3	D	C	now in
entry 4	A	D	sequence)

The program in Fig. 11-15 illustrates the use of straight insertion to sort a table of five 5-byte entries into ascending sequence. This example equates the name J to register 6, the name I to register 7, and the name LEN to the length of each entry. At the end of the sort, the program dumps the contents of the table.

Many other sort routines are available, with various degrees of complexity. However, many tables are relatively short, and assembler programs sort them especially fast.

BINARY SEARCH

You normally open a telephone directory toward the center and flip the pages forward and backward as you close in on the required name. An equivalent programming technique called binary search is used for searching through large tables.

If a table contains 100 entries, a standard table search requires an average of 50 comparisons to find an entry. A binary search can reduce this number considerably. This technique first tests the middle of the table to determine which half contains the required entry. The next step checks the midpoint of the half, and so forth, thereby quickly closing in on the required entry. For a binary search to work correctly, the table entries must be in sequence.

Consider the table of 20 job numbers and their associated rates-of-pay in Fig. 11-16. To locate the position of the table's middle entry, average the sum of the first position (starting at zero) and the last position (20):

$$\text{Midpoint} = \frac{0 + 20}{2} = 10$$

The calculation tells you to begin the search at the tenth entry, which contains job 27. Comparing the search argument to the value 27 discloses the following:

SEARCH ARGUMENT	RESULT
Equal	The required entry is found.
Lower	The required entry is in the lower half of the table.
Higher	The required entry is in the upper half of the table.

If a search argument contains job 47, the first comparison of 47 to 27 is high, and you can eliminate searching the lower half of the table. Now compute the midpoint of the upper half: (10 + 20)/2 = entry 15, which contains job 52. A comparison of job 47 to 52 gives a low condition, indicating that the required entry is in the third quarter of the table.

ENTRY	JOB	RATE	ENTRY	JOB	RATE
1	01	8.50	11	30	9.25
2	03	9.25	12	32	9.95
3	04	9.35	13	47	10.30
4	06	9.35	14	50	8.50
5	07	9.25	15	52	10.30
6	13	9.25	16	56	10.30
7	15	9.25	17	63	10.20
8	16	10.30	18	72	9.95
9	20	10.30	19	74	9.95
10	27	10.30	20	76	9.35

Figure 11-16 Table of job numbers and rates of pay.

The midpoint of the third quarter is (10 + 15)/2 = 12.5, rounded to 13. Because entry 13 contains job number 47, an equal comparison occurs. The rate of pay for job 47, $10.30, was located with only three comparisons, whereas a sequential search would have required 13.

You can initialize the calculation of the midpoint in either of two ways:

1. (0 + highest entry)/2, rounding this and all subsequent calculations.
2. (1 + highest entry + 1)/2, with no rounding of this or subsequent calculations. The initial calculation in the preceding example could have been (1 + 21)/2 = 11.

Either rule works for a table with any number of entries. Any deviation, such as not rounding by method 1 or rounding by method 2, causes the search to miss the first or last entry in the table.

The formula to calculate each midpoint is

$$\text{MID} = \frac{\text{LO} + \text{HI}}{2} \quad \text{(rounded)}$$

where LO is the position of the low entry and HI is the position of the high entry. To move up or down the table, place the previously calculated midpoint (MID) in LO or HI. If the comparison of the search argument to the table is low, place MID in HI to check lower in the table. If the comparison of the search argument to the table is high, place MID in LO to check higher in the table.

For example, the preceding binary search initially calculated MID as (0 + 20)/2 = 10. The first comparison of job 47 to entry 10 (job 27) was high. Therefore, to check higher in the table, store the contents of MID (10) in LO. The next comparison is then (10 + 20)/2 = 15.

Missing Entry

A possibility is that a required entry is not in the table. A conventional search, which progresses sequentially through a table, can detect a missing entry by a low comparison. For a binary search, if two successive calculations result in the same midpoint, the entry is not in the table. For example, consider the same table of job numbers and rates of pay discussed earlier and an input record containing job 12. The calculations and comparisons are as follows:

STEP	MIDPOINT: (LO + HI)/2	SEARCH:TABLE	RESULT
1	(0 + 20)/2 = 10	12:27	Low
2	(0 + 10)/2 = 5	12:07	High
3	(5 + 10)/2 = 7.5 or 8	12:16	Low
4	(5 + 8)/2 = 6.5 or 7	12:15	Low
5	(5 + 7)/2 = 6	12:13	Low
6	(5 + 6)/2 = 5.5 or 6	12:13	Quit!

The routine has now calculated midpoint 6 twice in a row and will continue to do so unless you provide a test.

Maximum Number of Comparisons

The following chart compares the use of the sequential search to that of the binary search for tables of various sizes. The maximum number of comparisons for a sequential search is always the number of entries in the table. On the average, a sequential search requires processing halfway through the table.

NUMBER OF ENTRIES	MAXIMUM SEQUENTIAL	AVERAGE SEQUENTIAL	MAXIMUM BINARY
20	20	10	5
50	50	25	6
100	100	50	7
400	400	200	9
800	800	400	10
2,000	2,000	1,000	11
10,000	10,000	5,000	14

The figures for the maximum number of comparisons for a binary search are based on the formula

$$2^n > \text{number of table entries}$$

where n is the maximum number of comparisons required. For example, if there are 50 table entries, select the smallest necessary n:

$$2^5 = 32 \text{ (too small, because } 32 < 50)$$

$$2^6 = 64 \text{ (correct, because } 64 > 50)$$

As a result, a binary search of a table containing 32 to 63 entries involves a maximum of six comparisons. The worst case for a binary search (the maximum number of comparisons) is much better even than the average number of sequential comparisons. But a binary search does require more machine instructions and is perhaps better suited for tables containing, say, 30 or more entries.

The routine in Fig. 11-17 uses the same table of job numbers as Fig. 11-9. COUNT contains the number of entries in the table (plus 1), and SEARCH contains the search argument. The routine initializes register 6 with 1 for the low entry point and initializes register 10 with COUNT for the high address. It uses these two values to calculate the midpoint, which is initially $(1 + 51)/2 = 26$. Since the length of each entry is 5, the routine multiplies the midpoint by 5 to determine a displacement and adds it to the starting address of JOBTABLE (actually JOBTABLE-5) for the direct address of the midpoint.

Try using JOBTABLE as defined in Fig. 11-17, and work through the binary search using a number of arguments.

```
                STM    5,10,SAVEREGS          SAVE REGISTERS 5 -- 10
                LA     6,1                    LOAD INITIAL LOW ENTRY
                L      10,COUNT               LOAD INITIAL HIGH ENTRY
                LA     8,0                    CLEAR MID-POINT

C10LOOP         LR     9,6                    LOAD LOW ENTRY IN CALC'N REG.
                AR     9,10                   ADD HIGH ENTRY TO CALC'N REG.
                SRA    9,1                    MID = 1/2 SUM
                CR     8,9                    NEW MID = PREV. MID?
                BE     R10ERR                 *  YES - ENTRY NOT IN TABLE

                LR     8,9                    MID NEW MID INTO PREVIOUS
                LA     5,JOBTABLE-5           LOAD ADDR OF TAB MINUS ENTRY LEN
                MH     9,=H'5'                DISPLACEMENT = MID X ENTRY LEN
                AR     5,9                    ADD DISPLACEMENT TO ADDRESS
                CLC    SEARCH,0(5)            COMPARE SEARCH TO TABLE ARG:
                BE     D10FOUND               *  EQUAL - FOUND
                BL     C20LOW                 *  LOW

                LR     6,8                    *  HIGH - LOAD MID INTO LOW
                B      C10LOOP

C20LOW          LR     10,8                   *  LOW  - LOAD MID INTO HIGH
                B      C10LOOP

D10FOUND LM     5,10,SAVEREGS                 RESTORE REGISTERS 5 -- 10
                ...                           ROUTINE FOR FOUND CONDITION
R10ERR          ...                           ROUTINE FOR NOT FOUND
                ...
COUNT    DS     F                             1 + NO. ENTRIES IN TABLE
SEARCH   DS     CL3                           SEARCH ARGUMENT
SAVEREGS DS     6F                            REGISTER SAVEAREA
```

```
Register Usage:
        5       For calculation of the table address.
        6       Low entry number for the table; initialized to 1.
        8       Midpoint number for the table.
        9       For calculation of the table displacement.
        10      High entry no. for table; init'd with # of entries.
```

Figure 11-17   Binary search.

SAMPLE PROGRAM: CALCULATING SALES VALUES

The hierarchy chart in Fig. 11-18 and the program in Fig. 11-19 illustrate the use of many features in Chapters 10 and 11. The objective is to calculate the cost of inventory stock sold for each stock item in a sales file.

Input. The program reads two types of data records: stock table records first, followed by inventory sales records.

Stock table records in unique sequence:

```
01-02 Record code (06)
03-06 Stock number
07-11 Price
12-18 Description
```

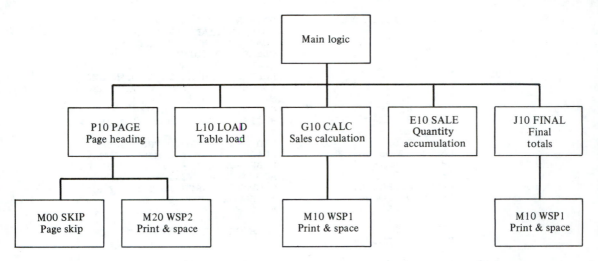

Figure 11-18　Hierarchy chart for inventory program.

Inventory sales records in sequence, any number per stock number:

```
01-02 Record code (12)
03-06 Stock number
07-11 Quantity sold
```

Input data consists of the following records:

```
Stock table:    Code Stock    Price Description
                06   1234      00100   GIDGETS
                06   2468      01525   WIDGETS
                06   2470      10017   MIDGETS
                06   2844      02000   FIDGETS
                06   9999

Stock records: Code Stock    Qty.
                12   1234      125
                12   2844      076
                12   2844      096
                12   2470      035
                12   2844      020
```

The program defines a dynamic table, that is, one with no initial entries. The table provides for up to ten entries for stock number, price, and description with the following definition:

```
COSTABLE DC 10X'FFFFFFFF00000C40404040404040'
```

　　　　　　　　　stock no.　price　　description

```
  2              PRINT ON,NOGEN,NODATA
  4 PROG11       START
  5              BALR  3,0                      INITIALIZE
  6              USING *,3,4                    *   BASE REGS
  7              LA    4,2048                   *   3 & 4
  8              LA    4,2048(3,4)
  9              OPEN  FILEIN,PRTR
 18              LH    10,=H'55'                SET LINE COUNT PAST MAXIMUM
 19              BAL   9,P10PAGE                PRINT HEADING FOR PAGE 1
 20              BAL   9,L10LOAD                LOAD TABLE
 22              GET   FILEIN,STRECIN           READ 1ST STOCK RECORD
 28              MVC   PREVSTK,STOCKIN          INIT'ZE SEQ

 30 A10LOOP      CLC   STOCKIN,PREVSTK          NEW STOCK : PREVIOUS?
 31              BE    A30                      *    EQUAL - PROCESS RECEIPT
 32              BL    R10SEQ                   *    LOW   - OUT-OF-SEQUENCE
 33 *                                          *    HIGH  - NEW STOCK NO.
 34              BAL   9,P10PAGE                CHECK FOR PAGE OVERFLOW
 35              BAL   9,G10CALC                CALC. & PRINT UNIT COST
 37 A30          BAL   9,E10SALE                PROCESS INPUT RECORD
 38              GET   FILEIN,STRECIN           READ NEXT RECORD
 44              B     A10LOOP                  LOOP

 46 A90END       BAL   9,G10CALC                EOF - CALC & PRINT UNIT COST
 47              BAL   9,J10FINAL               *     PRINT FINAL TOTAL
 48              CLOSE FILEIN,PRTR
 57              EOJ                            TERMINATE

 61 *                    P R O C E S S     S A L E S
 62 *                    ------------------------------
 63 E10SALE      PACK  QTYPK,QTYSALIN
 64              AP    QTYPKDW,QTYPK            ADD QUANTITY SOLD TO STOCK
 65              BR    9

 67 *                    C O S T   C A L C U L A T I O N
 68 *                    ---------------------------------
 69 G10CALC      LA    2,COSTABLE               INITIALIZE TABLE SEARCH
 70 G20          CLC   PREVSTK,0(2)             INPUT STOCK# : TABLE STOCK#?
 71              BE    G30                      *    EQUAL - FOUND
 72              BL    R20NOSTK                 *    LOW   - NOT IN TABLE
 73              AH    2,=H'14'                 *    HIGH  - TEST NEXT ENTRY
 74              B     G20

 76 G30          ZAP   COSTPKDW,4(3,2)          EXTRACT UNIT COST FROM TABLE
 77              CVB   1,COSTPKDW               CONVERT UNIT COST,
 78              CVB   0,QTYPKDW                *    QUANTITY   TO BINARY
 79              MR    0,0                      MULT UNIT COST BY QUANTITY
 80              CVD   1,COSTPKDW               CONVERT COST TO PACKED
 81              MVC   COSTPR,EDCOS             EDIT:
 82              ED    COSTPR,COSTPKDW+4        *    STOCK COST
 83              MVC   UNCOSPR,EDUNIT
 84              ED    UNCOSPR,4(2)             *    UNIT COST (FROM TABLE)
 85              MVC   QTYPR,EDQTY
 86              ED    QTYPR,QTYPKDW+5          *    QUANTITY

 88              MVC   DESCRIPR,7(2)            MOVE DESCRIPTION (FROM TABLE)
 89              MVC   STOCKPR,PREVSTK          *    STOCK NO.
 90              BAL   11,M10WSP1               PRINT STOCK LINE
 91              AP    FINCOSPK,COSTPKDW+4(4)   ADD COST TO FINAL TOTAL
 92              ZAP   QTYPKDW,=P'0'            CLEAR STOCK QUANTITY
 93              MVC   PREVSTK,STOCKIN          STORE STOCK IN PREV
 94              BR    9
```

Figure 11-19   Program: calculation of sales costs.

```
 96 *                    F I N A L   T O T A L S
 97 *                    ----------------------
 98 J10FINAL  LA      1,PRINT+69            ADDRESS OF SIGNIF. START + 1
 99          MVC     COSTPR(L'EDCOS+2),EDCOS  EDIT FINAL TOTAL COST
100          EDMK    COSTPR,FINCOSPK       *    WITH FLOATING $ SIGN
101          SH      1,=H'1'               *    DECREMENT REGISTER-1
102          MVI     0(1),C'$'             *    INSERT $ SIGN
103          MVC     DESCRIPR(12),=C'FINAL  TOTAL'
104          BAL     11,M10WSP1            PRINT FINAL TOTAL
105          BR      9

107 *                    T A B L E   L O A D   R O U T I N E
108 *                    ----------------------------------
109 L10LOAD   LA      2,COSTABLE            INIT TABLE ADDRESS
110          LA      11,10                 MAX. NO. ENTRIES
112 L20       GET     FILEIN,TABRECIN       GET TABLE RECORD
118          CLC     TABCODIN,=C'06'       TABLE CODE?
119          BNE     R50CODE               * NO - ERROR
120          CLC     TABSTKIN,PREVSTK      STOCK# IN SEQ?
121          BNH     R30TSEQ               *  NO - ERROR
123          BCT     11,L30                TOO MANY ENTRIES?
124          B       R40OVER               *  YES - ERROR
125 L30       MVC     0(4,2),TABSTKIN       STORE STOCK#
126          PACK    4(3,2),TABPRCIN       PACK PRICE
127          MVC     7(7,2),TABDESIN       STORE DESCR'N
128          AH      2,=H'14'              SET NEXT TABLE ENTRY
129          MVC     PREVSTK,TABSTKIN      SET SEQ TEST
130          CLC     TABSTKIN,=C'9999'     LAST ENTRY?
131          BNE     L20                   *  NO - CONTINUE
132          BR      9                     *  YES - RETURN

134 *                    P R I N T   R O U T I N E
135 *                    ------------------------
136 M00SKIP   MVI     CTLPR,X'8B'           SKIP TO PAGE
137          SR      10,10                 CLEAR LINE COUNT
138          B       M90PRINT
139 M10WSP1   MVI     CTLPR,X'09'           WRITE, SPACE 1
140          AH      10,=H'1'              ADD 1 TO LINE COUNT
141          B       M90PRINT
142 M20WSP2   MVI     CTLPR,X'11'           WRITE, SPACE 2
143          AH      10,=H'2'              ADD 2 TO LINE COUNT
144          B       M90PRINT
145 M50SPC1   MVI     CTLPR,X'0B'           SPACE, NO WRITE
146          AH      10,=H'1'              ADD TO LINE COUNT
147 M90PRINT  PUT     PRTR,PRINT
153          MVC     PRINT,BLANK
154          BR      11

156 *                    P A G E   H E A D I N G
157 *                    ----------------------
158 P10PAGE   CH      10,=H'55'             END OF PAGE?
159          BL      P20                   * NO - BYPASS PAGE OVERFLOW
160          BAL     11,M00SKIP            SKIP TO A NEW PAGE
161          MVC     PRINT,PRHEAD1
162          BAL     11,M20WSP2            PRINT REPORT HEADING-1
163          MVC     PAGEPR,EDPAGE         SET UP
164          ED      PAGEPR,PAGEPK         *  PAGE NO.
165          MVC     PRINT,PRHEAD2
166          BAL     11,M20WSP2            PRINT REPORT HEADING-2
167          AP      PAGEPK,=P'1'
168 P20       BR      9
```

Figure 11-19 (*continued*)

```
170 *                   E R R O R   R O U T I N E S
171 *                   ----------------------------
172 R10SEQ   MVC    MSGPR(L'ERRSEQ),ERRSEQ     OUT OF SEQUENCE STOCK
173          B      R90

175 R20NOSTK MVC    MSGPR(L'ERRSTK),ERRSTK     STOCK ITEM NOT IN TABLE
176          B      R90

178 R30TSEQ  MVC    MSGPR(L'TABSEQ),TABSEQ     TABLE OUT OF SEQ
179          B      R90

181 R40OVER  MVC    MSGPR(L'TABOVER),TABOVER   TOO MANY TABLE ENTRIES
182          B      R90
183 R50CODE  MVC    MSGPR(L'ERRCDE),ERRCDE     INVALID RECORD CODE
185 R90      MVC    STOCKPR,PREVSTK
186          BAL    11,M20WSP2                 PRINT ERROR MESSAGE
187          CLOSE  FILEIN,PRTR
196          CANCEL ALL                        ABNORMAL END-OF-JOB

201 *                   D E C L A R A T I V E S
202 *                   -------------------------
203 FILEIN   DTFCD  BLKSIZE=80,                DEFINE INPUT FILE       +
                    DEVADDR=SYSIPT,                                    +
                    DEVICE=2540,                                       +
                    EOFADDR=A90END,                                    +
                    IOAREA1=INBUFF1,                                   +
                    TYPEFLE=INPUT,                                     +
                    WORKA=YES

227 INBUFF1  DC     CL80' '                    INPUT BUFFER-1

229 TABRECIN DS     0CL80                      TABLE RECORD:
230 TABCODIN DS     CL02                       *   RECORD CODE
231 TABSTKIN DS     CL04                       *   STOCK #
232 TABPRCIN DS     ZL05                       *   PRICE
233 TABDESIN DS     CL07                       *   DESCRIPTION
234          DS     CL62                       *

236          ORG    TABRECIN
237 STRECIN  DS     0CL80                      STOCK RECORD:
238 CODEIN   DS     CL02                       01-02 RECORD CODE
239 STOCKIN  DS     CL04                       05-08 STOCK NO.
240          DS     CL02                       09-10 UNUSED
241 QTYSALIN DS     ZL03                       11-13 QUANTITY SOLD
242          DS     CL69                       14-80 UNUSED

244 PRTR     DTFPR  BLKSIZE=133,               DEFINE PRINTER FILE     +
                    CTLCHR=YES,                                        +
                    DEVADDR=SYSLST,                                    +
                    DEVICE=3203,                                       +
                    IOAREA1=PRBUFF1,                                   +
                    WORKA=YES

270 PRBUFF1  DC     CL133' '                   PRINTER BUFFER-1

272 PRHEAD1  DS     0CL133                     HEADING-1 AREA:
273          DC     CL29' '                    *
274          DC     CL104'I N V E N T O R Y  S A L E S   R E P O R T'

276 PRHEAD2  DS     0CL133                     HEADING-2 AREA
277          DC     CL22' '                    *
```

Figure 11-19 *(continued)*

```
278            DC     CL22'STOCK'                  *
279            DC     CL42'QUANTITY UNITCOST       COST'
280            DC     CL09'PAGE'                   *
281 PAGEPR     DS     CL04                         *
282            DC     CL34' '                      *

284 BLANK      DC     C' '                         BLANK FOR CLEARING PRINT
285 PRINT      DS     0CL133                       REPORT PRINT AREA
286 CTLPR      DS     XL01                         *
287            DC     CL21' '                      *
288 STOCKPR    DS     CL04                         *    STOCK NO.
289            DC     CL02' '                      *
290 DESCRIPR   DS     CL07                         *    DESCRIPTION
291            DC     CL09' '                      *
292 QTYPR      DS     ZL08                         *    QUANTITY
293            DC     CL01' '                      *
294 UNCOSPR    DS     ZL07                         *    UNIT COST
295            DC     CL01' '                      *
296 COSTPR     DS     ZL12                         *    COST
297 MSGPR      DC     CL60' '                      *

299            DS     0D                           ALIGNED DOUBLEWORD:
300 COSTPKDW   DC     PL8'0'                       *
301 QTYPKDW    DC     PL8'0'                       *

303 QTYPK      DC     PL2'0'                       NORMAL PACKED DECLARES:
304 FINCOSPK   DC     PL4'0'                       *
305 PAGEPK     DC     PL2'1'                       *

307 ERRCDE     DC     C'INVALID RECORD CODE'
308 ERRSEQ     DC     C'RECORD OUT OF SEQUENCE ON STOCK'
309 ERRSTK     DC     C'STOCK ITEM NOT IN TABLE'
310 TABSEQ     DC     C'TABLE ENTRY OUT OF SEQUENCE'
311 TABOVER    DC     C'TOO MANY TABLE ENTRIES'
313 PREVSTK    DC     XL4'00'
314 EDCOS      DC     X'4020206B2020214B2020C3D9',C'**'
315 EDUNIT     DC     X'402020214B2020'
316 EDQTY      DC     X'402020202020C3D9'
317 EDPAGE     DC     X'40202020'
319 COSTABLE   DC     10X'FFFFFFFF00000C40404040404040'
320            LTORG
337            END    PROG11
```

Output:-

INVENTORY SALES REPORT

STOCK		QUANTITY	UNITCOST	COST	PAGE 1
1234	GIDGETS	125	1.00	125.00	
2468	WIDGETS	76	15.25	1,159.00	
2470	MIDGETS	96	100.17	9,616.32	
2844	FIDGETS	35	20.00	700.00	
	FINAL TOTAL			$11,600.32	**

Figure 11-19 (*continued*)

The program first loads the stock table records one after another into a table. The last table record contains nines in stock number. Once the program has loaded the stock table records, it processes the inventory stock records. Note that for loading tables, it is a good idea to allow for expansion—define the table large enough to accept more entries than you would normally ever expect.

Processing. The program is organized as follows:

Main logic. The routine opens the files, links to P10PAGE for the first headings, links to L10LOAD to load the table, and reads the first stock record. It then performs a loop: Compare the new stock number to the previously processed number. A low sequence is an error. A high sequence means link to G10CALC to calculate and print the last stored stock quantity. Equal and high sequences link to E10SALE to process the new input record. The routine then reads the next record. At end-of-file, the routine links to G10CALC to calculate and print the last stored stock quantity and links to J10FINAL for final totals.

E10SALE. The routine accumulates quantity sold for a stock item.

G10CALC. The routine performs a table search on the stored stock number. An item not in the table is an error. If found, the routine uses the stored unit cost to calculate and print amount of sale (quantity × unit cost) and adds to a final total.

J10FINAL. The routine prints the final total.

L10LOAD. The routine is performed only once, at initialization. It sets the address of COSTABLE and then performs a loop that reads a table record and, if a stock table code (06), performs the following:

1. Checks that the stock number is in ascending sequence.
2. Checks that the table is not about to be overloaded—that is, that the table is large enough to contain the new entry.
3. Moves stock number into the first 4 bytes, replacing the X'FF's; packs price into the next 3 bytes, replacing X'00000C'; and moves the description into the next 7 bytes, replacing the X'40's.
4. Increments for the address of the next table entry.
5. Exits on either of two conditions: The record code is not 06 or the table stock number is 9999.

P10PAGE. The routine handles the page headings.

Error routines. The program checks for sales records out of sequence, stock items not in the table, table records out of sequence, too many table records, and invalid record codes. Since errors involving table records are especially serious, the program cancels on any error.

REGISTER USAGE

0,1	Calculation of cost
1	For EDMK instruction
2	Table search on stock table
3	Base register for program addressing
9	Subroutine linkage
10	Line count for page overflow
11	Count for entries loaded in the table

KEY POINTS

- You may use explicit base addressing for any operand that references main storage.
- Instructions such as MVC and CLC provide an explicit length only for operand 1, whereas packed instructions permit lengths for both operands.
- The communication region is a storage area in the supervisor. The first 8 bytes contain today's date, which the DOS COMRG and the OS TIME macros may access.
- Tables contain a set of related data arranged so that each item can be referenced according to its location in the table. A static table contains defined data, such as income tax steps and inventory stock prices. A dynamic table consists of a series of adjacent blank or zero fields defined to store or accumulate related data.
- The contents of a table may be descriptive (such as the names of departments in a company), numeric (as in an income tax table), or a combination of descriptive and numeric.
- A table often consists of arguments and functions. In a table search, a search argument is compared against the table argument to determine if the required function is in the table.
- If table arguments are both sequential and consecutive, you could omit defining the arguments in the table, and you can use direct table addressing.

PROBLEMS

11-1. For a program, a field containing "SPACE AGE" is subject to base register 3 and a displacement of 0024. What is the effect of the following instruction?

```
MVC       24(6,3),25(3)
```

11-2. What is the effect of the following AP instruction?

```
                              LA        7,TOTAL
                              LA        8,AMOUNT
                              AP        0(5,7),0(4,8)
                              . . .
            AMOUNT    DS      PL4
            TOTAL     DS      PL5
```

11-3. Provide the instructions to extract today's date from the communication region for (a) DOS; (b) OS.

11-4. What two ways may an assembler program use to terminate a table search? What may be the result if no provision is made to terminate if the argument is (a) character; (b) packed; (c) binary?

11-5. In each of the following cases, register 5 is initialized to zero. Based on the contents of FW1 and FW2, explain the instructions and determine the contents of register 5:

```
        FW1       DC      F'25'
        FW2       DC      F'250'
(a)               L       7,FW1
        A20       A       5,=F'2'
                  BCT     7,A20
(b)               LA      6,100
                  LM      8,9,FW1
        B20       A       5,=F'3'
                  BXLE    6,8,B20
```

11-6. What do the following unrelated routines accomplish?

```
(a)               LA      7,X30
                  LA      6,10
                  BCTR    6,7
(b)               LA      9,25
                  BALR    10,0
                  BCTR    9,10
(c)               LA      9,25
        C20       BCT     9,C20
```

11-7. Define the table named TAXTAB required to calculate the current federal income tax and define a field named TAXINC for taxable income.

11-8. A payroll table contains consecutive job numbers from 021 through 047. Each job number has an associated rate of pay (xx.xx) as its function. Job numbers are 3 characters, hours worked have the format xx.x, and wages have the format xxxx.xx. Define the table and code the instructions to perform a direct table search. Calculate wages as hours worked times the located rate, rounded to two decimal places.

11-9. Use the defined linked list in Fig. 11-13 to perform a search on part number. Provide for items that are not in the list.

11-10. Revise the routines to sort the tables in descending sequence in (a) Fig. 11-14; (b) Fig. 11-15.

11-11. Revise Fig. 11-19 as follows: (a) Allow for storing table entries in random sequence.

(b) After loading the table, sort the entries into ascending sequence.   (c) Instead of a sequential search, use a binary search.

11-12. A program contains a table of job numbers and rates of pay:

JOB	RATE
1046	12.25
1053	13.75
1073	15.35

...

Users enter job numbers and hours worked, and the program is to calculate pay = hours × rate, rounded.   For convenience, treat each entered job number and number of hours worked as a record.   However, job number (four digits) can begin at any position, and hours worked can begin at any position following, including immediately.   Hours may contain a decimal point (one only), such as 4.5.   Because of correcting entries, hours may occasionally be negative, entered as −4.5 or 4.5−. Lack of a minus sign implies a positive value.   A blank erminates the hours field.

Eliminate any decimal point, but keep track of its position.   Convert hours to binary.   Find the rate in the table and calculate pay, rounded.   Convert the binary pay to edited character, and insert a decimal point in the correct position.   Print the results for each record, and print total pay at the end.

```
       Sample input data (job followed by hours):
              1046 0
          1073                       12
              1046 -2.25
        1088                6.5
```

12

LOGICAL OPERATIONS
AND
BIT MANIPULATION

OBJECTIVE

To explain the operation and uses of the computer's logical instructions.

Certain operations such as CLC, CLI, MVC, and LA treat data as "logical." The operations assume that the fields contain no sign and act nonalgebraically on each byte as a string of 8 bits. Similarly, certain binary operations such as AL, CL, and SRL treat all 32 bits of the binary fullword as unsigned (logical) data.

The first part of this chapter discusses the logical operations that add, subtract, compare, and shift. These instructions are useful when numeric fields are of such magnitude that they require double precision, a 63-bit field plus a sign bit. Double precision involves an even-odd pair of registers: The left register contains the sign and the leftmost 31 data bits; the right register contains the rightmost 32 data bits:

sign ———— data ————	———— data ————
even register	odd register

Of greater use are the other logical operations: TM (test under mask), TR

(Translate), and TRT (Translate and Test). Although technically a branch operation, EX (Execute) is also included. These instructions provide a repertoire of powerful techniques to manipulate bits, to translate bits to other codes, and to handle variable-length records. Another use for logical operations is to translate binary (fixed-point) data to floating-point format.

LOGICAL OPERATIONS

Add and Subtract Logical (AL, ALR, SL, SLR)

These add and subtract instructions treat binary fields as unsigned logical data.

Name	Operation	Operand
[label]	AL	R1,X2 *or* R1,D2(X2,B2)
[label]	ALR	R1,R2
[label]	SL	R1,X2 *or* R1,D2(X2,B2)
[label]	SLR	R1,R2

AL, ALR, SL, and SLR are similar to A, AR, S, and SR, with the following differences:

- Since the operation treats the data as logical, it assumes no sign, and adds or subtracts all 32 bits.
- There may be a carry out of the leftmost bit (bit 0). For subtraction, if the carry out of bit 0 differs from bit 1, an overflow occurs.
- The condition code is set as follows:

CODE	ADD	SUBTRACT
0	Zero sum	Zero difference
1	Nonzero sum	Minus
2	Zero sum with carry	Plus
3	Nonzero sum with carry	Overflow

Double-Precision Addition

Double-precision fields contain a sign bit and 63 data bits. Because a register can handle only 32 bits, you have to give such fields special programming consideration.

Figure 12-1 defines two 64-bit fields named DBL1 and DBL2 that are to be added, with the result stored in DBL1. The program has to split each field into two 32-bit fields. The leftmost 32 bits of DBL1 are loaded into register 6 and the rightmost 32 bits into register 7. (The example shows two 5-bit registers for ease of understanding.) The sign is the left bit of register 6. An AL instruction adds

```
 6 *                                 Reg-6: Reg-7:
 8            L       6,DBL1          00101           LOAD LEFTMOST   32 BITS
 9            L       7,DBL1+4        00101 11010     LOAD RIGHTMOST  32 BITS
10            AL      7,DBL2+4        00101 10000     ADD  RIGHTMOST  32 BITS
11            BC      12,NOFLOW       BRANCH IF COND CODE 0 OR 1
12 *                                 NO BRANCH IF CARRY SUM OR
13 *                                     NON-ZERO SUM.
14            AH      6,=H'1'         00110 10000     ADD 1 TO LEFTMOST FIELD
15 NOFLOW     A       6,DBL2          01001 10000     ADD  LEFTMOST   32 BITS
16            ST      6,DBL1                          STORE LEFTMOST  32 BITS
17            ST      7,DBL1+4                        STORE RIGHTMOST 32 BITS
18 *            ...
19 DBL1       DS      D               00101 11010     ASSUME 10-BIT FIELD 186
20 DBL2       DS      D               00011 10110     ASSUME 10-BIT FIELD 118
```

Figure 12-1   Addition of double-precision binary fields.

the rightmost 32 bits of DBL2 to register 7—a logical add because register 7 has no sign bit.   If an overflow occurs, a bit has been lost; adding 1 to register 6 remedies this situation.   Then an A instruction adds the leftmost 32 bits of DBL2 to register 6.   Check the binary values for each step.

Compare Logical (CL, CLR)

The CL and CLR instructions are similar to C and CR.   However, CL and CLR compare logically all 32 bits from left to right regardless of the sign.   Consequently, if the leftmost bit of operand 1 is 1 and the leftmost bit of operand 2 is 0, the comparison is high.   (C and CR would compare as low.)   An unequal compare terminates the operation.   The usual condition code is set to equal (0), low (1), and high (2).

Name	Operation	Operand
[label]	CL	R1,X2 *or* R1,D2(X2,B2)
[label]	CLR	R1,R2

Shift Logical (SRL, SLL, SRDL, SLDL)

These instructions shift bits right or left logically regardless of sign and treat the entire 32 or 64 bits as a single unsigned field.   Operand 1 of SRDL and SLDL references the even register of an even-odd pair.

Name	Operation	Operand
[label]	SRL	R1,S2 *or* R1,D2(B2)
[label]	SLL	R1,S2 *or* R1,D2(B2)
[label]	SRDL	R1,S2 *or* R1,D2(B2)
[label]	SLDL	R1,S2 *or* R1,D2(B2)

The rules for SRL, SLL, SRDL, and SLDL are similar to those for SRA, SLA, SRDA, and SLDA, with these exceptions:

- All 32 or 64 bits shift.
- Zero bits replace bits shifted off the left or right.
- The condition code is not set, and no overflow occurs.

The following two examples illustrate logical shift operations.

1. Shift register 6 contents 12 bits to the right:

```
SRL    6,12
```

2. Shift registers 6 and 7 contents 12 bits to the left:

```
SLDL   6,12
```

DATA COMPRESSION

The following routine illustrates shifting logical data in registers. Frequently, a file consists of thousands or hundreds of thousands of records stored on disk or tape. One way to conserve storage is to compress fields in binary format. Consider customer records for an electric utility. The following shows four numeric fields at present defined in character format and the number of bits that could be used to store the fields in binary format:

	NUMBER OF CHARACTERS	NUMBER OF BITS FOR BINARY REPRESENTATION
District	3	10
Account	5	17
Rate code	1	1
Service code	+1	+2
	10 bytes	30 bits, or 4 bytes

You can store the contents of district in 3 characters or alternatively in a 10-bit binary field, which can store a value up to 1,023. Similarly, account, with a maximum value of 99,999, can be stored in a 17-bit binary field. Rate code requires only a 1-bit field: 0 for domestic or 1 for commercial rate. Service code can contain four possibilities requiring 2 bits:

	CODE	BITS
None	0	00
Budget	1	01
Meter rental	2	10
Both	3	11

```
24 *                              Reg:          Binary Format:
25 BINPACK  PACK   DOUBWORD,DISTRICT
26         CVB    6,DOUBWORD       6: --   --22 zeros--    --1101000110
28         PACK   DOUBWORD,ACCOUNT
29         CVB    7,DOUBWORD       7: -- 15zeros --   00100010100010011
30         SLL    7,15             7: 00100010100010011--  15 zeros --
31         SLDL   6,17             6: 00000110100011000100010100010011
33         PACK   DOUBWORD,RATE
34         CVB    7,DOUBWORD       7: ----     --31 zeros--      ---1
35         SLL    7,31             7: 1---     --31 zeros--      ----
36         SLDL   6,1              6: 00001101000110001000101000100111
38         PACK   DOUBWORD,SERVICE
39         CVB    7,DOUBWORD       7: ----     --30 zeros--      --10
40         SLL    7,30             7: 10 -     --30 zeros--      ---
41         SLDL   6,2              6: 00110100011000100010100010011110
42         ST     6,FULLWORD
43 *         ...

44 *                   Assumed Values- Char: Binary:
45 DISTRICT DC   CL3'838'           838   1101000110
46 ACCOUNT  DC   CL5'17683'       17683   00100010100010011
47 RATE     DC   CL1'1'               1   1
48 SERVICE  DC   CL1'2'               2   10
49 DOUBWORD DS   D
50 FULLWORD DS   F
```

Figure 12-2   Binary data compression.

Whereas character format requires 10 bytes to store the data, binary format here requires only 30 bits, or one fullword of 4 bytes.   If there are 400,000 records stored on a disk file, the saving is 400,000 × 6 = 2,400,000 bytes of disk storage (not main storage).   You have to condense or compress these fields into one binary fullword prior to writing the data on disk.

The coding in Fig. 12-2 performs this compression using logical shift operations because there are no signs.   The compressed binary format is to be as follows:

Unused	00–01
District	02–11
Account	12–28
Rate	29–29
Service	30–31

BOOLEAN LOGIC: AND, OR, EXCLUSIVE OR

Boolean logic was devised by George Boole (1815–1864).   Practical applications have been in switches for telephone circuits and in the design of electronic computers.   Boolean logic uses only digits 0 and 1 and has two arithmetic functions: addition and multiplication.   The following shows the four possible results for both addition and multiplication:

	ADDITION					MULTIPLICATION		
0	0	1	1		0	0	1	1
+0	+1	+0	+1		×0	×1	×0	×1
0	1	1	1		0	0	0	1

Assembler language uses Boolean logic for the logical functions AND, OR, and XOR (Exclusive OR) to perform bit manipulation. For each of the three logical functions there are four instructions, in RR, RX, SI, and SS format.

AND	OR	XOR	Instruction Format	Data Processed
NR	OR	XR	RR	Two registers
N	O	X	RX or R1,D2(X2,B2)	Register and storage
NI	OI	XI	SI or D1(B1),I2	Register and immediate
NC	OC	XC	SS or D1(L,B1),D2(B2)	Storage and storage

For all 12 instructions, operand 1 is called the *target* field and operand 2 is the *mask*. The operations compare the bits in the mask against those in the target, one at a time from left to right. The target bits are modified to 0 or 1 according to the bit contents and the logical operation. The condition code is set as follows:

0 if all target bits are set to 0. Test with BZ or BNZ.

1 if any target bit is set to 1. Test with BM or BNM.

The following shows two 4-bit fields, named MASK and TARGET. The three unrelated cases illustrate AND, OR, and XOR. Each case sets the condition code to 1:

FIELD	AND	OR	XOR
MASK	0011	0011	0011
TARGET	0101	0101	0101
Result	0001	0111	0110

The AND Operation

The logical AND operation is equivalent to Boolean multiplication. If both the mask and the target bit are 1, the target bit is set to 1. All other cases set the target bit to zero.

The following four examples use these declaratives to illustrate the AND operations:

```
          DS    0F                    Force fullword alignment
MASK      DC    B'00110111001010011111000011001101'
TARGET    DC    B'01010101110010011000011110011110'
```

1. AND the contents of register 8 (the mask) with register 9 (the target):

```
L    8,MASK      Load MASK value
L    9,TARGET    Load TARGET value
NR   9,8         AND TARGET with MASK
```

2. AND the contents of MASK in storage (a fullword) with the target in register 8:

```
L    8,TARGET    Load TARGET value
N    8,MASK      AND TARGET with MASK
```

3. AND the single immediate byte with the first byte of TARGET:

```
NI    TARGET,B'01010101'      AND 1st byte of TARGET
```

4. AND the first 2 bytes of MASK and TARGET:

```
NC    TARGET(2),MASK     AND 1st 2 bytes
```

The OR Operation

The logical OR operation is equivalent to Boolean addition. If either the mask or the target bit is 1 (or both), the target bit is set to 1. Where both bits are zero, the target bit is set to zero.

The following four examples use these declaratives to illustrate the OR operations:

```
          DS    0F                        Force fullword alignment
MASK      DC    B'00110111001010011111000011001101'
TARGET    DC    B'01010101110010011000011110011110'
```

1. OR the contents of register 8 (the mask) with the target in register 9:

```
L    8,MASK      Load MASK value
L    9,TARGET    Load TARGET value
OR   9,8         OR TARGET with MASK
```

2. OR the contents of MASK in storage (a fullword) with the target in register 8:

```
L    8,TARGET    Load TARGET value
O    8,MASK      OR TARGET with MASK
```

3. OR the single immediate byte with the first byte of TARGET:

```
OI    TARGET,B'01010101'      OR 1st byte of TARGET
```

4. OR the first 2 bytes of MASK and TARGET:

```
OC      TARGET(2),MASK        OR 1st 2 bytes
```

The Exclusive OR (XOR) Operation

If either the mask or the target bit (but not both) is 1, XOR sets the target bit to 1. Where both are 0 or 1, the target is set to 0.

The following four examples use these declaratives to illustrate the XOR operations:

```
        DS    0F                              Force fullword alignment
MASK    DC    B'00110111001010011111000011001101'
TARGET  DC    B'01010101110010011000011110011110'
```

1. XOR the contents of register 8 (the mask) with the target in register 9:

```
        L     8,MASK      Load MASK value
        L     9,TARGET    Load TARGET value
        XR    9,8         XOR TARGET with MASK
```

2. XOR the contents of MASK in storage (a fullword) with the target in register 8:

```
        L     8,TARGET    Load TARGET value
        X     8,MASK      XOR TARGET with MASK
```

3. XOR the single immediate byte with the first byte of TARGET:

```
        XI      TARGET,B'01010101'      XOR 1st byte of TARGET
```

4. XOR the first 2 bytes of MASK and TARGET:

```
        XC      TARGET(2),MASK      XOR 1st 2 bytes
```

Common Uses for Boolean Operations

Figure 12-3 shows several applications of Boolean operations. In CLEAR, the Exclusive OR clears an area to hex zeros. Since both mask and target contain the same bits, Exclusive OR sets all bits to zero and clears a binary field to X'00's, all binary zeros. Some programmers use XC to clear the print area, as XC PRINT,PRINT, although X'40' is the normal and recommended blank character.

SIGN corrects the sign in an unpacked field. In Chapter 8 you saw that a packed field such as | 23 | 4C | when unpacked becomes | F2 | F3 | C4 |, which prints incorrectly as 23D. The solution used MVZ to insert an F sign in place of

```
  5 *                       Clear a Field to Hex Zeros:
    *                       --------------------------
  6 CLEAR   XC    FULLWD,FULLWD                 CLEAR BINARY VALUE
  7 *       ...
  8 FULLWD  DS    F                             BINARY FULLWORD

 10 *                       Correct Sign For Printing:
    *                       --------------------------
 11 SIGN    UNPK  PRINT+91(3),PAGENO            UNPACK PAGE COUNTER
 12         OI    PRINT+93,X'F0'                FORCE F-SIGN
 13 *       ...
 14 PAGENO  DC    PL2'1'                        PAGE COUNTER

 16 *                       Exchange 2 Registers:    7: 1010   8: 1001
    *                       ---------------------
 17 REVERSE XR    7,8                            7: 0011   8: 1001
 18         XR    8,7                            7: 0011   8: 1010
 19         XR    7,8                            7: 1001   8: 1010

 21 *                       Change NOP to Branch
    *                       --------------------
 22 SWITCH  NOP   CHANGE                        NO-OP INSTRUCTION
 23 *       .
 24 *       .
 25         OI    SWITCH+1,X'F0'                CHANGE SWITCH MASK TO
 26 *       .                                     X'F' (B)
 27 *       .
 28         B     SWITCH
 29 CHANGE  NI    SWITCH+1,X'0F'                CHANGE SWITCH MASK TO
 30 *       .                                     X'0' (NOP)
 31 *       .
 33 *                       Test Bits On For Customer Code:
    *                       ------------------------------
 34 CODES   MVC   TEST,CUSCODE                  MOVE CODE TO TEST
 35         NI    TEST,B'11100000'              'AND' FIRST 3 BITS
 36 *       BNZ   ...                           BRANCH ANY BIT IS ON
 37 *       .
 38 *       .
 39 CUSCODE DS    BL1
 40 TEST    DS    BL1

 42 *                       Test Characters For F-Zone
    *                       --------------------------
 43 ZONES   MVC   STORE,FIELD                   MOVE CHAR FIELD TO STORE
 44         NC    STORE,=X'F0F0F0F0F0'          'AND' WITH X'F0'S
 45         CLC   STORE,=X'F0F0F0F0F0'          UNEQUAL?  SOME BYTE
 46 *       BNE   ...                           HAS NO F-ZONE
 47 *       .
 48 *       .
 49 FIELD   DS    CL5
 50 STORE   DS    CL5
```

Figure 12-3 Sample uses of Boolean operators.

the C sign, changing the field to │ F2 │ F3 │ F4 │ . This example unpacks a page counter, PAGENO, in the print area. OI forces all 4 sign bits to be turned on, thereby adjusting the sign to X'F'. For example, C4 ORed with F0 gives F4.

REVERSE shows how XR may interchange two registers without the use of an intermediary register. The 4-bit areas illustrate how the example works.

SWITCH illustrates switching. You may manipulate the mask in the BC (branch on condition) instruction to change the program flow. BC 15 (unconditional branch) is commonly written as B. BC 0 is a no-operation condition that performs no branch at all; the extended mnemonic is NOP. The mask is in bits 8–11 of the object code. The example switches the mask from X'0' to X'F' (NOP becomes B), and vice versa—clever, but not good programming practice.

CODES uses bits that represent yes or no conditions for customers. In the example, a utility company customer has an 8-bit code designed as follows:

Bit 0	Electric account	Bit 4	Electric heating
Bit 1	Gas account	Bit 5	30 days delinquent
Bit 2	Budget account	Bit 6	Rented meter
Bit 3	Industrial	Bit 7	Not used

A 1 bit means the condition exists, and more than one bit may be validly on. The example tests whether the customer has any of the electric, gas, or budget conditions. The NI operation tests bits 0, 1, and 2; any equal bits set the condition code to 1.

ZONES tests for F zones in a character field. This is a useful check for validity of input data, such as date, account number, and amounts (except the units portion of minus amounts, such as F1F2F3F4D5).

The TM instruction in the next section is usually more effective for testing bits.

OTHER OPERATIONS: TM, IC, STC, EX, TR, TRT

This section examines some of the more advanced and powerful operations for manipulating data.

Test under Mask (TM)

We have been using bits as switches or indicators. An efficient instruction to test bit conditions is TM (Test Under Mask).

Name	Operation	Operand
[label]	TM	S1,I2 *or* D1(B1),I2

TM is an immediate instruction (like MVI) with two operands: Operand 1 refers to one byte in storage, containing the bits to be tested; operand 2 is the 8-bit mask in immediate format. One bits in the mask indicate which bits to test in operand 1. TM compares the one-bits in the mask against the selected bits in operand 1, bit for bit. For example, if the immediate operand is B'01001100', TM tests only bits 1, 4, and 5 of operand 1. Operand 1 is unchanged. The condition code is set as follows:

SELECTED BITS IN OPERAND 1	CONDITION CODE	TEST USING
All selected bits are 0	0	BZ (Branch Zeros) or BNZ
Bits are mixed, 0 and 1	1	BM (Branch Mixed) or BNM
All selected bits are 1	3	BO (Branch Ones) or BNO

TM tests only the bit positions of the mask that contain 1 and ignores positions that contain 0. (Boolean operators, however, process all bit positions regardless of contents.) The extended mnemonics for testing the condition code, BZ, BM, and BO, are the same but are described differently for TM. Branch Minus is called Branch Mixed, and Branch Overflow becomes Branch Ones.

In our recent example CODES, an 8-bit code represented yes or no conditions for utility customers. The three examples in Fig. 12-4 use BZ, BM, and BO to test this code.

TESTZERO. To determine whether a customer has an industrial account with a rented meter, test bits 3 and 6 of CODE. In the example, the selected bits in CODE are both 0. Because the condition code is set to 0, BZ causes a branch. To determine whether customers have an electric account, electric heating, and are 30 days delinquent in paying their bill, test bits 0, 4, and 5 of CODE.

TESTMIX. The status of the selected bits is as follows: Bit 0 is on, bit 4 is off, and bit 5 is on. Because the bits are mixed off and on, the condition code is set to 1, and BM causes a branch.

TESTONES. To determine whether a customer has electric, gas, and budget, test bits 0, 1, and 2. The selected bits in CODE all contain 1. The condition code is set to 3, and BO causes a branch.

```
 7 TESTZERO TM    CODE,B'00010010'        SELECTED BITS ALL 0
 8 *        BZ    ...                     BRANCH ON ZEROS

10 TESTMIX  TM    CODE,B'10001100'        SELECTED BITS MIXED
11 *        BM    ...                     BRANCH ON MIXED

13 TESTONES TM    CODE,B'11100000'        SELECTED BITS ALL 1
14 *        BO    ...                     BRANCH ON ONES
15 *        ...
16 CODE     DC    B'11100100'
```

Figure 12-4   Sample uses of TM.

Insert Character (IC) and Store Character (STC)

IC moves a single byte (8 bits) from storage into a register, and STC moves a byte from a register into storage.

Name	Operation	Operand
[label]	IC	R1,X2 *or* R1,D2(X2,B2)
[label]	STC	R1,X2 *or* R1,D2(X2,B2)

For both IC and STC, operand 1 references the rightmost 8 bits of a register (bits 24–31). Operand 2 references one byte of storage. IC, like LH, transfers data from operand 2 (storage) to operand 1 (register). STC, like STH, transfers data from operand 1 (register) to operand 1 (register). However, the IC and STC operations do not affect the other bits (0–23) of the register. Further, operand 2 can specify any storage position, odd or even.

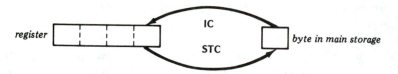

Extended IC and STC Example

Figure 12-5 illustrates both IC and STC and introduces variable-length fields. This example reads a record from an input device. The record, named NAMEADDR,

```
24              XR    1,1                  CLEAR REG 1
25              LA    9,NAMADDR            ADDR OF 1ST LENGTH
26              IC    1,0(0,9)             LENGTH OF NAME IN REG 1
27              LR    8,1                  LOAD REG 1 INTO REG 8
28              BCTR  1,0                  DECREMENT REG 1 BY 1
30              STC   1,M10MOVE+1          STORE DECREMENTED LENGTH
31              LA    9,1(0,9)             INCREMENT FOR NAME FIELD
32  M10MOVE     MVC   PRINT+20(0),0(9)     MOVE NAME TO PRINT
33              AR    9,8                  ADDR OF NAME + LENGTH FOR
34  *                                         2ND LENGTH INDICATOR
35              IC    1,0(0,9)             LENGTH OF ADDR IN REG 1
36              BCTR  1,0                  DECREMENT REG 1 BY 1
37              STC   1,M20MOVE+1          STORE DECREMENTED LENGTH
38              LA    9,1(0,9)             INCREMENT FOR ADDR FIELD
39  M20MOVE     MVC   PRINT+50(0),0(9)     MOVE ADDRESS TO PRINT
40  *           .
41  *           .
42  NAMADDR     DS    CL42                 VARIABLE NAME & ADDRESS
43  PRINT       DC    CL133' '             PRINT AREA
```

Figure 12-5 Use of IC and STC to move variable name and address.

consists of two fields, name and address, both of which may be of any length. The length of each field is defined by a one-byte binary number preceding the field, as shown here:

name   address

0A	ADAM SMITH	0C	423 BASIN ST

hex character hex character

Since the name is 10 characters long, the preceding length indicator contains X'0A'. The address is 12 characters long, and its preceding length indicator contains X'0C'. The entire record consists of 1 + 10 + 1 + 12 = 24 bytes. Other records would vary in length accordingly. The maximum record length is assumed to be 42 bytes.

  The purpose is to move the name and the address separately to the print area. IC extracts the length indicator, and STC inserts the length indicator (minus 1) into the second byte, the length, of the MVC instruction. (At execute time, the computer adds 1 to the instruction length.) At the end of execution the print area looks like this:

print area: | ADAM SMITH | 423 BASIN ST |
       | |
      PRINT + 20   PRINT + 50

The next section uses the EX instruction to handle the same example.

Execute (EX)

Although generally the declarative section is separate from instructions, under certain unique circumstances an instruction may be coded within the declaratives or at least outside the normal execute flow. This is called a *subject instruction*, which you may execute by means of the EX (Execute) operation.

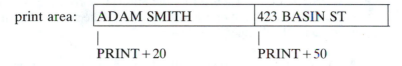

Name	Operation	Operand
[label]	EX	R1,X2 *or* R1,D2(X2,B2)

  The ability of EX to modify the second byte of a subject instruction gives you the power, depending on the instruction format, to change a register reference, an immediate operand, or an operand length. The following shows each instruction format, in which the second byte (in machine object code) that is subject to change is underlined:

FORMAT	OPERANDS	
RR	R1,R2	
RS	R1,R3,D2(B2)	
RX	R1,D2(X2,B2)	
SI	D1(B1),I2	
SS (1)	D1(L,B1),D2(B2)	(one length)
SS (2)	D1(L1,B1),D2(L2,B2)	(two lengths)

The rules for EX are as follows:

- Operand 1 designates a register containing a value used to modify the second byte of the subject instruction. However, if register 0 is specified, no modification is done.

- Operand 2 refers to the subject instruction, defined elsewhere in storage, to be executed by EX. Any instruction except another EX may be subject to EX.

- EX ORs bits 8–15 (byte 2) of the subject instruction with bits 24–31 (the rightmost byte) of the operand 1 register. The subject instruction, however, is not actually changed in storage.

After executing the subject instruction, the program resumes either with the instruction following the EX or, if the subject instruction is a branch, where the branch is directed.

The next section examines the five instruction formats, RR, RS, RX, SI, and SS, subject to EX. (In practice, the contents of the operand 1 register would generally be a result of a calculation.) In each case, the second byte of the subject instruction (ADDREG, STOREGS, etc.) is defined as zero because the byte is to be ORed. These examples are intended to illustrate how EX works but not necessarily how you would use it in practice.

RR format. The following RR example inserts '14' into register 5 and ORs byte 2 of ADDREG with X'14'. This process causes the second byte of ADDREG to reference registers 1 and 4 temporarily. ADDREG executes out of line as "add the contents of register 4 to register 1."

```
EXRR    IC   5,=X'14'      Insert X'14' in register 5
        EX   5,ADDREG      Add register 4 to register 1
        ...
        DS   0H            Force even address
ADDREG  AR   0,0           RR subject instruction
```

RS format. The RS example ORs the second byte of STOREGS with X'DF'. This process causes byte 2 of STOREGS to reference registers 13 and 15.

STOREGS executes out of line as "store the contents of registers 13, 14, and 15 in SAVEREGS."

```
            IC    6,=X'DF'          Insert X'DF' in register 6
            EX    6,STOREGS         Store registers 13, 14, 15
            . . .
SAVEREGS    DS    3F                3 fullwords
            DS    0H                Force even address
STOREGS     STM   0,0,SAVEREGS      RS subject instruction
```

RX format. The RX example ORs the second byte of STORCH with X'20'. This process causes byte 2 of STORCH to reference base register 2 and index register 0. STORCH executes as "store the rightmost 8 bits of register 2 in SAVEBYTE."

```
            IC    7,=X'20'          Insert X'20' in register 7
            EX    7,STORCH          Store right byte of register 2
            . . .
SAVEBYTE    DS    C                 One byte
            DS    0H                Force even address
STORCH      STC   0,SAVEBYTE        RX subject instruction
```

SI format. The SI example ORs the second byte of MOVIMM with X'5B' ($). (Remember that the subject instruction is not physically changed.) MOVIMM then moves X'5B' to PRINT+20, and the instruction can thus move any immediate value.

```
            IC    8,=X'5B'          Insert X'5B' in register 8
            EX    8,MOVIMM          Move $ to print area
            . . .
PRINT       DC    CL133' '          Print area
            DS    0H                Force even address
MOVIMM      MVI   PRINT+20,X'00'    SI subject instruction
```

SS format. Using EX on SS format causes it to modify operand lengths. Remember that when executing an SS instruction, the computer adds 1 to the length. The first example uses MOVECHAR to move a specified number of asterisks (up to three) to the print area and could be used to print one, two, or three asterisks to denote the total level:

```
            IC    9,=X'02'          Insert X'02' in register 9
            EX    9,MOVECHAR        Move *** to print area
            . . .
PRINT       DC    CL133' '          Print area
            DS    0H                Force even address
MOVECHAR    MVC   PRINT+30(0),=C'***'   SS subject instruction
```

```
LOC     OBJECT CODE  STMT  SOURCE STATEMENT
003802  1711           6   XR   1,1            CLEAR REG 1
003804  4190 4026      7   LA   9,NAMADDR      ADDR 1ST LENGTH INDICATOR
003808  4310 9000      8   IC   1,0(0,9)       LENGTH OF NAME IN REG 1
00380C  1881           9   LR   8,1            SAVE LENGTH IN REG 8
00380E  0610          11   BCTR 1,0            DECREMENT REG 1 BY 1
003810  4190 9001     12   LA   9,1(0,9)       INCREMENT FOR NAME FIELD
003814  4410 40D6     13   EX   1,M30MOVE      EXECUTE M30MOVE INSTR'N
003818  1A98          14   AR   9,8            ADDR OF NAME + LENGTH FOR
                      15   *                     2ND LENGTH INDICATOR
00381A  4310 9000     16   IC   1,0(0,9)       LENGTH OF ADDR IN REG 1
00381E  0610          17   BCTR 1,0            DECREMENT REG 1 BY 1
003820  4190 9001     18   LA   9,1(0,9)       INCREMENT FOR ADDR FIELD
003824  4410 40DC     19   EX   1,M40MOVE      EXECUTE M40MOVE INSTR'N
                      20   *
                      21   *
                      22   *
003828                23   NAMADDR DS  CL42              VARIABLE NAME & ADDRESS
003852                24   PRLINE  DS  CL133             PRINT AREA
0038D7  00
0038D8  D200 4064 9000  26  M30MOVE MVC PRLINE+20(0),0(9)   MOVE NAME TO PRINT
0038DE  D200 4082 9000  27  M40MOVE MVC PRLINE+50(0),0(9)   MOVE ADDRESS TO PRINT
```

Figure 12-6 Use of EX to move variable-length fields.

The second example executes an AP operation in which byte 2 contains a length code for both operands:

```
          IC      10,=X'32'           Insert X'32' in register 10
          EX      10,ADDPK            Add FLD2 to FLD1
          ...
FLD1      DS      PL4
FLD2      DS      PL3
          DS      0H                  Force even address
ADDPK     AP      FLD1(0),FLD2(0)     SS subject instruction
```

Extended EX Example

Figure 12-5 earlier illustrated variable-length move operations. Figure 12-6 uses EX to code the same example. Carefully compare the two examples to see how EX is used. A later section uses the same example to illustrate the TRT instruction.

Centering a Variable String

Let's say that a program is to move any number of dashes (-) up to 80 and is to center these dashes on a screen or page. Thus 80 dashes would fill the entire screen, but 20 dashes would fill positions 30–49. In this example, register 5 contains the actual number of dashes to display, and the receiving field is named LINE. Before checking the example in Fig. 12-7, see whether you can solve the problem.

Assume that register 5 contains a length of 20. The example in Fig. 12-7 would calculate the starting location in LINE as follows:

Initial value:	80
Subtract 20:	60
Divide by 2:	30
Add address of LINE:	A(LINE + 30)

```
31              LH      9,=H'80'        CALC SCREEN POS'N
32              SR      9,5             * 80 - LENGTH
33              SRA     9,1             * DIVIDE BY 2
34              A       9,=A(LINE)      * ADD ADDRESS
35              BCTR    5,0             DECR LENGTH
36              EX      5,M10MOVE       MOVE N DASHES
37  *                  .
38  *                  .
39  *                  .
40  LINE        DC      CL80' '
41  M10MOVE     MVC     0(0,9),=80C'-'  SUBJECT INSTRUCTION
```

Figure 12-7 Centering a variable string.

The routine therefore moves the 20 dashes beginning at LINE + 30. Note that if the line is 80, the starting location in LINE is (as it should be) LINE + 0. You could also make the routine more general; for example, by means of base/displacement addressing, operand 2 of M10MOVE could contain a reference to the address of any defined string. If the routine loads the address into register 10, the MVC instruction would appear as:

```
M10MOVE     MVC  0(0,9),0(10)
```

Translate (TR)

At times data introduced into a program is not in standard EBCDIC code (the 8-bit code on the 370-series computers). Or you may have to translate certain EBCDIC characters into some other characters. Here are some instances when you may need to translate code:

- Some systems use ASCII mode. If delivered as input to the 370 series (by magnetic tape or data communications), ASCII must be translated to EBCDIC.
- Input records may contain invalid characters in numeric fields that the program is to pack for arithmetic. For example, a 3-byte field that contains asterisks, X'5C5C5C', when packed becomes X'CCC5'. Because the field does not contain valid packed data, an operation such as AP or SP would cause a data exception.
- Responses from a terminal keyboard may require only alphabetic letters or numeric characters with optional decimal point and minus sign.
- It may be necessary to translate lower-case characters entered from a keyboard into upper case, or upper-case letters to lower case to display on a screen or on a printer.

The instruction that translates code from one format to another is TR (Translate).

Name	Operation	Operand
[label]	TR	S1,S2 *or* D1(L,B1),D2(B2)

The rules for TR are as follows:

- Operand 1 references the address of the argument: the byte or bytes to be translated. TR may translate a field or record up to 256 bytes long, such as a record coded in ASCII.
- Operand 2 references a table of functions, which contains the required new code, such as the correct EBCDIC code. The definition of the table is the key to the use of TR (and TRT, to be discussed later).

- TR starts processing with the leftmost byte of the argument. A byte can contain any value from X'00' through X'FF', which TR adds to the address of the table, giving a range of addresses from table + X'00' through table + X'FF'. The contents of the table address make up the function that TR uses to replace the argument byte. The operation continues, then, with the next argument, proceeding from left to right one byte at a time until completing the argument length.

Our next example translates hex numbers to alphabetic characters. The number 1 (X'01') is to be translated to the first character, A (X'C1'); 10, or X'0A', to the tenth character, J; 19, or X'13', to the nineteenth character, S, and so on. The only valid expected values are 0 through 26 (X'1A'). The table is defined as TABLE, with a blank followed by the letters A through Z. Assume that the argument ARGUMENT contains X'0104010D':

```
            TR      ARGUMENT,TABLE          Translate argument
            ...
ARGUMENT    DS      CL4                     Assume X'0104010D'
TABLE       DC      C' ABCDEFGHIJKLMNOPQRSTUVWXYZ'
```

The example works as follows:

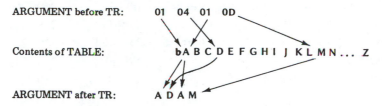

1. TR adds the first byte of ARGUMENT containing X'01' to the address of TABLE. At TABLE + 1 is the letter A (X'C1'), which replaces X'01' in ARGUMENT.

2. TR adds the second byte of ARGUMENT containing X'04' to the address of TABLE. At TABLE + 4 is the letter D, which replaces X'04' in AR-GUMENT.

3. TR adds the third byte of ARGUMENT containing X'01' to TABLE. The letter A replaces X'01' in ARGUMENT.

4. TR adds the fourth and last byte of ARGUMENT containing X'0D' to TABLE. At TABLE + 13 is the letter M, which replaces the X'0D'. ARGUMENT is now correctly translated to 'ADAM'.

Question: Why does TABLE begin with a blank byte rather than the letter A?

Warning: An argument may be invalid with respect to the table of functions. For example, if ARGUMENT contains X'28' (decimal 40), TR will access the address TABLE + 40, which yields a "function" that is outside the bounds of the table. Validating an argument prior to a TR is recommended. For many types of translations where almost any argument is valid, you have to define a table with all possible 256 EBCDIC codes, as illustrated in the next section.

Extended TR Example

A character field that is to be packed should contain only numbers 0–9 and sign. Our next example in Fig. 12-8 translates invalid bytes in an input amount field. When read in character format, these bytes should contain only two sets of values:

-0 through -9, represented by X'D0' through X'D9'
$+0$ through $+9$, represented by X'F0' through X'F9'

These valid hex values are to stay the same, whereas all other hex values are to translate arbitrarily to X'F0'. A table of functions could therefore define all possible EBCDIC codes that "translate" valid argument bytes to the same value and translate invalid bytes to X'F0'. Note the positioning of the table functions:

TABLE FUNCTIONS		REFERENCES	HEX VALUE	DECIMAL VALUE	TRANSLATE TO
First	208	Invalid hex arguments	00–CF	000–207	X'F0'
Next	10	−0 through −9	D0–D9	208–217	not changed
Next	22	Invalid	DA–EF	218–239	X'F0'
Next	10	+0 through +9	F0–F9	240–249	not changed
Last	6	Invalid	FA–FF	250–255	X'F0'

The example shows how invalid bytes in INAREA, assumed to be a numeric field, are translated to X'F0'. Devise some examples of valid and invalid data to check the operation.

Next is an approach that checks whether all bytes are numeric. The example translates all numeric (0–9) bytes to asterisks and checks whether the TR changed

```
45              TR      INAREA+10(6),TABLE2      TRANSLATE INPUT AREA
46              PACK    AMTPK,INAREA+10(6)       PACK VALIDATED FIELD
47   *          ...
48   *                                           POSITION:
49   TABLE2     DC      208X'F0'                 000-207   208 BYTES INVALID
50              DC      X'D0D1D2D3D4D5D6D7D8D9'   208-217    10 BYTES -0 THRU -9
51              DC      22X'F0'                  218-239    22 BYTES INVALID
52              DC      X'F0F1F2F3F4F5F6F7F8F9'   240-249    10 BYTES +0 THRU +9
53              DC      6X'F0'                   250-255     6 BYTES INVALID

55   INAREA     DS      CL80                     INPUT AREA
56   AMTPK      DS      PL4                      PACK AREA
```

Figure 12-8 Use of TR to translate invalid bytes.

every byte. (Checking that the rightmost byte contains a minus sign requires special treatment.)

```
        MVC   TEST,INAREA      Move numeric amount
        TR    TEST,TABLE       Translate numerics to *
        CLC   TEST,=6C'*'      All asterisks?
        BNE   error            No - perform error routine
        ...
TEST    DS    CL6              Test field
TABLE   DC    240X'00'         Translate table
        DC    10C'*'           *
        DC    6X'00'           *
```

Design a table for TR with care. A byte offset in the wrong table position can cause infrequent, subtle errors. One common error is forgetting that the first table position is numbered zero. Another error is failure to account for all 256 possible positions.

If you have to know which record positions contain an invalid character, use the TRT instruction (covered next).

Translate and Test (TRT)

It is sometimes necessary to scan input data to detect an invalid character (as in the TR example) or to detect a unique character, such as a "delimiter" that terminates a variable-length record. TRT (Translate and Test) conveniently serves this purpose.

Name	Operation	Operand
[label]	TRT	S1,S2 *or* D1(L,B1),D2(B2)

TRT is similar to TR in these ways. (1) Operand 1 references the address of the argument, up to 256 bytes in length. (2) Operand 2 references a table of functions containing the required new code. (3) The operation begins with the first byte of the argument and processes one byte at a time. TRT adds the value of each argument byte to the address of the table to find each function in the table.

TRT differs from TR in these ways. (1) If the value of the table function is zero, TRT continues with the next argument byte. (2) If the value of the table function is nonzero, TRT inserts into register 1 the address of the argument in bits 8–31 (bits 0–7 are unchanged), inserts into register 2 the contents of the function in bits 24–31 (bits 0–23 are unchanged). (3) The argument byte is unchanged; there is no translation since, in effect, TRT is a scan operation. (4) TRT terminates on finding a nonzero function or on reaching the end of the argument.   (5) The condition code is set as follows:

CODE	CAUSED BY	TEST WITH
0	All functions found were zero	BZ, BNZ
1	A nonzero function was found, but not at the end of the argument	BM, BNM
2	A nonzero function was found at the end of the argument	BP, BNP

The next three examples illustrate the condition codes set by TRT and assume the same argument, ARG.

Example 1.   The TRT scans each byte (pair of hex digits) of ARG.   For instance, X'02' is directed to TABLEA + 2, and so forth.   Since all function bytes are found to be zero, the condition code is set to zero, and registers 1 and 2 remain unchanged.

```
SCAN1     TRT     ARG,TABLEA
          . . .
ARG       DC      X'0203000604'
TABLEA    DC      X'005C0000005C00'
```

Graphically, the foregoing TRT operation looks like this:

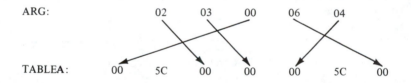

Example 2.   X'02', X'03', and X'00' in ARG direct the operation to zero functions in TABLEB.   X'06' in ARG, however, directs the operation to TABLEB + 6, which contains X'5C'.   Therefore, TRT does the following: (1) inserts the address of ARG + 3 in register 1, (2) inserts the table function X'5C' in register 2, and (3) sets the condition code to 1.

```
SCAN2     TRT     ARG,TABLEB
          . . .
ARG       DC      X'0203000604'
TABLEB    DC      X'004B0000004B5C'
```

Example 3.   The first 4 bytes of ARG locate zero functions in TABLEC. The last byte, X'04', however, directs the operation to TABLEC + 4, which contains

```
60              MVC     NAMEOUT,SURNAME
61              MVC     SPACEOUT,=CL5' '
62              TRT     NAMEOUT,TABLNK           SCAN FOR BLANK
63              BZ      S20                      NOT FOUND - EXIT
64              MVI     0(1),C','                INSERT COMMA,
65              MVC     2(1,1),INITIALS              INITIAL,
66              MVI     3(1),C'.'                    & PERIOD
68              CLI     INITIALS+1,C' '          2ND INITIAL?
69              BE      S20                      *  NO - EXIT
70              MVC     4(1,1),INITIALS+1        INSERT INITIAL
71              MVI     5(1),C'.'                    & PERIOD
72 S20          EQU     *
73 *            ...
74 TABLNK       DC      64X'00'                  SCAN TABLE:
75              DC      X'40'                    *   BLANK POS'N
76              DC      191X'00'                 *

78 SURNAME  DS      CL20                         SURNAME
79 INITIALS DS      CL02                         INITIALS
80 NAMEOUT  DC      CL20' '
81 SPACEOUT DC      CL05' '
```

Figure 12-9   Scanning for a blank.

X'5B'.   TRT does the following: (1) inserts the address of ARG + 4 in register 1, (2) inserts the table function X'5B' in register 2, and (3) because the last byte of ARG was processed, sets the condition code to 2.

```
SCAN3       TRT     ARG,TABLEC
            ...
ARG         DC      X'0203000604'
TABLEC      DC      X'004B00005B5C00'
```

Scanning for a Blank

At the beginning of Chapter 11, Fig. 11-3 described a routine that inserted a comma, initials, and periods to the right of surnames, as Brown, J.L.   The program used base/displacement addressing to scan the surname for a blank.   In the next example, in Fig. 12-9, a TRT instruction replaces the earlier technique.

The scan table contains all hex zeros except for one in the blank (hex '40') position.   An MVC instruction moves the surname to NAMEOUT, and another MVC moves blanks to a 5-byte field that immediately follows.   This space ensures that at least one blank follows the name and provides positions for inserting the initials.

TRT scans NAMEOUT for a blank, and if found, the routine uses the address in register 1 to insert the commas, initials, and periods.   The situation in which a blank is not found should never occur.

Checking for Positive and Negative Numbers

Let's now see how to use TRT to scan an input field for valid positive numbers in all positions and valid negative numbers only in the units position.

```
 5              TRT     VALUEIN,POSTAB       TEST FOR POS CHARS.
 6              BZ      G200K                * ALL CHARS ARE 0-9
 7              BM      R95INV               * INVALID BEFORE LAST
 8    *                                      * LAST CHAR NOT POS
 9              TRT     VALUEIN+6(1),NEGTAB  TEST LAST FOR NEG
10              BNZ     R95INV               * INVALID LAST CHAR
11    *                                      * LAST IS NEG.
12 G200K        EQU     *                    PROCESS VALID FIELD
13    *                 ...
14 R95INV       EQU     *                    ERROR ROUTINE
15    *                 ...
16      *                                    POSITION:
17 POSTAB       DC      240X'FF'             000-239   240 BYTES INVALID
18              DC      10X'00'              240-249    10 BYTES +0 THRU +9
19              DC      06X'FF'              250-255     6 BYTES INVALID

21    *                                      POSITION:
22 NEGTAB       DC      208X'FF'             000-207   208 BYTES INVALID
23              DC      10X'00'              208-217    10 BYTES -0 THRU -9
24              DC      38X'FF'              218-255    38 BYTES INVALID

26 VALUEIN      DS      ZL7
```

Figure 12-10   Checking for positive and negative numbers.

In the example in Fig. 12-10, the input field is VALUEIN. The table named POSTAB defines the valid positive numbers X'F0' through X'F9' as hex zeros and NEGTAB defines the valid negative numbers X'D0' through X'D9' as hex zeros.

- The first TRT scans VALUEIN for positive numbers. If all numbers are positive, the routine performs no further checking.
- If an invalid number occurs before the units position, the program branches to an error routine.
- If the units position contains a nonpositive character, the second TRT checks the position for a valid negative number.

Scanning Variable-Length Fields

The next example, for variable-length fields, is similar to the examples for IC, STC, and EX in Figs. 12-5 and 12-6. This example has no length indicator preceding the name and address. Instead, a delimiter character, in this case an asterisk (*), indicates the end of the variable-length field:

                    ADAM SMITH*423 BASIN ST*

In Fig. 12-11, TRT scans the record to find the asterisk delimiter and then uses the address of the delimiter to calculate the length of the name and the address and to determine the address of the next field. The program uses two TRT and two EX operations to move the name and address to the print area. Both TRT instructions assume a maximum length of 21. The table, TABSCAN, contains a nonzero function only for the X'5C' (*) position and zero functions for all other

```
10              SR    1,1                CLEAR REG 1
11              LA    9,NAMADD           LOAD ADDR OF VARIABLE RECORD
12              TRT   0(21,9),TABSCAN    SCAN FOR NAME DELIMITER
13  *           BZ    ...                *      NOT FOUND, ERROR

15              LR    7,1                SAVE ADDR OF DELIMITER
16              SR    1,9                CALCULATE LENGTH OF NAME
17              BCTR  1,0                DECREMENT LENGTH BY 1
18              EX    1,M50MOVE          EXECUTE M50MOVE INSTR'N
19              LA    9,1(0,7)           INCREMENT FOR ADDR FIELD

21              TRT   0(21,9),TABSCAN    SCAN FOR ADDR DELIMITER
22  *           BZ    ...                *      NOT FOUND, ERROR
23              SR    1,9                CALCULATE LENGTH OF ADDR
24              BCTR  1,0                DECREMENT LENGTH BY 1
25              EX    1,M60MOVE          EXECUTE M60MOVE INSTR'N
26  *           ...
27  *                                    POSITION:
28  TABSCAN     DC    92X'00'            000-091    92 ZERO FUNCTIONS
29              DC    X'5C'              092-092     1 ASTERISK *
30              DC    163X'00'           093-255   163 ZERO FUNCTIONS
32  NAMADD      DS    CL42               VARIABLE NAME & ADDRESS
33  PRINT       DS    CL133

35  *           Subject Instructions For EX:
36  M50MOVE     MVC   PRINT+20(0),0(9)   MOVE NAME TO PRINT
37  M60MOVE     MVC   PRINT+50(0),0(9)   MOVE ADDRESS TO PRINT
```

Figure 12-11   Use of TRT to move variable-length fields.

codes.   The example assumes, perhaps unwisely, that a delimiter always follows both name and address.

Further examples of EX, TRT, and variable-length records can be found in Chapter 18.

MASKED BYTE OPERATIONS: ICM, STCM, CLM

The ICM, STCM, and CLM instructions provide for handling 1 to 4 selected bytes. ICM inserts up to 4 bytes from storage into a register, STCM stores up to 4 bytes from a register into storage, and CLM makes a logical comparison of 4 bytes between a register and storage.

Name	Operation	Operand
[label]	ICM	R1,S2 *or* R1,M3,D2(B2)
[label]	STCM	R1,S2 *or* R1,M3,D2(B2)
[label]	CLM	R1,S2 *or* R1,M3,D2(B2)

- Operand 1 designates any one of the 16 general registers.
- Operand 2 supplies the name of a data field in storage.   There is no required alignment, and although you may define the field in any format, the instruction

can reference only the first 4 bytes.   The number of one-bits in the mask determines the length in bytes of operand 2.

- Operand 3 defines a mask that can be any value 0–15 (hex 0–F).   Each one-bit bit specifies a byte position in the register from left to right.   Thus a mask of 10 (bits 1010) indicates the first and third bytes of the register.

Insert Characters under Mask (ICM)

The ICM instruction begins with the leftmost byte of storage and inserts up to 4 bytes into the designated register according to the mask.   In the following examples, each ICM is unrelated:

		Mask:	Register 7:
SR	7,7		00 00 00 00
ICM	7,1,FLDA	0001	00 00 00 31
ICM	7,3,FLDA	0011	00 00 31 32
ICM	7,9,FLDA	1001	31 00 00 32
ICM	7,15,FLDA	1111	31 32 33 34

```
          . . .
FLDA   DC    X'31323334'
```

If the mask is 0, the operation acts like NOP, except that the condition code is set to 0.   Otherwise, ICM sets the condition code according to the leftmost bit of the storage field—a value of 0 sets the code to 2 (positive), and 1 sets the code to 1 (negative).   Note that the mask in the last ICM example, 15, acts like an LTR with no alignment requirement.

Store Characters under Mask (STCM)

The STCM instruction is the reverse of ICM.   The instruction begins with the leftmost byte of the register and stores into storage up to 4 bytes, according to the mask.   STCM does not set the condition code.

In the following unrelated examples, assume that register 8 contains X'41424344':

		Mask:	FLDB:
STCM	8,1,FLDB	0001	00 00 00 41
STCM	8,5,FLDB	0101	00 41 00 42
STCM	8,11,FLDB	1011	41 00 42 43

```
          . . .
FLDB   DC    X'00000000'
```

Compare Logical under Mask (CLM)

The CLM instruction performs a logical (not algebraic) comparison left to right of bytes in a register with bytes in storage, according to the mask.   The condition code settings are as follows:

0 if compared bytes are equal or mask is 0

1 if compared bytes in the register are low

2 if compared bytes in the register are high

In the following example, assume that register 9 contains X'51525354'.   The example compares the 3 leftmost bytes of register 9 (X'515253') to the 3 leftmost bytes of FLDC (X'515240'), from left to right.   The third byte of register 9 is higher:

			Bits:	Condition Code:
	CLM	9,14,FLDC	1110	high (02)
	...			
FLDC	DC	X'51524040'		

KEY POINTS

- Binary operations such as AL, CL, and SRL treat all 32 bits of the binary fullword as unsigned (logical) data.
- The logical AND function is equivalent to Boolean multiplication.   If both the mask and the target bit are 1, the target bit is set to 1.   In all other cases, the target bit is set to zero.
- The logical OR function is equivalent to Boolean addition.   If either the mask or the target bit (or both) is 1, the target bit is set to 1.   If both bits are zero, the target bit is set to zero.
- If either the mask or the target bit (but not both) is 1, XOR sets the target bit to 1.   If both are zero or 1, the target is set to zero.
- Operand 1 of TM refers to one byte in storage, containing the bits to be tested, and operand 2 is the 8-bit mask in immediate format.   TM compares one-bits in the mask against the selected bits in operand 1, bit for bit.   The condition code is set to 0, 1, or 3 and is tested with BZ, BM, and BO.
- IC moves a single byte (8 bits) from storage into a register, and STC moves a byte from a register into storage.
- The EX (Execute) operation modifies the second byte of a subject instruction, defined elsewhere, and allows you to change a register reference, an immediate operand, or an operand length.
- The TR instruction translates code from one format to another.   Operand 1 references the address of the argument: the byte or bytes to be translated.   Operand 2 references a table of functions, which contains the required new code.
- TRT allows you to scan a record in order to detect an invalid character or a unique character, such as a delimiter that terminates a variable-length record.

TRT delivers values to both registers 1 (the address of the located byte) and 2 (the byte value).

- ICM inserts up to 4 bytes from storage into a register, STCM stores up to 4 bytes from a register into storage, and CLM makes a logical comparison of 4 bytes between a register and storage.

PROBLEMS

12-1. Figure 12-2 compressed four fields into one binary fullword. Assume that the fullword has been read from tape into storage field FULLWORD DS FL4. Write the coding to decompress the fullword into four individual character fields named DIST, ACCOUNT, RATE, and SERVICE.

12-2. STC stores the rightmost 8 bits of a register into a field named BOOL. Use Boolean operations (a) to force the leftmost 4 bits of BOOL to be zeros; (b) to reverse all 8 bits, zeros to ones and vice versa; (c) to force the leftmost 4 bits of BOOL to be ones.

12-3. Figure 12-4 showed how to test bit values. Code the instruction to test whether a customer has both gas and industrial accounts.

12-4. Figure 12-5 illustrated variable-length name and address. Change NAMADDR to 63 bytes, allowing for a third variable field, city. Revise the coding to move this field to PRINT + 80. Also, recode the routine as a loop so that there is one set of instructions executed three times, one for each field. *Hint:* Change operand 1 of the MVC to explicit base register format. Expand the code to include a read and print, then test the program.

12-5. Recode Fig. 12-6 using one EX for the same changes required in Problem 12-4.

12-6. Design a table for TR to translate upper-case letters $(A-Z)$ to lower-case $(a-z)$. Leave characters 0–9, comma, and period unchanged. Convert all other characters to X'40'.

12-7. ASCII code is given in the table in Appendix F. Design two tables of functions to translate (a) ASCII to EBCDIC; (b) EBCDIC to ASCII.

12-8. In Fig. 12-8, TR translated invalid bytes in an input field to character zero. Change the example so that the program prints the column where the invalid code occurred. A record may contain more than one invalid column.

12-9. Translate hex into character format. Each 4 bits (hex digit) of register 9 is to print as a single character, just like a storage dump. Hex zero should print as character zero, X'9' as character 9, X'A' as character A, and so on. Since register 9 contains 32 bits, 8 characters are required, printing from PRINT + 11 to PRINT + 18. *Suggestion:* Shift the 4 leftmost bits of register 9 into register 8. Store these in a one-byte field and use TR to translate from hex to character. Repeat the loop eight times. You can define the table as quite short.

12-10. Recode Fig. 12-12 using one TRT for the same changes required in Problem 12-4.

12-11. A program polls external devices for inquiries and delivers them to a "stack" defined in the program—in effect, a table. The first entry in the stack provides the total number (in binary) of the inquiries. Subsequently, each entry in the stack begins with a destination code followed by an inquiry and terminates with hex FF. The last entry terminates with two hex FFs, as follows:

```
05 [FF]
759 Check discount on customer 63246[FF]
672 Send current product prices to Cleveland office[FF]
645 Backorder needed on endrails in Klamath Falls[FF]
632 Arrange flight schedule for Miller [FF][FF]
672 Reroute delivery 563 to route 54[FF]
```

For this program exercise, you'll have to define the table and its actual contents. The program is to sort these inquiries into ascending sequence by destination code. (In practice, it would route the messages to their proper destinations.) For sorting, note that lengths are variable—use some imagination to solve this.

Define a second table consisting of destination codes and names of the recipients of messages at that destination. Print (or display) the names of the recipients and their messages.

12-12. A program receives ASCII data from a communications line and is to convert it into EBCDIC format for processing. For convenience, we'll define the ASCII data in a declarative. Each field within a record terminates with an asterisk, ASCII 2A. The last field in a record terminates with two asterisks, and hex FF indicates end-of-file. (Appendix F of the text lists all ASCII and EBCDIC codes. Note that ASCII blank is hex 20.)

The table in ASCII format is as follows:

```
ASCTAB    DC     X'454C7454C4C20454C454354524F4E4943532A2A'
                 X'4241524220454C4C49532A3037303938392A2A'
                 X'41434520535550504C4945532A3038303938392A2A'
                 X'4D4F4F52455320464F524D532A3037303938392A2A'
                 X'FF'
```

Convert each entry in the table into EBCDIC format, and print each record with fields separated by two blanks. Assume that each record fits on a standard 132-character line.

13

SUBPROGRAM LINKAGE

OBJECTIVE

To describe the various ways to link separately
assembled programs and the ways to transfer data
between them.

One of the common uses of assembler programs is as subprograms called by large
main programs written in a high-level language. This chapter uses the general
term *subprogram* to mean a section of coding that comprises a separate part of the
program, such as a control section (CSECT) or a phase. The link-edit step combines the separate subprograms into a single executable program. You may want
to code a program in more than one subprogram for the following reasons:

- Several programmers can work separately on subprograms.
- Breaking a program into logical components simplifies the problem.
- It is easier to debug small sections.
- There may not be enough base registers available for a large program.
- Main storage may be too small for an entire program. The use of virtual

storage, however, provides automatic program sectioning and overlays and to a large degree reduces the need for programmers to design such programs.

- A program may involve linking two different languages, such as COBOL and assembler.

CONTROL SECTION: CSECT

Chapters 3 and 6 introduced the term *control section* (CSECT). A CSECT is a block of coding that can be relocated without affecting the operating logic of the program. Both the assembler and the linkage editor process control sections, not programs. You may assemble CSECTs as separate object modules, each with its own unique base registers. Then you link-edit the object modules into one or more phases, and a phase may consist of one or more control sections. Here are two ways to organize a program into subprograms:

1. The program may consist of a single phase containing one or more control sections. You assemble the CSECTs separately or together and link-edit them into a single phase. For execution, the system loads the entire phase into storage.

2. The program may consist of more than one phase, each with one or more CSECTs. Each phase is separately assembled, then link-edited together. At execution time, the system loads the first (root) phase into storage. The root phase loads the other phases into storage as required.

Two main considerations are associated with the use of subprograms:

1. Some data is common to more than one subprogram, but data is defined in only one subprogram. Because subprograms are assembled separately, the assembler treats each subprogram as a completely different program. Data defined in one subprogram is not therefore automatically known in another. There are two methods of transferring data between programs. In the first method, *call by reference*, you make the address in the main program known to the subprogram. In the second method, *call by value*, the calling program delivers the actual values as parameters.

2. A subprogram must be able to link to another subprogram, its register contents must be saved (especially base registers), and there must be some means of returning and restoring the register contents. The assembler macros that provide this linkage are CALL, SAVE, and RETURN. The assembler requires a standard savearea for registers and a standard linkage convention.

This chapter first examines a simple case of how a dummy section works. Then it shows you how to assemble and link two CSECTs for execution. The last example combines three separately assembled phases into one program consisting of a root phase and two overlay phases. The last section explains how to link a COBOL program with an assembler program.

DUMMY SECTION: DSECT

You may need to *describe* a data area without actually reserving any storage. For example, a main subprogram, SUBPROGA, contains the main data and certain other coding, including instructions to link to SUBPROGB. SUBPROGB is a separately assembled control section. Within SUBPROGB you want to reference the main data that is defined and exists in SUBPROGA. This method is a call by reference, since it provides the address of the common data. You may describe this main data in SUBPROGB so that when assembling SUBPROGB, the assembler knows the names, lengths, formats, and relative position of each field in SUBPROGA. The special assembler directive, for this purpose, is DSECT (Dummy Section).

Name	Operation	Operand
label	DSECT	blank

The name of a DSECT refers to the first byte of the section. Instead of reserving storage, DSECT gives the assembler a mask or image of data defined elsewhere. Figure 13-1 illustrates a DSECT defined within a CSECT. The partial program reads records with two buffers and no workarea (IOREG = 5). Rather than transfer the current buffer to a workarea with MVC RECDIN,0(5), the program processes input records directly in the buffer and defines the fields.

The DSECT, named DATAIN, generates no object code. The fields defined within the DSECT tell the assembler the names and formats. The directive USING DATAIN,5 assigns register 5 as a base register for DATAIN, because the buffers for RECDIN are under register 5 (IOREG = 5). Register 5 therefore acts as a base register with respect to DATAIN. For the instruction CLC CODEIN, = C'03', the assembler treats CODEIN under base register 5. The operand for CODEIN in object code is 5000 (base register 5 and no displacement, because CODEIN is the first byte within DATAIN). Assume that for the first input record, the system has loaded register 5 with the address of buffer 1 (INBUFF1). Since register 5 contains the address of INBUFF1, a reference to CODEIN is to the first 2 bytes of INBUFF1. On the next read operation, the system loads the address of INBUFF2 into register 5, and a reference to CODEIN is now to the first 2 bytes of that buffer.

In this program, base register 5 is to apply to the fields within the DSECT. The directive DROP 5 tells the assembler to discontinue applying base register 5, and in this example the assembler resumes addressing under base register 3. The

```
LOC    OBJECT CODE        ADDR1 ADDR2  STMT  SOURCE STATEMENT
                                         1         PRINT ON,NODATA,NOGEN
000000                                   3   TESTA CSECT                     CONTROL SECTION
000000 0530                              4         BALR  3,0
                          00002          5         USING *,3
                          00000          6         USING DATAIN,5

                                         8         OPEN  FILEIN
                                        16         GET   FILEIN              READ A RECORD
00001E D501 5000 3132     00000 00134   21         CLC   CODEIN,=C'03'       VALID RECORD?
000024 4770 303E                00040   22         BNE   R10CODE          *  NO - ERROR

000028 D205 303E 5002     00040 00002   24         MVC   PREVACCT,ACCTIN
                                        25   *
                                        26   *
                                        27   B10END CLOSE FILEIN
                                        35         EOJ

000040 000000000000                     39  R10CODE EQU  *                   ERROR ROUTINE

000040 000000000000                     41  PREVACCT DC  XL6'00'             PREV ACCOUNT #

                                        43  FILEIN DTFCD BLKSIZE=80,                      +
                                                         DEVADDR=SYSIPT,                  +
                                                         DEVICE=2540,                     +
                                                         EOFADDR=B10END,                  +
                                                         IOAREA1=INBUFF1,                 +
                                                         IOAREA2=INBUFF2,                 +
                                                         RECFORM=FIXUNB,                  +
                                                         TYPEFLE=INPUT,                   +
                                                         IOREG=(5)

00007A 4040404040404040              68  INBUFF1 DC   CL80' '                INPUT BUFFER-1
0000CA 4040404040404040              69  INBUFF2 DC   CL80' '                INPUT BUFFER-2
```

Figure 13-1 CSECT and DSECT example.

continued

```
000000       71 DATAIN   DSECT  ,            DATA DUMMY SECTION:
000000       72 RECDIN   DS     0CL80        * INPUT RECORD
000000       73 CODEIN   DS     CL2          * RECORD CODE
000002       74 ACCTIN   DS     CL6          * ACCOUNT NO.
000008       75          DS     CL72         * REST OF RECORD

                         76          DROP   5

00011A                   78 TESTA   CSECT  ,            RESUME CTL SECTION
000120                   79          LTORG
000120 5B5BC2D6D7C5D540  80                  =C'$$BOPEN '
000128 5B5BC2C3D3D6E2C5  81                  =C'$$BCLOSE'
000130 00000048          82                  =A(FILEIN)
000134 F0F3              83                  =C'03'
00000                    84          END    TESTA
```

Figure 13-1 (*continued*)

CSECT following the DROP terminates the DSECT, and because the CSECT is named TESTA, tells the assembler to resume the initial CSECT named TESTA.

Under OS, Locate Mode involves register 1. The changes necessary to convert the DOS example to OS are as follows:

- OS linkage for initialization and return to the supervisor
- A DCB specifying MACRF=(GL)
- After the GET, load the contents of register 1 into register 5, as in the example:

```
GET     FILEIN
LR      5,1
```

You may also use register 1 as the DSECT base register, provided that the program executes no macro that destroys the base address while it is still required.

SUBPROGRAM LINKAGE

You may use DSECTs to make data known between separately assembled subprograms. In addition, you use standard linkage and saveareas to link between subprograms and to save the contents of registers. The following discussion uses the term *calling program* for the program that calls a subprogram, the *called* (sub)program. A called subprogram may call a lower-level subprogram, which may in turn call a lower-level subprogram, and so forth.

Linkage Registers

Linkage to subprograms requires the calling program to know the entry address of the called program and the called program to know the return address of the calling program. As well, since the called program has to preserve the calling program's registers, it must know the address of the calling program's savearea. The standard linkage registers are 0, 1, 13, 14, and 15:

REGISTER	USE
0, 1	Parameter registers, used by CALL to pass parameters (such as addresses of data) to the called program
13	Savearea register, containing the address of the calling program's savearea
14	Return register, containing the address of the calling program, to which the called program is to return
15	Entry point register, containing the address of the called program's entry point, where you link to begin execution.

Standard Savearea

Each calling program requires definition of a savearea to preserve the contents of its registers. The savearea contains 18 fullwords (or 9 doublewords), aligned on a doubleword boundary. The savearea provides for an additional condition: One subprogram may call another subprogram, which in turn may call yet another subprogram. Figure 13-2 gives the savearea format.

Word	Displacement	Contents of Each Fullword
1	0	Used by PL/I programs.
2	4	Address of the savearea of the calling program. The called program saves this in its own savearea.
3	8	Address of the savearea of the called program.*
4	12	Contents of register 14, return address to the calling program.*
5	16	Contents of register 15, the address of the entry point to the called program.*
6	20	Contents of register 0.*
7-18	24	Contents of registers 1 through 12.*

*The called program stores these in the calling program's savearea.

Figure 13-2   Standard savearea words.

Linkage Macros

The CALL, SAVE, and RETURN macros link subprograms. Assume that SUBPROGA is the subprogram, loaded in storage and being executed. SUBPROGA calls SUBPROGB for execution (SUBPROGB must also be in storage). SUBPROGA is the calling program, and SUBPROGB is the called program.

   The CALL macro.   The CALL macro in a calling program links to a called subprogram.

Name	Operation	Operand
[label]	CALL	entrypoint,(parameter,...)

The operand entrypoint is the name of the first executable instruction of the called program. (Following entrypoint is an optional parameter list, and parameters are symbolic addresses that you want known in the called program.) CALL loads the address of the next sequential instruction in register 14 to facilitate return and branches to the called program.

The SAVE macro. When linking to a called program, you must save the contents of the registers of the calling program. The calling program defines the standard savearea for this purpose.

Name	Operation	Operand
[label]	SAVE	(r1,r2)

Before issuing the CALL macro, first load the address of the savearea in register 13. At the beginning of the called program, code SAVE (14,12) to save the contents of the registers, except 13.

The RETURN macro. You code RETURN (14,12) to restore the original contents of the calling program's registers and to return to the calling program.

Name	Operation	Operand
[label]	RETURN	(r1,r2)

In Fig. 13-3, PROG1 is the calling program and PROG2 is the called program.

PROG1	LA	13,SAVEAREA
	CALL	PROG2
	...	
SAVEAREA	DS	9D
PROG2	SAVE	(14,12)
	...	
	RETURN	(14,12)

Figure 13-3 CALL, SAVE, and RETURN.

Next we examine the generated code for the macros and the additional instructions needed to complete the linkage.

LINKING TWO CONTROL SECTIONS

Figure 13-4 gives skeleton coding for two separately assembled CSECTs: a calling subprogram, PROGA, and a called subprogram, PROGB. The savearea in PROGA defines common data under DATA (immediately at the start). DATA is subject to base register 4, and the rest of the program following BEGINA is under base register 3. Before calling PROGB, the program loads register 13 with the address of the savearea, SAVEA. For the macro CALL PROGB, the assembler generates the following:

```
L    15,=V(PROGB)        Load address of PROGB in register 15
BALR 14,15               Load next instruction address in register
                         14 and branch to PROGB
```

```
// EXEC ASSEMBLY

                EXTERNAL SYMBOL DICTIONARY
SYMBOL        TYPE          ID  ADDR  LENGTH LD-ID
PROGA         SD (CSECT)    001 000000 000090
PROGB         ER (EXTRN)    002

  LOC   OBJECT CODE      STMT   SOURCE STATEMENT
                         1             PRINT ON,NOGEN
000000                   3     PROGA   CSECT  ,            MAIN CONTROL SECTION

                         4     *       COMMON DECLARATIVES:
000000                   5     DATA    DS     0CL1         AREA UNDER REG 3
000000 125C              6     HRSPK   DC     PL2'12.5'    |XX|.XC|
000002 01125C            7     RATEPK  DC     PL3'11.25'   |XX|X.X|XC|
000005                   8     WAGEPK  DS     PL5          |00|XX|XX|X.X|XC|

00000A 0530              10    BEGINA  BALR   3,0          INIT BASE REGISTER-3
                         11            USING  *,3
                         12            USING  DATA,4       ASSIGN BASE REG-4
00000C 5840 307C         13            L      4,=A(DATA)   LOAD BASE REG-4
                         14    *         .
                         15    *         .
000010 F841 4005 4000    16            ZAP    WAGEPK,HRSPK SET UP MULTIPL'D
                         17    *         .
                         18    *         .
000016 41D0 3024         19            LA     13,SAVEA     ADDR OF SAVEAREA
                         20            CALL   PROGB        LINK TO PROGB
                         24    A10RTN  EQU    *            ANY INSTR'N HERE
                         25    *         .
                         26    *         .
                         27    *         .
                         28            PDUMP  DATA,BEGINA
                         34            EOJ

000030                   38    SAVEA   DS     9D           PROGA REG SAVEAREA
000078                   39            LTORG
000078 5B5BC2D7C4E4D4D7  40                   =CL8'$$BPDUMP'
000080 000000000000000A  41                   =A(DATA,BEGINA)
000088 00000000          42                   =A(DATA)
00008C 00000000          43                   =V(PROGB)
                         45            END    BEGINA
```

Figure 13-4 Linkage between a main program and a subprogram.

```
// EXEC ASSEMBLY
                        EXTERNAL SYMBOL DICTIONARY
        SYMBOL    TYPE          ID   ADDR   LENGTH  LD-ID
        PROGB     SD (CSECT)   001  000000  000074
                        DUMMY SECTION DICTIONARY
        SYMBOL      ID  LENGTH
        DATAB      1FF  00000A

   LOC   OBJECT CODE      STMT    SOURCE STATEMENT
                            1               PRINT  ON,NOGEN
```

LOC	OBJECT CODE	STMT	SOURCE STATEMENT			
000000		3 DATAB	DSECT	,		PROGB COMMON DATA:
000000		4 HRSPK	DS	PL2		|XX| .XC|
000002		5 RATEPK	DS	PL3		|XX|X.X|XC|
000005		6 WAGEPK	DS	PL5		|00|XX|XX|X.|XC|

```
   000000              8 PROGB    CSECT
                       9               SAVE   (14,12)        SAVE REGS 14-12
   000004 0590        12               BALR   9,0            INIT BASE REG-9
                      13               USING  *,9
                      14               USING  DATAB,4        ASSIGN BASE REG-4

   000006 50D0 902A   16               ST     13,SAVEB+4     SAVE ADDR OF SAVEA
   00000A 18CD        17               LR     12,13
   00000C 41D0 9026   18               LA     13,SAVEB
   000010 50DC 0008   19               ST     13,8(12)       SAVE ADDR OF SAVEB
                      20 *        .
                      21 *        .
                      22 *        .
   000014 FC42 4005 4002  23           MP     WAGEPK,RATEPK  MULT HOURS X RATE
   00001A F045 4005 003F  24           SRP    WAGEPK,63,5    SHIFT & ROUND WAGE
                      25 *.
                      26 *        .
   000020 58D0 902A   27               L      13,SAVEB+4     ADDR OF SAVEA
                      28               RETURN (14,12)        RETURN TO PROGA

   00002C             33 SAVEB    DS     18F                 PROGB SAVEAREA
                      35               END    PROGB
```

Figure 13-4 *(continued)*

The literal = V(PROGB) is an *external address constant*. Since the assembler does not know the address of PROGB, you tell it that this address is external to this assembly. The assembler inserts an address of X'0000', and the linkage editor inserts the correct address. BALR loads the address of the next instruction, A10RTN, in register 14 and branches to PROGB. PROGB immediately saves PROGA's registers. The SAVE macro here generates the following instruction:

```
                STM 14,12,12(13)
```

In effect, SAVE stores registers 14 through 12 beginning at SAVEA + 12 (words 4 through 18).

Next, PROGB initializes base register 9. (This could be any available register except register 4, which still contains the address of the common data area DATA, as loaded in PROGA). You still need this address in order to reference the fields in the common data area, which in PROGB is named DATAB. Since register 4 is already loaded, you need only code the directive

```
USING DATAB,4
```

to inform the assembler to assign base register 4 to DATAB. For any subsequent reference to the fields within the DSECT for DATAB, the assembler assigns base register 4.

PROGB must now save the contents of register 13, which contains the address of PROGA's savearea. You have to store the contents of register 13 in SAVEB+4 (word 2) because before returning, you must reload PROGA's registers. The next three instructions store the address of SAVEB in SAVEA+8 (word 3). This is done because if there are other subprograms, you can refer to this field for debugging and tracing if the program does not work correctly. The linkage routine has now stored the following:

SAVEA			SAVEB		
Word	Displacement	Contents	Word	Displacement	Contents
1	0		1	0	
2	4		2	4	A(SAVEA)
3	8	A(SAVEB)	3	8	
4	12	A(A10RTN)	4	12	
5	16	A(PROGB)	5	16	
6-18	20	Registers 0-12	6-18	20	

Now PROGB may perform required processing and reference the fields defined in the DATAB DSECT (actually DATA in PROGA). To return to the calling program, PROGA, simply reload register 13 with SAVEB+4, the address of SAVEA.

The RETURN macro next generates

```
LM   14,12,12(13)      Reload registers 14-12 with SAVEA+12
BR   14                Branch to A10RTN in PROGA
```

RETURN restores the original SAVEA registers (14 through 12). Since register 14 now contains the return address (A10RTN), BR branches to this address. You now resume normal processing in PROGA, with base registers reinitialized.

The question may arise: Why doesn't PROGA save its own registers in SAVEA before linking to PROGB? Assume that this is done, and PROGB then initializes its own register values. When PROGB returns to PROGA, PROGA's base registers are not loaded, and without a base register PROGA has no way to reload its own registers.

In this example, SAVEB does not require a full savearea, but you would define SAVEB this way if PROGB were to link to another subprogram. If so, the called program would store PROGB's registers, linkage address, and savearea in SAVEB.

Technical Note on the USING Directive

One rule of the assembler is "in calculating the base register to be used, the assembler always uses the available register giving the smallest displacement." This rule sometimes causes the assembler to override a DROP or another USING. Suppose that the program uses two base registers, 3 and 4. The common data is under register 5 and is defined toward the end of the CSECT:

```
        BALR   3,0
        USING  *,3,4          3 and 4 are base registers for the program
        USING  DATA,5         5 is base register for common data
        . . .
DATA    DS     0C             Common data area
        . . .
```

Depending on the size of the program preceding DATA, the assembler may apply register 4 to DATA rather than the specified register 5. For this reason, the program in Fig. 13-4 defines the common data before the BALR/USING, where the assembler is sure to apply the correct base register.

PASSING PARAMETERS

Another way to make data known between subprograms is call by value, in which the main program passes the actual values as parameters. The CALL statement contains a parameter list of all addresses to be passed to the called program:

```
        CALL subprogram,(parameter-list)
```

Each parameter generates a fullword address, one after the other. CALL loads into register 1 the address of the first parameter in the list. Since the parameter is itself an address, register 1 will contain the address of the first address. The called program can load the address of the first parameter into an available register.

Figure 13-5 provides the same simple example as the previous one, converted to parameters. In the calling program, the instruction

```
        CALL PROGB,(HRSPK)
```

loads the address of HRSPK's address into register 1 and links to PROGB. Here is part of the code that the CALL generates:

```
L    15,=V(PROGB)      Load address of PROGB in register 15
LA   14,*+10           Load return address in register 14
BALR 1,15             Load address of HRSPK address in register 1
DC   A(HRSPK)              and link to PROGB
```

```
// EXEC ASSEMBLY,SIZE=128K
                        EXTERNAL SYMBOL DICTIONARY
        SYMBOL      TYPE            ID ADDR   LENGTH LD-ID
        PROGA       SD (CSECT)      001 000000 000074
        PROGB       ER (EXTRN)      002

   LOC   OBJECT CODE    STMT     SOURCE STATEMENT
                          1               PRINT ON,NODATA,NOGEN
 000000                   3 PROGA    CSECT
 000000 0530              4          BALR  3,0
                          5          USING *,3
                          6 *          .
                          7 *          .
 000002 41D0 3016         8          LA    13,SAVEA         ADDR OF SAVEAREA
                          9          CALL  PROGB,(HRSPK)    LINK TO PROGB
                         19 *          .
                         20 *          .
                         21          EOJ

 000018                  25 SAVEA    DS    18F              PROGA REG SAVEAREA
 000060                  26 HRSPK    DS    PL2              |XX|.XC|
 000062                  27 RATEPK   DS    PL3              |XX|X.|XC|
 000065                  28 WAGEPK   DS    PL5              |00|XX|XX|X.X|XC|

 000070                  30          LTORG
 000070 00000000         31                =V(PROGB)
                         32          END   PROGA


// EXEC ASSEMBLY,SIZE=128K

                        EXTERNAL SYMBOL DICTIONARY
        SYMBOL      TYPE            ID ADDR   LENGTH LD-ID
        PROGB       SD (CSECT)      001 000000 00007C

   LOC   OBJECT CODE    STMT     SOURCE STATEMENT
                          1               PRINT ON,NOGEN
 000000                   3 PROGB    CSECT
                          4          SAVE  (14,12)          SAVE REGS 14-12
 000004 0590              7          BALR  9,0              INIT BASE REG-9
                          8          USING *,9
 000006 50D0 9032         9          ST    13,SAVEB+4       SAVE ADDR SAVEA
 00000A 18CD             10          LR    12,13
 00000C 41D0 902E        11          LA    13,SAVEB
 000010 50DC 0008        12          ST    13,8(12)

 000014 5880 1000        14          L     8,0(0,1)         LOAD ADDR HRSPK
 000018 F841 8005 8000   15          ZAP   5(5,8),0(2,8)    RATE IN PROD
 00001E FC42 8005 8002   16          MP    5(5,8),2(3,8)    MULT HOURS X RATE
 000024 F045 8005 003F   17          SRP   5(5,8),63,5      SHIFT & ROUND WAGE
                         18 *          .
                         19 *          .
 00002A 58D0 9032        20          L     13,SAVEB+4       LOAD ADDR OF SAVEA
                         21          RETURN (14,12)         RETURN TO PROGA

 000034                  26 SAVEB    DS    18F              PROGB SAVEAREA
                         28          END   PROGB
```

Figure 13-5 Passing parameters.

The called program uses this address to load the actual address of HRSPK into register 8 with the instruction L 8,0(0,1). The program can use this address explicitly as a base address reference. In the following instruction, operand 1 references WAGEPK (containing hours), and operand 2 references RATEPK (containing rate):

```
        MP        5(4,8),2(3,8)
```

The example provides standard program linkage, although there are shortcut methods. For example, PROGB could assume register 15 as a base register, since it contains the starting address of PROGB. You could omit the standard BALR/USING and code USING *,15 at its start. Also, you need not store the contents of register 13 in the savearea and reload it on return. These practices may be shortsighted, however, because any input/output or CALL executed in PROGB destroys the contents of registers 13 and 15, causing a subsequent execution error.

LINKING PHASES

You may assemble and link-edit one or more control sections and may arrange the assembly so that the linkage editor output is one or more *phases*. Up to now our programs have consisted of only one phase. The linkage editor writes the object code phase into the core image or load library. The job control command // EXEC causes the first or only phase to load into main storage and to begin execution. If you have organized the program into additional phases, the system does not load them into storage. Instead, you use the LOAD or FETCH macro to load subsequent phases during execution. There are two reasons for organizing a program into phases:

1. Some phases may be separately assembled and cataloged. A useful example is data common to many programs, such as file declarations and record definitions. You need not reassemble these phases each time you need them; you can use the INCLUDE command to link-edit them into your program.

2. The entire program may not fit into main storage. You may arrange the program into separate logical phases.

The main (root) phase is first, followed by as many additional (overlay) phases as required. After the link edit, the EXEC job command loads the root phase into storage and begins its execution. The root phase generally contains the common data and the main program logic. It may load (with LOAD or FETCH) the various phases as they are required. (The system loads phases, not programs or CSECTs.) Such phases are called overlays because when they load into storage, they may overlay previously loaded phases. The root phase generally remains intact and is not overlaid.

The PHASE Control Statement

Linkage editor control commands include PHASE, INCLUDE, ENTRY, and AC-TION. The PHASE command tells the linkage editor that a section of coding is to link-edit as a separate phase. If the code is to be assembled, insert the PHASE command ahead of // EXEC ASSEMBLY.

Name	Operation	Operand
[label]	PHASE	name,origin

The *name* gives the symbolic name of the phase, up to 8 characters. If the program consists of more than one phase, the first 4 characters of each phase name must be identical. The *origin* gives the address of where the phase is to load at execute time. These are among the most commonly used entries:

- **PHASE name,ROOT.** The phase is the root phase, to be always in storage during execution of the program. Only the first phase may be ROOT. Under a simple operating system, the root phase begins at a doubleword address immediately following the supervisor. In a multiprogramming system, the root phase loads at the beginning of a partition.
- **PHASE name,*.** The * references the linkage editor location counter (similar to that of the assembler). If not the first phase, the linkage editor assigns it to begin at a doubleword address following the previous phase. If the first phase, it is assigned a starting location like the root phase.
- **PHASE name,symbol.** You may instruct the linkage editor that at execute time this phase is to be overlaid in storage beginning at the same address as a previously defined phase.

The LOAD and FETCH Macros

The LOAD and FETCH macros are used to load a phase into storage during program execution.

Name	Operation	Operand
[label]	LOAD	phasename *or* (1)
[label]	FETCH	phasename *or* (1)

The LOAD macro. The operand of LOAD contains the name of the phase to be loaded. You may use the phase name or load the phase name into register 1. LOAD causes the phase to load into storage and returns control to the calling phase. LOAD also stores in register 1 the entry point address of the called phase. This address is required because you later use it to CALL the overlay phase for execution. Place LOAD in the program where the overlay phase does not erase it.

The FETCH macro. The operand of FETCH contains the name of the phase to be loaded. You may use the phase name or load the phase name into register 1. FETCH loads the phase into storage and branches to its entry point address. In effect, FETCH acts as a combined LOAD and CALL, but with no automatic return.

AN OVERLAY PROGRAM

Figure 13-6 illustrates a simple overlay program that links three phases. The first phase initializes hours (HRSPK) in a product field (WAGEPK) and links to the second phase. This phase multiplies hours by rate of pay (RATEPK) to calculate wage and returns to phase 1. Next, phase 1 loads phase 3 over phase 2 and links to phase 3, which prints the wage.

The three phases are organized as follows:

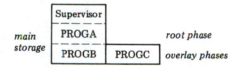

The PHASE statements are:

PHASE PROGA,ROOT defines PROGA as the root phase, always in storage during execution.
PHASE PROGB,∗ tells the linkage editor to begin the phase PROGB following the previous phase (PROGA).
PHASE PROGC,PROGB tells the linkage editor to assign and overlay the phase PROGC at the same storage location as PROGB.

After assembly and link edit, the EXEC job command loads the first phase, PHASA, into storage. The first statements define the common data area. At BEGINA, base register 3 for the program and register 4 for the common data area are loaded. Then LOAD causes PHASB, the second phase, to load into storage, following PHASA. LOAD also places in register 1 the address of the entry point to PHASB. The program stores this entry point in ADDRESB for later use. The program then initializes WAGEPK with HRSPK and links to PHASB.

PHASB saves the registers of PHASA and initializes its own registers. Then

```
// LIBDEF PHASE,CATALOG=libname.name      (catalog phases
// OPTION CATAL,ERRS,NOXREF,LOG            in system library)
        ACTION MAP
        PHASE PHASA,ROOT
// EXEC ASSEMBLY,SIZE=256K
```

LOC	OBJECT CODE	STMT	SOURCE STATEMENT			
		1		PRINT	ON,NODATA,NOGEN	
000000		3	PROGA	CSECT		
000000		4	DATA	DS	0CL1	COMMON DATA:
000000	125C	5	HRSPK	DC	PL2'12.5'	|XX|.XC|
000002	01125C	6	RATEPK	DC	PL3'11.25'	|XX|X.X|XC|
000005		7	WAGEPK	DS	PL5	
00000A	0530	9	BEGINA	BALR	3,0	
		10		USING	*,3	
		11		USING	DATA,4	
00000C	5840 3204	12		L	4,=A(DATA)	BASE REG FOR DATA
		13		OPEN	PRTR	
		21		LOAD	PHASB	LOAD PHASB IN STORAGE
000026	5010 3098	26		ST	1,ADDRESB	SAVE ENTRY TO PHASB
		27	*	.		
00002A	F841 4005 4000	28		ZAP	WAGEPK,HRSPK	SET UP MULTIPLICAND
		29	*	.		
000030	41D0 3050	30		LA	13,SAVEA	LOAD ADDR OF SAVEAREA
000034	58F0 3098	31		L	15,ADDRESB	LOAD ADDR OF PHASB
		32		CALL	(15)	LINK TO PHASB ENTRY
		35	*	.		
		36	*	.		
		37	*	.		
		38		LOAD	PHASC	LOAD PHASC IN STORAGE
000042	18F1	43		LR	15,1	LOAD PHASC ENTRY POINT
000044	41D0 3050	44		LA	13,SAVEA	LOAD ADDR OF SAVEAREA
		45		CALL	(15)	LINK TO PHASC ENTRY
		48	*	.		
		49	*	.		
		50		CLOSE	PRTR	
		58		EOJ		
00005C		62	SAVEA	DS	18F	SAVEAREA FOR PHASE
0000A4		63	ADDRESB	DS	F	ADDR OF PHASEB ENTRY
		65	PRTR	DTFPR	BLKSIZE=133,	+
					CTLCHR=YES,	+
					DEVADDR=SYSLST,	+
					DEVICE=3203,	+
					IOAREA1=IOARPRT1,	+
					IOAREA2=IOARPRT2,	+
					RECFORM=FIXUNB,	+
					IOREG=(5)	
0000E1	4040404040404040	92	IOARPRT1	DC	CL133' '	PRINT BUFFER-1
000166	4040404040404040	93	IOARPRT2	DC	CL133' '	PRINT BUFFER-2
		94		ENTRY	PRTR	
0001F0		95		LTORG		
0001F0	5B5BC2D6D7C5D540	96			=C'$$BOPEN '	
0001F8	D7C8C1E2C2404040	97			=CL8'PHASB'	
000200	D7C8C1E2C3404040	98			=CL8'PHASC'	
000208	5B5BC2C3D3D6E2C5	99			=C'$$BCLOSE'	
000210	00000000	100			=A(DATA)	
		101		END	BEGINA	

Figure 13-6 Linkage of three phases.

// EXEC ASSEMBLY

LOC	OBJECT CODE	STMT	SOURCE STATEMENT	
		1	PRINT ON,NODATA,NOGEN	
000000		2 DATAB	DSECT ,	COMMON DATA:
000000		3 HRSPK	DS PL2	XX .XC
000002		4 RATEPK	DS PL3	XX X.X XC
000005		5 WAGEPK	DS PL5	
000000		7 PROGB	CSECT	
		8 BEGINB	SAVE (14,12)	SAVE REGS IN SAVEA
000004	0530	11	BALR 3,0	INIT PROGB BASE REG
		12	USING *,3	
		13	USING DATAB,4	
000006	50D0 302A	15	ST 13,SAVEB+4	SAVE ADDR OF SAVEA
00000A	18CD	16	LR 12,13	
00000C	41D0 3026	17	LA 13,SAVEB	
000010	50DC 0008	18	ST 13,8(12)	STORE ADDR OF SAVEB
000014	FC42 4005 4002	20	MP WAGEPK,RATEPK	MULT HOURS X RATE
00001A	F045 4005 003F	21	SRP WAGEPK,63,5	SHIFT & ROUND
000020	58D0 302A	23	L 13,SAVEB+4	LOAD ADDR OF SAVEA
		24	RETURN (14,12)	RETURN TO PROGA
00002C		29 SAVEB	DS 18F	PROGB SAVEAREA
		30	END BEGINB	

// EXEC ASSEMBLY

LOC	OBJECT CODE	STMT	SOURCE STATEMENT	
		1	PRINT ON,NODATA,NOGEN	
000000		2 DATAC	DSECT ,	COMMON DATA:
000000		3 HRSPK	DS PL2	XX .XC
000002		4 RATEPK	DS PL3	XX X.X XC
000005		5 WAGEPK	DS PL5	
000000		7 PROGC	CSECT	
		8 BEGINC	SAVE (14,12)	SAVE REGS IN SAVEA
000004	0530	11	BALR 3,0	INIT PROGC BASE REG
		12	USING *,3	
		13	USING DATAC,4	
000006	50D0 303A	15	ST 13,SAVEC+4	SAVE ADDR OF SAVEA
00000A	18CD	16	LR 12,13	
00000C	41D0 3036	17	LA 13,SAVEC	
000010	50DC 0008	18	ST 13,8(12)	STORE ADDR OF SAVEC
000014	D209 3093 307E	20	MVC WAGEPR,EDWORD	
00001A	DE09 3093 4006	21	ED WAGEPR,WAGEPK+1	
000020	D284 5000 3088	22	MVC 0(133,5),PRINT	MOVE TO BUFFER
		23	PUT PRTR	PRINT WAGE

Figure 13-6 *(continued)*

```
000032 58D0 303A      29          L      13,SAVEC+4      LOAD ADDR OF SAVEA
                      30          RETURN (14,12)         RETURN TO PROGA

00003C                35 SAVEC    DS     18F             SAVEC SAVEAREA
000084 4020202021204B20 36 EDWORD DC     X'4020202021204B202060'
00008E                37 PRINT    DS     0CL133          PRINT LINE:
00008E 09             38          DC     XL01'09'        *
00008F 4040404040404040 39        DC     CL10' '         *
000099                40 WAGEPR   DS     ZL10            *
0000A3 4040404040404040 41        DC     CL112' '        *

                      43          EXTRN  PRTR
000118                44          LTORG
000118 00000000       45                 =A(PRTR)
                      47          END    BEGINC
```

`// EXEC LNKEDT`

                    LINKAGE EDITOR DIAGNOSTIC OF INPUT

ENTRY PHASE	XFR-AD	LOCORE	HICORE	CSECT/ ENTRY	LOADED AT	RELOC. FACTOR	PARTIT. OFFSET	PHASE OFFSET	TAKEN FROM
PHASA	02C082	02C078	02C2F3						
				PROGA	02C078	02C078	000000	000000	SYSLNK
				+PRTR	02C128				
				IJDFYZIZ	02C290	02C290	000218	000218	IJDFYZIZ
PHASB	02C2F8	02C2F8	02C36B						
				PROGB	02C2F8	02C2F8	000280	000000	SYSLNK
PHASC	02C2F8	02C2F8	02C413						
				PROGC	02C2F8	02C2F8	000280	000000	SYSLNK

Figure 13-6 (*continued*)

it multiplies WAGEPK by RATEPK (DSECT entries, defined in PHASA) and returns to PHASA.

PHASA next loads and links to PHASC, which saves the registers, prints WAGEPK, and returns to PHASA. At this point, PHASA and the program terminate.

Note that PHASA contains the definition of the DTFPR macro, PRTR, which PHASC also uses. The assembler directive ENTRY PRTR makes PRTR known outside PHASA. In PHASC, EXTRN PRTR tells the assembler that PRTR is defined outside this phase. The link editor completes the address linkage.

Under OS, the relative location of each CSECT appears in the cross reference table following the last assembled CSECT. Look for CONTROL SECTION, which could appear with such entries as these:

```
CONTROL       SECTION
  Name        ORIGIN            LENGTH
  PHASA         00               . . .
  PHASB        280               . . .
  PHASC        280               . . .
```

If the load point address of the first CSECT, PHASA, is 02C078, the load point of both PHASB and PHASC in this case is

Load point of PHASA:	X'02C078'
Origin of PHASB and PHASC:	+ 280
Load point of PHASB and PHASC:	X'02C2F8'

You can locate any field in a storage dump through use of the load point plus the contents of the location counter (LOC) on the program printout.

Note also that execution diagnostics show the contents of the registers under SA (savearea) in the same 18-fullword format as explained in this chapter.

The Linkage Editor Map

In Fig. 13-6, each phase name begins with the same first 4 characters, PROG. At the end of the program is the linkage editor map, which you may cause to print with the DOS control command ACTION MAP. The map lists the starting address of each phase and CSECT in the program. In large programs, the map is a useful debugging and tracing device.

In the map, RELOC. FACTOR means relocation factor. PROGA loaded for execution beginning at location X'02C078', PROGB loaded beginning at X'02C2F8', and PROGC overlaid PROGB also at X'02C2F8'.

The heading PARTIT. OFFSET indicates the displacement of a module from the initial load point, PROGA. Thus the offset for PROGA is 000000. PROGB and PROGC are offset X'280' bytes from PROGA, as follows:

Load point of PROGA:	X'02C078'
Offset of PROGB and PROGC:	X'000280'
Load point of PROGB and PROGC:	X'02C2F8'

The CSECT beginning IJD in the linkage editor map represents a printer module, which IOCS generated for the DTFPR macro in the program. Details of modules are in the IBM supervisor services and macro instructions manual. DOS modules include the following:

FILE	DTF MACRO	IBM MODULE	
System reader	DTFCD	CDMOD	IJCxxxx
Printer	DTFPR	PRMOD	IJDxxxx
Magnetic tape	DTFMT	MTMOD	IJFxxxx
Sequential disk	DTFSD	SDMOD	IJGxxxx
Indexed sequential	DTFIS	ISMOD	IJHxxxx
Direct access	DTFDA	DAMOD	IJIxxxx

OVERLAY CONSIDERATIONS

LOAD brings a phase into storage, where it remains until overlaid by another phase. Therefore, once you LOAD a phase, you may CALL it any number of times. To load and immediately execute a phase once, you may use FETCH. If there is insufficient storage, large programs may require loading and reloading phases. Here is a common procedure using overlays:

1. The ROOT phase contains all common declaratives and basic main logic. It loads (or fetches) the initialize phase.
2. The initialize phase contains routines executed only once, such as OPEN files and extract the date from the communications region.
3. The ROOT phase then overlays the initialize phase with the general processing phase, which includes calculations and input/output. (Storage restrictions may require overlaying some of these phases.)
4. At the end of processing, the ROOT phase overlays the general processing phase with an end-of-file phase, which includes final totals and closing the files.

There are countless ways to handle program overlays. However, in all programming problems, the simplest way is generally the best way. Simplification may involve dividing a problem not into phases but into completely separate programs.

LINKING COBOL AND ASSEMBLER PROGRAMS

Linking a COBOL program and an assembler program is similar to linking two assembler programs. Figure 13-7 provides an example, for brevity once again defining hours, rate, and wage and multiplying hours times rate. After compilation of the COBOL program and assembly of the assembler program, both are linked into one executable module.

The COBOL defines hours, rate, and wage in a group item named COMMON-DATA. Its format is COMP-3, which is equivalent to packed format in assembler. Understandably, the sequence and format of common data items must be identical, although their names need not be. Remember also that the data in this example exists only in the COBOL program, which passes its address to the assembler program.

The CALL statement in the COBOL program is:

```
CALL 'PROG13D' USING COMMON-DATA.
```

PROG13D happens to be the name of the CSECT in the assembler program, although it could be any valid assembler name. COMMON-DATA is the name

```
// OPTION LINK,LOG,NOSYM,ERRS,NOXREF
   ACTION MAP
// EXEC FCOBOL,SIZE=256K
```

```
00001          IDENTIFICATION DIVISION.
00002          PROGRAM-ID. COBLINK.
00003        *OBJECTIVE: TO LINK COBOL WITH ASSEMBLER PROGRAM.
00004
00005          ENVIRONMENT DIVISION.
00006
00007          DATA DIVISION.
00008          WORKING-STORAGE SECTION.
00009
00010      01  WAGE-OUT             PIC ZZZZZ9.99- USAGE DISPLAY.
00011
00012      01  COMMON-DATA                      USAGE COMP-3.
00013          05  HOURS        PIC S99V9       VALUE +12.5.
00014          05  RATE         PIC S999V99     VALUE +11.75.
00015          05  WAGE         PIC S9(7)V99.
00016
00017          PROCEDURE DIVISION.
00018      *
00019      *
00020      *
00021          MOVE RATE TO WAGE.
00022          CALL 'PROG13D' USING COMMON-DATA.
00023          MOVE WAGE TO WAGE-OUT.
00024          DISPLAY 'AMOUNT OF WAGE  ', WAGE-OUT.
00025      *    ...
00026          STOP RUN.
```

CROSS-REFERENCE DICTIONARY

DATA NAMES	DEFN	REFERENCE	
COMMON-DATA	000012	000022	
HOURS	000013		
RATE	000014	000021	
WAGE	000015	000021	000023
WAGE-OUT	000010	000023	000024

```
// EXEC ASSEMBLY

  LOC   OBJECT CODE   STMT    SOURCE STATEMENT
                       1            PRINT ON,NOGEN

000000                 3 DATAB  DSECT  ,         PROGB COMMON DATA:
000000                 4 HRSPK  DS     PL2       XX |.XC|
000002                 5 RATEPK DS     PL3       XX|X.X|XC|
000005                 6 WAGEPK DS     PL5       |0X|XX|XX|X.X|XC|

000000                 8 PROG13D CSECT
                       9         SAVE   (14,12)  SAVE REGISTERS 14-12
000004 0590           12         BALR   9,0      INIT BASE REGISTER-9
                      13         USING  *,9
                      14         USING  DATAB,4  BASE REG-4 FOR DATAB
000006 5841 0000      15         L      4,0(1)   ADDR OF COMMON DATA

00000A 50D0 902E      17         ST     13,SAVEB+4 SAVE ADDR OF SAVEA
```

Figure 13-7   Linkage between COBOL and assembler.

```
00000E 18CD              18           LR      12,13
000010 41D0 902A         19           LA      13,SAVEB
000014 50DC 0008         20           ST      13,8(12)         STORE ADDR OF SAVEB
000018 FC41 4005 4000    22           MP      WAGEPK,HRSPK     MULT HOURS X RATE
00001E F045 4005 003F    23           SRP     WAGEPK,63,5      SHIFT & ROUND
000024 58D0 902E         25           L       13,SAVEB+4       LOAD ADDR OF SAVEA
                         26           RETURN (14,12)           RETURN TO PROGA

000030                   31 SAVEB     DS      18F              PROGB SAVEAREA

                         33           END     PROG13D
```

Figure 13-7 (*continued*)

of the COBOL group item (any valid COBOL name) that is to be known to the
called assembler program. The COBOL CALL generates an address constant for
COMMON-DATA, inserts its address in register 1, and transfers to the specified
CSECT address, PROG15D. This procedure is similar to passing parameters
between two assembler programs.

The COBOL program needs to make known only the address of the defined
data area. The assembler program defines the common data as a DSECT with
the name DATAB. Hours, rate, and wage are in the same sequence and format
as in the COBOL program. A USING directive assigns register 4 as base register
for DATAB and loads the address constant of the common data into register 4:

```
                    USING DATAB,4
                    L     4,0(1)
```

Here's a pictorial representation of this load (L) instruction:

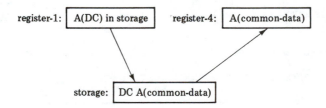

The assembler program performs the usual business about saving registers,
multiplies hours times rate, rounds the result, and exits with the usual return
operation.

Figure 13-8 shows the link editor map for this program. The two CSECT
entries, COBLINK and PROG15D, designate the starting locations of each of
these modules. The CSECT entries beginning with ILBD are modules that the
COBOL compiler has included, in the extravagant manner of a compiler. Note
that the resulting executable module is considerably larger than one comprised of
two assembler programs.

The alarming entry indicating "unresolved external references" as WXTRN
("weak externals") does not in this case indicate a true linkage error. The state-

```
// EXEC LNKEDT

                    LINKAGE EDITOR DIAGNOSTIC OF INPUT
ENTRY
PHASE    XFR-AD  LOCORE  HICORE  CSECT/     LOADED    RELOC.  PARTIT. PHASE    TAKEN
                                 ENTRY      AT        FACTOR  OFFSET  OFFSET   FROM
PHASE***02C078 02C078 02E4E3
                                 COBLINK    02C078    02C078  000000  000000   SYSLNK
                                 PROG13D    02C550    02C550  0004D8  0004D8   SYSLNK
                                 ILBDDBG0   02C5C8    02C5C8  000550  000550   ILBDDBG0
                                +ILBDDBG4   02CBF2
                                +ILBDDBG3   02CBE8
                                *ILBDDBG1   02C798
                                *ILBDDBG2   02C906
                                *ILBDDBG5   02CB6E
                                *ILBDDBG6   02CC02
                                *STXITPSW   02CCD8
                                +ILBDDBG7   02CC40
                                *SORTEP     02CE88
                                +ILBDDBG8   02CC14
                                 IJJCPDV    02D138    02D138  0010C0  0010C0   IJJCPDV
                                +IJJCPDV1   02D138
                                *IJJCPDV2   02D138
                                 ILBDDSP0   02D4E8    02D4E8  001470  001470   ILBDDSP0
                                +ILBDDSP1   02D8F8
                                 ILBDDSS0   02DA30    02DA30  0019B8  0019B8   ILBDDSS0
                                +ILBDDSS1   02DC88
                                +ILBDDSS2   02DC7C
                                +ILBDDSS3   02DD40
                                +ILBDDSS4   02DA54
                                +ILBDDSS5   02DB04
                                +ILBDDSS6   02DB56
                                +ILBDDSS7   02DB2C
                                +ILBDDSS8   02DA84
                                 ILBDMNS0   02DD50    02DD50  001CD8  001CD8   ILBDMNS0
                                 ILBDPRM0   02DD60    02DD50  001CE8  001CE8   ILBDMNS0
                                 ILBDSTN0   02DEC8    02DEC8  001E50  001E50   ILBDSTN0
                                 ILBDTC20   02E3F0    02E3F0  002378  002378   ILBDTC20


UNRESOLVED EXTERNAL REFERENCES     WXTRN        ILBDFLW0
                                   WXTRN        ILBDFLW2
                                   WXTRN        ILBDSRT0
                                   WXTRN        ILBDTEF3
                                   WXTRN        ILBDTC00
                                   WXTRN        ILBDTC01
                                   WXTRN        ILBDTC30
UNRESOLVED ADCON   AT OFFSET 0002CE78
UNRESOLVED ADCON   AT OFFSET 0002CD34
UNRESOLVED ADCON   AT OFFSET 0002CD38
UNRESOLVED ADCON   AT OFFSET 0002CD2C
UNRESOLVED ADCON   AT OFFSET 0002CE7C
UNRESOLVED ADCON   AT OFFSET 0002CE80
UNRESOLVED ADCON   AT OFFSET 0002E4A8
UNRESOLVED ADCON   AT OFFSET 0002E4AC
UNRESOLVED ADCON   AT OFFSET 0002E4A4

009 UNRESOLVED ADDRESS CONSTANTS

// EXEC

     Output:-

AMOUNT OF WAGE        146.88
```

Figure 13-8 Linkage editor map.

ment at the bottom, "009 unresolved address constants," also refers to these non-errors. The linkage editor signals a true error as EXTRN, not WXTRN; your program would generate such an error if the linkage editor cannot find a required module. One cause would be if the COBOL program calls the assembler program using the wrong name, such as PROG14D instead of PROG13D.

KEY POINTS

- A CSECT is a block of coding that can be relocated without affecting the operating logic of the program.
- The two methods of transferring data between two programs are call by reference, in which you make the address in the main program known to the subprogram, and call by value, in which the calling program delivers the actual values as parameters.
- The special assembler directive DSECT (Dummy Section) describes a data area without actually reserving any storage. DSECT gives the assembler a mask or image of data defined elsewhere.
- The directive DROP tells the assembler to discontinue applying a base register.
- You may use DSECTs to make data known between separately assembled subprograms and use standard linkage and saveareas to link between subprograms and to save the contents of registers. A calling program calls a subprogram, the called (sub)program. A called subprogram may call a lower-level subprogram, which may in turn call a lower-level subprogram, and so forth.
- The standard linkage registers are 0, 1, 13, 14, and 15.
- Each calling program requires definition of a savearea to preserve the contents of its registers. The savearea contains 18 fullwords (or 9 doublewords), aligned on a doubleword boundary.
- The CALL macro in a calling program links to a called subprogram. At the beginning of the called program, code SAVE (14,12) to save the contents of the registers, except 13. RETURN (14,12) restores the original contents of the calling program's registers and returns to the calling program.
- Linkage editor control commands include PHASE, INCLUDE, ENTRY, and ACTION. The PHASE command tells the linkage editor that a section of coding is to link-edit as a separate phase.
- The LOAD and FETCH macros are used to load a phase into storage during program execution.

PROBLEMS

13-1. For what reasons would it be useful to organize a program into subprograms?

13-2. What is the difference (if any) between a CSECT and a DSECT?

13-3. USING tells the assembler to apply a base register to a particular section of code. What directive tells it to discontinue applying the base register?

13-4. Recode and test an earlier program using locate mode for input and output, with buffers defined under a DSECT.

13-5. Why is it an especially dangerous practice to use register 13 as a base register?

13-6. For subprogram linkage, what is the purpose of registers 0, 1, 13, 14, and 15?

13-7. What three macros are required to link to another subprogram, to preserve register contents, and to return? What is their purpose?

13-8. Revise and test any earlier program into two separately assembled CSECTs. Use a DSECT for common data.

13-9. Revise Problem 13-8, changing the common data from a DSECT to passing parameters.

13-10. What is the difference between the LOAD and CALL macros? Between LOAD and FETCH?

13-11. Revise and test any previously written program into four phases. Phase 1 (ROOT) calls phase 2 for initialization and OPEN. Phase 1 then overlays phase 2 with phase 3 for processing. At end-of-job, phase 1 overlays phase 3 with phase 4 for final processing.

14

MACRO WRITING

OBJECTIVE

To cover the uses and requirements for writing
assembler macros.

The Greek word *makros* means "long," and in programming, *macro* means a "long" instruction, one that causes the generation of several or many instructions. For each macro, the assembler generates one or more instructions. Most programmers suppress the generated code, but the examples in this chapter use PRINT GEN to cause it to print. There are two sources of macros:

1. *Manufacturer-supplied Macros.* IBM macros such as OPEN, GET, EOF, DTF, and DCB facilitate complex supervisor and input/output operations and simplify much difficult but repetitious coding. They are cataloged in the system library for assembling with source programs.

2. *User-defined Macros.* You may code as your own macro any routine commonly used in a program or in other programs. You may then include it with the source program at assembly time or assemble and catalog it in the

system library.   Common examples are multiplication, division, program and base register initialization, and table searching.

Macros and Subroutines

Subroutines have a significantly different use from macros.   In a subroutine, the program branches out of the main logic into a separately coded routine.   This routine is performed identically each time it is executed.   A macro, however, generates one or more assembler instructions wherever it is coded.   Depending on how the macro is coded, the generated instructions each time may be identical or different.

You then have to assess which technique is more efficient for any given situation.   Subroutines are more easily coded and use less storage; macros are more versatile.

WRITING MACROS

The three basic types of macros are positional, keyword, and mixed.

1. *Positional Macros.*   For positional macros, you code the entries or parameters in a predetermined sequence; for example:

```
PUT PRTR,PRINT
```

Depending on the way the macro has been defined, in some cases a parameter may be omitted, as PUT PRTR.   A positional macro is illustrated in Fig. 14-1.

2. *Keyword Macros.*   For keyword macros, you code the entries in any sequence. The assembler recognizes the presence of the parameter, followed by an equal sign (=).   A familiar example is

```
FILEIN    DTFCD      TYPEFLE=INPUT,                    +
                     WORKA=YES,                        +
                     . . .
```

TYPEFLE and WORKA, which the assembler recognizes as keywords, may be in any sequence.   In some cases you may omit keywords; the assembler then assumes default values.   A keyword macro is depicted in Fig. 14-3.

3. *Mixed Macros.*   A macro definition may combine both positional and keyword types.   Under DOS, positional entries are specified first, in sequence. Mixed types are shown in Fig. 14-9.

Certain rules govern writing and assembling macros. The simple positional macro in Fig. 14-1 performs packed division and shows the basic terminology for a *macro definition*:

symbolic parameters

(a) Header:	`MACRO`		
(b) Prototype:	`DIVID`	`&QUOT,&DIVDEND,&DIVISOR`	
(c) Model statements:	`ZAP`	`&QUOT,&DIVDEND`	`Move DIVDEND to QUOT`
	`DP`	`&QUOT,&DIVISOR`	`Divide by DIVISOR`
(d) Trailer:	`MEND`		

Figure 14-1   Definition of the positional divide macro DIVID.

(a) The first statement of a macro definition is the *header* statement, containing the operation MACRO. This instruction tells the assembler that a macro is being defined next.

(b) The *prototype* statement tells the assembler the name of the macro (in this example, DIVID) and how the macro instruction will be coded. The operand contains *symbolic parameters* (names preceded by an ampersand) for quotient, dividend, and divisor.

(c) The assembler uses the *model statements* to generate assembler instructions. (You may also include comments and conditional assembly instructions, covered later.)

(d) The *trailer* statement, MEND, terminates a macro definition.

In the partial program in Fig. 14-2, DIVID is the macro instruction coded once for execution. DIVID was the only instruction coded; the ZAP and DP instructions are the generated code or *macro expansion*. The assembler generated these instructions based on (1) the macro definition and (2) the operands coded in the macro instruction. The assembler inserts a plus sign (+) beside the statement number for all instructions that it generates.

The three entries in the macro instruction operand, MILEAGE, MILES, and GALS, match the three parameters in the prototype, &QUOT, &DIVDEND, and

```
14            DIVID MILEAGE,MILES,GALS   MACRO-INSTRUCTION
15+           ZAP   MILEAGE,MILES        MOVE DIVIDEND TO QUOT
16+           DP    MILEAGE,GALS         DIVIDE BY DIVISOR
17 *                .
18 *                .
19 MILEAGE   DS    PL6                   QUOTIENT - MILES/GAL
20 MILES     DS    PL3                   DIVIDEND - MILES
21 GALS      DS    PL3                   DIVISOR  - GALLONS
```

Figure 14-2   Use of the positional DIVID macroinstruction.

&DIVISOR.   For a positional macro, the macro instruction operands correspond exactly with the prototype.   The assembler replaces each parameter in the macro definition:

MACRO INSTRUCTION		MACRO DEFINITION
MILEAGE	replaces	&QUOT
MILES	replaces	&DIVDEND
GALS	replaces	&DIVISOR

You have to define MILEAGE, MILES, and GALS in the source program. The assembler uses their addresses and lengths when producing the generated code.   (See the generated ZAP and DP instructions.)

You insert macro definitions before the main source program.   Only comments and the assembler control directives EJECT, PRINT, SPACE, TITLE, ICTL, and ISEQ may precede the MACRO header.   You may define more than one macro, one after another, but you may not define a macro within another macro.   Also, a macro may be separately assembled and cataloged for use in other programs.

Within the program, you may use the macro instruction any number of times, using either the same labels or labels of any other valid fields.   However, the assembler performs no automatic checking for validity.   For example, if a macro instruction is wrongly coded with character instead of packed operands, the assembler generates character operands.   To check for validity, use conditional assembly instructions (covered later).

Variable Symbols

In a macro definition, a variable symbol begins with an ampersand (&) followed by one to seven letters or digits, the first of which must be a letter.   Examples are &NAME and &DIVISOR.   There are three types of variable symbols.

1. *Symbolic Parameters.*   You may use symbolic parameters in a macro definition name field and operand.   In the prototype DIVID, one symbolic parameter is &QUOT.   The macro instruction contained a value MILEAGE, which the assembler assigned to the symbolic parameter &QUOT.

2. *System Variable Symbols.*   The assembler automatically assigns values to system variable symbols.   The three symbols are &SYSECT, &SYSLIST, and &SYSNDX (all covered later).

3. *Set Symbols.*   Set symbols permit you to define temporary storage and work-areas to be used within a macro definition.   They are defined and processed by conditional assembly instructions (covered later).

Explanation of the Macro Definition

The general format for the macro definition is as follows:

	Name	Operation	Operand
Header:	blank	MACRO	blank
Prototype:	symbolic parameter or blank	symbol	symbolic parameter(s)
Model:	ordinary, sequence, or variable symbol, or blank	instruction or variable symbol	ordinary or variable symbols
Trailer:	sequence symbol or blank	MEND	blank

Header.   The MACRO header statement is blank in the name or operand field.   It tells the assembler that a macro is to be defined.

Prototype.   The name field may be blank, as in Fig. 14-1, or it may contain a symbolic parameter (a name preceded by an ampersand, as explained earlier). The operation is a unique symbolic name, such as DIVID, which is not the name of another macro or assembler instruction.   The operand may contain zero to 100 symbolic parameters separated by commas.   OS permits up to 200 parameters.

Model statements.   Model statements define the assembler statements that are to be generated.   There may be many model statements or none.   The name field may be blank (as in Fig. 14-1), or it may contain an ordinary symbol, a variable symbol, or a sequence symbol (a name preceded by a period, explained later). The operation may contain an assembler instruction, a macro instruction, or a variable symbol.   The operand may contain ordinary symbols (such as AMTPK) or variable symbols (such as &QUOT).   Use any nonblank character in column 72 to indicate continuation.

Trailer.   MEND is a required entry to terminate the macro definition.   The name may be blank or may contain a sequence symbol (a name preceded by a period).

Comments.   Comments may begin anywhere after a blank following the operand, as shown in Fig. 14-1.   Also, you may code an entire line as a comment, and you may include comment lines anywhere in a macro definition following the prototype statement.   There are two ways to define a comment:

1. An asterisk (*) in column 1 causes the assembler to print the comment along with the generated code.   (See Figs. 14-5 and 14-6.)

2. A period in column 1 followed by an asterisk (*) tells the assembler not to print the comment with the generated code. (See Figs. 14-5 and 14-6.)

Keyword Macros

Keyword macros have two advantages over positional macros:

1. You may code keyword parameters in any sequence.
2. The symbolic parameters in the prototype statement may contain standard (default) values that allow you to omit the parameter when using the macro instruction.

Other than the prototype statement, keyword macros are defined the same as positional macros. The parameters of a keyword prototype are immediately followed by an equal sign (=) and an optional standard value.

The macro in Fig. 14-3 is similar to the one in Fig. 14-1. The keyword prototype is coded as

```
DIVID &QUOT=QUOTIENT,&DIVDEND=,&DIVISOR=
```

Figure 14-4 uses the macro twice, depicting two ways to code keyword macros. The first operand, &QUOT=, is followed by a standard value, QUOTIENT. When using the macro instruction, you may omit the parameter &QUOT. In this case, the assembler assumes that the name to be used by &QUOT is always QUOTIENT. (See B10DIV in Fig. 14-4.) Alternatively, you may override the standard value by coding a different label, such as QUOT=SPEED. (See B20DIV in Fig. 14-4.)

The other prototype parameters, &DIVDEND and &DIVISOR, have no standard values. You code the name to be used in the macro instruction as

```
DIVDEND=DIST, ...
```

In B20DIV in Fig. 14-4, the operands are not coded in sequence.

Except for operands that have standard values, you code the keyword each time you use the macro. Unless there are a number of standard values, a keyword macro instruction could cause more coding for a programmer.

```
2          MACRO
3          DIVID &QUOT=QUOTIENT,&DIVDEND=,&DIVISOR=
4          ZAP    &QUOT,&DIVDEND        MOVE DIVIDEND TO QUOT
5          DP     &QUOT,&DIVISOR        DIVIDE BY DIVISOR
6          MEND
```

Figure 14-3 Definition of the keyword divide macro DIVID.

```
13 B10DIV    DIVID DIVDEND=DIST,DIVISOR=TIME
14+          ZAP   QUOTIENT,DIST          MOVE DIVIDEND TO QUOT
15+          DP    QUOTIENT,TIME          DIVIDE BY DIVISOR

17 B20DIV    DIVID DIVISOR=TIME,DIVDEND=DIST,QUOT=SPEED
18+          ZAP   SPEED,DIST             MOVE DIVIDEND TO QUOT
19+          DP    SPEED,TIME             DIVIDE BY DIVISOR
20 *          .
21 *          .
22 QUOTIENT  DS    PL7                    QUOTIENT
23 DIST      DS    PL4                    DIVIDEND - DISTANCE
24 TIME      DS    PL3                    DIVISOR  - TIME
25 SPEED     DS    PL7                    QUOTIENT - SPEED
```

Figure 14-4   Use of the keyword DIVID macroinstruction.

Concatenation

Concatenation means linking as in a chain.   In model statements it is possible to concatenate a symbolic parameter with another symbolic parameter or with characters.

1. *Concatenate Symbolic Parameters*.   The macro in Fig. 14-5 generates a load operation that varies according to the type of data to be loaded.   You code L concatenated with a symbolic parameter, here called &TYPE, as L&TYPE. If &TYPE contains blank, H, E, or D, the assembler generates L, LH, LE, or LD, respectively.

2. *Concatenate Characters*.   If you concatenate a symbolic parameter with digits, letters, left bracket, or a period, code a period joining the two fields.   Consider a symbolic parameter &AREA.   If it references a label named FIELD, then &AREA.A results in generated code FIELDA.   Figure 14-5 illustrates concatenation with a bracket &PRIN.(&LEN) to permit different lengths.

The macro in Fig. 14-5 multiplies both binary fullword or halfword fields and illustrates symbolic parameters, comments, and concatenation.   The prototype, MPY, contains a symbolic parameter &LABEL1 in the name field.   When using

```
 2            MACRO
 3 &LABEL1    MPY   &REG1,&REG2,&MULTCAN,&MULTPLR,&TYP,&LEN,&PRIN
 4 .*               LOAD REGISTERS WITH MULTIPLICAND & MULTIPLIER
 5 &LABEL1    L&TYP &REG2,&MULTCAN            LOAD MULTIPLICAND
 6            L&TYP &REG1,&MULTPLR            LOAD MULTIPLIER

 7 *                MULTIPLY TWO REGISTERS
 8            MR    &REG1,&REG1               MULTIPLY REGISTERS

 9 .*               CONVERT PRODUCT TO DECIMAL
10            CVD   &REG2,DBLEWORD            STORE PRODUCT
11            UNPK  &PRIN.(&LEN),DBLEWORD     UNPACK IN PRINT AREA
12            MEND
```

Figure 14-5   Definition of the multiply macro MPY with concatenation.

MPY as a macro instruction, you may code a label such as M10MULT, which the assembler includes in the generated code. The symbolic parameters in the prototype operand are as follows:

&REG1	The even-numbered register of an even-odd pair
&REG2	The odd-numbered register
&MULTCAN	The multiplicand field, fullword or halfword
&MULTPLR	The multiplier field, fullword or halfword
&TYP	The type of operation, blank for fullword or H for halfword
&LEN	The length in the print area where the product is unpacked
&PRIN	The name of the print area

The first model statement contains the same symbolic parameter &LABEL1 as the prototype, because the assembler is to generate this label for this statement. The operation loads the fullword or halfword multiplicand into the odd register. The second model statement loads the fullword or halfword multiplier into the even register. The third model statement multiplies the contents of the two registers. (Operand 1 of MR is the even register of an even-odd pair.)

The fourth model statement converts the product in the odd register to decimal format in DBLEWORD, defined in the main source program. Finally, the decimal product is unpacked in the print area. Note the concatenation &PRIN.(&LEN) to append the length code in operand 1.

The program in Fig. 14-6 tests the macro instruction twice. M10MULT,

```
19 M10MULT  MPY   8,9,FIELDH1,FIELDH2,H,6,PRINT+10
20+M10MULT  LH    9,FIELDH1              LOAD MULTIPLICAND
21+         LH    8,FIELDH2              LOAD MULTIPLIER
22+*              MULTIPLY TWO REGISTERS
23+         MR    8,8                    MULTIPLY REGISTERS
24+         CVD   9,DBLEWORD             STORE PRODUCT
25+         UNPK  PRINT+10(6),DBLEWORD   UNPACK IN PRINT AREA

27 M20MULT  MPY   0,1,FIELDF1,FIELDF2,,10,PRINT+25
28+M20MULT  L     1,FIELDF1              LOAD MULTIPLICAND
29+         L     0,FIELDF2              LOAD MULTIPLIER
30+*              MULTIPLY TWO REGISTERS
31+         MR    0,0                    MULTIPLY REGISTERS
32+         CVD   1,DBLEWORD             STORE PRODUCT
33+         UNPK  PRINT+25(10),DBLEWORD  UNPACK IN PRINT AREA
34 *              .
35 *              .
36 DBLEWORD  DS    D                     DOUBLEWORD PRODUCT
37 FIELDH1   DS    H                     HALFWORD MULTIPLICAND
38 FIELDH2   DS    H                     HALFWORD MULTIPLIER
39 FIELDF1   DS    F                     FULLWORD MULTIPLICAND
40 FIELDF2   DS    F                     FULLWORD MULTIPLIER
41 PRINT     DC    CL133' '              PRINT AREA
```

Figure 14-6 Use of the MPY macroinstruction.

which designates H in the &TYP position, generates LH for L&TYP.   M20MULT omits the &TYP position by means of two commas and generates the instruction L for L&TYP.

This example is still relatively simple.   The conditional assembly instructions in the next section test for validity and permit more variations.

CONDITIONAL ASSEMBLY INSTRUCTIONS

Conditional assembly instructions permit you to test such attributes as data format, value, and field length and to define fields and change values.   They do not generate any code in themselves; rather, they help determine which assembler instructions to generate.   There are two main groups:

1. *Branching and Testing*.   AGO, ANOP, AIF, and ACTR permit testing attributes and branching to different locations within a macro definition.
2. *Defining Set Symbols and Varying Their Values*.   Local set symbols, LCLA, LCLB, and LCLC, provide defining within a macro expansion.   Global set symbols, GBLA, GBLB, and GBLC, enable symbols to be known in other macro expansions.   The values in the SET symbols are modified by SETA, SETB, and SETC instructions.

Attributes

For each assembler constant or instruction, the assembler assigns attributes such as field length and packed format.   You may reference these attributes by conditional assembly instructions.   There are six kinds of attributes:

SYMBOL	ATTRIBUTE	NOTATION
L'	Length	Length of symbolic parameter
I'	Integer	Integer attribute of fixed-point, floating-point, or decimal number
S'	Scaling	Scale attribute of fixed-point, floating-point, or decimal number
K'	Count	Number of characters in a macro instruction operand
N'	Number	Number of operands coded in the macro instruction
T'	Type	Type of DC or DS, such as P, C, X, F

Length.   Only AIF, SETA, and SETB statements may reference the length of a variable symbol. For example,

```
&X  SETA  L'&Y
```

means store the length of &Y in the field defined by the SET symbol &X.

Integer and scaling. A macro may check the defined integer and scaling attributes of fixed-point (binary), floating-point, and decimal numbers with AIF, SETA, and SETB. In the statement

```
AMT DC P'1234.56'
```

the integer attribute is 4 (four digits left of the decimal point), and the scale is 2 (two digits right of the decimal point). The IBM assembler manual contains further details.

Count and number. The count attribute refers to the number of characters in a macro instruction operand. The number attribute refers to the number of operands in a macro instruction. They may be referenced with AIF, SETA, and SETB; for example:

```
DIVID MPG,MILES,GALS
```

Since GALS has 4 characters, the count attribute is 4. And since the macro has three operands, the number attribute is 3. The IBM assembler manual contains further details.

Type. The type attribute refers to the type of DC, DS, or instruction. Among the types are these:

A	A-type address	F	Fullword	P	Packed		
B	Binary	H	Halfword	V	V-type address		
C	Character	I	Machine instruction	X	Hexadecimal		
D	Long float	M	Machine code	Y	Y-type address		
E	Short float	O	Omitted operand	Z	Zoned		

The type attribute may be referenced by AIF, SETC, and SETB. Both the next section under AIF and Fig. 14-7 give examples.

Branching and Testing (AGO and AIF)

The AGO and AIF instructions make use of *sequence symbols*. A sequence symbol begins with a period (.) followed by one to seven letters or digits, the first of which is a letter. Examples are .B25, .AROUND, and .P. Since a name field of a model statement may contain a sequence symbol, you may use it to branch to different statements.

Name	Operation	Operand
sequence symbol *or* blank	AGO	sequence symbol
sequence symbol *or* blank	AIF	(logical expression) sequence symbol

AGO (unconditional branch). AGO branches unconditionally to a statement with a sequence symbol for its name, such as

```
         AGO       .B25
         . . .
 .B25    MVC       DATEPR,DATEIN
```

AIF (conditional branch). AIF means "ask if." The operand consists of two parts: (1) a logical expression in parentheses and (2) immediately following, a sequence symbol. The AIF logical expression may use the following *relational operators*:

EQ	Equal to	NE	Not equal to
LT	Less than	LE	Less than or equal to
GT	Greater than	GE	Greater than or equal to

Five AIF examples follow. The testing occurs when the assembler converts the macro to generated code, since the assembler cannot test the contents of a field at execution time. The first example tests whether &AMT is defined as packed, not what the field actually contains. (These macros may be cataloged for use by other programs.)

1. If the type of &AMT equals packed, branch to .B25PAK:

```
    AIF (T'&AMT EQ 'P').B25PAK
```

2. If the length of &AMT is greater than 16, branch to .E35ERR:

```
    AIF (L'&AMT GT 16).E35ERR
```

3. If the type of &LINK is not an instruction, branch to .R45ERR:

```
    AIF (T'&LINK NE 'I').R45ERR
```

```
 2              MACRO
 3 &LABEL2      DIVID  &QUOT,&DIVDEND,&DIVISOR
 4 .*                  TEST IF DIVIDEND & DIVISOR BOTH DEFINED PACKED
 5              AIF    (T'&DIVDEND NE T'&DIVISOR).NOTPAK
 6              AIF    (T'&DIVDEND NE 'P').NOTPAK
 7 .*                  TEST IF QUOTIENT LENGTH ADEQUATE
 8              AIF    (L'&DIVDEND+L'&DIVISOR GT L'&QUOT).WRONLN
 9              AGO    .DIVE                    VALID PACKED FIELDS
10 .NOTPAK      MNOTE  'PARAMETER NOT DEFINED AS PACKED'
11              MEXIT
12 .WRONLN      MNOTE  'LENGTH OF DIVIDEND + DIVISOR EXCEEDS QUOTIENT'
13              MEXIT
14 .*                  PERFORM DIVISION
15 .DIVE        ANOP
16 &LABEL2      ZAP    &QUOT,&DIVDEND           MOVE DIVIDEND TO QUOTIENT
17              DP     &QUOT,&DIVISOR           DIVIDE BY DIVISOR
18              MEND
```

Figure 14-7   Definition of the divide macro DIVID with validity tests.

4. Logical operators AND, OR, and NOT combine terms in a logical expression. If the contents of &TAB are blank and &ARG is omitted, branch to .R65. This is a way of checking whether a macroinstruction operand is omitted, intentionally or accidentally:

```
AIF ('&TAB' EQ ' ' and T'&ARG EQ 'O').R65
```

5. Finally, arithmetic operators, + (add), − (subtract), * (multiply), and / (divide), may combine terms of an expression. If the length of product is greater than or equal to the length of &MULTCD plus &MPR plus 1, branch to .VALID. This test ensures that a defined product area is large enough for an MP operation:

```
AIF (L'PROD GE (L'&MULTCD+L'&MPR+1)).VALID
```

Examine the AGO and AIF instructions in Fig. 14-7. This example is similar to Fig. 14-1, with the additional checks that the dividend and divisor are defined as packed and that the quotient area is at least as large as the dividend plus divisor. Figure 14-8 tests the macro. D10DIV shows valid operands that generate

```
25 D10DIV    DIVID MILEAGE,MILES,GALS     VALID DIVISION
26+D10DIV    ZAP   MILEAGE,MILES          MOVE DIVIDEND TO QUOTIENT
27+          DP    MILEAGE,GALS           DIVIDE BY DIVISOR
29 D20DIV    DIVID MILEAGE,MILES,PRINT    INVALID DIVISION
30+PARAMETER NOT DEFINED AS PACKED

32 D30DIV    DIVID MILES,MILEAGE,GALS     INVALID DIVISION
33+LENGTH OF DIVIDEND + DIVISOR EXCEEDS QUOTIENT
34 *           .
35 *           .
36 MILES     DS    PL3                    DIVIDEND - MILES
37 GALS      DS    PL3                    DIVISOR  - GALLONS
38 MILEAGE   DS    PL6                    QUOTIENT - MILES PER GALLON
```

Figure 14-8   Use of the DIVID macroinstruction.

the correct instructions.   D20DIV and D30DIV illustrate invalid operands that generate error messages.

OTHER INSTRUCTIONS

There are three instructions still to be covered: ANOP, MNOTE, and MEXIT.

ANOP (No Operation)

AGO and AIF require a sequence symbol as a branch operand but may require branching to an instruction whose name is an ordinary or variable symbol. If so, AGO and AIF must branch to an ANOP, a convenience instruction, immediately before the statement.

Name	Operation	Operand
sequence symbol	ANOP	blank

Figure 14-7 illustrates the use of ANOP, where AGO has to branch to &LABEL2.   Since AGO cannot branch to a variable symbol, it goes to .MULT, containing the ANOP operation, immediately preceding &LABEL2.

MNOTE and MEXIT

You may use the MNOTE and MEXIT operations to print error messages and to exit from a macro.

Name	Operation	Operand
sequence symbol, variable symbol, or blank	MNOTE	any message, between apostrophes
sequence symbol or blank	MEXIT	blank

MNOTE (macro error message).   MNOTE is used to print programmer macro messages at assembly time. The message is written between apostrophes. To print an ampersand or an apostrophe as part of the message, you code two adjacent ampersands or apostrophes, as in the following example:

```
MNOTE 'CAIN && ABEL''S'
```

Two MNOTE messages in Fig. 14-7 warn that the dividend or divisor is not in packed format and that the quotient length is too short. In Fig. 14-8, when the error condition occurs, the assembler statements are not generated. Before program execution, first check for and correct any assembly errors.

MEXIT (macro definition exit). MEXIT provides a convenient way to terminate processing of a macro. It acts like MEND, although MEND must be the last statement of the macro definition. Figure 14-7 shows exit and termination of the macro. You could alternatively code the exit as follows:

```
                MNOTE    'message'
                AGO      .FINISH (or any sequence symbol)
                ...
.FINISH         MEND
```

SET SYMBOLS

You may need to define and assign values within a macro, and you may then use them to test values and to build instructions. These are SET symbols, which are assigned values when you code SETA, SETB, or SETC conditional assembly instructions. They must first have been defined by an LCL (load) or GBL (global) instruction. Under DOS, you code GBLs and then LCLs in the macro definition immediately following the prototype statement. OS allows you to code them in any sequence.

Name	Operation	Operand
[blank]	LCLA	one or more variable
[blank]	LCLB	(SET) symbols,
[blank]	LCLC	separated by commas

LCLA defines a SETA symbol that creates a 32-bit field initialized with zero. LCLB defines a SETB symbol that creates a 1-bit field initialized with zero. LCLC defines a SETC symbol that creates a "null character value," that is, a field with no defined length.

GBLA, GBLB, and GBLC similarly define SET symbols for values that are to be known in other macro expansions in the same assembly. A later section discusses global instructions.

LCL instructions merely define SET symbols, whereas the SET operations, SETA, SETB, and SETC, assign actual values to them.

SETA (Set Arithmetic)

SETA assigns an arithmetic value to a SETA symbol.

Name	Operation	Operand
SETA symbol	SETA	arithmetic expression

The maximum and minimum values of the expression are $+2^{31}-1$ and -2^{31}. An expression consists of a term or an arithmetic combination of terms. These terms are valid:

- Self-defining terms, which have an inherent value that is not assigned a value by the assembler. These may be decimal (as 11), hexadecimal (as X'B'), and binary (as B'1011').
- Variable symbols, such as &AMT.
- Attributes for count, integer, length, number, and scale.

Here are some examples of SETA arithmetic:

```
1.            LCLA      &FLD1,&FLD2
2. &FLD1      SETA      15
3. &FLD2      SETA      &FLD1+L'&AMT+25
```

1. LCLA defines &FLD1 and &FLD2 as SETA symbols.
2. The value 15 (a self-defining term) is assigned to &FLD1.
3. The expression contains an arithmetic combination of terms.

If &AMT is defined elsewhere with a length of 6, the assembler calculates the expression as follows:

TERM		VALUE
&FLD1	(variable symbol)	15
L'&AMT	(length attribute)	6
25	(self-defining term)	+ 25
Value assigned to &FLD2:		46

The maximum number of terms in the expression is 16. Also, parentheses may contain terms in an expression, such as (&COUNT-X'1B')*3.

Figure 14-9 illustrates LCLA and SETA. In this mixed-type macro, the first

```
 3              MACRO
 4  &NAME       HEDNG   &HEAD,&PAGE,&DAT=DATE,&PRT=PRINT
 5              LCLA    &LEN,&MID               LENGTH & MID-POINT
 6              LCLC    &LIT,&L1,&L2            AREA FOR CHARS.
 7  .*                  TEST VALIDITY OF PARAMETERS
 8              AIF     (T'&PAGE NE 'P').ERRPACK
 9              AIF     (T'&HEAD NE 'C').ERRCHAR
10              AIF     (L'&HEAD GT 90).ERRSIZE HEADING > 90 CHARS?
11  .*                  SET VALUES
12  &LEN        SETA    L'&HEAD                LENGTH OF HEADING
13  &MID        SETA    (120-&LEN)/2           CENTER HEADING
14  &LIT        SETC    '=C''PAGE'''           LITERAL FOR 'PAGE'
15  &L1         SETC    'L'''                  LENGTH CODE
16  &L2         SETC    '&DAT'                 DATE
17  .*
18  &NAME       UNPK    &PRT+115(3),&PAGE      UNPK PAGE CTR.
19              OI      &PRT+117,X'F0'         CLEAR UNITS ZONE
20              MVC     &PRT+110(4),&LIT       MOVE PAGE LITERAL,
21              MVC     &PRT+&MID.(&LEN),&HEAD   HEADING,
22              MVC     &PRT+1(&L1&L2),&DAT      DATE
23              MEXIT
24  .*                  ERROR MESSAGES
25  .ERRPACK MNOTE 'PAGE COUNT NOT DEFINED AS PACKED'
26              MEXIT
27  .ERRCHAR MNOTE 'HEADING NOT DEFINED AS CHARACTER'
28              MEXIT
29  .ERRSIZE MNOTE 'LENGTH OF HEADING EXCEEDS PRINT AREA'
30              MEND
```

Figure 14-9 Definition of the heading macro HEDNG with conditional assembly instructions.

two parameters are positional, whereas the third and fourth are keyword. This macro prints a heading line containing a heading title, page number, and the date, centered on a page.

PARAMETER	SPECIFIES	LENGTH IN BYTES
&HEAD	Heading	Up to 90 characters
&PAGE	Page number	2 packed bytes
&DAT	Date	Not defined
&PRT	Print area	121

&LEN and &MID in Fig. 14-9 define two SETA symbols. AIF checks that the length of the heading does not exceed 90 bytes. (Assume 120 print positions with space for date and page number.) SETA assigns the length of &HEAD to &LEN. The title is centered by calculating the first print position of &HEAD; for example:

L'&HEAD	EXPRESSION	FIRST POSITION
23	$(120 - 23)/2 = 97/2 =$	48
16	$(120 - 16)/2 = 104/2 =$	52
11	$(120 - 11)/2 = 109/2 =$	54

```
37 P10HED      HEDNG HEADG1,PAGEPK
38+P10HED      UNPK  PRINT+115(3),PAGEPK        UNPK PAGE CTR.
39+            OI    PRINT+117,X'F0'            CLEAR UNITS ZONE
40+            MVC   PRINT+110(4),=C'PAGE'      MOVE PAGE LITERAL,
41+            MVC   PRINT+48(23),HEADG1            HEADING,
42+            MVC   PRINT+1(L'DATE),DATE           DATE

44 P20HED      HEDNG HEADG2,PAGEPK,DAT=DATOT
45+P20HED      UNPK  PRINT+115(3),PAGEPK        UNPK PAGE CTR.
46+            OI    PRINT+117,X'F0'            CLEAR UNITS ZONE
47+            MVC   PRINT+110(4),=C'PAGE'      MOVE PAGE LITERAL,
48+            MVC   PRINT+52(16),HEADG2            HEADING,
49+            MVC   PRINT+1(L'DATOT),DATOT         DATE

51 P30HED      HEDNG HEADG3,PAGEPK,PRT=OUTAREA,DAT=DATOT
52+P30HED      UNPK  OUTAREA+115(3),PAGEPK      UNPK PAGE CTR.
53+            OI    OUTAREA+117,X'F0'          CLEAR UNITS ZONE
54+            MVC   OUTAREA+110(4),=C'PAGE'    MOVE PAGE LITERAL,
55+            MVC   OUTAREA+54(11),HEADG3          HEADING,
56+            MVC   OUTAREA+1(L'DATOT),DATOT       DATE

58 P40HED      HEDNG HEADG4,PAGEPK
59+LENGTH OF HEADING EXCEEDS PRINT AREA
61 *               .
62 *               .
63 PRINT     DC    CL121' '                    PRINT AREA
64 OUTAREA   DC    CL121' '                    PRINT AREA
65 PAGEPK    DC    PL2'0'                       PAGE COUNTER
66 HEADG1    DC    CL23'HOTROD CUSTOM IMPORTERS'
67 HEADG2    DC    CL16'ABC DISTRIBUTORS'
68 HEADG3    DC    CL11'BAKER CORP.'
69 HEADG4    DS    CL100                        LONG HEADING
70 DATE      DS    CL12                         DATE AREA
71 DATOT     DS    CL12                         DATE AREA
```

Figure 14-10   Use of the HEDNG macroinstruction.

These lengths are used in Fig. 14-10 to center the heading.   Figure 14-10 also illustrates the SETC symbol, covered next.

SETC (Set Character)

SETC assigns a character value to a SETC symbol, written between apostrophes. The DOS limit is 8 characters, and the OS limit is 255.   The operand generally defines a character expression.

Name	Operation	Operand
SETC symbol	SETC	one character

Here are some examples of SETC character operations:

```
1.             LCLC    &CHAR1,&CHAR2,&CHAR3
2. &CHAR1      SETC    'SAM''S'
```

```
3. &CHAR2        SETC     '&TYPE.A'
4. &CHAR3        SETC     'L'FLOAT'
```

1. LCLC defines three SETC symbols, &CHAR1, &CHAR2, and &CHAR3.
2. The character value SAM'S is assigned to the SETC symbol &CHAR1. Two apostrophes within the expression denote a single apostrophe.
3. If &TYPE contains the value FIELD, the expression concatenates FIELD with A and assigns FIELDA to &CHAR2.
4. The value L'FLOAT is assigned to the SETC symbol &CHAR3.

In Fig. 14-9, SETC defines three symbols, &LIT, &L1, and &L2. One SETC assigns &LIT with a character expression to be used as a literal. Note the literal, =C'PAGE', in the generated code in Fig. 14-10. Instead of using &LIT in the macro definition, the example could have coded the literal itself:

```
MVC  &PRT+110(4),=C'PAGE'
```

&L1 and &L2 are used to create a symbolic length reference for moving the date to the print area. Note the macro definition and generated code for this example.

We have now covered all the features used in the macro HEDNG. Some remaining items, SETB symbols, system variable symbols, and global SET symbols are covered next.

SETB (Set Binary)

SETB assigns the binary value 0 or 1 to a SETB symbol to help determine whether a condition is false (0) or true (1). One use for SETB is as a switch indicator in a macro definition.

Name	Operation	Operand
SETB symbol	SETB	0 *or* 1 (0) *or* (1) (logical expression)

A logical expression, enclosed in parentheses, consists of one term (arithmetic relationship, character relationship, or SETB symbol) or a logical combination of terms connected by AND, OR, or NOT.

In the following SETB examples, assume that &SYM1 is type C (character) containing the value 6, &SYM2 is type C, and &SYM3 contains the word YES.

```
1.      LCLB  &B1,&B2,&B3,&B4
2. &B1  SETB  1
```

```
3. &B2    SETB    (&SYM1 LT 7)
4. &B3    SETB    ('&SYM3' EQ 'NO')
5. &B4    SETB    ('&SYM3' EQ 'YES' and T'&SYM1 NE T'&SYM2)
```

The following explains the SETB examples:

1. LCLB defines four SETB symbols, &B1, &B2, &B3, and &B4.
2. SETB assigns an arithmetic term (1 = true) to &B1.
3. The arithmetic relationship is true, so 1 is assigned to &B2.
4. The character relationship is false, so 0 is assigned to &B3.
5. The logical combination of terms is false, so 0 is assigned to &B4.

In Fig. 14-11, SETB is a switch &ERRB that determines whether the assembler has located any errors in a macro instruction. If an error is found, the assembler prints the appropriate message, and the switch is set. The macro then continues with the next test. Only after all validity testing does the macro terminate processing. In this way, you fully test the macro instruction each time it is used.

Note that SETB symbols such as &ERRB can contain only 0 or 1. In the instruction AIF (&ERRB).A30, AIF branches to A30 if &ERRB contains 1.

SYSTEM VARIABLE SYMBOLS

The assembler automatically assigns values to the local system variable symbols &SYSLIST, &SYSNDX, &SYSECT, &SYSDATE, and &SYSTIME.

&SYSLIST (Macro-Instruction Operand)

You may use &SYSLST as an alternative way of referencing a positional macro operand. In the HEDNG macro in Fig. 14-9, you could have coded the UNPK instruction as

```
UNPK &PRT+115(3),&SYSLIST(2)
```

The subscript (2) refers to the second parameter in the prototype (&PAGE).

&SYSNDX (Macro-Instruction Index)

For the first macro instruction processed in an assembly, the assembler initializes &SYSNDX with 0001. For each succeeding macro instruction, the assembler increments &SYSNDX by 1. In Fig. 14-10, the macro HEDNG is used four times. Since this is the only macro instruction in the assembly, at P10HED, &SYSNDX is set to 0001; at P20HED, &SYSNDX is set to 0002, and so forth.

&SYSNDX can prevent a macro from generating duplicate labels. This situation did not occur in any examples up to this point. However, in Fig. 14-11, the macro LOOKP requires that the macro generate several labels. If the macro instruction is coded more than once, it generates labels with the same name, causing assembler error messages. To avoid these errors, the macro uses labels such as R&SYSNDX. In the generated code in Fig. 14-12, this label becomes R0001 for L10LK and R0002 for L20LK.

&SYSECT (Macro-Instruction Control Section)

This variable symbol delivers the name of the control section currently being assembled. A possible use for &SYSECT is within a macro that defines a DSECT (dummy section). A DSECT ends with a CSECT statement (or another DSECT). You could code &SYSECT in the macro to generate and resume the original CSECT.

&SYSDATE (Macro-Instruction System Date—OS)

The OS TIME macro delivers the date when a program is executed, whereas &SYSDATE delivers it when the macro is assembled, in the form mm/dd/yy. You may code it simply as

```
DC  C'&SYSDATE'
```

The purpose is to date-stamp the object program for identification purposes.

&SYSTIME (Macro-Instruction System Time—OS)

The OS TIME macro delivers the time of day when a program is executed, whereas &SYSTIME delivers it when the macro is assembled, in the form hh.mm.

GLOBAL SET SYMBOLS

LCLA, LCLB, and LCLC define local SET symbols for use within the same macro definition. GBLA, GBLB, and GBLC define global SET symbols for communicating values between different macro definitions.

Name	Operation	Operand
[blank]	GBLA	one or more variable
[blank]	GBLB	(SET) symbols,
[blank]	GBLC	separated by commas

```
 2              MACRO
 3 &LOOK        LOOKP  &TABLE,                        ADDR OF TABLE                    +
                       &SERARG,                       ADDR OF SEARCH ARG'T             +
                       &FUNCTN,                       ADDR TO STORE FUNCTION           +
                       &NOTFND                        ADDR IF ARG'T NOT FOUND
 4              GBLB   &SAVIND                         SAVE AREA INDICATOR
 5              LCLA   &LSER,&LENTRY                   LENGTH OF SEARCH & ENTRY
 6              LCLB   &ERRB                           ERROR SWITCH INDICATOR
 7              LCLC   &H,&HALF                        HALFWORD LITERAL
 8 &ERRB        SETB   (1)                             SET ERROR INDICATOR = 1
 9 .*                  TEST FOR VALIDITY
10              AIF    (T'&NOTFND EQ 'I').A10          NOTFND A VALID ADDRESS?
11              MNOTE  'ADDRESS FOR NOTFOUND IS INVALID'
12 &ERRB        SETB   (0)                             SET ERROR INDICATOR TO 0
13 .A10         AIF    (T'&TABLE EQ 'C' AND T'&SERARG EQ 'C').A20
14              AIF    (T'&TABLE EQ 'P' AND T'&SERARG EQ 'P').A20
15              MNOTE  'TABLE && SEARCH NOT BOTH CHAR OR PACKED'
16 &ERRB        SETB   (0)                             SET ERROR INDICATOR TO 0
17 .A20         AIF    (&ERRB).A30                     ERROR INDICATOR = 1?
18              MNOTE  'MACRO CANNOT BE RESOLVED - TERMINATED'
19              MEXIT

20 .*                  SET VALUES
21 .A30         ANOP
22 &LSER        SETA   L'&SERARG                       LENGTH OF SEARCH ARG'T
23 &LENTRY      SETA   &LSER+L'&FUNCTN                 LENGTH OF SEARCH + FUNC'N
24 &H           SETC   '=H'                            SET UP HALFWORD
25 &HALF        SETC   '''&LENTRY'''                   *   CONSTANT
26 &LOOK        ST     10,SAVREG                       SAVE REGISTER-10
27              LA     10,&TABLE                       LOAD ADDR OF TABLE
28              AIF    (T'&TABLE EQ 'P').B10           TABLE DEFINED AS PACKED?
29 .*                  COMPARE SEARCH TO TABLE ARGUMENT
30 R&SYSNDX     CLC    &SERARG,0(10)                   COMPARE CHARACTER
31              AGO    .B20
32 .B10         ANOP
33 R&SYSNDX     CP     &SERARG,0(&LSER,10)             COMPARE PACKED
34 .B20         BE     T&SYSNDX                        *   EQUAL - FOUND
35              BL     S&SYSNDX                        *   LOW   - NOT IN TABLE
36              AH     10,&H&HALF                      INCREMENT NEXT ENTRY
37              B      R&SYSNDX
38 .*                  DEFINE SAVEAREA FIRST TIME ONLY
39              AIF    (&SAVIND).B30                   IS SAVIND DEFINED?
40 SAVREG       DS     F                               REGISTER SAVE AREA
41 &SAVIND      SETB   (1)                             SET INDICATOR ON (1)
42 .B30         ANOP
43 .*                  ARGUMENT NOT FOUND
44 S&SYSNDX     L      10,SAVREG                       RESTORE REG-10
45              B      &NOTFND                         GO TO ERROR ROUTINE
46 .*                  ARGUMENT FOUND
47 T&SYSNDX     MVC    &FUNCTN,&LSER.(10)              MOVE FUNCTION FROM TABLE
48              L      10,SAVREG                       RESTORE REG-10
49              MEND
```

Figure 14-11   Definition of the table search macro LOOKP.

The global operations GBLA, GBLB, and GBLC define the same initial values as local operations.   However, they are initialized only once, the first time the assembler encounters them.   Under DOS (but not OS), you define global instructions immediately after the prototype statement.

Figure 14-11 gives an example in which GBLB defines and initializes

&SAVIND to zero and prevents the assembler from defining SAVREG DS F more than once.   The macro tests whether &SAVIND contains zero.   If so, it permits SAVREG to be defined and sets &SAVIND to 1.   &SAVIND is now permanently set to 1, through all succeeding macro instructions, and the assembler, by means of the AIF statement, bypasses generating more than one DS for SAVREG.   (Consider how &SYSNDX could achieve the same result.)

EXTENDED EXAMPLE: TABLE SEARCH MACRO

The table search macro LOOKP in Fig. 14-11 permits you to code in one statement a table search routine that initializes a register with the table address and compares a search argument to the table argument.

```
56 L10LK       LOOKP  JOBTABPK,JOBNOPK,RATEPK,R10NOFND
57+L10LK       ST     10,SAVREG                  SAVE REGISTER-10
58+            LA     10,JOBTABPK                LOAD ADDR OF TABLE
59+R0001       CP     JOBNOPK,0(4,10)            COMPARE PACKED
60+            BE     T0001                 *    EQUAL - FOUND
61+            BL     S0001                 *    LOW   - NOT IN TABLE
62+            AH     10,=H'7'                   INCREMENT NEXT ENTRY
63+            B      R0001
64+SAVREG      DS     F                          REGISTER SAVE AREA
65+S0001       L      10,SAVREG                  RESTORE REG-10
66+            B      R10NOFND                   GO TO ERROR ROUTINE
67+T0001       MVC    RATEPK,4(10)               MOVE FUNCTION FROM TABLE
68+            L      10,SAVREG                  RESTORE REG-10

70 L20LK       LOOKP  JOBTABCH,JOBNOCH,RATECH,R10NOFND
71+L20LK       ST     10,SAVREG                  SAVE REGISTER-10
72+            LA     10,JOBTABCH                LOAD ADDR OF TABLE
73+R0002       CLC    JOBNOCH,0(10)              COMPARE CHARACTER
74+            BE     T0002                 *    EQUAL - FOUND
75+            BL     S0002                 *    LOW   - NOT IN TABLE
76+            AH     10,=H'9'                   INCREMENT NEXT ENTRY
77+            B      R0002
78+S0002       L      10,SAVREG                  RESTORE REG-10
79+            B      R10NOFND                   GO TO ERROR ROUTINE
80+T0002       MVC    RATECH,5(10)               MOVE FUNCTION FROM TABLE
81+            L      10,SAVREG                  RESTORE REG-10

83 L30LK       LOOKP  JOBTABPK,JOBNOCH,RATEPK,R20NOFND
84+ADDRESS FOR NOTFOUND IS INVALID
85+TABLE & SEARCH NOT BOTH CHAR OR PACKED
86+MACRO CANNOT BE RESOLVED - TERMINATED
88 R10NOFND MVC    PRINT+10(21),=C'ARGUMENT NOT IN TABLE'
89 *           .
90 *           .
91 PRINT       DC     CL133' '                   PRINT AREA
92 JOBTABPK DS     25PL7                      TABLE OF PACK JOBS & RATES
93 JOBNOPK  DS     PL4                        SEARCH ARG - JOB NUMBER
94 RATEPK   DS     PL3                        TO STORE FOUND TABLE RATE

96 JOBTABCH DS     15CL9                      TABLE OF CHAR JOBS & RATES
97 JOBNOCH  DS     CL5                        SEARCH ARG - JOB NUMBER
98 RATECH   DS     CL4                        TO STORE FOUND TABLE RATE
```

Figure 14-12   Use of the LOOKP macroinstruction.

- If equal, it branches to an address where the table function is extracted.
- If low, it branches to the address of an error routine.
- If high, it increments for the next argument and returns to the compare.

The macro allows for either character or packed arguments. It requires that the table contain discrete arguments (unique numbers such as job or stock numbers, rather than table ranges as in income tax), in ascending sequence. The comments beside each parameter explain the symbolic parameters in the prototype operand. You code as the fourth parameter in the macro instruction the address to which the lookup routine branches if the search argument cannot be found. The program must contain the address of this error routine. The routine should provide the usual error handling, such as the printing of a message.

Figure 14-12 shows how the LOOKP macro is used.

KEY POINTS

- You may code as a macro any commonly used routine. You may then include it with the source program at assembly time or assemble and catalog it in the system library.
- For positional macros, you code the entries or parameters in a predetermined sequence. For keyword macros, you code the entries in any sequence. A macro definition may combine both positional and keyword types.
- The first statement of a macro definition is the header statement, containing the operation MACRO.
- The prototype statement tells the assembler the name of the macro and how the macro instruction will be coded.
- The assembler uses the model statements to generate assembler instructions.
- The trailer statement, MEND, terminates a macro definition.
- In a macro definition, a variable symbol begins with an ampersand (&) followed by one to seven letters or digits, the first of which must be a letter. The three types of variable symbols are symbolic parameters, system variable symbols, and set symbols.
- Local set symbols, LCLA, LCLB, and LCLC, provide defining within a macro expansion. Global set symbols, GBLA, GBLB, and GBLC, enable symbols to be known in other macro expansions.
- Conditional assembly instructions permit you to test such attributes as data format, value, and field length and to define fields and change values. There are two main groups. AGO, ANOP, AIF, and ACTR permit testing attributes and branching to different locations within a macro definition. SETA, SETB, and SETC instructions modify values in SET symbols.

- MNOTE allows you to print error messages.
- MEXIT allows you to exit from a macro.

PROBLEMS

14-1. (a) What is the first statement of a macro definition?   (b) What is the last statement?

14-2. What is a prototype statement?

14-3. Distinguish between a positional macro and a keyword macro.

14-4. What is the difference between using a variable symbol and using a sequence symbol?

14-5. Revise Figs. 14-5 and 14-6 so that the operation is DR (Divide Register).   Change the names to suit.

14-6. Revise Figs. 14-7 and 14-8 so that the operation is DR (Divide Register).   Change the names to suit.

14-7. Revise Figs. 14-9 and 14-10 for the following: Print area = 133 positions (change other lengths accordingly); add 1 to the page counter; edit (ED) the page counter.

14-8. Write a macro that provides for MP and SRP with round and shift to two decimal places.

14-9. Expand the macro in Problem 14-8 to provide for M and MH as well.

14-10. Write a macro to initialize a program with three base registers.

14-11. Write a macro to test given character fields for blank positions.   (Assume that the fields are input fields, to be packed.)   Replace any blank position with a zero.

15

DEBUGGING STRATEGY

OBJECTIVE

To describe the various common coding and execution bugs and the means to debug programs.

One common error in an early assembly is a result of spelling an instruction or operand incorrectly. For example, the assembler generates hex zeros for machine code, which, when executed, cause an operation exception. Most program bugs, however, are not so easily recognized.

One of the more charming features of an assembler program is that every instruction can be wrong, either syntactically or logically. A syntactical error involves failure to follow the rules of an instruction, such as coding an instruction incorrectly or failing to code a required explicit length. A logical error involves a failure to follow the objective of the program, such as branching to an incorrect address or making a wrong computation.

This chapter covers syntactical errors that can occur during program execution by general category, such as character data, packed data, addressing, and input/output, and then explores reading of storage dumps. For handling logical errors, your best bet is to provide input data that tests the program logic thoroughly.

DEBUGGING CHARACTER DATA

A common error that occurs in handling character data arises from the use of the MVC instruction. Since MVC can move up to 256 bytes of any type of data, the error may appear during execution of a subsequent instruction. In the following MVC instruction, because operand 1, PRINT, has no explicit length, the assembler assumes a length of 133 from the declarative:

```
        MVC     PRINT+115,=C'MEGABYTE CORP'
        . . .
PRINT   DS      CL133
```

Now assume that the literal pool contains the following two literals:

```
        =C'MEGABYTE CORP'
        =C'AKRON OHIO'
        . . .
```

The MVC moves 133 bytes in all: the 13-byte literal plus the 120 bytes following in the literal pool. The data moves beginning at PRINT + 115, as follows:

```
        MEGABYTE CORPAKRON OHIO . . .
        |                   |
     PRINT+115          PRINT+132
```

In effect, the MVC fills the print record with 18 bytes and moves an additional 115 bytes into the area following. The system generates no error message based on the MVC. An unpredictable error occurs when you subsequently attempt to process one of the damaged fields, but the precise type of error depends on the data that is erased. For example, erasure of packed data may cause a data exception, and erasure of the first part of the literal pool may cause an input/output error. This type of error is often difficult to locate because another instruction is the indirect cause of the error. A check of a storage dump (if any) can help shed light on the cause of the error.

A remedy is to avoid relative addressing or to double-check that such operands contain an explicit length.

Another example of errors in the use of literals is coding = CL5'0' when you mean = CL5'00000' and coding = C' ' when you mean = 5CL' '.

See also Appendix B for program check interrupts: 1 (operation exception), 2 (privileged exception), 5 (addressing exception), and 6 (specification exception).

DEBUGGING PACKED DECIMAL DATA

The use of packed decimal data may cause a variety of errors because of the requirements: a valid sign in the leftmost half-byte and digits 0–9 in all other half-bytes.

Data Exception

A data exception is particularly common because there are so many clever ways to cause one. Here's a common example:

```
                AP      LINECTR,=P'1'
                . . .
        LINECTR DS      PL3
```

As you may have noticed, LINECTR does not contain an initial value. Since its contents are unpredictable, the AP will likely cause a data exception.

Another common error is caused by a blank input field, as in the following example:

```
                PACK    RATEPK,RATEIN
                ZAP     MULTPR,RATEPK
                . . .
        RATEIN  DS      ZL5
        RATEPK  DS      PL3
        MULTPR  DS      PL6
```

If RATEIN is blank, its contents are 4040404040. After the PACK, RATEPK contains 000004. The ZAP instruction causes a data exception because its second operand must contain valid packed data. Although you may have no control over the initial contents of input fields, you could replace blanks with zeros. In fact, you may prefer to use TR to translate any invalid character to zero.

The next example manages to cause a data exception on packed fields even when the data is valid:

```
        ZAP     WAGEPK,RATEPK       | 00 | 00 | 01 | 23 | 5C |
        MP      WAGEPK,HOURSPK      | 01 | 48 | 20 | 00 | 0C |
        . . .
HOURSPK DC      PL3'120.00'
RATEPK  DC      PL3'12.35'
WAGEPK  DS      PL5
```

A quick calculation discloses that a 5-byte product should be adequate for the product, but the MP fails on a data exception. The reason? Violation of a rule of MP: The product field must contain a byte of zeros to the left for each byte in the multiplier. This example requires 3 bytes of zeros, and consequently WAGEPK must be at least 6 bytes long.

Divide by Zero

Attempting to divide by zero is another popular error that causes a decimal-divide exception. The error is easy to locate because most programs contain few DP operations.

Decimal Overflow

An arithmetic operation can easily lose leftmost significant digits. Consider the following definition:

```
LINEPK      DC        PL1'0'
```

Once LINEPK reaches the value 9 (hex 9C), the next instruction that adds 1 now has no space for the carried 1, and a decimal overflow occurs. The contents of LINEPK (after the add) in a storage dump is hex 0C.

See Appendix B for program check interrupts 7 (data exception), A (decimal-overflow exception), and B (decimal-divide exception).

DEBUGGING BINARY DATA

Because technically all data is in binary format, you cannot get program checks on referencing binary data. But you can perform binary arithmetic operations that generate invalid results and cause program checks. One way is to generate a value that exceeds the capacity of a register, a fixed-point-overflow exception.

See Appendix B for program check interrupts 8 (fixed-point-overflow exception) and 9 (fixed-point-divide exception).

ENDLESS LOOPING

There are a number of ways to incur an endless loop. One way is to perform a loop that has no exit, as in the following:

```
B50       . . .
          B     B50
```

You can avoid this type of error by branching only forward, although there are exceptions. For example, a table search and a table sort typically require looping backward; be especially careful when coding these routines.

You can also cause an endless loop in a table search by branching back to the instruction that initializes the address of the table or by failing to increment the register that addresses the table.

A difficult error to trace is one that involves BAL and BR. If you BAL to a subroutine via register 9, you must return via register 9, with the original address still intact. A BR that returns via the wrong register may cause an endless loop. (It may also cause an unpredictable error, depending on the contents of the referenced register.)

ADDRESSING ERRORS

For base registers, you cannot use register 0 at all, and you should avoid the use of registers 1, 13, 14, and 15 because I/O operations and subprogram linkage change their contents. Also, the TRT instruction uses register 2. Assume that a program 10K in size is to initialize three base registers. It doesn't matter which of registers 3 through 12 you use as long as you reserve them for that exclusive purpose. The following example uses registers 10, 11, and 12:

```
BALR    10,0
USING   *,10,11,12
LA      12,2048
LA      11,2048(10,12)
LA      12,2048(11,12)
```

BALR and USING must specify the same register. The second register must contain an address that is 4,096 (X'1000') more than the first, and the third register must contain an address that is 4,096 more than the second. Any minor change can make the coding incorrect and cause curious results during program execution.

If your program loads one of these base registers for another purpose, its base address is lost. A subsequent attempt using that base register will reference the wrong storage location, with unpredictable results. This type of error is very difficult to trace.

INPUT/OUTPUT ERRORS

One common input/output error involves printing: failure to initialize the print control character or initializing it with an incorrect value. (This error could occur using PUT but not PUTPR.) For example, the control character for skipping to a new page is X'8B'; many programmers have misread the code as X'88'. Regardless of the cause, the system generates a message such as

```
INVALID INPUT/OUTPUT
```

When you get such a diagnostic, first check your PUT routines. In fact, you may minimize output bugs by coding one common print subroutine.

An I/O error may also occur because of an incorrect definition of a file or an improper reference to it. For example, the assembler does not recognize the error in the transposed operands in GET RECDIN,FILEIN. Subsequently, when the first GET executes, the program links to the RECDIN area expecting to find the file definition instructions.

If you cannot locate the macro that caused an I/O error, check the contents of register 14, provided that there was a storage dump. Examine the second line of registers beginning with GR 0–F (general registers 0–15). Consider the following registers:

```
GR 8-F    ...   x————x    00051268    x————x
                  |           |          |
                reg-13      reg-14     reg-15
```

When your program performs an I/O operation, it exits and links to the supervisor program. But before leaving, it loads into register 14 the address of the instruction following the GET or PUT. This action enables the supervisor to return to your program after the I/O is completed. If the program crashes on the I/O operation, the supervisor issues a diagnostic and (if directed) dumps the contents of the registers and storage. An examination of register 14 indicates the address of the instruction immediately following the GET or PUT, in this case X'00051268'. You may have to calculate the location of the macro in the program listing by subtracting the program's load point (also known as entry point). You can determine the load point either from the contents of the base register or by an OS diagnostic that indicates EPA (entry point address). Let's assume that the load point is X'051210'; subtract that value from the address in register 14:

Address in register 14:	X'051268'
Load point of program:	X'051210'
Location in listing:	X'000058'

In this case, the instruction at LOC X'58' should immediately follow the GET or PUT that caused the error.

A common way of causing an I/O error is to erase a file definition (DTF or DCB) or the literal pool. The literal pool contains such vital information as addresses for handling the I/O macros. In either case, an attempt to perform an I/O operation may cause a mysterious execution error that confuses both the system and you!

There are three common ways to erase file definitions (DTFs or DCBs) and literal pools. First, if an input workarea or buffer area is defined smaller than the actual record length, an input operation fills the area plus the bytes immediately following. If this damaged area contains a file definition or literal pool, a subsequent I/O operation could fail.

Second, an instruction such as MVC PRINT + 100,HEADING (missing explicit length) could erase data following PRINT, such as a file definition or literal pool.

Third, a program could build a table, as follows:

```
NAMETAB     DS      10CL20      Table of names
            LTORG               Literal pool
```

In this case, the program could store names successively in the table. There is provision for only ten names; if the program stores an eleventh name, it will erase the first 20 bytes of the literal pool. However, how about defining the literal pool before the table, like this?

```
                        LTORG
        NAMETAB         DS      10CL20
```

Storing 11 names no longer erases the literal pool; instead, it now erases input/output modules that the link editor has coupled to the end of the program. Once again, program execution will terminate on an unpredictable error. The solution is to increase the size of the table and to check the number of entries that are stored.

UNCATALOGED I/O MODULES

Another type of error for which you should be alert is related to the coding of a DTF or DCB. One symptom of this error (although other errors may also cause it) is that the supervisor displays a diagnostic message such as

```
PROGRAM CHECK INTERRUPT HEX LOCATION 000008 CONDITION CODE x
    OPERATION EXCEPTION
```

A system programmer must catalog all the expected I/O modules, such as a module for handling a terminal. Under DOS, the macro is DTFCN (console). If you code this macro in a program and the module is not cataloged or if it is cataloged in a different version from the one that you have coded, the assembler has no way of knowing that it does not exist. It simply leaves an address in the external symbol dictionary for the linkage editor to complete. When the linker fails to locate the module, it inserts a diagnostic in the link edit map:

```
        UNRESOLVED EXTERNAL REFERENCES    EXTRN   xxxxxxx
        001 UNRESOLVED ADDRESS CONSTANTS
```

Take note of EXTRN addresses that the linkage editor cannot locate and ignore references to WXTRN (weak external) addresses. But if your system defaults to ACTION NOMAP, you won't get the message (code ACTION MAP). To remedy the error, have the systems programmer catalog the I/O module, or define a file definition macro that is already cataloged.

Often, examination of a diagnostic message, the assembled program listing, and the link edit map does not disclose the cause of an error, and the only resort is to study a storage dump.

STORAGE DUMPS

One of the main debugging tools of experienced programmers is the storage dump. Indeed, a dump is often the easiest and only way to locate a bug. You can force a dump on an execution error by coding your job control as follows:

DOS: `// OPTION LINK,DUMP`   (or PARTDUMP if partitioned)

OS: `//GO.SYSUDUMP DD SYSOUT=A`   (include after the source program with other //GO entries)

The computer cannot process an invalid instruction, an invalid address, or invalid packed data. In such cases, the supervisor interrupts program execution and prints the location of the failing instruction and the type of error. Unless you provide for error recovery with the DOS STXIT or SPIE macros, the supervisor produces the dump, terminates execution, and begins execution of the next job. The diagnostic messages vary by operating system.

Dumps under DOS

On a processing error, the DOS supervisor prints an error message such as the following:

```
PROGRAM CHECK INTERRUPTION--HEX LOCATION 051340--
     CONDITION CODE 3--DATA EXCEPTION
```

"Hex location" is the address of the instruction in error, in this case X'051340'. The condition code is seldom useful, but knowing the type of program check, in this case a data exception, is very useful.

If your program's START directive specifies the program's actual load point (starting location for execution), you simply have to check the program listing for the failed instruction. Consider the following instruction at X'51340':

```
51340     ZAP   AMTPK,AMTIN
```
(instruction causing the error)

Assume also that the defined fields are the following:

```
AMTIN     DS    ZL6
```
(in input record)

```
AMTPK     DS    PL4
```
(with packed declaratives)

You may realize immediately that AMTIN is supposed to be an input field containing zoned data, whereas ZAP requires that operand 2 reference packed data. The instruction code presumably should be PACK.

If the START directive does not supply the program's load point (that is, if START has a blank or zero operand), you have to calculate the storage address. If the supervisor has printed a dump of the registers and storage, check the address in the base register. Since the INIT macro in this text initializes base register 3, it contains the starting address, and the first line of the dump beginning with GR 0–F (general registers 0–15) would appear as follows:

```
GR 0-F    x———x  x———x  x———x   40051212  ...
           |       |       |            |
         reg-0   reg-1   reg-2        reg-3
```

In this case, register 3 contains the address X'051212' (ignore the 40 to the left— except on the most recent supercomputers, addresses have six digits). Deduct 2 from this address: X'051212' − 2 = X'051210', the true load point for this program. Subtract this load point from the hex location in the supervisor diagnostic:

Location of interrupt:	X'051340'
Load point of program:	− X'051210'
Location of error in list:	X'000130'

Now check X'130' in the printout of the assembled program, which could appear as follows:

```
130          ZAP AMTPK,AMTIN
```

The ZAP instruction is the one in error, as shown earlier. In the dump example in the next section, you will see how to get the load point from a link edit map as well.

Dumps under OS

OS provides a mass of diagnostic messages, telling you more than you may ever want to know. Provided that you have inserted a SYSUDUMP job control entry, the system will supply the entry (or load) point of your program, the address of the failed instruction, and a hex dump of the registers and storage area. If your program encounters a program check interrupt, examine the printout following the program listing and output (if any). The first diagnostics could appear as follows:

```
JOB jobname STEP GO
COMPLETION CODE SYSTEM 0C7                (7 is the code for data exception)
PSW AT ENTRY TO ABEND FFB5000D C0051346  (051346 is instruction address)
```

"Completion code" indicates the type of program check. In this case, code 7 is a data exception—see Appendix B for all codes. The PSW (program status word) indicates the instruction address in the rightmost six hex digits, in this case 051346, the address following the failed instruction. Since you don't know where an OS program will load for execution, the START or CSECT directives contain a zero operand. You can determine the entry point in the diagnostics under the CDE section. The first statement there could appear as follows:

```
... NM MAIN (or NM GO) USE 01 EPA 051210
```

The entry point address (EPA, or relocation factor) is therefore 051210. You can now determine the failed instruction in the program listing:

Address in the PSW:	X'51346'
Entry point address:	−X'51210'
Location of instruction following the error:	X'00136'

An examination of the program listing discloses the following at this location:

LOCATION	INSTRUCTION
130	ZAP AMTPK,AMTIN
136	...

The instruction preceding 136 is the ZAP at 130. The data exception indicates invalid packed data, once again the contents of AMTIN, as discussed in the previous section.

Error Recovery

Program checks cause a program to terminate; however, when testing, you usually want to push the program through to detect as many errors as possible. The special macros that provide for error recovery are STXIT under DOS and SPIE under OS.

DUMP EXAMPLE

The program in Fig. 15-1 reads stock records and calculates unit cost (cost ÷ quantity). The output consists of a heading, the first detail line, an error diagnostic caused by a program check, and, finally, a storage dump.

The diagnostics disclose that a data exception occurred at hex location X'02C166':

```
OS03I PROGRAM CHECK INTERRUPTION - HEX LOCATION
   02C166 - CONDITION CODE 0 - DATA EXCEPTION
```

You can use this address to locate the actual instruction that caused the data

```
                EXTERNAL SYMBOL DICTIONARY
SYMBOL    TYPE          ID   ADDR   LENGTH  LD-ID
PRDUMP    SD (CSECT)    001  000000 00047C
IJCFZIWO  ER (EXTRN)    002
IJDFYZIW  ER (EXTRN)    003

LOC      OBJECT CODE          ADDR1 ADDR2   STMT  SOURCE STATEMENT
000000                                       3  PRDUMP  START
000000   0530                                4          BALR  3,0                 INITIALIZE
                                             5          USING *,3
                                             6          OPEN  FILEIN,PRTR
                              00002          15         PUTPR PRTR,HDGLINE,SK1     SKIP NEW PAGE
                                             22         PUTPR PRTR,HDGLINE,WSP2    PRINT HEADING
                                             29         GET   FILEIN,RECDIN       1ST RECORD

00004E   4560 307A          0007C            36  A10LOOP BAL  6,B10CALC           PROCESS RECORD
                                             37          GET   FILEIN,RECDIN      READ NEXT
000062   47F0 304C          0004E            43          B    A10LOOP             LOOP

                                             45  A90EOF CLOSE FILEIN,PRTR         TERMINATE
                                             54          EOJ
                                             58  *
                                             59  *      C A L C U L A T E   U N I T   C O S T

00007C   F236 341D 32D9     0041F 002DB     60  B10CALC PACK COSTPK,COSTIN        *
000082   F223 3421 32D5     00423 002D7     61          PACK QTYPK,QTYIN          *
000088   F822 3421 3421     00423 00423     62          ZAP  QTYPK,QTYPK          QUANTITY = 0?
00008E   4780 30A8          000AA           63          BZ   B20                  * YES - BYPASS
000092   F873 3424 341D     00426 0041F     64          ZAP  UNCOSTPK,COSTPK      CALCULATE
000098   F070 3424 0001     00426 00001     65          SRP  UNCOSTPK,1,0         * UNIT COST
00009E   FD72 3424 3421     00426 00423     66          DP   UNCOSTPK,QTYPK       *
0000A4   F045 3424 003F     00426 0003F     67          SRP  UNCOSTPK(5),63,5     *
0000AA   D20B 33D9 3434     003DB 00436     69  B20      MVC  COSTPR,EDCOST        EDIT FIELDS
0000B0   DE0B 33D9 341D     003DB 0041F     70          ED   COSTPR,COSTPK        * COST
0000B6   D206 33D1 3440     003D3 00442     71          MVC  UNCOSPR,EDUNIT        *
0000BC   DE06 33D1 3426     003D3 00428     72          ED   UNCOSPR,UNCOSTPK+2   * UNIT COST
0000C2   D207 33C5 3447     003C7 00449     73          MVC  QTYPR,EDQTY           *
0000C8   DE07 33C5 3421     003C7 00423     74          ED   QTYPR,QTYPK          * QUANTITY
0000CE   D20F 33B5 32C5     003B7 002C7     75          MVC  DESCRPR,DESCRIN       *
0000D4   D203 33AF 32C1     003B1 002C3     76          MVC  STOCKPR,STOCKIN       *
                                            78          PUTPR PRTR,STKLINE,WSP1   PRINT RECORD
0000EE   FA73 342C 341D     0042E 0041F     85          AP   FINCSTPK,COSTPK      ADD TO TOTAL
0000F4   07F6                               86          BR   6                    RETURN
```

Figure 15-1 Program interrupt and dump.

```
                              D E C L A R A T I V E S
                              ------------------------
           88   *
           89   *
000000F8   90   FILEIN   DEFIN  A90EOF                              INPUT FILE
0000...    116  PRTR     DEFPR                                      PRINTER

0002C3    146  RECDIN    DS    0CL80                                INPUT RECORD:
0002C3    147  STOCKIN   DS    CL04                                 *  STOCK NO.
0002C7    148  DESCRIN   DS    CL16                                 *  DESCRIPTION
0002D7    149  QTYIN     DS    ZL04                                 *  QUANTITY
0002DB    150  COSTIN    DS    ZL07                                 *  COST
0002E2    151            DS    CL51                                 *

000315 4040404040404040      153  HDGLINE  DC  CL22' '              HEADING:
00032B E2E3D6C3D2404040      154           DC  CL23'STOCK'
000342 D8E4C1D5E3C9E3E8      155           DC  CL88'QUANTITY    UNITCOST     COST'

00039A                157  STKLINE  DS  0CL133                      PRINT LINE:
00039A 4040404040404040 158           DC  CL23' '                  *
0003B1 4040            159  STOCKPR  DS  CL04                       *  STOCK NO.
0003B5 4040            160           DC  CL02' '                    *
0003B7                 161  DESCRPR  DS  CL16                       *  DESCRIPTION
0003C7 40404040        162  QTYPR    DS  ZL08                       *  QUANTITY
0003CF                 163           DC  CL04' '                    *
0003D3 40              164  UNCOSPR  DS  ZL07                       *  UNIT COST
0003DA                 165           DC  CL01' '                    *
0003DB                 166  COSTPR   DS  ZL12                       *     COST
0003E7 4040404040404040 167          DC  CL56' '                    *

00041F 0000000C             169  COSTPK    DC  PL4'0'               PACKED FIELDS:
000423 00000C               170  QTYPK     DC  PL3'0'               *
000426 00000000000000000C   171  UNCOSTPK  DC  PL8'0'               *
00042E                      172  FINCSTPK  DS  PL8                  *
                            173  *                                 EDIT WORDS :
000436 4020206B2020214B2020C3D9  174  EDCOST  DC  X'4020206B2020214B2020C3D9'
000442 402020214B2020            175  EDUNIT  DC  X'402020214B2020'
000449 40202020120C3D9           176  EDQTY   DC  X'40202020120C3D9'
000458                           177          LTORG
000458 5B5BC2D6D7C5D540               =C'$$BOPEN '
000460 5B5BC2C3D3D6E2C5               =C'$$BCLOSE'
000468 00000188                       =A(PRTR)
00046C 00000315                       =A(HDGLINE)
000470 000000F8                       =A(FILEIN)
000474 000000C3                       =A(RECDIN)
000478 0000039A                       =A(STKLINE)
                                       PRDUMP
00000                            185          END
```

Figure 15-1 (continued)

Output:-

STOCK	QUANTITY	UNITCOST	COST
1234 PLYWOOD 1/4	50	3.05	152.50

0S03I PROGRAM CHECK INTERRUPT - HEX LOCATION 02C166 - CONDITION CODE 0 - DATA EXCEPTION
0S00I JOB ABEL   CANCELED.
0S07I PROBLEM PROGRAM PSW   031D00000002C16C

PSW AND REGISTERS OF ENDING TASK
PSW=   031D0000 0002C16C   register 3
                                    |
GR 0-F 0002C412 0002C200 0004BFFF 4002C07A 001A5FFF 00000000 8002C0CA 0002C0E0
        40BD45AA 00000608 00000000 0004BFFF 0002C078 0004C080 A002C166 00C17680
FP 0-3 40404040 40404040 40404040 40404040 40404040 40404040 40404040 40404040

BG PARTITION

```
...
02C160  001045EF  000CFA73  342C341D  07F60000  00008000  0C000001  0002C190  0002C198
02C180  0002C4F8  02810202  0002C1A2  0002C0E0  0202C1A2  20000050  47000000  47000000
02C1A0  0000F1F2  F3F4D7D3  E8E6D6D6  C440F161  F4404040  4040F0F0  F5F0F0F0  F1F5F2F5
02C1C0  F0404040  40404040  40404040  40404040  40404040  00000000  40404040  40404040
02C1E0  40404040  40404040  40404040  40404040  40400000  00010000  0002C230  0002C230
02C200  00008001  0C000003  0902C2B7  0004C118  01C17680  08B60909  00000000  00000000
02C220  07004700  00000000  20000084  0004C110  0C000000  0002C232  0002C232  40404040
02C240  40404040  40404040  F1F2F3F4  4040D7D3  E8E6D6D6  C440F161  F4404040  40404040
02C260  4040F5F0  40404040  40F34BF0  40404040  F5404040  4040F1F5  F24BF5F0  40404040
02C280  40404040  --SAME--
02C2C0  40404040  E4C1D5E3  C9E3E840  404040E4  D5C9E3C3  D6E2E340  40404040  40C3D6E2
02C2E0  40404040  40BD45E3  40404040  40404040  40404040  40404040  40404040  40404040
02C300  E3404040  40404040  40404040  40404040  40400000  40404040  40404040  40404040
02C320  40404040  40404040  40404040  40404040  40404040  404040F1  F2F3F4D7  40404040
02C340  D3E8E6D6  D6C440F1  61F44040  40404040  F0F5F0F0  F0F1F5F2  F5F04040  40404040
02C360  40404040  --SAME--
02C380  40404040  40404000  00114040  40404040  40404040  40404040  C1D5E3C9  40404040
02C3A0  40404042  E3D6C3D2  40404040  40404040  40404040  4040D8E4  40404040  QUANTI*
02C3C0  E3E84040  4040E4D5  C9E3C3D6  E2E34040  40404040  C3D6E2E3  40404040  40404040
02C3E0  40404040  --SAME--
02C400  40404040  40404040  40404040  40404040  40400940  40404040  40404040  40404040
02C420  40404040  40F1F2F3  F4404040  40404040  D3E8E6D6  D6C440F1  61F44040  40404040
02C440  40404040  F0404040  40404040  4040F34B  F0404040  F5F24BF5  F0404040  40404040
02C460  40404040  --SAME--
02C480  40404040  40404040  40404040  40404040  40404040  40404040  15250F00  050C0000
02C4A0  00305C00  000C0000  00000000  00000000  206B2020  214B2020  C3D94020  20214B20
02C4C0  20402020  202120C3  D9000000  00000000  5B5BC2D6  D7C5D540  5B5BC2C3  D3D6E2C5
02C4E0  0002C200  0002C38D  0002C170  0000C933B  5B5BC2C5  F7C5D540  0A320000  0A320000
02C500  47F0F06C  0A320000  C9D1C3C6  E9C9E6F0  C8F0F7F0  F5F6F6F6  60F3F0F1  40C3D6D7
...
```

Figure 15-1 (continued)

exception.   You have to know the program's load point, which you can derive
from the dump:

1. `PSW AND REGISTERS OF ENDING TASK`
2. `PSW=       031D0000 0002C16C`
3. `GR 0-F  0002C412 0002C200 0004BFFF 4002C07A    001A5FFF ...`
4. `        40BD45AA 00000608 00000000 0004BFFF    0002C078 ...`
5. `FP 0-3  40404040 40404040 40404040 40404040    40404040 ...`

- Line 2 shows the contents of the PSW at the time of the interrupt.   The word
  to the right contains the address following the failed instruction, X'0002C16C'.
- Lines 3 and 4 display the hex contents of the 16 general-purpose registers
  (GR 0–F or 0–15), each containing eight hex digits.
- Line 5 displays the contents of the floating-point (FP) registers.

Following is the hexadecimal dump of storage, reduced in size here for brevity.
Each line displays 32 (hex 20) bytes, collected in groups of 4 bytes for readability.
To the extreme left is the address of the leftmost byte on the line, always at an
address evenly divisible by hex 10 (decimal 16).   The first line contains

```
        02C160   001045EF ...
```

02C160 is the address of the first pair of hex digits, 00.   The left half of the first
line provides the contents of locations 02C160 through 02C16F, and the right half
provides the contents of 02C170 through 02C17F.

The extreme right displays the character contents of the dump, where printable.   This information is a guide only to fast identification of character constants
and input/output records.

The base register in the program is register 3, whose contents you can use to
determine where the program loaded.   According to the dump, the first line contains the contents of the general registers, as follows:

```
GR 0-F   0002C412   0002C200   0004BFFF   4002C07A      ...
            |          |          |          |
          reg-0      reg-1      reg-2      reg-3
```

Ignore the hex 40 to the left in register 3 because addresses have six hex digits.
Also, because the initial BALR at statement 4 loads the starting address plus 2,
subtract 2 from this address: 02C07A − 2 = 02C078, the program's true load
point.   Register 12 also contains the load point, stored there by the supervisor.
(An OS program supplies the load point as EPA, entry point address, as explained
earlier.)   Now you can locate the failed instruction in the listing as follows:

Address of the failed instruction:	02C166
Minus load point of the program:	−02C078
Location in the listing:	0000EE

A check of location (LOC) 0000EE to the left of the program printout discloses that the instruction is

```
        0000EE              AP    FINCSTPK,COSTPK
```

Either operand of an AP may cause a data exception. Let's check the contents of the operands in the dump. To determine their locations in storage, add the load point address and the displacement values under ADDR1 and ADDR2 on the listing:

	FINCSTPK	COSTPK
Load point:	02C078	02C078
ADDR of operand:	+ 42E	+ 41F
Storage location:	02C4A6	02C497

Now trace these two locations in the dump in Fig. 15-1. The contents of FINCSTPK begins at 02C4A6. Trace down the leftmost column of the dump until you reach an address that is close—02C4A0. Now trace horizontally across the line. Count each pair of hex digits as one byte, and count across seven pairs (or count fours, as 4, 8, C). FINCSTPK is an 8-byte field beginning at 02C4A6.

As you can see, FINCSTPK does not contain valid packed data. A check back in the program listing shows that FINCSTPK is defined as a DS instead of a DC. That explains the data exception, and the correction is easy to make. Since the program doesn't even print final totals, a solution is to delete both the DS and the AP instruction.

Before leaving, it might be wise to check the contents of COSTPK. Trace the storage address of 02C497 in the dump. You'll have to step up one line beginning at 02C480, then advance to the center of the line, which is 02C490. Now count across eight pairs of hex digits until you reach 02C497. As you can see, COSTPK contains a valid packed value, 0015250F.

The program contains another error that the test data did not detect. Later we explain how to dump a selected area of storage to help locate the error.

LINK EDIT MAP

The program in Fig. 15-1 also produced a link edit map following the assembled listing. The system may generate a map depending on the system defaults or your request of ACTION MAP. As shown in Fig. 15-2, the map contains the following:

XFR-AD   The address where the loader program is to transfer for the start of program execution. The address in the base register is normally 2 bytes higher than this address.

Link Edit Map:-

```
              LINKAGE EDITOR DIAGNOSTIC OF INPUT
ACTION TAKEN  MAP
ENTRY
PHASE    XFR-AD  LOCORE  HICORE    CSECT/    LOADED   RELOC.   PARTIT.  PHASE    TAKEN
                                   ENTRY     AT       FACTOR   OFFSET   OFFSET   FROM
PHASE*** 02C078  02C078  02C5E7
                                   PRDUMP    02C078   02C078   000000   000000   SYSLNK
                                   IJCFZIW0  02C4F8   02C4F8   000480   000480   IJCFZIW0
                                   IJDFYZIW  02C598   02C598   000520   000520   IJDFYZIW
```

Figure 15-2   Link edit map.

LOCORE	The lowest address of the program.
HICORE	The highest address of the program. (You can calculate a program's size by the difference between HICORE and LOCORE.)
CSECT/ENTRY	The names of external addresses in the program, in this example PRDUMP (the name of the program), and the I/O modules for system reader and printer that the linker has included.
LOADED AT	The storage location of each module.
RELOC. FACTOR	The relocation factor that you may use to add to the starting value to locate addresses, in this case 02C078.
PARTIT. OFFSET	The number of bytes from the lowest address in the partition. For example, PRDUMP is offset zero bytes and IJCFZIW0 is offset X'480' bytes from the lowest address.
TAKEN FROM	The source where the linker located the module.

PARTIAL DUMPS OF STORAGE: PDUMP AND SNAP

Both DOS and OS have provision for intentional dumps of storage during program execution. The DOS macro is PDUMP and the OS macro is SNAP. Both let you view the contents of any storage area. When your program encounters a dump macro, it transfers control to the supervisor, which produces a hexadecimal printout of the contents of the registers and the specified storage area. At termination of the dump, control returns to the statement immediately following the dump macro. In effect, it produces a snapshot of storage.

Often a program that executes to completion produces the wrong results. If a check of the program listing and input data cannot reveal the cause of the error, a common practice is to insert the dump macro (one or more) in the executable part of your program where you want to see the changed contents of one or more declaratives, I/O areas, or buffers. Once you have located and corrected all errors, be sure to take the dump macros out.

The DOS PDUMP Macro

The PDUMP macro has the following format:

Name	Operation	Operand
[label]	PDUMP	address1,address2
		or (reg),(reg)

address1 and address2 specify the start and end positions of an area to be dumped, as RECDIN,TOTALPAY + 10. You may also supply the addresses in registers and code them, for example, as (6),(9). In either event, PDUMP executes only if the second address is higher and generates the hexadecimal contents of the registers and the defined storage area. The operation changes the contents of registers 0 and 1; the other registers still contain the contents that your own program generated.

Refer now to the program in Fig. 15-3, which is the same as the one in Fig. 15-1 with the DS and AP instructions deleted. Statement 54 displays the contents of storage from RECDIN through EDCOST:

```
PDUMP RECDIN,EDCOST
```

The program still contains an error, which PDUMP can help to locate. The program was run with only two input records:

```
Stock  Description      Qty    Cost
|1234|Plywood 1/4     |0050|0015250
|1234|Plywood 1/4     |0000|0026730
```

You can detect the problem in the output. The first detail line provides a correct calculation of unit cost, but the second line appears to be incorrect. Although quantity is zero, unit cost prints as 3.05 but should be zero. Let's check the dump for the contents of cost, quantity, and unit cost.

Line 1 shows the contents of the PSW at the time of the dump. Lines 2 and 3 display the hex contents of the 16 general registers, GR 0–F or 0–15, each containing eight hex digits. Line 4 contains the contents of the floating-point (FP) registers.

Note that general register 3 (the fourth one on the first line) contains 4002C07A. Since the program initialized register 3 with the base address, you can tell where in storage the program has loaded for execution. Since an address consists of only the rightmost 24 bits (six hex digits) of a register, you can ignore the X'40' to the left, and the address is 02C07A. The first instruction is BALR 3,0, which loads the storage address of the following instruction into register 3.

```
LOC     OBJECT CODE     ADDR1   ADDR2   STMT   SOURCE STATEMENT
000000
000000  0530                             3 PRDUMP  START
                                         4         BALR  3,0                     INITIALIZE
                        00002            5         USING *,3
                                         6         OPEN  FILEIN,PRTR
                                        15         PUTPR PRTR,HDGLINE,SK1         SKIP NEW PAGE
                                        22         PUTPR PRTR,HDGLINE,WSP2        PRINT HEADING
                                        29         GET   FILEIN,RECDIN           1ST RECORD

00004E  4560 3084               00086   36 A10LOOP BAL   6,B10CALC               PROCESS RECORD
                                        37         GET   FILEIN,RECDIN           READ NEXT
000062  47F0 304C               0004E   43         B     A10LOOP                 LOOP

                                        45 A90EOF  CLOSE FILEIN,PRTR             TERMINATE
                                        54         PDUMP RECDIN,EDCOST           PDUMP MACRO
                                        60         EOJ

                                        64 *                 C A L C U L A T E   U N I T   C O S T
                                        65 *
000086  F236 3425 32E1  00427  002E3    66 B10CALC PACK  COSTPK,COSTIN           *
00008C  F223 3429 32DD  0042B  002DF    67         PACK  QTYPK,QTYIN             *
000092  F822 3429 3429  0042B  0042B    68         ZAP   QTYPK,QTYPK             QUANTITY = 0?
000098  4780 30B2       000B4           69         BZ    B20                     * YES - BYPASS
00009C  F873 342C 3425  0042E  00427    70         ZAP   UNCOSTPK,COSTPK         CALCULATE
0000A2  F070 342C 0001  0042E  00001    71         SRP   UNCOSTPK,1,0            * UNIT COST
0000A8  FD72 342C 3429  0042E  0042B    72         DP    UNCOSTPK,QTYPK          *
0000AE  F045 342C 003F  0042E  0003F    73         SRP   UNCOSTPK(5),63,5        *

0000B4  D20B 33E1 3434  003E3  00436    75 B20     MVC   COSTPR,EDCOST           EDIT FIELDS
0000BA  DE0B 33E1 3425  003E3  00427    76         ED    COSTPR,COSTPK           * COST
0000C0  D206 33D9 3440  003D9  00442    78         MVC   UNCOSPR,EDUNIT          *
0000C6  DE06 33D9 342E  003DB  00430    79         ED    UNCOSPR,UNCOSTPK+2      * UNIT COST
0000CC  D207 33CD 3447  003CF  00449    81         MVC   QTYPR,EDQTY             *
0000D2  DE07 33CD 3429  003CF  0042B    82         ED    QTYPR,QTYPK             * QUANTITY
0000D8  D20F 33BD 32CD  003BF  002CF    84         MVC   DESCRPR,DESCRIN         *
0000DE  D203 33B7 32C9  003B9  002CB    85         MVC   STOCKPR,STOCKIN         *

0000F8  07F6                            87         PUTPR PRTR,STKLINE,WSP1       PRINT RECORD
                                        94         BR    6                       RETURN
```

Figure 15-3 Partial dump of storage.

```
                                        D E C L A R A T I V E S

                    96  *                                                 DECLARATIVES
                    97  *
0002CB              98  FILEIN   DEFIN  A90EOF                            INPUT FILE
                   124  PRTR     DEFPR                                    PRINTER

0002CB             154  RECDIN   DS   0CL80                               INPUT RECORD:
0002CB             155  STOCKIN  DS   CL04                                  STOCK NO.
0002CF             156  DESCRIN  DS   CL16                                  DESCRIPTION
0002DF             157  QTYIN    DS   ZL04                                  QUANTITY
0002E3             158  COSTIN   DS   ZL07                                  COST
0002EA             159           DS   CL51                                    *
00031D 404040404040404040  161  HDGLINE  DC  CL22' '                     HEADING:
000333 E2E3D6C3D2404040    162           DC  CL23'STOCK'
00034A D8E4C1D5E3C9E3E8    163           DC  CL88'QUANTITY   UNITCOST    COST'

0003A2             165  STKLINE  DS   0CL133                              PRINT LINE:
0003A2             166           DC   CL23' '                            *------------
0003B9             167  STOCKPR  DS   CL04                               * STOCK NO.
0003BD 4040        168           DC   CL02' '                            *
0003BF             169  DESCRPR  DS   CL16                               * DESCRIPTION
0003CF             170  QTYPR    DS   ZL08                               * QUANTITY
0003D7 40404040    171           DC   CL04' '                            *
0003DB             172  UNCOSPR  DS   ZL07                               * UNIT COST
0003E2 40          173           DC   CL01' '                            *
0003E3             174  COSTPR   DS   ZL12                               * COST
0003EF 404040404040404040  175           DC  CL56' '                     *

000427 0000000C    177  COSTPK   DC   PL4'0'                             PACKED FIELDS:
00042B 00000C      178  QTYPK    DC   PL3'0'                             *
00042E             179  UNCOSTPK DS   PL8                                *
                   180  *                                                EDIT WORDS  :
000436 4020206B2020214B  181  EDCOST  DC  X'4020206B2020214B2020C3D9'
000442 402020214B2020    182  EDUNIT  DC  X'402020214B2020'
000449 402020202120C3D9  183  EDQTY   DC  X'402020202120C3D9'
000458             184           LTORG
000458 5B5BC2D6D7C5D540  185          =C'$$BOPEN '
000460 5B5BC2C3D3D6E2C5  186          =C'$$BCLOSE'
000468 5B5BC2D7C4E4D4D7  187          =CL8'$$BPDUMP'
000470 000002CB00000436  188          =A(RECDIN,EDCOST)
000478 00000190          189          =A(PRTR)
00047C 0000031D          190          =A(HDGLINE)
000480 00000100          191          =A(FILEIN)
000484 000002CB          192          =A(RECDIN)
000488 000003A2          193          =A(STKLINE)
00000              194           END  PRDUMP
```

Figure 15-3 (continued)

```
Link Edit Map:-    LINKAGE EDITOR DIAGNOSTIC OF INPUT

ACTION TAKEN MAP

PHASE    XFR-AD  LOCORE  HICORE  CSECT/    LOADED  RELOC.   PARTIT.  PHASE    TAKEN
                                 ENTRY     AT      FACTOR   OFFSET   OFFSET   FROM

PHASE*** 02C078  02C078  02C5F7  PRDUMP    02C078  02C078   000000   000000   SYSLNK
                                 IJCFZIWO  02C508  02C508   000490   000490   IJCFZIWO
                                 IJDFYZIW  02C5A8  02C5A8   000530   000530   IJDFYZIW

Output:-

               STOCK          QUANTITY   UNITCOST   COST

               1234 PLYWOOD 1/4    50      3.05     152.50
               1234 PLYWOOD 1/4     0      3.05     267.30

PSW=  031D3000 0002C0FC

GR 0-F  0002C4E8 0002C4E0 0004BFFF 4002C07A   001A5FFF 00000000 8002C0CA 0002C0E0
        40BD45AA 00000608 00000000 0004BFFF   0002C078 0004C080 0002C0E0 0002C508

FP 0-3  40404040 40404040 40404040 40404040   40404040 40404040 40404040 40404040

02C340  40404040 F2F3F4D7 D3E8E6D6 D6C440F1   61F44040 404040F0 F0F0F0F0 F0F2F6F7  *1234PLYWOOD 1/4  000000267*
02C360  F3F04040 40404040 40404040 40404040   40404040 40404040 40404040 40404040  *30                        *
02C380  40404040 40404040 40404040 404040E2   40404000 00114040 40404040 40404040  *                         *
02C3A0  40404040 4040D8E4 C1D5E3C9 E3D6C3D2   C9E3C3D6 E2E34040 40404040 C3D6E2E3  *        STOCK            *
02C3C0  4040D8E4 C1D5E3C9 E3E84040 4040E4D5   40404040 40404040 40404040 40404040  * QUANTITY  UNITCOST  COST*
02C3E0  40404040 --SAME--                                                          *                         *
02C400  40404040 40404040 40404040 40404040   40404040 40404040 40400940 40404040  *                         *
02C420  40404040 40404040 40404040 40404040   40F1F2F3 F44040D7 D3E8E6D6 D6C440F1  *           1234 PLYWOOD 1*
02C440  61F44040 40404040 4040F040 40404040   40404040 4040F34B F0F54040 40404040  */4      0        3.05    2*
02C460  F6F74BF3 F0404040 40404040 40404040   40404040 40404040 40404040 40404040  *67.30                    *
02C480  40404040 40404040 40404040 40404040   40404040 40404040 40404040 40404040  *                         *
02C4A0  26730F00 000C0000 00305C00 000C4020   40404040 40404040 40404040 40404000  *                         *
```

Figure 15-3 (continued)

409

Since BALR is 2 bytes long, the address of the program's load point is 2 bytes less than the address in register 3:

Base address in register 3:	02C07A
Less 2 bytes for BALR:	− 2
Load point of program:	02C078

Register 12 also contains the load point address. As you can see, the supervisor has loaded the executable program into storage beginning at 02C078. In this example, the declaratives that PDUMP displays begin at 02C380.

Following the registers is the contents of storage that PDUMP specified, in the same format as the dump in Fig. 15-1. At the extreme left is the hex address of the first byte of the line, an address evenly divisible by X'10' (decimal 16). Each line (except for the first and last) lists 64 hex digits (32 bytes) with a space every eight hex digits for readability. To the right is the character representation for each byte, if the character is printable. For example, X'F0' displays as a zero, but X'00' appears as a blank.

Note the line beginning at 02C3E0, which contains all the same character, X'40'. PDUMP minimizes printing and displays --SAME--.

Now let's locate COSTPK in the dump. According to the assembler listing, COSTPK is at relative location (LOC) 000427:

Load point of the program:	02C078
Relative location of COSTPK:	+ 427
Actual location of COSTPK:	02C49F

Scan down the leftmost column of the dump and stop at 02C480. The center part separated by three spaces begins with the address X'02C490':

```
02C480: ...    40404040 40404040 40404040 40404000
                 |                                  |
               02C490                            02C49F
```

Count 15 bytes (30 hex digits) across the line beginning at 02C490 until you reach 02C49F. COSTPK is a 4-byte field containing 0026730F beginning at this address and continuing on the next line. You can derive the contents of QTYPK and UNCOSTPK by the same method.

UNCOSTPK is defined as 8 bytes but now contains two packed fields: a quotient (000000305C) and a remainder (00000C). Although the quotient is incorrect, the divide operation presumably did not calculate it incorrectly; the error must be in the program logic.

As you probably noticed, the unit cost 305 is the same as that for the previously printed stock item. The second stock item differs from the first item in that it contains a zero quantity. A check of program logic following B10CALC shows a test for zero QTYPK and a branch to B20. Consequently, if QTYPK is zero, the routine does not calculate unit cost. But since there is no value stored in unit cost, the field still contains the previously calculated unit cost. A solution is to initialize UNCOSTPK to zero immediately before the instruction at statement 68 that tests for zero quantity.

Smaller DOS systems may load programs at a predictable location. You could therefore set the START directive to this value and relate addresses on the assembled listing directly to addresses in the dump.

DOS supports two other dump macros: DUMP and JDUMP, both of which have blank operands. DUMP terminates the job step and produces a hexadecimal dump of the registers, the supervisor, and the entire partition in which the program was executing. JDUMP terminates the entire job and produces a similar dump. Since a dump of the supervisor can be enormous and of little value to a production programmer, normally only a systems programmer is concerned with these macros.

The OS SNAP Macro

The OS SNAP macro requires that you define a related output file. Place the SNAP macro (one or more) in the executing part of your program where you want the dump to occur, and insert the DCB (data control block) macro in your declarative section. The general formats for SNAP and its associated DCB are as follows:

[label]	SNAP	DCB=dcbname, ID=n, PDATA=(PSW,REGS), STORAGE=(from,to)	+ + +
dcbname	DCB	DSORG=PS, DDNAME=ddname, RECFM=VBA, MACRF=(W), LRECL=125, BLKSIZE=1632	+ + + + +

The following describes SNAP parameters:

DCB   Provides the name of a DCB macro that handles output for the SNAP.

ID=n   Optionally specifies a number between 0 and 127 that SNAP

uses for identification on output.   You could use this option
if your program is executing a number of SNAP macros.

PDATA   Optionally directs SNAP to generate the contents of the PSW
and registers.

STORAGE   Optionally identifies the storage addresses where the dump is
to begin and end.   You may actually identify more than one
pair of beginning and ending addresses, as (address1, address2,
address3, address4, . . .).   The second address of each pair
must be higher.

For the DCB, the dcbname must agree with that for the DCB entry in the
SNAP macro.   DDNAME relates to a job control entry that specifies the system
listing device:

```
//ddname DD SYSOUT=A
```

You OPEN the SNAP file prior to executing the first SNAP and CLOSE the
file on termination.   The dump is in the same format as a regular dump and a
PDUMP.   Note that any dump changes the contents of registers 0 and 1.   Figure
15-4 provides a skeleton of SNAP logic.

```
progname CSECT
         . . .
         OPEN        (OSSNAP,(OUTPUT))
         . . .
         SNAP        DCB=OSSNAP,ID=3,PDATA=(PSW,REGS),               +
                     STORAGE=(SNBEG,SNEND)
         . . .
         CLOSE       (OSSNAP)
         . . .
***                  D E C L A R A T I V E S

OSSNAP   DCB         DSORG=PS,DDNAME=SNAPIT,RECFM=VBA,MACRF=(W),     +
                     LRECL=125,BLKSIZE=1632
         . . .
SNBEG    EQU         *
         .
         .           (Declaratives to be dumped)
         .
SNEND    EQU         *
         . . .
         END         progname
/*
//SNAPIT  DD SYSOUT=A
```

Figure 15-4   Use of the OS SNAP macro.

THE STXIT MACRO: SET EXIT

Without a recover procedure, a program check such as a data exception causes the supervisor to interrupt processing, display an error diagnostic, and terminate the program.   One way to force your program to resume processing after a supervisor message is to code a special recovery macro, STXIT under DOS and SPIE under OS.

The STXIT macro has three operands:

- Operand 1 provides the type of exit, coded as PC, OC, IT, or AB. PC (the common entry) is for program checks, OC is for an operator (external) check, IT is for an interval timer check, and AB is for an abnormal task termination.
- Operand 2 provides the storage address where you want the supervisor to branch after its message. The routine could print a message or issue a PDUMP of the declarative area.
- Operand 3 references a savearea of 18 fullwords in which the supervisor stores

```
PROG15   START
         BALR   12,0
         USING  *,12
         STXIT  PC,X10PC,SAVEPC          Set error recovery
         OPEN   files
         .                               *
         .                               Processing
         .                               *
         CLOSE  files
         EOJ

X10PC    PDUMP  STDECL,ENDECL            Dump declaratives
         EXIT   PC


*          D E C L A R A T I V E S

filename DTFxx  ...                      Define files
STDECL   EQU    *
SAVEPC   DC     18F'0'                   *
         .                               Declaratives
         .                               *
ENDECL   EQU    *
         END    PROG15
```

Figure 15-5   Use of the DOS STXIT macro.

the old interrupt status information and the contents of registers 0–15, in that order.

Use the EXIT macro to return from your own recovery routine. The operand for EXIT matches the type of interrupt:

[label]	EXIT	PC *or* OC *or* IT

The skeleton program in Fig. 15-5 gives an example of recovery from a program check. Assume that an AP instruction has caused a data exception. The supervisor displays an error diagnostic and then branches to X10PC, where the routine dumps the declarative area (there is usually no advantage to dumping the contents of file definition macros). The EXIT macro causes a return to the address immediately following the AP.

Although your calculations will be incorrect, your program can process more instructions and provide more thorough testing.

KEY POINTS

- A syntactical error involves failure to follow the rules of an instruction, such as coding an instruction incorrectly or failing to code a required explicit length. A logical error involves a failure to follow the objective of the program, such as branching to an incorrect address or making a wrong computation.

- A common error that occurs with handling character data stems from the use of the MVC instruction, such as omission of an explicit length.

- Packed decimal data may cause a variety of errors because of the requirements: a valid sign in the leftmost half-byte and digits 0–9 in all other half-bytes. A data exception is particularly common.

- An error using binary arithmetic operations is to generate a value that exceeds the capacity of a register, a fixed-point-overflow exception.

- For base registers, do not use register 0, and avoid the use of registers 1, 13, 14, and 15 because I/O operations and subprogram linkage change their contents. Also avoid the use of register 2 because the TRT instruction uses it.

- A common input/output error involves printing: failure to initialize the print control character or initializing it with an incorrect value. An I/O error may also occur because of an incorrect definition of a file or an improper reference to it.

- If you code a DTF or DCB in a program and the module is not cataloged, the linkage editor will fail to locate the module and will insert a diagnostic in the link edit map.

- One of the main debugging tools is the storage dump. You can force a dump on an execution error by coding your job control with OPTION PARTDUMP (DOS) or SYSUDUMP (OS).
- The DOS PDUMP macro and the OS SNAP macro have provision for intentional dumps of storage during program execution.

PROBLEMS

15-1. *Character Data.* Identify and correct the following unrelated bugs based on the definition of RATEIN.

```
        RATEIN    DS    CL5
(a)               CLC   RATEIN,=C' '        RATEIN blank?
(b)               MVC   RATEIN,=C'0'        Move zeros to RATEIN
(c)               CLI   RATEIN,C'0'         RATEIN = zero?
(d)               MVC   RATEIN+3,=C'  '     Move 2 blanks
```

15-2. *Packed Data.* Identify and correct the following unrelated bugs based on the definitions.

```
        HOURIN    DS    ZL5
        HOURPK    DS    PL3'25'
        HOURTOT   DS    PL5
        PAGENO    DC    PL1'1'
(a)               AP    HOURTOT,HOURPK
(b)               AP    PAGENO,=P'9'
(c)               CP    HOURIN,=P'0'
(d)               CLC   HOURPK,=P'0'
(e)               DP    HOURPK,=P'0'
```

15-3. *Branch and Link.* Identify and correct the following bug.

```
                  BAL   7,H10HDG
                  BAL   8,C10CALC
                  ...
        C10CALC   ...
                  BR    7
        H10HDG    ...
                  BR    7
```

15-4. *Input/Output.* Identify and correct the following unrelated bugs.

```
        PRTR      DTF or DCB (assume correct
                              definition)
        PRINT     DS    CL133

(a)               OPEN  PRINT
(b)               MVI   PRINT,X'40'
                  PUT   PRTR,PRINT
```

15-5. *Explicit Base Addressing.*   Identify and correct the following unrelated bugs. Assume the same declaratives as in Problem 15-2, and assume that HOURIN contains valid numeric data.

   (a)

```
           LA        7,HOURIN
           PACK      HOURPK,0(7)
```

   (b)

```
           LA        8,HOURIN
           LA        9,HOURPK
           PACK      0(3,8),0(5,9)
```

15-6. *Storage Dump.*   A dump displays a data exception at address X'56894' and the contents of the base register as X'4005684A.'

   (a) Assuming the directive START 0, what would be the location on the assembled listing of the instruction that failed?

   (b) Assume that the failed instruction is AP ACCUM,VALUE. The assembled listing shows the address of the operands as follows:

LOC	NAME	OPERATION	OPERAND
7A	ACCUM	DS	PL5
7F	VALUE	DS	PL3

What are the locations of the two fields in the dump?

   (c) The dump displays the following for line 368C0:

```
      368C0       F0F10000 00000000 00040426 7C404040 ...
```

Locate the two fields in the dump and determine the two errors in the data.

16

FLOATING-POINT OPERATIONS

OBJECTIVE

To cover the definitions of floating-point data and the use of the floating-point instruction set.

Up to now, this text has discussed arithmetic data in two formats: packed decimal and binary or fixed-point. Two disadvantages may derive from performing arithmetic in these formats: (1) The maximum and minimum values may be inadequate for the calculation being performed, and (2) the programmer is fully responsible for maintaining decimal and binary point precision. Assembler floating-point format has its own unique set of instructions designed to overcome these disadvantages. Its most common use is for calculations in aerodynamics, weather forecasting, and electronics design that require extremely high or low values.

Most programs requiring floating-point arithmetic are written in high-level languages such as FORTRAN and PL/I, which replace much of the tedious detail that assembler programming requires. However, studying the assembler floating-point instructions gives a better understanding of the high-level languages and results in better programming performance.

FLOATING-POINT DATA FORMATS

First we'll examine floating point in base 10 format and then see how to convert it into base 16.

Base 10 Floating Point

Floating-point format perhaps can be explained best in terms of decimal (base 10) values. Any decimal value can be expressed by the formula

$$n = 10^e \times f$$

where

n = the decimal value

e = exponent, or power, to which the base 10 is raised

f = fraction

Consider the following decimal values:

Decimal value $n = 10^e \quad \times f$

123.45	= 10^3	× 0.12345 =	1,000	× 0.12345
1.2345	= 10^1	× 0.12345 =	10	× 0.12345
0.12345	= 10^0	× 0.12345 =	1	× 0.12345
0.0012345	= 10^{-2}	× 0.12345 =	0.01	× 0.12345

A floating-point value omits the base (10) and stores only the exponent (e) and the fraction (f). The system could store the floating-point fullword as

03		123450

                 exponent   fraction

meaning $10^3 \times 0.123450$.

Converting Base 10 to Base 16

The 370-series computers store floating-point values in base 16. The following technique converts decimal value 123.45 into hexadecimal.

1. Use the decimal-to-hexadecimal conversion table in Appendix A to convert the integer portion 123 to base 16 as 7B.0000.

2. Convert the fraction portion as follows:

			7B.0000
0.45			
×16	Multiply by 16		
7.20	Extract the 7	=	.7000
0.20			
×16	Multiply by 16		
3.20	Extract the 3	=	.0300
0.20			
×16	Multiply by 16		
3.20	Extract the 3	=	.0030
0.20			
×16	Multiply by 16		
3.20	Extract the 3	=	.0003
	Hexadecimal value:		7B.7333

This result is stored as 6 digits in single precision as 7B.7333 or, more accurately, as 14 digits in double precision as 7B.733333333333. As you can see, there is no exact hex representation for the decimal value 123.45.

Base 16 Floating Point

The previous example converted 123.45 to X'7B.7333'. This hex number can be represented in the following way:

$$n_{16} = 16^e \times f_{16}$$

$$7B.7333 = 16^0 \times 7B.7333$$

$$= 16^1 \times 7.B7333$$

$$= 16^2 \times .7B7333$$

You may therefore store this floating-point number without the base (16) as

02		7B7333
exponent		fraction

meaning $16^2 \times$ X'.7B7333'.

Floating-point data, like binary data, may be defined in storage or loaded in registers. Either way, you may represent floating-point values in three formats:

FORMAT	PRECISION	LENGTH
Short	Single	Fullword
Long	Double	Doubleword
Extended long	Extended	Two doublewords

A float number consists of a *sign, characteristic* (exponent), and *fraction*, shown in bit format:

Format	Sign	Characteristic	Fraction
Single precision	0	1 — 7	8 — 31
Double precision	0	1 — 7	8 —— 63
Extended precision	0	1 — 7	8 ——— 127

Sign. The sign, in bit position 0, applies to the fraction. A zero-bit means plus, and a one-bit means minus fraction.

Characteristic. In a value such as 16^3, 16 is the fraction, and 3 is the exponent. 16^3 means $16 \times 16 \times 16$, or 4,096. The computer stores the exponent as a characteristic in *excess-64 notation* by adding 64 (X'40') to the stored exponent, as the following examples show.

DECIMAL REPRESENTATION

Exponent + 64 = characteristic
03 + 64 = 67
00 + 64 = 64
−03 + 64 = 61

HEXADECIMAL REPRESENTATION

Exponent + 40 = characteristic
03 + 40 = 43
00 + 40 = 40
−03 + 40 = 3D

The exponent is incremented by 64 (X'40') and stored in hex format in bit positions 1–7. The lowest exponent, X'−40', is stored as X'−40' + X'40' = X'00'. The highest exponent, X'3F', is stored as X'3F' + X'40' = X'7F'. This maximum exponent is stored with all 7 bits on. The characteristic has an implicit sign; for example, the exponent −2 is stored as X'−02' + X'40' = X'3E'. Under base 16, this exponent means 16^{-2}.

Fraction. You may represent the fraction as single precision, double precision, or extended precision. Single precision processes faster and requires less storage, whereas double and extended precision provide greater accuracy.

Single precision stores the fraction in hex in bits 8–31, double precision in bits 8–63, and extended precision in bits 8–127. (Bit 0 is the sign.) Negative fractions are stored the same as positive fractions (unlike binary, which uses two's complement for negatives). The radix point (in base 10, the decimal point) is immediately to the left of the fraction.

Here are three examples of floating-point values.

Example 1: Positive exponent, positive fraction. The decimal value 128.0 equals X'80', or 16^2 x X'.8'. It is stored in single precision as

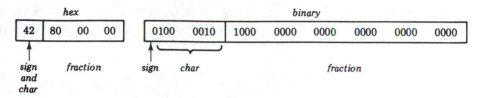

Based on $16^2 \times$ X'.8', the characteristic is calculated as $02 + 40 =$ X'42'. Because the fraction is positive, the sign bit becomes 0. The fraction with the radix point to the left is represented as X'.8'. You may now use the exponent 2 and the fraction to compute its value as

$$16^2 \times \text{X'.8'} = 256 \times 0.5 = 128.$$

Example 2: Positive exponent, negative fraction. The decimal value $-2,816.0$ equals X'$-$B00', or $16^3 \times$ X'$-$.B'. It is stored in single precision as

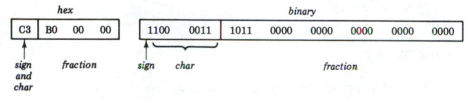

The characteristic is calculated as $03 + 40 =$ X'43'. Because the fraction is negative, the characteristic is stored as X'C3', and the fraction becomes X'$-$.B0'. You may use exponent 3 and fraction to compute its value as

$$16^3 \times \text{X'}-.\text{B0'} = 16^3 \times \frac{-11}{16} = 16^2 \times -11 = -2,816$$

Example 3: Negative exponent, positive fraction. Consider a floating-point value stored in single precision as

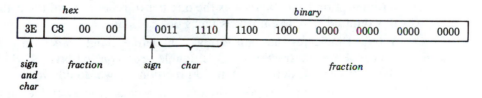

The characteristic is calculated as X'3E' − X'40' = −02. You may compute the value as

$$16^{-2} \times X'.68' = \frac{1}{16^2} \times \left(\frac{12}{16} + \frac{8}{16^2} \right) = \text{approximately } 0.0030517$$

Normalization

Precision is maintained more accurately by means of *normalization*. The normalization procedure left-adjusts the floating-point fraction until the leftmost hex digit is nonzero and decrements the characteristic by 1 for each fraction digit shifted. For example, consider the floating-point value

$$\boxed{43 \mid 00 \mid 88 \mid 00} = 16^3 \times \left(\frac{8}{16^3} + \frac{8}{16^4} \right) = 8 + \frac{8}{16} = 8.5$$

To normalize, shift the fraction left two digits and decrement the characteristic by 2:

$$\boxed{41 \mid 88 \mid 00 \mid 00} = 16^1 \times \left(\frac{8}{16} + \frac{8}{16^2} \right) = 8 + \frac{8}{16} = 8.5$$

Certain float operations involve prenormalizing (before the operation) and postnormalizing (after the operation). These practices are discussed later along with the instructions.

DECLARATIVES

You define floating-point data in decimal format, which the assembler converts to float. You may define data as single precision (E format), double precision (D format), or extended precision (L format). (We used D format earlier as a DS to facilitate the CVB and CVD operations.)

Name	Operation	Operand
[name]	DC	dTLn'constant'

d (duplication factor) indicates the number of repetitions of the constant. If it is omitted, the assembler assumes one constant.

T (type) indicates the data format. E defines single precision (32 bits, of which 24 are the fraction). D is double precision (64 bits, of which 56 are the fraction). L defines extended precision as two doublewords.

Ln (length in bytes) is normally omitted because the assembler aligns E on a fullword and D on a doubleword boundary, the required format for floating-point RX instructions. If Ln is specified, this alignment is not done.

'constant' is defined as a decimal value, with a preceding minus sign if necessary. You may also code a decimal point; if omitted, it is assumed to be to the right. The assembler uses the decimal point in the conversion to floating point. To modify constants further, you may code exponent modifiers and scale modifiers.

Exponent Modifier

The exponent modifier has the form (En). For example, 3.1416 may be coded as .31416E1 (meaning 0.31416×10^1) or as 3141.6E-3 (meaning $3141.6 \times 10-3$). The assembler rounds and normalizes the constant if necessary.

Scale Modifier

For an unnormalized constant, the scale modifier has the form Sn. The n tells the assembler how many hex digits to right-shift the fraction so that there are hex zeros to the left.

Examples of Floating-Point Declaratives

Figure 16-1 illustrates various floating-point declaratives. Note the alignment and the generated object code in each case. The first group defines single-precision declaratives.

FLOATE1 simply defines a 4-byte DS aligned on a fullword boundary.

FLOATE2 defines a positive constant.

FLOATE3 defines the same constant as negative.

FLOATE4 has a duplication factor of 3, causing definition of three identical constants.

FLOATE5 illustrates a multiple declaration in which one statement defines three different constants. The third constant, 0, defines true zero—a zero fraction and characteristic.

FLOATE6, FLOATE7, and **FLOATE8** depict the exponent modifier, and each generates the same float constant.

FLOATE9 uses a scale modifier, S3, to prevent normalization. The S3 causes the assembler to shift the fraction three positions to the right. The generated constant, 450007B7, is interpreted as

$$16^5 \times \left(\frac{7}{16^4} + \frac{11}{16^5} + \frac{7}{16^6} \right)$$

Note that compared to FLOATE6, this constant has lost some precision.

```
                              6  *      --------------------
                              7  *      SINGLE-PRECISION
                              8  *      --------------------
003804                        9  FLOATE1  DS    E              DEFINE FULLWORD AREA
003808  427B7333             10  FLOATE2  DC    E'123.45'      POSITIVE VALUE
00380C  C27B7333             11  FLOATE3  DC    E'-123.45'     NEGATIVE VALUE
003810  413243FE413243FE     12  FLOATE4  DC    3E'3.1416'     3 CONSTANTS
003818  413243FE
00381C  4164FDF4BD9D4952     13  FLOATE5  DC    E'6.312,-.00015,0'  MULTIPLE DECLARE
003824  00000000
003828  427B7333             14  FLOATE6  DC    E'123.45E0'    123.45 X 1   = 123.45
00382C  427B7333             15  FLOATE7  DC    E'1.2345E2'    1.2345 X 100 = 123.45
003830  427B7333             16  FLOATE8  DC    E'12345E-2'    12345  X .01 = 123.45
003834  450007B7             17  FLOATE9  DC    ES3'123.45'    UNNORMALIZED, USE OF
                             18  *                                SCALE MODIFIER

                             19  *      --------------------
                             20  *      DOUBLE-PRECISION
                             21  *      --------------------
003838                       22  FLOATD1  DS    0D             DOUBLEWORD BOUNDARY
003838  427B733333333333     23  FLOATD2  DC    D'123.45'      POSITIVE VALUE
003840  475912BC00000000     24  FLOATD3  DC    D'93.4E6'         93,400,000
003848  450007B733333333     25  FLOATD4  DC    DS3'123.45'    UNNORMALIZED, USE OF
                             26  *                                SCALE MODIFIER

                             28  *      --------------------
                             29  *      EXTENDED-PRECISION
                             30  *      --------------------
003850  427B733333333333     31  FLOATX   DC    L'123.45'
003858  3433333333333333
```

Figure 16-1   Floating-point declaratives.

The second group defines double-precision declaratives.

FLOATD1 is a DS with a zero duplication factor to force alignment on a doubleword boundary.

FLOATD2 and **FLOATD3** define double-precision constants.   FLOATD2 gives more precision than the same constant defined as single precision in FLOATE2.

FLOATD4 uses a scale modifier and defines the same constant as FLOATE9.

FLOATX in the last statement defines an extended-precision constant.

FLOATING-POINT REGISTERS

From the context it should be clear where *register* in this chapter means floating-point register and where it means general register.   The four floating-point registers are numbered 0, 2, 4, and 6, and each is a doubleword in length (8 bytes or 64 bits).   The type of instruction determines that it is a floating-point and not a general register.   For example, AR references two general registers, whereas ADR references two floating-point registers.

A floating operand may specify one-half of a register, a full register, or two adjacent registers, depending on the format:

Single precision:	Leftmost 32 bits
Double precision:	A full 64-bit register
Extended precision:	Two adjacent registers: 0 and 2 or 4 and 6

FLOATING-POINT INSTRUCTIONS

The floating-point instruction set, although less extensive, is similar to that for binary. The instructions are in RR and RX format, where R references a register and X references a storage address subject to the usual base and index register. These instructions permit data manipulation between registers and between registers and storage. Operations include load, store, add, subtract, compare, halve, multiply, and divide. The operations are named to describe their purpose. Consider the following three load operations:

```
operation:          LE      LER     LTER
                    ||      |||     Y||
position:           12      123     1 23
```

Position 1 indicates the type of operation, such as L for load or A for add. Exceptions are LC, LN, LP, LT, and ST, which require two letters.

Position 2 defines the length of the operation. E as in AER means single precision, D as in ADR means double precision, and X as in AXR means extended precision. U as in AUR implies single precision unnormalized, and W as in AWR implies double precision unnormalized.

Position 3 for RX format is blank. For RR, the letter R indicates a register, as in LER and LTER.

Load Instructions

The load instructions load floating-point values from storage into a register or between registers, similar to binary L and LR. The most common load instructions are

Name	Operation	Operand
[label]	LE	R1,X2 or R1,D2(X2,B2)
[label]	LD	R1,X2 or R1,D2(X2,B2)
[label]	LER	R1,R2
[label]	LDR	R1,R2

```
35 *           ------------------------------------
36 *           LE & LER   LOAD SINGLE-PRECISION
37 *           ------------------------------------
38 LOADE1      LE      2,FLOATEP1              REG-2: 434D28F6
39 LOADE2      LER     4,2                     REG-4: 434D28F6

41 *           ------------------------------------
42 *           LD & LDR   LOAD DOUBLE PRECISION
43 *           ------------------------------------
44 LOADD1      LD      0,FLOATDP1              REG-0: C27B74BC 6A7EF9DB
45 LOADD2      LDR     6,0                     REG-6: C27B74BC 6A7EF9DB
46 *          ...

47 FLOATDP1 DC         D'-123.456'
48 FLOATEP1 DC         E'1234.56'
```

Figure 16-2   Floating-point load operations: LE, LER, LD, LDR.

The rules are as follows:

- The operations load the floating-point number referenced by the operand 2 address (storage or register) into the operand 1 register without normalization.
- For LE, operand 2 is an aligned fullword in storage; for LD, operand 2 is an aligned doubleword.
- LE and LER, being single precision, process only the leftmost 32 bits of the register; the right half is not affected.
- These load instructions do not set the condition code.

Refer now to Fig. 16-2.   In LOADE1, LE loads a single-precision constant called FLOATEP1 into register 2.   In LOADE2, LER loads the contents of register 2 into register 4.   Only the leftmost 32 bits of both operands engage in these operations, and the rightmost 32 bits are undisturbed.

In LOADD1, LD loads a double-precision constant named FLOATDP1 into register 0.   In LOADD2, LDR loads the contents of register 0 into register 6.   All 64 bits of both operands engage in these operations.

Special Load Instructions

You may use certain load operations, for example, to reverse the sign or to set the condition code.   (The binary correlates are LCR, LNR, LPR, and LTR.)

Name	Operation	Operand
[label]	LCER	R1,R2
[label]	LCDR	R1,R2
[label]	LNER	R1,R2
[label]	LNDR	R1,R2
[label]	LPER	R1,R2
[label]	LPDR	R1,R2
[label]	LTER	R1,R2
[label]	LTDR	R1,R2

These instructions are similar to the previous load operations. Additionally, each sets the condition code: 0 = zero fraction, 1 = less than zero (except LPER and LPDR), and 2 = greater than zero (except LNER and LNDR).

Load Complement: LCER AND LCDR load the operand 2 register into operand 1 and reverse the sign bit: 0 becomes 1 and 1 becomes 0.

Load Negative: LNER AND LNDR load the operand 2 register into operand 1 and set the sign bit to 1, for minus.

Load Positive: LPER AND LPDR load the operand 2 register into operand 1 and set the sign bit to 0, for positive.

Load and Test: LTER AND LTDR load the operand 2 register into operand 1. These work the same as LER and LDR but also set the condition code.

Store Instructions

STE and STD store the contents of a floating-point register into a storage address. (The binary correlates are STH and ST.) The rules are (1) STE and STD store the contents of the operand 1 register in the operand 2 storage address without normalization; (2) STE stores the leftmost 32 bits of the register; the storage address must be an aligned fullword; (3) STD stores the entire 64 bits into an aligned doubleword address.

Name	Operation	Operand
[label]	STE	R1,X2 *or* R1,D2(X2,B2)
[label]	STD	R1,X2 *or* R1,D2(X2,B2)

In Fig. 16-3, LD loads a double-precision value into register 0. STE stores the leftmost 32 bits of register 0 in the fullword area, STORSING. STD stores the entire 64 bits of register 0 in the doubleword area, STORDOUB.

Addition and Subtraction

There are instructions for both normalized and unnormalized addition and subtraction. Subtraction inverts the sign of operand 2 and then adds the operands. The first step in add and subtract ensures that the characteristics of both operands are equal. If unequal, the field with the smaller characteristic is adjusted by shifting

```
55              LD      0,FLTD1            REG-0:     44392800 00000000
56              STE     0,STORSING         STORSING:  44392800
57              STD     0,STORDOUB         STORDOUB:  44392800 00000000
58  *           ...
59  FLTD1   DC      D'146.32E2'        DOUBLEWORD CONSTANT
60  STORDOUB DS     D                  DOUBLEWORD AREA
61  STORSING DS     E                  FULLWORD   AREA
```

Figure 16-3 Floating-point store operations; STE and STD.

its fraction to the right and incrementing the characteristic by 1 until the characteristics are equal.

Example: Simple addition of single precision.   The characteristics differ for the following values:

```
   41 290000  =    41 290000
 +40 120000  =  +41 012000        shift right and add 1
                  ─────────
                  41 2A2000
```

Example: Fraction overflow.   If the fraction overflows because of addition, the operation shifts the fraction right one hex digit and increments the characteristic by 1.   (If the characteristic overflows, a program interrupt occurs.)

```
 41   940000
 41   760000
 ───────────
 41 11A0000      fraction overflows
 42 011A000      shift fraction right, add 1 to characteristic
```

Example: Guard digit and normalization.   Normalized addition and subtraction perform postnormalization; that is, they normalize the result after the operation.   Also, single-precision add and subtract maintain improved precision by means of a guard digit.   When the operation shifts the fraction, this guard digit saves the last digit shifted.   The digit is restored during postnormalization.

```
 42 0B2584  =  42 0B2584          guard digit
 40 114256  =  42 001142(5)       shift right 2 digits
 Add:          42 0B36C6(5)
 Normalize:    41 B36C65          shift left 1 digit
```

Add and Subtract Normalized

The normalized add and subtract instructions are

Name	Operation	Operand
[label]	AE	R1,X2 *or* R1,D2(X2,B2)
[label]	AD	R1,X2 *or* R1,D2(X2,B2)
[label]	AER	R1,R2
[label]	ADR	R1,R2
[label]	SE	R1,X2 *or* R1,D2(X2,B2)
[label]	SD	R1,X2 *or* R1,D2(X2,B2)
[label]	SER	R1,R2
[label]	SDR	R1,R2

Each operation sets the condition code as follows: 0 = zero fraction in the result, 1 = fraction less than zero, 2 = fraction greater than zero, and 3 = exponent overflow in the result.

Add normalized. AE, AD, AER, and ADR add the contents of operand 2 to operand 1 and normalize the result. The single-precision operations AE and AER process only the leftmost 32 bits of the register, and the rightmost 32 bits are unaffected.

Subtract normalized. SE, SD, SER, and SDR subtract the contents of operand 2 from operand 1 and normalize the result. The single-precision operations SE and SER process only the leftmost 32 bits of a register, and the rightmost 32 bits are unaffected.

Figure 16-4 provides examples of addition and subtraction of both single and double precision.

ADDFLTE depicts single-precision add. An LD operation loads a doubleword into register 2, and AE adds the left half of a doubleword to register 2. A

```
65 *       -------------------------------------------------
66 *       AE & AER   ADD SINGLE-PRECISION NORMALIZED
67 *       -------------------------------------------------
68 ADDFLTE LD     2,AMTFLT1              REG-2: 427B7333 33333333
69         AE     2,AMTFLT2              REG-2: 429AB603 33333333
70         LD     4,AMTFLT3              REG-4: 435C0999 9999999A
71         AER    4,2                    REG-4: 4365B4F9 9999999A

73 *       -------------------------------------------------
74 *       AD & ADR   ADD DOUBLE-PRECISION NORMALIZED
75 *       -------------------------------------------------
76 ADDFLTD LD     2,AMTFLT1              REG-2: 427B7333 33333333
77         AD     2,AMTFLT2              REG-2: 429AB604 189374BC
78         LD     4,AMTFLT3              REG-4: 435C0999 9999999A
79         ADR    4,2                    REG-4: 4365B4F9 DB22D0E5

81 *       -------------------------------------------------
82 *       SE & SER   SUBTRACT SINGLE-PRECISION NORMALIZED
83 *       -------------------------------------------------
84 SUBFLTE LD     2,AMTFLT1              REG-2: 427B7333 33333333
85         SE     2,AMTFLT2              REG-2: 425C3063 33333333
86         LD     4,AMTFLT3              REG-4: 435C0999 9999999A
87         SER    4,2                    REG-4: 43564692 9999999A

89 *       -------------------------------------------------
90 *       SD & SDR   SUBTRACT DOUBLE-PRECISION NORMALIZED
91 *       -------------------------------------------------
92 SUBFLTD LD     2,AMTFLT1              REG-2: 427B7333 33333333
93         SD     2,AMTFLT2              REG-2: 425C3062 4DD2F1AA
94         LD     4,AMTFLT3              REG-4: 435C0999 9999999A
95         SDR    4,2                    REG-4: 43564693 74BC6A7F
96 *       ...
97 AMTFLT1 DC     D'123.45'             DOUBLEWORD
98 AMTFLT2 DC     D'31.261'             DOUBLEWORD
99 AMTFLT3 DC     D'1472.6'             DOUBLEWORD
```

Figure 16-4 Floating-point normalized add and subtract operations.

third doubleword is loaded into register 4, and AER adds the left half of register 2 to register 4. The right half contents of the registers are undisturbed.

ADDFLTD is similar to ADDFLTE except that it uses double precision. All 64 bits engage in the operations, and the results (shown in comments) are more precise.

SUBFLTE is similar to ADDFLTE except that it performs single-precision subtraction.

SUBFLTD is similar to SUBFLTE but uses double-precision subtraction for a more precise answer.

Add and Subtract Unnormalized

You may want to control precision by preventing normalization. Unnormalized operations are desirable, for example, in converting between floating-point and binary formats (illustrated later). Unnormalized add and subtract set the condition code but omit use of the guard digit and the postnormalization step.

Name	Operation	Operand
[label]	AU	R1,X2 *or* R1,D2(X2,B2)
[label]	AW	R1,X2 *or* R1,D2(X2,B2)
[label]	AUR	R1,R2
[label]	AWR	R1,R2
[label]	SU	R1,X2 *or* R1,D2(X2,B2)
[label]	SW	R1,X2 *or* R1,D2(X2,B2)
[label]	SUR	R1,R2
[label]	SWR	R1,R2

In these operations, U stands for single precision unnormalized and W for double precision. Examples in Fig. 16-5 are similar to those just given for normalized add and subtract and should be compared.

ADDFLTU illustrates single-precision unnormalized addition. An LD operation loads a doubleword into register 2. AU adds a short unnormalized constant to register 2. Another doubleword is loaded into register 4, and AUR adds the left half of register 2 to register 4. The right half of the registers are undisturbed, and the results are unnormalized.

ADDFLTW is similar to ADDFLTU except that it uses double precision and all 64 bits engage in the operation.

SUBFLTU is also similar to ADDFLTU except that it performs unnormalized subtraction.

SUBFLTW is similar to SUBFLTU but uses double precision. In this example, SWR shows a convenient way to clear a register to true zero, since the characteristic and fraction are both set to zero.

```
03 *       ------------------------------------------------
04 *       AU & AUR   ADD SINGLE-PRECISION UNNORMALIZED
05 *       ------------------------------------------------
06 ADDFLTU  LD    2,AMTFLU1              REG-2: 427B7333 33333333
07          AU    2,AMTFLU2              REG-2: 44009AB6 33333333
08          LD    4,AMTFLU3              REG-4: 435C0999 9999999A
09          AUR   4,2                    REG-4: 44065B4F 9999999A

11 *       ------------------------------------------------
12 *       AW & AWR   ADD DOUBLE-PRECISION UNNORMALIZED
13 *       ------------------------------------------------
14 ADDFLTW  LD    2,AMTFLU1              REG 2: 427B7333 33333333
15          AW    2,AMTFLU2              REG-2: 44009AB6 04189375
16          LD    4,AMTFLU3              REG-4: 435C0999 9999999A
17          AWR   4,2                    REG-4: 44065B4F 9DB22D0E

19 *       ------------------------------------------------
20 *       SU & SUR   SUBTRACT SINGLE-PRECISION UNNORMALIZED
21 *       ------------------------------------------------
22 SUBFLTU  LD    2,AMTFLU1              REG-2: 427B7333 33333333
23          SU    2,AMTFLU2              REG-2: 44005C30 33333333
24          LD    4,AMTFLU3              REG-4: 435C0999 9999999A
25          SUR   4,2                    REG-4: 44056469 9999999A

27 *       ------------------------------------------------
28 *       SW & SWR   SUBTRACT DOUBLE-PRECISION UNNORMALIZED
29 *       ------------------------------------------------
30 SUBFLTW  LD    2,AMTFLU1              REG-2: 427B7333 33333333
31          SW    2,AMTFLU2              REG-2: 44005C30 624DD2F1
32          SWR   4,4                    REG-4: 00000000 00000000
33 *       ...
34 AMTFLU1  DC    D'123.45'             DOUBLEWORD NORMALIZED
35 AMTFLU2  DC    DS2'31.261'           DOUBLEWORD UNNORMALIZED
36 AMTFLU3  DC    D'1472.6'             DOUBLEWORD NORMALIZED
```

Figure 16-5 Floating-point unnormalized add and subtract operations.

Compare

The following operations compare two floating-point fields:

Name	Operation	Operand
[label]	CE	R1,X2 or R1,D2(X2,B2)
[label]	CD	R1,X2 or R1,D2(X2,B2)
[label]	CER	R1,R2
[label]	CDR	R1,R2

The rules are as follows:

- The operation checks the characteristics of the two operands. The shorter one is incremented and its fraction shifted right, as for normalized subtract.
- The operation compares operand 1 algebraically to operand 2, including the

```
40 *          -------------------------------------
41 *          CE & CER   COMPARE SINGLE-PRECISION
42 *          -------------------------------------
43 COMPE      LE    2,COMP1
44            CE    2,COMP2               427B7333 > 421F42D0
45            LE    4,COMP3
46            CER   2,4                   427B7333 < 435C0999

48 *          -------------------------------------
49 *          CD & CDR   COMPARE DOUBLE-PRECISION
50 *          -------------------------------------
51 COMPD      LD    2,COMP1
52            CD    2,COMP2               427B7333 33333333 > 421F42D0
E5604189
53            LD    4,COMP3
54            CDR   2,4                   427B7333 33333333 < 435C0999
9999999A
55 *          ...
56 COMP1      DC    D'123.45'             DOUBLEWORD
57 COMP2      DC    D'31.261'             DOUBLEWORD
58 COMP3      DC    D'1472.6'             DOUBLEWORD
```

Figure 16-6 Floating-point compare operations.

sign, exponent, and fraction.   However, if both fractions are zero, the result
is equal regardless of sign and exponent.

- CE and CER compare only the leftmost 32 bits.
- For CE, operand 2 is an aligned fullword in storage.   For CD, operand 2 is
  an aligned doubleword.
- The condition is set for 0 (equal), 1 (low), and 2 (high).

In Fig. 16-6, COMPE compares single-precision values and COMPD compares double-precision values.

Halve

The Halve instructions permit convenient division of an operand by 2.

Name	Operation	Operand
[label]	HER	R1,R2
[label]	HDR	R1,R2

The rules are as follows:

- Operand 2 references a register containing the dividend that is to be divided
  by 2.
- The operations move operand 2 to operand 1 and the fraction one bit to the
  right.   The sign and characteristic are unaffected.   Operand 2 is not changed.

```
62 *           ------------------
63 *           HER & HDR  HALVE
64 *           ------------------
65 HALVE   LD    6,AMTHALF          REG-6: 434D28F5 C28F5C29
66         HER   4,6                REG-4: 4326947A
68         HDR   2,6                REG-2: 4326947A E147AE14
69 *             ...
70 AMTHALF DC    D'1234.56'         DOUBLEWORD
```

Figure 16-7   Floating-point halve operations.

- HER references only the leftmost 32 bits.
- The condition code is not set.
- There is no normalization or test for zero fraction.

In Fig. 16-7, an LD operation loads a doubleword in register 6. HER shifts only the left 8 hex digits one bit to the right, and HDR shifts all 16 hex digits.

Multiplication

The following instructions multiply floating-point values.

Name	Operation	Operand
[label]	ME	R1,X2 *or* R1,D2(X2,B2)
[label]	MD	R1,X2 *or* R1,D2(X2,B2)
[label]	MER	R1,R2
[label]	MDR	R1,R2

The multiply operation prenormalizes the field if necessary. Then it adds the characteristics and multiplies the fractions. The rules are as follows:

- The operand 1 register specifies the multiplicand.
- Operand 2 references the multiplier, either a storage address (ME and MD) or a register (MER and MDR).
- The operation normalizes the product, which replaces the multiplicand. Regardless of the operation, the product is a double-precision value.

Figure 16-8 provides examples of single- and double-precision multiplication. MULTE depicts single precision. An LE operation loads a fullword multiplicand into register 2. Then ME multiplies the left half of register 2 by the fullword multiplier in storage. Although the fields are defined as doublewords, only the left half engages in the operations. Next, another fullword is loaded into register 4, and MER multiplies the contents of register 4 by register 2. The final product is in register 4.

```
74 *          ------------------------------------
75 *          ME & MER  MULTIPLY SINGLE-PRECISION
76 *          ------------------------------------
77 MULTE    LE    2,MULTCAN1           REG-2: 4326D666
78         ME    2,MULTPLER           REG-2: 445CB979
79         LE    4,MULTCAN2           REG-4: 441205B8
80         MER   4,2                  REG-4: 476871CC
82 *          ------------------------------------
83 *          MD & MDR  MULTIPLY DOUBLE-PRECISION
84 *          ------------------------------------
85 MULTD    LD    2,MULTCAN1           REG-2: 4326D666 66666666
86         MD    2,MULTPLER           REG-2: 445CB97A E147AE13
87         LD    4,MULTCAN2           REG-4: 441205B8 51EB851F
88         MDR   4,2                  REG-4: 476871D0 639C0EBE
89 *          ...
90 MULTCAN1 DC    D'621.4'             DOUBLEWORD
91 MULTPLER DC    D'38.2'              DOUBLEWORD
92 MULTCAN2 DC    D'4613.72'           DOUBLEWORD
```

Figure 16-8 Floating-point multiplication.

MULTD uses double precision. All 16 hex digits participate and provide a more precise product than MULTE.

Division

The following instructions divide floating-point values:

Name	Operation	Operand
[label]	DE	R1,X2 *or* R1,D2(X2,B2)
[label]	DD	R1,X2 *or* R1,D2(X2,B2)
[label]	DER	R1,R2
[label]	DDR	R1,R2

The divide operation prenormalizes the fields if necessary. The rules are as follows:

- The operand 1 register specifies the dividend.
- Operand 2 references the divisor, either a storage address (DE and DD) or a register (DER and DDR).
- The operation normalizes the quotient, which replaces the dividend. For DE and DER, the quotient is single precision; for DD and DDR, the quotient is double precision.
- There is no remainder.
- A divisor containing a zero fraction causes a program interrupt.

Figure 16-9 provides examples of single- and double-precision division. DIVIDE depicts single precision. An LE instruction loads a fullword divi-

```
 96 *            --------------------------------------
 97 *            DE & DER   DIVIDE  SINGLE-PRECISION
 98 *            --------------------------------------
 99 DIVIDE    LE    2,DIVIDND1              REG-2: 4326D666
100           DE    2,DIVSOR               REG-2: 4210445B
101           LE    4,DIVIDND2             REG-4: 441205B8
102           DER   4,2                    REG-4: 4311B9FC

104 *            --------------------------------------
105 *            DD & DDR   DIVIDE  DOUBLE-PRECISION
106 *            --------------------------------------
107 DIVIDD    LD    2,DIVIDND1             REG-2: 4326D666 66666666
108           DD    2,DIVSOR               REG-2: 4210445B 24304055
109           LD    4,DIVIDND2             REG-4: 441205B8 51EB851F
110           DDR   4,2                    REG-4: 4311B9FC E537151B
111 *            ...
112 DIVIDND1  DC    D'621.4'               DOUBLEWORD
113 DIVSOR    DC    D'38.2'                DOUBLEWORD
114 DIVIDND2  DC    D'4613.72'             DOUBLEWORD
```

Figure 16-9 Floating-point division.

dend into register 2.   Then DE divides the left half of register 2 by the fullword divisor in storage.   Next, another fullword is loaded into register 4, and DER divides the contents of register 4 by register 2.   The final quotient is in register 4.

DIVIDD uses double precision.   All 16 hex digits participate and provide a more precise quotient.

EXTENDED PRECISION

Extended-precision values are developed and processed in adjacent registers, numbered 0 and 2 or 4 and 6.   You can expand a double-precision value to extended precision by loading a double-precision value into the first register of a pair and loading a zero fraction into the second register:

| double precision | | zero fraction |

The following instructions use floating-point registers 0 and 2 for this purpose:

```
LD  0,DBLAMT      Double-precision amount
LD  2,=D'0'       Zero  amount
```

Seven instructions are available for adding, subtracting, multiplying, and rounding extended-precision values.

Addition and Subtraction

AXR and SXR are RR-type instructions that add or subtract two extended-precision values and produce an extended-precision result.   The use of the condition code, guard digit, and normalization is the same as for single and double precision.

Name	Operation	Operand
[label]	AXR	R1,R2
[label]	SXR	R1,R2

Multiplication

There are three multiplication instructions in this group. MXD is an RX-type instruction that multiplies two double-precision values and produces an extended-precision product. MXDR is an RR-type instruction that multiplies two double-precision values and produces an extended-precision product. MXR is an RR-type instruction that multiplies two extended-precision values and produces an extended-precision product.

Name	Operation	Operand
[label]	MXD	R1,D2(X2,B2)
[label]	MXDR	R1,R2
[label]	MXR	R1,R2

Loading and Rounding

The two load and round instructions are LRER and LRDR, both RR format. LRER (Load and Round) loads and rounds a double-precision value from operand 2 to single-precision format in operand 1. This is not an extended-precision operation but is included here because it is part of the same group implemented some years after the regular floating-point group. LRDR (Load and Round Double) loads and rounds an extended-precision value from operand 2 to double precision in operand 1.

Name	Operation	Operand
[label]	LRER	R1,R2
[label]	LRDR	R1,R2

CONVERSION FROM PACKED TO FLOAT FORMAT

Although it is simple to define data in floating-point format, a number of steps are required to convert packed or binary data into floating point. The standard practice is to use CVB to convert packed to binary in a general register and

```
18 *                                          GENERAL REGISTERS:
19 PACKFLOT ZAP     DBLWD,AMTPK        8:          9:          10:
20          CVB     8,DBLWD         FFFBE91E
21          LPR     10,8           FFFBE91E                  000416E2
22          L       9,CHAR         FFFBE91E    4E000000      000416E2
23          SLDA    8,32           CE000000    00000000      000416E2
24          LR      9,8            CE000000    CE000000      000416E2
25          STM     9,10,SAVEUNOR
26 *                                       FLOATING-POINT REG-4:
27          SWR     4,4            00000000    00000000
28          AD      4,SAVEUNOR     C5416E20    00000000
29          STE     4,SAVENORM
30 *          ...
31 AMTPK    DC      PL6'-268002'   PACKED FIELD
32 DBLWD    DS      D              DOUBLEWORD AREA
33 SAVEUNOR DS      D              DOUBLEWORD AREA
34 SAVENORM DS      F              FULLWORD   AREA
35 CHAR     DC      X'4E000000'    CHARACTERISTIC
```

Figure 16-10 Conversion of packed to floating-point format.

there create the floating-point number. We'll use hexadecimal format to represent binary values. Consider the decimal number 268,002. Converted to binary it is X'000416E2'. With the fraction to the right, the double-precision float value is 4E000000 000416E2. You may load this number into a floating-point register and use a float operation to normalize the fraction.

Because negative binary numbers are in two's complement form, you must first convert them to positive. For the packed number 268,002-, the correct float value is CE000000 000416E2.

Figure 16-10 gives the programming steps to convert 268,002- to normalized single-precision floating point. When converted into binary in general register 8, 268,002- appears in two's complement as X'FFFBE91E'. But since a floating-point fraction is stored in absolute form, you may use LPR to adjust the binary number to its absolute value in register 10: X'000416E2'. Next, load the characteristic X'4E' into register 9 and algebraically shift it left 32 bits into register 8. Now the sign bit of the original binary number is the leftmost bit of the characteristic, X'CE' or binary 1100 1110. With the characteristic loaded into register 9 and the fraction in register 10, an STM operation stores the two registers in a doubleword.

To normalize the floating-point field, SWR clears the floating-point register and AD adds the double-precision value. The floating-point number now contains the correct characteristic and normalized fraction in single precision as C5416E20.

CONVERSION FROM FLOAT TO PACKED FORMAT

Because of the great magnitude of floating-point numbers, you must be careful in converting to packed format. If the absolute floating-point value is greater than $2^{31} - 1$ (or 2,147,483,647), its binary equivalent will exceed the capacity of a 32-bit general register. You may make use of a unique shortcut in the conversion.

Consider a normalized float value, 45416E20. Its correct unnormalized hexadecimal value is X'416E2', or decimal 268,002. You can use an unnormalized add operation, AW, with an operand containing a characteristic of 4E to shift the radix point from the left to the right as follows:

$$4E000000\ 00000000 = 4E000000\ 00000000$$
$$+45416E20\ 00000000 = \underline{4E000000\ 000416E2}$$
$$4E000000\ 000416E2$$

The rightmost 8 hex digits now contain the correct binary value, which you can convert to packed. If the float number had contained any significant digits to the right, the operation would have shifted them out.

If the float value is negative, convert it to two's complement in binary. A minor adjustment to the preceding routine gives correct results for either positive or negative values. The AW operation adds X'4E00000100000000'. The 1 in the fraction has no effect on positive numbers but forces two's complement on negative numbers. Assume a float value of C5416E20:

$$4E000001\ 00000000 = 4E000001\ 00000000$$
$$+C5416E20\ 00000000 = \underline{CE000000\ 000416E2}$$
$$CE000001\ FFFBE91E$$

The rightmost eight hex digits now contain the correct two's complement value, which you can now translate to packed.

Figure 16-11 converts normalized single-precision float to packed format. An LE instruction loads the float value just discussed, C5416E20, into floating-point register 4. The CE operation checks whether the value exceeds $2^{31} - 1$. Next, AW unnormalizes the number, and STD stores the entire 64-bit register in DOUBLE. Finally, the rightmost 4 bytes of DOUBLE are converted into packed.

Conversion rules can be much more involved. The examples given process only single-precision values with integers—that is, the implicit decimal point for

```
39 FLOTPACK LE    4,FLOAT                 FLT REG-4: C5416E20
40          LPER  6,4                     FLT REG-6: 45416E20
41          CE    6,MAXVAL                IF EXCEEDS MAXIMUM,
42          BNL   B10PASS                 THEN BYPASS
43          AW    4,ADJUST                FLT REG-4: 4E000000 FFFBE91E
44          STD   4,DOUBLE                STORE FLOAT DOUBLEWORD
45          L     9,DOUBLE+4              GEN REG-9: FFFBE91E BINARY
46          CVD   9,DOUBLE                DOUBLE:    -268,002 PACKED
47 *        ...
48 DOUBLE   DS    D                       DOUBLEWORD AREA
49 ADJUST   DC    X'4E000000100000000'    ADJUSTMENT FACTOR
50 MAXVAL   DC    E'2147483648'           MAXIMUM VALUE
51 FLOAT    DC    E'-268002'              FLOAT VALUE TO BE CONVERTED
```

Figure 16-11 Conversion of floating-point to packed format.

the number is to the right.   A binary or decimal number may be mixed, with an integer and fraction, such as 123.45, in which case you have to separate the integer portion from the fraction portion.

KEY POINTS

- You may represent floating-point values in three formats: single (fullword), double (doubleword), and extended (two doublewords).
- A floating-point value omits the base (16) and stores the sign, characteristic (exponent), and fraction.
- The computer stores the exponent (characteristic) in excess-64 notation by adding 64 (X'40') to the stored exponent.
- Single precision (E format) stores the fraction in hex in bits 8–31, double precision (D format) in bits 8–63, and extended precision (L format) in bits 8–127.   (Bit 0 is the sign.)   The radix point (in base 10, the decimal point) is immediately to the left of the fraction.
- Precision is maintained by means of normalization.   The normalization procedure left-adjusts the floating-point fraction until the leftmost hex digit is nonzero and decrements the characteristic by 1 for each fraction digit shifted.
- The four floating-point registers are numbered 0, 2, 4, and 6, and each is a doubleword in length.
- A floating operand may specify one-half of a register, a full register, or two adjacent registers, depending on the format.
- The floating-point instruction set is in RR and RX format, where R references a register and X references a storage address subject to the usual base and index register.   Operations include load, store, add, subtract, compare, halve, multiply, and divide.

PROBLEMS

16-1. Under what circumstances should you consider using a floating-point format?

16-2. Why is the characteristic represented in excess-64 notation?

16-3. Convert the binary numbers (represented in hex) to normalized single-precision float: (a) X'1520'; (b) X'9A.312'; (c) X'6B3.F2'.

16-4. Convert the following decimal numbers to normalized single-precision float: (a) 32,768; (b) 79.396; (c) 244.2166.

16-5. Code the decimal values in Problem 16-4 as DCs and assemble them.   Compare the assembler object code to your own calculations.

16-6. Code the decimal value 412.673 as a floating-point constant.   Assemble and check the results for (a) normalized single precision; (b) normalized double precision; (c) double precision with an exponent modifier E2; (d) unnormalized double precision with three hex digits preceding the first significant digit.

16-7. The slope m of a line joining two points (x_1, y_1) and (x_2, y_2) is $m = (y_2 - y_1)/(x_2 - x_1)$. Define four fields X1, Y1, X2, and Y2 containing single-precision constants. Calculate and store the slope as float in M. Code, assemble, and take a storage dump of the results. *Note*: What if X2 = X1?

16-8. Convert m in Problem 16-7 to character format so that it may be printed normally.

16-9. In Chapter 9, the program in Fig. 9-5 calculated finance charge rebates in binary format. Rewrite the routine using floating-point declaratives and instructions. Take a dump of the registers and storage to check your results.

17

EXTERNAL
STORAGE

OBJECTIVE

To explain the design and uses of magnetic tape and
disk storage devices.

A file, or data set, is a collection of related data records. Most data processing applications involve data files of such volume that they require large external magnetic tape and disk storage devices. Tape and disk provide mass external storage, extremely fast input/output, reusability, and records of almost any length.

This chapter introduces the various file organization methods and describes the architecture for magnetic tape and disk drives. The next three chapters cover the processing of files.

FILE ORGANIZATION METHODS

In any system, a set of related records is arranged into a file and organized according to the way in which programs are intended to process them. Once you create a file under a particular organization method, all programs that subsequently process the file must do so according to the requirements of the method.   Let's take a brief look at the most common organization methods.

Sequential File Organization

Under sequential organization, records are stored one after another.   They may be in ascending sequence (the usual) or descending sequence by a particular key or keys (control word), such as customer number or employee number within department, or, contrary to what the name sequential organization implies, records need not be in any particular sequence.

Transaction records may be accumulated into a file in random sequence. You can either use the file in its unsorted form for random updating of a master file or sort it into a specified order for sequential updating.

You can store a sequentially organized file on any type of device and for any type of file, such as master, transaction, and archival.

Indexed Sequential File Organization

Indexed sequential organization for master files lets you access records in ascending sequence and also supports indexes that enable you to access any record randomly by key, such as customer number.

Direct File Organization

Direct file organization facilitates direct access of any record in a master file.   The main advantage is that this method provides fast accessing of records and is thus particularly useful for online systems.

Virtual Storage Access Method

Virtual storage access method (VSAM) supports three organization types.   Entry-sequenced is equivalent to sequential organization, key-sequenced is equivalent to indexed, and relative-record is equivalent to direct.

Disk storage devices, but not tape, support indexed sequential, VSAM, and direct organization.   Chapters 18, 19, and 20 cover sequential, VSAM, and indexed sequential, respectively.

ACCESS METHODS

An access method is the means by which the system performs input/output requests. The methods depend on the file organization and the type of accessing required. DOS supports four methods and OS supports seven.

File Organization Method	DOS	OS
Sequential	SAM	QSAM *or* BSAM
Virtual	VSAM	VSAM
Indexed	ISAM	QISAM *or* BISAM
Direct	DAM	BDAM
Partitioned	–	BPAM

PROCESSING OF EXTERNAL STORAGE DEVICES

Major similarities between tape and disk are that records may be of virtually any length, of fixed or variable length, and clustered together into one or more records per block.

There are, however, two major differences in processing tape and disk. First, each time you read or write, the tape drive starts, transfers the data, and then stops, whereas a disk drive rotates continuously. Second, whenever you update (add, change, or delete) records on tape, you rewrite the entire changed file on another reel, whereas you can update disk records directly, in place.

Identification of External Devices

Both disk and tape have unique ways of identifying their contents to help in locating files and in protecting them from accidental erasure.

Tape file identification. At the beginning of the tape reel is a volume label, which is a record that identifies the reel being used. Immediately preceding each file on the tape is a *header label*, which describes the file that follows. This record contains the name of the file (for example, INVENTORY FILE) and the date the file was created. Following the header label are the records that comprise the data file.

The last record following the file is a *trailer label*, which is similar to the header label but also contains the number of blocks written on the reel. The operating system automatically handles the header and trailer labels.

Disk file identification. To keep track of all the files it contains, a disk device uses a special directory (*volume table of contents*, VTOC) at the beginning of its storage area. The directory includes the names of the files, their locations on disk, and their present status.

Packed and Binary Data

Tape and disk records can contain numeric fields defined as zoned, binary, or packed. Packed format involves two digits per byte plus a half-byte for the sign, such as

PAYMENT DS PL4

In this case, the field length is 4 bytes, stored as dd | dd | dd | ds, where d is a digit and s is the sign.

If the field is defined as binary, watch out for erroneous alignment of the field when you read it into main storage. The following binary fields are both 4 bytes long:

Aligned on a fullword boundary: PAYMENT1   DS   F
Not aligned on a boundary: PAYMENT2   DS   FL4

The assembler automatically aligns PAYMENT1 on a fullword boundary, whereas the assembler defines PAYMENT2 at its proper (unaligned) location.

Unblocked and Blocked Records

Disk and tape devices recognize *blocks* of data, which consist of one or more records. A blank space, known as an interblock gap (IBG), separates one block from another. The length of an IBG on tape is 0.3 to 0.6 inches depending on the device, and the length of an IBG on disk varies by device and by track location. The IBG has two purposes: (1) to define the start and end of each block of data and (2) to provide space for the tape when the drive stops and restarts for each read or write of a block.

Records that are stored one to a block are called *unblocked*. As shown in Fig. 17-1(a), following each block is an IBG.

To reduce the amount of tape and disk storage and to speed up input/output, you may specify a *blocking factor*, such as three records per block, as shown in

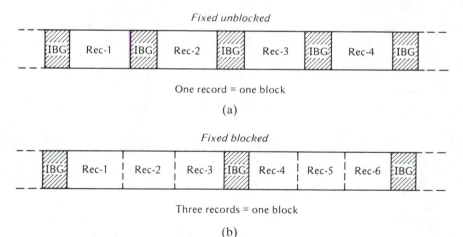

Fixed unblocked

One record = one block

(a)

Fixed blocked

Three records = one block

(b)

Figure 17-1   (a) Unblocked records. (b) Blocked records.

Fig. 17-1(b). In this format, the system writes an entire block of three records from main storage onto the device. Subsequently, when the system reads the file, it reads the entire block of three records from the device into storage. All programs that subsequently read the file must specify the same record length and block length.

Blocking records makes better use of disk and tape storage but requires a larger buffer area in main storage to hold the block.

Input Buffers

The action of an input operation depends on whether records are unblocked or blocked. If unblocked, the operation transfers one record (block) at a time from the device into the input/output buffer in your program.

The following example of blocked records assumes three records per block. Initially, the input operation transfers the first block from the device into the buffer (I/O area) in your program and delivers the first record to your program's workarea:

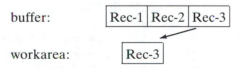

For the second input executed, the operation does not have to access the device. Instead, it simply delivers the second record from the buffer to your program's workarea:

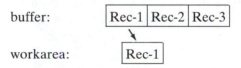

And for the third input executed, the operation delivers the third record from the buffer to your program's workarea:

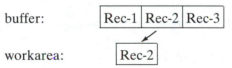

While the program processes the third record in the workarea, the system can read ahead and transfer the second block from the device into the buffer in your program. For the fourth input executed, the operation delivers the first record from the buffer to your program's workarea:

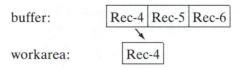

Output Buffers

The action of an output operation depends on whether records are unblocked or blocked. If unblocked, the output operation transfers one record (block) at a time from your workarea to the buffer in your program and then to the output device.

The following example of blocked records assumes three records per block. The first output operation writes the record in the workarea to the first record location in the output buffer:

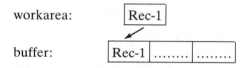

No actual physical writing to the output device occurs at this time. The second output operation writes the record in the workarea to the second record location in the buffer:

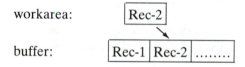

Similarly, the third output operation writes the record in the workarea to the third record location in the buffer. Now that the buffer is full, the system can physically write the contents of the buffer, the block of three records, to the external device.

The CLOSE operation automatically writes the last block of data, which may validly contain fewer records than the blocking factor specifies.

Fixed-Length and Variable-Length Records

Records and blocks may be fixed in length, where each has the same length throughout the entire file, or variable in length, where the length of each record and the blocking factor are not predetermined. There are five formats:

1. *Fixed, unblocked:* one record of fixed length per block
2. *Fixed, blocked:* more than one fixed-length record per block
3. *Variable, unblocked:* one variable-length record per block
4. *Variable, blocked:* more than one variable-length record per block
5. *Undefined:* contents of no defined format (Not all systems support this format.)

MAGNETIC TAPE STORAGE

The magnetic tape used in a computer system is similar to the tape used by conventional audiotape recorders; both use a similar coating of metallic oxide on flexible plastic, and both can be recorded and erased. Its large capacity and its reusability make tape an economical storage medium.

Data records on tape are usually, but not necessarily, stored sequentially, and a program that processes the records starts with the first record and reads or writes each record consecutively.

The main users of tape are installations such as department stores and utilities that require large files that they process sequentially. Many installations use disk for most general processing and use tape for backing up the contents of the disk master files at the end of each workday. Consequently, if it is necessary to rerun a job because of errors or damage, backup tapes are always available.

Characteristics of Tape

The most common width of a reel of magnetic tape is 1/2 inch, and its length ranges from 200 feet to the common 2,400 feet, with lengths as long as 3,600 feet. A tape drive records data as magnetic bits on the oxide side of the tape.

Storage format. Data is stored on tape according to tracks. The tape in Fig. 17-2 shows nine horizontal tracks, each of which represents a particular bit position. Each vertical set of 9 bits constitutes a byte, of which 8 bits are for data and 1 bit is for parity.

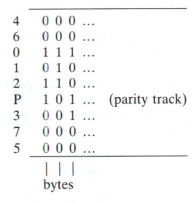

```
4    0 0 0 ...
6    0 0 0 ...
0    1 1 1 ...
1    0 1 0 ...
2    1 1 0 ...
P    1 0 1 ...   (parity track)
3    0 0 1 ...
7    0 0 0 ...
5    0 0 0 ...
     | | |
     bytes
```

Figure 17-2   Data on tape.

As you can see, the tracks for each of the bits are not in the expected sequence. The tracks for bits 4 and 5, the least used, are in the outer area where the tape is more easily damaged. The first byte, on the left, would appear in main storage as follows:

| Bit value: | 1 0 1 0 0 0 0 1 |
| Bit number: | 0 1 2 3 4 5 6 7 P |

Storage density. Tape density is measured by the number of stored characters, or bytes, per inch (bpi), such as 800, 1,600, or 6,250 bpi. Therefore, a 2,400-foot reel with a recording density of 1,600 bpi could contain 46 million bytes, which is equal to over a half-million 80-byte records.

Double-density tape stores data on 18 tracks, representing 2 bytes for each set of 18 vertical bits.

Tape speed. Tape read/write speeds vary from 36 to 200 or more inches per second. Thus a tape drive that reads 1,600 bpi records at 200 inches per second would be capable of reading 320,000 bytes per second. Other high-speed cartridge drives transfer data at up to 3 million bytes per second.

Tape markers. A reflective strip, called a load point marker, located about 15 feet from the beginning of a tape reel, indicates where the system may begin reading and writing data. Another reflective strip, an end-of-tape marker, located about 14 feet from the end of the reel, warns the system that the end of the reel is near and that the system should finish writing data. Both the load point marker and the end-of-tape marker are on the side of the tape opposite the recording oxide.

Tape File Organization

A file or data set on magnetic tape is typically stored in sequence by control field or key, such as inventory number. For compatibility with disks, a reel of tape is know as a *volume*. The simplest case is a one-volume file, in which one file is entirely and exclusively stored on one reel (volume).

An extremely large file, known as a *multivolume file*, requires more than one reel. Many small files may be stored on a *multifile volume*, one after the other, although you may have to rewrite the entire reel just to update one of the files.

Unblocked and Blocked Tape Records

As an example of the effect of blocking records on tape, consider a file of 1,000 records each 800 bytes long. Tape density is 1,600 bytes per inch, and each IBG is 0.6 inches. How much space does the file require given (a) unblocked records and (b) a blocking factor of 5? Calculate the size of a record of 800 bytes as $800 \div 1,600 = 0.5$ inches.

(a) Unblocked records

One block = one record = 800 bytes
Length of one block = 800 bytes/1,600 bpi =   0.5"
Length of one IBG =   0.6

Space required for one block   1.1"
Space required for file = 1,000 blocks × 1.1" = 1,100"

(b) Blocked records

One block = five records = 4,000 bytes
Length of one block = 4,000 bytes/1,600 bpi =   2.5"
Length of one IBG =   0.6

Space required for one block   3.1"
Space required for file = 200 blocks × 3.1" = 620"

As can be seen, the blocked records require considerably less space because there are fewer IBGs.

Standard Labels

Under the various operating systems, tape reels require unique identification. Each reel, and each file on a reel, usually contains descriptive standard labels supported by the operating systems (1) to uniquely identify the reel and the file for each program that processes it and (2) to provide compatibility with other IBM systems and (to some degree) with systems of other manufacturers.

Installations typically use standard labels. Nonstandard labels and unlabeled tapes are permitted but are not covered in this text. The two types of standard labels are volume and file labels. Figure 17-3 illustrates standard labels for one file on a volume, a multivolume file, and a multifile volume. In the figure, striped lines indicate IBGs, and TM (for tape mark) is a special marker that the system writes to indicate the end of a file or the end of the reel.

Volume Labels

The volume label is the first record after the load point marker and describes the volume (reel). The first 3 bytes contain the identification VOL. Although some systems support more than one volume label, this text describes only the common situation of one label.

On receipt of a new tape reel, an operator uses an IBM utility program to write a volume label with a serial number and a temporary header file label. When

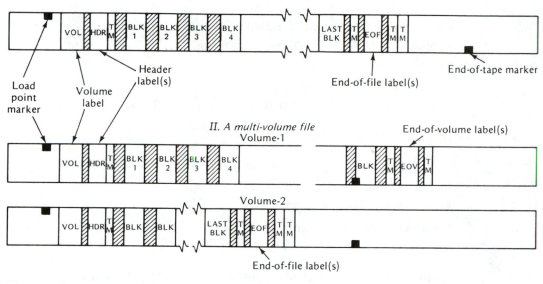

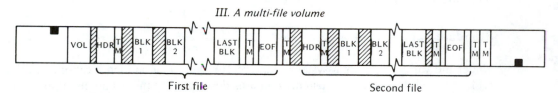

Figure 17-3   Magnetic tape standard labels.

subsequently processing the reel, the system expects the volume label to be the first record.   It checks the tape serial number against the number supplied by the job control command, TLBL under DOS or DD under OS.

The following describes each field in the 80-byte standard volume label:

POSITIONS	NAME	DESCRIPTION
01–03	Label identifier	Contains VOL to identify the label.
04	Volume label number	Some systems permit more than one volume label; this field contains their numeric sequence.
05–10	Volume serial number	The permanent unique number assigned when the reel is

POSITIONS	NAME	DESCRIPTION
		received. (The number also becomes the file serial number in the header label.)
11	Volume security code	A special security code, supported by OS.
12–41	Unused	Reserved.
42–51	Owner's identification	May be used under OS to identify the owner's name and address.
52–80	Unused	Reserved.

File Labels

A tape volume contains a file of data, part of a file, or more than one file. Each file has a unique identification to ensure, for example, that the system is processing the correct file and that the tape being used to write on is validly obsolete. Two file labels for each file, a header label and a trailer label, provide this identification.

Header label. A header label precedes each file. If the file requires more than one reel, each reel contains a header label, numbered from 001. If a reel contains more than one file, a header label precedes each file.

The header label contains HDR in the first 3 bytes, the file identification (such as CUSTOMER RECORDS), the date the file may be deleted, and so forth. The system expects a header label to follow the volume label immediately and checks the file identification, date, and other details against information supplied by job control.

OS supports two header labels, HDR1 and HDR2, with the second label, also 80 bytes, immediately following the first. Its contents include the record format (fixed, variable, or undefined), block length, record length, and density of writing on the tape.

Trailer label. A trailer label is the last record of every file. (OS supports two trailer labels.) The first 3 bytes contain EOV if the file requires more than one reel and the trailer label is the end of a reel but not end of the file. The first 3 bytes contain EOF if the trailer label is the end of the file.

The trailer label is otherwise identical to the header label except for a block count field. The system counts the blocks as it writes them and stores the total in the trailer label. Subsequently, when reading the reel, the system counts the blocks and checks its count against the number stored in the trailer label.

The following describes each field in the standard file label for both header and trailer labels.

POSITIONS	NAME	DESCRIPTION
01–03	Label identifier	Contains HDR if a header label, EOF if the end of a file, or EOV if the end of a volume.
04	File label number	Specifies the sequence of file labels for systems that support more than one. OS supports two labels each for HDR, EOF, and EOV.
05–21	File identifier	A unique name that describes the file.
22–27	File serial number	The same identification as the volume serial number for the first or only volume of the file.
28–31	Volume sequence number	The sequence of volume numbers for multivolume files. The first volume for a file contains 0001, the second 0002, and so on.
32–35	File sequence number	The sequence of file numbers for multifile volumes. The first file in a volume contains 0001, the second 0002, and so on.
36–39	Generation number	Each time the system rewrites a file, it increments the generation number by 1 to identify the edition of the file.
40–41	Version number of generation	Specifies the version of the generation of the file.
42–47	Creation date	The year and day when the file was written. The format is byyddd, where b means blank.

POSITIONS	NAME	DESCRIPTION
48–53	Expiration date	The year and day when the file may be overwritten. The format is byyddd, where b means blank.
54	File security code	A special security code used by OS.
55–60	Block count	Used in trailer labels for the number of blocks since the previous header label.
61–73	System code	An identification for the operating system.
74–80	Unused	Reserved.

IOCS FOR MAGNETIC TAPE

The system (IOCS for DOS and data management for OS) performs the following functions for input and for output.

Reading a Tape File

The processing for reading a tape file is as follows:

1. *Processing the Volume Label.* On OPEN, IOCS reads the volume label and compares its serial number to that on the TLBL or DD job control entry.
2. *Processing the Header Label.* IOCS next reads the header label and checks that the file identification agrees with that on the job control entry to ensure that it is reading the correct file. For a multivolume file, the volume sequence numbers are normally in consecutive, ascending sequence.
3. *Reading Records.* The GET macro reads records, specifying either a work-area or IOREG. If the tape records are unblocked, each GET reads one record (a block) from tape into storage. If records are blocked, IOCS performs the required deblocking.
4. *End-of-Volume.* If IOCS encounters the end-of-volume label before the end-of-file (meaning that the file continues on another reel), IOCS checks that the block count is correct. It rewinds the reel, opens a reel on an alternate tape drive, checks the labels, and resumes reading this new reel.
5. *End-of-File.* Each GET operation causes IOCS to transfer a record to the workarea. Once every record has been transferred and processed and you

attempt to perform another GET, IOCS recognizes an end-of-file condition. It then checks the block count, (usually) rewinds the reel, and transfers control to your end-of-file address designated in the DTFMT or DCB macro. You should now CLOSE the tape file. To attempt further reading of a rewound tape file, you must perform another OPEN.

Writing a Tape File

The processing for writing a tape file is as follows:

1. *Processing the Volume Label.* On OPEN, IOCS checks the volume label (VOL) and compares its serial number to the serial number (if any) on the job control entry.

2. *Processing the Header Label.* IOCS next checks the header label for the expiration date. If this date has passed, IOCS backspaces the tape and writes a new header (HDR) over the old one, based on data in job control. If this is a multivolume file, IOCS records the volume sequence number for the volume. It then writes a tape mark.

3. *Writing Records.* If the tape records are unblocked, each PUT writes one record (a block) from tape into storage. If records are blocked, IOCS performs the required blocking.

4. *End-of-Volume.* If IOCS detects the end-of-tape marker near the end of the reel, it writes an EOV trailer label, which includes a count of all blocks written, followed by a tape mark. Since the reflective marker is on the opposite side of the tape, data may be recorded through its area. If an alternate tape drive is assigned, IOCS opens the alternate volume, processes its labels, and resumes writing this new reel.

5. *End-of-File.* When a program closes the tape file, IOCS writes the last block of data, if any. The last block may contain fewer records than the blocking factor specifies. IOCS then writes a tape mark and an EOF trailer label with a block count. Finally, IOCS writes two tape marks and deactivates the file from further processing.

DISK STORAGE

A direct access storage device (DASD), which includes magnetic disk storage and the less common drum storage, is a device that can access any record on a file directly. Diskettes, a common and familiar storage medium on micro- and mini-computers, store data in a similar manner. This section describes the details of the larger magnetic disk devices used in data processing installations.

Each disk storage device contains a number of thin circular plates (or disks)

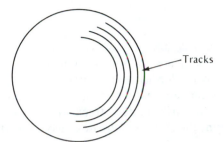

Figure 17-4   Disk surface and tracks.

stacked one on top of the other.   Both sides of each plate (except the outer top and bottom on some devices) have a coat of ferrous oxide material to permit recording.   As Fig. 17-4 shows, each disk contains circular tracks for storing data records as magnetized bits.   Each track contains the same number of bits (and bytes) because the bits are spaced more closely together on the innermost tracks.

The disks are constantly rotating on a vertical shaft.   As Fig. 17-5 shows, the disk device has a set of access arms that move read/write heads from track to track. The heads read data blocks from a disk track into main storage and write data blocks from main storage onto a disk track.   Because the disks spin continually, the system has to wait for a required data block to reach the read/write heads.

Disk storage devices permit processing of records both sequentially and randomly (directly).   As a result, programs can read unsorted records from a transaction file and use them to randomly update matching master records on disk. Disk storage therefore facilitates online processing where users can at any time make inquiries into a file and can enter transactions for updating as they occur.

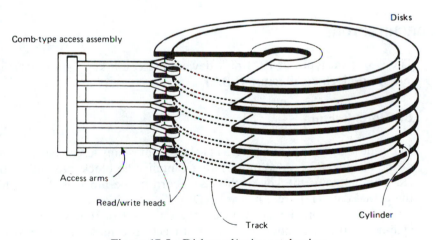

Figure 17-5   Disk read/write mechanism.

Disk Format

The amount of data that a disk device can store varies considerably by model, ranging from small disks with a few million bytes to large disks with more than one billion bytes. Some disk models use fixed-length sectors on each track to store one or more records; the system addresses a record by disk number, track number, and sector number. On other disk models, tracks are not sectored, and records may be of almost any length; the system addresses records by disk surface number and track number.

Like magnetic tape, disk storage contains gaps between one block of data and the next, but the size of the gap is greater on the outermost tracks and smaller on innermost tracks. You may also store records on disk as unblocked or blocked. However, because of the fixed capacity of a disk track, the optimum blocking factor depends on the record length and track capacity. Special formulas are available for calculating optimum blocking factors for different disk devices.

As a simplified example, consider a file containing 1,000-byte records and a disk track with a capacity of 10,000 bytes. If the blocking factor is 5, one block is 5,000 bytes and you can store two blocks (ten records) on a track. If the blocking factor is 6, one block is 6,000 bytes and a track has space for only one block (six records).

The storage of data on disk begins with the top outermost track (track 0) and continues consecutively down, surface by surface, through to the bottom outermost track. Storage of data then continues with the next inner set of tracks (track 1), starting with the top track through to the bottom track. The set of vertical tracks is known as a *cylinder*. As a result, for sequential processing the system reduces access motion of the read/write heads: It reads and writes blocks, for example, on track 5 of every surface (cylinder 5) before moving the arm to cylinder 6.

DISK ARCHITECTURE

The two main types of IBM disk devices are count-key-data (CKD) architecture and fixed-block architecture (FBA).

CKD Architecture

In this design, records and blocks may be of almost any length, subject to limitations of the disk device. A count (C) area contains the block size and an optional key (K) area contains the key of the last record in the block, both of which precede the actual data (D) area; hence CKD.

If a disk contains 20 surfaces, the outer set of tracks (all track 0) is called cylinder 0, the next inner vertical set of tracks is cylinder 1, the next is cylinder 2, and so forth. If the device contains 200 sets of tracks, there are 200 cylinders numbered 0 through 199, each with 20 tracks.

Examples of disk devices using CKD architecture include IBM models 3330, 3340, 3350, and 3380.

The basic format for a track on a CKD device is

Index Point (a)	Home Address (b)	Track Descriptor Record (R0) (c)	Data Record (R1)	Data Record (R2) (d)

(a) *Index Point.* The index point tells the read/write device that this point is the physical beginning of the track.

(b) *Home Address.* The home address tells the system the address of the track (the cylinder, head, or surface number) and whether the track is primary, alternate, or defective.

(c) *Track Descriptor Record (R0).* This record stores information about the track and consists of two separate fields: a count area and a data area. The count area contains 0 for record number and 8 for data length and is otherwise similar to the count area described next for data record under item (d). The data area contains 8 bytes of information used by the system. The track descriptor record is not normally accessed by user programs.

(d) *Data Record Formats (R1 through Rn).* The users' data records, or technically, blocks, consist of the following:

Address Marker	Count Area	Key Area (optional)	Data Area

The I/O control unit stores the 2-byte address marker before each block of data, which it uses subsequently to locate the beginning of data.

The count area includes the following:

- An identifier field that provides the cylinder and head number (like that in the home address) and the sequential block number (0–255) in binary, representing R0 through R255. (The track descriptor record, R0, contains 0 for record number.)
- The key length (to be explained shortly).
- The data length, a binary value 0 through 65,535 that specifies the number of bytes in the data area field (the length of your data block). For end-of-file, the system generates a last dummy record containing a length of 0 in this field. When the system reads the file, the zero length indicates that there are no more records.
- The optional key area contains the key, or control field, for the records in the file, such as part number or customer number. The system uses the key area to locate records randomly. If the key area is omitted, the file is said

Device	CAPACITY				SPEED		
	Bytes per track	Tracks per cylinder	Number of cylinders	Total bytes	Ave. seek time (ms)	Ave. rot'l delay (ms)	Data rate KB/sec.
3340-1	8368	12	348	35,000,000			
3340-2	8368	12	696	70,000,000	25	10.1	885
3344	8368	12	4 × 696	280,000,000			
3330-1	13030	19	404	100,000,000			
3330-11	13030	19	808	200,000,000	30	8.4	806
3350	19069	30	555	317,500,000	25	8.4	1200
3375	35616	12	2 × 959	819,738,000	19	10.1	1859
3380	47476	15	2 × 885	1,260,500,000	16	8.3	3000

Figure 17-6   Capacity table for CKD devices.

to be formatted without keys and is stored as count-data format. The key length in the count area contains 0. If the file is formatted with keys, it is stored as count-data format. The key length in the count area contains the length of the key area.

- The data area contains the users' data blocks, in any format, such as unblocked or blocked and fixed or variable length. The system stores as many blocks on a track as possible, usually complete and intact on a track. A record overflow feature permits the overlapping of a record from one track to the next.

Figure 17-6 provides the capacities and speeds of a number of IBM CKD devices.

Under normal circumstances, you won't be concerned with the home address, the track descriptor record, or the address marker, count area, and key area portions of the data record field. You simply provide appropriate entries in your file definition macros and job control commands.

Fixed-Block Architecture

In this design, the recording tracks contain equal-length blocks of 512 bytes, although your records and blocks need not fit a sector exactly.

Figure 17-7 provides the details for two disk models using fixed-block architecture, the 3310 and 3370.

Device	Bytes per Block	Blocks per Track	Number of Cylinders	Tracks per Cylinder	Total Bytes
3310	512	32	358	11	64,520,192
3370	512	62	2 × 750	12	571,392,000

Figure 17-7   Capacity table for FBA devices.

DISK CAPACITY

Knowing the length of records and the blocking factor, you can calculate the number of records on a track and on a cylinder. Knowing the number of records, you can also calculate the number of cylinders for the entire file. Based on the values in Fig. 17-8, the formula for the number of blocks of data per track is

$$\text{Blocks per track} = \frac{\text{track capacity}}{\text{overhead} + C + KL + DL}$$

In the formula, C is a constant overhead value for keyed records, KL means key length, and DL is data (block) length. These values vary by disk device, as shown in Fig. 17-8.

Device	Maximum Capacity (bytes)	One Data Block	Key Overhead		Track Capacity
3330	13,030	135 + C + KL + DL	C = 0 when KL = 0		13,165
			C = 56 when KL = 0		
3340	8,368	167 + C + KL + DL	C = 0 when KL = 0		8,535
			C = 75 when KL = 0		
3350	19,069	185 + C + KL + DL	C = 0 when KL = 0		19,254
			C = 82 when KL = 0		

Figure 17-8 Track capacity table.

The following two examples illustrate.

Example 1.   Device is a 3350, records are 242 bytes, five records per block (block size = 1,210), and formatted without keys:

$$\text{Blocks per track} = \frac{19,254}{185 + (5 \times 242)} = \frac{19,254}{1,395} = 13.8$$

$$\text{Records per track} = \text{blocks per track} \times \text{blocking factor}$$

$$= 5 \times 13 = 65$$

Example 2.   Same as Example 1, but formatted with keys (key length is 12):

$$\text{Blocks per track} = \frac{19,254}{185 + 82 + 12 + 1,210} = \frac{19,254}{1,489} = 12.93$$

$$\text{Records per track} = 5 \times 12 = 60$$

Note that a disk stores a full block, not a fraction of one. Therefore, even if you calculate 13.8 or 12.9 blocks per track, the disk stores only 13 or 12 blocks, respectively.

To determine the number of records on a cylinder, refer to Fig. 17-6, which discloses that a 3350 has 30 tracks per cylinder. Based on Example 1 where the number of records per track is 65, a cylinder on the 3350 could contain $65 \times 30 = 1{,}950$ records.

Using these figures, you can now calculate how much disk storage a file of, say, 100,000 of these records would require. Based on the figure of 1,950 records per cylinder, the file would require $100{,}000 \div 1{,}950 = 51.28$ cylinders.

DISK LABELS

Disks, like magnetic tape, also use labels to identify a volume and a file. The system reserves cylinder 0, track 0 for standard labels, as Fig. 17-9 shows. The following describes the contents of track 0:

Record 0: The track descriptor, R(0) record.

Records 1 and 2: If the disk is SYSRES, which contains the operating system, certain devices reserve R(1) and R(2) for the initial program load (IPL) routine. For all other cases, R(1) and R(2) contain zeros.

Record 3: The VOL1 label. OS supports more than one volume label, from R(3) through R(10).

Record 4 through the end of the track: The standard location for the volume table of contents (VTOC). The VTOC contains the file labels for the files on the device. Although you may place a VTOC in any cylinder, its standard location is cylinder 0, track 0.

Volume Labels

The standard volume label uniquely identifies a disk volume. A 4-byte key area immediately precedes the 80-byte volume data area. The volume label is the fourth record (R3) on cylinder 0. The 80 bytes are arranged like a tape volume label, with one exception: Positions 12–21 are the "data file directory," containing the starting address of the VTOC.

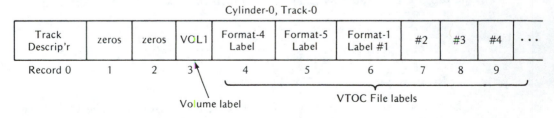

Figure 17-9 Disk volume layout.

File Labels

File labels identify and describe a file, or data set, on a volume. The file label is 140 bytes long, consisting of a 44-byte key area and a 96-byte file data area. Each file on a volume requires a file label for identification. In Fig. 17-9, all file labels for a volume are stored together in the VTOC. There are four types of file labels:

1. The format 1 label is equivalent to a file label on tape. The format 1 label differs, however, in that it defines the actual cylinder and track addresses of each file's beginning and end (its extent). Further, a file may be stored intact in an extent or in several extents in the same volume. Format 3 is used if a file is scattered over more than three extents.

2. The format 2 label is used for indexed sequential files.

3. The format 3 label is stored if a file occupies more than three extents.

4. The format 4 label is the first record in the VTOC and defines the VTOC for the system.

The format 1 file label contains the following information:

POSITION	NAME	DESCRIPTION
01–44	File identification	Unique identifier consisting of file ID, optional generation number, and version number, separated by periods.
45	Format identifier	'1' for format 1.
46–51	File serial number	Volume serial number from the volume label.
52–53	Volume sequence number	Sequence number if the file is stored on more than one volume.
54–56	Creation date	ydd (binary): y = year (0–99) and dd = day (1–366).
57–59	Expiration date	Same format as creation date.
60	Extent count number	Number of extents for this file on this volume.
61	Bytes used in last block of directory	Used by OS.
62	Unused	Reserved.
63–75	System code	Name of the operating system.
76–82	Unused	Reserved.
83–84	File type	Code to identify if SD (sequential),

POSITION	NAME	DESCRIPTION
		DA (direct), or IS (indexed) file organization.
85	Record format	Used by OS.
86	Option codes	ISAM—indicates if master index is present and type of overflow area.
87–88	Block length	ISAM—length of each block.
89–90	Record length	ISAM—length of each record.
91	Key length	ISAM—length of key area.
92–93	Key location	ISAM—position of key within the record.
94	Data set indicators	SD—indicates if last volume.
95–98		Used by OS.
99–103	Last record pointer	Used by OS.
104–105	Unused	Reserved.
106	Extent type	
107	Extent sequence number	Descriptors for the first or only extent for the file.
108–111	Extent lower limit	
112–115	Extent upper limit	
116–125		Descriptors for a second extent.
126–135		Descriptors for a third extent.
136–140	Pointer	Address of the next label.

KEY POINTS

- Sequential file organization provides only for sequential processing of records. Indexed and direct organization provides for both sequential and random processing of records.

- At the beginning of the tape reel is a volume label, which identifies the reel being used. Immediately preceding each file on the tape is a header label, which contains the name of the file and the date the file was created. Following the header label are the records that comprise the data file. The last record is a trailer label, which is similar to the header label but also contains the number of blocks written on the reel.

- To keep track of all the files it contains, a disk device uses a special directory (volume table of contents, VTOC) at the beginning of its storage area. The directory includes the names of the files, their locations on disk, and their present status.

- If you define a tape or disk field as packed on an IBM system, the field contains two digits per byte plus a half-byte for the sign.

- The set of vertical tracks on a disk device is known as a cylinder.

- An interblock gap (IBG) separates each block of data from the next on tape and disk. The length of an IBG on tape is 0.3 to 0.6 inches depending on the device, and the length of an IBG on disk varies by device and by track location. The IBG defines the start and end of each block of data and provides space for the tape when the drive stops and restarts for each read or write.

- Blocking of records helps conserve space on storage devices and reduces the number of input/output operations. The number of records in a block is known as the blocking factor.

- The system reads an entire block into the computer's storage and transfers one record at a time to the program.

- All programs that process a file should use the same record length and blocking factor.

- Records and blocks may be fixed in length, where each has the same length throughout the entire file, or variable in length, where the length of each record and the blocking factor are not predetermined.

- The two main types of disk devices are count-key-data (CKD) architecture, which stores records according to count, key, and data area, and fixed-block architecture (FBA), which stores data in fixed-length blocks.

PROBLEMS

17-1. Distinguish the differences among sequential, direct, and indexed sequential organization methods.

17-2. Explain each of the following: (a) tape density; (b) tape markers; (c) IBG; (d) fixed length and variable length; (e) blocking factor.

17-3. Give an advantage and a disadvantage of increasing the blocking factor.

17-4. What is the purpose of each of the following: (a) volume label; (b) header label; (c) trailer label?

17-5. Distinguish between each of the following: (a) EOV and EOF on a trailer label; (b) a multifile volume and a multivolume file; (c) volume sequence number and file sequence number.

17-6. What is the advantage of disk storage over magnetic tape?

17-7. Based on Fig. 17-6, how many bytes can be stored on a cylinder for each device listed?

17-8. Why does a disk device store data vertically by cylinder rather than by tracks across a surface?

17-9. Explain the purpose of (a) the home address; (b) the track descriptor record; (c) the key area.

17-10. What is the difference between a CKD disk and an FBA disk?

17-11. What are the purpose, location, and contents of the VTOC?

17-12. What is the disk equivalent of the magnetic tape header label; that is, what is its location and how does it differ?

17-13. Assume disk device 3350, record length 300 bytes, and six records per block. Based on the data in Fig. 17-8, calculate the number of records that a track can store for the following: (a) records formatted without keys; (b) records formatted with keys, key length = 10.

18

SEQUENTIAL FILE ORGANIZATION

OBJECTIVE

To cover sequential file organization and its processing requirements.

In this chapter, you examine sequential file organization for DOS and OS and learn how to create and read such files. You will also examine the definition and processing of variable-length records.

The processing of sequential files involves the same imperative macros used up to now: OPEN, CLOSE, GET, and PUT. IOCS (data management) handles all the necessary label processing and blocking and deblocking of records. Other than job control commands, the only major difference is the use of blocked records.

An installation has to make a (perhaps arbitrary) choice of a blocking factor when a file is created, and all programs that subsequently process the file define the same blocking factor. A program may also define one or more I/O buffers; if records are highly blocked, a second buffer involves more space in main storage with perhaps little gained in processing speed.

CREATING A TAPE FILE

The first two examples create a tape file for DOS and OS. The programs accept input data from the system reader and write four records per block onto tape.

For both programs, OPEN checks the volume label and header label, and CLOSE writes the last block (even if it contains fewer than four records) and writes a trailer label.

DOS Program to Create a Tape File

The DOS DTFMT file definition macro defines a magnetic tape file. You define a DTFMT macro with a unique name for each tape input or output file that the program processes. The parameters that you code are similar to those for the DTFCD and DTFPR macros covered earlier.

In Fig. 18-1, the program reads records into RECDIN and transfers required fields to a tape workarea named TAPEWORK. The program then writes this workarea to a tape output file named FILOTP. Based on the BLKSIZE entry in the DTFMT, IOCS blocks four records before physically writing the block onto tape. Thus for every four input records that the program reads, IOCS writes one block of four records onto tape.

```
 1             PRINT ON,NODATA,NOGEN
 2 PROG18A     START
 3             BALR  3,0                      INITIALIZE BASE REGISTER
 4             USING *,3
 5             OPEN  FILEIN,FILEOTP           ACTIVATE FILES
14             GET   FILEIN,RECDIN            READ 1ST RECORD
20 A10LOOP     BAL   9,B10PROC
21             GET   FILEIN,RECDIN            READ NEXT
27             B     A10LOOP

29 *                E N D - O F - F I L E
30 A90EOF      CLOSE FILEIN,FILEOTP           DE-ACTIVATE FILES
39             EOJ                            NORMAL END-OF-JOB

43 ***               M A I N   P R O C E S S I N G
45 B10PROC     MVC   ACCTTPO,ACCTIN          MOVE INPUT FIELDS
46             MVC   NAMETPO,NAMEIN          *   TO WORK AREA
47             MVC   ADDRTPO,ADDRIN          *
48             PACK  BALNTPO,BALNIN          *
49             MVC   DATETPO,DATEIN          *
50             PUT   FILEOTP,TAPEWORK        WRITE TAPE WORKAREA
56             BR    9                       RETURN

58 *                 D E C L A R A T I V E S
60 FILEIN      DTFCD DEVADDR=SYSIPT,         INPUT FILE            +
                     IOAREA1=IOARIN1,                              +
                     BLKSIZE=80,                                   +
                     DEVICE=2540,                                  +
                     EOFADDR=A90EOF,                               +
                     TYPEFLE=INPUT,                                +
                     WORKA=YES                                     +
```

Figure 18-1   Program: writing a tape file under DOS.

```
85 IOARIN1   DC      CL80' '                     INPUT BUFFER 1
87 RECDIN    DS      0CL80                       INPUT AREA:
88 CODEIN    DS      CL02                        01-02   RECORD CODE
89 ACCTIN    DS      CL06                        03-08   ACCOUNT NO.
90 NAMEIN    DS      CL20                        09-28   NAME
91 ADDRIN    DS      CL40                        29-68   ADDRESS
92 BALNIN    DS      ZL06'0000.00'               69-74   BALANCE
93 DATEIN    DS      CL06'DDMMYY'                75-80   DATE
95 FILEOTP   DTFMT   BLKSIZE=360,                 TAPE FILE                +
                     DEVADDR=SYS025,                                      +
                     FILABL=STD,                                         +
                     IOAREA1=IOARTPO1,                                   +
                     IOAREA2=IOARTPO2,                                   +
                     RECFORM=FIXBLK,                                     +
                     RECSIZE=90,                                         +
                     TYPEFLE=OUTPUT,                                     +
                     WORKA=YES
132 IOARTPO1 DS      CL360                       TAPE BUFFER-1
133 IOARTPO2 DS      CL360                       TAPE BUFFER-2

135 TAPEWORK DS      0CL90                       TAPE WORK AREA:
136 ACCTTPO  DS      CL06                        01-06   ACCOUNT NO.
137 NAMETPO  DS      CL20                        07-26   NAME
138 ADDRTPO  DS      CL40                        27-66   ADDRESS
139 BALNTPO  DS      PL04                        67-70   BALANCE
140 DATETPO  DS      CL06                        71-76   DATE
141          DC      CL14' '                     77-90   RESERVED

143          LTORG
144                  =C'$$BOPEN '
145                  =C'$$BCLOSE'
146                  =A(FILEIN)
147                  =A(RECDIN)
148                  =A(FILEOTP)
149                  =A(TAPEWORK)
150          END     PROG18A
```

Figure 18-1   (continued)

The following explains the DTFMT entries:

BLKSIZE = 360 means that each block to be written from the IOAREA is 360 bytes long, based on four records at 90 bytes each.

DEVADDR = SYS025 denotes the logical address of the tape device that is to write the file.

FILABL = STD indicates that the tape file contains standard labels, as described in Chapter 17.

IOAREA1 and **IOAREA2** are the two IOCS buffers, each defined with the same length (360) as BLKSIZE.   If your blocks are especially large, you may omit defining a second buffer to reduce program size.

RECFORM = FIXBLK defines output records as fixed-length and blocked. Records on tape and disk may also be variable-length or unblocked.

RECSIZE = 90 means that each fixed-length record is 90 bytes in length, the same as the workarea.

TYPEFLE = OUTPUT means that the file is output, that is, for writing only. Other options are INPUT and WORK (for a work file).

WORKA = YES means that the program is to process output records in a workarea. In this program, TAPEWORK is the workarea and has the same length as RECSIZE, 90 bytes. Alternatively, you may code IOREG and use the macro PUT FILEOTP with no workarea coded in the operand.

The DTFMT file definition macro for tape input requires an entry EOFADDR = address to indicate the name of the routine where IOCS links on reaching the end of the tape file.

OS Program to Create a Tape File

For OS, you define a DCB macro with a unique name for each tape input or output file that the program processes. The parameters that you code are similar to those for the DCB macros covered earlier.

In Fig. 18-2, the program reads records into RECDIN and transfers required fields to a tape workarea named TAPEWORK. The program then writes this workarea to a tape output file named FILOTP. Based on the BLKSIZE entry in job control, the system blocks four records before physically writing the block onto tape. Thus for every four input records that the program reads, the system writes one block of four records onto tape.

```
//GO.TAPEOT   DD DSNAME=TRFILE,DISP=(NEW,PASS),UNIT=3420,              +
                DCB=(BLKSIZE=360,RECFM=FB,DEN=3)
                                             ▽_____ DD for tape
                                                     output data set
//GO.SYSIN    DD *           <--- DD for input file
PROG18B   START
          SAVE   (14,12)
          BALR   3,0
          USING  *,3
          ST     13,SAVEAREA+4
          LA     13,SAVEAREA
          OPEN   (FILEIN,(INPUT),FILEOTP,(OUTPUT))
          GET    FILEIN,RECDIN           READ 1ST RECORD

***              M A I N   P R O C E S S I N G
A10LOOP   MVC    ACCTTPO,ACCTIN          MOVE INPUT FIELDS TO TAPE
          MVC    NAMETPO,NAMEIN          *      WORK AREA
          MVC    ADDRTPO,ADDRIN          *
          PACK   BALNTPO,BALNIN          *
          MVC    DATETPO,DATEIN          *
          PUT    FILEOTP,TAPEWORK        WRITE WORK AREA ONTO TAPE
          GET    FILEIN,RECDIN           READ NEXT RECORD
          B      A10LOOP

*                E N D - O F - F I L E
A90EOF    CLOSE  (FILEIN,,FILEOTP)
          L      13,SAVEAREA+4
          RETURN (14,12)
```

Figure 18-2 Program: writing a tape file under OS.

```
*                   D E C L A R A T I V E S
FILEIN    DCB       DDNAME=SYSIN,                DCB FOR INPUT DATA SET      +
                    DEVD=DA,                                                 +
                    DSORG=PS,                                                +
                    EODAD=A90EOF,                                            +
                    MACRF=(GM)

RECDIN    DS        0CL80                         INPUT RECORD AREA:
CODEIN    DS        CL02                          01-02   RECORD CODE
ACCTIN    DS        CL06                          03-08   ACCOUNT NO.
NAMEIN    DS        CL20                          09-28   NAME
ADDRIN    DS        CL40                          29-68   ADDRESS
BALNIN    DS        ZL06'0000.00'                 69-74   BALANCE
DATEIN    DS        CL06'DDMMYY'                  75-80   DATE

FILEOTP   DCB       DDNAME=TAPEOT,                DCB FOR TAPE DATA SET       +
                    DSORG=PS,                                                +
                    LRECL=90,                                                +
                    MACRF=(PM)

TAPEWORK  DS        0CL90                         TAPE WORK AREA:
ACCTTPO   DS        CL06                          01-06   ACCOUNT NO.
NAMETPO   DS        CL20                          07-26   NAME
ADDRTPO   DS        CL40                          27-66   ADDRESS
BALNTPO   DS        PL04                          67-70   BALANCE(PACKED)
DATETPO   DS        CL06                          71-76   DATE
          DC        CL14' '                       77-90   RESERVED

SAVEAREA  DS        18F                           REGISTER SAVE AREA
          LTORG
          END       PROG18B
```

Figure 18-2   (continued)

The DD job commands for the files appear first in the job stream and provide some entries that could also appear in the DCB. This common practice enables users to change entries without reassembling programs. The DD entries for the tape file, TAPEOT, are as follows:

DSNAME = TRFILE provides the data set name.

DISP = (NEW,PASS) means that the file is new (to be created) and is to be kept temporarily.

UNIT = 3420 provides the tape drive model.

BLKSIZE = 360 means that each block to be written from the IOAREA is 360 bytes long, based on four records at 90 bytes each.

RECFM = FB defines output records as fixed-length and blocked. Records on tape and disk may also be variable-length (V) or unblocked.

DEN = 3 indicates tape density as 1,600 bpi. (DEN = 2 would mean 800 bpi.)

The following explains the DCB entries:

DDNAME = TAPEOT relates to the same name in the the DD job control command:

```
//GO.TAPEOT ...
```

DSORG = PS defines output as physical sequential.

LRECL = 90 provides the logical record length for each record.

MACRF = (PM) defines the type of output operation as put and move from a workarea. MACRF = (PL) would allow you to use locate mode to process records directly in the buffers.

The DCB file definition macro for tape input requires an entry EOFADDR = address to indicate the name of the routine where IOCS links on reaching the end of the tape file.

Also, another DCB entry, EROPT, provides for an action if an input operation encounters problems. The options are as follows:

=ACC	Accept the possibly erroneous block of data.
=SKP	Skip the data block entirely and resume with the next one.
=ABE	Abend (abnormal end of program execution), the standard default if you omit the entry.

ACC and SKP can use a SYNAD entry for printing an error message and continue processing. If the error message routine is named R10TPERR, the DCB coding could be

```
EROPT=SKP,
SYNAD=R10TPERR
```

Since the use of ACC and SKP may cause invalid results, it may be preferable for important production jobs to use ABE (or allow it to default). See the OS supervisor manuals for other DCB options.

CREATING A SEQUENTIAL DISK FILE

The next two examples create a disk file for DOS and OS. The programs accept input data from the system reader and write four records per block onto disk.

For both programs, OPEN checks the disk label, and CLOSE writes the last data block (even if it contains fewer than four records) and writes a last dummy block with zero length.

DOS Program to Create a Sequential Disk File

The DOS file definition macro that defines a sequential disk file is DTFSD. The parameters that you code are similar to those for the DTFMT macro.

The program in Fig. 18-3 reads the tape records from the file created in Fig. 18-1 and transfers required fields to a disk workarea named DISKWORK. The program then writes this workarea to a disk output file named SDISK. Based on

```
 1                PRINT ON,NODATA,NOGEN
 2  PROG18B       START
 3                BALR  3,0
 4                USING *,3
 5                OPEN  TAPE,SDISK
14                GET   TAPE,TAPEIN          READ 1ST RECORD
20  A10LOOP       BAL   9,B10PROC
21                GET   TAPE,TAPEIN          READ NEXT RECORD
27                B     A10LOOP

29  *                   M A I N   P R O C E S S I N G
30  B10PROC       MVC   ACCTDKO,ACCTIN       MOVE FIELDS TO DISK
31                MVC   NAMEDKO,NAMEIN       *     WORK AREA
32                MVC   ADDRDKO,ADDRIN       *
33                ZAP   BALNDKO,BALNIN       *
34                MVC   DATEDKO,DATEIN       *
35                PUT   SDISK,DISKWORK       WRITE WORK AREA
41                BR    9

43  *                   E N D - O F - F I L E
44  A90END        CLOSE TAPE,SDISK
53                EOJ

57  *                   D E C L A R A T I V E S
58  TAPE          DTFMT BLKSIZE=360,         TAPE FILE              +
                        DEVADDR=SYS025,                             +
                        EOFADDR=A90END,                             +
                        ERROPT=IGNORE,                              +
                        FILABL=STD,                                 +
                        IOAREA1=IOARTPI1,                           +
                        RECFORM=FIXBLK,                             +
                        RECSIZE=090,                                +
                        TYPEFLE=INPUT,                              +
                        WORKA=YES
96  IOARTPI1 DS         CL360                INPUT TAPE BUFFER
98  TAPEIN   DS         0CL90                TAPE INPUT AREA:
99  ACCTIN   DS         CL6                  *   ACCOUNT NO.
100 NAMEIN   DS         CL20                 *   NAME
101 ADDRIN   DS         CL40                 *   ADDRESS
102 BALNIN   DS         PL4                  *   BALANCE
103 DATEIN   DS         CL6'DDMMYY'          *   DATE
104          DS         CL14                 *   UNUSED
106 SDISK    DTFSD      BLKSIZE=368,         DISK FILE              +
                        DEVADDR=SYS015,                             +
                        DEVICE=3380,                                +
                        IOAREA1=IOARDK,                             +
                        RECFORM=FIXBLK,                             +
                        RECSIZE=90,                                 +
                        TYPEFLE=OUTPUT,                             +
                        VERIFY=YES,                                 +
                        WORKA=YES
172 IOARDK   DS         CL368                DISK BUFFER

174 DISKWORK DS         0CL90                DISK WORK AREA:
175 ACCTDKO  DS         CL06                 *   ACCOUNT NO.
```

Figure 18-3 Program: writing a sequential disk file under DOS.

```
176 NAMEDKO   DS    CL20                  *   NAME
177 ADDRDKO   DS    CL40                  *   ADDRESS
178 BALNDKO   DS    PL04                  *   BALANCE
179 DATEDKO   DS    CL06                  *   DATE
180           DC    CL14' '               *   RESERVED
181           LTORG
182                 =C'$$BOPEN '
183                 =C'$$BCLOSE'
184                 =A(TAPE)
185                 =A(TAPEIN)
186                 =A(SDISK)
187                 =A(DISKWORK)
188           END   PROG18B


// EXEC LNKEDT
// TLBL    TAPE,'CUST REC TP',0,100236
// ASSGN   SYS015,DISK,VOL=SVSE03,SHR
// DLBL    SDISK,'CUSTOMER RECORDS SD',0,SD
// EXTENT  SYS015,ATMP70,1,0,3,4
```

Figure 18-3   (continued)

the BLKSIZE entry in the DTFMT and DTFSD, the system both reads and writes blocks of four records, although the two blocking factors need not be the same.

The following explains the DTFSD entries:

BLKSIZE = 368 means that the blocksize for output is 360 bytes (4 x 90) plus 8 bytes for the system to construct a count field.   You provide for the extra 8 bytes only for output; for input, the entry would be 360.

DEVICE = 3380 means that the program is to write blocks on a 3380 disk device.

VERIFY = YES tells the system to reread each output record to check its validity.   If the record when reread is not identical to the record that was supposed to be written, the system rewrites the record and performs another reread.   If the system eventually cannot perform a valid write, it may advance to another area on the disk surface.   Although this operation involves more accessing time, it helps ensure the accuracy of the written records.

DEVADDR, IOAREA1, RECFORM, RECSIZE, TYPEFLE, and **WORKA** are the same as for previous DTFs.   You omit the FILABL entry because disk labels must be standard.

If you omit the entry for DEVADDR, the system uses the SYSnnn address from the job control entry.

OS Program to Create a Sequential Disk File

For OS, you define a DCB macro with a unique name for each disk input or output file that the program processes.   The parameters that you code are similar to those for the DCB macros covered earlier.

The program in Fig. 18-4 reads the tape records from the file created in Fig.

```
//GO.TAPEIN DD DSNAME=TRFILE,DISP=(OLD,PASS),UNIT=3420,           +
              DCB=(BLKSIZE=360,RECFM=FB,DEN=3)
//GO.DISKOT DD DSNAME=&TEMPDSK,DISP=(NEW,PASS),UNIT=3380,SPACE=(TRK,10), +
              DCB=(BLKSIZE=360,RECFM=FB)

PROG18D   START 0
          SAVE  (14,12)
          BALR  3,0
          USING *,3
          ST    13,SAVEAREA+4
          LA    13,SAVEAREA
          OPEN  (TAPE,(INPUT),SDISK,(OUTPUT))
          GET   TAPE                      READ 1ST TAPE RECORD

***             M A I N   P R O C E S S I N G
A10LOOP   MVC   TAPEIN,0(1)               MOVE FROM TAPE BUFFER
          MVC   ACCTDKO,ACCTIN            MOVE TAPE FIELDS TO DISK
          MVC   NAMEDKO,NAMEIN            *     WORK AREA
          MVC   ADDRDKO,ADDRIN            *
          ZAP   BALNDKO,BALNIN            *
          MVC   DATEDKO,DATEIN            *
          PUT   SDISK,DISKWORK            WRITE WORK AREA ONTO DISK
          GET   TAPE                      READ NEXT TAPE RECORD
          B     A10LOOP

***             E N D - O F - F I L E
A90END    CLOSE (TAPE,,SDISK)
          L     13,SAVEAREA+4
          RETURN (14,12)

***             D E C L A R A T I V E S
TAPE      DCB   DDNAME=TAPEIN,            TAPE INPUT DATA SET        +
                DSORG=PS,                                           +
                EODAD=A90END,                                       +
                LRECL=90,                                           +
                MACRF=(GL)

TAPEIN    DS    0CL90                     TAPE INPUT AREA:
ACCTIN    DS    CL06                      *   ACCOUNT NO.
NAMEIN    DS    CL20                      *   NAME
ADDRIN    DS    CL40                      *   ADDRESS
BALNIN    DS    PL04                      *   BALANCE (PACKED)
DATEIN    DS    CL06'DDMMYY'              *   DATE
          DS    CL14                      *   UNUSED

SDISK     DCB   DDNAME=DISKOT,            DISK OUTPUT DATA SET       +
                DSORG=PS,                                           +
                LRECL=90,                                           +
                MACRF=(PM)

DISKWORK  DS    0CL90                     DISK WORK AREA:
ACCTDKO   DS    CL06                      *   ACCOUNT NO.
NAMEDKO   DS    CL20                      *   NAME
ADDRDKO   DS    CL40                      *   ADDRESS
BALNDKO   DS    PL04                      *   BALANCE (PACKED)
DATEDKO   DS    CL06                      *   DATE
          DC    CL14' '                   *   RESERVED FOR EXPANSION

SAVEAREA  DS    18F                       REGISTER SAVE AREA
          LTORG
          END   PROG18D
```

Figure 18-4 Program: writing a sequential disk file under OS.

18-2 and transfers required fields to a disk workarea named DISKWORK. The program then writes this workarea to a disk output file named SDISK. Based on the BLKSIZE entry in job control, the system both reads and writes blocks of four records, although the two blocking factors need not be the same.

The DD entries for the disk file, DISKOT, are as follows:

DSNAME = &TEMPDSK provides the data set name.

DISP = (NEW,PASS) means that the file is new and is to be kept temporarily.

UNIT = 3380 provides the disk drive model.

SPACE = (TRK,10) allocates ten tracks for this file.

BLKSIZE = 360 means that each block to be written from the buffer is 360 bytes long, based on four records at 90 bytes each.

RECFM = FB defines output records as fixed-length and blocked. Records on disk may also be variable-length (V) or unblocked.

The following explains the DCB entries:

DDNAME = DISKOT relates to the same name in the the DD job control command:

```
//GO.DISKOT ...
```

DSORG = PS defines output as physical sequential.

LRECL = 90 provides the logical record length for each record.

MACRF = (PM) defines the type of output operation as put and move from a workarea. MACRF = (PL) would allow you to use locate mode to process records directly in the buffers.

The DCB file definition macro for disk input requires an entry EOFADDR = address to indicate the name of the routine where the system links on reaching the end of the disk file.

VARIABLE-LENGTH RECORDS

Tape and disk files provide for variable-length records, either unblocked or blocked. The use of variable-length records may significantly reduce the amount of space required to store a file. However, beware of trivial applications in which variations in record size are small or the file itself is small, because the system generates overhead that may defeat any expected savings.

A record may contain one or more variable-length fields or a variable number of fixed-length fields.

1. *Variable-Length Fields.* For fields such as customer name and address that vary considerably in length, a program could store only significant characters

and delete trailing blanks.   One approach is to follow each variable field with a special delimiter character such as an asterisk.

The following example illustrates fixed-length name and address of 20 characters each, compressed into variable length with an asterisk replacing trailing blanks:

Fixed length: `Norman Bates.......Bates Motel.........`
Variable length: `Norman Bates*Bates Motel*`

To find the end of the field, the program may use a TRT instruction to scan for the delimiter.   Another technique stores a count of the field length immediately preceding each variable-length field.   For the preceding record, the count for the name would be 12 and the count for the address would be 11:

`| 12 | Norman Bates | 11 | Bates Motel |`

2. *Variable Number of Fixed-Length Fields.*   Records may contain a variable number of fields.   For example, an electric utility company may maintain a large file of customer records with a fixed portion containing the customer name and address and optional subrecords for their electric account, natural gas account, and budget account.

VARIABLE-LENGTH RECORD FORMAT

Immediately preceding each variable-length record on tape or disk is a 4-byte record control word (RCW) that supplies the length of the record.   Immediately preceding each block is a 4-byte block control word (BCW) that supplies the length of the block.   As a consequence, both records and blocks may be variable length.   You have to supply a maximum block size into which the system is to fit as many records as possible.

Unblocked Records

Variable-length records that are unblocked contain a BCW and an RCW before each block.   Here are three unblocked records:

`| BCW | RCW | record 1 | ... | BCW | RCW record 2 | ... | BCW | RCW record 3 |`

Suppose that three records are to be stored as variable-length unblocked.   Their lengths are 310, 260, and 280 bytes, respectively:

Field:	BCW	RCW	record	BCW	RCW	record	BCW	RCW	record
Length:	4	4	310	4	4	260	4	4	280
Contents:	318	314	record 1	268	264	record 2	288	284	record 3

The RCW contains the length of the record plus its own length of 4. Since the first record has a length of 310, its RCW contains 314. The BCW contains the length of the RCW(s) plus its own length of 4. Since the only RCW contains a length of 314, the BCW contains 318.

Blocked Records

Variable-length records that are blocked contain a BCW before each block and an RCW before each record. The following shows a block of three records:

```
| BCW | RCW | record 1 | RCW | record 2 | RCW | record 3
```

Suppose that the same three records with lengths of 310, 260, and 280 bytes are to be stored as variable-length blocked and are to fit into a maximum block size of 900 bytes:

Field:	BCW	RCW	record	RCW	record	RCW	record
Length:	4	4	310	4	260	4	280
Contents:	866	314	record 1	264	record 2	284	record 3

The length of the block is the sum of one BCW, the RCWs, and the record lengths:

Block control word:	4 bytes
Record control words:	12
Record lengths:	+850
Total length:	866 bytes

The system stores as many records as possible in the block up to (in this example) 900 bytes. Thus a block may contain any number of bytes up to 900, and both blocks and records are variable length. The system automatically handles all blocking, unblocking, and control of BCWs.

Your BLKSIZE entry tells the system the maximum block length. For example, if the BLKSIZE entry in the preceding example specified 800, the system would fit only the first two records in the block, and the third record would begin the next block.

Programming for Variable-Length Records

Although IOCS performs most of the processing for variable-length records, you have to provide the record length. The additional programming steps are concerned with the record and block length:

Record length.   As with fixed-length records, a program may process variable-length records in a workarea or in the buffers (I/O areas).   You define the workarea as the length of the largest possible record, including the 4-byte record control word.   When creating each record, calculate and store the record length in the record control word field.   This field must be 4 bytes long, with the contents in binary format, as

```
          VARRCW  DS      F
```

DOS uses only the first 2 bytes of this field.

Block length.   You define the I/O area as the length of the largest possible block, including the 4-byte block control word.   On output, IOCS stores as many complete records in the block as will fit.   IOCS performs all blocking and calculating of the block length.   On input, IOCS deblocks all records, similar to its deblocking of fixed-length records.

Sample Program: Reading and Printing Variable-Length Records

Consider a file of disk records that contains variable-length records, with fields defined as follows:

01–04	Record length
05–09	Account number
10–82	Variable name and address

To indicate the end of a name, it is immediately followed by a delimiter, in this case a plus sign (hex '4E').   Another delimiter terminates the next field, the address, and a third terminates the city.   Here is a typical case:

```
JP Programmer+1425 North Basin Street+Kingstown+
```

The program in Fig. 18-5 reads and prints these variable-length records.   Note that in the DTFSD, RECFORM = VARBLK specifies variable blocked.   The program reads each input record and uses TRT and a loop to scan each of the three variable-length fields for the record delimiter.   It calculates the length of each field and uses EX to move each field to the output area.   The program also checks for the absence of a delimiter.

   Output would appear as

```
JP Programmer
1425 North Basin Street
Kingstown
```

```
  1              PRINT ON,NODATA,NOGEN
  2 PROG18C      START
  3              BALR  3,0
  4              USING *,3
  5              OPEN  FILEIDK,FILEOPR
 14              GET   FILEIDK,WORKAREA        READ 1ST RECORD

 21 ***              M A I N   P R O C E S S I N G
 23 A10LOOP      BAL   5,B10SCAN               SCAN
 24              GET   FILEIDK,WORKAREA        READ RECORD
 30              B     A10LOOP
 32 *                E N D - O F - F I L E
 34 A90EOF       CLOSE FILEIDK,FILEOPR         TERMINATE
 43              EOJ

 47 *                P R O C E S S   V A R I A B L E   R E C O R D
 49 B10SCAN      LA    6,IDENTIN               ADDR OF INPUT IDENT
 50              LR    7,6                     ESTABLISH ADDRESS OF
 51              AH    7,RECLEN                   END OF RECORD
 52              SH    7,=H'9'
 53              MVC   PRINT+10(5),ACCTIN      MOVE ACCOUNT TO PRINT
 55 B20          TRT   0(73,6),SCANTAB         SCAN FOR DELIMITER
 56              BZ    B30                     *  NO DELIMITER FOUND
 57              LR    4,1                     SAVE ADDR OF DELIMITER
 58              SR    1,6                     CALC. LENGTH OF FIELD
 59              BCTR  1,0                     DECREMENT LENGTH BY 1
 60              EX    1,M10MOVE               MOVE VAR LENGTH FIELD
 61              MVI   CTLCHPR,WSP1
 62              PUT   FILEOPR,PRINT           PRINT, SPACE 1
 68              MVC   PRINT,BLANKPR           CLEAR PRINT AREA
 69              LA    6,1(0,4)                INCREMENT FOR NEXT FIELD
 70              CR    6,7                     PAST END OF RECORD?
 71              BL    B20                     *  NO  - SCAN NEXT
 72 *                                         *  YES - END
 73 B30          MVI   CTLCHPR,WSP2
 74              PUT   FILEOPR,PRINT           PRINT 3RD LINE
 80              BR    5                       RETURN

 82 M10MOVE      MVC   PRINT+20(0),0(6)        MOVE VAR FIELD TO PRINT

 84 *                D E C L A R A T I V E S
 86 SCANTAB      DC    78X'00'                 TRT TABLE:
 87              DC    X'4E'                   * DELIMITER POSITION
 88              DC    177X'00'                * REST OF TABLE

 90 FILEIDK      DTFSD BLKSIZE=300,            DISK FILE                    +
                       DEVICE=3380,                                         +
                       DEVADDR=SYS025,                                      +
                       EOFADDR=A90EOF,                                      +
                       IOAREA1=IOARDKI1,                                    +
                       IOAREA2=IOARDKI2,                                    +
                       RECFORM=VARBLK,                                      +
                       TYPEFLE=INPUT,                                       +
                       WORKA=YES
154              DS    0H                      ALIGN ON EVEN BOUNDARY
155 IOARDKI1 DS        CL300                   BUFFER-1 DISK FILE
156 IOARDKI2 DS        CL300                   BUFFER-2 DISK FILE

158 *                                         INPUT AREA:
159              DS    0H                      * ALIGN EVEN BOUNDARY
```

Figure 18-5 Program: printing variable-length records.

```
160 WORKAREA DS    0CL82                * MAX. RECORD + LENGTH
161 RECLEN   DS    H                    * 2-BYTE RECORD LENGTH
162          DC    H'0'                 * 2 BYTES UNUSED IN DOS
163 ACCTIN   DS    CL05                 * ACCOUNT NUMBER
164 IDENTIN  DS    CL73                 * AREA FOR VAR. NAME|ADDR

166 FILEOPR  DTFPR BLKSIZE=133,           PRINTER FILE            +
                   CTLCHR=YES,                                    +
                   DEVADDR=SYSLST,                                +
                   DEVICE=3203,                                   +
                   IOAREA1=IOARPR1,                               +
                   IOAREA2=IOARPR2,                               +
                   WORKA=YES
192 IOARPR1  DC    CL133' '             BUFFER-1 PRINT FILE
193 IOARPR2  DC    CL133' '             BUFFER-2 PRINT FILE

195 WSP1     EQU   X'09'                CTL CHAR: PRINT, SPACE 1
196 WSP2     EQU   X'13'                *         PRINT, SPACE 2

198 BLANKPR  DC    C' '
199 PRINT    DS    0CL133               PRINT AREA
200 CTLCHPR  DS    XL1                  *
201          DC    CL132' '             *
202          LTORG
203                =C'$$BOPEN '
204                =C'$$BCLOSE'
205                =A(FILEIDK)
206                =A(WORKAREA)
207                =A(FILEOPR)
208                =A(PRINT)
209                =H'9'
210          END   PROG18C
```

Figure 18-5   (continued)

The DTFSD omits RECSIZE because IOCS needs to know only the maximum block length.   For OS, the DCB entry for variable blocked format is RECFM = VB.
You could devise some records and trace the logic of this program step by step.

KEY POINTS

- Entries in a program file definition macro should match the job control commands.
- The block size for a file must be a multiple of record size, and all programs that process the file must specify the same record and block size.
- For variable-length files, the workareas and buffers should be aligned on an even boundary.   When creating the file, you calculate and store the record length, whereas the system calculates the block length.   Your designated maximum block size must equal or exceed the size of any record.

PROBLEMS

18-1. For blocked disk or tape records, under what circumstances would it be advisable to define only one buffer for the file?

18-2. Revise the program in Fig. 18-1 or 18-2 for six records per block and the use of locate mode.

18-3. Revise the file definition macro entries and I/O areas in Fig. 18-3 or 18-4 for the following. Input records are 90 bytes long and have six records per block. Output records have three records per block, to be loaded on a 3350 disk device as SYS017. Assemble and test.

18-4. Revise the job control for Fig. 18-3 for the following: The filename is DISKOUT, the file ID is ACCTS.RECEIVABLE, retention is 30 days, to be run on SYS017, serial number 123456, using a 3380 on cylinder 15, track 0 for 15 tracks.

18-5. Revise the job control for Figure 18-4 for the following. The filename is DISKOUT, the file ID is ACCTS.RECEIVABLE, retention is 30 days, to be run on SYS017, serial number 123456, using a 3380 on cylinder 15, track 0 for 15 tracks.

18-6. Code the file definition macro for DTFMT. The input file name is TAPFLIN, record size is fixed-length 500 bytes, the blocking factor is 5, on SYS030, two buffers, use of a workarea, and standard labels. The end-of-file address is X10EOF.

18-7. Code the file definition macro for DCB. The input file name is TAPFLIN, record size is fixed-length 500 bytes, the blocking factor is 5, use of a workarea, and standard labels. The end-of-file address is X10EOF.

18-8. Code the file definition macro for DTFSD. The input file name is DSKFLIN, record size is fixed-length 500 bytes, the blocking factor is 5, on SYS030, disk device 3380, two buffers, and use of a workarea. The end-of-file address is X10EOF.

18-9. Code the file definition macro for DCB. The input file name is DSKFLIN, record size is fixed-length 500 bytes, the blocking factor is 5, disk device 3380, and use of a workarea. The end-of-file address is X10EOF.

18-10. A file contains variable-length records with the following lengths: 326, 414, 502, 384, 293, 504. The maximum block length is 1,200 bytes. Arrange the records in blocks and show RCWs and BCWs.

18-11. Write a program that creates a supplier file on disk from the following input records:

```
01-05   Supplier number
06-25   Supplier name
26-46   Street
47-67   City
68-74   Amount payable
75-80   Date of last purchase (yymmdd)
```

Store name, street, and city as variable-length fields, with hex 'FF' as a delimiter after each field. Store the amount payable in packed format.

19

VIRTUAL STORAGE ACCESS METHOD (VSAM)

OBJECTIVE

To explain the design of the virtual storage access
method and its processing requirements.

Virtual storage access method (VSAM) is a relatively recent file organization method
for users of IBM OS/VS and DOS/VS. VSAM facilitates both sequential and
random processing and supplies a number of useful utility programs.

The term *file* is somewhat ambiguous since it may reference an I/O device or
the records that the device processes. To distinguish a collection of records, IBM
OS literature uses the term *data set*.

VSAM provides three types of data sets:

1. *Key-sequenced Data Set (KSDS).* KSDS maintains records in sequence of
   key, such as employee or part number, and is equivalent to indexed sequential
   access method.
2. *Entry-sequenced Data Set (ESDS).* ESDS maintains records in the sequence
   in which they were initially entered and is equivalent to sequential organization.

Feature	Key-Sequenced	Entry-Sequenced	Relative-Record
Record sequence	By key	In sequence in which entered	In sequence of relative record number
Record length	Fixed or variable	Fixed or variable	Fixed only
Access of records	By key via index or RBA	By RBA	By relative record number
Change of address	Can change record RBA	Cannot change record RBA	Cannot change relative record number
New records	Distributed free space for records	Space at end of-data set	Empty slots in data set
Recovery of space	Reclaims space if record is deleted	No delete but can overwrite an old record	Can reuse deleted space

Figure 19-1 Features of VSAM organization methods.

3. *Relative-Record Data Set (RRDS).* RRDS maintains records in order of relative record number and is equivalent to direct file organization.

Both OS/VS and DOS/VS handle VSAM the same way and use similar support programs and macros, although OS has a number of extended features.

Thorough coverage of assembler VSAM would require an entire textbook. However, this chapter supplies enough information to enable you to code programs that create, retrieve, and update a VSAM data set. For complete details, see the IBM Access Methods Services manual and the IBM DOS/VSE Macros or OS/VS Supervisor Services manuals.

CONTROL INTERVALS

For all three types of data sets, VSAM stores records in groups (one or more) of control intervals. You may select the control interval size, but if you allow VSAM to do so, it optimizes the size based on the record length and the type of disk device being used. The maximum size of a control interval is 32,768 bytes.

At the end of each control interval is control information that describes the data records:

Rec-1	Rec-2	Rec-3	. . .	Control Information

A control interval contains one or more data records, and a specified number of control intervals comprise a control area. VSAM addresses a data record by relative byte address (RBA)—its displacement from the start of the data set. Consequently, the first record of a data set is at RBA 0, and if records are 500 bytes long, the second record is at RBA 500.

The list in Fig. 19-1 compares the three types of VSAM organizations.

ACCESS METHOD SERVICES (AMS)

Before physically writing (or "loading") records in a VSAM data set, you first catalog its structure. The IBM utility package, Access Method Services (AMS), enables you to furnish VSAM with such details about the data set as its name, organization type, record length, key location, and password (if any). Since VSAM subsequently knows the physical characteristics of the data set, your program need not supply as much detailed information as would a program accessing an ISAM file.

The following describes the more important features of AMS. Full details are in the IBM OS/VS and DOS/VS Access Methods Services manual.   You catalog a VSAM structure using an AMS program named IDCAMS, as follows:

```
OS:       //STEP EXEC PGM=IDCAMS
DOS:      // EXEC IDCAMS,SIZE=AUTO
```

Immediately following the command are various entries that DEFINE the data set.   The first group under CLUSTER provides required and optional entries that describe all the information that VSAM must maintain for the data set.   The second group, DATA, creates an entry in the catalog for a data component, that is, the set of all control area and intervals for the storage of records.   The third group, INDEX, creates an entry in the catalog for a KSDS index component for the handling of the KSDS indexes.

Figure 19-2 provides the most common DEFINE CLUSTER entries.   Note that to indicate continuation, a hyphen (-) follows every entry except the last.

Cluster level

```
DEFINE    CLUSTER
          ( NAME(data-set-name) -
          {CYLINDERS(primary[ secondary])|
           BLOCKS(primary[ secondary])|          (choose
           RECORDS( primary[ secondary])|          one)
           TRACKS(primary[ secondary])} -
          [INDEXED|NONINDEXED|NUMBERED] -         (choose one)
          [KEYS(length offset)] -
          [RECORDSIZE(average maximum)] -
          [VOLUMES(vol-ser[ vol-ser ...])]
```

Data component level

```
          [DATA
          ([CONTROLINTERVALSIZE(size)] -
          [NAME(data-name)] -
          [VOLUMES(vol-ser[ vol-ser ...])]
          )]
```

Index component level

```
          [INDEX
          ([NAME(index-name)] -
          [VOLUMES(vol-ser[ vol-ser ...])]
          )]
```

Figure 19-2   Entries for defining a VSAM data set.

Note:	SYMBOL	MEANING
	[ ]	Optional entry, may be omitted
	{ }	Select one of the following options
	( )	You must code these parentheses
	|	"or"

Figure 19-2 (continued)

- DEFINE CLUSTER (abbreviated DEF CL) provides various parameters all contained within parentheses.
- NAME is a required parameter that supplies the name of the data set. You can code the name up to 44 characters with a period after each 8 or fewer characters, as EMPLOYEE.RECORDS.P030. The name corresponds to job control, as follows:

```
OS:      //FILEVS DD DSNAME=EMPLOYEE.RECORDS.P030 ...
DOS:     // DLBL FILEVS,'EMPLOYEE.RECORDS.P030',0,VSAM
```

The name FILEVS in this example is whatever name you assign to the file definition (ACB) in your program, such as

```
filename ACB DDNAME=FILEVS ...
```

- BLOCKS. You may want to load the data set on an FBA device (such as 3310 or 3370) or on a CKD device (such as 3350 or 3380). For FBA devices, allocate the number of 512-byte BLOCKS for the data set. For CKD devices, the entry CYLINDERS (or CYL) or TRACKS allocates space. The entry RECORDS allocates space for either FBA or CKD. In all cases, indicate a primary allocation for a generous expected amount of space and an optional secondary allocation for expansion if required.
- Choose one entry to designate the type of data set: INDEXED designates key-sequenced, NONINDEXED is entry-sequenced, and NUMBERED is relative-record.
- KEYS for INDEXED only defines the length (from 1 to 255) and position of the key in each record. For example, KEYS (6 0) indicates that the key is 6 bytes long beginning in position 0 (the first byte).
- RECORDSIZE (or RECSZ) provides the average and maximum lengths in bytes of data records. For fixed-length records and for RRDS, the two entries are identical. For example, code (120b120) for 120-byte records.
- VOLUMES (or VOL) identifies the volume serial number(s) of the DASD volume(s) where the data set is to reside. You may specify VOLUMES at

any of the three levels; for example, the DATA and INDEX components may reside on different volumes.

DEFINE CLUSTER supplies a number of additional specialized options described in the IBM AMS manual.

ACCESSING AND PROCESSING

VSAM furnishes two types of accessing, keyed and addressed, and three types of processing, sequential, direct, and skip sequential. The following chart shows the legal accessing and processing by type of organization:

Type	Keyed Access	Addressed Access
KSDS	Sequential Direct Skip sequential	Sequential Direct
ESDS		Sequential Direct
RRDS	Sequential Direct Skip sequential	

In simple terms, *keyed accessing* is concerned with the key (for KSDS) and relative record number (for RRDS). For example, if you read a KSDS sequentially, VSAM delivers the records in sequence by key (although they may be in a different sequence physically).

Addressed accessing is concerned with the RBA. For example, you can access a record in an ESDS using the RBA by which it was stored. For either type of accessing method, you can process records sequentially or directly (and by skip sequential for keyed access). Thus you always use addressed accessing for ESDS and keyed accessing for RRDS and may process either type sequentially or directly. KSDS, by contrast, permits both keyed access (the normal) and addressed access, with both sequential and direct processing.

KEY-SEQUENCED DATA SETS

A key-sequenced data set (KSDS) is considerably more complex than either ESDS or RRDS but is more useful and versatile. You always create ("load") a KSDS in ascending sequence by key and may process a KSDS directly by key or sequentially. Since KSDS stores and retrieves records according to key, each key in the data set must be unique.

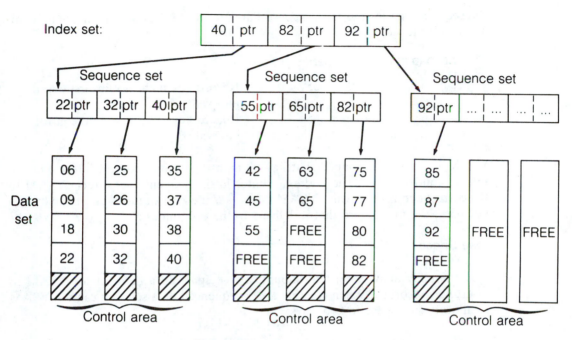

Figure 19-3 Key-sequenced organization.

Figure 19-3 provides a simplified view of a key-sequenced data set. The control intervals that contain the data records are depicted vertically, and for this example three control intervals comprise a control area. A *sequence set* contains an entry for each control interval in a control area. Entries within a sequence set consist of the highest key for each control interval and the address of the control interval; the address acts as a pointer to the beginning of the control interval. The highest keys for the first control area are 22, 32, and 40, respectively. VSAM stores each high key along with an address pointer in the sequence set for the first control area.

At a higher level, an *index set* (various levels depending on the size of the data set) contains high keys and address pointers for the sequence sets. In Fig. 19-3, the highest key for the first control area is 40. VSAM stores this value in the index set along with an address pointer for the first sequence.

When a program wants to access a record in the data set directly, VSAM locates the record first by means of the index set and then the sequence set. For example, a program requests access to a record with key 63. VSAM first checks the index set as follows:

RECORD KEY	INDEX SET	
63	40	Record key high, not in first control area.
63	82	Record key low, in second control area.

VSAM has determined that key 63 is in the second control area. It next examines

the sequence set for the second control area to locate the correct control interval.
These are the steps:

RECORD KEY	SEQUENCE SET	
63	55	Record key high, not in first control interval.
63	65	Record key low, in second control interval.

VSAM has now determined that key 63 is in the second control interval of the
second control area. The address pointer in the sequence set directs VSAM to
the correct control interval. VSAM then reads the keys of the data set and locates
key 63 as the first record that it delivers to the program.

Free Space

You normally allow a certain amount of free space in a data set for VSAM to
insert new records. When creating a key-sequenced data set, you can tell VSAM
to allocate free space in two ways:

1. Leave space at the end of each control interval.
2. Leave some control intervals vacant.

If a program deletes or shortens a record, VSAM reclaims the space by shifting
to the left all following records in the control interval. If the program adds or
lengthens a record, VSAM inserts the record in its correct space and moves to the
right all following records in the control interval. VSAM updates RBAs and
indexes accordingly.

A control interval may not contain enough space for an inserted record. In
such a case, VSAM causes a *control interval split* by removing about half the records
to a vacant control interval in the same control area. Although records are now
no longer *physically* in key order, for VSAM they are *logically* in sequence. The
updated sequence set controls the order for subsequent retrieval of records.

If there is no vacant control interval in a control area, VSAM causes a control
area split, using free space outside the control area. Under normal conditions,
such a split seldom occurs. To a large degree, a VSAM data set is self-organizing
and requires reorganization less often than an ISAM file.

ENTRY-SEQUENCED DATA SETS

An entry-sequenced data set (ESDS) acts like sequential file organization but has
the advantages of being under control of VSAM, some use of direct processing,
and password facilities. Basically, the data set is in the sequence in which it is

created, and you normally (but not necessarily) process from the start to the end of the data set.   Sequential processing of an ESDS by RBA is known as addressed access, which is the method you use to create the data set.   You may also process ESDS records directly by RBA.   Since ESDS is not concerned with keys, the data set may legally contain duplicate records.

Assume an ESDS containing records with keys 001, 003, 004, and 006.   The data set would appear as follows:

| 001 | 003 | 004 | 006 |

You may want to use ESDS for tables that are to load into programs, for small files that are always in ascending sequence, and for files extracted from a KSDS that are to be sorted.

RELATIVE-RECORD DATA SETS

A relative-record data set (RRDS) acts like direct file organization but also has the advantages of being under control of VSAM and offering keyed access and password facilities.   Basically, records in the data set are located according to their keys.   For example, a record with key 001 is in the first location, a record with key 003 is in the third location, and so forth.   If there is no record with key 002, that location is empty, and you can subsequently insert the record.

Assume an RRDS containing records with keys 001, 003, 004, and 006.   The data set would appear as follows:

| 001 | ... | 003 | 004 | ... | 006 |

Since RRDS stores and retrieves records according to key, each key in the data set must be unique.

You may want to use RRDS where you have a small to medium-sized file and keys are reasonably consecutive so that there are not large numbers of spaces. One example would be a data set with keys that are regions or states, and contents are product sales or population and demographic data.

You could also store keys after performing a computation on them.   As a simple example, imagine a data set with keys 101, 103, 104, and 106.   Rather than store them with those keys, you could subtract 100 from the key value and store the records with keys 001, 003, 004, and 006.

VSAM MACRO INSTRUCTIONS

VSAM uses a number of familiar macros as well as a few new ones to enable you to retrieve, add, change, and delete records.   In the following list, for macros marked with an asterisk (*), see the IBM DOS/VS or OS/VS Supervisor and I/O Macros manual for details.

- To relate a program and the data:
  ACB   (access method control block)
  EXLST   (exit list)

- To connect and disconnect a program and a data set:
  OPEN   (open a data set)
  CLOSE   (close a data set)
  TCLOSE*   (temporary close)

- To define requests for accessing data:
  RPL   (request parameter list)

- To request access to a file:
  GET   (get a record)
  PUT   (write or rewrite a record)
  POINT*   (position VSAM at a record)
  ERASE   (erase a record previously retrieved with a GET)
  ENDREQ*   (end request)

- To manipulate the information that relates a program to the data:
  GENCB*   (generate control block)
  MODCB*   (modify control block)
  SHOWCB   (show control block)
  TESTCB*   (test control block)

A program that accesses a VSAM data set requires the usual OPEN to connect the data set and CLOSE to disconnect it, the GET macro to read records, and PUT to write or rewrite records. An important difference in the use of macros under VSAM is the RPL (request for parameter list) macro. As shown in the following relationship, a GET or PUT specifies an RPL macro name rather than a file name. The RPL in turn specifies an ACB (access control block) macro, which in its turn relates to the job control entry for the data set:

```
Imperative macro:
                        GET RPL = RPLname
                                         ↗
    Define request:                    ↙
                        RPLname     RPL ACB = VSAMname . . .
                                                         ↗
    Define Access Control Block:          ↙
                        VSAMname    ACB DDNAME = filename . . .
                                                      ↗
    Job control:            ↙
                        //filename DD    DSNAME = EMPLOYEE . RECORDS . P030 . . .
```

The ACB macro is equivalent to the OS DCB or DOS DTF file definition macros. As well, the OPEN macro supplies information about the type of file organization, record length, and key. Each execution of OPEN, CLOSE, GET, PUT, and ERASE causes VSAM to check its validity and to insert a code into register 15 that you can check. A return code of X'00' means that the operation was successful. You can use the SHOWCB macro to determine the exact cause of the error.

THE ACB MACRO: ACCESS METHOD CONTROL BLOCK

The ACB macro identifies a data set that is to be processed. Its main purpose is to indicate the proposed type of processing (sequential or direct) and the use of exit routines, if any. The DEFINE CLUSTER command of AMS has already stored much of the information about the data set in the VSAM catalog. When a program opens the data set via the ACB, VSAM delivers this information to virtual storage.

Entries for an ACB macro may be in any sequence, and you may code only those that you need. Following is the general format, which you code like a DCB or DTF, with a comma following each entry and a continuation character in column 72. All operands are optional.

```
name      ACB     AM=VSAM,                              +
                  DDNAME=filename,                      +
                  EXLST=address,                        +
                  MACRF=([ADR][,KEY]
                        [,DIR][,SEQ][,SKP]
                        [,IN][,OUT]
                        [,NRM|AIX]),                    +
                  STRNO=number
```

name	The name indicates the symbolic address for the ACB when assembled. If you omit the DDNAME operand from the ACB definition, this name should match the filename in your DLBL or DD job statement.
AM=VSAM	Code this parameter if your installation also uses VTAM; otherwise, the assembler assumes VSAM.
DDNAME	This entry provides the name of your data set that the program is to process. This name matches the filename in your DLBL or DD job statement.
EXLST	The address references a list of your addresses of routines that provide exits. Use the EXLST macro to generate the list, and enter its name as the address. A common use is to code an

entry for an end-of-file exit for sequential reading.　If you have no exit routines, omit the operand.

MACRF　　　The options define the type of processing that you plan.　In the following, an underlined entry is a default:

ADR | <u>KEY</u>	Use ADR for addressed access (KS and ES) and KEY for keyed access (KS and RR).
DIR | <u>SEQ</u> | SKP	DIR provides direct processing, SEQ provides sequential processing, and SKP means skip sequential (for KS and RR).
<u>IN</u> | OUT	IN retrieves records and OUT permits retrieval, insertion, add-to-end, or update for keyed access and retrieval, update, or add-to-end for addressed access.
<u>NRM</u> | AIX	The DDNAME operand supplies the name of the data set (or path).　NRM means normal processing of the data set, whereas AIX means that this is an alternate index.

Other MACRF options are RST | <u>NRS</u> for resetting catalog information and <u>NUB</u> | UBF for user buffers.

STRNO　　　The entry supplies the total number of RPLs (request parameter lists) that your program will use at the same time (the default is 1).

ACB also has provision for parameters that define the number and size of buffers; however, the macro has standard defaults.

In the program example in Fig. 19-4, the ACB macro VSMFILOT has only two entries and allows the rest to default.　Access is keyed (KEY), processing is sequential (SEQ), and the file is output (OUT).　There is no exit list, STRNO defaults to 1, and MACRF defaults to NRM (normal path).

The assembler does not generate an I/O module for an ACB, nor does the linkage editor include one.　Instead, the system dynamically generates the module at execute time.

THE RPL MACRO: REQUEST PARAMETER LIST

The request macros GET, PUT, ERASE, and POINT require a reference to an RPL macro.　For example, the program in Fig. 19-4 issues the following GET macro:

```
GET   RPL=RPLISTIN
```

The operand supplies the name of the RPL macro that contains the information needed to access a record. If your program is to access a data set in different ways, you can code an RPL macro for each type of access; each RPL keeps track of its location in the data set.

The standard format for RPL is as follows. The name for the RPL macro is the one that you code in the GET or PUT operand. Every entry is optional.

```
RPLname      RPL      AM=VSAM,              +
                      ACB=address,          +
                      AREA=address,         +
                      AREALEN=length,       +
                      ARG=address,          +
                      KEYLEN=length,        +
                      OPTCD=(options),      +
                      RECLEN=length
```

AM	The entry VSAM specifies that this is a VSAM (not VTAM) control block.
ACB	The entry gives the name of the associated ACB that defines the data set.
AREA	The address references an I/O workarea in which a record is available for output or is to be entered on input.
AREALEN	The entry supplies the length of the record area.
ARG	The address supplies the search argument—a key, including a relative record number or an RBA.
KEYLEN	The length is that of the key if processing by generic key. (For normal keyed access, the catalog supplies the key length.)
OPTCD	Processing options are SEQ, SKP, and DIR; request options are UPD (update) and NUP (no update). For example, a direct update would be (DIR,UPD).
RECLEN	For writing a record, your program supplies the length to VSAM, and for retrieval, VSAM supplies the length to your program. If records are variable length, you can use the SHOWCB and TESTCB macros to examine the field (see the IBM Supervisor manual).

THE OPEN MACRO

The OPEN macro ensures that your program has authority to access the specified data set and generates VSAM control blocks.

```
[label]  OPEN  address[,address ... ]
```

The operand designates the address of one or more ACBs, which you may code either as a macro name or as a register notation (registers 2–12); for example:

```
       OPEN VSFILE
or  LA   6,VSFILE
       OPEN (6)
```

You can code up to 16 filenames in one OPEN and can include both ACB names and DCB or DTF names. Note, however, that to facilitate debugging, avoid mixing them in the same OPEN. OPEN sets a return code in register 15 to indicate success (zero) or failure (nonzero), which your program can test:

X'00'   Opened all ACBs successfully.

X'04'   Opened all ACBs successfully but issued a warning message for one or more.

X'08'   Failed to open one or more ACBs.

On a failed OPEN or CLOSE, you can also check the diagnostics following program execution for a message such as OPEN ERROR X'6E', and check Appendix K of the IBM Supervisor manual for an explanation of the code.

THE CLOSE MACRO

The CLOSE macro completes any I/O operations that are still outstanding, writes any remaining output buffers, and updates catalog entries for the data set.

```
[label] CLOSE address[,address ... ]
```

You can code up to 16 names in one CLOSE and can include both ACB names and DCB or DTF names. CLOSE sets a return code in register 15 to indicate success or failure, which your program can test:

X'00   Closed all ACBs successfully.

X'04'   Failed to close one or more ACBs successfully.

X'08'   Insufficient virtual storage space for close routine or could not locate modules.

THE REQUEST MACROS: GET, PUT, ERASE

The VSAM request macros are GET, PUT, ERASE, POINT, and ENDREQ. For each of these, VSAM sets register 15 with a return code to indicate success or failure of the operation, as follows:

X'00'   Successful operation.

X'04'   Request not accepted because of an active request from another
         task on the same RPL.   End-of-file also causes this return code.

X'08'   A logical error; examine the specific error code in the RPL.

X'0C'   Uncorrectible I/O error; examine the specific error code in the
         RPL.

The GET Macro

GET retrieves a record from a data set.   The operand specifies the address of an
RPL that defines the data set being processed.   The entry may either (1) cite the
address by name or (2) use register notation, any register 2–12, in parentheses.
You may use register 1; its use is more efficient, but GET does not preserve its
address.

```
1. GET   RPL=RPLname
2. LA    reg,RPLname
   GET   RPL=(reg)
```

The RPL macro provides the address of your workarea where GET is to
deliver an input record.   Register 13 must contain the address of a savearea defined
as 18 fullwords.

Under sequential input, GET delivers the next record in the data set.   The
OPTCD entry in the RPL macro would appear, for example, as
OPTCD=(KEY,SEQ) or OPTCD=(ADR,SEQ).   You have to provide for end-
of-file by means of an EXLST operand in the associated ACB macro; see Fig. 19-
4 for an example.

For nonsequential accessing, GET delivers the record that the key or relative
record number specifies in the search argument field.   The OPTCD entry in the
RPL macro would appear, for example, as OPTCD=(KEY,SKP) or
OPTCD=(KEY,DIR), or as an RBA in the search argument field, as
OPTCD=(ADR,DIR).

You also use GET to update or delete a record.

The PUT Macro

PUT writes or rewrites a record in a data set.   The operand of PUT specifies the
address of an RPL that defines the data set being processed.   The entry may either
(1) cite the address by name or (2) use register notation, any register 2–12, in
parentheses.   You may use register 1; its use is more efficient, but PUT does not
preserve its address.

```
1. PUT   RPL=RPLname
2. LA    reg,RPLname
   PUT   RPL=(reg)
```

The RPL macro provides the address of your workarea containing the record that PUT is to add or update in the data set. Register 13 must contain the address of a savearea defined as 18 fullwords.

To create (load) or extend a data set, use sequential output. The OPTCD entry in the RPL macro would appear, for example, as OPTCD = (SEQ or SKP). SKP means "skip sequential" and enables you to start writing at any specific record.

For writing a KSDS or RRDS, if OPTCD contains any of the following, PUT stores a new record in key sequence or relative record sequence:

```
OPTCD=(KEY,SKP,NUP)      Skip, no update
OPTCD=(KEY,DIR,NUP)      Direct, no update
OPTCD=(KEY,SEQ,NUP)      Sequential, no update
```

Note that VSAM does not allow you to change a key in a KSDS (delete the record and write a new one). To change a record, first GET it using OPTCD = UPD, change its contents (but not the key), and PUT it, also using OPTCD = UPD. To write a record in ESDS, use OPTCD = (ADR, . . .).

The ERASE Macro

The purpose of the ERASE macro is to delete a record from a KSDS or an RRDS. To locate an unwanted record, you must previously issue a GET with an RPL specifying OPTCD = (UPD. . .).

```
[label]   ERASE   RPL=address or =(register)
```

For ESDS, a common practice is to define a delete byte in the record. To "delete" a record, insert a special character such as X'FF'; all programs that process the data set should bypass all records containing the delete byte. You can occasionally rewrite the data set, dropping all deletes.

THE EXLST MACRO

If your ACB macro indicates an EXLST operand, code a related EXLST macro. EXLST provides an optional list of addresses for user exit routines that handle end-of-file and error analysis. All operands in the macro are optional.

[label]	EXLST	AM=VSAM, EODAD=address, LERAD=address, SYNAD=address	+ + +

When VSAM detects the coded condition, the program enters your exit routine. Register 13 must contain the address of your register savearea. For example, if you are reading sequentially, supply an end-of-data address (EODAD) in the EXLST macro—see the ACB for VSMFILIN in Fig. 19-4.

Here are explanations of the operands for EXLST:

VSAM Indicates a VSAM control block.

EODAD Supplies the address of your end-of-data routine. You may also read sequentially backward, and VSAM enters your routine when reading past the first record. The request return code for this condition is X'04'.

LERAD Indicates the address of the routine that analyzes logical errors that occurred during GET, PUT, POINT, and ERASE. The request return code for this condition is X'08'.

SYNAD Provides the address of your routine that analyzes physical I/O errors on GET, PUT, POINT, ERASE, and CLOSE. The request return code for this condition is X'0C'.

Other operands are EXCPAD and JRNAD.

THE SHOWCB MACRO

The original program in Fig. 19-4 contained an error that caused it to fail on a PUT operation. The use of the SHOWCB macro in the error routine for PUT (R30PUT) helped determine the actual cause of the error.

The purpose of SHOWCB is to display fields in an ACB, EXLST, or RPL. Code SHOWCB following a VSAM macro where you want to identify errors that VSAM has detected. The SHOWCB in the PUT error routine in Fig. 19-4 is as follows:

```
        SHOWCB  RPL=RPLISTOT,AREA=FDBKWD,FIELDS=(FDBK),LENGTH=4
        ...
FDBKWD  DC      F'0'
```

AREA Designates the name of a fullword where VSAM is to place an error code.

FIELDS Tells SHOWCB the type of display; the keyword FDBK (feedback) causes a display of error codes for request macros.

LENGTH Provides the length of the area in bytes.

On a failed request, VSAM stores the error code in the rightmost byte of the fullword area. These are some common error codes:

08 Attempt to store a record with a duplicate key.

0C Out-of-sequence or duplicate record for KSDS or RRDS.

10   No record located on retrieval.

1C   No space available to store a record.

Your program can test for the type of error and display a message. For nonfatal errors, it could continue processing; for fatal errors, it could terminate.

The original error in Fig. 19-4 was caused by the fact that the RPL macro RPLISTOT did not contain an entry for RECLEN; the program terminated on the first PUT error, with register 15 containing X'08' (a "logical error"). Insertion of the SHOWCB macro in the next run revealed the cause of the error in FDBKWD: 00006C. Appendix K of the IBM Supervisor manual explains the error (in part) as follows: "The RECLEN value specified in the RPL macro was [either] larger than the allowed maximum [or] equal to zero. . . ." Coding a RECLEN operand in the RPL macro solved the problem, and the program then executed through to normal termination. One added point: Technically, after each SHOWCB, you should test register 15 for a successful or failed operation.

SAMPLE PROGRAM: LOADING A KEY-SEQUENCED DATA SET

The program in Fig. 19-4 reads records from the system reader and sequentially creates a key-sequenced data set. A DEFINE CLUSTER command has allocated space for this data set as INDEXED (KSDS), with three tracks, a 4-byte key starting in position 0, and an 80-byte record size. The program loads the entire data set and closes it on completion. For illustrative (but not practical) purposes, it reopens the data set and reads and prints each record.

The PUT macro that writes records into the data set is:

```
PUT RPL=RPLISTOT
```

RPLISTOT defines the name of the ACB macro (VSMFILOT), the address of the output record, and its length. Although the example simply duplicates the records into the data set, in practice you would probably define various fields and store numeric values as packed or binary.

The ACB macro defines VSMFILOT for keyed accessing, sequential processing, and output. The DDNAME, VSAMFIL, in this example relates to the name for the data set in the DLBL job control entry (DD under OS).

For reading the data set, the GET macro is

```
GET RPL=RPLISTIN
```

RPLISTIN defines the name of the ACB macro (VSMFILIN), the address in which GET is to read an input record, and the record length.

The ACB macro defines VSMFILIN for keyed access, sequential processing, and input. The DDNAME, VSAMFIL, relates to the name for the data set in

```
IDCAMS   SYSTEM SERVICES

    DELETE (VSAMFIL.ABEL) CLUSTER PURGE
IDC0550I ENTRY (C) VSAMFIL.ABEL DELETED
IDC0550I ENTRY (D) VSAMFIL.DATA DELETED
IDC0550I ENTRY (I) VSAMFIL.INDEX DELETED
IDC0001I FUNCTION COMPLETED, HIGHEST CONDITION CODE WAS 0

    DEFINE CLUSTER (NAME(VSAMFIL.ABEL) -
                   TRACKS(3) -
                   VOLUME(SVSE03) -
                   INDEXED -
                   KEYS(4 0) -
                   RECORDSIZE(80 80) ) -
            DATA (NAME(VSAMFIL.DATA) ) -
            INDEX (NAME(VSAMFIL.INDEX) )

IDC0001I FUNCTION COMPLETED, HIGHEST CONDITION CODE WAS 0

IDC0002I IDCAMS PROCESSING COMPLETE. MAXIMUM CONDITION CODE WAS 0

// OPTION LINK,PARTDUMP,NOXREF,LOG
   ACTION NOMAP
// EXEC ASSEMBLY,SIZE=256K

    3              PRINT NOGEN,NODATA
    4 *                   M A I N   P R O C E S S I N G
    5 *                   ----------------------------
    6 PROGVSM   START
    7              BALR  12,0                      INITIALIZE
    8              USING *,12                        BASE REG &
    9              LA    13,VSAMSAVE                 VSAM SAVEAREA
   10              OPEN  FILEIN,VSMFILOT
   19              LTR   15,15                     SUCCESSFUL OPEN?
   20              BNZ   R10OPEN                     NO - TERMINATE
   21              GET   FILEIN,VSMREC             READ 1ST RECORD
   28 A10LOOP   BAL   6,B10LOAD                  CREATE FILE
   29              GET   FILEIN,VSMREC             READ NEXT
   35              B     A10LOOP

   37 A80EOF    CLOSE FILEIN,VSMFILOT
   46              LA    13,VSAMSAVE
   47              OPEN  FILEPRT,VSMFILIN
   56              LTR   15,15                     SUCCESSFUL OPEN?
   57              BNZ   R10OPEN                     NO -- TERMINATE
   58              BAL   6,C10PRINT                READ & PRINT VSAM FILE
   60 A90EOF    CLOSE FILEPRT,VSMFILOT
   69              EOJ                             NORMAL TERMINATION

   73 *                   L O A D   V S A M   F I L E
   74 *                   -------------------------
   75 B10LOAD   PUT   RPL=RPLISTOT               WRITE VSAM RECORD
   82              LTR   15,15                     SUCCESSFUL WRITE?
   83              BNZ   R30PUT                      NO --ERROR
   84              BR    6                         RETURN

   86 *                   R E A D   &   P R I N T   V S A M   F I L E
   87 *                   ---------------------------------------
   88 C10PRINT  GET   RPL=RPLISTIN
   95              LTR   15,15                     SUCCESSFUL READ?
   96              BNZ   R40GET                      NO - TERMINATE
```

Figure 19-4 Loading a key-sequenced data set.

```
 97           MVC    PRREC,VSMREC
 98           PUT    FILEPRT,PRINT                PRINT RECORD
104           B      C10PRINT

106 *                E R R O R   R O U T I N E S
107 *                -------------------------
108 R10OPEN  MVI    ERRCDE,C'O'                  OPEN ERROR
109          B      R90DUMP
110 R30PUT   MVI    ERRCDE,C'P'                  PUT ERROR
111          ST     15,SAVE15
112          SHOWCB RPL=RPLISTOT,AREA=FDBKWD,FIELDS=(FDBK),LENGTH=4
164          CLOSE  FILEIN,VSMFILOT
173          B      R90DUMP
174 R40GET   MVI    ERRCDE,C'G'                  GET ERROR
175          ST     15,SAVE15
176          SHOWCB RPL=RPLISTIN,AREA=FDBKWD,FIELDS=(FDBK),LENGTH=4
228          CLOSE  FILEPRT,VSMFILOT
237 R90DUMP  EQU    *
238          PDUMP  ERRCDE,PRINT+133
244          EOJ                                 ABNORMAL TERMINATION

248 *                -------------------------
249 *                D E C L A R A T I V E S
250 *                -------------------------
252 FILEIN   DEFIN  A80EOF                       DEFINE INPUT FILE
278 FILEPRT  DEFPR                               DEFINE PRINTER FILE
308 VSMFILOT ACB    DDNAME=VSAMFIL,              DEFINE VSAM O/P FILE    +
                    MACRF=(KEY,SEQ,OUT)

341 RPLISTOT RPL    ACB=VSMFILOT,                RPL FOR VSMFILOT        +
                    AREA=VSMREC,                                         +
                    AREALEN=80,                                          +
                    RECLEN=80,                                           +
                    OPTCD=(KEY,SEQ,NUP)

371 VSMFILIN ACB    DDNAME=VSAMFIL,              DEFINE VSAM I/P FILE    +
                    MACRF=(KEY,SEQ,IN),                                  +
                    EXLST=EOFDCB

404 EOFDCB   EXLST  EODAD=A90EOF                 EOF EXIT FOR VSAM I/P
416 RPLISTIN RPL    ACB=VSMFILIN,                RPL FOR VSMFILIN        +
                    AREA=VSMREC,                                         +
                    AREALEN=80,                                          +
                    OPTCD=(KEY,SEQ,NUP)

446 VSAMSAVE DS     18F                          VSAM SAVEAREA
447 ERRCDE   DC     X'00'                        ERROR CODE
448 SAVE15   DS     F
449 FDBKWD   DC     F'0'
450 VSMREC   DS     0CL80                        INPUT/OUTPUT RECORD
451 RECKEY   DS     CL04                         *
452          DS     CL76                         *

454 PRINT    DS     0CL133                       PRINT RECORD
455          DC     X'09'                        *
456 PRREC    DC     CL80' '                      *
457          DC     CL52' '                      *
458          LTORG
459                 =C'$$BOPEN '
460                 =C'$$BCLOSE'
461                 =CL8'IKQVTMS'
```

Figure 19-4 (continued)

```
462                     =CL8'$$BPDUMP'
463                     =A(ERRCDE,PRINT+133)
464                     =A(FILEIN)
465                     =A(VSMREC)
466                     =A(RPLISTOT)
467                     =A(RPLISTIN)
468                     =A(FILEPRT)
469                     =A(PRINT)
470           END       PROGVSM


// EXEC LNKEDT,SIZE=128K

// DLBL VSAMFIL,'VSAMFIL.ABEL',,VSAM
// EXTENT SYS008,SVSE03
// ASSGN SYS008,X'303'
// EXEC ,SIZE=128K

Output:-

   0034AES PROCESSORS              (Output from
   0047MICROTEL INDUSTRIES          printing contents
   0065ACE ELECTRONICS              of loaded data set)
```

Figure 19-4   (continued)

the DLBL job control entry.   Note that there is an ACB and RPL macro for both
input and output, but both ACB macros specify the same DDNAME: VSAMFIL.

Error routines are for failures on OPEN, GET, and PUT.   These rather
primitive routines supply an error code and the contents of the declaratives; in
practice, you may want to enlarge these routines.   If you fail to provide error
routines, your program may crash with no clear cause.

During testing, you may have changed the contents of a VSAM data set and
now want to reload (re-create) the original data set.   Except for updating with
new keys, VSAM does not permit overwriting records in a data set.   You have to
use IDCAMS to DELETE and again DEFINE the data set as follows:

```
          DELETE(data-set-name) CLUSTER PURGE ...
          DEFINE CLUSTER(NAME(data-set-name) -
          ...
```

Loading an ESDS

To convert the program in Fig. 19-4 from KSDS to ESDS, change DEFINE CLUS-
TER from INDEXED to NONINDEXED and delete the KEYS and INDEX
entries.   Change the ACB MACRF from KEY to ADR, and change the RPL
OPTCD from KEY to ADR—that's all.

KEYED DIRECT RETRIEVAL

Key-sequenced data sets provide for both sequential and direct processing by key.
For direct processing, you must supply VSAM with the key of the record to be
accessed.   If you use a key to access a record directly, it must be the same length

as the keys in the data set (as indicated in the KEYS operand of DEFINE CLUS-
TER), and the key must actually exist in the data set.   For example, if you request
a record with key 0028 and there is no such record, VSAM returns an error code
in register 15.

Using the data set in Fig. 19-4, assume that a program is to access records
directly.   A user enters record key numbers via a terminal, and the program is to
display the record on the screen.   In this partial example, the RPL macro specifies
the name (ARG) of the key to be in a 4-byte field named KEYFLD.   These are
the specific coding requirements for the ACB, RPL, and GET macros:

```
VSMFILE   ACB   DDNAME=name,                        +
                MACRF=(KEY,DIR,IN)

RPLIST    RPL   ACB=VSMFILE,                         +
                AREA=DCBREC,                         +
                AREALEN=80,                          +
                ARG=KEYFLD,                          +
                OPTCD=(KEY,DIR,NUP)
KEYFLD    DS    CL4
DCBREC    DS    CL80
          ...
          [Accept a key number from the terminal]
          MVC   KEYFLD,keyno
          GET   RPL=RPLIST
          LTR   15,15
          BNZ   error
          [Display the record on the screen]
```

For updating a KSDS record, change the MACRF from IN to OUT, and
change the OPTCD from NUP to UPD.   GET the record, make the required
changes to it (but not the key!), and PUT the record using the same RPL.

SORTING VSAM FILES

You can sort VSAM records into either ascending or descending sequence.   You
must first use DEFINE CLUSTER to allocate a vacant data set (NONINDEXED)
for SORT to write the sorted data set.   Here is a typical SORT specification:

```
// EXEC SORT,SIZE=256K
     SORT FIELDS=(1,4,CH,A,9,4,PD,D)
     RECORD TYPE=F,LENGTH=(150)
     INPFIL VSAM
     OUTFIL ESDS
     END
/*
```

SORT causes the SORT program to load into storage and begin execution.

SORT FIELDS defines the fields to be sorted, indicated by major control to minor, from left to right. In this example, the major sort field begins in position 1 (the first position), is 4 bytes long, is in character (CH) format, and is to be sorted in ascending (A) sequence. The minor sort field begins in position 9, is 4 bytes long, is in packed (PD) format, and is to be sorted in descending (D) sequence. The example could be a sort of departments in ascending sequence, and within each department are employee salaries in descending sequence.

RECORD TYPE indicates fixed (F) length and record length (150 bytes).

INPFIL informs SORT that the input file is VSAM; SORT can determine the type of data set from the VSAM catalog.

OUTFIL defines the type of output file, in this case entry-sequenced. This entry should match the DEFINE CLUSTER for this data set, NONIN-DEXED.

Job control commands for SORTIN and SORTOUT provide the names of the data sets. Since job control varies by operating system and by installation requirements, check with your installation before attempting the SORT utility.

VSAM UTILITY PRINT

IDCAMS furnishes a convenient utility program named PRINT that can print the contents of a VSAM, SAM, or ISAM data set. The following provides the steps for OS and for DOS:

```
OS:     //STEP EXEC PGM=IDCAMS
           PRINT INFILE(filename) CHARACTER or HEX or DUMP
        /*
DOS:    // EXEC IDCAMS,SIZE=256K
           PRINT INFILE(filename) CHARACTER or HEX or DUMP
        /*
```

The options for PRINT indicate the format of the printout, in character, hexa-decimal, or both (DUMP prints hex on the left and character format on the right).

INFILE(filename) matches the name in the OS DD or DOS DLBL job statement with any valid filename as long as the two are identical. The DD or DLBL statement notifies VSAM which data set is to print.

PRINT lists KSDS and ISAM data sets in key sequence and lists ESDS, RRDS, and SAM data sets in physical sequence. You can also print beginning and ending at a specific record.

KEY POINTS

- A key-sequenced data set (KSDS) maintains records in sequence of key, such as employee or part number, and is equivalent to indexed sequential access method.

- An entry-sequenced data set (ESDS) maintains records in the sequence in which they were initially entered and is equivalent to sequential organization.

- A relative-record data set (RRDS) maintains records in order of relative record number and is equivalent to direct file organization.

- For the three types of data sets, VSAM stores records in groups (one or more) of control intervals. At the end of each control interval is control information that describes the data records.

- Before physically writing (loading) records in a VSAM data set, you must first catalog its structure. Access method services (AMS) enables you to furnish VSAM with such details about the data set as its name, organization type, record length, key location, and password (if any).

- VSAM furnishes two types of accessing, keyed and addressed, and three types of processing, sequential, direct, and skip sequential.

- The most common errors in processing VSAM data sets occur because of the need to match definitions in the program, job control, and the cataloged VSAM data set.

- The data-set-name in job control (such as CUSTOMER.INQUIRY) must agree with the NAME(data-set-name) entry in DEFINE CLUSTER. This name is the only one by which VSAM recognizes the data set. VSAM relates the ACB DDNAME in the program to the job control name and the job control name to the data-set-name.

- If a data set is cataloged as KSDS, ESDS, or RRDS, each program must access it accordingly.

- For KSDS, the length and starting position of the key in a record must agree with the KEYS entry in DEFINE CLUSTER and, for direct input, with the defined ARG in the OPTCD.

- Every program that references the data set defines the fields with identical formats and lengths in the same positions; the actual field names need not be identical. You may define as character any input field in a record that the program does not reference. The simplest practice is to catalog all record definitions in the assembler source library and COPY the definition into the program during assembly.

- After each OPEN, CLOSE, GET, PUT, and SHOWCB, test register 15 for success or failure, and use SHOWCB (as well as TESTCB) as a debugging aid.

PROBLEMS

19-1. What are the three types of VSAM data sets, and how do they differ?

19-2. Explain control interval, control interval split, and RBA.

19-3. Assume a KSDS that contains records with keys in two control areas as follows:

Control area 1:	360, 373, 385
	390, 412, 415
Control area 2:	420, 475, 480
	512, 590, 595

What are the contents of (a) the two sequence sets; (b) the index set?

19-4. What is the program that catalogs the structure of a VSAM data set, and what are its three component levels?

19-5. Code DEFINE CLUSTER for the data-set-name CUSTOMER.FILE, assuming 20 blocks, ESDS, and 100-byte records.

19-6. Code job control (OS DD and DOS DLBL) for the data set in Problem 19-5 with filename CUSTVS.

19-7. Code the ACB macro named CUSVSIN for the data set in Problem 19-6 for addressed sequential input and an EXLST macro named EOFCUS for end-of-file.

19-8. Code the RPL macro named RPLCUSIN for the ACB in Problem 19-7 with an input area named CUSVSREC.

19-9. Code the GET macro to read the data set in Problem 19-8.

19-10. Write a program that creates a KSDS supplier file from the following input records:

```
01-05    Supplier number
06-25    Supplier name
26-46    Street
47-67    City
68-74    Amount payable
75-80    Date of last purchase (yymmdd)
```

Store the amount payable in packed format.

20

INDEXED SEQUENTIAL
ACCESS METHOD
(ISAM)

OBJECTIVE

To explain the design of indexed sequential access
method and its processing requirements.

Indexed sequential access method (ISAM) is available in many variations on microcomputers, minicomputers, and mainframes, although the preferred method under DOS/VS and OS/VS is the newer VSAM.

A significant way in which ISAM (and other nonsequential file organization methods) differs from sequential organization is that the record keys in an indexed file must be unique; this is a system requirement, not just a programming practice. Consequently, an indexed file is typically a master file. Also, there is a clear difference between updating a sequential file and updating an indexed file. When you update a sequential file, you rewrite the entire file; this practice leaves the original file as a convenient backup in case the job must be rerun. When you update an indexed file, the system rewrites records in the file directly in place, thereby providing no automatic backup file. To create a backup, you periodically copy the file onto another device.

The flexibility of indexed sequential access method is realized at some cost

506

in both storage space and accessing time. First, the system requires various levels of indexes to help locate records in the file. Second, the system stores new, added records in special reserved overflow areas.

Check that your system supports ISAM before attempting to use it.

CHARACTERISTICS OF INDEXED SEQUENTIAL FILES

ISAM initially stores records sequentially and permits both sequential and random processing. The features that provide this flexibility are indexes to locate a correct cylinder and track and keys to locate a record on a track.

Keys

A key is a record control field such as customer number or stock number. Records in an indexed file are in sequence by key to permit sequential processing and to aid in locating records randomly, and blocks are formatted with keys. That is, ISAM writes each block immediately preceded by the highest key within the block, namely, the key of the last or only record in the block. The key is usually also embedded within each data record, as normal.

Unblocked Records

This is the layout of keys for unblocked records:

key 201	record 201	key 205	record 205	key 206	record 206

The records could represent, for example, customer numbers, and the keys could be for customer numbers 201, 205, and 206. In this example, the key is 3 characters long and the data record is the conventional size. Under unblocked format, a key precedes each block containing one record.

Blocked Records

This is the layout of keys for blocked records based on the preceding unblocked example:

key 206	record 201	record 205	record 206

Under blocked format, the key for the last record in the block, 206, precedes the block.

ISAM automatically handles this use of keys, and when you perform a read operation, the system delivers the block, not the separate key, to main storage.

Indexes

To facilitate locating records randomly, ISAM maintains three levels of indexes on disk: track index, cylinder index, and an optional master index.

Track index.　When ISAM creates a file, it stores a track index in track 0 of each cylinder that the file uses.　The track index contains the highest key number for each track on the cylinder.　For example, if track 4 on cylinder 12 contains records with keys 201, 205, 206, and 208, the track index contains an entry for key 208 and a reference to cylinder 12, track 4.　If a disk device has ten tracks per cylinder, there are ten key entries for each track index, in ascending sequence.

Cylinder index.　When ISAM creates a file, it stores a cylinder index on a separate cylinder containing the highest key for each cylinder.　For example, if the file is stored on six cylinders, the cylinder index contains six entries.

Master index.　An optional master index facilitates locating an appropriate cylinder index.　This index is recommended if the entries in the cylinder index exceed four cylinders—a very large file.

PROCESSING AN INDEXED FILE

Consider a small indexed file containing 14 records on cylinder 5, with tracks 1 and 2 containing five records and track 3 containing four.　This area is known as the *prime data area*.　Track 1, for example, contains records with keys 205, 206, 208, 210, and 213.　Assume that records are suitably blocked.

TRACK	DATA RECORDS ON CYLINDER 5
1	205　206　208　210　213
2	214　219　220　222　225
3	226　227　230　236　unused

Track 0 of cylinder 5 contains the track index, with an entry indicating the high key for each track.　The track index entries specify that the highest keys on cylinder 5, tracks 1, 2, and 3 are 213, 225, and 236, respectively:

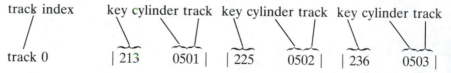

The cylinder index contains an entry for each cylinder that contains data, indicating the high key for each cylinder.   In this case, the only index entry is key 236 on cylinder 5 (the track number is not important in this index):

key   cylinder

Cylinder index | 236 0500 |

As an example of processing, a program has to locate randomly a record with key 227.   The read statement directs the system to perform the following steps:

1. Check the cylinder index (assuming no master index), comparing key 227 against its first entry, 236.   Since 227 is lower, the required record should be on cylinder 5.
2. Access the track index in cylinder 5, track 0, comparing key 227 successively against each entry: 213 (high), 225 (high), and 236 (low).   According to the entry for 236, the required record should be on cylinder 5, track 3.
3. Check the keys on track 3; find key 227 and deliver the record to the program's input area.   If the key and the record do not exist, ISAM signals an error.

As you can see, locating a record randomly involves a number of additional processing steps, although little extra programming effort is required.   Even more processing steps are involved if a new record has to be added.   If ISAM has to insert the record within the file, it may have to "bump" a record into an overflow area.

Overflow Areas

When a program first creates a file, ISAM stores the records sequentially in a prime data area.   If you subsequently add a new record, ISAM stores it in an overflow area and maintains links to point to it.

There are two types of overflow areas: cylinder and independent:

1. For a *cylinder overflow area*, each cylinder has its own overflow track area. ISAM reserves tracks on the same cylinder as the prime data for all of its overflow records stored on a specific cylinder.   The advantage of cylinder overflow is that less disk seek time is required to locate records on a different cylinder.   The disadvantage is an uneven distribution of overflow records: Some of the overflow cylinders may contain many records, whereas other overflow cylinders may contain few or none.
2. For an *independent overflow area*, ISAM reserves a number of separate cylinders for all overflow records in the file.   The advantage is that the distribution of overflow records is unimportant.   The disadvantage is in the additional access time to locate records in the overflow area.

A system may adopt both types: the cylinder overflow area for initial overflows and the independent overflow area in case cylinder overflow areas overflow.

In our most recent example, adding a record with key 209 causes ISAM to bump record 213 from track 1 into an overflow area, move 210 in its place, and insert 209 in the place vacated by 210. The following assumes a cylinder overflow area in track 9:

TRACK	DATA RECORDS ON CYLINDER 5	
1	205 206 208 209 210	prime data area
2	214 219 220 222 225	
3	226 227 230 236 unused	
...		
9	213	overflow area

The track index now becomes 210, with a pointer (not shown) to key 213 in the overflow area:

	key cylinder track	key cylinder track	key cylinder track
track index	| 210 0501 |	| 225 0502 |	| 236 0503 |

Reorganizing an Indexed File

Because a large number of records in overflow areas cause inefficient processing, an installation can use a program periodically to rewrite or reorganize the file. The program simply reads the records sequentially and writes them into another disk area. ISAM automatically follows its indexes for the input file and delivers the records sequentially from the prime and overflow areas. It stores all the output records sequentially in the new prime data area and automatically creates new indexes. At this time, the program may drop records coded for deletion.

PROCESSING DOS INDEXED SEQUENTIAL FILES

Since ISAM automatically handles indexes and overflow areas, little added programming effort is involved in the use of indexed files. There are four approaches to processing:

1. *Load or Extend.* The initial creation of an ISAM file is known as loading. Once a file is loaded, you may extend it by storing higher-key records at the end of the file.
2. *Adding Records.* New records have keys that do not currently exist on the file. You have to insert or add these records within the file.

3. *Random Retrieval.* To update an ISAM file with data (such as sales and payments on customer records), you use the key to locate the master record randomly and rewrite the updated record.

4. *Sequential Processing.* If you have many records to update and the new transactions are in sequence, you can sequentially read, change, and rewrite the ISAM master.

Load or Extend a DOS ISAM File

Loading a file creates it for the first time, and extending involves storing records at the end. Input records must be in ascending sequence by a predetermined key, and all keys must be unique. For load and extend, you code the usual OPEN and CLOSE to activate and deactivate the file. Figure 20-1 uses sequential input records to load an ISAM file named DISKIS. The new macros for this purpose are SETFL, WRITE, ENDFL, and DTFIS.

Name	Operation	Operand
[label]	SETFL	filename
[label]	WRITE	filename,NEWKEY
[label]	ENDFL	filename

Let's examine the imperative macros and the DTFIS file definition macro.

SETFL (set file load mode). SETFL initializes an ISAM file by preformatting the last track of each track index. The operand references the DTFIS name of the ISAM file to be loaded. In Fig. 20-1, SETFL immediately follows the OPEN macro.

WRITE. The WRITE macro loads a record into the ISAM file. Operand 1 is your DTFIS filename, and operand 2 is the word NEWKEY. You store the key and data area in a workarea (named ISAMOUT in Fig. 20-1). DTFIS knows this area through the entry WORKL = ISAMOUT. For the WRITE statement, ISAM checks that the new key is in ascending sequence. ISAM then transfers the key and data area to an I/O area (named IOARISAM in the figure and known to DTFIS by IOAREAL = IOARISAM). Here ISAM constructs the count area:

WORKL = ISAMOUT: | key | data |

IOAREAL = IOARISAM: | count | key | data |

ENDFL (end file load mode). After all records are written and before the CLOSE, ENDFL writes the last data block (if any), an end-of-file record, and any required index entries.

```
 1              PRINT ON,NODATA,NOGEN
 2 PROG20A     START
 3             BALR  3,0
 4             USING *,3
 5             OPEN  DISKSD,DISKIS
14             SETFL DISKIS                  SET ISAM LIMITS
20             TM    DISKISC,B'10011000'     ANY SETFL ERRORS?
21             BO    R10ERR                       YES - ERROR ROUTINE
22             GET   DISKSD,SDISKIN          GET 1ST SEQ'L RECORD

29 *                 M A I N   P R O C E S S I N G
30 A10LOOP     MVC   ISKEYNO,ACCTIN          SET UP KEY NUMBER
31             MVC   ISRECORD,SDISKIN        SET UP ISAM DISK RECORD
32             WRITE DISKIS,NEWKEY           WRITE ISAM RECORD
37             TM    DISKISC,B'11111110'     ANY WRITE ERRORS?
38             BO    R10ERR                       YES - ERROR ROUTINE
39             GET   DISKSD,SDISKIN          GET NEXT SEQ'L RECORD
45             B     A10LOOP                      NO  - CONTINUE

47 *                 E N D - O F - F I L E
48 A90END      ENDFL DISKIS                  END ISAM FILE LIMITS
60             TM    DISKISC,B'11000001'     ANY ENDFL ERRORS?
61             BO    R10ERR                       YES - ERROR ROUTINE
62             CLOSE DISKSD,DISKIS           NORMAL TERMINATION
71             EOJ

75 *                 D I S K   E R R O R   R O U T I N E S
76 R10ERR      EQU   *                       DISK ERROR
77 *             .                           RECOVERY ROUTINES
78 *             .
79             CLOSE DISKSD,DISKIS           ABNORMAL TERMINATION
88             EOJ

92 *                 D E C L A R A T I V E S
93 DISKSD      DTFSD BLKSIZE=360,            SEQUENTIAL DISK INPUT    +
                     DEVADDR=SYS015,                                  +
                     EOFADDR=A90END,                                  +
                     DEVICE=3340,                                     +
                     IOAREA1=IOARSD1,                                 +
                     RECFORM=FIXBLK,                                  +
                     RECSIZE=90,                                      +
                     TYPEFLE=INPUT,                                   +
                     WORKA=YES
154 IOARSD1    DS    CL360                   SEQ'L DISK BUFFER-1

156 SDISKIN    DS    0CL90                   SEQ'L DISK INPUT AREA
157 ACCTIN     DS    CL06                    *     KEY
158            DS    CL84                    *     REST OF RECORD

160 DISKIS     DTFIS CYLOFL=1,               INDEXED SEQ'L LOAD       +
                     DEVICE=3340,                                     +
                     DSKXTNT=2,                                       +
                     IOAREAL=IOARISAM,                                +
                     IOROUT=LOAD,                                     +
                     KEYLEN=6,                                        +
                     KEYLOC=1,                                        +
                     NRECDS=3,                                        +
                     RECFORM=FIXBLK,                                  +
                     RECSIZE=90,                                      +
                     VERIFY=YES,                                      +
                     WORKL=ISAMOUT
209 IOARISAM   DS    CL284                   ISAM BUFFER AREA
```

Figure 20-1   Program: loading a DOS ISAM file.

```
211 ISAMOUT   DS    0CL96              ISAM WORKAREA
212 ISKEYNO   DS    CL06               *      KEY LOCATION
213 ISRECORD  DS    CL90               *      DATA AREA

215           LTORG
216                 =C'$$BOPEN '
217                 =C'$$BSETFL'
218                 =C'$$BENDFL'
219                 =C'$$BCLOSE'
220                 =A(DISKIS)
221                 =A(DISKSD)
222                 =A(SDISKIN)
223           END   PROG20A
```

Figure 20-1   (continued)

The DTFIS Macro

The maximum length for an ISAM filename is 7.   In Fig. 20-1, the DTFIS entries
for the file being loaded are as follows:

CYLOFL = 1 gives the number of tracks on each cylinder to be reserved for
each cylinder overflow area (if any).

DEVICE = 3340 is the disk device containing the prime data area or overflow
area.

DSKXTNT = 2 provides the number of extents that the file uses: one for each
data extent and one for each index area and independent overflow area extent.
The program in Fig. 20-1 has one extent for the prime data area and one for
the cylinder index.

IOAREAL = IOARISAM provides the name of the ISAM I/O load area.   The
symbolic name, IOARISAM, references the DS buffer area.   For loading
blocked records, you calculate the field length as

Count area (8) + key length (6) + block length (90 $\times$ 3) = 284

IOROUT = LOAD tells the assembler that the program is to load an ISAM
file.

KEYLEN = 6 gives the length of each record's key.

KEYLOC = 1 tells ISAM the starting location of the key in the record, where
1 is the first position.

NRECDS = 3 provides the number of records per block.

RECFORM = FIXBLK indicates fixed, blocked record format.

RECSIZE = 90 gives the length of each record.

VERIFY = YES tells the system to check the parity of each record as it is
written.

WORKL = ISAMOUT gives the name of your load workarea, which is a DS
defined elsewhere in the program.   For blocked records, you calculate the

field length as

$$\text{Key length (6)} + \text{data area } (90 \times 3) = 284$$

For unblocked records, you would calculate the field length as

Count area (8) + key length + "sequence link field" (10) + record length

Status Condition

On execution, ISAM macros may generate error conditions, which you may test. After each I/O operation, ISAM places its status in a one-byte field named filenameC. For example, if your DTFIS name is DISKIS, ISAM calls the status byte DISKISC. Following is a list of the 8 bits in filenameC that the system may set when loading an ISAM file:

BIT	LOAD STATUS ERROR CONDITION
0	Any uncorrectable disk error except wrong length record.
1	Wrong length record detected on output.
2	The prime data area is full.
3	SETFL has detected a full cylinder index.
4	SETFL has detected a full master index.
5	Duplicate record—the current key is the same as the one previously loaded.
6	Sequence error—the current key is lower than the one previously loaded.
7	The prime data area is full, and ENDFL has no place to store the end-of-file record.

The program in Fig. 20-1 uses TM operations to test DISKIS after execution of the macros SETFL, WRITE, and ENDFL. After SETFL, for example, TM tests whether bits 0, 3, and 4 are on. If any of the conditions exist, the program executes an error routine (not coded) where the program may isolate the error and issue an error message.

The job control commands also vary. First, the DLBL job entry for "codes" contains ISC, meaning indexed sequential create, and second, there is an EXTENT command for both the cylinder index and the data area.

Random Retrieval of an ISAM File

The main purpose of organizing a file as indexed sequential is to facilitate the random accessing of records. For this, there are a number of special coding requirements. The program in Fig. 20-2 randomly retrieves records in the file created in Fig. 20-1. The program reads a file of modification records in random sequence, with changes to the ISAM master file. For each modification record, the program uses the account number (key) to locate the correct ISAM record, corrects it, and then updates the record on the ISAM file.

ISAM macros for random retrieval. The new macros for random retrieval are

Name	Operation	Operand
[label]	READ	filename,KEY
[label]	WAITF	filename
[label]	WRITE	filename,KEY

READ causes ISAM to access a required record from the file. Operand 1 contains the DTFIS filename, and operand 2 contains the word KEY. You store the key in the field referenced by the DTFIS entry KEYARG. In Fig. 20-2, KEYARG = KEYNO. For each modification record processed, the program transfers the account key number to KEYNO.

WAITF allows completion of a READ or WRITE operation before another is attempted. Since a random retrieval reads and rewrites the same record, you must ensure that the operation is finished. Code WAITF anywhere following a READ or WRITE and preceding the next READ or WRITE.

```
 1             PRINT ON,NODATA,NOGEN
 3 PROG20B    START
 4            BALR  3,0
 5            USING *,3
 6            OPEN  FILEIN,DISKIS
15            GET   FILEIN,RECDIN          READ 1ST INPUT RECORD

22 *               M A I N   P R O C E S S I N G
23 A10LOOP   MVC   ISKEYNO,ACCTIN         SET UP KEY NUMBER
24           READ  DISKIS,KEY             READ ISAM RANDOMLY
29           TM    DISKISC,B'11010101'    ANY READ ERROR?
30           BO    R10ERR                     YES - ERROR ROUTINE
31           WAITF DISKIS                 COMPLETE READ OPERATION
36           MVC   ACCTDKO,ACCTIN         MOVE FIELDS
37           MVC   NAMEDKO,NAMEIN         *   TO DISK
38           MVC   ADDRDKO,ADDRIN         *   WORKAREA
39           PACK  BALNDKO,BALNIN         *
40           MVC   DATEDKO,DATEIN         *
42           WRITE DISKIS,KEY             WRITE NEW ISAM RECORD
47           TM    DISKISC,B'11000000'    ANY WRITE ERROR?
48           BO    R10ERR                 *   YES - ERROR ROUTINE
49           GET   FILEIN,RECDIN          READ NEXT INPUT RECORD
55           B     A10LOOP                *   NO  - CONTINUE
```

Figure 20-2 Program: random retrieval of a DOS ISAM file.

```
57 *                    E N D - O F - F I L E
58 A90END    CLOSE FILEIN,DISKIS              TERMINATION
67           EOJ

71 *                    D I S K   E R R O R   R O U T I N E S
72 R10ERR    EQU   *                          DISK ERROR
73 *          .                                RECOVERY ROUTINES
74           B     A90END

76 *                    D E C L A R A T I V E S
77 FILEIN    DTFCD DEVADDR=SYSIPT,             INPUT FILE               +
                   IOAREA1=IOARIN1,                                     +
                   BLKSIZE=80,                                          +
                   DEVICE=2540,                                         +
                   EOFADDR=A90END,                                      +
                   TYPEFLE=INPUT,                                       +
                   WORKA=YES
101 IOARIN1  DS    CL80                        INPUT BUFFER 1

103 RECDIN   DS    0CL80                       INPUT AREA:
104 CODEIN   DS    CL02                        *   RECORD CODE '01'
105 ACCTIN   DS    CL06                        *   ACCOUNT NO.
106 NAMEIN   DS    CL20                        *   NAME
107 ADDRIN   DS    CL40                        *   ADDRESS
108 BALNIN   DS    ZL06'0000.00'               *   BALANCE
109 DATEIN   DS    CL06'DDMMYY'                *   DATE
```

```
111 DISKIS    DTFIS CYLOFL=1,                   ISAM RANDOM RETRIEVAL +
                    DEVICE=3340,                                       +
                    DSKXTNT=2,                                         +
                    IOAREAR=IOARISAM,                                  +
                    IOROUT=RETRVE,                                     +
                    KEYARG=ISKEYNO,                                    +
                    KEYLEN=6,                                          +
                    KEYLOC=1,                                          +
                    NRECDS=3,                                          +
                    RECFORM=FIXBLK,                                    +
                    RECSIZE=90,                                        +
                    TYPEFLE=RANDOM,                                    +
                    VERIFY=YES,                                        +
                    WORKR=ISAMOUT
193 IOARISAM DS    CL270                        ISAM BUFFER AREA
```

```
195 ISAMOUT  DS    0CL90                       ISAM WORKAREA:
196 ISKEYNO  DS    CL06                        *   KEY AREA
197 ACCTDKO  DS    CL06                        *   ACCOUNT NO.
198 NAMEDKO  DS    CL20                        *   NAME
199 ADDRDKO  DS    CL40                        *   ADDRESS
200 BALNDKO  DS    PL04                        *   BALANCE
201 DATEDKO  DS    CL06                        *   DATE
202          DC    CL14' '                     *   RESERVED

204          LTORG
205                =C'$$BOPEN '
206                =C'$$BCLOSE'
207                =A(FILEIN)
208                =A(RECDIN)
209                =A(DISKIS)
210          END   PROG20B
```

Figure 20-2   (continued)

WRITE rewrites an ISAM record. Operand 1 is the DTFIS filename, and operand 2 is the word KEY, which refers to your entry in KEYARG.

The DTFIS Macro

In Fig. 20-2, the DTFIS entries for the random retrieval include these:

IOAREAR = IOARISAM provides the name of the ISAM I/O retrieval area. The symbolic name, IOARISAM, references the DS retrieval area for un-blocked records. For blocked records, the buffer size is

Record length (including keys) × blocking factor

For unblocked records, the buffer size is:

Key length + "sequence link field" (10) + record length

TYPEFLE = RANDOM means that the system is to retrieve records randomly by key. Other entries are SEQNTL for sequential and RANSEQ for both random and sequential.

WORKR = ISAMOUT gives the name of your retrieval workarea.

Status Condition

The status byte for add and retrieve is different from load. Following is a list of the 8 bits in filenameC that the system may set:

BIT	ADD AND RETRIEVE STATUS CONDITION
0	Any uncorrectable disk error except wrong length record.
1	Wrong length record detected on an I/O operation.
2	End-of-file during sequential retrieval (not an error).
3	The requested record is not in the file.
4	The ID given to SETFL for SEQNTL is outside the prime data limits.
5	Duplicate record—an attempt to add a record that already exists in the file.
6	The cylinder overflow area is full.
7	A retrieval operation is trying to process an overflow record.

The program in Fig. 20-2 uses TM operations to test DISKIS after execution of the macros READ and WRITE. Once again, the program would isolate the error and issue an error message.

Sequential Reading of an ISAM File

Sequential reading of an ISAM file involves the use of the SETL, GET, and ESETL macros. SETL (Set Low) establishes the starting point of the first record to be processed. Its options include these:

- Set the starting point at the first record in the file:

```
SETL filename,BOF
```

- Set the starting point at the record with the key in the field defined by the DTFIS KEYARG entry:

```
SETL filename,KEY
```

- Set the starting point at the first record within a specified group. For example, the KEYARG field could contain "B480000" to indicate all records with key beginning with B48:

```
SETL filename,GKEY
```

The ESETL macro terminates sequential mode and is coded as ESETL, filename.

DTFIS entries include these:

IOAREAS = buffername for the name of the buffer area. You calculate the buffer size just as you do for random retrieval.

IOROUT = RETRVE to indicate sequential retrieval.

TYPEFLE = SEQNTL or **RANDOM** for sequential or random retrieval.

KEYLOC = n to indicate the first byte of the key in a record, if processing begins with a specified key or group of keys and records are blocked.

To delete a record, you may reserve a byte in the record and store a code in it. A practice is to use the first byte to match OS requirements. Subsequently, your program may test for the code when retrieving records and when reorganizing the file.

PROCESSING OS INDEXED SEQUENTIAL FILES

Processing ISAM files under OS is similar to DOS processing, except that QISAM (queued indexed sequential access method) is used for sequential processing and BISAM (basic indexed sequential access method) is used for random processing.

The Delete Flag

Under OS, the practice is to reserve the first byte of each record with a delete flag, defined with a blank when you create the file. You also code OPTCD = L in the DCB macro or the DD command. When you want to delete a record, store X'FF' in this byte. QISAM subsequently will not be able to retrieve the record. QISAM automatically drops the record when the file is reorganized.

Let's examine some features of OS ISAM processing.

Load an ISAM File

The OS imperative macros concerned with loading an ISAM file are the conventional OPEN, PUT, and CLOSE. DCB entries are as follows:

DDNAME	Name of the data set.
DSORG	IS for indexed sequential.
MACRF	(PM) for move mode or (PL) for locate mode.
BLKSIZE	Length of each block.
CYLOFL	Number of overflow tracks per cylinder.
KEYLEN	Length of the key area.
LRECL	Length of each record.
NTM	Number of tracks for the master index, if any.
OPTCD	Options required, such as MYLU in any sequence: M establishes a master index (or omit M). Y controls use of cylinder overflow areas. I controls use of an independent area. L is a delete flag to cause bypassing records with X'FF' in the first byte. U (for fixed length only) establishes the track index in main storage.
RECFM	Record format for fixed/variable and unblocked/blocked: F, FB, V, and VB.
RKP	Relative location of the first byte of the key field, where 0 is the first location. (For variable-length records, the value is 4 or greater.)

Sequential Retrieval and Update

Under OS, sequential retrieval and update involve the OPEN, SETL, GET, PUTX, ESETL, and CLOSE macros. Once the data set has been created with standard labels, many DCB entries are no longer required. DDNAME and DSORG=IS are still used, and the following entries are available:

MACRF=(entry)   The entries are
                       (GM) or (GL) for input
                       (PM) or (PL) for output
                       (GM,SK,PU) if read and rewrite in place, where
                       S is use of SETL, K is key or key class, and PU is
                       use of PUTX macro
EODAD=eofaddress   Used for input, if reading to end-of-file.
SYNAD=address   Requests optional error checking.

The SETL macro. SETL (Set Low address) establishes the first sequential record to be processed anywhere within the data set. The general format is the following:

Name	Operation	Operand
[label]	SETL	dcb-name,start-position,address

The start-position operand has the following options:

B   Begin with the first record in the data set. (Omit operand 3 for B or BD.)

K   Begin with the record with the key in the operand 3 address.

KC   Begin with the first record of the *key class* in operand 3. A key class is any group of keys beginning with a common value, such as all keys H48xxxx. If the first record is "deleted," begin with the first non-deleted record.

I   Begin with the record at the actual device address in operand 3.

BD, KD, KDH, KCD, and ID cause retrieval of only the data portion of a record.

Here are some examples of SETL to set the first record in a file named DISKIS, using a 6-character key:

• Begin with the first record in the data set:

                    SETL   DISKIS,B

• Begin with the record with the key 012644:

               SETL   DISKIS,K,KEYADD1

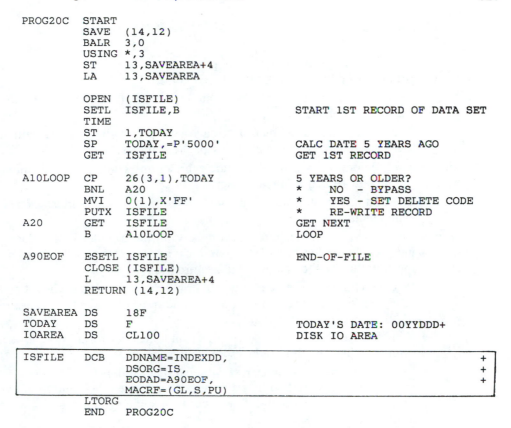

```
PROG20C    START
           SAVE    (14,12)
           BALR    3,0
           USING   *,3
           ST      13,SAVEAREA+4
           LA      13,SAVEAREA

           OPEN    (ISFILE)
           SETL    ISFILE,B              START 1ST RECORD OF DATA SET
           TIME
           ST      1,TODAY
           SP      TODAY,=P'5000'        CALC DATE 5 YEARS AGO
           GET     ISFILE                GET 1ST RECORD

A10LOOP    CP      26(3,1),TODAY         5 YEARS OR OLDER?
           BNL     A20                   *    NO  - BYPASS
           MVI     0(1),X'FF'            *    YES - SET DELETE CODE
           PUTX    ISFILE                *       RE-WRITE RECORD
A20        GET     ISFILE                GET NEXT
           B       A10LOOP               LOOP

A90EOF     ESETL   ISFILE                END-OF-FILE
           CLOSE   (ISFILE)
           L       13,SAVEAREA+4
           RETURN  (14,12)

SAVEAREA   DS      18F
TODAY      DS      F                     TODAY'S DATE: 00YYDDD+
IOAREA     DS      CL100                 DISK IO AREA

ISFILE     DCB     DDNAME=INDEXDD,                                    +
                   DSORG=IS,                                          +
                   EODAD=A90EOF,                                      +
                   MACRF=(GL,S,PU)
           LTORG
           END     PROG20C
```

Figure 20-3 Program: sequential retrieval of an OS ISAM file.

- Begin with the first record of the key class 012:

```
           SETL      DISKIS,KC,KEYADD2
           ...
KEYADD1    DC        C'012644'        6-character key
KEYADD2    DC        C'012',XL3'00'   3-character key class
```

The ESETL macro, used as ESETL dcb-name, terminates sequential retrieval. If there is more than one SETL, ESETL must precede each one.

The program in Fig. 20-3 reads an ISAM file sequentially and inserts a delete code in any record that is more than five years old. The TIME macro delivers the standard date from the communication region as packed 00yyddd+, and the date in the record (positions 26–28) is in the same format. The PUTX macro rewrites an obsolete record with a delete byte in the first position.

KEY POINTS

- The indexed system writes a key preceding each block of records. The key is that of the highest record in the block.
- The track index, cylinder index, and master index help the system locate records randomly.
- The track index is in track 0 of each cylinder of the file and contains the highest key number for each track of the cylinder.
- The cylinder index is on a separate cylinder and contains the key number of the highest record on the cylinder.
- The optional master index is recommended if the cylinder index exceeds four cylinders in size.
- The master index facilitates locating keys in the cylinder index, the cylinder index facilitates locating keys in the track index, and the track index facilitates locating the track containing the required record.
- ISAM creates a file sequentially in a prime data area. Subsequent additions of higher keys append to the end, and additions of lower keys cause records to bump into an overflow area.
- Cylinder overflow areas reserve tracks on a cylinder for all overflows in that cylinder. This method reduces disk access time.
- Independent overflow areas reserve separate cylinders for overflows from the entire file. This method helps if there is an uneven distribution of overflow records—that is, many overflow records in some cylinders and few or none in others.

PROBLEMS

20-1. What is the purpose of (a) the master index; (b) the cylinder index; (c) the track index?

20-2. An indexed file contains three records per block. For a block containing records with keys 542, 563, and 572, what is the key for the block?

20-3. An indexed file contains unblocked records on cylinder 8 beginning with track 1. Assuming four records per track, show the organization of the records on the tracks for keys 412, 413, 415, 417, 419, 420, 424, 425, 432, 433.

20-4. For the file in Problem 20-3, show the contents of (a) the track index; (b) the cylinder index.

20-5. For the file in Problem 20-3, show the records on the tracks if a program adds a record with key 422. Assume that track 20 handles overflow records.

20-6. What are the two overflow areas and their advantages and disadvantages? Under what circumstances would you recommend use of both types of overflow areas?

20-7. What is the normal procedure to remove records from an overflow area into proper sequence in the prime data area?

20-8. What is the common method for deleting records from an indexed file for (a) DOS; (b) OS?

20-9. What are the different ways to process an ISAM file? What is the difference between extending and adding records?

20-10. Write a program that creates an ISAM supplier file on disk from the following input records:

01-05	Supplier number
06-25	Supplier name
26-46	Street
47-67	City
68-74	Amount payable
75-80	Date of last purchase (yymmdd)

Store the amount payable in packed format.

21

OPERATING SYSTEMS

OBJECTIVE

To introduce basic operating systems for DOS and OS
and job control requirements.

This chapter introduces material that is suitable for more advanced assembler programming. The first section examines general operating systems and the various support programs. Subsequent sections explain the functions of the program status word and the interrupt system. Finally, there is a discussion of input/output channels, physical IOCS, and the input/output system.

These topics provide an introduction to systems programming and the relationship between the computer hardware and the manufacturer's software. A knowledge of these features can be a useful asset when serious bugs occur and when a solution requires an intimate knowledge of the system.

In an installation, one or more systems programmers, who are familiar with the computer architecture and assembler language, provide support for the operating system. Among the software that IBM supplies to support the system are language translators such as assembler, COBOL, and PL/I and utility programs for cataloging and sorting files.

OPERATING SYSTEMS

Operating systems were developed to minimize the need for operator intervention during the processing of programs. An operating system is a collection of related programs that provide for the preparation and execution of a user's programs. The system is stored on disk, and part of it, the supervisor program, is loaded into the lower part of main storage.

You submit job control commands to tell the system what action to perform. For example, you may want to assemble and execute a source program. To this end, you insert job control commands before and after the source program and submit it as a job to the system. In simple terms, the operating system performs the following steps:

1. Preceding the source program is a job control command that tells the operating system to assemble a program. The system loads the assembler program from a disk library into storage and transfers control to it for execution.

2. The assembler reads and translates the source program into an object program and stores it on disk.

3. Another job control command tells the system to link-edit the object program. The system loads the linkage editor from a disk library into storage and transfers control to it for execution.

4. The linkage editor reads and translates the object program, adds any required input/output modules, and stores it on disk as an executable module.

5. Another job control command tells the system to execute the executable module. The system loads the module into storage and transfers control to it for execution.

6. The program executes until normal or abnormal termination, when it returns processing control to the system.

7. A job command tells the system that this is the end of the job, since a job may consist of any number of execution steps. The system then terminates that job and prepares for the next job to be executed.

Throughout the processing, the system continually intervenes to handle all input/output, interrupts for program checks, and protecting the supervisor and any other programs executing in storage.

IBM provides various operating systems, depending on users' requirements, and they differ in services offered and the amount of storage they require. These are some major operating systems:

DOS	Disk Operating System	Medium-sized systems
DOS/VSE	Disk Operating System	Medium-sized systems with virtual storage
OS/VS1	Operating System	Large system

OS/VS2   Operating System   Large system
OS/MVS   Operating System   Large system

Systems Generation

The manufacturer typically supplies the operating system on reels of magnetic tape, along with an extensive set of supporting manuals. A systems programmer has to tailor the supplied operating system according to the installation's requirements, such as the number and type of disk drives, the number and type of terminals to be supported, the amount of processing time available to users, and the levels of security that are to prevail. This procedure is known as *systems generation*, abbreviated as *sysgen*.

Operating System Organization

Figure 21-1 shows the general organization of Disk Operating System (DOS), on which this text is largely based. The three main parts are the control program, system service programs, and processing programs.

Control Program

The control program, which controls all other programs being processed, consists of initial program load (IPL), the supervisor, and job control. Under OS, the functions are task management, data management, and job management.

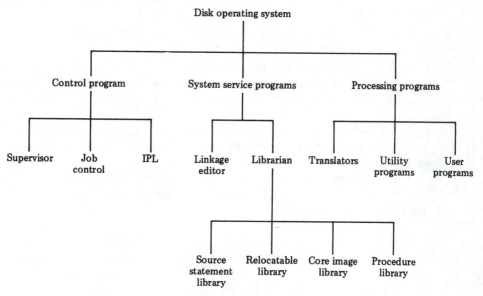

Figure 21-1   Disk operating system organization.

IPL is a program that the operator uses daily or whenever required to load the supervisor into storage. On some systems, this process is known as booting the system.

Job control handles the transition between jobs run on the system. Your job commands tell the system what action to perform next.

The supervisor, the nucleus of the operating system, resides in lower storage, beginning at location X'200'. The system loads user (problem) programs in storage following the supervisor area, resulting in at least two programs in storage: the supervisor program and one or more problem programs. Only one is executing at any time, but control passes between them.

The supervisor is concerned with handling interrupts for input/output devices, fetching required modules from the program library, and handling errors in program execution. An important part of the supervisor is the input/output control system (IOCS), known under OS as data management.

Figure 21-2 (not an exact representation) illustrates the general layout of the supervisor in main storage. Let's examine its contents.

1. *Communication Region.* This area contains the following data:

LOCATION	CONTENTS
00–07	The current date, as mm/dd/yy or dd/mm/yy
08–11	Reserved
12–22	User area, set to zero when a JOB command is read to provide communication within a job step or between job steps
23	User program status indicator (UPSI)
24–31	Job name, entered from job control
32–35	Address: highest byte of problem program area
36–39	Address: highest byte of current problem program phase
40–43	Address: highest byte of phase with highest ending address
44–45	Length of label area for problem program

2. *Channel Scheduler.* The channels provide a path between main storage

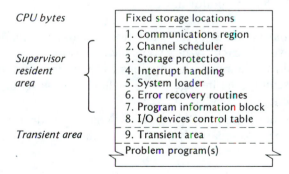

Figure 21-2 Supervisor areas.

and the input/output devices for all I/O interrupts and permit overlapping of program execution with I/O operations. If the requested channel, control unit, and device are available, the channel operation begins. If they are busy, the channel scheduler places its request in a queue and waits until the device is available. The channel notifies the scheduler when the I/O operation is complete or that an error has occurred.

3. *Storage Protection.* Storage protection prevents a problem program from erroneously moving data into the supervisor area and destroying it. Under a multiprogramming system, this feature also prevents a program in one partition from erasing a program in another partition.

4. *Interrupt Handling.* An interrupt is a signal that informs the system to interrupt the program that is currently executing and to transfer control to the appropriate supervisor routine. A later section on the program status word covers this topic in detail.

5. *System Loader.* The system loader is responsible for loading programs into main storage for execution.

6. *Error Recovery Routines.* A special routine handles error recovery for each I/O device or class of devices. When an error is sensed, the channel scheduler invokes the required routine, which attempts to correct the error.

7. *Program Information Block (PIB).* The PIB contains information tables that the supervisor needs to know about the current programs in storage.

8. *I/O Devices Control Table.* This area contains a table of I/O devices that relate physical unit addresses (X'nnn') with logical addresses (SYSxxx).

9. *Transient Area.* This area provides temporary storage for less used routines that the supervisor loads as required, such as OPEN, CLOSE, DUMP, end-of-job handling, some error recovery, and checkpoint routines.

System Service Programs

System service programs include the linkage editor and the librarian.

Linkage editor. The linkage editor has two main functions:

1. To include input/output modules. An installation catalogs I/O modules in the system library (covered next). When you code and assemble a program, it does not yet contain the complete instructions for handling input/output. On completion of assembly, the linkage editor includes all the required I/O modules from the library.
2. To link together separately assembled programs. You may code and assemble a number of subprograms separately and link-edit these subprograms into

one executable program.   The linkage editor enables data in one subprogram to be recognized in another and facilitates transfer of control between subprograms at execution time.

Librarian.   The operating system contains libraries on a disk known as SYSRES to catalog both IBM programs and the installation's own commonly used programs and subroutines.   DOS/VS supports four libraries:

1.   The source statement library (SSL) catalogs as a book any program, macro, or subroutine still in source code.   You can use the assembler directive COPY to include cataloged code into your source program for subsequent assembling.
2.   The relocatable library (RL) catalogs frequently used modules that are assembled but not yet ready for execution.   The assembler directs the linkage editor to include I/O modules automatically, and you can use the INCLUDE command to direct the linkage editor to include your own cataloged modules with your own assembled programs.
3.   The core image library (CIL) contains phases in executable machine code, ready for execution.   The CIL contains, for example, the assembler, COBOL, PL/I, and other translator programs, various utility programs such as LINK and SORT, and your own production programs ready for execution.   To request the supervisor to load a phase from the CIL into main storage for execution, use the job control command // EXEC phasename.
4.   The procedure library (PL) contains cataloged job control to facilitate automatic processing of jobs.

The OS libraries vary by name according to the version of OS, but basically the OS libraries equivalent to the DOS source statement, relocatable, and core image are, respectively, source library, object library, and load library, and they serve the same functions.

Processing Programs

Processing programs are cataloged on disk in three groups:

1.   Language translators that IBM supplies with the system include assembler, PL/I, COBOL, and RPG.
2.   Utility programs that IBM supplies include such special-purpose programs as disk initialization, copy file-to-file, and sort/merge.
3.   User-written programs that users in the installation write and that IBM does not support.   All the programs in this text are user-written programs.

For example, the job command // EXEC ASSEMBLY causes the system to load the assembler from the CIL into an available area ("partition") in storage and begins assembling a program. The job command // OPTION LINK directs the assembler to write the assembled module on SYSLNK in the relocatable library.

Once the program is assembled and stored on SYSLNK, the job command // EXEC LNKEDT tells the linkage editor to load the module from SYSLNK into

FIXED STORAGE LOCATIONS

AREA, dec.	Hex addr	EC only	Function
0– 7	0		Initial program loading PSW, restart new PSW
8– 15	8		Initial program loading CCW1, restart old PSW
16– 23	10		Initial program loading CCW2
24– 31	18		External old PSW
32– 39	20		Supervisor Call old PSW
40– 47	28		Program old PSW
48– 55	30		Machine-check old PSW
56– 63	38		Input/output old PSW
64– 71	40		Channel status word (see diagram)
72– 75	48		Channel address word (0–3 key, 4–7 zeros, 8–31 CCW address)
80– 83	50		Interval timer
88– 95	58		External new PSW
96–103	60		Supervisor Call new PSW
104–111	68		Program new PSW
112–119	70		Machine-check new PSW
120–127	78		Input/output new PSW
132–133	84		CPU address assoc'd with external interruption, or unchanged
132–133	84	X	CPU address assoc'd with external interruption, or zeros
134–135	86	X	External interruption code
136–139	88	X	SVC interruption (0–12 zeros, 13–14 ILC, 15:0, 16–31 code)
140–143	8C	X	Program interrupt (0–12 zeros, 13–14 ILC, 15:0, 16–31 code)
144–147	90	X	Translation exception address (0–7 zeros, 8–31 address)
148–149	94		Monitor class (0–7 zeros, 8–15 class number)
150–151	96	X	PER interruption code (0–3 code, 4–15 zeros)
152–155	98	X	PER address (0–7 zeros, 8–31 address)
156–159	9C		Monitor code (0–7 zeros, 8–31 monitor code)
168–171	A8		Channel ID (0–3 type, 4–15 model, 16–31 max. IOEL length)
172–175	AC		I/O extended logout address (0–7 unused, 8–31 address)
176–179	B0		Limited channel logout (see diagram)
185–187	B9	X	I/O address (0–7 zeros, 8–23 address)
216–223	D8		CPU timer save area
224–231	E0		Clock comparator save area
232–239	E8		Machine-check interruption code
248–251	F8		Failing processor storage address (0–7 zeros, 8–31 address)
252–255	FC		Region code*
256–351	100		Fixed logout area*
352–383	160		Floating-point register save area
384–447	180		General register save area
448–511	1C0		Control register save area
512†	200		CPU extended logout area (size varies)

*May vary among models: see system library manuals for specific model

†Location may be changed by programming (bits 8–28 of CR 15 specify address)

Figure 21-3   Fixed storage locations.

storage, to complete addressing, and to include I/O modules from the RL.   Assuming that there was no job command to catalog it, the linkage editor writes the linked phase in the CIL in a noncatalog area.   If the next job command is // EXEC with no specified phasename, the supervisor loads the phase from the noncatalog area into storage for execution.   The next program that the linkage editor links overlays the previous one in the CIL noncatalog area.

The job command // OPTION CATAL instead of // OPTION LINK tells the system both to link the program and to catalog the linked phase in the catalog area of the CIL.   You normally catalog production programs in the CIL and for immediate execution use the job command // EXEC phasename.

FIXED STORAGE LOCATIONS

As mentioned earlier, the first X'200' bytes of storage are reserved for use by the CPU.   Figure 21-3 lists the contents of these fixed storage locations.

MULTIPROGRAMMING

Multiprogramming is the concurrent execution of more than one program in storage.   Technically, a computer executes only one instruction at a time, but because of the fast speed of the processor and the relative slowness of I/O devices, the computer's ability to service a number of programs at the same time makes it appear that processing is simultaneous.   For this purpose, an operating system that supports multiprogramming divides storage into various *partitions* and is consequently far more complex than a single-job system.

The number and size of partitions vary according to the requirements of an installation.   One job in each partition may be subject to execution at the same time, although only one program is actually executing.   Each partition may handle jobs of a particular nature.   For example, one partition handles relatively short jobs of high priority, whereas another partition handles large jobs of lower priority.

The job scheduler routes jobs to a particular partition according to its class.   Thus a system may assign class A to certain jobs, to be run in the first partition.

In Fig. 21-4, the job queue is divided into four classes, and main storage is divided into three user partitions.   Jobs in class A run in partition 1, jobs in classes B and C run in partition 2, and jobs in class P run in partition 3.

Depending on the system, storage may be divided into many partitions, and a job class may be designated to run in any one of the partitions.   Also, a partition may be designated to run any number of classes.

When an operator uses the IPL procedure to boot the system, the supervisor is loaded from the CIL into low storage.   The supervisor next loads job control from the CIL into the various partitions.   The supervisor then scans the system readers and terminals for job control commands.

When a job completes processing, the job scheduler selects another job from

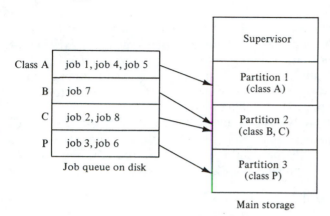

Main storage

Figure 21-4 Job queue and partitions.

the queue to replace it. For example, if partition 1 is free, the job scheduler in Fig. 21-4 selects from the class A queue either the job with the highest priority or, if all jobs have the same priority, the first job in the queue.

The system has to provide a more or less equitable arrangement for processing jobs in each partition. Under time slicing, each partition is allotted in turn a time slice of so many milliseconds of execution. Control passes to the next partition when the time has expired, the job is waiting for an I/O operation to complete, or the job is finished.

VIRTUAL STORAGE

In a multiprogramming environment, a large program may not fit entirely in a partition. As a consequence, both DOS/VS and OS/VS support a virtual storage system that divides programs into segments of 64K bytes, which are in turn divided into pages of 2K or (usually) 4K bytes. On disk, the entire program is contained as pages in a page data set, and in storage VS arranges a page pool for as much of the program as it can store, as shown in Fig. 21-5. As a consequence, a program that is 100K in size could run in a 64K partition. If the executing program references an address for a part of the program that is not in storage, VS swaps an unneeded page into the page data set on disk and pages in the required page from

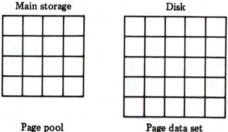

Figure 21-5 Page pool.

disk into the page pool in storage. (Actually, VS swaps onto disk only if the program has not changed the contents of the page.) The 16 control registers handle much of the paging operations.

Since a page from disk may map into any page in the pool, VS has to change addresses; this process is known as dynamic address translation (DAT).

When running a realtime application such as process control, a data communications manager, or an optical scan device, you may not want VS to page it out. It is possible to assign an area of nonpageable (real) storage for such jobs or use a "page fix" to lock certain pages into real storage.

PROGRAM STATUS WORD: PSW

The PSW is a doubleword of data stored in the control section of the CPU to control an executing program and to indicate its status. The two PSW modes are *basic control (BC) mode* and *extended control (EC) mode*. A 0 in PSW bit 12 indicates BC mode, and a 1 indicates EC mode. EC mode provides an extended control facility for virtual storage.

One of the main features of the PSW is to control the state of operation. Users of the system have no concern with certain operations such as storage management and allocation of I/O devices, and if they were allowed access to every instruction, they could inadvertently access other users' partitions or damage the system. To provide protection, certain instructions, such as Start I/O and Load PSW, are designated as privileged.

The PSW format is the same in only certain positions for each mode. Figure 21-6 illustrates the two modes, in which the bits are numbered 0 through 63 from left to right. Some of the more relevant fields are explained next.

> **Bit 14: Wait state.** When bit 14 is 0, the CPU is in running state executing instructions. When bit 14 is 1, the CPU is in wait state, which involves waiting for an action such as an I/O operation to be completed.
>
> **Bit 15: State.** For both modes, 0 = supervisor state and 1 = problem state. When the computer is executing the supervisor program, the bit is 0 and all instructions are valid. When in the problem state, the bit is 1 and privileged instructions cannot be executed.
>
> **Bits 16–31: Program interrupt code (BC mode).** When a program interrupt occurs, the computer sets these bits according to the type. The following list shows the interrupt codes in hex format:

0001	Operation exception
0002	Privileged operation exception
0003	Execute exception
0004	Protection exception
0005	Addressing exception

PROGRAM STATUS WORD (BC Mode)

Channel masks	E	Protect'n key	CMWP	Interruption code
0 6	7	8 11	12 15	16 23 24 31

ILC	CC	Program mask	Instruction address
32	34	36 39	40 47 48 55 56 63

0–5 Channel 0 to 5 masks   32–33 (ILC) Instruction length code
6 Mask for channel 6 and up   34–35 (CC) Condition code
7 (E) External mask   36 Fixed-point overflow mask
12 (C–0) Basic control mode   37 Decimal overflow mask
13 (M) Machine-check mask   38 Exponent underflow mask
14 (W–1) Wait state   39 Significance mask
15 (P–1) Problem state

PROGRAM STATUS WORD (EC Mode)

0R00 0TIE	Protect'n key	CMWP	00	CC	Program mask	0000 0000
0 7	8 11	12 15	16	18	20 23	24 31

0000 0000	Instruction address
32 39	40 47 48 55 56 63

1 (R) Program event recording mask   15 (P–1) Problem state
5 (T–1) Translation mode   18–19 (CC) Condition code
6 (I) Input/output mask   20 Fixed-point overflow mask
7 (E) External mask   21 Decimal overflow mask
12 (C–1) Extended control mode   22 Exponent underflow mask
13 (M) Machine-check mask   23 Significance mask
14 (W–1) Wait state

Figure 21-6   PSW format for BC and EC modes.

0006	Specification exception
0007	Data exception
0008	Fixed-point overflow exception
0009	Fixed-point divide exception
000A	Decimal overflow exception
000B	Decimal divide exception
000C	Exponent overflow exception
000D	Exponent underflow exception
000E	Significance exception
000F	Floating-point divide exception

0010	Segment translation exception
0011	Page translation exception
0012	Translation specification exception
0013	Special operation exception
0040	Monitor event
0080	Program event (may be combined with another code)

Bits 34–35: Condition code. BC mode only; the condition code under EC mode is in bits 18–19. Comparisons and certain arithmetic instructions set this code.

Bits 40–63: Instruction address. This area contains the address of the next instruction to be executed. The CPU accesses the specified instruction from main storage, decodes it in the control section, and executes it in the arithmetic/logic section. The first 2 bits of a machine instruction indicate its length. The CPU adds this length to the instruction address in the PSW, which now indicates the address of the next instruction. For a branch instruction, the branch address may replace the PSW instruction address.

INTERRUPTS

An interrupt occurs when the supervisor has to suspend normal processing to perform a special task. The six main classes of interrupts are as follows:

1. *Program Check Interrupt.* This interrupt occurs when the computer cannot execute an operation, such as performing arithmetic on invalid packed data. This is the common type of interrupt when a program terminates abnormally. Appendix B lists the various types of program interrupts.

2. *Supervisor Call Interrupt.* A problem program may issue a request for input/output or to terminate processing. A transfer from the problem program to the supervisor requires a supervisor call (SVC) operation and causes an interrupt.

3. *External Interrupt.* An external device may need attention, such as the operator pressing the request key on the console or a request for communications.

4. *Machine Check Interrupt.* The machine-checking circuits may detect a hardware error, such as a byte not containing an odd number of on bits (odd parity).

5. *Input/Output Interrupt.* Completion of an I/O operation making a unit available or malfunction of an I/O device (such as a disk head crash) cause this interrupt.

6. *Restart Interrupt.* This interrupt permits an operator or another CPU to invoke execution of a program.

The supervisor region contains an interrupt handler for each type of interrupt. On an interrupt, the system alters the PSW as required and stores the PSW in a fixed storage location, where it is available to any program for testing.

The PSW discussed to this point is known as the current PSW. When an interrupt occurs, the computer stores the current PSW and loads a new PSW that controls the new program, usually the supervisor. The current PSW is in the control section of the CPU, whereas the old and new PSWs are stored in main storage, as the following indicates:

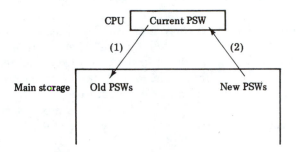

The interrupt replaces the current PSW in this way. (1) It stores the current PSW into main storage as the old PSW, and (2) it fetches a new PSW from main storage, to become the current PSW. The old PSW now contains in its instruction address the location following the instruction that caused the interrupt. The computer stores PSWs in 12 doubleword locations in fixed storage; 6 are for old PSWs and 6 are for new PSWs, depending on the class of interrupt:

	OLD PSW	NEW PSW
Restart	0008	0000
External	0024	0088
Supervisor call	0032	0096
Program old PSW	0040	0104
Machine check	0048	0112
Input/output	0056	0120

Let's trace the sequence of events following a supervisor interrupt. Assume that the supervisor has stored in the six new PSWs the address of each of its interrupt routines. (The old PSWs are not required yet.) Remember also that when an instruction executes, the computer updates the instruction address and the condition code in the current PSW as required.

1. A program requests input from disk. The GET or READ macro contains a supervisor call to link to the supervisor for input/output. This is a supervisor interrupt.

2. The instruction address in the current PSW contains the address in the program immediately following the SVC that caused the interrupt. The CPU stores this current PSW in the old PSW for supervisor interrupt, location 32. The new PSW for supervisor interrupt, location 96, contains supervisor state bit = 0 and the address of the supervisor interrupt routine. The CPU moves this new PSW to the current PSW and is now in the supervisor state.

3. The PSW instruction address contains the address of the supervisor I/O routine, which now executes. The channel scheduler requests the channel for disk input.

4. To return to the problem program, the supervisor loads the old PSW from location 32 back into the current PSW. The instruction links to the PSW instruction address, which is the address in the program following the original SVC that caused the interrupt. The system switches the PSW from supervisor state back to problem state.

In the event of a program check interrupt, the computer sets its cause on PSW bits 16–31, the program interrupt code. For example, if the problem program attempts arithmetic on invalid data, the computer senses a data exception and stores X'0007' in PSW bits 16–31. The computer then stores the current PSW in old PSW location 0040 and loads the new PSW from 0104 into the current PSW. This PSW contains the address of the supervisor's program check routine, which tests the old PSW to determine what type of program check caused the interrupt.

The supervisor displays the contents of the old PSW in hexadecimal and the cause of the program check (data exception), flushes the interrupted program, and begins processing the next job. Suppose that the invalid operation is an MP at location X'6A320'. Since MP is 6 bytes long, the instruction address in the PSW and the one printed will be X'6A326'. You can tell from the supervisor diagnostic message that the error is a data exception and that the invalid operation immediately precedes the instruction at X'6A326'.

CHANNELS

A channel is a component that functions as a separate computer operated by channel commands to control I/O devices. It directs data between devices and main storage and permits attaching a great variety of I/O devices. The more powerful the computer model, the more channels it may support. The two types of channels are multiplexer and selector.

1. *Multiplexer channels* are designed to support simultaneous operation of more than one device by interleaving blocks of data. The two types of multiplexer channels are byte-multiplexer and block-multiplexer. A byte-multiplexer channel typically handles low-speed devices, such as printers and terminals.

A block-multiplexer can support higher-speed devices, and its ability to interleave blocks of data facilitates simultaneous I/O operations.

2. *Selector channels*, no longer common, are designed to handle high-speed devices, such as disk and tape drives. The channel can transfer data from only one device at a time, a process known as burst mode.

Each channel has a 4-bit address coded as in the following example:

CHANNEL	ADDRESS	TYPE
0	0000	byte-multiplexer
1	0001	block-multiplexer
2	0010	block-multiplexer
3	0011	block-multiplexer
4	0100	block-multiplexer
5	0101	block-multiplexer
6	0110	block-multiplexer

A *control unit*, or controller, is required to interface with a channel. A channel is basically device-independent, whereas a control unit is device-dependent. Thus a block-multiplexer channel can operate many type of devices, but a disk drive control unit can operate only a disk drive. Figure 21-7 illustrates a typical configuration of channels, control units, and devices.

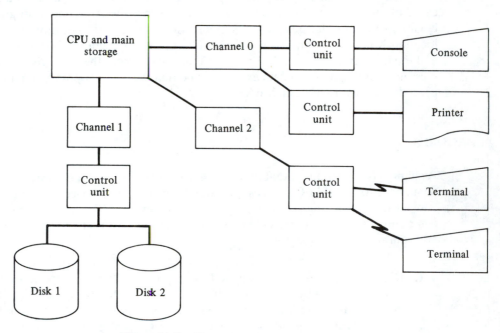

Figure 21-7   Channels, control units, and devices.

For example, a computer uses a multiplexer channel to connect it to a printer's control unit. The control unit has a 4-bit address. Further, each device has a 4-bit address and is known to the system by a physical address. The device address is therefore a 12-bit code that specifies:

DEVICE	CODE
Channel	0CCC
Control unit	UUUU
Device	DDDD

If the printer's device number is 1110 (X'E') and it is attached to channel 0, control unit 1, then to the system its physical address is 0000 0001 1110, or X'01E'. Further, if two disk devices are numbered 0000 and 0001 and they are both attached to channel 1, control unit 9, their physical addresses are X'190' and X'191', respectively. This physical address permits the attaching of 2^8, or 256 devices.

Symbolic Assignments

Although the supervisor references I/O devices by their physical numbers, your programs use symbolic names. You may assign a symbolic name to any device temporarily or (more or less) permanently, and a device may have more than one symbolic name assigned. The operating system uses certain names, known as system logical units, that include the following:

SYSIPT	The terminal, system reader, or disk device used as input for programs
SYSRDR	The terminal, system reader, or disk device used as input for job control for the system
SYSIN	The system name to assign both SYSIPT and SYSRDR to the same terminal, system reader, or disk device
SYSLST	The printer or disk used as the main output device for the system
SYSPCH	The device used as the main unit for output
SYSOUT	The system name to assign both SYSLST and SYSPCH to the same output device
SYSLNK	The disk area used as input for the linkage editor
SYSLOG	The console or printer used by the system to log operator messages and job control statements
SYSRES	The disk device where the operating system resides
SYSRLB	The disk device for the relocatable library
SYSSLB	The disk device for the system library

In addition, you may reference programmer logical units, SYS000–SYSnnn.

For example, you may assign the logical address SYS025 to a disk drive with physical address X'170'. The supervisor stores the physical and logical addresses in an I/O devices control table in order to relate them. A simplified table could contain the following:

I/O DEVICE	PHYSICAL ADDRESS	LOGICAL UNITS
Reader	X'00C'	SYSIPT, SYSRDR
Printer	X'00E'	SYSLST
Disk drive	X'170'	SYSLNK, SYSRES, SYS025
Tape drive	X'280'	SYS031, SYS035

A reference to SYSLST is to the printer, and a reference to SYSLNK, SYSRES, or SYS025, depending on its particular use, is to disk device X'170'. You may assign a logical address permanently or temporarily and may change logical addresses from job to job. For instance, you could use an ASSGN job control command to reassign SYS035 for a program from a disk device X'170' to another disk device X'172'.

I/O LOGIC MODULES

Consider a program that reads a tape file named TAPEFL. The program would require a DTFMT or DCB file definition macro to define the characteristics of the file and tape device to generate a link to an I/O logic module. The assembler determines which particular logic module, based on (1) the kind of DTF and (2) the specifications within the file definition, such as device number, an input or output file, the number of buffers, and whether processing is in a workarea (WORKA) or a buffer (IOREG). In the following example, the assembler has generated a logic module named IJFFBCWZ (the name would vary depending on specifications within the DTFMT).

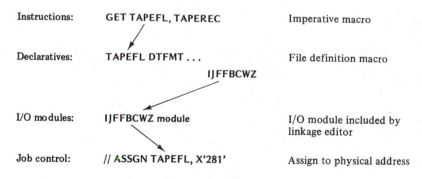

Instructions:	GET TAPEFL, TAPEREC	Imperative macro
Declaratives:	TAPEFL DTFMT ...	File definition macro
	IJFFBCWZ	
I/O modules:	IJFFBCWZ module	I/O module included by linkage editor
Job control:	// ASSGN TAPEFL, X'281'	Assign to physical address

When linking a program, the linkage editor searches for addresses in the external symbol dictionary that the assembler generates. For this example, the ESD would contain entries at least for the program name and IJFFBCWZ. The linker accesses the named module cataloged on disk (provided it was ever cataloged) and includes it at the end of the assembled object program. One role of a system programmer is to define and catalog these I/O modules.

On execution of the program, the GET macro links to the specified file definition macro, DTFMT. This macro contains the address of the I/O logic module at the end of the object program where the linker included it. The module, combined with information from the DTFMT, contains all the instructions necessary to notify the supervisor as to the actual type of I/O operation, device, block size, and so forth.

The only remaining information is to determine which tape device; the supervisor derives it from the job control entry, which in this example assigns X'281' as the physical address. The supervisor then (at last) delivers the physical request for input via a channel command.

For example, the printer module, PRMOD, consists of three letters (IJD) and five option letters (abcde), as IJDabcde. The options are based on the definitions in the DTFPR macro, as follows:

a	RECFORM: FIXUNB (F), VARUNB (V), UNDEF (U)
b	CTLCHR: ASA (A), YES (Y), CONTROL (C)
c	PRINTOV = YES and ERROPT = YES (B), PRINTOV = YES and ERROPT not specified (Z), plus 14 other options
d	IOAREA2: defined (I), not defined (Z)
e	WORKA: YES (W), YES and RDONLY = YES (V), neither specified (Z)

A common printer module for IBM control character, two buffers, and a workarea would be IJDFYZIW. For one buffer, the module is IJDFYZZW.

PHYSICAL IOCS

Physical IOCS (PIOCS), the basic level of IOCS, provides for channel scheduling, error recovery, and interrupt handling. When using PIOCS, you write a channel program (the channel command word) and synchronize the program with completion of the I/O operation. You must also provide for testing the command control block for certain errors, for checking wrong-length records, for switching between I/O areas where two are used, and, if records are blocked, for blocking and deblocking.

PIOCS macros include CCW, CCB, EXCP, and WAIT.

Channel Command Word (CCW)

The CCW macro causes the assembler to construct an 8-byte channel command word that defines the I/O command to be executed.

Name [label]	Operation CCW	Operand command-code,data-address,flags,count-field

- command-code defines the operation to be performed, such as 1 = write, 2 = read, X'09' = print and space one line.
- data-address provides the storage address of the first byte where data is to be read or written.
- flag bits determine the next action when the channel completes an operation defined in a CCW. You can set flag bits to 1 to vary the channel's operation (explained in detail later).
- count-field provides an expression that defines the number of bytes in the data block that is to be processed.

Command Control Block (CCB)

You define a CCB macro for each I/O device that PIOCS macros reference. The CCB comprises the first 16 bytes of most generated DTF tables. The CCB communicates information to PIOCS to cause required I/O operations and receives status information after the operation.

Name blockname	Operation CCB	Operand SYSnnn,command-list-name

- blockname is the symbolic name associated with the CCB, used as an old PSW for the EXCP and WAIT macros.
- SYSnnn is the symbolic name of the I/O device associated with the CCB.
- command-list-name is the symbolic name of the first CCW used with the CCB.

Execute Channel Program (EXCP)

The EXCP macro requests physical IOCS to start an I/O operation, and PIOCS relates the blockname to the CCB to determine the device. When the channel and the device become available, the channel program is started. Program control then returns to your program.

Name	Operation	Operand
[label]	EXCP	blockname *or* (1)

The operand gives the symbolic name of the CCB macro to be referenced.

The WAIT Macro

The WAIT macro synchronizes program execution with completion of an I/O operation, since the program normally requires its completion before it can continue execution. (When bit 0 of byte 2 of the CCB for the file is set to 1, the WAIT is completed and processing resumes.) For example, if you have issued an EXCP operation to read a data block, you now WAIT for delivery of the entire block before you can begin processing it.

Name	Operation	Operand
[label]	WAIT	blockname *or* (1)

The operand gives the symbolic name of the CCB macro to be referenced.

CCW Flag Bits

You may set and use the flag bits in the CCW as follows:

- Bit 32 (chain data flag), set by X'80', specifies *data chaining*. When the CCW has processed the number of bytes defined in its count field, the I/O operation does not terminate if this bit is set. The operation continues with the next CCW in storage. You may use data chaining to read or write data into or out of storage areas that are not necessarily adjacent.

  In the following three CCWs, the first two use X'80' in the flag bits, operand 3, to specify data chaining. An EXCP and CCB may then reference the first CCW, and as a result, the chain of three CCWs causes the contents of an 80-byte input record to be read into three separate areas in storage: 20 bytes in NAME, 30 bytes in ADDRESS, and 30 bytes in CITY.

```
DATCHAIN CCW   2,NAME,X'80',20      Read 20 bytes into NAME, chain.
         CCW   ,ADDRESS,X'80',30    Read 30 bytes into ADDRESS, chain.
         CCW   ,CITY,X'00',30       Read 30 bytes into CITY, terminate.
```

- Bit 33 (chain command flag), set by X'40', specifies *command chaining* to enable the channel to execute more than one CCW before terminating the I/O operation. Each CCW applies to a separate I/O record.

   The following set of CCWs could provide for reading three input blocks, each 100 bytes long:

```
COMCHAIN CCW   2,INAREA,X'40',100        Read record-1 into
                                         INAREA, chain.
         CCW   2,INAREA+100,X'40',100   Read record-2 into
                                         INAREA+100, chain.
         CCW   2,INAREA+200,X'00',100   Read record-3 into
                                         INAREA+200, terminate.
```

- Bit 34 (suppress length indication flag), set by X'20', is used to suppress an error indication that occurs when the number of bytes transmitted differs from the count in the CCW.
- Bit 35 (skip flag), set by X'10', is used to suppress transmission of input data. The device actually reads the data, but the channel does not transmit the record.
- Bit 36 (program controlled interrupt flag), set by X'08', causes an interrupt when this CCW's operation is complete. (This is used when one supervisor SIO instruction executes more than one CCW.)
- Bit 37 (indirect data address flag), as well as other features about physical IOCS, is covered in the IBM Principles of Operation manual and the appropriate supervisor manual for your system.

Sample Physical IOCS Program

The program in Fig. 21-8 illustrates many of the features of physical IOCS we have discussed. It performs the following operations:

- At initialization, prints three heading lines by means of command chaining (X'40').
- Reads input records one at a time containing salesman name and company.
- Prints each record.
- Terminates on reaching end-of-file.

   Note that the program defines a CCB/CCW pair for each type of record, and the EXCP/WAIT operations reference the CCB name—INDEVIC for the reader, OUTDEV1 for heading lines, and OUTDEV2 for sales detail lines. Each CCB contains the name of the I/O device, SYSIPT or SYSLST, and the name of an associated CCW: INRECD, TITLES, and DETAIL, respectively.

```
LOC     OBJECT CODE           STMT    SOURCE STATEMENT
                                1             PRINT NODATA,NOGEN
000000                          2  PIOCSPRG START 0                    INITIALIZE
000000  0530                    3             BALR  3,0                *
                                4             USING *,3                *

                                6             EXCP  OUTDEV1            PRINT TITLES
                               10             WAIT  OUTDEV1            *

                               17  A100READ EXCP  INDEVIC            READ RECORD
                               21             WAIT  INDEVIC            *

00002A  D501 3076 3332         28             CLC   RECORD(2),=C'/*'  END FILE?
000030  4780 305C              29             BE    A900END                 YES
000034  D213 32B8 3076         31             MVC   SURNOUT,SURNAME   LOAD
00003A  D213 32CD 308A         32             MVC   GIVENOUT,GIVENAME * PRINT
000040  D21D 32E2 309E         33             MVC   COMPOUT,COMPANY   * LINE

                               35             EXCP  OUTDEV2            PRINT
                               39             WAIT  OUTDEV2            *
00005A  47F0 3014              45             B     A100READ          RETURN

                               47  A900END  EOJ                       END OF JOB

                               51  *         ----------------------
                               52  *         D E C L A R A T I V E S
                               53  *         ----------------------
                               54  INDEVIC  CCB   SYSIPT,INRECRD     I/P DEVICE
000070  0200007820000050       65  INRECRD  CCW   X'02',RECORD,X'20',80

000078                         67  RECORD   DS    0CL80             I/P RECORD
000078                         68  SURNAME  DS    CL20              *
00008C                         69  GIVENAME DS    CL20              *
0000A0                         70  COMPANY  DS    CL40              *

                               72  OUTDEV1  CCB   SYSLST,TITLES     O/P DEVICE

0000D8  8B0000D860000001       84  TITLES   CCW   X'8B',*,X'60',1
0000E0  110000F840000085       85           CCW   X'11',PRIMARY,X'40',133
0000E8  1900017D40000085       86           CCW   X'19',SECONDRY,X'40',133
0000F0  1100020200000085       87           CCW   X'11',TERTIARY,X'00',133

0000F8                         89  PRIMARY  DS    0CL133            TITLE #1
0000F8  4040404040404040       90           DC    CL37' '
00011D  E340D640D7404040       91           DC    CL16'T O P   S A L E'
00012D  E240D440C540D540       92           DC    CL80'S M E N   O F'

00017D                         94  SECONDRY DS    0CL133            TITLE #2
00017D  4040404040404040       95           DC    CL34' '
00019F  E340C840C5404040       96           DC    CL14'T H E   W E S'
0001AD  E340C540D940D540       97           DC    CL14'T E R N   R E'
0001BB  C740C940D640D540       98           DC    CL71'G I O N'

000202                        100  TERTIARY DS    0CL133            TITLE #3
000202  4040404040404040      101           DC    CL26' '
00021C  E2E4D9D5C1D4C540      102           DC    CL21'SURNAME'
000231  C7C9E5C5D540D5C1      103           DC    CL21'GIVEN NAME'
000246  C3D6D4D7C1D5E840      104           DC    CL65'COMPANY'
```

Figure 21-8   Program: physical IOCS.

```
                                  106 OUTDEV2  CCB   SYSLST,OUTRECRD   O/P DEVICE
000297 00
000298 090002A020000085 118 OUTRECRD CCW   X'09',DETAIL,X'20',133

0002A0                            120 DETAIL   DS   0CL133           DETAIL
0002A0 4040404040404040 121          DC   CL26' '          * LINE
0002BA                            122 SURNOUT  DS   CL20
0002CE 40                         123          DC   CL01' '
0002CF                            124 GIVENOUT DS   CL20
0002E3 40                         125          DC   CL01' '
0002E4                            126 COMPOUT  DS   CL30
000302 4040404040404040 127          DC   CL35' '

000328                            129          LTORG ,
000328 000000C8                   130               =A(OUTDEV1)
00032C 00000060                   131               =A(INDEVIC)
000330 00000287                   132               =A(OUTDEV2)
000334 615C                       133               =C'/*'
                                  134          END  PIOCSPRG
```

Output:-
```
          T O P   S A L E S M E N   O F
        T H E   W E S T E R N   R E G I O N

    SURNAME              GIVEN NAME          COMPANY

    RUTH                 GEORGE HERMAN       LASER CORP.
    JOHNSON              WALTER              AMX ELECTRONICS
    COLLINS              EDDIE               B M I
    COBB                 TYRUS RAYMOND       AUDIO SHACK
    SPEAKER              TRIS                PACKLETT HEWARD
    SIMMONS              AL                  VIDEO DUMP
    SISLER               GEORGE              COMPUTER HEAP
    WAGNER               HANS                DIGITAL CORP.
```

Figure 21-8   (continued)

KEY POINTS

- Systems generation (sysgen) involves tailoring the supplied operating system to the installation's requirements, such as the number and type of disk drives, the number and type of terminals to be supported, the amount of process time available to users, and the levels of security that are to prevail.

- The control program, which controls all other programs being processed, consists of initial program load (IPL), the supervisor, and job control. Under OS, the functions are task management, data management, and job management.

- Initial program load (IPL) is a program that the operator uses daily or whenever required to load the supervisor into storage. The system loader is responsible for loading programs into main storage for execution.

- The supervisor resides in lower storage, beginning at location X'200'. The supervisor is concerned with handling interrupts for input/output devices, fetching required modules from the program library, and handling errors in program execution.

- Channels provide a path between main storage and the input/output devices and permit overlapping of program execution with I/O operations. The channel scheduler handles all I/O interrupts.

- Storage protection prevents a problem program from erroneously moving data into the supervisor area and destroying it.

- An interrupt is a signal that informs the system to interrupt the program that is currently executing and to transfer control to the appropriate supervisor routine.

- The source statement library (SSL) catalogs as a book any program, macro, or subroutine still in source code.

- The relocatable library (RL) catalogs frequently used modules that are assembled but not yet ready for execution.

- The core image library (CIL) contains phases in executable machine code, ready for execution.

- Multiprogramming is the concurrent execution of more than one program in storage. An operating system that supports multiprogramming divides storage into various partitions. One job in each partition may be subject to execution at the same time, although only one program is actually executing.

- The PSW is stored in the control section of the CPU to control an executing program and to indicate its status. The two PSW modes are basic control (BC) mode and extended control (EC) mode.

- Certain instructions such as Start I/O and Load PSW are privileged to provide protection against users' accessing the wrong partitions.

- An interrupt occurs when the supervisor has to suspend normal processing to perform a special task. The supervisor region contains an interrupt handler for each type of interrupt.

- A channel is a component that functions as a separate computer operated by channel commands to control I/O devices. It directs data between devices and main storage and permits the attachment of a variety of I/O devices. The two types are multiplexer and selector.

- The operating system uses certain names, known as system logical units, such as SYSIPT, SYSLST, and SYSLOG. Programmer logical units are referenced as SYS000–SYSnnn.

- Physical IOCS (PIOCS), the basic level of IOCS, provides for channel scheduling, error recovery, and interrupt handling. When using PIOCS, you write a channel program (the channel command word) and synchronize the program with completion of the I/O operation.

- The CCW macro causes the assembler to construct an 8-byte channel command word that defines the I/O command to be executed.

PROBLEMS

21-1. What is the purpose of an operating system?

21-2. Where is the supervisor located in storage?

21-3. What is a sysgen?

21-4. What is the purpose of the supervisor transient area?

21-5. Where is the channel scheduler and what is its function?

21-6. In which libraries are the following stored (a) phase; (b) module; (c) book?

21-7. What are the two main functions of the linkage editor?

21-8. Explain the role of partitions and the job scheduler.

21-9. What is dynamic address translation?

21-10. What do the first 512 bytes of main storage contain?

21-11. What are the two modes and the two states of the PSW?

21-12. Where in the PSW (the name and bit positions) is the next sequential instruction located?

21-13. What are the classes of interrupts and their causes?

21-14. What is the purpose of channels? What are the two types and their differences?

21-15. A printer, number 1101, is attached to control unit 0010 and a multiplexer channel. What is the printer's physical address in hex?

21-16. Distinguish between physical address and logical address.

21-17. What are system logical units and programmer logical units?

21-18. Revise a simple program and substitute physical IOCS for input/output.

APPENDIX

HEXADECIMAL-DECIMAL CONVERSION

This appendix provides the steps in converting between hexadecimal and decimal formats. The first section shows how to convert hex A7B8 to decimal 42,936 and the second section shows how to convert 42,936 back to hex A7B8.

CONVERTING HEXADECIMAL TO DECIMAL

To convert hex number A7B8 to a decimal number, start with the leftmost hex digit (A), continuously multiply each hex digit by 16, and accumulate the results. Since multiplication is in decimal, convert hex digits A through F to decimal 10 through 15.

First digit, A (10):	10
Multiply by 16:	$\times$ 16
	160
Add next digit, 7:	+ 7
	167
Multiply by 16:	$\times$ 16
	2672
Add next digit, B (11):	+ 11
	2683
Multiply by 16:	$\times$ 16
	42,928
Add next digit, 8:	+ 8
Decimal value	42,936

You can also use the conversion table in Fig. A-1.   For hex number A7B8, think of the rightmost digit (8) as position 1, the next digit to the left (B) as position 2, the next digit (7) as position 3, and the leftmost digit (A) as position 4.   Refer to the figure and locate the value for each hex digit:

For position 1 (8), column 1 equals	8
For position 2 (B), column 2 equals	176
For position 3 (7), column 3 equals	1,792
For position 4 (A), column 4 equals	40,960
Decimal value:	42,936

CONVERTING DECIMAL TO HEXADECIMAL

To convert decimal number 42,936 to hexadecimal, first divide the original number 42,936 by 16; the remainder becomes the rightmost hex digit, 6.   Next divide the new quotient 2,683 by 16; the remainder, 11 = B, becomes the next hex digit to the left.   Develop the hex number from the remainders of each step of the division. Continue in this manner until the quotient is zero.

DIVISION	QUOTIENT	REMAINDER	HEX	
42,936 ÷ 16	2,683	8	8	(rightmost)
2,683 ÷ 16	167	11	B	
167 ÷ 16	10	7	7	
10 ÷ 16	0	10	A	(leftmost)

Hex	Dec	Hex	Dec	Hex	Dec	Hex	Dec	Hex	Dec	Hex	Dec	Hex	Dec	Hex	Dec
0	0	0	0	0	0	0	0	0	0	0	0	0	0	0	0
1	1	1	16	1	256	1	4,096	1	65,536	1	1,048,576	1	16,777,216	1	268,435,456
2	2	2	32	2	512	2	8,192	2	131,072	2	2,097,152	2	33,554,432	2	536,870,912
3	3	3	48	3	768	3	12,288	3	196,608	3	3,145,728	3	50,331,648	3	805,306,368
4	4	4	64	4	1,024	4	16,384	4	262,144	4	4,194,304	4	67,108,864	4	1,073,741,824
5	5	5	80	5	1,280	5	20,480	5	327,680	5	5,242,880	5	83,886,080	5	1,342,177,280
6	6	6	96	6	1,536	6	24,576	6	393,216	6	6,291,456	6	100,663,296	6	1,610,612,736
7	7	7	112	7	1,792	7	28,672	7	458,752	7	7,340,032	7	117,440,512	7	1,879,048,192
8	8	8	128	8	2,048	8	32,768	8	524,288	8	8,388,608	8	134,217,728	8	2,147,483,648
9	9	9	144	9	2,304	9	36,864	9	589,824	9	9,437,184	9	150,994,944	9	2,415,919,104
A	10	A	160	A	2,560	A	40,960	A	655,360	A	10,485,760	A	167,772,160	A	2,684,354,560
B	11	B	176	B	2,816	B	45,056	B	720,896	B	11,534,336	B	184,549,376	B	2,952,790,016
C	12	C	192	C	3,072	C	49,152	C	786,432	C	12,582,912	C	201,326,592	C	3,221,225,472
D	13	D	208	D	3,328	D	53,248	D	851,968	D	13,631,488	D	218,103,808	D	3,489,660,928
E	14	E	224	E	3,584	E	57,344	E	917,504	E	14,680,064	E	234,881,024	E	3,758,096,384
F	15	F	240	F	3,840	F	61,440	F	983,040	F	15,728,640	F	251,658,240	F	4,026,531,840
1		2		3		4		5		6		7		8	

Figure A-1

You can also use Fig. A-1 to convert decimal to hexadecimal. For decimal number 42,936, locate the number that is equal or next smaller. Note the equivalent hex number and its position in the table. Subtract the decimal value of that hex digit from 42,936, and locate the difference in the table. The procedure works as follows:

	DECIMAL		HEX
Starting decimal value:	42,936		
Subtract next smaller number:	− 40,960	=	A000
Difference:	1,976		
Subtract next smaller number:	− 1,792	=	700
Difference:	184		
Subtract next smaller number:	− 176	=	B0
Difference:	8	=	8
Final hex number:			A7B8

APPENDIX

B

PROGRAM INTERRUPTS

A program interrupt occurs when a program attempts an operation that requires special attention. These are the program interrupts, listed by hex code number.

1. Operation Exception

The CPU has attempted to execute an invalid machine operation, such as hexadecimal zeros. Possible causes: (a) missing branch instruction, and the program has entered a declarative area; (b) the instruction, such as a floating-point operation, is not installed on the computer; (c) during assembly, an invalid instruction has caused the assembler to generate hexadecimal zeros in place of the machine code. For a 6-byte instruction, such as MVC with an invalid operand, the assembler generates 6 bytes of hex zeros. At execute time, the computer tries to execute the zero operation code, causing an operation exception. (Since the computer attempts to execute 2 bytes at a time, the system may generate three consecutive operation exceptions.) See also the causes for an addressing exception.

2. Privileged-Operation Exception

An attempt has been made to execute a privileged instruction that only the supervisor is permitted to execute. Possible causes: See operation (1) and addressing

(5) exceptions.   Since there are many causes, it may be necessary to take a hexadecimal dump of the program to determine the contents of I/O areas and other declaratives to discover at what point during execution the error occurred.

3. Execute Exception

An attempt has been made to use the EX instruction on another EX instruction.

4. Protection Exception

A storage protection device prevents programs from erroneously moving data into the supervisor area or other partitions.   Such attempts (for example, by MVC and ZAP) cause the computer to signal the error.   Possible causes: (a) the program has erroneously loaded data into one of its base registers; (b) improper explicit use of a base register.

5. Addressing Exception

The program is attempting to reference an address that is outside available storage. Possible causes: (a) a branch to an address in a register containing an invalid value; (b) an instruction, such as MVC, has erroneously moved a data field into program instructions; (c) improper use of a base register, for example, loaded with a wrong value; (d) a BR instruction has branched to an address in a register and the wrong register was coded or its contents were changed.

6. Specification Exception

The program has violated a rule of an instruction.   (a) For any type of operation, an attempt has been made to execute or branch to an instruction that does not begin on an even storage address (possibly an incorrect base register).   (b) For packed operations DP and MP, a multiplier or divisor exceeds 8 bytes, or the length of the operand 1 field is less than or equal to that of operand 2.   (c) For binary operations D, DR, M, MR, SLDA, SLDL, SRDA, and SRDL, the instruction does not reference an even-numbered register.   (d) A floating-point operation does not reference register 0, 2, 4, or 6, or an extended-precision instruction does not reference a proper pair of registers, 0 and 2 or 4 and 6.   (e) CLCL or MVCL does not reference an even-numbered register.

7. Data Exception

An attempt has been made to perform arithmetic on an invalid packed field.   (a) For AP, CP, CVB, DP, ED, EDMK, MP, SP, SRP, or ZAP, the digit or sign positions contain invalid data.   Possible causes: An input field contains blanks or other nondigits that pack invalidly; failure to pack, or an improper pack; an AP has added to an accumulator that was not initialized with valid packed data; improper use of relative addressing; an MVC has erroneously destroyed a packed field; improper explicit use of a base register. (b) The multiplicand field for an MP is too short. (c) The operation fields for AP, CP, DP, MP, SP, or ZAP overlap improperly due to incorrect use of relative addressing.

8. Fixed-Point Overflow Exception

A binary operation (A, AH, AR, LCR, LPR, S, SH, SR, SLA, or SLDA) has caused the contents of a register to overflow, losing a leftmost significant digit. The maximum value that a register can contain is, in decimal notation, +2,147,483,647.

9. Fixed-Point Divide Exception

A binary divide (D or DR) or a CVB has generated a value that has exceeded the capacity of a register. A common cause for divide operations is dividing by a zero value. The maximum value that a register can contain is, in decimal notation, +2,147,483,647.

A. Decimal-Overflow Exception

The result of a decimal packed operation (AP, SP, SRP, or ZAP) is too large for the receiving field. Solution: Redefine the receiving field so that it can contain the largest possible value, or perform a right shift to reduce the size of the value.

B. Decimal-Divide Exception

The generated quotient/remainder for a DP operation is too large for the defined area. Possible causes: (a) failure to follow the rules of DP; (b) the divisor contains a zero value.

C. Exponent-Overflow Exception

A floating-point arithmetic operation has caused an exponent to overflow (exceed +63).

D. Exponent-Underflow Exception

A floating-point arithmetic operation has caused an exponent to underflow (less than −64).

E. Significance Exception

A floating-point add or subtract has caused a zero fraction. All significant digits are lost, and subsequent computations may be meaningless.

F. Floating-Point Divide Exception

A floating-point operation has attempted a division using a zero divisor.

In each case, the system issues an error message, giving the type of program interrupt and the address where the interrupt occurred. Sometimes an error causes a program to enter a declarative area or another invalid area outside the program. (The computer may even find a valid machine code there.) In debugging, determine how the program arrived at the invalid address. In many cases, a dump of the program's registers and storage area is essential in tracing the cause of the error.

Another common error, though not a program interrupt, is generated by the operating system: INVALID STATEMENT. The system is attempting to read an invalid job control command. A common cause is a program that has terminated before reading all its data in the job stream, and the system is trying to read its remaining data records as job commands. Possible causes are (a) missing branch instructions causing the program inadvertently to enter its end-of-file routine; (b) branching to the end-of-file routine on an error condition without flushing remaining records in the job stream.

APPENDIX

C

ASSEMBLER INSTRUCTION SET

MACHINE INSTRUCTIONS

NAME	MNEMONIC	OP CODE	FORMAT	OPERANDS
Add (c)	AR	1A	RR	R1,R2
Add (c)	A	5A	RX	R1,D2(X2,B2)
Add Decimal (c)	AP	FA	SS	D1(L1,B1),D2(L2,B2)
Add Halfword (c)	AH	4A	RX	R1,D2(X2,B2)
Add Logical (c)	ALR	1E	RR	R1,R2
Add Logical (c)	AL	5E	RX	R1,D2(X2,B2)
AND (c)	NR	14	RR	R1,R2
AND (c)	N	54	RX	R1,D2(X2,B2)
AND (c)	NI	94	SI	D1(B1),I2
AND (c)	NC	D4	SS	D1(L,B1),D2(B2)
Branch and Link	BALR	05	RR	R1,R2
Branch and Link	BAL	45	RX	R1,D2(X2,B2)
Branch on Condition	BCR	07	RR	M1,R2
Branch on Condition	BC	47	RX	M1,D2(X2,B2)
Branch on Count	BCTR	06	RR	R1,R2
Branch on Count	BCT	46	RX	R1,D2(X2,B2)
Branch on Index High	BXH	86	RS	R1,R3,D2(B2)
Branch on Index Low or Equal	BXLE	87	RS	R1,R3,D2(B2)
Clear I/O (c,p)	CLRIO	9D01	S	D2(B2)
Compare (c)	CR	19	RR	R1,R2
Compare (c)	C	59	RX	R1,D2(X2,B2)
Compare and Swap (c)	CS	BA	RS	R1,R3,D2(B2)
Compare Decimal (c)	CP	F9	SS	D1(L1,B1),D2(L2,B2)
Compare Double and Swap (c)	CDS	BB	RS	R1,R3,D2(B2)
Compare Halfword (c)	CH	49	RX	R1,D2(X2,B2)
Compare Logical (c)	CLR	15	RR	R1,R2
Compare Logical (c)	CL	55	RX	R1,D2(X2,B2)
Compare Logical (c)	CLC	D5	SS	D1(L,B1),D2(B2)
Compare Logical (c)	CLI	95	SI	D1(B1),I2
Compare Logical Characters under Mask (c)	CLM	BD	RS	R1,M3,D2(B2)
Compare Logical Long (c)	CLCL	0F	RR	R1,R2
Convert to Binary	CVB	4F	RX	R1,D2(X2,B2)
Convert to Decimal	CVD	4E	RX	R1,D2(X2,B2)
Diagnose (p)		83		Model-dependent
Divide	DR	1D	RR	R1,R2
Divide	D	5D	RX	R1,D2(X2,B2)
Divide Decimal	DP	FD	SS	D1(L1,B1),D2(L2,B2)
Edit (c)	ED	DE	SS	D1(L,B1),D2(B2)
Edit and Mark (c)	EDMK	DF	SS	D1(L,B1),D2(B2)
Exclusive OR (c)	XR	17	RR	R1,R2
Exclusive OR (c)	X	57	RX	R1,D2(X2,B2)

MACHINE INSTRUCTIONS (Contd)

NAME	MNEMONIC	OP CODE	FORMAT	OPERANDS
Exclusive OR (c)	XI	97	SI	D1(B1),I2
Exclusive OR (c)	XC	D7	SS	D1(L,B1),D2(B2)
Execute	EX	44	RX	R1,D2(X2,B2)
Halt I/O (c,p)	HIO	9E00	S	D2(B2)
Halt Device (c,p)	HDV	9E01	S	D2(B2)
Insert Character	IC	43	RX	R1,D2(X2,B2)
Insert Characters under Mask (c)	ICM	BF	RS	R1,M3,D2(B2)
Insert PSW Key (p)	IPK	B20B	S	
Insert Storage Key (p)	ISK	09	RR	R1,R2
Load	LR	18	RR	R1,R2
Load	L	58	RX	R1,D2(X2,B2)
Load Address	LA	41	RX	R1,D2(X2,B2)
Load and Test (c)	LTR	12	RR	R1,R2
Load Complement (c)	LCR	13	RR	R1,R2
Load Control (p)	LCTL	B7	RS	R1,R3,D2(B2)
Load Halfword	LH	48	RX	R1,D2(X2,B2)
Load Multiple	LM	98	RS	R1,R3,D2(B2)
Load Negative (c)	LNR	11	RR	R1,R2
Load Positive (c)	LPR	10	RR	R1,R2
Load PSW (n,p)	LPSW	82	S	D2(B2)
Load Real Address (c,p)	LRA	B1	RX	R1,D2(X2,B2)
Monitor Call	MC	AF	SI	D1(B1),I2
Move	MVI	92	SI	D1(B1),I2
Move	MVC	D2	SS	D1(L,B1),D2(B2)
Move Long (c)	MVCL	0E	RR	R1,R2
Move Numerics	MVN	D1	SS	D1(L,B1),D2(B2)
Move with Offset	MVO	F1	SS	D1(L1,B1),D2(L2,B2)
Move Zones	MVZ	D3	SS	D1(L,B1),D2(B2)
Multiply	MR	1C	RR	R1,R2
Multiply	M	5C	RX	R1,D2(X2,B2)
Multiply Decimal	MP	FC	SS	D1(L1,B1),D2(L2,B2)
Multiply Halfword	MH	4C	RX	R1,D2(X2,B2)
OR (c)	OR	16	RR	R1,R2
OR (c)	O	56	RX	R1,D2(X2,B2)
OR (c)	OI	96	SI	D1(B1),I2
OR (c)	OC	D6	SS	D1(L,B1),D2(B2)
Pack	PACK	F2	SS	D1(L1,B1),D2(L2,B2)
Purge TLB (p)	PTLB	B20D	S	
Read Direct (p)	RDD	85	SI	D1(B1),I2
Reset Reference Bit (c,p)	RRB	B213	S	D2(B2)
Set Clock (c,p)	SCK	B204	S	D2(B2)
Set Clock Comparator (p)	SCKC	B206	S	D2(B2)

MACHINE INSTRUCTIONS (Contd)

NAME	MNEMONIC	OP CODE	FOR-MAT	OPERANDS
Set CPU Timer (p)	SPT	B208	S	D2(B2)
Set Prefix (p)	SPX	B210	S	D2(B2)
Set Program Mask (n)	SPM	04	RR	R1
Set PSW Key from Address (p)	SPKA	B20A	S	D2(B2)
Set Storage Key (p)	SSK	08	RR	R1,R2
Set System Mask (p)	SSM	80	S	D2(B2)
Shift and Round Decimal (c)	SRP	F0	SS	D1(L1,B1),D2(B2),I3
Shift Left Double (c)	SLDA	8F	RS	R1,D2(B2)
Shift Left Double Logical	SLDL	8D	RS	R1,D2(B2)
Shift Left Single (c)	SLA	8B	RS	R1,D2(B2)
Shift Left Single Logical	SLL	89	RS	R1,D2(B2)
Shift Right Double (c)	SRDA	8E	RS	R1,D2(B2)
Shift Right Double Logical	SRDL	8C	RS	R1,D2(B2)
Shift Right Single (c)	SRA	8A	RS	R1,D2(B2)
Shift Right Single Logical	SRL	88	RS	R1,D2(B2)
Signal Processor (c,p)	SIGP	AE	RS	R1,R3,D2(B2)
Start I/O (c,p)	SIO	9C00	S	D2(B2)
Start I/O Fast Release (c,p)	SIOF	9C01	S	D2(B2)
Store	ST	50	RX	R1,D2(X2,B2)
Store Channel ID (c,p)	STIDC	B203	S	D2(B2)
Store Character	STC	42	RX	R1,D2(X2,B2)
Store Characters under Mask	STCM	BE	RS	R1,M3,D2(B2)
Store Clock (c)	STCK	B205	S	D2(B2)
Store Clock Comparator (p)	STCKC	B207	S	D2(B2)
Store Control (p)	STCTL	B6	RS	R1,R3,D2(B2)
Store CPU Address (p)	STAP	B212	S	D2(B2)
Store CPU ID (p)	STIDP	B202	S	D2(B2)
Store CPU Timer (p)	STPT	B209	S	D2(B2)
Store Halfword	STH	40	RX	R1,D2(X2,B2)
Store Multiple	STM	90	RS	R1,R3,D2(B2)
Store Prefix (p)	STPX	B211	S	D2(B2)
Store Then AND System Mask (p)	STNSM	AC	SI	D1(B1),I2
Store Then OR System Mask (p)	STOSM	AD	SI	D1(B1),I2
Subtract (c)	SR	1B	RR	R1,R2
Subtract (c)	S	5B	RX	R1,D2(X2,B2)
Subtract Decimal (c)	SP	FB	SS	D1(L1,B1),D2(L2,B2)
Subtract Halfword (c)	SH	4B	RX	R1,D2(X2,B2)
Subtract Logical (c)	SLR	1F	RR	R1,R2
Subtract Logical (c)	SL	5F	RX	R1,D2(X2,B2)
Supervisor Call	SVC	0A	RR	I
Test and Set (c)	TS	93	S	D2(B2)
Test Channel (c,p)	TCH	9F00	S	D2(B2)
Test I/O (c,p)	TIO	9D00	S	D2(B2)
Test under Mask (c)	TM	91	SI	D1(B1),I2
Translate	TR	DC	SS	D1(L,B1),D2(B2)
Translate and Test (c)	TRT	DD	SS	D1(L,B1),D2(B2)
Unpack	UNPK	F3	SS	D1(L1,B1),D2(L2,B2)
Write Direct (p)	WRD	84	SI	D1(B1),I2
Zero and Add Decimal (c)	ZAP	F8	SS	D1(L1,B1),D2(L2,B2)

Floating-Point Instructions

NAME	MNEMONIC	OP CODE	FOR-MAT	OPERANDS
Add Normalized, Extended (c,x)	AXR	36	RR	R1,R2
Add Normalized, Long (c)	ADR	2A	RR	R1,R2
Add Normalized, Long (c)	AD	6A	RX	R1,D2(X2,B2)
Add Normalized, Short (c)	AER	3A	RR	R1,R2
Add Normalized, Short (c)	AE	7A	RX	R1,D2(X2,B2)
Add Unnormalized, Long (c)	AWR	2E	RR	R1,R2
Add Unnormalized, Long (c)	AW	6E	RX	R1,D2(X2,B2)
Add Unnormalized, Short (c)	AUR	3E	RR	R1,R2
Add Unnormalized, Short (c)	AU	7E	RX	R1,D2(X2,B2)
Compare, Long (c)	CDR	29	RR	R1,R2
Compare, Long (c)	CD	69	RX	R1,D2(X2,B2)
Compare, Short (c)	CER	39	RR	R1,R2
Compare, Short (c)	CE	79	RX	R1,D2(X2,B2)
Divide, Long	DDR	2D	RR	R1,R2
Divide, Long	DD	6D	RX	R1,D2(X2,B2)
Divide, Short	DER	3D	RR	R1,R2
Divide, Short	DE	7D	RX	R1,D2(X2,B2)
Halve, Long	HDR	24	RR	R1,R2
Halve, Short	HER	34	RR	R1,R2
Load and Test, Long (c)	LTDR	22	RR	R1,R2
Load and Test, Short (c)	LTER	32	RR	R1,R2
Load Complement, Long (c)	LCDR	23	RR	R1,R2
Load Complement, Short (c)	LCER	33	RR	R1,R2
Load, Long	LDR	28	RR	R1,R2

Floating-Point Instructions (Contd)

NAME	MNEMONIC	OP CODE	FOR-MAT	OPERANDS
Load, Long	LD	68	RX	R1,D2(X2,B2)
Load Negative, Long (c)	LNDR	21	RR	R1,R2
Load Negative, Short (c)	LNER	31	RR	R1,R2
Load Positive, Long (c)	LPDR	20	RR	R1,R2
Load Positive, Short (c)	LPER	30	RR	R1,R2
Load Rounded, Extended to Long (x)	LRDR	25	RR	R1,R2
Load Rounded, Long to Short (x)	LRER	35	RR	R1,R2
Load, Short	LER	38	RR	R1,R2
Load, Short	LE	78	RX	R1,D2(X2,B2)
Multiply, Extended (x)	MXR	26	RR	R1,R2
Multiply, Long	MDR	2C	RR	R1,R2
Multiply, Long	MD	6C	RX	R1,D2(X2,B2)
Multiply, Long/Extended (x)	MXDR	27	RR	R1,R2
Multiply, Long/Extended (x)	MXD	67	RX	R1,D2(X2,B2)
Multiply, Short	MER	3C	RR	R1,R2
Multiply, Short	ME	7C	RX	R1,D2(X2,B2)
Store, Long	STD	60	RX	R1,D2(X2,B2)
Store, Short	STE	70	RX	R1,D2(X2,B2)
Subtract Normalized, Extended (c,x)	SXR	37	RR	R1,R2
Subtract Normalized, Long (c)	SDR	2B	RR	R1,R2
Subtract Normalized, Long (c)	SD	6B	RX	R1,D2(X2,B2)
Subtract Normalized, Short (c)	SER	3B	RR	R1,R2
Subtract Normalized, Short (c)	SE	7B	RX	R1,D2(X2,B2)
Subtract Unnormalized, Long (c)	SWR	2F	RR	R1,R2
Subtract Unnormalized, Long (c)	SW	6F	RX	R1,D2(X2,B2)
Subtract Unnormalized, Short (c)	SUR	3F	RR	R1,R2
Subtract Unnormalized, Short (c)	SU	7F	RX	R1,D2(X2,B2)

c. Condition code is set.   p. Privileged instruction.
n. New condition code is loaded.   x. Extended precision floating-point.

EXTENDED MNEMONIC INSTRUCTIONS[†]

Use	Extended Code* (RX or RR)	Meaning	Machine Instr.* (RX or RR)
General	B or BR	Unconditional Branch	BC or BCR 15,
	NOP or NOPR	No Operation	BC or BCR 0,
After Compare Instructions (A:B)	BH or BHR	Branch on A High	BC or BCR 2,
	BL or BLR	Branch on A Low	BC or BCR 4,
	BE or BER	Branch on A Equal B	BC or BCR 8,
	BNH or BNHR	Branch on A Not High	BC or BCR 13,
	BNL or BNLR	Branch on A Not Low	BC or BCR 11,
	BNE or BNER	Branch on A Not Equal B	BC or BCR 7,
After Arithmetic Instructions	BO or BOR	Branch on Overflow	BC or BCR 1,
	BP or BPR	Branch on Plus	BC or BCR 2,
	BM or BMR	Branch on Minus	BC or BCR 4,
	BNP or BNPR	Branch on Not Plus	BC or BCR 13,
	BNM or BNMR	Branch on Not Minus	BC or BCR 11,
	BNZ or BNZR	Branch on Not Zero	BC or BCR 7,
	BZ or BZR	Branch on Zero	BC or BCR 8,
After Test under Mask Instruction	BO or BOR	Branch if Ones	BC or BCR 1,
	BM or BMR	Branch if Mixed	BC or BCR 4,
	BZ or BZR	Branch if Zeros	BC or BCR 8,
	BNO or BNOR	Branch if Not Ones	BC or BCR 14,

*Second operand not shown; in all cases it is D2(X2,B2) for RX format or R2 for RR format.

[†]For OS/VS and DOS/VS; source: GC33-4010.

EDIT AND EDMK PATTERN CHARACTERS (in hex)

20—digit selector	40—blank	5C—asterisk
21—start of significance	4B—period	6B—comma
22—field separator	5B—dollar sign	C3D9—CR

CONDITION CODES

Condition Code Setting	0	1	2	3
Mask Bit Value	8	4	2	1
General Instructions				
Add, Add Halfword	zero	<zero	>zero	overflow
Add Logical	zero, no carry	not zero, no carry	zero, carry	not zero, carry
AND	zero	not zero	—	—
Compare, Compare Halfword	equal	1st op low	1st op high	—
Compare and Swap/Double	equal	not equal	—	—

CONDITION CODES (Contd)

Compare Logical	equal	1st op low	1st op high	—
Exclusive OR	zero	not zero	—	—
Insert Characters under Mask	all zero	1st bit one	1st bit zero	—
Load and Test	zero	<zero	>zero	—
Load Complement	zero	<zero	>zero	overflow
Load Negative	zero	<zero	—	—
Load Positive	zero	—	>zero	overflow
Move Long	count equal	count low	count high	overlap
OR	zero	not zero	—	—
Shift Left Double/Single	zero	<zero	>zero	overflow
Shift Right Double/Single	zero	<zero	>zero	—
Store Clock	set	not set	error	not oper
Subtract, Subtract Halfword	zero	<zero	>zero	overflow
Subtract Logical	—	not zero, no carry	zero, carry	not zero, carry
Test and Set	zero	one	—	—
Test under Mask	zero	mixed	—	ones
Translate and Test	zero	incomplete	complete	—

Decimal Instructions

Add Decimal	zero	<zero	>zero	overflow
Compare Decimal	equal	1st op low	1st op high	—
Edit, Edit and Mark	zero	<zero	>zero	—
Shift and Round Decimal	zero	<zero	>zero	overflow
Subtract Decimal	zero	<zero	>zero	overflow
Zero and Add	zero	<zero	>zero	overflow

Floating-Point Instructions

Add Normalized	zero	<zero	>zero	—
Add Unnormalized	zero	<zero	>zero	—
Compare	equal	1st op low	1st op high	—
Load and Test	zero	<zero	>zero	—
Load Complement	zero	<zero	>zero	—
Load Negative	zero	<zero	—	—

CONDITION CODES (Contd)

Load Positive	zero	—	>zero	—
Subtract Normalized	zero	<zero	>zero	—
Subtract Unnormalized	zero	<zero	>zero	—

Input/Output Instructions

Clear I/O	no oper in progress	CSW stored	chan busy	not oper
Halt Device	interruption pending	CSW stored	channel working	not oper
Halt I/O	interruption pending	CSW stored	burst op stopped	not oper
Start I/O, SIOF	successful	CSW stored	busy	not oper
Store Channel ID	ID stored	CSW stored	busy	not oper
Test Channel	available	interruption pending	burst mode	not oper
Test I/O	available	CSW stored	busy	not oper

System Control Instructions

Load Real Address	translation available	ST entry invalid	PT entry invalid	length violation
Reset Reference Bit	R=0, C=0	R=0, C=1	R=1, C=0	R=1, C=1
Set Clock	set	secure	—	not oper
Signal Processor	accepted	stat stored	busy	not oper

CNOP ALIGNMENT

DOUBLEWORD							
WORD				WORD			
HALFWORD		HALFWORD		HALFWORD		HALFWORD	
BYTE	BYTE	BYTE	BYTE	BYTE	BYTE	BYTE	BYTE
0,4		2,4		0,4		2,4	
0,8		2,8		4,8		6,8	

D

DOS AND OS JOB CONTROL

This appendix provides some typical examples of job control under DOS and OS.

DOS JOB CONTROL

Here is an example of conventional job control to assemble and execute a program under DOS:

```
// JOB jobname
// OPTION DUMP,LIST,LOG,XREF



            ACTION MAP
```

Jobname may be 1–8 characters.

DUMP: Print contents of storage on abnormal execute error (or NODUMP).

LIST: List the assembled program (or NOLIST).

LOG: Print the job control statements (or NOLOG).

XREF: Print a cross-reference of symbolic names after the assembly (or NOXREF).

Print a map of the link-edited program (or NOMAP).

```
// EXEC ASSEMBLY              Load assembler and begin assembly.
     ... (source program here)
/*                            End of assembly.
// EXEC LNKEDT                Perform link edit.
// EXEC                       Load linked module into storage; begin
                              execution.
     ... (input data here)
/*                        .   End of input data.
/&                            End of job; return to supervisor.
```

Larger DOS systems provide for cataloging commonly used job control on disk in the procedure library. The preceding example of job control could be cataloged, for example, to provide for automatic assembly, link edit, and execute through the use of only a few job commands, as follows:

```
* $$ JOB jobname              Jobname may be 1-8 characters.
// EXEC PROC=ASSEMBLY         Cataloged procedure ASSEMBLY con-
                              tains assembly, link-edit, and execute job
                              commands.

     ... (source program here)

/*                            End of assembly.
     ... (input data here)

/*                            End of input data.
/&                            End of job.
* $$ EOJ
```

DOS Job Control for Magnetic Tape

The job commands for magnetic tape are similar to those for the system reader and printer. However, tape files require additional information on a TLBL job command to provide greater control over the file.

```
// TLBL filename,'file-ID',date,file-serial-no.,volume-sequence
no.,file-sequence-no.,generation-no.,version-no.
```

filename	Name of the DTFMT, the only required entry.
'file-ID'	The file identifier in the file label, 1–17 characters.
retention date	One of two formats for output files: (1) yy/ddd, the date of retention; e.g., 95/030 tells the system to retain the file until Jan. 30, 1995; (2) dddd, a retention period in days.
file serial number	1–6 characters, the volume serial number for the first or only volume of the file.

volume sequence number	1–4 digits for the volume number in a multi-volume file.
file sequence number	1–4 digits for the file number in a multifile volume.
generation number	1–4 digits for the generation number.
version number	1–2 digits for the version number.

If you omit any of the last four entries, the system assumes 1 if output and ignores if input.

DOS Job Control for Direct Access Storage Devices

Each extent (disk area) for a disk file requires two job control commands, DLBL and EXTENT, equivalent to the magnetic tape TLBL job command. Note that you may store a file on more than one extent. DLBL and EXTENT follow the LNKEDT command, coded as follows:

```
// EXEC LNKEDT
// DLBL filename...
// EXTENT symbolic-unit...
```

Here are details for the DLBL and EXTENT commands:

```
// DLBL filename,'file-ID',date,codes
```

filename	Name of the DTFSD, 1–7 characters.
'file-ID'	1–44 characters, between apostrophes. This is the first field of the format 1 label. You can code the file ID and optionally generation and version number. If you omit this entry, the system uses the filename.
retention date	One of two formats for output: (1) dddd = retention period in days; (2) yy/ddd = date of retention; e.g., 95/030 means retain file until January 30, 1995. If you omit this entry, the system assumes 7 days.
codes	Type of file label: SD is sequential disk; ISC is index sequential create; ISE is index sequential extend; DA is direct access. If you omit this entry, the system assumes SD.

```
// EXTENT symbolic-unit,serial-no.,type,sequence-no.,relative-
track,number-of-tracks,split-cylinder-track
```

| symbolic unit | The symbolic unit SYSnnn for the file. If you omit this entry, the system assumes the unit from the preceding EXTENT, if any. |

serial number	The volume serial number for the volume. If you omit this entry, the system uses the number from the preceding EXTENT, if any.
type	The type of extent, where 1 is data area with no split cylinder; 2 is independent overflow area for IS; 4 is index area for IS; 8 is data area, split cylinder. If omitted, the system assumes type 1.
sequence number	The sequence number (0–255) of this extent in a multiextent file. Not required for SD and DA, but if used, the extent begins with 0. For IS with a master index, the number begins with 0; otherwise IS files begin with extent 1.
relative track	1–5 digits to indicate the sequential track number, relative to 0, where the extent begins. The formula to calculate the relative track is

$$RT = \text{tracks per cylinder} \times \text{cylinder number}$$
$$+ \text{ track number}$$

Example for a 3350 (30 tracks/cylinder), on cylinder 3, track 4:

$$RT = (30 \times 3) + 4 = 94$$

| number of tracks | 1–5 digits to indicate the number of tracks allocated for the file on this extent. |
| split cylinder track | Digits 0–19 to signify the upper track number for split cylinders in SD files. (There may be more than one SD file within a cylinder.) |

OS JOB CONTROL

There are different versions of OS job control language. The following illustrates one version, providing for assembly, link edit, and execution of test data. The program uses the system reader and a printer file, both of which require a DD (data definition) job command.

```
//jobname JOB [optional account#,acctg-information,programmer-name]

//stepname EXEC ASMGCLG          .Use ASMG to assemble, with no execute.
                  ││││           ─Level of assembler, e.g., F or G.
                  │││└────────────Compile (assemble).
                  ││└─────────────Link-edit the assembled program.
                  │└──────────────Go, or execute the linked program.
//ASM.SYSIN DD *                 The * means that the source program
                                 immediately follows in the job stream.
```

```
   ...(source program here)
/*                              End of assembly.
//GO.SYSUDUMP DD SYSOUT=A        Causes printing of execution error
                                diagnostics.
//GO.printername DD SYSOUT=A    Data definition for printer in program
                                DCB. (A is class of output for printer.)
//GO.readername DD *           Data definition for system reader.  (*
                                indicates that input data immediately follows.)
   ...(input data here)
/*                              End of input data.
//                              Optional entry for end of job.
```

Descriptions of the OS EXEC and DD commands follow. As a convention:

- Braces { } indicate a choice of one entry.
- Brackets [ ] indicate an optional entry from which you may choose one entry or none.
- Parentheses ( ), where they appear, must be coded.

The OS EXEC Command

The general format for the OS EXEC command is the following:

$$
//\text{[stepname] EXEC} \left\{ \begin{array}{l} \texttt{PGM=programname} \\ \texttt{PGM=*.stepname.ddname} \\ \texttt{PGM=*.stepname.procstepname.ddname} \\ \texttt{[PROC=]procedure-name} \\ \texttt{[other options]} \end{array} \right\}
$$

Other options for EXEC include ACCT (accounting information), COND, DPRTY (for MVT), PARM (parameter), RD (restart definition), REGION (for MVT), ROLL (for MVT), and TIME (to assign CPU time limit for a step).

```
ACCT[.procstepname]=(accounting information)
```

$$
\texttt{COND[.procstepname]=} \left[\begin{array}{l} \texttt{(code,operator)} \\ \texttt{(code,operator,stepname)} \\ \texttt{(code,operator,stepname,procstepname)} \end{array} \right]
$$

```
DPRTY[.procstepname]=(value1,value2)

PARM[.procstepname]=value

RD[.procstepname]=R or RNC or NC or NR

REGION[.procstepname]=(valueK[,value1K])
```

$$ROLL[.procstepname]=\left(\begin{Bmatrix} YES \\ NO \end{Bmatrix} \begin{Bmatrix} ,YES \\ ,NO \end{Bmatrix}\right)$$

TIME[.procstepname]=(mins,secs)

The OS DD Command

The DD (data definition) command defines the name and property of each device that the program requires. Its general format is the following:

```
//ddname        DD  operand
      procstepname.ddname
```

The operand for DD permits a variety of options, as follows:

$\begin{bmatrix} * \\ DATA \end{bmatrix}$ Define a data set in the input stream.

```
[DCB=(attributes)
 DCB=(dsname[,attributes])
 DCB=(*.ddname[,attributes])
 DCB=(*.stepname.ddname[,attributes])
 DCB=(*.stepname.procstep.ddname[,attributes])]
```
Completion of data control block.

[DDNAME=ddname]   Postpones definition of the data set.

$$DISP=\left(\begin{bmatrix} NEW \\ OLD \\ SHR \\ MOD \end{bmatrix}\begin{bmatrix} ,DELETE \\ ,KEEP \\ ,PASS \\ ,CATLG \\ ,UNCATLG \end{bmatrix}\begin{bmatrix} ,DELETE \\ ,KEEP \\ ,CATLG \\ ,UNCATLG \end{bmatrix}\right)$$

Assigns status, disposition, and conditional disposition of the data set.

$$DSNAME=\begin{Bmatrix} dsname \\ dsname(areaname) \\ dsname(membername) \\ dsname(generation\#) \\ \&\&dsname \\ \&\&dsname(areaname) \\ \&\&dsname(membername) \\ *.ddname \\ *.stepname.ddname \\ *.stepname.procstepname.ddname \end{Bmatrix}$$

Abbreviated as DSN. Assign name to new or existing data set.

$$FCB=\left(image-id \begin{bmatrix} ,ALIGN \\ ,VERIFY \end{bmatrix}\right)$$

Forms control for 3211 printer.

[LABEL=([data set seq#][parameters])   [Label information (see below).

[SPACE=(parameters)]   Allocate space on disk for a new data set (see below).

[SYSOUT=(classname[,programname][,form#])[OUTLIM=no.]]
                                               Route a data set through the output job stream.

[UNIT=(parameters)]   Unit information.

[VOLUME=(parameters)]   Also VOL. Provide information about the volume (see below).

The following describes in detail the parameters for LABEL, UNIT, and VOLUME.

$$
\text{LABEL=}\left([\text{dataset seq\#}]
\begin{bmatrix} ,SL \\ ,SUL \\ ,AL \\ ,AUL \\ ,NSL \\ ,NL \\ ,BLP \end{bmatrix}
\begin{bmatrix} ,PASSWORD \\ ,NOPWREAD \end{bmatrix}
\begin{bmatrix} ,IN \\ ,OUT \end{bmatrix}
[,]
\begin{bmatrix} EXPDT=yymmdd \\ RETPD=nnnn \end{bmatrix}
\right)^{*}
$$

$$
\text{SPACE=}\left(\begin{Bmatrix} TRK \\ CYL \\ blocksize \end{Bmatrix}
\left(,primary \begin{bmatrix} ,secondary \\ , \end{bmatrix}
\begin{bmatrix} ,directory \\ ,index \end{bmatrix} \right)
\begin{bmatrix} ,RLSE \\ , \end{bmatrix}
\begin{bmatrix} ,CONTIG \\ ,MXIG \\ ,ALX \end{bmatrix} [,ROUND] \right)
$$

$$
\text{SPACE=}\left(ABSTR, \left(primary\ qty,\ address \begin{bmatrix} ,directory \\ ,index \end{bmatrix} \right) \right)
$$

$$
\text{UNIT=}\left(\begin{bmatrix} unit-address \\ device-type \\ group-name \end{bmatrix}
\begin{bmatrix} ,count \\ ,P \\ , \end{bmatrix}
[,DEFER][,SEP=(ddname1, ...)] \right)
$$

UNIT=AFF=ddname

$$
\begin{aligned}
\text{VOLUME=} \\ \text{(or VOL)}
\end{aligned}
\left([PRIVATE] \begin{bmatrix} ,RETAIN \\ , \end{bmatrix}
\begin{bmatrix} ,volseq\# \\ , \end{bmatrix} [,volcount][,]
\begin{bmatrix} SER=serial\#,... \\ REF=dsname \\ REF=*.ddname \end{bmatrix} \right)
$$

*EXPDT is expiration date and RETPD is retention period.

For REF, other entries are

```
REF=*.stepname.ddname
REF=*.stepname.procstepname.ddname
```

Other DD operands include these:

DUMMY	Bypass I/O on a data set under BSAM and QSAM.
DYNAM	Request dynamic allocation under MVT with TSO.
AFF=ddname	Request channel separation.
OUTLIM=number	Limit the number of logical records to be included in an output data set.
SPLIT=operand	Assign space for a new data set on a disk device and to share cylinders.
SUBALLOC=operand	Request part of the space on a disk device that the job assigned earlier.
TERM=TS	Inform the system that data is transferring to or from a timesharing terminal.

APPENDIX

E

SPECIAL MACROS: INIT, PUTPR, DEFIN, DEFPR, EOJ

This appendix describes the special macros INIT, PUTPR, DEFIN, DEFPR, and EOJ used at the beginning of this text to handle program initialization and input/output. The macros are simple to implement and to use, and anyone is free to catalog them. Beginners often have trouble coding the regular full macros, making punctuation and spelling errors and omitting entries. The use of macros such as the ones in this appendix can avert a lot of initial coding errors and can free beginners to concentrate on programming logic.

The INIT macro, which is used for initializing base register addressing, requires versions for both DOS and OS, shown in Figs. E-1 and E-2, respectively. A further recommended refinement could include the DOS STXIT or OS SPIE macro for error recovery.

```
          MACRO
&INITZE   INIT
&INITZE   BALR   3,0                  LOAD BASE REGISTER 3
          USING  *,3,4,5              ASSIGN BASE REGS 3,4 & 5
          LA     5,2048               LOAD X'800' (1/2 OF X'1000')
          LA     4,2048(3,5)          LOAD BASE REG 4
          LA     5,2048(4,5)          LOAD BASE REG 5
          MEND
```

Figure E-1 The DOS INIT macro.

```
            MACRO
&INITZE     INIT
&INITZE     SAVE    (14,12)             SAVE REGS FOR SUPERVISOR
            BALR    3,0
            USING   3,4,5
            ST      13,SAVEAREA+4       SAVE ADDRESSES FOR RETURN
            LA      13,SAVEAREA            TO SUPERVISOR
            LA      5,2048              LOAD X'800' (1/2 OF X'1000')
            LA      4,2048(3,5)         LOAD BASE REG 4
            LA      5,2048(4,5)         LOAD BASE REG 5
            B       SAVEAREA+18*4
            SPACE
SAVEAREA    DS      18F                 SAVE AREA FOR INTERRUPTS
            MEND
```

Figure E-2   The OS INIT macro.

```
            MACRO
&WRITE      PUTPR   &FILE,&PRAREA,&CTLCHR
            LCLC    &CTL
.*
.VALAREA    AIF     ('&CTLCHR' NE 'WSP1').NEXT1    PRINT & SPACE 1?
&CTL        SETC    'X''09'''
            AGO     .NEXT9
.*
.NEXT1      AIF     ('&CTLCHR' NE 'WSP2').NEXT2    PRINT & SPACE 2?
&CTL        SETC    'X''11'''
            AGO     .NEXT9
.*
.NEXT2      AIF     ('&CTLCHR' NE 'WSP3').NEXT3    PRINT & SPACE 3?
&CTL        SETC    'X''19'''
            AGO     .NEXT9
.*
.NEXT3      AIF     ('&CTLCHR' NE 'SP1').NEXT4     SPACE 1, NO PRINT?
&CTL        SETC    'X''0B'''
            AGO     .NEXT9
.*
.NEXT4      AIF     ('&CTLCHR' NE 'SP2').NEXT5     SPACE 2, NO PRINT?
&CTL        SETC    'X''13'''
            AGO     .NEXT9
.*
.NEXT5      AIF     ('&CTLCHR' NE 'SP3').NEXT6     SPACE 3, NO PRINT?
&CTL        SETC    'X''1B'''
            AGO     .NEXT9
.*
.NEXT6      AIF     ('&CTLCHR' NE 'SK1').NEXT7     SKIP TO NEW PAGE?
&CTL        SETC    'X''8B'''
            AGO     .NEXT9
.*
.NEXT7      AIF     ('&CTLCHR' NE 'WSP0').NEXT8    PRINT & SPACE 0?
&CTL        SETC    'X''01'''
            AGO     .NEXT9
.*
.NEXT8      MNOTE   1,'INVALID PRINT CONTROL - DEFAULT TO WSP1'
&CTL        SETC    'X''09'''
.*
.NEXT9      ANOP
&WRITE      MVI     &PRAREA,&CTL                MOVE CTL CHAR TO PRINT
            PUT     &FILE,&PRAREA        *      & PRINT
.NEXT10     ANOP
            MEND
```

Figure E-3   The PUTPR macro.

The PUTPR macro, shown in Fig. E-3, generates two instructions, of the form:

```
MVI PRINT,X'nn'        Insert control character
PUT PRTR,PRINT         Print line
```

If the control character is invalid, the macro instruction defaults to write and space one line.

The DEFIN macro defines the system reader and assume the use of a workarea for input.   (That is, you code GET filename,workarea.)   The macro usefully checks the validity of the supplied end-of-file address.   The DOS version, shown in Fig. E-4, generates a DTFCD, whereas the OS version, shown in Fig. E-5, generates a DCB.   The particular entries may vary by installation.

```
             MACRO
&FILEIN      DEFIN &EOF
             AIF    (T'&EOF EQ 'I' OR T'&EOF EQ 'M').A10   EOF ADDRESS VALID?
             MNOTE 1,'EOF ADDRESS NOT DEFINED'   NO -
&EOF         CLOSE &FILEIN                    *      GENERATE EOF ROUTINE
             EOJ
.A10         ANOP
&FILEIN      DTFCD BLKSIZE=80,                  DEFINE INPUT FILE        +
                   DEVADDR=SYSIPT,                                       +
                   DEVICE=2540,                                          +
                   EOFADDR=&EOF,                                         +
                   IOAREA1=INBUFF1,                                      +
                   IOAREA2=INBUFF2,                                      +
                   TYPEFLE=INPUT,                                        +
                   WORKA=YES
             SPACE
INBUFF1      DC     CL80' '                     INPUT BUFFER-1
INBUFF2      DC     CL80' '                     INPUT BUFFER-2
             MEND
```

Figure E-4   The DOS DEFIN macro.

```
             MACRO
&FILEIN      DEFIN &EOF
             AIF    (T'&EOF EQ 'I' OR T'&EOF EQ 'M').A10   EOF ADDRESS VALID?
             MNOTE 1,'EOF ADDRESS NOT DEFINED'   NO -
&EOF         CLOSE &FILEIN                    *      GENERATE EOF ROUTINE
             EOJ
.A10         ANOP
&FILEIN      DCB    DDNAME=SYSIN,               DEFINE INPUT FILE        +
                    DEVD=DA,                                             +
                    DSORG=PS,                                            +
                    EODAD=&EOF,                                          +
                    MACRF=(GM)
             MEND
```

Figure E-5   The OS DEFIN macro.

```
            MACRO
&PRFILE     DEFPR
&PRFILE     DTFPR  BLKSIZE=133,                 DEFINE OUTPUT FILE           +
                   CTLCHR=YES,                                               +
                   DEVADDR=SYSLST,                                           +
                   DEVICE=3203,                                              +
                   IOAREA1=PRBUFF1,                                          +
                   IOAREA2=PRBUFF2,                                          +
                   WORKA=YES
            SPACE
PRBUFF1     DC     CL133' '                     OUTPUT BUFFER-1
PRBUFF2     DC     CL133' '                     OUTPUT BUFFER-2
            SPACE
            MEND
```

Figure E-6   The DOS DEFPR macro.

```
            MACRO
&PRFILE     DEFPR
&PRFILE     DCB    DDNAME=SYSPRINT,                                          +
                   DEVD=DA,                                                  +
                   DSORG=PS,                                                 +
                   RECFM=FBSM,                                               +
                   MACRF=(PM)
SYSPRINT    EQU    &PRFILE
            ENTRY  SYSPRINT
            MEND
```

Figure E-7   The OS DEFPR macro.

```
            MACRO
&LABEL      EOJ
&LABEL      L      13,SAVEAREA+4                END-OF-JOB
            RETURN (14,12)                      RETURN TO SUPERVISOR
            MEND
```

Figure E-8   The OS EOJ macro.

The DEFPR macro defines the printer and assumes the use of a workarea
for output. (That is, you code PUT filename,workarea.) The DOS version,
shown in Fig. E-6, generates a DTFPR, whereas the OS version, shown in Fig.
E-7, generates a DCB. The particular entries may vary by installation.

DOS already has a simple EOJ macro. The OS EOJ macro, shown in Fig.
E-8, generates the load savearea and return and ties in with the OS INIT macro.

APPENDIX

F

EBCDIC CODE REPRESENTATION

CODE TRANSLATION TABLE

Dec.	Hex	Instruction (RR)	BCDIC	EBCDIC(1)	ASCII	EBCDIC Card Code	Binary
0	00			NUL	NUL	12-0-1-8-9	0000 0000
1	01			SOH	SOH	12-1-9	0000 0001
2	02			STX	STX	12-2-9	0000 0010
3	03			ETX	ETX	12-3-9	0000 0011
4	04	SPM		PF	EOT	12-4-9	0000 0100
5	05	BALR		HT	ENQ	12-5-9	0000 0101
6	06	BCTR		LC	ACK	12-6-9	0000 0110
7	07	BCR		DEL	BEL	12-7-9	0000 0111
8	08	SSK			BS	12-8-9	0000 1000
9	09	ISK			HT	12-1-8-9	0000 1001
10	0A	SVC		SMM	LF	12-2-8-9	0000 1010
11	0B			VT	VT	12-3-8-9	0000 1011
12	0C			FF	FF	12-4-8-9	0000 1100
13	0D			CR	CR	12-5-8-9	0000 1101
14	0E	MVCL		SO	SO	12-6-8-9	0000 1110
15	0F	CLCL		SI	SI	12-7-8-9	0000 1111
16	10	LPR		DLE	DLE	12-11-1-8-9	0001 0000
17	11	LNR		DC1	DC1	11-1-9	0001 0001
18	12	LTR		DC2	DC2	11-2-9	0001 0010
19	13	LCR		TM	DC3	11-3-9	0001 0011
20	14	NR		RES	DC4	11-4-9	0001 0100
21	15	CLR		NL	NAK	11-5-9	0001 0101
22	16	OR		BS	SYN	11-6-9	0001 0110
23	17	XR		IL	ETB	11-7-9	0001 0111
24	18	LR		CAN	CAN	11-8-9	0001 1000
25	19	CR		EM	EM	11-1-8-9	0001 1001
26	1A	AR		CC	SUB	11-2-8-9	0001 1010
27	1B	SR		CU1	ESC	11-3-8-9	0001 1011
28	1C	MR		IFS	FS	11-4-8-9	0001 1100
29	1D	DR		IGS	GS	11-5-8-9	0001 1101
30	1E	ALR		IRS	RS	11-6-8-9	0001 1110
31	1F	SLR		IUS	US	11-7-8-9	0001 1111
32	20	LPDR		DS	SP	11-0-1-8-9	0010 0000
33	21	LNDR		SOS	!	0-1-9	0010 0001
34	22	LTDR		FS	"	0-2-9	0010 0010
35	23	LCDR			#	0-3-9	0010 0011
36	24	HDR		BYP	$	0-4-9	0010 0100
37	25	LRDR		LF	%	0-5-9	0010 0101
38	26	MXR		ETB	&	0-6-9	0010 0110
39	27	MXDR		ESC	'	0-7-9	0010 0111

CODE TRANSLATION TABLE (Contd)

Dec.	Hex	Instruction (RX)	BCDIC	EBCDIC(1)	ASCII	EBCDIC Card Code	Binary
40	28	LDR			(	0-8-9	0010 1000
41	29	CDR			)	0-1-8-9	0010 1001
42	2A	ADR		SM	*	0-2-8-9	0010 1010
43	2B	SDR		CU2	+	0-3-8-9	0010 1011
44	2C	MDR			,	0-4-8-9	0010 1100
45	2D	DDR		ENQ	-	0-5-8-9	0010 1101
46	2E	AWR		ACK	.	0-6-8-9	0010 1110
47	2F	SWR		BEL	/	0-7-8-9	0010 1111
48	30	LPER			0	12-11-0-1-8-9	0011 0000
49	31	LNER			1	1-9	0011 0001
50	32	LTER		SYN	2	2-9	0011 0010
51	33	LCER			3	3-9	0011 0011
52	34	HER		PN	4	4-9	0011 0100
53	35	LRER		RS	5	5-9	0011 0101
54	36	AXR		UC	6	6-9	0011 0110
55	37	SXR		EOT	7	7-9	0011 0111
56	38	LER			8	8-9	0011 1000
57	39	CER			9	1-8-9	0011 1001
58	3A	AER			:	2-8-9	0011 1010
59	3B	SER		CU3	;	3-8-9	0011 1011
60	3C	MER		DC4	<	4-8-9	0011 1100
61	3D	DER		NAK	=	5-8-9	0011 1101
62	3E	AUR			>	6-8-9	0011 1110
63	3F	SUR		SUB	?	7-8-9	0011 1111
64	40	STH	Sp	Sp	@	no punches	0100 0000
65	41	LA			A	12-0-1-9	0100 0001
66	42	STC			B	12-0-2-9	0100 0010
67	43	IC			C	12-0-3-9	0100 0011
68	44	EX			D	12-0-4-9	0100 0100
69	45	BAL			E	12-0-5-9	0100 0101
70	46	BCT			F	12-0-6-9	0100 0110
71	47	BC			G	12-0-7-9	0100 0111
72	48	LH			H	12-0-8-9	0100 1000
73	49	CH			I	12-1-8	0100 1001
74	4A	AH	¢	¢	J	12-2-8	0100 1010
75	4B	SH	.	.	K	12-3-8	0100 1011
76	4C	MH	⌑	<	L	12-4-8	0100 1100
77	4D		[	(	M	12-5-8	0100 1101
78	4E	CVD	<	+	N	12-6-8	0100 1110
79	4F	CVB	≠	‖	O	12-7-8	0100 1111

CODE TRANSLATION TABLE (Contd)

Dec.	Hex	Instruction and Format	BCDIC	EBCDIC(1)	ASCII	EBCDIC Card Code	Binary
80	50	ST	& +	&	&	P	12	0101 0000
81	51					Q	12-11-1-9	0101 0001
82	52					R	12-11-2-9	0101 0010
83	53					S	12-11-3-9	0101 0011
84	54	N				T	12-11-4-9	0101 0100
85	55	CL				U	12-11-5-9	0101 0101
86	56	O				V	12-11-6-9	0101 0110
87	57	X				W	12-11-7-9	0101 0111
88	58	L	.			X	12-11-8-9	0101 1000
89	59	C				Y	11-1-8	0101 1001
90	5A	A		!	!	Z	11-2-8	0101 1010
91	5B	S	$	$	$	[	11-3-8	0101 1011
92	5C	M	•	•	•	\	11-4-8	0101 1100
93	5D	D	]	)	)	]	11-5-8	0101 1101
94	5E	AL	;	;	;	¬ ^	11-6-8	0101 1110
95	5F	SL	Δ	¬	¬	_	11-7-8	0101 1111
96	60	STD	-	-	-	`	11	0110 0000
97	61		/	/	/	a	0-1	0110 0001
98	62					b	11-0-2-9	0110 0010
99	63					c	11-0-3-9	0110 0011
100	64					d	11-0-4-9	0110 0100
101	65					e	11-0-5-9	0110 0101
102	66					f	11-0-6-9	0110 0110
103	67	MXD				g	11-0-7-9	0110 0111
104	68	LD				h	11-0-8-9	0110 1000
105	69	CD				i	0-1-8	0110 1001
106	6A	AD		¦		j	12-11	0110 1010
107	6B	SD		¦		k	0-3-8	0110 1011
108	6C	MD	%(	%	%	l	0-4-8	0110 1100
109	6D	DD	V			m	0-5-8	0110 1101
110	6E	AW	\	>	>	n	0-6-8	0110 1110
111	6F	SW	⇔	?	?	o	0-7-8	0110 1111
112	70	STE				p	12-11-0	0111 0000
113	71					q	12-11-0-1-9	0111 0001
114	72					r	12-11-0-2-9	0111 0010
115	73					s	12-11-0-3-9	0111 0011
116	74					t	12-11-0-4-9	0111 0100
117	75					u	12-11-0-5-9	0111 0101
118	76					v	12-11-0-6-9	0111 0110
119	77					w	12-11-0-7-9	0111 0111
120	78	LE				x	12-11-0-8-9	0111 1000
121	79	CE		`		y	1-8	0111 1001
122	7A	AE	♭	:	:	z	2-8	0111 1010
123	7B	SE	♯ •	#	#	{	3-8	0111 1011
124	7C	ME	@ '	@	@	¦	4-8	0111 1100
125	7D	DE	:	'	'	}	5-8	0111 1101
126	7E	AU	>	=	=	~	6-8	0111 1110
127	7F	SU	✓	"	"	DEL	7-8	0111 1111
128	80	SSM -S					12-0-1-8	1000 0000
129	81			a	a		12-0-1	1000 0001
130	82	LPSW -S		b	b		12-0-2	1000 0010
131	83	Diagnose		c	c		12-0-3	1000 0011
132	84	WRD SI		d	d		12-0-4	1000 0100
133	85	RDD		e	e		12-0-5	1000 0101
134	86	BXH		f	f		12-0-6	1000 0110
135	87	BXLE		g	g		12-0-7	1000 0111
136	88	SRL		h	h		12-0-8	1000 1000
137	89	SLL		i	i		12-0-9	1000 1001
138	8A	SRA					12-0-2-8	1000 1010
139	8B	SLA RS			{		12-0-3-8	1000 1011
140	8C	SRDL			≤		12-0-4-8	1000 1100
141	8D	SLDL			[		12-0-5-8	1000 1101
142	8E	SRDA			•		12-0-6-8	1000 1110
143	8F	SLDA			+		12-0-7-8	1000 1111
144	90	STM					12-11-1-8	1001 0000
145	91	TM		j	j		12-11-1	1001 0001
146	92	MVI SI		k	k		12-11-2	1001 0010
147	93	TS -S		l	l		12-11-3	1001 0011
148	94	NI		m	m		12-11-4	1001 0100
149	95	CLI		n	n		12-11-5	1001 0101
150	96	OI SI		o	o		12-11-6	1001 0110
151	97	XI		p	p		12-11-7	1001 0111
152	98	LM -RS		q	q		12-11-8	1001 1000
153	99			r	r		12-11-9	1001 1001
154	9A						12-11-2-8	1001 1010
155	9B				}		12-11-3-8	1001 1011

CODE TRANSLATION TABLE (Contd)

Dec.	Hex	Instruction (SS)	BCDIC	EBCDIC(1)	ASCII	EBCDIC Card Code	Binary
156	9C	SIO, SIOF			¤		12-11-4-8	1001 1100
157	9D	TIO, CLRIO ⎫S			)		12-11-5-8	1001 1101
158	9E	HIO, HDV			±		12-11-6-8	1001 1110
159	9F	TCH ⎭			■		12-11-7-8	1001 1111
160	A0				¯		11-0-1-8	1010 0000
161	A1			~	°		11-0-1	1010 0001
162	A2			s	s		11-0-2	1010 0010
163	A3			t	t		11-0-3	1010 0011
164	A4			u	u		11-0-4	1010 0100
165	A5			v	v		11-0-5	1010 0101
166	A6			w	w		11-0-6	1010 0110
167	A7			x	x		11-0-7	1010 0111
168	A8			y	y		11-0-8	1010 1000
169	A9			z	z		11-0-9	1010 1001
170	AA						11-0-2-8	1010 1010
171	AB				L		11-0-3-8	1010 1011
172	AC	STNSM ⎫SI			⌐		11-0-4-8	1010 1100
173	AD	STOSM ⎭			[		11-0-5-8	1010 1101
174	AE	SIGP -RS			≥		11-0-6-8	1010 1110
175	AF	MC -SI			•		11-0-7-8	1010 1111
176	B0				°		12-11-0-1-8	1011 0000
177	B1	LRA -RX			¹		12-11-0-1	1011 0001
178	B2	See below			²		12-11-0-2	1011 0010
179	B3				³		12-11-0-3	1011 0011
180	B4				⁴		12-11-0-4	1011 0100
181	B5				⁵		12-11-0-5	1011 0101
182	B6	STCTL ⎫RS			⁶		12-11-0-6	1011 0110
183	B7	LCTL ⎭			⁷		12-11-0-7	1011 0111
184	B8				⁸		12-11-0-8	1011 1000
185	B9				⁹		12-11-0-9	1011 1001
186	BA	CS ⎫RS					12-11-0-2-8	1011 1010
187	BB	CDS ⎭			⌐		12-11-0-3-8	1011 1011
188	BC				¬		12-11-0-4-8	1011 1100
189	BD	CLM			]		12-11-0-5-8	1011 1101
190	BE	STCM ⎫RS			÷		12-11-0-6-8	1011 1110
191	BF	ICM ⎭			¯		12-11-0-7-8	1011 1111
192	C0		?	{			12-0	1100 0000
193	C1		A	A	A		12-1	1100 0001
194	C2		B	B	B		12-2	1100 0010
195	C3		C	C	C		12-3	1100 0011
196	C4		D	D	D		12-4	1100 0100
197	C5		E	E	E		12-5	1100 0101
198	C6		F	F	F		12-6	1100 0110
199	C7		G	G	G		12-7	1100 0111
200	C8		H	H	H		12-8	1100 1000
201	C9		I	I	I		12-9	1100 1001
202	CA						12-0-2-8-9	1100 1010
203	CB						12-0-3-8-9	1100 1011
204	CC			⌠			12-0-4-8-9	1100 1100
205	CD						12-0-5-8-9	1100 1101
206	CE			⊬			12-0-6-8-9	1100 1110
207	CF						12-0-7-8-9	1100 1111
208	D0		!	}			11-0	1101 0000
209	D1	MVN	J	J	J		11-1	1101 0001
210	D2	MVC	K	K	K		11-2	1101 0010
211	D3	MVZ	L	L	L		11-3	1101 0011
212	D4	NC	M	M	M		11-4	1101 0100
213	D5	CLC	N	N	N		11-5	1101 0101
214	D6	OC	O	O	O		11-6	1101 0110
215	D7	XC	P	P	P		11-7	1101 0111
216	D8		Q	Q	Q		11-8	1101 1000
217	D9		R	R	R		11-9	1101 1001
218	DA						12-11-2-8-9	1101 1010
219	DB						12-11-3-8-9	1101 1011
220	DC	TR					12-11-4-8-9	1101 1100
221	DD	TRT					12-11-5-8-9	1101 1101
222	DE	ED					12-11-6-8-9	1101 1110
223	DF	EDMK					12-11-7-8-9	1101 1111
224	E0		‡	\			0-2-8	1110 0000
225	E1				¯		11-0-1-9	1110 0001
226	E2		S	S	S		0-2	1110 0010
227	E3		T	T	T		0-3	1110 0011
228	E4		U	U	U		0-4	1110 0100
229	E5		V	V	V		0-5	1110 0101
230	E6		W	W	W		0-6	1110 0110
231	E7		X	X	X		0-7	1110 0111

CODE TRANSLATION TABLE (Contd)

Dec.	Hex	Instruction and Format	Graphics and Controls BCDIC	EBCDIC(1)	ASCII	EBCDIC Card Code	Binary
232	E8		Y	Y	Y	0-8	1110 1000
233	E9		Z	Z	Z	0-9	1110 1001
234	EA					11-0-2-8-9	1110 1010
235	EB					11-0-3-8-9	1110 1011
236	EC			rl		11-0-4-8-9	1110 1100
237	ED					11-0-5-8-9	1110 1101
238	EE					11-0-6-8-9	1110 1110
239	EF					11-0-7-8-9	1110 1111
240	F0	SRP	0	0	0	0	1111 0000
241	F1	MVO	1	1	1	1	1111 0001
242	F2	PACK	2	2	·2	2	1111 0010
243	F3	UNPK	3	3	3	3	1111 0011

CODE TRANSLATION TABLE (Contd)

Dec.	Hex	Instruction (SS)	Graphics and Controls BCDIC	EBCDIC(1)	ASCII	EBCDIC Card Code	Binary
244	F4		4	4	4	4	1111 0100
245	F5		5	5	5	5	1111 0101
246	F6		6	6	6	6	1111 0110
247	F7		7	7	7	7	1111 0111
248	F8	ZAP	8	8	8	8	1111 1000
249	F9	CP	9	9	9	9	1111 1001
250	FA	AP		l		12-11-0-2-8-9	1111 1010
251	FB	SP				12-11-0-3-8-9	1111 1011
252	FC	MP				12-11-0-4-8-9	1111 1100
253	FD	DP				12-11-0-5-8-9	1111 1101
254	FE					12-11-0-6-8-9	1111 1110
255	FF				EO	12-11-0-7-8-9	1111 1111

G

SUMMARY
OF ASSEMBLER
DECLARATIVES

Here is a list of the assembler data types for defining DC and DS declaratives.

Type	Format	Implied length	Maximum length	Alignment	Truncation/ padding
A	address	4	4	word	left
B	binary digits	—	256	byte	left
C	character[1]	—	256	byte	right
D	floating-point — — long	8	8	doubleword	right
E	floating-point — — short	4	8	word	right
F	fixed-point binary	4	8	word	left
H	fixed-point binary	2	8	halfword	left
L	floating-point — — extended	16	16	doubleword	right
P	packed decimal	—	16	byte	left
Q	symbol naming a DXD or DSECT[2]	4	4	word	left
S	address in base/ displacement format	2	2	halfword	—
V	external defined address	4	4	word	left
X	hexadecimal digits[1]	—	256	byte	left
Y	address	2	2	halfword	left
Z	zoned decimal	—	16	byte	left

[1]For DS, C and X type declaratives may have a defined length up to 65,535. [2]Q-type declaratives are available only for F-level Assembler.

APPENDIX

SUMMARY
OF ASSEMBLER
DIRECTIVES

Here is a list of the various assembler directives in each general category. Directives marked with an asterisk (*) are available only under OS/VS or VM.

Program sectioning and linking

COM	Identify beginning of a common control section.
CSECT	Identify start or resumption of a control section.
CXD*	Cumulative length of an external dummy section.
DSECT	Identify start or resumption of a dummy control section.
DXD*	Define an external dummy section.
ENTRY	Identify an entry point, referenced in another assembly.
EXTRN	Identify an external symbol, defined in another assembly.
START	Define start of the first control section in a program.
WXTRN	Identify a weak external symbol (suppresses search of libraries).

Base register assignment

DROP	Discontinue use of a base register.
USING	Indicate sequence of base registers to use.

Listing control

EJECT	Start assembled listing on next page.
PRINT	Control assembled listing (operands are ON/OFF, GEN/NO-GEN, and DATA/NODATA).
SPACE	Space *n* lines in the assembled listing.
TITLE	Provide a title at the top of each page of listing.

Program control

CNOP	Conditional no-operation (see next section).
COPY	Copy code from an assembler source library.
END	Signal end of an assembly module.
EQU	Equate name or number to a symbol.
ICTL	Define the format of following source statements.
ISEQ	Start or end sequencing of source input statements.
LTORG	Begin the literal pool.
OPSYN*	Equate a name operation code with an operand op code.
ORG	Set the location counter.
POP*	Recover status of PRINT/USING directives saved by last PUSH.
PUNCH	Provide output on cards.
PUSH*	Save current PRINT/USING status.
REPRO	Reproduce the following card.

Macro definition

MACRO	Begin a macro definition.
MEND	Terminate a macro definition.
MEXIT	Exit from a macro definition.
MNOTE	Display a macro note.

Conditional assembly

ACTR	Set loop counter for conditional assembly.
AGO	Branch to sequence symbol.
AIF	Conditional branch to sequence symbol.
ANOP	Assembly no-operation.
GBLA	Define global SETA symbol.
GBLB	Define global SETB symbol.
GBLC	Define global SETC symbol.
LCLA	Define local SETA symbol.
LCLB	Define local SETB symbol.

LCLC   Define local SETC symbol.

SETA   Set an arithmetic variable symbol.

SETB   Set a binary variable symbol.

SETC   Set a character variable symbol.

Conditional No-Operation (CNOP)

The purpose of CNOP is to enable you to align instructions on integral boundaries. You would most likely use CNOP where you have defined local declaratives at the end of a subroutine and want to ensure that the first instruction for the next subroutine begins on an even boundary.

There are six variations on CNOP, depending on whether you want alignment based on fullword or doubleword boundaries. Operand 2 designates fullword (4) or doubleword (8) alignment. Operand 1 determines the particular location in the fullword or doubleword. To force the correct alignment, CNOP generates from one to three NOP instructions, each 2 bytes long.

Fullword alignment

CNOP 0,4   On fullword boundary

CNOP 2,4   On address aligned on halfword boundary in middle of aligned fullword

Doubleword alignment

CNOP 0,8   On doubleword boundary

CNOP 2,8   On second halfword immediately following doubleword boundary

CNOP 4,8   On fullword boundary in middle of aligned doubleword

CNOP 6,8   On fourth halfword boundary in aligned doubleword

A common requirement for alignment on a fullword boundary is simply CNOP 0,4. If the assembler location counter was at X'762', this CNOP would generate one NOP so that the following instruction begins at X'764'. Note, however, that if the location counter is at an odd-numbered address, the assembler forces normal alignment before processing the CNOP.

Relevant IBM reference manuals

GC33-4010 OS/VS-DOS/VS-VM/370 Assembler Language

GC24-3414 DOS Assembler Language

APPENDIX

I

ANSWERS TO SELECTED PROBLEMS

Chapter 1

1-4. (a) 7;   (c) 25.

1-5. (a) 110;   (c) 10010.

1-6. (a) A;   (c) 12;   (e) 20.

1-7. (a) B;   (c) 12;   (e) 1A.

1-11. (a) $64 \times 1,024 = 65,536$.

1-18. (a) binary = 1111 0101; hex = F5.

1-19. (a) 370 F3F7F0 11110011 11110111 11110000
   (c) Sam E28194 11100010 10000001 10010100 (lowercase)

1-21. (a) PAT D7C1E3 11010111 11000001 11100011

Chapter 2

2-1. (a) A unit of data, such as employee number or rate of pay.

2-2. (a) The instruction that a computer executes.

2-5. (a) The program as written in symbolic language, prior to assembly.

Chapter 3

3-2. An asterisk in column 1 means a comment and in column 72 would mean continuation.

3-4. The START or CSECT directive.

3-6. During assembly.

3-9. With PRINT GEN.

3-12. The following are invalid: (b) no hyphen; (c) maximum is 8 characters; (e) no blanks; (f) asterisk; (g) leading digit.

3-13. By means of its location counter.

3-15. (a) Location counter.

3-17. (a) RR (register-to-register) format.

Chapter 4

4-1. BALR and USING.

4-5. Printer control character.

4-8. (a) The original symbolic program prior to assembly.

4-9. (a) Loads the assembler program and begins its execution.

4-17. You could name the input record RECDIN, for example, and move its contents to RECOUT.

Chapter 5

5-1. (a) SAM1   DS   CL12
     (c) SAM3   DS   H
     (e) DAN2   DC   C'SPACE AGE CORP.' (or CL15)

5-2. (a) MVC;   (c) L;   (e) LR;   (g) CP.

5-3. Condition code is 1 for minus.

5-4. (a) Mixed data types, and operand lengths differ.
     (c) Operand 1 references a storage location.   Operation could be L.
     (e) Operation should be L.
     (g) Mixed data types, and operand lengths differ.

5-5. (a) X'352C8 and X'352CC'.

5-6. Define the input record, for example, as CUSRECIN DS CL80, followed by its contained fields up to 80 bytes.

Chapter 6

6-6. (a) At assembly time.

6-8. (a) 1A C5;   (c) 5A C0 42E3.

6-9. BAL 3,P10PAGE destroys the address in base register 3.

6-10. The subroutine returns to the address in the base register, causing the program to restart at its initialization.

6-11. (a) BE   C50
      (c) BNL   E50

6-12. (a) B   B30   47 F0 3A38
      (c) BAL   5,B30   47 50 3A38

6-13. (a) Since a reference in machine code to a register is 4 bits long, the range is 0 through F (0–15).

6-14. BALR loads the address of the next instruction (BR) in register 8. BR then branches to the address in register 8—to itself. The BR becomes an endless loop.

Chapter 7

7-1. (a) OUT   DS   CL80
      (c)   DS   5CL10

7-2. (a) ASTER DC   C'*'
      (c)   DC   C'SAM''S'

7-3. (a)   MVC   B+1(2),C
      (c)   MVC   B+2(3),A
      (e)   MVC   A(6),A+1

7-4. (a)   CLC   E,F
                 BNH   X40

7-5. (a) Low;   (c) low;   (e) high.

Chapter 8

8-1. (a) MVN HAM,TOAST   (hex = C9C2D4, char = IBM).

8-2. (a) PK1 = 12 3C
      (c) PK2 = 01 02 3C
      (g) PK2 = 00 12 3D
      (j) PK2 = 01 23 9C

8-3. (a) Low;   (c) data exception (operand 1 is not packed).

8-4. (a) Any character.

8-5. (a)   MVC   PRINT+20(L'EDWD1),EDWD1
                    ED   PRINT+20(L'EDWD1),VALUE1
           EDWD1   DC   X'4020206B2020214B202060'

8-6. (a)   ZAP   PRODUCT,AMT1
                    MP   PRODUCT,AMT2
                    SRP   PRODUCT,63,5
        or   AP   PRODUCT,PRODUCT+4(1)
                    MVO   PRODUCT,PRODUCT(4)
           PRODUCT DS   PL5
      (c)   ZAP   PRODUCT,AMT2   *(or MVO/AP/MOV)*
                    MP   PRODUCT,AMT4
                    SRP   PRODUCT,62,5
           PRODUCT DS   PL6

8-7. **(a)**

```
            ZAP    RESULT,AMTB           (or MP by =P'10')
            SRP    RESULT,1,0
            DP     RESULT,AMTA           (2 decimal places)
            SRP    RESULT(3),63,5        (or AP/MVO)
     RESULT DS     PL5
```

(c)

```
            ZAP    RESULT,AMTD           (3 decimal places)
            DP     RESULT,AMTA
            SRP    RESULT(4),62,5        (or MVO/AP/MVO)
     RESULT DS     PL6
```

Chapter 9

9-1. **(a)**   00000111   **(c)**   00001001
             +00000100   +11111010
             ─────────   ─────────
              00001011   00000011

9-3. **(a)** Loads contents of FULLWD1 into register 7.

(c) Operand 2 should reference a doubleword.

(e) Operand 2 is a displacement, as 5000(0,0), but the maximum displacement is 4,095.

(g) Operand 1 is a displacement that references storage location 7; the result is a storage protection exception on computers with that feature.

(l) Loads the first 2 bytes of FULLWD1 into register 9.

9-4. **(a)** Subtracts 7 from register 9.

(c) Subtracts the contents of register 8 from register 7.

(e) Compares the contents of register 8 to the contents of FULLWD2.

(g) Subtracts the first 2 bytes of FULLWD2 from register 9.

(i) Multiplies the contents of register 9 by a halfword.

(k) Shifts the contents of register 7 8 bits to the right.

9-6. **(a)** Multiplies the contents of register 7 by itself; the result is 625.

(c) Shifts the contents of FULLA 3 digits to the left; in effect, multiplies by 8.

9-7. **(a)** Divides the contents of FULLWD1 into the contents of register 7.

Chapter 10

10-2. Only the supervisor can execute a privileged instruction.

10-3. Permits overlapping input/output with processing.

10-8.

```
                        MVI    PRINT,X'19'
                        PUT    PRTR,PRINT
```

Chapter 11

11-2. Adds AMOUNT to TOTAL.

11-5. **(a)** Loops 25 times; register 5 contains 50.

11-6. **(a)** Decrements register 6 by 1 (becomes 9), and since the result is nonzero, branches to X30.

(c) Executes the BCT 25 times until register 9 is decremented to zero.

Chapter 12

12-2. (a) AND BOOL,=X'0F'
     (c) OR   BOOL,=X'F0'

12-4.

	SR	1,1	Clear register 1.
	LA	9,NAMADDR	Initialize address of
	LA	10,PRINT+20	name and print area.
LOOP	IC	1,0(0,9)	Get length.
	LR	8,1	Save length.
	BCTR	1,0	Decrement length.
	STC	1,MOVE+1	Set length of MVC.
	LA	9,1(0,9)	Increment address.
MOVE	MVC	0(0,10),0(9)	Move field to print.
	AR	9,8	Add length to address.
	AH	10,=H'30'	Increment print address.
	C	10,=A(PRINT+80)	Past 3rd field?
	BNH	LOOP	yes - print.
	...		
NAMADDR	DS	0CL63	
	DC	X'0D'	Length of name
	DC	C'JP PROGRAMMER'	
	DC	X'13'	Length of address
	DC	C'3700 WILLINGDON AVE'	
	DC	X'07'	Length of city
	DC	C'CHICAGO'	
PRINT	DC	CL133' '	

12-6.

TRANTAB	DC	75X'40',X'4B'
	DC	31X'40',X'6B'
	DC	85X'40',X'818283848586878889'
	DC	07X'40',X'919293949596979899'
	DC	08X'40',X'A2A3A4A5A6A7A8A9'
	DC	06X'40',X'F0F1F2F3F4F5F6F7F8F9'
	DC	06X'40'

12-9. Assume that register 9 contains eight hex digits to be converted and printed.

	LH	10,=H'8'	Initialize count and
	LA	7,PRINT+11	address of PRINT.
LOOP	SR	8,8	Clear register 8.
	SLDL	8,4	Shift digit into 8.
	STC	8,BYTE	Store digit as 0n.
	TR	BYTE,TABLE	Translate to character.
	MVC	0(1,7),BYTE	Move to print.
	AH	7,=H'1'	Increment print address.
	BCT	10,LOOP	Loop if not 8 times.
	...		
BYTE	DS	C	
TABLE	DC	X'F0F1F2F3F4F5F6F7F8F9'	
	DC	X'C1C2C3C4C5C6'	

Chapter 13

13-1. The program may be extremely large, or the subprograms may be common to a number of other programs.

13-3. DROP reg.

13-5. The system uses register 13 for linkage on input/output operations.

13-7. CALL (call the subprogram), SAVE (save the calling program's registers), and RETURN (return to the calling program).

13-10. LOAD loads a module from disk into storage, whereas CALL links to the module for execution; FETCH both loads a module and links to it for execution but does not provide a path for return.

Chapter 14

14-1. (a) MACRO (header).

14-3. A positional macro contains entries in a predetermined sequence, whereas keyword macro entries may be in any sequence.

Chapter 15

15-1. (a) The literal should be =CL5' '.
   (c) Tests only the first byte of RATEIN; change to (a).

15-2. (a) Data exception; HOURTOT should be a DC.
   (c) Data exception: To test a zoned field, use CLC and a character literal.
   (e) Decimal divide exception (divides by 0).

15-3. The BAL to C10CALC loads register 8 but returns via register 7. Since register 7 contains the return address for the BAL to H10HDG, the program executes C10CALC endlessly.

15-4. (a) OPEN should specify PRTR.

15-5. (a) Operand 2 of PACK should specify an explicit length.

15-6. (a) X'004C';   (b) X'568C2' and X'568C7';   (c) ACCUM contains hex zeros and VALUE contains packed blanks. Either will cause a data exception.

Chapter 16

16-2. To enable both positive and negative characteristics.

16-3. (b) X'9A.312' = 42 9A3120

16-4. (b) X'4F.6560' = 42 4F6560

Chapter 17

17-2. (a) Number of bytes per inch; (c) a gap that separates blocks of records; (e) number of records per block.

17-3. Advantage: more records on tape and faster input/output; disadvantage: larger program space for buffer(s).

17-4. **(a)** To identify the volume (reel).

17-5. **(a)** EOV indicates end of data on the reel, and the file continues on another reel; EOF indicates end of the data file.

17-8. To reduce disk access motion for sequential processing.

17-10. CKD stores records of any length by tracks and cylinders; FBA stores records in fixed-length blocks.

17-12. The volume table of contents (VTOC).

17-13. **(a)**

$$\text{Blocks per track} = \frac{19{,}254}{185 + 6(300)} = \frac{19{,}254}{1{,}985} = 9.69 = 9$$

$$\text{Records per track} = 9 \times 6 = 54$$

(b)

$$\text{Blocks per track} = \frac{19{,}254}{185 + 82 + 10 + 1{,}800} = 9.27 = 9$$

$$\text{Records per track} = 9 \times 6 = 54$$

Chapter 18

18-1. Where the need for program space is greater than any expected gains in input/output speed.

18-10.

								Total:
Block 1:	4	4	326	4	414			752
Block 2:	4	4	502	4	384	4	293	1195
Block 3:	4	4	504					512

Chapter 19

19-1. KSDS permits sequential and direct processing by key; ESDS permits sequential and direct processing by RBA; RRDS permits sequential and direct processing by relative record number.

19-3. **(a)** 385/415 and 480/595.

19-5.
```
DEFINE CLUSTER
     (NAME(CUSTOMER.FILE) -
      BLOCKS(no.) -
      VOLUME(name) -
      NONINDEXED -
      RECORDSIZE(100) ) -
     DATA (NAME(data.name) )
```

19-7.
```
CUSVSIN ACB   DDNAME=CUSTVS,              +
              EXLST=EOFCUS,               +
              MACRF=(ADR,SEQ,IN)
```

19-8.
```
RPLCUSIN RPL ACB=CUSVSIN,                 +
             AREA=CUSVSREC,               +
             AREALEN=100,                 +
             OPTCD=(ADR,SEQ,NUP)
```

Chapter 20

20-1. (a) If the cylinder index occupies more than four tracks, a master index reduces the time required to search the cylinder index.

20-2. The key for a block is always the highest one.

Chapter 21

21-2. During execution, in lower main storage.

21-7. Includes any required input/output modules into the assembled program and links separate subprograms.

21-10. The fixed storage locations.

21-11. The two PSW modes are basic control (BC) and extended control (EC). The two PSW states are supervisor and problem state.

21-12. In the instruction address, bits 40–63.

21-14. Channels provide a path between main storage and input/ output devices. The types are multiplexer (byte-multiplexer for slow devices and block-multiplexer for fast devices) and selector for fast devices.

21-15. X'02D'.

21-16. A physical address is the actual hex address by which an operating system accesses a device; a logical address is a name such as SYSLST by which a programmer can reference a device. The supervisor relates the devices by means of its I/O devices control table.

INDEX

Q

R